# INDIA'S
## Lost Frontier

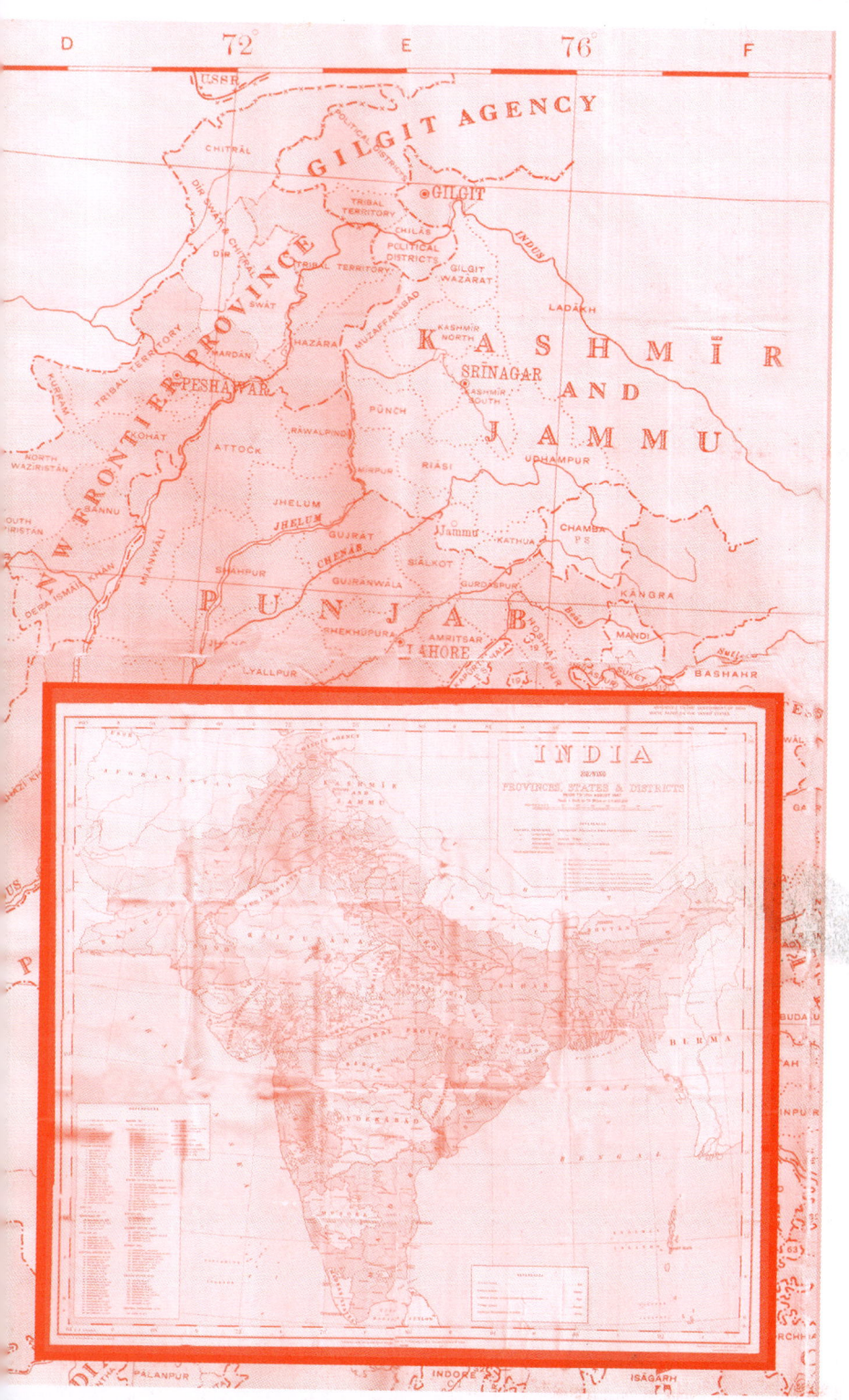

# INDIA'S
## Lost Frontier

### THE STORY OF THE NORTH-WEST FRONTIER PROVINCE

## Raghvendra Singh

RUPA

Published by
Rupa Publications India Pvt. Ltd 2019
7/16, Ansari Road, Daryaganj
New Delhi 110002

*Sales Centres:*

Allahabad Bengaluru Chennai
Hyderabad Jaipur Kathmandu
Kolkata Mumbai

Copyright © Raghvendra Singh 2019

Photos courtesy: author archives

The views and opinions expressed in this book are the author's own and the facts are as reported by him which have been verified to the extent possible, and the publishers are not in any way liable for the same.

While every effort has been made to trace copyright holders and obtain permission, this has not been possible in all cases. References of the works consulted by the author has been provided, but it is possible that it may contain unintentional omissions. Any error brought to our attention will be remedied in future editions.

All rights reserved.
No part of this publication may be reproduced, transmitted, or stored in a retrieval system, in any form or by any means, electronic, mechanical, photocopying, recording or otherwise, without the prior permission of the publisher.

ISBN: 978-81-291-3462-2

Second impression 2019

10 9 8 7 6 5 4 3 2

The moral right of the author has been asserted.

Printed at Parksons Graphics Pvt. Ltd, Mumbai

This book is sold subject to the condition that it shall not, by way of trade or otherwise, be lent, resold, hired out, or otherwise circulated, without the publisher's prior consent, in any form of binding or cover other than that in which it is published.

*Time has taught me that
erasing memory is an exceptional inexcuse.*

# Contents

*Prefatory Note* ix

1. India's Partition: A Strategic Necessity for Britain — 1
2. Convoyed through the Land of Insolence — 22
3. Between One Great War and Another — 95
4. Sometimes Badly Served: Wavell's Viceroyalty — 144
5. The 'Not Entirely Accidental' Role of Viceroy Mountbatten — 162
6. The Wise Man of the NWFP: Governor Sir George Cunningham — 194
7. A Paladin Himself: Governor Sir Olaf Caroe — 215
8. Nehru's Kamerad — 247
9. The Muslim League Punch — 288
10. Malang Baba's Abounding Optimism: Gandhi — 308
11. The Pathan Jeremiad: Khan Abdul Ghaffar Khan — 326
12. The Kafir King: Dr Khan Saheb — 351
13. Kestrel of Kashmir: Abdul Qayyum Khan — 372
14. Difficult under Difficult Conditions: Muhammad Ali Jinnah — 381
15. An Epoch, an Episode and an Epitaph: Britain, Afghanistan and NWFP — 409
16. The Danger of Little Knowledge — 443

*References* 471
*Index* 479

# Prefatory Note

THE NORTH-WEST FRONTIER Province (NWFP)[1] in Pakistan is arduous territory. Ask an Indian about this expanse and chances are that he will shrug his shoulders and claim ignorance. For most Indians, this dangerous flashpoint is remote, and to the generations born after 1947, certainly not part of a common geography.

On the eve of India's partition and independence, Muhammad Ali Jinnah's[2] Muslim League came to power in the newly created state of Pakistan. The Union Jack was brought down for the last time in Karachi on 14 August and in New Delhi on 15 August 1947. In India, a Congress ministry headed by Jawaharlal Nehru replaced the last Viceroy's interim government. But in the NWFP (Pakistan), surprisingly, the Congress administration continued to be in place. Overwhelmingly Muslim, the NWFP had voted for the Congress, a party which the Muslim League accused of being Hindu. One of Jinnah's earliest executive decrees as Pakistan's first Governor General was to dismiss the constitutionally elected NWFP cabinet. The Muslim League ministry that succeeded the Congress government lacked a majority in the Provincial Legislature. *India's Lost Frontier* is about how this province ceased to be a part of India after the country's independence.

Jinnah spearheaded the Muslim League movement for the ten years preceding the formation of Pakistan. The logic behind his demand for Pakistan was the incompatibility of two communities (nations)—Hindu and Muslim. To coexist, he asked for a separate territorial state, assuming, in the process, the mantle of 'sole spokesman'[3] for India's Muslims. For the NWFP, where 92 per cent of the population was Muslim, to then be governed by a Congress ministry was a complete denial of Jinnah's logic. It was, therefore, imperative for the Muslim League to win over the NWFP for Pakistan.

Then British Prime Minister Clement Attlee's announcement on 20 February 1947 of a final date of withdrawal from India, set a time limit—June 1948—for the Muslim League to accomplish this task. The chain of events unleashed by the Calcutta killings of August 1946,[4] followed by Noakhali, Bihar, Bombay and the riots in Punjab, sharply raised the communal temperature in the NWFP. The bloodletting at Dera Ismail Khan, Hazara and many other places resulted in an exodus of Hindus and Sikhs from the NWFP.

Why did India's partition come about? What made Jinnah's demand for a nation and a separate territorial state so appealing to the Muslims? Though numerically so, India's Muslims never considered themselves a 'minority' until after 1857, when the last symbol of Mughal power, Bahadur Shah Zafar, was banished to Burma (now Myanmar). Their social dominance diminished thereafter. The disarming of the general populace by the British in 1858 adversely impacted the Muslims, dependent as they were on the use of weaponry as compared to the Hindus, who maintained primacy in business. The shift in the power balance took place while the British consolidated their rule in India. The resultant effect was the rise of a Hindu elite at a pan-Indian level. And it was this Hindu elite that came in conflict with its Muslim counterpart at the provincial and district levels. The nature of politics in India changed. It became communally competitive—separate electorates, weightages and special reservations. The United Provinces,[5] home to divisive Indian politics, was a prime case in point.

Jinnah believed that Muslims would forever be subjected to an inferior status if they chose to be with Hindus in independent India. However, in provinces like Bengal and Punjab, they had numerical superiority. Why not then have a distinct territory carved out of India which the Muslims could dominate? The NWFP was just one such area which was predominantly Muslim. For this reason, a dominant Hindu elite was conspicuous by its absence there. The people of the NWFP could never conceive of Hindu supremacy. The provincial elections held in 1946 brought a Congress ministry to power in the NWFP. Within almost a year of the ministry's formation, the NWFP opted for Pakistan. Why?

Mahatma Gandhi and Jawaharlal Nehru, two prominent Congress leaders, perhaps failed to appreciate the situation. To Gandhi, the

Hindu–Muslim problem was that of the essential unity of two religions; for Nehru, it was a consequence of poverty and exploitation within India. Both steadfastly denied that the problem, or the conflict, was civilizational. The strong appeal of Islam as a religion in the NWFP, over and above any regional or ethnic appeal, was ignored. What escaped them was the ability of Islam to use tribal and local allegiances in its favour. In the penultimate year of partition, the plea for Pakistan was made to the people of the NWFP in the name of Islam. And it was in the name of Islam that the Muslim League made good political use of spatial kinship.

Jinnah had unrelentingly accused the Indian National Congress of espousing 'Hindu nationalism' on the grounds that it was a Hindu body—which it was by virtue of its ethos, if not by ideology and composition—and he pitted 'Muslim nationalism' against it. If at all, it was the concept of 'Islamic nationhood' which brooked religion (Jain 1994: 11). This, of course, played out advantageously for Jinnah in the NWFP. 'Islam is in danger,' the clarion call of the Muslim League in 1946–47, was a far bigger draw than ethnic or regional fidelity. Loyalty to Islam triumphed.

With the ceding of Jinnah's demand, India stood divided in August 1947. The curse of communalism stayed, however. The issue of Muslim minoritism refused to get resolved. But the Muslims were not in a minority in NWFP. Then why did the issue come up there? No other community raised this issue. This question begs enquiry.

The Ottomans, the Safavids and the Mughals, together, had contributed significantly to the splendour, power and stability of the Islamic world order. When Jinnah raised the demand for a separate state for India's Muslims, the days of the three dynastic empires were long over. Jinnah's demand, therefore, caught the imagination of the Indian Muslims. It offered the romantic possibility of creating another Islamic order, a *qaum* with a territorial boundary in South Asia, in the wake of the ebbing away of the three Muslim empires.

One is prone to look at the idea of the state, the nation or any closely connected concept of identity only through a western prism. But does this approach suit South Asia? Pivotal changes—the Muslim League gaining sudden popularity in the NWFP or the partition of Punjab—can be explained accurately even without resorting to

European notions of nationhood. The Islamic theory of state and nation varies significantly from its western ideal. India, in fact, had its own indigenous concept of nationalism, quite distinct from the Islamic and the western. The British ignored it, preoccupied as they were with their own nineteenth-century liberal beliefs. Even Al Beruni, the philosopher-astronomer (who had occasion to study Indian civilization), was immediately struck by a distinct 'group consciousness' among the Hindus when he arrived in India in the early eleventh century—nearly a millennium ago.. The society that existed then in the Indian subcontinent forbade interaction with foreigners, who were considered impure; the feelings of 'purity' and 'impurity' became more severe with the passage of time. Since Al Beruni's times, the Hindu law-givers increasingly tightened the rules of commensality and social interaction (Chaudhuri 1964: 484). Is it difficult to conceive of 'group consciousness' as 'nationalism' because it is not inclusive? Or are we to use only a single hypothesis of 'nationhood'? The 'group consciousness' of Hindus flourished on a plain where it could not be attacked militarily or politically. The loyalty of the Hindus could only be counted upon as long as a Muslim ruler was able to command it. The moment he lost that power, he also lost the loyalty (Chaudhuri 1964: 485). At the time when Hindus lost power to the Muslims, they displayed a disaffection similar to that displayed by the Muslims when they lost power to the British (Chaudhuri 1964: 559–61).

In the West one could easily identify with terms like 'patriotism' or 'country', but not necessarily so in the Muslim Ottoman empire. Writing in 1862 to his Ambassador in Paris, the Ottoman Foreign Minister sought to clarify this difference:

> In times of need how could the colonel of a mixed battalion [meaning mixed religions] arouse the zeal of his soldiers. Amongst us, if you say the word 'country,' all that would come to the minds of our soldiers is their village squares. If we were to adopt the word 'country' now, and if, in the course of time, it were to establish itself in men's minds and acquire the power that it has in Europe, even then it would not be as potent as 'religious zeal,' nor could it take its place. And even that would take a long time, and in the meantime our armies, would be left without spirit (Lewis 1986: 30–31).

The titles that the Muslim sovereigns used were not territorial. Until influenced by the European spirit, the Sultan of Turkey never called himself by that name, the case being no different with Egypt and Iran. The pattern of statehood, set up especially after the Great War, was different, as also the majority of names appearing on the map. The Turks evidently did not have a word for Turkey—the name given to that country being a Western innovation (Lewis 1986: 32). The old names stood abolished with the Ottoman empire.[6] But even with the changed set-up, the older realities remained, the most important being the religio-political community—of which a particularly dominant one had lasted for fourteen centuries: Islam. Theoretically, 'Islam is one state under one chief with its identity being defined neither by territory (Islam is not a place) nor by nationality' (Lewis 1986: 32). Islam is not limited to those born to it, as is the case with Hindus, but is defined by the acceptance of a minimum religious belief under recognition, at least in theory, of the authority of Islamic law and of the Islamic state that upholds the Islamic law (Lewis 1986: 33). Historically in Islam, there was no separation of religion and state. Religion was state and state was religion—this status certainly lasted until the nineteenth century. The question of relations between one Muslim state and another could not arise, since all Islam was one state. The Ottomans always spoke of themselves as the realm of Islam and not as Turkey, using the term 'Ottoman' empire only when specifically required to identify themselves from amongst others in the Islamic world. Even during times of struggle between two Muslim rulers, the notion of a territorial title did not come into play. The way Europeans perceived the history of a country or a nation was also not quite the way in which it was perceived in Islamic society. For the believers of Islam, history began only with the advent of Islam. Even in countries of ancient civilizations like Egypt and Iran, the pre-Islamic past has been often ignored (Lewis 1986: 33).

The Muslims identified with dynastic traditions like those of the Ottomans. But simultaneously, they also held on to local allegiances. At that (local) level, ties of kinship became important. This allegiance included in itself a variety of regional and sectarian groupings. This is also a level at which personal relationships acquire significance. What about the Muslim communities which display linguistic or ethnic affinity? The Arabs, the Persians and also the Turks are all bound by strong cultural ties. But this has not come in the way while determining their nationality. Europe has, no doubt, made a distinct impact on Islamic concepts, but the influence has not been profound. Gradually, European ideas of patriotism and nationalism did come to find a place within Islamic concepts. The Ottomans, much impressed by the unification of Germany and Italy, attempted to create a greater unity within their empire on similar lines. What they strove for, of course, was not pan-Turkism or pan-Arabism but pan-Islamism. After the Great War and with the infiltration of European concepts, the Muslim states acquired the territorial connotations of a nation state. The first to go down this path was the Turkish Republic. Being a new concept, it proved difficult for the Muslims to accept it (Lewis 1986: 33).

Despite the European influence, Islam never ceased to operate as an organizing principle of unity (Ahmad 1983: 32). Take the case of the NWFP. It has consistently shown Islamic solidarity. In 1947 it chose Pakistan in the name of religion over Pathanistan, an ethnic construct. The Muslim League sought Islamic fealty in local groups—in regional and sectarian groupings, in kinship ties and at levels where personal relationships acquire importance. They were highly successful. Islamic identity, by tradition, was always perpetuated through allegiance of the local groups, particularly in the tribal society of the NWFP. Kinship linkages and personal relationships were always very important. The mullahs and *sajjadanashins*[7] forever provided a fulcrum around which Islamic solidarity came to be built. In 1946–47 there were people like the Pir of Manki Sharif[8] and the Pir of Zakori.[9] Nearer to our times, there have been many others. Mullah Baitullah Mahsud[10] and Mullah Fazlullah,[11] Taliban[12] leaders, are some recent examples.

The NWFP and Afghanistan have a shared past. This swathe of territory, of immense strategic importance, lies at the crossroads of three different geographical regions—the West and Central and South Asia. Coincidentally, it also borders three cultural zones—Islamic, Hindu and Chinese. The region has always been restive. Because of the tension it generates, it has ended up involving Russia, China, Persia, Turkey, France, Britain and now, the United States of America. Britain, till now, can boast of the closest engagement. What led to Britain's involvement in this region, and why? What prompted Lord Salisbury,[13] the British Foreign Secretary, to say in 1900, 'We cannot conquer it; we cannot leave it alone?' Throughout, Britain's relationship with Kabul was the function of its politics in the land of the Pakhtuns, the NWFP (Ahmad 1983: 32). That 'function of politics' was dictated by the region; this still remains a fact. Britain, the Soviet Union and now the US have had to deal with Afghanistan and the NWFP simultaneously. The reason, as mentioned earlier, lies in their collective history. What existed a century ago still holds good. It is seldom realized that Kabul is just 50 miles from the borders of Kurram Agency in the NWFP. The area of the NWFP was first retained by Britain under Punjab until Lord Curzon created a separate province for it in 1901. The British continued to govern Afghan foreign policy till the Great War ended. A dedicated cadre of servicemen drawn from the Indian army and the Indian Civil Service administered the NWFP and monitored Afghanistan's foreign policy. The legacy, the tradition and the reservoir of experience of these administrators remains unmatched. The level of Soviet engagement in the 1970s and 1980s, and subsequently that of the US, in Afghanistan and the NWFP falls far short of the British experience. The Americans should have drawn upon Britain's past experience and vast knowledge of this region. The context is reminiscent of the famous rebel, the Fakir of Ipi.[14] For twenty-five years, first the British and thereafter the Pakistan government tried to capture him, but to no avail. A Torikhel Wazir, the Fakir remained free until he died in 1960. The areas on both sides of the Durand Line[15] remain as challenging as they were during the Fakir of Ipi's time. And so are the territories of Chitral[16] and Swat.[17]

The phenomenon of mullahs in the Islamic social order peculiar to this region is noteworthy. These territories have had a strong tradition of mullahs. That a new 'Mullah Omar'[18] had emerged in the South Waziristan Agency is old news, for Baitullah Mahsud's influence in South Waziristan did come to be widely acknowledged. The first time we took notice of this thirty-four-year-old Taliban leader was when Pakistan's former Prime Minister Benazir Bhutto's[19] convoy was attacked on the night of 18 October 2007. Juxtapose this with a letter that the then President of Afghanistan, Hamid Karzai[20] had written to the reclusive Taliban leader, Mullah Mohammad Omar, requesting a meeting for peace talks. Referring to him as 'Esteemed Mullah Sir',

President Karzai promised Mullah Omar and his followers positions in the government to bring them on board. The Taliban refused. Things did not augur well both for Pakistan and Afghanistan. The portents were numerous. Benazir Bhutto was assassinated. The Pakistan government's very swift and perhaps convenient conclusion was that Baitullah Mahsud had had a hand in Benazir's assassination. Most US experts agreed that Baitullah was the likely culprit. Baitullah is long since dead—the Americans got to him.

It is from the region of Waziristan that I draw analogies. The Durand Line that divides Afghanistan and Pakistan constitutes the border of the South Waziristan Agency. An age-old British refrain still helps appreciate realities: 'In the North they have monarchy (Dir, Swat and Chitral), next a feudal aristocracy, then a fairly well working democracy and finally down south in the Waziristan, anarchy.' So turbulent was Waziristan in the 1930s that the troops stationed there were far greater in number than in the rest of the Indian subcontinent. In 1937, an entire British brigade was wiped out trying to contain the unrest in Waziristan. Traditionally, steel, rather than glass, was used for the tenement windows by the forces as protection against sniping.

The Wazirs and Mahsuds are the two main tribes of Waziristan. The mullahs of Waziristan have had a history of leading revolts[21] against the establishment. Mullah Powindah, the Fakir of Ipi and Noor Mohammad have all been part of the belt's so-called 'romantic' folklore. Who exactly are these mullahs? With no formal priesthood, where do they fit in in Islamic society?

Take the case of Mullah Powindah, who rapidly attained political influence in Waziristan. A leader of the Mahsuds, he led a prolonged rebellion against the British in the early twentieth century. Efforts were then made to seize the British garrison at Wana and proclaim Mullah Powindah as an independent king of Waziristan. Like the Mahsuds, the Wazirs too had a famous priest who troubled the British throughout the 1930s. He was Mirza Ali Khan, the Torikhel Wazir, better known as the Fakir of Ipi. Of more recent vintage is Noor Muhammad, another mullah of the South Waziristan Agency. His story begins in the 1920s when Maulvi Khan, a Wazir, established himself at Wana, accepting the task of looking after a mosque. Noor Muhammad, his son, succeeded him as the mullah of that mosque in 1963. Securing a religious base among the Wazirs, he soon started testing the political waters of the Agency. His authority established, he also interfered in the internal affairs of the Agency through his *talibs*, quickly appropriating the role of a traditional elder.

The mullahs are not part of any broadly defined Islamic religious group—Ulema, Sufi, Sharif, Sayyid or Mian. Ambiguity surrounds their social role. Not quite the learned mufti, nor the Sufi, the mullah is forced to define and create his own status. A mullah could in fact borrow from all these categories. Though the word 'mullah' does not signify superior status, his religion does enter the minutest detail of everyday Frontier and Afghan life. To the people of this region who are Muslim and pride themselves on their religious zeal, the mullah is the embodiment of what is most rational and sacred. Experience had taught the British that to ignore these mullahs was to court trouble.

It was around 1971, the year Bangladesh gained independence from Pakistan, when some 18,000 tribesmen—mostly Mahsuds—from South Waziristan Agency were held as prisoners of war in Bangladesh. These were critical times of crisis and of despair in Pakistan. Mullah Noor Mohammad's dominance over the Wazirs was complete. Visits by the Governors and other high-level government functionaries had already bestowed a national stature upon him. In the mid-1970s, the mullah ordered a complete boycott of the administration, which led to his arrest and thereafter his immediate release on account of the strong feelings of the 'Wazir nation'.

Afghanistan, all along, had kept an attentive eye on developments in Waziristan. Ideal material was at hand for their 'Pakhtunistan' propaganda. Kabul therefore adopted a pro-Wazir stance, casting the affair as a revolt of the Pakhtuns against the authority of Pakistan. On 26 May 1976, Pakistani authorities razed to the ground the areas around the mullah's mosque at Wana. Raids were conducted on the mullah's houses and also those of his men. Though the mullah escaped, he surrendered some months later and was incarcerated. The action in Wana was perceived as a Pakhtun struggle for autonomy against a Punjabi-dominated central government. Not since the merger of the NWFP states of Swat, Chitral, Dir and Amb[22] in 1969 had such a live issue presented itself to Kabul. The propaganda emphasized the ethnic nature of the mullah's struggle and portrayed the key men in the drama, the central Interior Minister, the Chief Secretary of the province and the Political Agent, all as non-Pakhtuns.

Consider now the primary motivation behind Noor Mohammad's action. Was it religious? Though he employed a specifically religious idiom, his objective was political. He wished to control Islam rather than be controlled by it. His involvement in the religious affairs of the mosque provided him an ideal platform—to be seen and heard. His next logical step was to convert students in madrassas to disciples and then extend his influence to adjacent areas. But political ambition was not his only motivation. His aspirations remained somewhat clouded, for they changed with the situation. Though Noor Mohammad's movement was an act of ethnic assertion, as a religious leader he could not espouse an overtly ethnic secessionist cause. Therein lay the paradox. The more successful a mullah becomes in advocating a parochially ethnic philosophy, the further he moves away from the position of being a religious leader. This dilemma was reflected both in the Fakir of Ipi's as well as in Noor Mohammad's actions. Immediately following the destruction of the marketplace around his mosque, Noor Mohammad escaped but he did not cross the border into Afghanistan. This crossing would have identified him as being pro-Pakhtun and therefore anti-Pakistan. His political and cultural moorings would have been altered then (Ahmad 1983: 86–89). The Fakir of Ipi had to face a similar dilemma after 1947. Mullah Powindah, however, was not put in such a quandary. Baitullah Mahsud was also in no such doubt. For him the jihad was against the US. For Mullah Powindah it was against the British, as also for the Fakir of Ipi till 1947. In fighting Pakistani forces, Baitullah Mahsud was seen to be fighting the forces helping Americans. Noor Mohammad had no such luck; the Soviet Union had not yet occupied Afghanistan then.[23]

For quite some time after the Noor Mohammad episode, the Mahsud elders firmly kept the mullahs 'in their place', asserting that '*mizh charta mullah predo*', which, roughly translated, means, 'We would never allow a mullah to emerge.' Yet that is exactly what keeps on happening even now.

Compared to the Soviets and the Americans, British involvement in the NWFP has been far more intensive. They once directly administered these areas. In comparison, the Americans only exerted an indirect influence through the ruling elite of Pakistan. If history is anything to go by, the experience of the Russian occupation of Afghanistan and the help meted out to the resistance from the NWFP should have long made the Americans uneasy. After all, it was the Americans who were involved in providing help against Soviet occupation. The events have come full circle. Pakistan's efficacy in persecuting terrorists in the NWFP is doubtful. Events playing out in the NWFP amply bear this out. The main obstacle is overcoming the religious fervour of the Pathans, and more importantly, nurturing a feeling of respect and admiration sufficient for the Pathans to abandon their deeply ingrained feelings of antipathy towards an aggressor.

A notable feature of the tribes of this area is that they find it difficult to coalesce. Seldom have they come together, except when they have risen in popular revolt. Their loathing for the Americans gave them sufficient reason to unite. I have no means of assessing the success achieved by the Americans in playing the tribes against one another through financial and other such incentives, amounting to direct bribes. The problem has also been that of tactics of war. This has changed little over the past decades, the only difference being the introduction of satellite technology. The Pathans, though short on weaponry, excel in the warfare native to their country. Invariably, attempts at capture prove abortive.

Then there are areas like Chitral, which even the Pakistanis admit are remote. The name 'Chitral', sounding more like 'a shot from a rifle echoing down the slopes of a frontier gorge' (Harris 1975: 4) is on the main and shortest line of communication between Punjab (Pakistan), Afghanistan and the Central Asian region of the Oxus. It lies close to the passes over the Hindu Kush,[24] a circumstance that gives it outstanding strategic importance. The dominant feature of Chitral is its size and desolation. This is how Sir George Scott Robertson,[25] the British Political Agent, described the area in 1895:

> It takes time for the mind to recover from the depression which the stillness and melancholy of the landscape at first compels. The startling sensation of the immensity, in comparison to man's minuteness, strikes home with almost stunning effect while cruelty, the predominant emotion in Chitral gets symbolized

in those circling eagles and the straight purposeful flight of the hawks (Harris 1975: 5).

It is said of Chitral that once food was so scarce there that 'a fat man had never been seen and even the upper classes looked underfed, and the most effective of bribes was a good meal' (Harris 1975: 6).

The Chitralis are non-Pathan people. They may have come from Wakhan[26] and the Pamirs. Like the Pathans, they are Muslims. Sir Olaf Caroe, who spent half his life in the Frontier, talking of the old enemies of the British—the Pathans—admired their courage, gallant bearing and courtesy and their enchant for fighting honourably to the bitter end. Caroe wrote that the Chitralis, who were their next-door neighbours but not Pathans themselves, had inherited all of their (the Pathans') inherent cruelty and none of their honesty, and the early history of their country was 'a monstrous tale of murder and perfidy' (Harris 1975: 7). Sir Francis Edward Younghusband,[27] once a political agent in Chitral, said the Chitralis 'were like children—impulsive, gay, careless, easily roused and easily soothed. Their bad points were the same as children's, always wanting presents and the more they were given the more they wanted' (Harris 1975: 8).

Within easy reach of Chitral lies Badakhshan,[28] the northernmost province of Afghanistan. Also in close proximity lies Nuristan/Kafiristan, whose people long remained infidels in the eyes of Islam, practising a religion that idolized horses and figures carved from wood. Chitral was one part of the world where polo only came second to religion as a popular obsession. The hard climate may have made it difficult to breed horses and therefore, traditionally, the horses came from Badakhshan, except during the period of Russian occupation when Chitral and other places in the north had to make do with what Punjab (Pakistan) could offer (Harris 1975: 243). Through the Durah Pass,[29] trails of ponies would make the journey to Chitral. But before they were sold to the Chitralis, a valuable cargo, opium, would be unloaded. The opium would then make its journey down to Naushera,[30] on the way to the ports in Pakistan. It was a trade that seemed harmless to the Chitralis, whose need for ponies for polo far outweighed all other considerations. I wonder if this trade still continues. In all likelihood, it does.

How inaccessible is India to Chitral? With the Line of Control intervening now, and no road connectivity to boot, things have not changed much. From Srinagar to the Yasin valley,[31] adjoining Chitral, is a journey through inhospitable passes and glaciers. Beginning with the Woolar lake, then to Bandipur through Kamri and Traghal passes each 12,000 feet high into the Pamirs (Kilik Pass) via the Batura glacier[32] to Gilgit, from where Chitral is about 220 miles.

More than a hundred years ago, in 1903 to be precise, the British had raised an outfit specifically meant for this region—the Chitral Scouts,[33] with 1,200 men under British officers. The object was to create a body of trained marksmen to defend the passes into Chitral. Each one of the 1,200 soldiers was a born cragsman, and none ever saw service outside Chitral in normal circumstances. The scouts' knowledge of the local mountains was unequalled. They only spoke 'Khowar',[34] a language no one else could understand. They rarely left their mountains and valleys, a tradition maintained even after the British left. They have always kept watch on their mountain passes, honed their shooting skills and exercised on the familiar crags with preposterous ease (Moorhouse 1986: 254–55). As for their mountain warfare tactics, in which they are rated amongst the best, they are quite simple—'gain and maintain height, that way one can have the enemy the way one wants him, impotent' (Moorhouse 1986: 256). Drosh, a town near Chitral, has been their headquarters. From the terrace of the headquarters can be seen that famous ridge, the Durand Line, with Afghanistan on the other side. The Scouts regularly exercise on this ridge. There are forty-two passes between Chitral and Afghanistan and it is their job to keep an eye on each one of them (Moorhouse 1986: 247).

Chitral's suitability as a good hideaway, a safe haven for militants, cannot be doubted. It is remote, with a difficult terrain and so located that keeping vigil on its numerous entry and exit points is onerous. If the Pakistan government wanted to check infiltration, it would find the Chitral Scouts peerlessly placed to deal with it. As for the US, getting to know more about the Chitral Scouts should have become an imperative long ago.

## Notes

1. The NWFP or Khyber-Pakhtoonkhwa of Pakistan is home to a majority of the Pakhtuns in Pakistan. The province borders Afghanistan to the west and north. The provincial capital is Peshawar. The province is also referred to as *sarhad*, meaning 'frontier'.
2. Muhammad Ali Jinnah (1876–1948) was a lawyer and politician who fought for the creation of Pakistan. He entered politics in India in 1905 and within a decade, acquired the stature of a national leader. He was initially the most visible supporter of Hindu–Muslim unity. His belief in the constitutional form of agitation was in contrast to Gandhi's civil disobedience strategies. In 1920, Jinnah broke away from the Indian National Congress. In 1940 he demanded the separate nation of Pakistan and by 1947 had achieved this goal. He was the first Governor General of Pakistan. He died on 11 September 1948, within eleven months of taking office.
3. Ayesha Jalal, a historian from Pakistan, has made this term popular.
4. The Calcutta riots, also known as the 'Great Calcutta Killings', were four days of communal bloodletting in the capital of Bengal, India, between 16 and 19 August 1946. Different interpretations are put forward on the exact sequence of events, its various actors and the long-term political consequences.
5. The United Provinces of Agra and Oudh, now Uttar Pradesh, was called thus during British rule.
6. The Ottoman empire centred around Anatolia. It was named after Osman I (1259–1326), a Turkish Muslim who conquered the neighbouring regions once held by the Seljuq dynasty. Ottoman troops first invaded Europe in 1345. The Ottomans triumphed over the Byzantine empire and captured its capital Constantinople (now Istanbul), which henceforth served as the Ottoman capital. Ottoman sultans also held the title of Caliph, the spiritual head of Islam.
7. *Sajjadanashin* or a descendant of a *pir* (saint) or his disciple. Usually men, *Sajjadanashin* are dedicated to religion and piety as understood in Islam.
8. Born in 1923 at Manki Sharif, Aminul Hasanat came to be known as the 'Pir Sahib of Manki Sharif'. He commanded great influence among the Muslims in the Indian subcontinent. He toured the NWFP to win support for the Muslim League and worked indefatigably for the cause of

Pakistan. For his scathing criticism of the Indian National Congress, he was imprisoned by Dr Khan Saheb, the then Chief Minister of the NWFP. He played a pivotal role in securing success for the Muslim League in the referendum held in the NWFP in July 1947. He retired from active politics in 1955 and died in a road accident on 28 January 1960.

9. Mohammad Abdul Latif, Pir Sahib Zakori Sharif (1914–78), was born in a well-known religious family of Dera Ismail Khan. He joined the Muslim League in 1935 and led the campaign concerning the incident of Islam Bibi in the NWFP in 1936. Jinnah nominated Pir Sahib to the Parliamentary Board of the Muslim League from the NWFP in 1945. He played a leading role in the 1946 NWFP Assembly elections. During the Muslim League civil disobedience movement in 1947, he hoisted the Pakistan Muslim League flag after removing the Union Jack from the Deputy Commissioner's house in Bannu and was arrested. His arrest caused great public resentment and a large number of his followers turned up for voluntary arrest, which filled the jails of the NWFP. As a result, temporary prison houses had to be arranged at Bannu and at places nearby to lodge the protestors.

10. Baitullah Mahsud (1974–2009) was a leading tribal militia leader in Waziristan, Pakistan. He was sympathetic to al-Qaeda and was the leader of the Pakistani Taliban umbrella group, Tehrik-i-Taliban, formed in December 2007. Mahsud was suspected of masterminding the assassination of Pakistani politician Benazir Bhutto. The media reported his death on 30 September 2008 at the age of thirty-four.

11. Maulana Fazlullah, nicknamed 'Radio Mullah', is the leader of the Tehreek-e-Nafaz-e-Shariat-e-Mohammadi, a banned Pakistani Islamic fundamentalist militant group which aims to enforce Sharia in the country. He is the son-in-law of the group's founder, Sufi Mohammad.

12. Talib (pl. Taliban) is an Arabic word meaning 'one who is seeking' but the word has evolved to mean 'someone who is seeking religious knowledge'. The Taliban emerged in 1994 and aimed to enforce Islamic law over Afghanistan. By February 1995, the Taliban militia had captured half of the southern provinces of Afghanistan and in September 1996 it took over Kabul, the capital city, establishing a strict Islamic rule of law. It was driven out of Afghanistan by North Atlantic Treaty Organization (NATO) forces in the wake of the 9/11 attack on the US in 2001.

13. Lord Robert Salisbury (1830–1903) was known best for his expansion

of British imperial power in Africa. A three-time Prime Minister and four-time Foreign Secretary of Great Britain, he became the Marquess of Salisbury in 1868 when his father died.
14. The Fakir of Ipi was born Mirza Ali Khan (1897–1960) and was venerably addressed as 'Haji Sahib'. The village of Ipi is located near Mirali camp in North Waziristan Agency from where the Fakir of Ipi started his self-styled jihad against the British government. He waged a highly effective guerrilla warfare against the British empire throughout the 1930s and 1940s until the British departure in 1947. Though some 40,000 British and Indian troops were reported at one time to be in the field trying to capture him, he succeeded in evading them. His own force of armed tribesmen perhaps never exceeded 1,000, fielded as it always was against a much larger British Indian army equipped with modern artillery, tanks and aircraft. The Fakir of Ipi was always short on ammunition, had no radio communication and relied on a traditional network of informants and messengers for his intelligence. When he died in 1960, *The Times* (of London) of 20 April described him as 'a doughty and honourable opponent…a man of principle and saintliness…a redoubtable organizer of tribal warfare…' The obituary also claimed that 'many retired Army officers and Political Agents…will hear the news with the tribute of wistful regret'.
15. The present border between Afghanistan and Pakistan was agreed upon in a treaty signed on 12 November 1893 in Kabul by Sir Mortimer Durand, representing British India, and Abdur Rahman, the Amir of Afghanistan. After the communist takeover of Afghanistan in 1978, the government of Noor Mohammad Taraki and Hafizullah Amin actively challenged the legitimacy of the Durand Line, largely because of their strong Pakhtun sentiments. For this reason, the Afghan government formally repudiated the Durand Agreement in 1979. In 1993, a hundred years since the signing of the agreement, the Durand Agreement formally lapsed. Afghanistan refused to renew the treaty. But the border still remains.
16. A former princely state of Pakistan and British India which ceased to exist in 1969. The area of the state now forms part of Chitral district in the NWFP. The town of the same name is situated on the west bank of the Kunar river at the foot of Tirich Mir which, at 25,289 feet, is the highest peak of the Hindu Kush.
17. A district in Malakand division, the NWFP, with Saidu Sharif as its

headquarters. The region is reached by air and through mountain passes from the south and east. Archaeological evidence indicates that Swat for long had a strong Buddhist presence. In recent times, fighting took place in 2007 between Pakistani troops and Islamic militants in Swat.
18. Mullah Mohammad Omar (born c. 1959, Nodeh, near Kandahar) was often simply called Mullah Omar. He was the reclusive leader of the Taliban of Afghanistan and was Afghanistan's de facto head of state from 1996 to 2001. Post the 9/11 war in Afghanistan, he was in hiding. Not much is publicly known about him. A few photos, none of them official, exist but the authenticity of the existing images is questioned too.
19. Daughter of Zulfikar Ali Bhutto, she became the Prime Minister of Pakistan in 1988. Only two years into her first term, she was dismissed from office to be once more re-elected to the same office in 1993. In 1996, she was again dismissed from office on charges of mismanagement. For many years she lived in exile and returned to Pakistan in December 2007. Her prospects of regaining the prime ministership in the elections of January 2008 were bright. But she was assassinated in Rawalpindi in December 2007 while participating in a political gathering.
20. Hamid Karzai (born 24 December 1957) was the President of Afghanistan from 2004 to 2014.
21. The Waziristan Revolt (1919–20) was sparked by the Afghan invasion of British India in 1919. Though the British quickly defeated the Afghans, the Waziri tribesmen gave the colonial forces a tough fight.
22. Amb, originally known as Tanawal, is the tribal homeland of the Tanoli people. The Nawabs of the Tanolis were best known for fighting against the Sikhs under Ranjit Singh. Amb became a 'non-salute' princely state under the British. In 1947 the Nawab of Amb, Mohammad Farid Khan, acceded to Pakistan. In 1969, the state was incorporated in the NWFP and in 1971 the royal status of the Nawab was abolished by the Government of Pakistan. The construction of Tarbela Dam across the Indus river in the early 1970s resulted in much of Amb state being submerged by the reservoir.
23. The Soviet invasion of Afghanistan was a nine-year conflict involving Soviet forces supporting the Marxist People's Democratic Party government of Afghanistan against mujahidin resistance. The latter group found support from a variety of sources including the US, Saudi Arabia, Pakistan and other Muslim nations. Soviet troops finally withdrew in February 1989.

24. A mountain range of south-west Asia extending westward from northern Pakistan to north-eastern Afghanistan. It is crossed by several high-altitude passes used as invasion and trade routes since ancient times. The highest elevation is Tirich Mir, at 7,695.2 metres (25,230 feet), in Pakistan. Its passes have historically been of great military significance, providing access to the northern plains of the Indian subcontinent.
25. Sir George Scott Robertson (22 October 1852 to 1 January 1916) was a British soldier, author and administrator, best known for his journey to Kafiristan (now called Nuristan) in what is now north-eastern Afghanistan. He chronicled his Kafiristan experience in the book *The Kafirs of the Hindu-Kush* (published in 1896).
26. The Wakhan corridor is a mountainous part of the Pamir and Karakoram region, which extends to connect the extreme north-east of Afghanistan with China and separates the Gorno-Badakhshan region of Tajikistan from the NWFP and the northern areas of Pakistan. It contains the headwaters of the Amu Darya (Oxus river) and was an ancient corridor for travellers from the Tarim Basin to Badakhshan.
27. Sir Francis Edward Younghusband (1863–1942) was an English soldier, explorer and leader of an expedition to Lhasa.
28. Badakhshan is one of the thirty-four provinces of Afghanistan, consisting of twenty-nine districts. It is located in the north-east of the country, between the Hindu Kush and the Amu Darya.
29. The Durah Pass connects Badakhshan in Afghanistan with Chitral in Pakistan. The Dorah Pass is more than 14,000 feet (4,300 metres) high and crosses the Hindu Kush. It became famous during the Soviet invasion of Afghanistan for the Soviets were unable to stop the flow of arms and men back and forth across the pass.
30. Naushera is a district town in the NWFP of Pakistan.
31. The Yasin valley is a high mountain valley in the Hindu Kush mountains, in the north-west region of Gilgit (now called Baltistan) of the Northern Areas of Pakistan.
32. The Batura glacier (57 km long) is one of the largest and longest glaciers outside the Polar Regions. It lies in the Gojal region of the Northern Areas of Pakistan.
33. This infantry battalion was raised after the occupation of Chitral by the British in 1895. On the recommendation of Captain A.H. MacMahon, Political Agent of Dir, Swat and Chitral, a local corps was raised in 1903

and named the 'Chitral State Scouts'. When the army moved out of Chitral in 1942, the corps was redesignated as the Chitral Scouts. During the Third Afghan War of 1919, the force was mobilized for active service against the Afghans. It compelled the Afghans to retreat from the Chitral border.

34. Khowar, also known as Chitrali, is a Dardic language spoken by the people of Chitral, the Yasin valley, Gilgit, Hunza and parts of upper Swat. A small number of Khowar speakers also exist in Afghanistan, China and Tajikistan.

# 1

# India's Partition:
# A Strategic Necessity for Britain

WAS IT NOT axiomatic that a time should come when the British empire[1] faced a downturn? On a crest in 1945, it was at its widest ever, but after hitting a trough, within twenty years it stood liquidated. Imperial Britain had interests across the globe with India occupying centre stage. It was imperative that Britain follow an agenda that met its strategic requirements when its withdrawal from India became imminent. Was it not in Britain's strategic interest to partition India? Was it also not in its interest that the NWFP and Baluchistan, the two frontier provinces of India, join Pakistan? Why then, even after seven decades of India's independence, do we still question the inevitability of partition? What were the British strategic considerations?

The British responsibility had undoubtedly increased vastly in size and scope since World War I. There were new factors of air power and strategic routes to be secured, and most importantly, there was also the question of oil. The British mandate in Iraq[2] was drawing to a close. The union of Nejd[3] and Hejaz[4] (the new Saudi state) was creating problems for Britain. The territory in the Middle East[5] (with its own internal formal and informal relations), the Palestine[6] Mandate,[7] the Aden Protectorate,[8] Egypt and Iran presented growing challenges. After World War II, it was evident that the regional management of Britain's imperial affairs by the Government of India in Delhi would soon end. How best then to wrap up the 'Delhi' affairs so that Britain's strategic interests remained safe?

For the Government of India, developing strategic air links and the emerging importance of oil were secondary concerns—concerns that had become ever so crucial since the Great War. Whitehall needed to diminish this mismatch between Delhi and London. It therefore needed to curtail Delhi's role, and increase Whitehall's. Britain came to acquire substantial interest in oil in and around the Arab states. Securing air routes that passed through these states was consequently of prime importance. On the other hand, Britain's relations with Iran had deteriorated (Blyth 2000: 93–94). Could Britain afford to abandon the Iranian coast in favour of its oil interests in Arab states and secure air communications along that route? By June 1940, the Gulf had been brought well within the purview of British war planners. A perceived threat to Iraq led to British intervention in 1941. A similar fear over German activities in Iran resulted in an Anglo-Soviet engagement in Iran during the same year. Eventually, of course, the British clashed with the Soviets, each trying to secure their own sphere of influence in Iran. Commercial rivalries also brought Americans into the conflict. These commercial rivalries, which included oil, acquired a new prominence in the Middle East. British interests and prestige were already under threat from its wartime allies—the Soviets and the Americans. Accommodation of Arab and Iranian nationalism was another challenge that British statecraft faced in this region. This was alongside painful adjustments to be made with the impending arrival of Indian independence.

With India's freedom imminent, the British shifted their emphasis away from the subcontinent towards the Middle East. After the installation of an interim government in Delhi (September 1946), it became necessary that the Foreign Office (London) take sole charge of British interests in the Gulf. Delhi ceded control to the India Office on 1 April 1947, with the final transfer of charge to the Foreign Office being effected a year later. The Government of India's direct association with political affairs of the Gulf came to an end in March 1947. Removal of the Indian element from the British equation meant a loss in military power. This immediately impacted Britain's position throughout the Gulf region; it also impacted the balance of power vis-à-vis the US and Soviet Union. Britain's latitude for independent action in the Gulf and elsewhere in the Middle East now stood curbed (Blyth 2000: 95–96).

Although Britain's ability to direct the affairs of the Middle East diminished, the region remained at the centre of British strategy even after 1947. The Foreign Office tightened the existing network of treaties in the Gulf and strengthened British presence during the 1950s. In the 1960s, faced with escalating costs and the need to properly reappraise its strategic commitments, the British government took a decision to withdraw the bulk of its military forces from the east of Suez. It was only then that the direct legacy of the British–Indian connection disappeared (Blyth 2000: 105–06).

In February 1946, the India Office in London had circulated an important paper to a select few, like Sir Stafford Cripps[9] and A.V. Alexander,[10] on the subject of the viability of Pakistan. The paper was based on the assumption that Kalat[11] (a substantial part of Baluchistan) and the NWFP would opt for Pakistan. In the February 1946 provincial elections, the NWFP had returned a Congress ministry to power. The provincial legislature had a comfortable Congress majority. Why was the India Office then assuming that the NWFP, a Congress-ruled province, would opt for Pakistan? Elections in the provinces had just concluded. It could reasonably and comfortably be assumed that the Congress ministry would last its tenure. So then why would a Congress-governed province opt for Pakistan? Or were the India Office mandarins confident of their ability to change the destiny of the NWFP? In their forecast, however, the British officials were not off the mark. What they perceived to be theoretically possible could well turn into reality with the help of the NWFP Governor and the provincial bureaucracy. After all, the NWFP had never much been run along popular lines. Governor George Cunningham[12] ruled the province during the World War II years (1939–45), even though both the Congress[13] and the Muslim League[14] got a chance to form ministries. Baluchistan, bordering Persia and the sea and therefore strategically very important, proved a far easier game for the British.

The idea mooted in the India Office paper was of at least two Pakistans with no federal union, however loose. The paper was essentially an exercise in assessing the consequences of this division. If India's economic unity broke, so would the largest free trade area in the world. Calcutta was predicted to emerge as a major bone of contention between India and Pakistan.

Punjab had long enjoyed prosperity because of its predominance in the army and military. At the time World War II broke out, the

Punjabis formed more than 50 per cent of the Indian army. If the inhabitants of West Pakistan[15] were to find remunerative employment in military service in the future as they had in the past, it was assumed that it would be entirely at the expense of the area to which they belonged and not at the expense of the rest of India. Division of services like railways, posts, telegraphs, banking and currency would grievously hamper development unless goodwill prevailed. The effect of partition on civil aviation was difficult to foresee. Pakistan, soberly and realistically examined, was an unattractive proposition.

There weren't any prominent industrial or manufacturing areas in either wing of Pakistan. Karachi (a port city in Pakistan) would be the only port of importance in West Pakistan. In the east, Chittagong (Bangladesh's main seaport and its second-largest city) remained an indifferent port served only by a metre-gauge railway. There was no noticeable railhead except for the one at Lahore. The two divisions of Pakistan were only to be connected by sea, a two or three weeks' voyage, as long as no hostile power commanded the Indian Ocean. The military commitments and priorities of West and East Pakistan[16] differed greatly. A Soviet-aided Iran, the frontiers with Afghanistan, and the Soviet threat were all serious concerns that the armed forces in West Pakistan would have to contend with.

The paper laid special emphasis on assessing the requirements of the armed personnel, including air force squadrons, necessary to resist tribal and Afghan aggression. This requirement was in addition to the forces needed for aiding civil power. The war potential of Russia being immense, an estimate of the force needed by Pakistan to defeat a Soviet-aided Afghanistan was pointless. Strategically, Pakistan would not be safe even with bases in Afghanistan and Iran. Karachi, its one link with the outside world, stood exposed to air attacks and invasions from the sea. The single line of railway between Karachi and Multan[17] the sole means of communication between Karachi and Punjab—faced similar dangers. Lahore, the rail centre, was well within effective bombing range of Afghan/Persian airfields. Western Pakistan lacked the strategic depth necessary to enable the main bases to be located out of the effective range of enemy bombers. This factor assumed crucial importance because the mountainous NWFP could be an obstacle to the efficient functioning of radars.

The paper further contended that the experience of the two World Wars showed that the Bengalis and the Assamese did not make for good soldiers. The 60,000 Bengali Muslims recruited in World War II were assigned mostly to military labour. As for the Assamese Muslims, only 3,000 had been enlisted. The inhabitants of Sindh and Baluchistan (in West Pakistan) were omitted from the list of potential manpower, as they, even more than the Bengalis and the Assamese, did not take to army life. It was left to Punjab and the NWFP to provide the manpower necessary to meet the needs of a Pakistani army. Punjabi Muslims and Pathans lagged behind in education and it was highly doubtful whether the technical needs of the Pakistani army could be met without a prospective scheme of training, which was both time-consuming and expensive. Nor could Pakistan produce a sufficient number of officers necessary for a large army. Assistance from the United Kingdom would, therefore, certainly be required in the form of technical help and training. This shortage of officers and technicians was to affect the air force more seriously than the army. It was difficult to assemble more than one squadron for Pakistan from within the Royal Indian Air Force. The formation of the Pakistan Air Force[18] was to be a slow and laborious business. An almost complete lack of industry in Pakistan was militarily as serious as the shortage of officers and technicians. Practically everything needed for the clothing and equipment of the Pakistan armed forces would have to be imported.

The paper inferred that West and East Pakistan had different strategic problems and were separate entities. Assistance from the United Kingdom was necessary to make up for the shortfall in technicians and officers. Practically all arms and equipment would have to be imported, with a 50 per cent increase in the defence budget. Without strong allies, West Pakistan could not be defended against Russia. Britain was to prove just such an ally.

Maintaining oil stakes in the Middle East and securing air routes would become a major task for Britain once India was lost to it. Britain desperately needed a foothold in the Indian subcontinent where it could legitimize its presence as an ally of the newly created state of Pakistan. Leaders of the movement for Pakistan also appreciated the expediency of a British presence in the state. What could a militarily weak Pakistan do but allow British presence on its soil for a substantial period of time? It suited Britain to partition India. Apart from enabling Britain to sustain its position in the Middle East, the creation of the two dominions of India and Pakistan within the British Commonwealth also allowed for a continuity of sorts.

The Middle East was of critical importance to the containment of Soviet power. Lieutenant General Sir Archibald Nye, the Governor of Madras Presidency, gave voice to this concern while writing to the Viceroy on 2 May 1947.[19] Russia, to him, was a potential threat to world peace as also to India. His letter to Mountbatten was an objective assessment of India's strengths and weaknesses. This is how Lieutenant General Nye, who was later deputized as Britain's High Commissioner to India, summed up the situation:

> There is so much talk about the gallantry of Indian troops that there is a danger of people assuming that given a little time, the Indian armed forces would be very strong. But the military strength of any country is relative, relative to the threat that confronts it, and on that basis India will unquestionably be the weakest military country in the world. Putting aside its problems of turning captains into major generals overnight and ignorant coolies into highly qualified technicians, it has no scientific organization or knowledge that goes with it...its industrial potential is and will be for a very long time virtually non-existent. It will therefore be quite incapable of maintaining armed forces in action...this unfortunate country finds itself on the borders of Russia, the strongest military power in the world. If Russia chose to invade India, it would virtually be the process of taking toffee from a child...And if it becomes necessary to introduce some form of Pakistan, the situation of Hindustan is (if indeed that is possible) even more powerless than that of a unified India. Not only would the existing defence forces be truncated, but the natural frontiers of India (whether NWFP belongs to Pakistan or Hindustan) would be in the hands of a potentially hostile state who could quietly penetrate into the plains of India.[20]

This would undoubtedly threaten British communication in the Middle East, including sea communication. Nye felt that Nehru, whom he interestingly considered a combination of 'a clear-headed realist and a not so clear-headed idealist', would be well aware of this 'menace hanging over India'.[21] World War II was over. Though the threat of the Soviet Union loomed large, the Cold War era was yet to set in. Lieutenant General Nye's letter was a clear demonstration of British anxiety regarding the Middle East. How best then to deal with this peril? The solution lay in establishing British military presence in Pakistan. The creation of Pakistan was therefore a strategic necessity.

The partition plan was publicly announced by the British Prime Minister on 3 June 1947. Recalling his talks with Mountbatten in London in March 1947, Krishna Menon wrote him a letter on 14 June[22] particularly alluding to the fact that both of them had then thought it fundamental to keep the outer boundaries of India intact while effecting India's partition. All talk of secession was to be contingent on this. But the situation had changed after 3 June. The referendum in the NWFP would further alter the picture. The defence of India and Pakistan was to be in two separate hands. To quote the relevant excerpts from Krishna Menon's letter:

> Mr Bevin had said at Margate (the Labour Party[23] Annual Conference, 26–30 May 1947), that the withdrawal from India meant the consolidation of Britain in the Middle East. Is our frontier still the hinterland of this imperial strategy? Does Britain still think in terms of being able to use this territory and all that follows from it? There is a considerable amount of talking in this way and if Kashmir for one reason or the other chooses to be with Pakistan, there is a further development in [?] that direction—I do not know what the British Policy is in that matter. I do not know that you would know it either. [Only someone close enough can say this]... Perhaps I am wrong and Britain does not think in terms of an Empire.[24]

The letter proved prophetic. The dispute in Kashmir has since claimed a heavy toll. The NWFP still continues to be a region of instability. as well as, as Krishna Menon predicted, a hinterland of imperial strategy—earlier that of the British, then the Soviet Union and now America. It, however, arouses curiosity about why Krishna Menon voiced such sentiments. We all know he was present in the second week of May, a month before he wrote this letter in Simla, where Nehru and Mountbatten jointly decided on the revised partition plan subsequently carried by the latter to London for approval. The revised partition plan, Krishna Menon well knew when he wrote the letter, virtually signed away the NWFP to Pakistan even before the referendum was held.

Support for Zionism by countries of the West was a challenge to British statecraft, for it embittered relationships with Iran, Egypt and the Arabs. If the Soviets so desired, they could easily reach the Persian Gulf[25] without facing tough resistance. An increase in Soviet influence in the Middle East could seriously jeopardize the communication routes and Britain's oil interests. Nehru's position on all this was well known. He was likely to adhere to a policy of non-alignment in Britain and the United States' Middle Eastern affairs. Pakistan's participation in the defence of the Middle East was therefore the only 'desirable objective'[26] available to Britain. This was never hidden from the leaders of Pakistan.

The British government feared that an attempt to woo Pakistan and bypass India might drive India into the communist camp. In its view, India's neutrality was certainly preferable to its joining the other side, the Soviet Union. Without Indian support, the dispute over Pakhtunistan was not likely to pose serious problems. Sir Olaf Caroe, one-time Governor of the NWFP, stated unequivocally in his book *Wells of Power* that the western defence of the Middle East should be based on Pakistan, just as the British defence of the Middle East had previously been based on the control of the subcontinent. Caroe felt that Pakistan, with its Islamic heritage and strategic location, was in a unique position to play a significant role in a western alliance system aimed at containing communism.

Declassified US State Department documents suggest that even before Sir Olaf Caroe advanced his argument of a western defence based on Pakistan, Major A.E.G. Davy, a British officer, had voiced a similar opinion. Major Davy, who served for twenty years in the Government of India and was an advisor to the Nawab of Bhopal in the late 1940s, emphasized the importance of Pakistan in the East–West struggle in a memorandum prepared in 1948.[27] The crux of Major Davy's memorandum, titled 'The Strategic and Political Importance of Pakistan in the Event of War with the USSR', was that in the context of a possible conflict between the USSR, Great Britain and the US, Pakistan occupied the most vitally important strategic position on the face of the globe. In his view, the five most important bricks in the strategic wall dividing the Russian and non-Russian camps were Turkey, Iran, Afghanistan, Iraq and Pakistan. He contended that all these countries, in the event of outbreak of hostilities, would jointly and individually be under threat of immediate invasion by Soviet Union forces. Only in the region of the Indus valley, through the ocean port of Karachi, he argued, could the opponents of the Soviet Union take immediate and effective counter measures. Major Davy strongly recommended that the US and Great Britain assist in the development of the Indus valley, looking forward to the transformation of this region into an industrial area which would serve as a 'built-up area' for offensive action against the USSR (Afroz 1988: 175).

Although it would seem highly unlikely that Washington policymakers were influenced by Major Davy's arguments, the Soviet occupation of Afghanistan in 1979 and Pakistan's status as a 'frontline state' suggest that Major Davy presented a significant analysis of possible future developments in this area. It was not long after the creation of India and Pakistan that an effective defence system for the Middle East was created—which came to be known as the Baghdad Pact. Pakistan was one of its founding members, though ironically, the pact came into being mainly because of a US initiative. Afghanistan was not part of this strategic pact. With the USSR's increasing influence in Afghanistan, it could at best maintain a precarious neutrality.

## Churchill's Shadow over India's Partition

Historical records pertaining to the 'shameful flight', a premature hurried scuttle close to India's partition period are replete with references to British efforts at mediating for a united India. Britain maintained that it was the inability and intractability of the Congress and the Muslim League to arrive at a consensus that forced it to reluctantly formulate India's partition plan. This official view of the British government is, however, not borne out by events of that time, particularly the role of Sir Winston Churchill. By July 1945, Churchill was no longer the British Prime Minister, but he continued playing an indirect, albeit dominant, role in Britain's politics as the leader of the opposition. His international status was such that it was impossible for any British government of that time to ignore him on major policy issues. The Labour government that succeeded Churchill's well realized the importance of carrying him along on significant decisions, the decision to withdraw from India being one such.

Churchill had definite views about India. A die-hard imperialist, he did his best in the late 1920s and early 1930s to delay political reforms which eventually got introduced through the Government of India Act, 1935. During World War II, the political moves that Churchill made as Prime Minister of Britain are revealing of his intentions to divide India when granting it independence became necessary. The Cripps plan of 1942 had for the first time introduced the idea of India's balkanization. The provinces could secede from the Union if they so chose. Cripps was recalled by Churchill from India in April 1942 just when he found that Sir Cripps was going beyond his brief to settle with Indian leaders. After 1942 no opportunity came the Congress's way for negotiating India's freedom with the British. The launch of the Quit India movement in August 1942 saw most of the prominent Congressmen in jail for almost three years. The parliamentary election held in England in July 1945 brought the Labour Party into power and Clement Attlee[28] became the British Prime Minister. Even after relinquishing the prime ministership, Churchill did not stop taking an interest in Indian affairs. He continued to closely follow the Labour government's India policies. Churchill was in fact critical of quite a few decisions of the Labour government pertaining to India. He opposed the formation of an interim Indian government with Nehru as its de facto head. He was also against forming the Constituent Assembly, as he felt that it had been elected by an inadequate and unrepresentative franchise.

For the three years that Congress leaders were in jail (1942–45), the Muslim League quietly consolidated its position. Churchill purposely encouraged Jinnah's intransigence during the War years, allowing him a virtual veto whenever the Congress strove to come to terms with the Muslim League.

Churchill remained in close touch with Jinnah well after the former became the leader of the opposition in British Parliament.

In doing so, he continued to covertly interfere in Indian affairs. His comment that Jinnah 'was the one man who cannot do without British help' (Kothekar 1998) on hearing of Jinnah's reluctance to accept dominion status[29] and the 'personal message' he sent to Jinnah through Mountbatten pointing out the perils for Pakistan, denotes a certain ease and confidence in their relationship. Churchill informed Jinnah that 'it would be impossible for him to rule Pakistan without British help' (Kothekar 1998). With his faith in Churchill intact, Jinnah asked the Indian government to refer the case of the Andaman and Nicobar islands not only to the British cabinet but also to Churchill. Jinnah was staking claim to these islands in June 1947.

Churchill had begun to sound almost like Jinnah in his comments on India. When a communal carnage broke out in India in the wake of the Calcutta killings of August 1946, Churchill was voicing the same sentiments as the Muslim League. Prophesying a doomsday scenario in case unity was thrust upon India on the eve of British withdrawal, Churchill thundered:

> I must record my belief which I have long held and often expressed, that any attempt to establish the reign of a Hindu numerical majority in India will never be achieved without a civil war, proceeding, not perhaps at first on the fronts or armies of organized forces, but in thousands of separate and isolated places... any attempt by the Congress Party... will be fatal to any conception of the unity of India (Gilbert 1988).

With the purpose never in doubt, Churchill threw his entire weight behind Jinnah. Churchill continued to deliberately spout divisive comments, raising the issue of Harijans and Muslims while telling the House of Commons that whatever happened in India:

> We must not allow British troops or British officers in the Indian Army[30] to become the agencies and instruments of enforcing caste Hindu domination upon the 90 million Muslims and the 60 million untouchables; nor must the prestige or authority of the British power in India, even in its sunset, be used in partisanship on either side of these profound and awful cleavages...we feel that these issues should be placed bluntly and plainly before the

British and Indian peoples, even amid their present distresses and perplexities, that we thought it our bounden duty to ask for this debate.[31]

The civil war did after all rage when the exodus of millions began on the eve of partition. As Churchill had stated, British troops were not used to contain the conflagration.

On 20 February 1947, the British Labour government announced its intention to withdraw from India by June 1948. Another simultaneous announcement was the appointment of India's last Viceroy, Louis Mountbatten. For his personal staff, Mountbatten[32] chose General Ismay and Eric Mieville. It was no coincidence that these three important choices, Viceroy downwards, were made with Churchill's blessings. Churchill had been chiefly responsible for ensuring that Mountbatten's career did not flounder; Ismay had remained on Churchill's staff during World War II and it was well known that Eric Mieville 'carried influence with the Conservatives in England' (Kothekar 1998). In the months preceding partition, Ismay acted as a messenger between Churchill and Mountbatten. Mountbatten had called on Churchill immediately after being appointed India's Viceroy. Though no records exist of this meeting, it stands to reason that Churchill must have made known his ideas on India's partition. The observation of P.C. Joshi,[33] the General Secretary of the Communist Party of India, on this development that 'a Tory Field Marshall goes, but a Tory Admiral accompanied by one of the cleverest imperialist Generals, Ismay, both Churchill's favourites, comes' (Zeigler 1985) accurately points to the real nature of these appointments.

Within three weeks of his arrival, Mountbatten instructed his staff to work out the details of a plan for the transfer of power in India. Writing to his wife on 23 April 1947, Ismay observed: 'We have made almost innumerable alternative drafts…each formula was designed to achieve the same in a different way…to partition the country.'[34] Reacting to Attlee's statement of 20 February about the final date of British withdrawal from India, Churchill found Nehru's interim government to be 'a complete disaster'. To Churchill it was, and remained, a 'critical mistake' (Gilbert 1988) to entrust the Government of India in this interim period 'to the leader of the caste Hindus, Mr Nehru.' Mountbatten was being sent to India as Viceroy to secure within fourteen months a working agreement with Nehru on the future independence of India, in theory still a Dominion. 'Is he to make a new effort to restore the situation?' Churchill asked:

> Or is it merely 'Operation Scuttle' on which he [Mountbatten] and other distinguished officers have been dispatched?... In my view everyone will start to stake out their claims and prepare to defend them.... These fourteen months will not be used for the melting of hearts and the union of Muslim and Hindu all over India. They will be used in preparation for civil war; and they will be marked continually by disorders and disturbances such as are now going on in the great city of Lahore.[35]

As *Manchester Guardian* reported (7 March 1947), at this point Sir Stafford Cripps was seen 'smiling cynically' at Churchill's remarks in Parliament. This immediately prompted Churchill to say:

> The Right Hon'ble and learned Gentleman ought not to laugh. Although of fanatical disposition, he has a tender heart. I am sure that the horrors that have been going on since he put the Nehru Government in power, the spectacle we have seen in viewing these horrors, with the corpses of men, women and children littering the ground in thousands, have wrung his heart. I wonder that even his imagination does not guide him to review these matters searchingly in his own conscience (Hansard, 6 March 1947).

On 20 May 1947, Attlee and Mountbatten met Churchill and his senior Conservative colleagues, to propose an all-party accord on the government's final proposals for India's independence—that India should be partitioned into two states, the predominantly Hindu India and the predominantly Muslim Pakistan, both to be granted Dominion status, and both, after a period of time, free, if they wished, to declare full independence from the Crown. Churchill accepted the proposal. 'I am in a position to assure you,' Churchill wrote to Attlee on the following day 'that if those terms are made good, so that there is an effective acceptance of Dominion status for the several parts of a divided India, the Conservative Party will agree to facilitate the passage this session of the legislation necessary to confer Dominion status upon such several parts of India' (Hansard, 6 March 1947: 332–33).

Leading Conservative and Labour politicians now worked together for the final act of the severance of India from imperial rule. On 22 May, after a further talk with Mountbatten, Churchill suggested to Attlee that Anthony Eden,[36] Sir John Anderson,[37] Harold Macmillan[38] and 'possibly' Lord Simon meet Mountbatten to clarify some issues. Churchill had asked these colleagues to maintain secrecy, disallowing any consultation with private members of his party. This was very agreeable to Mountbatten (Gilbert 1988: 333).

On 26 May, with Attlee's approval, Mountbatten saw Sir John Anderson, Lord Salisbury, Harold Macmillan, Anthony Eden and Lord Simon, to explain the details of Attlee's partition plan. With Mountbatten was his chief of staff, General Ismay,[39] Churchill's friend and wartime advisor. The Conservatives accepted what they heard. Two days later, Mountbatten left for India (Gilbert 1988: 333).

Churchill had words of praise for Mountbatten while addressing the House of Commons on 3 June, the day India's partition was formally announced by Britain.

Four weeks later, learning that Attlee intended to call the new bill for India the 'India Independence Bill', Churchill wrote at once to protest: 'The essence of the Mountbatten proposals, and the only reason I gave support to them is because they establish the phase of Dominion Status.' He continued, 'Dominion Status is not the same as independence, although it may be freely used to establish independence.'

The India Independence Bill was presented to the House of Commons on 4 July. It provided that, as of 15 August 1947, His Majesty's Government in the United Kingdom would have no responsibility for the government of any of the territories then included in British India. Lord Mountbatten was to be Governor General both of India and Pakistan, whose prime ministers would be Jawaharlal Nehru and Muhammad Ali Jinnah respectively. Four days later, Churchill was consulted on a matter of the utmost urgency and sensitivity. In anticipation of the transfer of power in India, fixed for 15 August, and the creation on that day of two sovereign states, India and Pakistan, Muslim leader Muhammad Ali Jinnah insisted that his own position from the day of independence should be that of Governor General of

Pakistan, nothing less. Jinnah was willing to see Mountbatten remain Governor General of India, but not of Pakistan.

Would the Conservative Party accept this unexpected development? It was to seek immediate acceptance, if possible, that General Ismay flew to London. On 8 July, on Attlee's urging, Ismay travelled to Chartwell to seek Churchill's approval. That night Mountbatten's press officer, Alan Campbell-Johnson,[40] noted in his diary: 'Any expectations Ismay may have had of a difficult interview with the great man were quickly dispelled.' During his talk with Ismay, Churchill 'stressed in particular', Campbell-Johnson wrote, the 'political value' of Mountbatten's role in the months to come 'in mitigating communal tension, preserving the interests of the Princes and strengthening the ties of sentiment between India and the rest of the Commonwealth'. Campbell-Johnson added: 'Ismay, much relieved, came back to London post-haste and told Churchill's Conservative colleagues of the interview, also quickly relaying a message to Delhi.'[41] Churchill's friendship with Muhammad Ali Jinnah stood vindicated and in good time.

## Notes

1. The British empire was a worldwide system of dependencies—colonies, protectorates and other territories—that over a span of three centuries came under the British government. Territorial acquisition began in the early seventeenth century with a group of settlements in North America and West Indian, South Asian and African trading posts founded by private individuals and trading companies. In the eighteenth century the British took Gibraltar, established colonies along the Atlantic sea coast of North America and in the Caribbean Sea, and began to add territory in India. With its victory in the French and Indian War (1763), the empire secured Canada and the eastern Mississippi Valley and gained supremacy in India. From the late eighteenth century, it began to build power in Malaya and acquired the Cape of Good Hope, Ceylon (Sri Lanka) and Malta. The British settled Australia in 1788 and subsequently, New Zealand. Aden was secured in 1839, and Hong Kong in 1841. Britain then also went on to control the Suez Canal (1875–1956). In the nineteenth-century European partition of Africa, Britain acquired Nigeria, Egypt, the territories that would become British East Africa, and part of what would

become the Union (later republic) of South Africa. After World War I, Britain secured mandates to German East Africa, part of the Cameroons, Togo, German south-west Africa, Mesopotamia, Palestine and part of the German Pacific islands.
2. Called Mesopotamia in classical times, the region gave rise to the world's earliest civilizations, including those of Sumer, Akkad and Babylon. Conquered by Alexander the Great in 331 BC, the area later became a battleground between the Romans and Parthians, then between the Sasanians and Byzantines. Arab Muslims conquered it in the seventh century AD, and various Muslim dynasties ruled until the Mongols took over in 1258. The Ottoman empire gained control in the sixteenth century and ruled until the British occupied the country during World War I (1914–18). The British created the kingdom of Iraq in 1921 and occupied Iraq again during World War II (1939–45). The monarchy was restored following the war, but a revolution caused its downfall in 1958. Following a series of military coups, the socialist Ba'ath Party, eventually led by Saddam Hussein, took control and established totalitarian rule in 1968. The Iran–Iraq war in the 1980s and the Persian Gulf war in 1990–91 caused extensive death and destruction. The economy languished under a UN economic embargo imposed on Iraq in the 1990s. The embargo began to erode by the early twenty-first century, and in 2003 during the Iraq war, the Ba'ath Party was driven out of power.
3. A region of central Saudi Arabia, Nejd has been under the rule of the Saud dynasty almost continuously since 1824. It was united with Hejaz and became the independent kingdom of Saudi Arabia in 1932.
4. Hejaz is now part of Saudi Arabia on the Gulf of Aqaba and the Red Sea. Mecca is the chief city. After the fall of the Caliphate of Baghdad (1258), Hejaz came under Egyptian control. In 1517 it passed under Turkish suzerainty. In the early nineteenth century Hejaz was raided by the Wahhabis; peace was restored in 1817 by the Governor of Egypt. After 1845, Hejaz came again under direct Turkish control. To improve communications, the Turks built the Hejaz railway (completed in 1908) from Damascus to Medina. Hejaz, in 1916, was proclaimed independent by Hussein bin Ali, the Sharif of Mecca. Hussein himself was defeated in 1924 by Ibn Saud, ruler of Nejd and founder of Saudi Arabia, who annexed his domain. The formal union of Hejaz and Nejd into Saudi Arabia was proclaimed in 1932.

5. The geographical region where Europe, Africa and Asia meet. It is an unofficial and imprecise term that now generally encompasses the lands around the southern and eastern shores of the Mediterranean Sea—notably Egypt, Jordan, Israel, Lebanon, Syria, Iran, Iraq and the countries of the Arabian Peninsula. Afghanistan, Libya, Turkey and Sudan are sometimes also included. The term was formerly used by western geographers and historians to describe the region from the Persian Gulf to South-east Asia; Near East is sometimes used to describe the same area.
6. The region at the eastern end of the Mediterranean Sea. The political status and geographic area designated by the term have changed considerably over the course of three millennia. The region is sacred to Judaism, Christianity and Islam. Settled since early prehistoric times mainly by Semitic groups, it was occupied in Biblical times by the kingdoms of Israel, Judah and Judaea. It was subsequently held by virtually every power of the Middle East, including the Assyrians, Persians, Romans, Byzantines, Crusaders and Ottomans. It was governed by Britain under a League of Nations mandate from the end of World War I (in 1918) until 1948, when the state of Israel was proclaimed.
7. The Mandate for Palestine was a territory that included the modern territories of Israel, Jordan and the West Bank and Gaza strip, formerly belonging to the Ottoman empire, which the League of Nations entrusted to the United Kingdom to administer in the aftermath of World War I as a Mandate territory.
8. The Aden Protectorate was a British protectorate in southern Arabia in the early and middle twentieth century. Today the territory forms part of the Republic of Yemen.
9. Sir Richard Stafford Cripps (1889–1952) was a British statesman. A successful lawyer, he served British Parliament during 1930–50. He was on the extreme left of the Labour Party and helped found the Socialist League in 1932. After serving as Ambassador to Moscow (1940–42), he joined the British War Cabinet and led the Cripps Mission to India in 1942.
10. Albert Victor Alexander (1885–1965) was a British Labour politician. He was three times First Lord of the Admiralty, also during World War II, and then Minister of Defence under Clement Attlee. He was a member of the Cabinet Mission to India.
11. Kalat was a princely state located in the centre of the modern province of Baluchistan, Pakistan. The state capital was the town of Kalat.

12. Sir George Cunningham (1888–1964) was an administrator in British India. Cunningham served as Governor of the NWFP twice, once during the British Raj and later after the creation of Pakistan. A chapter of this book is dedicated to his eventful career.
13. The Indian National Congress was founded in 1885. Its leaders subsequently led the movement for Indian independence against British rule. After India's independence in 1947, it became the nation's dominant political party.
14. The Muslim League, founded in 1906 to safeguard the rights of Indian Muslims, led the movement calling for a separate Muslim nation to be created out of the partition of British India (1947).
15. West Pakistan was the western wing of Pakistan until 1971, when the eastern wing became independent as Bangladesh. The politically dominant western wing was composed of three Governors' provinces (the NWFP, Punjab and Sindh), one Chief Commissioner's province (Baluchistan), the Baluchistan States Union, several other princely states (notably Bahawalpur, Chitral, Dir, Hunza, Khairpur and Swat), the Federal Capital Territory (around Karachi) and Tribal Areas.
16. East Pakistan was a former province of Pakistan. Eastern Bengal chose to join Pakistan and became a province of Pakistan. East Bengal was renamed East Pakistan in 1955 and later became the independent country of Bangladesh after the bloody Bangladesh Liberation War of 1971.
17. Multan is a city in the Punjab province of Pakistan and is the headquarters of Multan district.
18. The Royal Pakistan Air Force (RPAF) was formed in 1947 following the partition of India and with it, the partition of the Royal Indian Air Force. The RPAF allegedly never received all the planes it was allotted at the time of partition of the subcontinent. It started with seven operational airbases scattered all over the provinces. The prefix 'royal' was removed when Pakistan gained the status of a republic on 23 March 1956. It has since been called the Pakistan Air Force (PAF).
19. Lieutenant General Sir A. Nye (Madras) to Mountbatten; r/3/1/152: ft. IB-3, 2 May 1947, *The Transfer of Power 1942–7*, HMSO 197–83, 1947 Vol., X pp.558–61.
20. Ibid.
21. Ibid.
22. Krishna Menon to Mountbatten, Mountbatten Papers, Demi-official

Correspondence Files: Krishna Menon; 14 June 1947, *The Transfer of Power*, Vol. XI, pp.390–91.
23. The Labour Party has been Britain's major democratic socialist party since the early twentieth century.
24. Krishna Menon to Mountbatten, Mountbatten Papers, Demi-official Correspondence Files: Krishna Menon; 14 June 1947, *The Transfer of Power*, Vol. XI, pp.390–91.
25. Around the Arabian Sea, it is about 990 km long and contains the island kingdom of Bahrain and is bordered by Iran, the United Arab Emirates, Oman, Saudi Arabia, Qatar, Kuwait and Iraq. It has long been a maritime trade route between the Middle East and South Asia; its modern economy is dominated by petroleum production. It gained added strategic significance after the discovery of oil in the Gulf states in the 1930s.
26. Possibility of Indian and Pakistani Cooperation in the Defence of the Canal Zone–Pritchard to the Prime Minister, London, undated FO 371/92876, PRO.
27. 'The Strategic and Political Importance of Pakistan in the Event of War with the USSR', prepared by Advisor to Nawab of Bhopal, Enclosure to Despatch No. 591, 29 May 1948, from Harward Donovan to Secretary of State, New Delhi, 845f.00/S-2948, Box 6014, Decimal files, Department of State, National Archives, Washington D.C.
28. Clement Richard Attlee (3 January 1883 to 8 October 1967) was a British politician who served as Prime Minister of the United Kingdom from 1945 to 1951 and leader of the Labour Party from 1935 to 1955. He served as Deputy Prime Minister under Winston Churchill in the wartime coalition government, before leading the Labour Party to a landslide election victory over Churchill in the 1945 general elections. His government presided over the decolonization of a large part of the British empire, a process by which India and the countries that are now Myanmar, Sri Lanka, Pakistan, Bangladesh, Jordan and Israel obtained independence.
29. The status, prior to 1939, of each of the British Commonwealth countries of Canada, Australia, New Zealand, the Union of South Africa, Eire and Newfoundland. Although there was no formal definition of Dominion status, a pronouncement by the Imperial Conference of 1926 described Great Britain and the Dominions as 'autonomous communities within the British empire, equal in status, in no way subordinate to another in any

aspect of their domestic or external affairs, though united by a common allegiance to the Crown and freely associated as members of the British Commonwealth of nations'.
30. The British Indian Army, officially called simply the Indian Army, was the army in India during the British Raj (1858–1947). The Indian Army also served in other areas during the World Wars. The term 'Indian Army' was used to collectively describe the presidency armies, particularly after the Indian Mutiny. However, the first army officially raised as the 'Indian Army' was in 1895. In 1903 the Indian Army absorbed the three presidency armies (the Bengal Army, the Madras Army and the Bombay Army). Between 1903 and 1947, the army of India consisted of two separate entities: the Indian Army and the British Army in India. The former consisted of Indian Army regiments originating in India, while the latter were British Army regiments originating in the United Kingdom which were sent to India on a tour of duty.
31. Speech of 12 December 1946, Hansard.
32. Admiral of the Fleet Louis Francis Albert Victor Nicholas Mountbatten (1900–1970) was a British admiral and statesman and an uncle of Prince Philip, Duke of Edinburgh. He was the last Viceroy of the British Indian empire (1947) and the first Governor General of independent India (1947–48). From 1954 until 1959 he was the First Sea Lord, a position that had been held by his father, Prince Louis of Battenberg some forty years earlier. Mountbatten was assassinated by the Provisional Irish Republican Army (IRA), which planted a bomb in his boat at Mullaghmore in the Republic of Ireland.
33. Puran Chand Joshi, one of the early leaders of the communist movement in India along with S.A. Dange and G.V. Ghate.
34. Ismay Papers iii 8/5A, cited by Philip Ziegler, *Mountbatten*, Collins, 1985.
35. Speech of 6 March 1947, Hansard.
36. Robert Anthony Eden (1897–1977) was a British Conservative politician who was Foreign Secretary as also Britain's Prime Minister.
37. John Anderson (1882–1958) was a Scottish politician who served under Winston Churchill as Lord President of the Council, Chancellor of the Exchequer and Home Secretary.
38. Harold Macmillan (1894–1986) was a British Conservative politician and Prime Minister of the United Kingdom from 10 January 1957 to 18 October 1963.

39. Born in India, Lord Ismay returned to India in 1907 where he began a distinguished military career serving initially in the NWFP. At the outbreak of World War II in 1939, Lord Ismay was made Deputy Secretary to the British War Cabinet, becoming the Chief of Staff to Winston Churchill and later to Clement Attlee when he became Prime Minister in 1945. In 1947 he was made Chief of Staff to Lord Mountbatten in the negotiations for India's independence.
40. Alan Campbell-Johnson (1913–1998): *Mission with Mountbatten* (Hamish Hamilton Ltd., 1951) is the day-to-day record of his third assignment on Lord Mountbatten's staff, this time in a civilian capacity as Press Attache to India's last Viceroy and first constitutional Governor General.
41. Campbell-Johnson, *Mission with Mountbatten*, 8 July 1947, p.132.

## 2

## Convoyed through the Land of Insolence

WITH INDIA'S PARTITION in 1947, the British again drew an artificial frontier, creating Pakistan. The earlier manmade line, the Durand Line, was also their handiwork. At one time, British India's land boundary was the longest in the world, touching China, Siam, Tibet, Russia, Persia, Nepal and Afghanistan. To India's north and west, the frontier comprised a series of dividing lines, five in number, some factitious, others natural. For the greater part of its length, the Oxus river[1] runs between the erstwhile Soviet Republic and Afghanistan. Anglo-Russian commissions in the closing decades of the nineteenth century resulted in this demarcation. A second perimeter is the Hindu Kush range. The third, fabricated by the British, is the Durand Line, that ran (still does) close to the Hindu Kush. It was drawn arbitrarily in the 1890s. East of the Durand Line lies the fourth border that once formed the contour of British India. This was separated from the Durand Line by a belt of country some 50 to 100 miles wide—a strip that was part of India, though not British India. And then there was the fifth and the last, corresponding to the other four, the line of the Indus river.

It was through these striations that invaders, from Alexander in 327–26 BC to Nadir Shah[2] in AD 1738–39 made their eastward march to reach the Indus and then India. The earliest contact with the Greeks was made when a group of Indian soldiers in the army of Xerxes invaded Greece. Xerxes, the son of Darius of Persia (ruler of the Achaemenid empire), had led the siege westward towards Greece in 480 BC. Within a century and a half of this invasion, Alexander, a Greek, had conquered Persia. It was upon his return from a campaign in Russian Turkestan[3] that Alexander crossed the Hindu Kush (327 BC).

After securing the Kabul[4] valley, he set out to annex the territory west of the Indus, thus asserting sovereignty over the Persian Empire where the Achaemenid influence had considerably weakened. The sources for this Macedonian invasion across the Hindu Kush are accounts left behind by Arrian Flavius, Quintus Curtius Rufus, Plutarch and Strabo. When Alexander began the invasion, his army was estimated at 1,20,000 men with an actual fighting force of 40,000, not all of whom were Macedonians. Alexander was to spend the entire winter of 327–26 BC fighting the tribes of Malakand[5] and Swat.[6]

Sir Aurel Stein, the explorer, set out in 1926, on his fourth expedition (having earlier embarked on three in 1904, 1906 and 1921), to trace the route of Alexander's[7] campaign in Swat. It was upper Swat that first witnessed Alexander's military offensive before Punjab was invaded. The most celebrated of his exploits in Swat was the siege of the mountain fortress of Aornos. The 1926 expedition of Stein was a search for this location.

Between the Hindu Kush and the open plains of Peshawar[8] lies the valley of Swat which extends along the river of the same name, a tributary of the Indus to the west. Swat in ancient times was known as 'Udyana'. It had once been a seat of Buddhist culture, replete with fine Graeco-Buddhist relics, vandalized, quarried and subsequently taken away from the ruined Buddhist shrines. The region figures prominently in the accounts of a number of Chinese pilgrims, beginning with Fa-Hsien (AD 400) and Hsuan-tsang, affirming the prominence this region was accorded in the Buddhist era.

Alexander came down the Kabul River to Peshawar valley and proceeded along the Kunar River to enter the Bajaur[9] territory. The Guraios river which the Macedonians crossed before Alexander led them to attack the Assakenois (people of Swat) is the same as the Panjkora river that divides Bajaur from Swat. Crossing the Swat valley during his 1926 expedition, Stein arrived at the hill of Birkot, an isolated rocky feature and a conspicuous landmark in the valley. On it was an imposing wall of stone slabs 50 feet high. Stein found this area in ruins, covered with pre-Islamic relics. The value of Birkot as a safe place was greatly enhanced by the assured supply of water. As long as the hilltop was defended, the enemy could not cut off its access to the river. Plenty of coins were found on the top and slopes of Birkot belonging to the times of the Greek rulers of Bactria[10] and the Indo-Scythian kings.

After crossing the Guraios River, Alexander entered the country of the powerful Assakenois. Instead of taking Alexander head on, the Assekenois dispersed their forces into several of their fortified towns, of which quite a few situated in the main Swat valley were successfully besieged by Alexander. The important town of Massaga, which Alexander first laid siege to, was situated in lower Swat. However, as Arrian does not furnish its definite topographical coordinates, the exact site of Massaga is difficult to locate. After capturing Massaga, Alexander despatched his forces to capture Bazira and invest Ora. When news of the slaughter at Ora reached Bazira, its people abandoned the town and took refuge along with other Assakenois in the rock fortress of Aornos. Stein identified the town of Birkot as the ancient stronghold town of Bazira. According to him, Birkot's natural strength fit Arrian's description of Bazira.

A short half-day march up the Swat valley brought Stein to a large habitation called Udaygram. In Arrian's account *The Anabasis of Alexander*, the town of Ora lay at a higher elevation than Bazira, up the main Swat valley. Stein believed Udaygram to be the place where the old town of Ora had earlier existed. Arrian also tells us that after abandoning the town of Bazira and some other boroughs, the Assakenois fled to Aornos, described by Arrian as a mighty mass of impregnable rock. Having established Macedonian garrisons at Massaga, Bazira and Ora, Alexander proceeded towards the Peshawar valley and thereafter headed east to the Indus to conquer Aornos instead of directly pursuing the Assakenois to their mountain refuge. A large part of his army had already preceded him into the Peshawar valley down the Kabul River. There, he set about organizing Macedonian control over the area before undertaking the eastward march towards the Indus. Arrian does not explicitly tell us that Aornos was situated on the right bank of the Indus, but the narrative of Curtius points to this distinct possibility. The main Swat valley had already been occupied by Macedonian posts, closing the option for the Assakenois to escape south or west. No safe refuge was available in the north, primarily because of severe winters and insufficient local resources on such high grounds. Conditions, however, were far more favourable for a retreat towards the east. The Assakenois sought help from the region of Hazara. They retreated, therefore, from the upper Swat valley towards the Indus. Alexander, for strategic reasons, proceeded south to the Peshawar valley before attacking Aornos. Once his hold was consolidated, he moved up the Indus and attacked the Assakenois as he was now in a position to simultaneously command the resources of the valley of the Indus and the broad plains of Peshawar. Besides, he also had the advantage of cutting the Assakenois off from a retreat to the east of the Indus and from such assistance as Abisares, the ruler of Hazara, might offer.

Aurel Stein's search for Aornos brought him to the Ghorband valley where he identified a raised feature, at an elevation of over 8,000 feet, as Aornos. Ptolemy, son of Lagos, one of Alexander's trusted generals (whom Arrian claims as his chief source), played an important role in the victory at Aornos. After securing towns on the Indus, Alexander reached Ambolima (Amb) to lay seige to Aornos. With a few select men, he thereafter attempted to reach the 'rocks', some 6,000 feet high. He sent Ptolemy to clear the path for a final assault. Though Ptolemy secured the position, it was only after much hard fighting on a steep ascent that Alexander could reach him. There was a deep ravine that divided the Macedonian position from the 'rocks'. Alexander directed a mound to be constructed across the ravine so that catapults and siege engines could be brought within range. According to Curtius, after seven days and nights of toil, the Assakenois, struck by the audacity of the Macedonians, abandoned resistance and started negotiations for surrender, which devolved into retreat and a rout for them. Alexander thus became the master of the 'rocks'. Historians like Diodorus and Curtius agree with Arrian on most points of the record of the capture of Aornos. After its capture, Arrian informs us that Alexander built a fortified post on the spur of Aornos. Stein found signs of a ruined fort at the spot. The capture of Aornos brought Alexander's campaign in the NWFP to an end. Alexander's invasion of Punjab has long fascinated popular imagination but in sheer physical terms, his success at Aornos provides a much better proof of his genius.

Chandragupta Maurya (320–298 BC), founder of the Mauryan empire, was the only Indian whose empire had secured its frontiers up to the Hindu Kush. Following Alexander's death, he managed to drive out the established Greek garrisons of north India, forcing them to surrender all control between the Indus and the Hindu Kush. The other great indigenous Indian empire, that of the Guptas, failed to push its boundaries so far into the north.

It suited the British to look for a certain pattern in the history of this region. Conveniently, they portrayed the conquest of western Punjab by the Persians in the sixth century BC and the crossing of the Hindu Kush by the Greeks under Demetrius in 184 BC as instances of India's invasion. Drawing on this analogy, they always emphasized that the Greek element in those invading forces was not so large; that in their method of governance, the ruling class consisted of a small body of foreigners. The Greek invasion came at a time when the fractured Mauryan empire had left northern India without a master. The empire of Demetrius did not last long. His involvement in India weakened his control north of the Hindu Kush. He had to return soon to Bactria to contend with revolts and rebellions, possibly in 168 BC. Unlike the British, the Greeks could not replenish their stocks; nor were they able to rely on support from their homeland. They were cut off from Europe, first by the Parthian[11] invasion of Persia and then from Bactria by the Saka penetration to Gandhara (Peshawar) and Kophene (Kabul).[12] Weakened, Greek rule in India ended somewhere between 141 and 128 BC. What overwhelmed it was the southern movement of the Sakas[13] and then of the Kushans.[14] Of the Yue-chi confederation, the Kushans first established themselves in Bactria and then, crossing the Oxus and other natural frontiers, descended on north India. The Kushan rule in North India lasted three hundred years, and was finally extinguished by the invasion of the Huns[15] in the fifth century AD.

According to standard British historiography, we now come to the period of the Arab invasion. Hazrat Mohammad, the founder of Islam, died in AD 632. Eight years after his death, the Arab Islamic armies had overrun Syria and Egypt, and within seventy years of it, North Africa and Spain. In the east, Persia was invaded in AD 637 and the whole of it, up to Herat,[16] lay annexed to the Arab empire in little over a decade by AD 650. Its northern frontiers would soon touch the Oxus. A hundred years after Mohammad's demise, the Arabs were knocking at the doors of central Europe. However, what is a little known fact is that it took four centuries and several failed attempts for the Arabs to make successful inroads into India.

The territory on both sides of the Durand Line has remained Muslim for over a millennium now. It is commonly believed that Islam arrived in India via Sind in the eighth century with Muhammad bin Qasim (late seventh or early eighth century AD), Mahmud of Ghazni (late tenth to early eleventh century AD) and Muhammad Ghori (1162–1206) proving to be the inceptors. The truth is that the first Arab invasion of North India took place during the caliphate of Mu'awiyah in AD 664–65. The two kingdoms of Kabul and Zabul valiantly withstood the Arab onslaughts. Kabul then comprised its river valley extending up to the Hindu Kush. The kingdom included the present areas of Lamghan, Jalalabad,[17] Peshawar and Charsadda in the south, bordering Kashmir in the north and Persia in the west. The kingdom of Zabul lay to the south of Kabul and north of Baluchistan (Gedrosia), and included the upper valley of the Helmand river with Seistan forming a part of this kingdom. In the seventh century AD, these two kingdoms were politically and culturally part of India, being Indian in language, literature and religion. In their efforts throughout the seventh century to subdue Kabul and Zabul, the Arabs gained notable successes but suffered serious reverses too. The Arabs soon realized that permanent conquest of these territories was beyond their power. They were, therefore, content merely to impose suzerainty over the area, but even this was achieved with difficulty and that too, for a very brief period (AD 700–14). For the next century and a half, Kabul and Zabul maintained their authority practically unimpaired.

Ahmad Ibn Yahya al Baladhuri's (a ninth-century Persian historian) *Kitab Futūh al-Buldan* is considered a major source for information on the Arab inroads into Sind, the Middle East and Transoxiana. In one of its chapters on Futuh al-Sind, he mentions: 'al-Muhallab-bin Abi Sufrah fought on this [the Indian] frontier in the days of Mu'awiyah in the year 44 (AD 664–65) and came up to Bannah and al-Ahwaz, which two places are between al-Multan and Kabul. He was met here by hostile forces whom he and his army fought.' It is also said in that chapter that the 'tribe of Al-Azd proved themselves to be the best troops of al-Muhallab on the night they raided Bannah'. Bannah has been identified with present-day Bannu[18] and Al-Ahwaz as al-Ahwar or Lahore.[19] Al-Ahwar of yesteryear is not the same at Lahore of today, as this city of Punjab is far too distant from the NWFP, the scene of the early Arab invasion. Besides it may not have been called Lahore at that time.

There is another Lahor that overlooks the banks of the upper Indus. About the Lahor of al-Baladhuri, Sir Olaf Caroe[20] says:

> There can be no doubt...that the reference is to the site near the present village of Lahor, in the neighbourhood of Hund in the Yusufzai[21] Samah of Peshawar...this surely is the place to be equated with this early Arab raid. It can be described as lying on one road from Kabul to Multan[22] via the Peshawar valley. I think it very possible also that this Lahor, and not the Punjab city, was the one mentioned by Farishta in the introduction to his history as the capital of Jaipal, the Hindushahaiya ruler.

This ancient Lahor was so situated that no aggressor with designs on 'Hindustan could miss it in those early days when the Indus was not bridged at Attock.'[23]

Alexander, on his way to India crossed the Indus at the same place. The spot is marked, on the river's western bank, by the ruins of the four-square fort of Hund. The surviving fortifications do not date from Alexander's time, but there is little doubt that there was always 'a fort here till Akbar put the present one out of commission by building his fortress at Attock.'[24]

No less an authority than al-Biruni himself testifies to the fact of a fortress of Lahor on the upper Indus. The Bannah of al-Baladhuri is the present-day Bannu of the NWFP, and an 'alluring oasis in the otherwise inhospitable, bleak and barren surrounding.'[25] Sir Olaf Caroe has also equated Bannah with Bannu. The importance of Bannah and Lahor lay in their strategic value as one of the main gateways to the Indo-Gangetic plains. It was here that the two most important land routes, the Peshawar valley–Kohat and the Paiwar–Kurram routes, converged.[26] It was through Bannu that Fa-hien entered India in the beginning of the fifth century AD. At the turn of the fourteenth century, Timurlane[27] invaded India through the Paiwar–Kurram route and passed through the Bannu valley. A century later, Bannu's fertile valley attracted the Mughal emperor, Babur,[28] who stayed there for some time on his way to the conquest of the Indian subcontinent.

Though al-Baladhuri's description is brief and sketchy, one may perhaps still infer that Muhallab attacked Lahor and Bannah, two distant places, at the same time. But if so, why? And why did his Indian campaign fail? A study of the military campaigns waged during the Umayyad days shows that the 'pincer movement' was the favourite military manoeuvre of their generals. The military campaigns of Muhallab were a culmination of big converging movements. Starting from Faras (Persia) by way of Kerman, he had initiated two operations: one, from the north through Nishapur to Herat, Merv and Balkh[29] (Bactria); the other in the southerly direction, by way of Sijistan (Sistan), to the Helmand and Bust (near modern Kandahar). Sir Olaf Caroe was of the view that Muhallab's Indian campaign, or raids as he calls them, were part of the southern operations. This also explains why a simultaneous attack was made on Lahor in the north and Bannu in the south of the Pathan territory. Probably the converging point was Multan, a great centre of Buddhist power in northern India at that time. But the stout resistance of the Pathans blunted the sharp edge of the Arab pincers.

Of the land routes, the Khyber Pass[30] was guarded by Kabul and Zabul while the Bolan Pass[31] was protected by the Jats. The Arabs had initially futilely endeavoured to enter India through these two great passes. The hardy hillmen of these regions, backed by the natural advantages of their hill country, offered stubborn resistance to the conquerors of the world, the Arabs. Even if defeated, they always refused to yield. Despite three centuries of unrelenting efforts by the Arabs one finds their dominion in India confined to the two petty states of Mansura and Multan. Compared to their spectacular military successes in other parts of the world, the comparatively insignificant results the Arabs achieved in India stand out in marked contrast. The cause for it does not lie in the religious or social peculiarities of India. The reason is undoubtedly the superior military strength and state organization of the Indians as compared to most other nations of the time.

It was not until AD 870 that both Kabul and Zabul were conquered by Yakub-ibn-Layth (AD 840–79), the founder of the Saffarid dynasty who was once a brigand in Seistan and ultimately became the ruler of Persia and the neighbouring regions in the east. Kabul may have regained independence to form part of the Hindu Shahaiya kingdom. The courageous resistance of the tiny states of Kabul and Zabul against the Arabs is yet to acquire its due place in India's history. They defied the conquerors of the world and ultimately succumbed not to the political power of the caliphate but to the local principalities. They carried on a prolonged and heroic resistance against Arab aggression for more than two hundred years before they ceased to belong to India either politically or culturally.

What had started during the caliphate of Mu'awiyah (AD 664–65), continued through the tenth century with the raids of Mir Qasim and Mahmud of Ghazni followed by Muhammad Ghori. Delhi came to be occupied by one foreign dynasty after another. The final conquest of northern India via these natural frontiers took place in 1526 by Babur. Though others like Nadir Shah and Ahmed Shah Abdali came to India by the same route, they did not establish themselves permanently in the country east of the Indus as the Mughals did.

Babur, the Barlas Chagatai Turk and founder of India's Mughal dynasty, hailed from Farghana in Turkestan. Strong on lineage, he took his ancestry from Ghenghis Khan and Timurlane. But why were he and his successors called the Mughals? Perhaps, the appellation 'Mughal' instilled fear. It meant much then, for the name brought to memory a historical recollection inspiring awe born of fear. By the time he was twenty, Babur was in possession of Kabul and Bactria. A descendant of Timurlane, he displayed a natural proclivity towards India. His efforts at dislodging the Ghilzai Afghan tribe that ruled Delhi did not initially prove successful. However, in December 1525, Babur did cross the Indus to ride into India and meet the Indianized Afghan (Pathan) Ibrahim Lodi on the fields of Panipat. Fifteen thousand Rohillas[32] fell in the battle. On 10 May 1526, Babur was proclaimed the emperor of India at Delhi.

This 'land of the insolent, NWFP and Afghanistan, has been inhabited by Pathans and Afghans who have long dwelt on India's western frontiers, their territories intersected by the Durand Line. Though they occupy a far larger area in Afghanistan, their population density is much higher in Pakistan. There was no Afghanistan before Ahmad Shah Abdali founded it. The territory of today's Afghanistan, then, was divided between the Persian and Mughal empires. This arrangement, having endured for more than two centuries, caused people inhabiting the western Afghan territories to Persianize. The Persian language became preferable to Pashtu in Kabul. The eastern Afghans, on the other hand, developed a bias towards Delhi over which they ruled thrice before the Mughals established themselves in India. The eastern Afghans retained Pashtu as their language. The Persian appellation 'Afghan' applies to the western tribes while Pathan, a Pakhtun appellation, is used for the eastern tribes. The Pakhtuns also consider themselves to be of a much older and indigenous stock. Distinct from the Pakhtuns of the hills, the Afghans of the open plains are considered to have descended from a mixed Turko-Iranian strain. They also differ in their dialect. The heartland of the Pathans is an area of which Thal, on the Kurram river, is the nodal point. These are the hill tribes that include the Afridis, Orakzais, Khattaks, Wazirs and Mahsuds. They are interposed between the Persianized Durranis and the Ghilzai Afghans to the west and the Peshawar tribes, Yusufzais and Mohmands[33] to the east. The terms Pathan and Afghan have been used interchangeably in this book, unless it is specifically required to distinguish the two.

Afghan or Pathan traits have since been variously described. The famous lines of despair spoken by a British soldier in Rudyard Kipling's writing provide one such description:

> When you're wounded and left on Afghanistan's plains,
> An' the women come out to cut up what remains,
> Jest roll to your rifle an' blow out your brains
> An' go to your Gawd like a soldier.

Theodore Pennel,[34] a nineteenth-century British missionary, also describes Afghan traits: 'The Afghan character is a strange medley of contradictions, qualities in which courage blends with stealth, the basest treachery with the most touching fidelity, intense religious fanaticism with an avarice which will even induce him to play false to his faith.'

There are about twenty million Pakhtuns in Afghanistan and Pakistan, together making for the largest tribal confederacy. Maintaining tribal unity for such huge numbers is naturally difficult. A Yusufzai Pakhtun from Swat and northern Pakistan is very different from his

Wazir cousin in the south. A Durrani from western Afghanistan would be ill at ease with the Afridis of Khyber.

During the seventeenth and eighteenth centuries, empire building was largely in the hands of the Persians to the west and the Mughals based in Delhi to the east. While some western Pakhtun tribes fought alongside the Safavid rulers of Persia against the Mughals, others could be found in Mughal armies fighting fellow Pakhtuns to regain territories around Kandahar[35] and present-day eastern Afghanistan. A few of them stayed neutral. Early enough, the Mughals discovered an expedient method of controlling the unruly Pakhtun areas by paying subsidies to the tribes rather than subjugating them militarily. However, even vast amounts paid by Aurangzeb could not guarantee peace. In the later part of Aurangzeb's reign, there was a considerable Pakhtun threat to his empire. This was an era of Pakhtun glory, recounted with much pride by Khushal Khan Khattak,[36] a seventeenth-century tribal chief. The Khattaks, his tribe, were eastern Pakhtuns, a formidable force and of considerable importance to the Mughals. They lived to the east and south of Peshawar, guarding the Mughals from the north-west. Like his forefathers, Khushal Khan first accepted Mughal wealth in return for protecting the roads between Attock and Peshawar. His forces fought for the Mughal emperor Shah Jahan in Turkistan and Badakhshan. Khushal Khan continued to support Aurangzeb, but for reasons not entirely clear, he was arrested and imprisoned by Aurangzeb, with disastrous results for the Mughals. Nearly five years after his arrest and on his release from prison in 1668, Khushal Khan led a successful tribal rebellion against the Mughals. In 1674, Aurangzeb had to personally intervene to crush the Pakhtun opposition, but Khushal Khan Khattak continued to defy the Mughals for the rest of his life.

The Pakhtun tribal organization was never made for unity. This was as true in the eighteenth century as it is today. Of the two larger Pakhtun tribes, the Ghilzai and the Abdali, the Ghilzais[37] registered many military successes against the Mughals but could never control areas they conquered. It was not a Pakhtun but an Afshar chief of a Turkish tribe in Persia, who took advantage of the weakening Mughal empire. This Afshar Turk, Nadir Shah, secured the throne of Persia by driving out the Afghans who had dominated the Persians. He then marched towards what is the Afghanistan of today and appeared at

Kabul, and thence proceeded to invade India via the Khyber Pass and adjoining routes. The throne of Delhi was tottering. The Mughals had been involved in a struggle with the Marathas. The loss of Kabul was accepted philosophically by the Mughals. Even after Nadir Shah crossed the Indus; only ineffective steps were taken to stop him. An army of Persian Turks, Afghan mercenaries and young Rohillas advanced leisurely to Delhi. There was no one to stop Nadir Shah.

In February 1739, Nadir Shah entered Delhi, to be received outside the city by the Mughals. Nadir Shah was to take away enormous booty and the famous Peacock Throne of the Mughals. A rumour that Nadir Shah was dead started a riot in Delhi. The city was sacked for three days by the Persians and its citizens massacred. At the end, Nadir Shah restored the throne of Delhi to his 'brother Turk', as he called the Mughal Mohammad Shah, though he left him with empty pockets, the graves of the dead and piles of heads in the capital to mourn. Nadir Shah also forced his 'brother Turk' to submit and agree to the annexation of Afghanistan, including Sind, Multan and the districts of Punjab near the Indus, by Persia.

Nadir Shah was murdered in 1747. One of his Afghan commanders founded an Afghan kingdom for the first time, a kingdom separate from India. The money and force at his disposal helped his fellow men choose him as the new ruler though his clan, the Saduzai, was not very important. To the Afghans or Abdalis he gave the name Durrani, 'The People of the Pearl', calling himself Dur-i-duran, 'Pearl of Pearls'. He turned the provinces that Nadir Shah had wrested from the Mughals into a Durrani empire. It included Sind, Multan, Peshawar, Hazara, Kashmir, Kandahar, Kabul and Ghazni,[38] and land on the far side of the Hindu Kush—Balkh, Oxus and even beyond.

Twice as big as France though it was, this territory was not enough for him. He made numerous attempts to cross the Indus into India and the Mughals were quite unable to resist. Ahmad Shah arrived near Delhi and fought the Third Battle of Panipat (1761).[39] The Maratha cavalry along with the remnant Mughals had assembled in opposition to meet Ahmad Shah. For some weeks the armies lay watching each other, and then hunger compelled the Marathas to leave their entrenched camp. A desperate battle followed in which the Marathas were routed.

The news of the Afghan victory at Panipat swept through India mostly through informed channels, particularly through the bankers' network, the cryptic content of it being, 'Two pearls of great price have been dissolved, twelve gold mohrs have been lost, and the silver and copper cannot be cast up.'[39] The story of this tragedy has been sung in the famous ballad, 'With Scindia to Delhi', by Rudyard Kipling. He wrote of the great battle of Panipat in 1890. The ballad tells the story of an Indian Maratha prince having ridden 50 miles after the day was lost with a beggar girl who loved him and followed him in all his camps on his saddle-bow. The prince lost the girl almost within sight of safety. Kipling had a Maratha trooper tell the story:

> Thrice thirty thousand men were we before the mists had cleared,
> The low white mists of morning heard the war-conch scream and bray;
> We called upon Bhowani and we gripped them by the beard,
> We rolled upon them like a flood and washed their ranks away.
> The children of the hills of Khost before our lances ran,
> We drove the black Rohillas back as cattle to the pen; 'Twas then we needed Mulhar Rao to end what we began,
> A thousand men had saved the charge; he fled the field with ten!
> ....
> I saw it fall in smoke and fire, the banner of the Bhao;
> I heard a voice across the press of one who called in vain:–
> 'Ho! Anand Rao Nimbalkhur, ride! Get aid of Mulhar Rao! Go shame his squadrons into fight–the Bhao–the Bhao is slain!'
> Now in that hour strength left my lord; he wrenched his mare aside;
> He bound the girl behind him and we slashed and struggled free.
> Across the reeling wreck of strife we rode as shadows ride
> From Paniput to Delhi town, but not alone were we.
> The wreath of banquet overnight lay withered on the neck,
> Our hands and scarfs were saffron-dyed for signal of despair,
> When we went forth to Paniput to battle with the Mlech, –
> Ere we came back from Panipat and left a kingdom there.

Ahmad Shah, the Durrani emperor, placed the Mughal, Ali Jauhar, with the famous title of Shah Alam,[40] back on the throne (no longer the peacock one), and fixed his frontier as far south as the Sutlej river,[41] where the British found it forty years later. Ahmad Shah died in 1773, not before he had returned to India several times trying to preserve Punjab from the rising power of the Sikhs. Timur Shah, his son, reigned on his prestige somewhat ineffectively till 1793, to be succeeded by his grandson, Shah Zaman. By now, Mughal and Pathan India was pressed on all sides by the Marathas, Sikhs and the British. The curtains had come down on one era with the dawn of another.

The arrival of Mountstuart Elphinstone[42] in Peshawar in February 1809 marked the first tentative British official involvement with India's NWFP and Afghanistan. This was necessitated because of the British apprehension that the French were attempting to forge alliances with the Ottomans and Persia to invade India. They feared Napoleon was entertaining visions of an eastern conquest. In 1808, the British in India sent a mission to Persia seeking to deter it from a French alliance. The mission failed. The head of the British mission found it impossible to seek an audience with the Shah of Persia. The alarm grew; panic seized the British as they planned a series of missions to Sind, Lahore and Kabul. The one that was sent to the kingdom of Kabul was headed by Elphinstone and had a contingent of four hundred soldiers. Peshawar was the winter town of the kingdom of Kabul. Elphinstone's brief was to forestall the French in Afghanistan in case they succeeded in Persia. He was to persuade the Amir of Kabul to a defensive alliance against a likely French invasion, and in the event of a French success, form a joint Anglo-Afghan defence of India, quite a far-fetched idea then.

The British knew little of the polity and geography of this region. In fact, they knew next to nothing of the country in between Persia and the British dominions in India. Since the death of Ahmad Shah Abdali, civil wars in Afghanistan were a common occurrence. Ranjit Singh's rise to power in Punjab had further muddled the politics of the frontier. When Elphinstone had set out, he did not even know where Shah Shuja,[43] the Amir of Afghanistan, was, and in what situation.

At the time the French General Gardanne[44] visited Persia in 1908, it seemed that the French intended to cross over into Asia. It was thought expedient then by the British government in India to send a mission to the king of Kabul. As the court of Kabul was known to be haughty, and to entertain a mean opinion of the European nations, it was decided that the Elphinston's mission should impress the Afghans with its 'great magnificence'.[45] With all preparations made at Delhi, the mission left on 13 October 1808.

The king of Kabul had always provided a sympathetic ear to those disaffected in India. Tipu Sultan,[46] Vazir Ali or the Marathas who had quarrelled with the British would usually confer with him. Uneasy of this British initiative, Ranjit Singh (1780–1839)[47] of Punjab contrived to dissuade the Amir of Kabul from entertaining this mission. The potentates of Sind and Multan along with Durrani overlords were averse to this alliance too. The Amir himself believed that the British would take advantage of the prevailing situation of disunity in the region. But he succumbed to the lure of 'magnificent presents', and allowed the British mission to be received in his court. Elphinstone was accorded a great reception at Peshawar. Eager to make an impression, the Amir ordered breakfast, lunch and dinner for over two thousand people, plus provisions for the mission's horses and elephants. It was with some difficulty and after considerable time that Elphinstone could convince the Amir 'to dispense with this expensive proof of his hospitality'.

Confusion over protocol prevented Elphinstone from calling on the Amir. But when the opportunity came, what shocked Elphinstone was the 'meanness and rapacity of the officers, who received charge of the presents.'[48] Even the camels on which those presents were brought were seized: 'They stripped the elephant's mahouts of their livery and gravely insisted that two English servants who were sent to put up the lustres, were part of the present.'[49] Shah Shuja had claimed the Amirship from his half-brother Shah Mahmood after deposing him. A minor rebellion mounted by Shah Mahmood had just been quelled before Elphinstone arrived. Feeling safe, Shah Shuja tried to reclaim Kashmir that had fallen in the hands of rebels. Within days of Elphinstone's arrival in Peshawar, news had arrived of the capture of Kandahar by the Shah's deposed brother. For the Amir, the Kashmir compaign did not yield the expected results. Intelligence was received on 23 April of the defeat and destruction of his army. Reports also arrived of the capture of Kabul, and the immediate advance of the enemy towards Peshawar.[50]

The situation becames untenable for Elphinstone when a Hindu, on his way to Kabul, was accosted in the passes. A rumour spread through Peshawar that he was Elphinstone's messenger tasked with a message for Shah Mahmood, 'begging him to push on to Peshawar and engage for the capture of the Balla Hissar, and the seizure of Shah Shuja'.[51] This gave rise to another story that the Amir was soon to allow the plunder of Elphinstone's retinue.

Perforce, Elphinstone had to retire further east of Peshawar for safety. Simultaneously, he also got orders for recall in the month of June 1809. His passage back entailed tough negotiations through the Sikh territories of Ranjit Singh. He was soon to hear of Shah Shuja's defeat on 4 July. His mission had failed and nothing tangible was achieved.

The mission was the first in a series of wrong assessments made by the British about the nature of Afghan politics. Though experienced in Persian and Indian affairs, Elphinstone lacked a proper understanding of Afghan tribal rivalries. Shah Shuja's friendship was born of desperation. He needed Britain as an ally in the continuing family and tribal feuds inherited from his father. It did not take long for Elphinstone to understand that an alliance would be futile in the face of continued strife in Afghanistan. While in Peshawar, he came to realize that like Ahmad Shah before him, Shah Shuja depended on a council of tribal chiefs, a *jirga*,[52] which, in turn, had a far from complete control over its tribesmen. The Amir could never expect complete submission from such independent-minded tribesmen. Elphinstone saw in 1809 what later generations of English politicians refused to accept: that control over the Pakhtuns could only be achieved if the tribesmen themselves wanted it.

Elphinstone got his paper alliance with Shah Shuja, but before he could reach British India, the Shah had lost his kingdom. Elphinstone saw no point in attempting to reach an alliance with Mahmud, the new Shah installed on the throne of Kabul. He returned to India to become the Governor of Bombay.

While Elphinstone moved to Bombay, Shah Shuja, with the help of the eastern Pakhtun tribes, made abortive attempts to regain his throne from Mahmud, who was in the process of losing all the Afghan lands east of the Indus to the Sikhs, under the leadership of Ranjit Singh. Taking advantage of the unstable situation in the region, Ranjit Singh united the various Sikh clans to establish one Sikh kingdom. Multan and Kashmir became Sikh territories. By 1820, even Peshawar fell to the Sikhs. This was followed by years of warfare between the Sikhs and Afghans for retention and capture of territory. The British intervened to end the strife at the Punjab border. Sir Mortimer Durand's poem 'Attar Singh' is a fine tribute to Sikh soldiery (Annexure). Shah Shuja, no more the ruler of Afghanistan, Ranjit Singh, the Maharaja of Lahore, and the British signed a tripartite treaty in Simla. In return for a friendly settlement on all outstanding disagreements between the three parties, Shah Shuja was to be restored to the 'throne of his fathers'.

### The Army of the Indus

It was the greatest disaster to afflict a British army (the Army of the Indus) in Asia. Hundred years hence, in 1942, another British army suffered a similar humiliation when Singapore capitulated. Sita Ram Pandey, a havaldar recruited in Shah Shuja's levy, participated in the Kabul campaign of the Army of the Indus. This British offensive was intended to restore Shah Shuja to the throne of Kabul. Havaldar Sita Ram Pandey[53] who retired as a subedar[54] recounted in Awadhi[55] language the story of this operation. His account was later translated into English by Lieutenant Colonel James Thomas Norgate of his regiment. I draw extensively from this first-hand account in reconstructing events of the doomed expedition of the 'Army of Indus'.

People of those days seldom referred to the territory the Afghans occupied as 'Afghanistan'. To Indians that area constituted the kingdom of Kabul. Kandahar, Jalalabad and Ghazni were all part of this kingdom. The British had decided to assemble a force at Ferozepur in October 1938 for the Kabul campaign. The original plan called for a force of two divisions from the Bengal army[56] and one from the Bombay army. The combined force under Lieutenant General Sir Henry Fane, Commander-in-Chief of the Bengal army, was to cross the Indus and enter Afghanistan via the Bolan Pass in Baluchistan. But in the interim, news came of the withdrawal of the Persian army besieging Herat. As a result, the strength of the Bengal army was reduced to just one division. Sir Henry was withdrawn from the overall command and replaced by Lieutenant General Sir John Keane,[57] Commander-in-Chief of the Bombay army. Shah Shuja was encouraged to recruit his own levy. When fully raised, it consisted of some artillery, two cavalry and six infantry regiments. At one stage it was commanded by General Abraham Roberts,[58] father of the soon to be famous Field Marshal Earl Roberts. Shah Shuja's levy suffered a general lack of discipline and intermittent pay. Much of the cash provided by the East India Company[59] was siphoned off by Shah Shuja and his minions. It was in Shah Shuja's levy that Havaldar Sita Ram Pandey was offered an appointment with the promise of a higher pay. The combined Army of the Indus crossed the Bolan and Khojak Passes[60] to arrive in Kandahar on 26 April 1839. It soon became clear to Pandey that the Afghans had not really yearned for Shah Shuja's return. Nevertheless, Shah Shuja was formally restored to his throne on 8 May 1839 upon entering Kandahar. That Shah Shuja had come with a foreign army offended several tribal chiefs. 'Having been shown the way into their country, these chiefs worried that the 'English would soon take possession of it as they had done all of Hindustan'.[61]

The Army of the Indus halted for two months at Kandahar. In doing so it gave Dost Mohammad,[62] Shah Shuja's adversary, enough time to consolidate. When the army did finally march towards the fortified town of Ghazni that lay between Kandahar and Kabul, for some inexplicable reason General Keane did not carry his 'siege artillery' which he had insisted on carrying all the way from Ferozepur. Ghazni was a tough impreganable fort against which Keane's light horse artillery guns proved ineffective. However, timely information that the British should attack the weakly defended Kabul Gate of the Ghazni fort enabled them, after severe fighting, to capture the fortress town. Ghazni was stormed by an all-European party in the early hours of 23 July 1839. Shah Shuja's levy was not involved in the initial assault but Sita Ram Pandey did take part in subsequent fighting within the walled city. Robert Sale commanded the troops that went into the city after the Kabul Gate was taken over. Later in the campaign, Robert Sale also commanded a brigade and successfully defended Jalalabad. He was killed during the Sikh wars in 1845. His wife Florentine, who joined him in Kabul, was later taken prisoner by the Afghans during the disastrous retreat of the Indus Army. The record of her experiences published later as *A Journal of the Disasters*, is perhaps the best narrative of the disaster that the Army of the Indus came to face.

No resistance was offered when the army entered Kabul at 4 p.m. on 7 August 1839. Shah Shuja made a regal entry into his capital, mounted on a white Persian horse looking every bit a king. What was ominous was the complete absence of jubilation on part of the spectators; 'the silence at the time of his entry hung like a storm cloud as he rode into the fortress palace of the Amirs of Kabul, the Bala Hissar.[63, 64] As in Kandahar, the people of Kabul had not taken part in the rejoicing. The situation was compounded by a folly Shah Shuja committed. Those taken prisoner at Ghazni were executed at an 'open durbar' on Shah Shuja's orders. Among them were some leading Afghan chiefs. The cold-blooded massacre took place in full view of the British officers, arousing great indignation. Sir William Hay Macnaghten,[65] the British envoy to Shah Shuja and his firm supporter was greatly angered. Soon after Shah Shuja became the Amir of Kabul, the Afghans began to resent the British occupation of their territory. The fact that many Afghan patricians had befriended British officers did not escape Havaldar Sita Ram Pandey's attention. Many of their ladies would visit the British officers secretly. In all his simplicity, Sita Ram Pandey believed that the Afghan women liked the foreigners because they were fair. 'There is no comprehending the fancies of women. They may have been sent in the first place to try to gain some knowledge of the designs of the British. But it was common gossip that they preferred the sahibs to their own husbands.'[66] To quote Sukhdeoji, a close acquaintance of Sita Ram Pandey's: 'Women of low degree leave their husbands. This is the custom all over the world and has been so for ever. But these were not women of low caste; some were wives of the Sardars themselves and they did not desert their husbands.'[67] Since several eyewitnesses had referred to the affairs between British officers and the Afghan ladies, some credence may be attached to Sukhdeoji's comments. Sir Alexander Burnes,[68] Macnaghten's able assistant, conducted parleys with Afghan women. There were several others who followed Burnes's example and all this greatly added to the bitterness harboured by the Afghans against the British.

In November 1840, Dost Mohammad surrendered to Sir William

Macnaghten and was banished to Calcutta. But his son Akbar Khan remained in Afghanistan to challenge the British. Shah Shuja continued to offend the Afghan chiefs with his high-handed behaviour. He had perhaps some of the 'worst rogues'[69] of Afghanistan for his ministers. It escaped Sir William Macnaghten's attention that 'Afghans preferred Dost Mohammad to Shah Shuja'.[70] Burnes, who had earlier headed a mission to Kabul and met Dost Mohammad, remained unimpressed with Shah Shuja. Burnes did try to convince Lord Auckland, the Governor General, to support Dost Mohammad but was prevailed upon by Macnaghten to support Shah Shuja instead. The situation, meanwhile, continued to deteriorate. In the middle of 1841, the Government of India, in an effort to downsize its expenditure, withdrew subsidies to the tribes that controlled the passes leading to India. The tribes rose in revolt, with the uprising coinciding with Macnaghten's appointment as the new Governor of Bombay. It was anticipated that Burnes would succeed him as the new British envoy in Kabul.

On 2 November 1841, a mob in Kabul attacked Burnes's house. Burnes, his brother and another British officer were murdered. Some of the Afghans utterly detested Burnes as they held him responsible for the British occupation of their country and also for the reputation that he carried with Afghan women of genteel descent.

By this time, Major General William Elphinstone,[71] a Waterloo veteran, had come to hold command of the army in Kabul. His Brigadier was a 'one-armed Peninsular War veteran called Shelton',[72] whose regiment had arrived in Kabul after a tiring campaign in Arakan. Neither Shelton nor his regiment was well suited for the future ordeal and both he and his general were reluctant to put up a fight. Attempts to bolster their position failed as garrisons from Kandahar and Ghazni could not reach Kabul. When Macnaghten was treacherously murdered by the Afghans, a complete sense of resignation overtook the remaining officials. It was decided that the Army of the Indus would withdraw from Kabul. Unfortunately, the officers on the spot committed the mistake of relying on the Afghan chiefs for providing them a safe passage back. The Army of the Indus commenced its retreat from Kabul on 6 January 1842, less than 5,000 strong and accompanied by 12,500 non-combatants. By 13 January 1842, all but one, Dr William Brydon,[73] were either killed or captured. The famous picture by Lady

Butler, 'The Last of an Army', shows surgeon Dr William Brydon, on a broken-down pony riding into Jalalabad, and a few mounted men coming out to meet him. He was the only survivor of Elphinstone's brigade, a force of four battalions, guns and horses, save the captives and the slaves carried off to Central Asia and a few frostbitten Indians who eked out a miserable existence as crippled beggars in Kabul. Many of them had once been Rajput soldiers.

The shock to British prestige was great. Lord Ellenborough,[74] who succeeded Lord Auckland as India's Governor General, ordered an avenging army to be assembled under Major General Pollock.[75] It was weeks before the avenging army set forth to relieve Jalalabad. Shah Shuja was assassinated. Before long, Dost Mohammad was invited back and went with British blessings as the Amir of Kabul.

## Melancholic Reflection of Tribal Treachery

It was Lord Auckland, the Indian Viceroy, who decided to place the fate of 4,500 troops and 12,500 camp followers at Kabul in the hands of Major General William Elphinstone and Sir William Macnaghten. Robert Sale was sent in advance to clear the road of the rebels blocking the main access from Kabul to Khyber. He embarked on this enterprise leaving behind in Kabul his fifty-four-year-old wife Florentine Sale, his daughter, and son-in-law, hoping his wife would soon join him in Jalalabad. Events dictated otherwise.

Sir Robert was cut off from Kabul. After Macnaghten was killed, the Army of the Indus was forced to begin a retreat from Kabul, a retreat that turned into a disaster. Lady Sale, part of the contingent returning from Kabul and later taken prisoner, maintained a diary of events that became a primary source for all subsequent narratives of the tragic retreat. It was fortuitous that her diary survived:

> I believe several people kept an account of these proceedings but all except myself lost all they had written; and had recourse to memory afterwards. I lost everything except the clothes I wore; and therefore it may appear strange that I should have saved these papers. The mystery is, however, easily solved. After everything was packed on the night before we left Kabul, I sat up to add a few

lines to the events of the day, and the next morning I put them in a small bag and tied them round my waist.[76]

This diary propelled Lady Sale to such prominence in England that porcelains were designed to her image. Lt Vincent Eyre, another survivor of the catastrophic retreat, also wrote a detailed journal, most of it from memory. No surprise that Lady Sale and Vincent Eyre were bitter critics of the British policy in 1841. They had survived to tell their tale.

The withdrawing army was surrounded by upwards of 20,000 armed Pakhtuns. These tribesmen were never before in such an overwhelmingly strong position. Sanctioned by Islam and with every chance of glory, most Pakhtun leaders were uncontrollable. On 6 January 1842, the retreat began—a distance of 116 miles from Kabul to Jalalabad where General Robert Sale's garrison waited. The army and its followers marched in deep snow through treacherous passes, with practically no supplies, surrounded by a hostile enemy.

Lady Sale's diary contained a daily record of events, often recorded hourly. Eerie, prophetic and one that would haunt her for long, Lady Sale chanced upon this verse before leaving the cantonment:

> Few, few shall part where many meet,
> The snow shall be their winding sheet;
> And every turf beneath their feet
> Shall be a soldier's sepulcher.

Far from being 'a believer in presentiments',[77] this verse was never absent from her thoughts. The fears were sadly realized, her premonitions coming true. Before the fourth day, 3,000 were dead and many wounded or suffering from frostbite. Her son-in-law died, and her daughter narrowly escaped a Pakhtun bullet.

Lady Sale preferred keeping the records objective:

> We left Cabul with five and a half days' rations to take us to Jellalabad and no forage for cattle…having no cover for officers or men, they are perfectly paralysed with the cold. The snow was more than a foot deep… On our arrival at Bhoodkhak, the enemy had very greatly increased… Scarcely any baggage of either officers or men now remained. No food for man or beast…

> Numbers of unfortunates have dropped, benumbed with cold, to be massacred by the enemy: yet, so bigoted are our rulers, that we are still told that the Sirdars are faithful.[78]

In two days' time the British force had become thoroughly disorganized.[79] Many had frozen to death and from those left alive, hardly anyone could 'hold his musket or move'. The Afghans had kept a hawk's eye on them. Very soon on that fateful day they had 'asembled in great numbers. Had they made a dash at us, we could have offered no resistance, and all would have been massacred.'[80] 'When the army had marched out of Kabul, each soldier had forty rounds of musket ammunition and hundred spare loads. Two days later they were left with not a single cartridge in pouch.'[81] Five hundred of their regular troops, and about 2,500 of the camp followers were dead. One of the army officers found two of his servants: 'The one has his hands and feet frostbitten, and had a fearful sword cut across one hand, and a musket ball in his stomach; the other had his right arm completely cut through the bone. Both are utterly destitute of covering, and have not tasted food for five days.'[82]

Mohammad Akbar Khan[83] had taken special delight in informing Lady Sale that only one man from the entire force had managed to reach Jalalabad fort which her husband commanded. And 'thus was verified what we were told before leaving Cabul: "that Mahommed Akbar would annihilate the whole army, except one man, who should reach Jellalabad to tell the tale."'[84]

The man who escaped to India was Dr William Brydon, the sole survivor from amongst the twelve officers who had left with the main party. In Jalalabad the men of Brigadier General Sale's brigade, watching for news of the retreating army from the town walls saw Brydon arrive. One of Sale's officers wrote:

> A little after noon on the 13th, one of the sentries on that part of the wall which faced Gandamak[85] and the road from Cabul called aloud that he saw a mounted man in the distance. In a moment glasses were leveled in that direction, and there, sure enough, could be distinguished, leaning rather than sitting upon a miserable pony, a European, faint, as it seemed, from travel, if not sick, or perhaps wounded. It is impossible to describe the

sort of thrill which ran through men's veins as they watched the movements of the stranger.... An escort of cavalry being sent out to meet the traveler, he was brought in bleeding and faint, and covered with wounds; grasping in his right hand the hilt and a small fragment of a sword which had broken in the terrible conflict from which he had come. He proved to be Dr Bryden, whose escape from the scene of slaughter had been marvelous, and who at the moment believes himself, and was so regarded by others, as the sole survivor of General Elphinstone's once magnificent little army.

The British hurriedly sent another army to salvage their lost prestige. But that is another episode in the continuing drama of the First Anglo-Afghan War. The next event in this strife-torn theatre took place fifteen years later, in 1857.

## 1857: Heroic Drama and British Perfidy

It was on 11 May 1857, that Herbert Edwardes[86] and John Nicholson,[87] Commissioner and Deputy Commissioner of Peshawar, first received the news of the Meerut uprising. Without wasting time, they firmed up an agenda for swift action in conjunction with Brigadier Sydney Cotton and Neville Chamberlain.[88] John Nicholson long expected just such a mutiny in the Bengal Army. According to him:

> Neither greased cartridges, the annexation of Oudh, nor the paucity of European officers were causes enough... I have watched the army and felt they only wanted an opportunity to try their strength with us... Mutiny is like small pox, it spreads quickly and must be crushed as soon as possible.[89]

At the time the mutiny occurred, the Bengal army had 23,000 European troops, of which half were stationed in Punjab.[90] It was therefore imminently necessary that the British 'regroup and consolidate European regiments based in North India'.[91] Punjab had, at the time, 36,000 Indian troops with eight of the regular Bengal army regiments stationed at Peshawar.[92] They all needed to be either disarmed or sufficiently overawed. On eight separate occasions between May and August 1857, twelve regiments of Indian troops mutinied in Punjab itself.[93] In its early stages, the mutiny appeared to be confined to the predominantly Hindu Brahmin and Rajput soldiery.[94] Hoping that Muslim tribal leaders and Sikh sardars may not support the mutiny, the administration in Peshawar sought immediate recruitment of Pakhtun soldiers. But the Pakhtuns did not come forward to enlist. The intelligence was ominous. A detachment of the 55th Bengal Native Infantry (BNI), sent from Naushera to Hoti Mardan,[95] was restive and ready to mutiny. Four of the eight Bengal army regiments quartered in Peshawar also showed signs of following suit. Nicholson's police intercepted a message from a Subedar Major of the 51st BNI calling on the 64th to join the uprising planned for 22 May. The Afridis with whom the Subedar Major sought refuge, handed him over to the Deputy Commissioner who, for effect, promptly ordered his 'death by hanging', in the presence of the entire garrison.[96]

Despite disarming and disbanding the suspect units in Peshawar on 21 May, the 55th Bengal Native Infantry mutinied at Hoti Mardan and marched off towards the nearby mountains. John Nicholson followed it in hot pursuit. Half the regiment perished in trying to escape and some were taken prisoner but about five hundred men survived to reach the safety of Swat. The Punjab British East India Company authorities decided to make a 'terrible example' of those taken prisoner by Nicholson. Nicholson had returned with 120 prisoners. They were all condemned to death. Execution by firing squad was the military norm. Later, it was decided to spare the Sikhs. The British designs, in dividing the prisoners along communal lines, were sinister. John Lawrence[97] wrote to Herbert Edwardes, the Commissioner of Peshawar:

> In respect to the mutineers of the fifty-fifth, they were taken fighting against us…and so far deserve little mercy…but, on full reflection, I would not put them all to death…I do not think that we should be justified in the eyes of the Almighty in doing so…a hundred and twenty men are a large number to put to death… our object is to make an example to terrify others…I think this object would be effectually gained by destroying from a quarter to a third of them…I would select all those against whom anything bad can be shown—such as general bad character, turbulence,

prominence in disaffection or in the fight, disrespectful demeanour. If these did not make up the required number, I would then add to them the oldest Soldiers...all these should be shot or blown away from guns, as may be most expedient... the rest I would divide into batches...some to be imprisoned ten years, some seven, some five, some three...I think a sufficient example will then be made, and that these distinctions will do good and not harm...the sepoys will see that we punish to deter and not for vengeance...public sympathy will not be on the side of the sufferers...otherwise, they will fight desperately to the last as feeling certain that they must die...[98]

On the morning of 10 June, the Indian troops in Peshawar were assembled to witness the punishment. Thousands gathered for the bloody spectacle of forty men being blown to bits. The fate meted out to the men of the 55th BNI was an exercise in Old Testament vengeance. Revenge was very much on John Nicholson's mind when he wrote to Herbert Edwardes:

> We are told in the Bible that stripes shall be meted out according to faults, and, if hanging is sufficient punishment for such wretches, it is too severe for ordinary mutineers. If I had them in my power today, and I knew that I were to die tomorrow, I would inflict the most excruciating tortures I could think of on them with a perfectly easy conscience.

On 10 June, 'Lawrence's instructions were implemented to the letter. The contemporary British opinion praised the barbaric act.'[99]

However, on the same day arrived a letter from John Lawrence addressed to Herbert Edwardes that depicted the mood of the top echelons of the British bureaucracy in India:

> I have done all I could to urge vigorous and prompt action at Delhi, and only stopped when I perceived that I might do more harm than good...if Delhi does not fall at once, or if any disaster occur there, all the Regular army, and probably all the irregular Cavalry will fall away...I think we must look ahead and consider what should be done, in the event of a disaster in Delhi. My decided opinion is that...we must concentrate. Our safety

depends on this. If we attempt to hold the whole country we shall be cut up in detail. The important points in the Punjab are Peshawar, Multan, and Lahore… But I do not think we can hold Peshawar and the other places also, in the event of disaster. We could easily retire from Peshawar early in the day. But, at the eleventh hour, it would be difficult, perhaps impossible.'[100]

John Lawrence suggested that Dost Mohammad, the Amir of Kabul, be asked to take possession of Peshawar. The letter was provocation enough for Herbert Edwardes to say that 'his chief, the titan of Punjab, had gone out of his mind'.[101] Lawrence was firm that the British must give away Peshawar, or otherwise give up the siege of Delhi. This view, he communicated to John Canning, the Governor General of India too.

For weeks the fate of Peshawar hung in balance, to be resolved only on 7 August when Canning asked Lawrence to hold on to Peshawar. 'Though the rebels in Delhi still held out, India was saved.'[102]

Fortunately for the British in Punjab, the Amir of Afghanistan chose not to support the uprising, a decision that Herbert Edwardes considered entirely timely. He did of course concede to Sir John Lawrence: 'It is clear that, if we had been on bad terms just now with Kabul, we should have lost, first Peshawar, and then the Punjab, and all India would have reeled under the blow.'[103] John Nicholson was thankful too, for Edwardes' policy of alliance with Dost Mohammad had the solid advantage of leaving them at liberty to contend with their own mutinous soldiers.

The men of the 55th batallion—those that escaped Nicholson and crossed into Swat—were mostly Awadhi Brahmins and Rajputs.[104] Unfortunately for them, the Padshah of the Swatis, Sayed Akbar Shah,[105] had died of natural causes on 11 May. His brother Sayed Umar Shah did not command quite the same respect from tribal elders. Despite this lack of support, Sayed Umar Shah offered the mutineers his protection and agreed to take them on as his standing army. The soldiers also enjoyed the sympathy of Gulab Singh's[106] Dogra Rajput Kashmiri troops. The Swatis' revered religious leader, the Akhund of Swat,[107] too welcomed them. The pro-mutiny Swat elements tried to persuade the frontier tribes to unite behind these soldiers. Facing great deprivation, the 55th mutineers first turned towards Kohistan with intent to cross over to Kashmir. However, a melancholic fate awaited them. Having crossed the Indus on rafts of inflated animal skins, they entered Hazara with letters from the unrecognized Padshah of Swat directing all good Muslims to help them and denouncing all who did not. But the letters did not impress the Hazariwals, who not only informed Major Becher, the British Assistant Commissioner, of their movement but harried them every foot of the way, hurling down boulders and picking off the stragglers. 'The Mahamedan women', recorded Becher, were shocked by these strange, dark men cooking and bathing almost naked; most of them were armed with muskets, or rifles and swords, but had little clothing and no cover from the rain and night dew…every step of their advance now brought new embarrassment: the knapsacks and bayonets and many of the muskets were cast down the rocks, and a large payment of silver could scarcely procure a seer [kilo] of flour.[108]

Going hungry for days, at least fifty of them perished. While fighting, these soldiers showed unparalleled discipline, especially in close line formation, beating back assaults from men who far outnumbered them, sometimes twenty to one; also fighting with bare hands when their ammunition finished. And, all this while, Major Becher was forever in their pursuit.

The 55th soldiers were unused to the terrain; they had all to abandon their knapsacks and bayonets. Desperate for help from the Muslim tribes, these Awadh sepoys had walked into a muddled political situation. Such was their resolve and revolutionary ardour that they persevered. On 5 July, while these soldiers halted at 'Nila Nadi' (a river), they were attacked by the Kohistanis. The fight was desperate—occupying the heights, pro-British Kohistanis kept up a constant fire with the exposed mutineers suffering heavy casualties. Resisting stubbornly, they defied the Kohistanis for an entire night. Several of them had bleeding fingers, yet they kept up a constant Brown Bess fire, only pausing to reload. At one point they saw more than 10,000 tribesmen charging at them with swords and carbines—yet even this final assault was beaten off.

This ever-dwindling band struggled through the country seeking the safety of Kashmir. It entered a deep nullah, a ravine at the head of which was a high mountain pass blocked by snow. Trapped, they had no option but to stand and fight as the tribesmen, Gujjars, Kohistanis and the locals, moved in for the kill:

> It was a rainy day, and as they appeared through the mists on the hills beating their drums and flaunting their pennons the hearts of the mutineers despaired. Checked everywhere, there seemed no hope and after a faint resistance and a slaughter of a few of their number, they surrendered their arms, and 124 more prisoners were afterwards made over to the escort which I [Major Becher] had dispatched to receive them.[109]

The prisoners were tried by Becher, found guilty of mutiny and executed in different parts of the district of Hazara. 'They met their deaths', concluded Becher, 'with the calmest bearing. Those who were hung spoke only to request that they might be blown from the guns instead ... Thus hunted to the last like wild beasts was consummated the miserable fate of the 55th Regiment.'[110] Their story is still spoken of locally as *Purabia Nar Sanghar Katha* (the story of the killing of the plainsmen).

John Nicholson prevented some other regiments from mutinying. The Akhund of Swat had communicated with 64th Bengal-Nagpur Infantry and 10th Irregular Cavalry soldiers to raise the banner of revolt. Stationed at Abayze, a fortress on the Swat river bank, the 64th and the 10th had decided to proceed with the 55th towards Swat. Ajun Khan, the Akhund emissary, had planned to include Peshawar regiments in the proposed march. Disarming and violent action against the 55th prevented this possibility yet Nicholson had to move personally to Abayze. He wrote: 'We arrived here alright yesterday, and found the 64th looking very villainous... they have been talking very disloyally...people of the country...have been rather hoping for a row in the midst of which they may escape paying revenue...'[111] The Abayze force was dispersed, and its detachments disarmed after European troops surrounded them. The uprising on the Indian frontiers was all but over.

## Gloomy Presentiments: Cavagnari Goes to Kabul

By the middle of nineteenth century, carving spheres of influence in Seistan had become a major bone of contention between Persia and Afghanistan.[112] In the early 1860s, the Persian Shah repeatedly complained to the British about Afghanistan's aggressive designs on Seistan. Nothing much came of it, since the British considered the Persian claim in Seistan disputed. They declined to interfere, leaving it 'to both parties to make good their possession by force of arms'. Immediately after consolidating his position in Kabul, Amir Sher Ali[113] threatened to attack Persia over the issue of Seistan. The British proposed arbitration. In 1870, Major General Sir Frederick Goldsmid[114] (he was credited with overseeing the construction of telegraph lines along the coast of British and Persian Makran, a great achievement in those days) was appointed to mediate on the Persian and Afghan claims. In his arbitral award, Goldsmid divided the area 'Seistan proper' and 'outer Seistan' between Persia and Afghanistan respectively. Though the British found the decision entirely just, both parties felt disappointed with the judgement.

The Russian advance in Central Asia was rapid after the First Anglo-Afghan War. In quick succession, the Khanates of Khokand, Khiva and Bokhara[115] were brought under Russian subjugation. Tashkent[116], Samarkand and Bokhara, the great Central Asian cities, stood occupied by Russia. The Russians were soon knocking on the doors of Afghanistan. The British were not in much of a hurry to accommodate the Amir's demands once they were assured by the Russians that Afghanistan lay outside their sphere of influence. By 1873, Britain and Russia agreed to a roughly drawn out boundary of influence in this region, this being reached without consulting Amir Sher Ali. Arbitration on Seistan had already annoyed Sher Ali. He considered the 'Seistan award' distinctly hostile. It did not help matters when Lord Northbrook,[117] India's Viceroy, refused to reopen this question. The Viceroy also refused to give any binding assurance of help in the event of Russian aggression. For the moment the British wanted to play the European diplomacy game.

In 1876, Lord Lytton[118] succeeded Lord Northbrook. He was clear about re-establishing British influence in Afghanistan. He asked the Commissioner of Peshawar to inform the Amir to expect a British mission. Amir Sher Ali feared that this could provoke Russia into sending its own envoy to Afghanistan. In a meeting of January 1877, between the British representative and the Afghan envoy at Peshawar, the Afghan representative declined the British request to station British officers in Afghan territory. Lord Lytton, however, was insistent on sending a mission to Kabul.

In April 1877, Russia declared war on Turkey. As a precautionary measure Britain ordered 5,000 Indian troops sent to Malta. Russia responded by despatching a mission to Kabul. This act was accompanied by Russian military activity on a large scale in Central Asia. Konstantin Petrovich Kaufmann,[119] the general who was responsible for conquering large Central Asian territory for the Russian empire, wrote to Amir Sher Ali in June 1878:

> I have deputed my agent, Major Stolietoff as an officer high in the favour of the emperor. He will inform you of all that is hidden in my mind. I hope that you will pay great attention to what he says and believe him as you would myself...the great advantage of a close alliance with the Russian Government will be permanently evident.

In truth, Kauffman had despatched Stolietoff to Kabul without any instructions from the Russian government. To increase the mission's threat perceptions, three columns of Russian troops took up positions along the Afghan frontier. Sher Ali was forced to receive Stolietoff. During his stay the Russian envoy did offer a Russian draft treaty of assistance to the Amir against an external enemy. How could it occur to Sher Ali to question the sanctity of such an offer? Later, the Russian government denied the offer ever having been made. The British were ever more insistent now that Sher Ali receive a similar mission from Britain. The letter to the Amir containing this announcement reached Kabul on 17 August 1878. Unfortunately, on the same day the heir apparent to the throne of Kabul died. Pleading this tragedy, the Amir asked for deferment of the arrival of the British mission which was not agreed to. The British mission, headed by Sir Neville Chamberlain, was despatched by Viceroy Lytton on 20 September. On the way to Kabul, the mission was stopped by the Afghans and had perforce to return to Peshawar. The British now issued an ultimatum allowing Kabul to respond by 20 November. No assistance was forthcoming when Sher Ali turned to Kaufmann for help. Instead, Kaufmann suggested that Sher Ali 'make terms with the British'.

Improper and faulty communication ensured that the British receive no reply until 20 November. As time ran out, the Indian Viceroy dispatched three columns of troops through Kandahar, Khurram and Khyber to march across the frontiers of Afghanistan. There was no opposition to the column that marched to Kandahar through Quetta and the Bolan Pass. The troops that marched across the Khurram valley engaged with the Afghan forces at Peiwar Kotal on 2 December 1878 and won the day for the British. The third column had no difficulty in advancing towards Jalalabad. Amir Sher Ali's sardars deserted him when news came of the British victory at Peiwar Kotal. Sher Ali released Yakub Khan, his son, from incarceration and appointed him regent before fleeing towards Balkh in the north. His forlorn hopes of Russian help never materialized. Kaufmann neither refused to send troops in Sher Ali's support nor permitted Sher Ali to visit St Petersberg. Disappointed and in ill-health, Sher Ali died at Mazar-i-Sharif[120] on 21 February 1879. Sir Alfred Lyall, a British civil servant, describes the nemesis of Amir Sher Ali in 'The Amir's Soliloquy':

> And yet when I think of Shir Ali, as he lies in his sepulcher low, How he died betrayed, heartbroken, 'twixt infidel friend and foe, Driven from his throne by the English, and scorned by the Russian, his guest, I am well content with the vengeance, and I see God works for the best.

Yakub Khan was forced to receive the British mission. The Treaty of Gandamak[121] resulted as a consequence. By its terms, Britain agreed to protect Afghanistan against external attacks on condition that Afghanistan would not deal directly with any other power. Kandahar and Jalalabad were restored to the Amir but, in return, Afghan control over the districts of Khurram, Pishin,[122] Sibi[123] and of the Khyber and Mishin Passes was ceded to the British. With Pishin and Sibi, both under British control now, Quetta and its lines of communication with India were secure. The occupation of the Khurram valley by the British afforded its own strategic advantage. The Shia[124] Muslims who resided in the Khurram valley supported the British move, fed up as they were of perpetual raids in their area by Sunni Pakhtuns. The arrangement of the passes also strengthened British control over the Afridis.

Sir Louis Cavagnari,[125] the head of the British mission reached

Kabul on 24 July 1879 and was appointed British envoy to Kabul. On 30 August, Cavagnari informed his government that six regiments from Herat, having arrived in Kabul in early August, were displaying mutinous tendencies. On 3 September, three of the six regiments asked for their pay. They were offered one month's salary which they refused. They then marched to the Residency where they asked Cavagnari to disburse the pay. When Cavagnari declined to intervene, they attacked the Residency. Cavagnari, his officers and men, were all killed and the Residency burnt. The British mission in Kabul had only been there for six weeks and five days when this tragedy occurred. There was a sense of tragic déjà vu, a cruel reminder of the days of late 1841. The Amir's complicity in the massacre could not be proven, but he could not escape the responsibility of his 'inaction'. The British overcame resistance in the field to again capture Kabul. Sir Fredrick Roberts[126] did the job for the British this time. During the First Afghan War, that responsibility had devolved upon General Pollock.

## Historical Millstone: The Durand Line

We all know how significantly the British contributed to surveying and map-making in India but on 15 August 1947, when independence came with India's partition, no one knew exactly where the new boundaries lay till three days later, the Radcliffe Line was announced, an act of near unbelievable insensitivity and administrative arbitrariness.

Britain, a maritime power, could not perceive of an attack on the Indian peninsula. The Himalayas provided a natural barrier in the north. What troubled them was not so much the threat of an actual invasion from the north-west by Russia, but the influence Russian agents might exert on the British Indian subjects, all this a classic component of the 'Great Game'.

No doubt the aspect of 'defence' played a dominant role in shaping the British Indian borders, but the practical issue of 'expense' had also to be sold to the British government. There were local factors too that affected the decision. The historical evolution of the British Indian frontier policy was therefore a mix of London's perception of its global strategy and localized problems arising out of the traditional relationship between the frontier tribes; frontier history made more fascinating by the interplay of these factors.[127]

The boundaries which the British secured on the NWFP were not traditional and customary. It was not that the British Raj inherited some well-defined boundary or that it, in turn, came as a heritage to the successor states of the British. For example, take the case of Baluchistan. Its borders did have a certain traditional basis, for the British roughly adopted the limits of those Baluch states which came under their protection. But then these borders did not mark an ethnic divide as Baluch were present on both sides of the Iran–Afghan border. At one time it appeared as if the British would extend their territory westwards to Iranian Baluchistan and Seistan. Had it not been for the need to hold Quetta, a vital cantonment town and a strategic key to the security of the Afghan frontier, it was possible that Baluchistan would never have entered the British empire at all. Had that been the case, Baluchistan today would be either part of Iran or Afghanistan, and the traditional, customary border would follow the line of the hills marking the western edge of the lower Indus valley.

In almost similar fashion, the NWFP too did not follow a traditional or customary line. Its border between the Afghan hills and the Indus plains had always seen wide fluctuations. At times Punjab had been ruled by Kabul or by Kabul-based dynasties in Delhi. A union, thus, of Afghan highlands and the lowlands of the Indus basin had not proved stable. The line of demarcation, falling in the hill tracts to the west of the Indus, had also not followed a single inevitable course. The British, in attempting to decide on a most appropriate alignment, had therefore to experiment with a number of possibilities ranging from the Indus river itself to the so-called 'scientific' frontier embracing Kandahar and Kabul deep within the Afghan highlands. The present border, the Durand Line, was a compromise solution based upon British strategic and administrative expediency, not upon tradition or custom. The persistently disputed nature of the Durand Line arises on account of the line not having a strong historical basis. It also marks a somewhat arbitrary division of Pathan tribal groups. The Durand Line has also not been part of an elaborate boundary system, for the British had a second border, the administrative boundary of the Russo-Afghan border, which they secured after painful negotiation over a long period, 1869-95. No part of this triple line could really be considered in isolation. Any attempt to extend the Russo-Afghan boundary to extend southward would inevitably produce a British desire for northward or westward extension of the Durand Line.[128]

Why and what would then involve Britain in Afghanistan? What would prompt Lord Salisbury to say in the year 1900: 'We cannot conquer it; we cannot leave it alone'?[129] For centuries, Afghanistan's affairs were interlocked with those of Persia whose Safavid kingdom (1501-1722) included both Seistan and Afghanistan with Herat and Kandahar as part of Persia when the Mughals dominated Kabul. The Afghans had hated the severe Persian rule and rebelled, seizing the Safavid capital, Isfahan, in 1722. This Afghan supremacy lasted till 1730 when the Turkoman conqueror and Persian ruler, Nadir Shah, invaded Afghanistan and Punjab. With Nadir Shah's assassination in 1747 and the resultant chaos, the Sadozai chief Ahmad Shah Abdali founded the Durrani dynasty, which lasted till 1818. Ahmad Shah's domain had then included Kabul, Punjab, Herat, Seistan, the districts between the Oxus and the Hindu Kush and Khorasan.[130]

As for the NWFP, it is the mix of legend and reality that sets it apart, for one is not quite certain where legend stops and reality begins. Many a career has been made and unmade in this fascinating land. Both the Alexanders, of Macedon and of Tunis, played themselves out here. And in between, some like Timurlane, Babur, Akbar, and with the coming of the British, Napier, Roberts, Churchill, Wavell and Auchinleck; also generations of administrators, politicians and statesmen, for example, Palmerston, Disraeli, Gladstone, Curzon, Gandhi, Nehru, Attlee, Jinnah and Mountbatten. The frontier directly concerned Britain, India and Afghanistan. Because of the pressure it generated, it ended up involving Russia, China, Persia, Turkey and even France.[131]

But why did the British find it necessary (at the turn of the last century) to formally create a buffer zone to be called the Tribal Areas between their empire and Afghanistan, and by extension of political strategy, imperial Russia? Reverting to the old theme, it was again the 'Great Game' which favoured the creation of a buffer in Afghanistan. The British found it convenient to have a buffer to a buffer and so created the Tribal Areas zone. The classical idea was to move pawns without actually escalating the Game into a full-fledged war, also not to lose important pieces. On the Central Asian board the pawns often moved of their own volition. To settle the problem of border Pakhtun tribes, the British created a defined zone, a no-man's land, which they officially designated as the Tribal Areas. This arrangement was formalized with the coming into being of the NWFP, a province carved out of Punjab during Curzon's viceroyalty in 1901.[132]

The dynamics of the 'Great Game' were not simple. Its complex nature was well understood in Moscow and Calcutta, for Calcutta then was the capital of the British Indian empire. The tribes between the administrative border and the Durand Line were a buffer to a buffer, with the Durand Line having none of the rigidity of other international frontiers. Each of the countries on either side had to realize that any attempt to enlarge its influence with the tribes would excite the suspicion of the other.[133] To sustain the 'Great Game', the creation of the Tribal Areas was found to be fundamental. Making a virtue of necessity, the Tribal Areas were recognized as special areas; if they had not existed, they would have had to be created.

Punjab was annexed to British India in 1849. Of the areas that broadly constituted the NWFP, Lord Lytton had patronizingly remarked:

> At least I know of no other spot where, after twenty-five years of peaceful occupation, a great civilised power has obtained so little influence over its semi-savage neighbours, and acquired so little knowledge of them, that the country within a day's ride of its most important garrison is an absolute *terra incognita*, and that there is absolutely no security for British life a mile or two beyond our border.

His statement was more of wishful thinking. The Uprising of 1857 or the Ambeyla campaign of 1863 could certainly not be cited as examples of peaceful occupation. How was Lytton to remedy the situation? He chose to disarm the populace and carry out military expeditions to achieve permanent peace. The remedies not only failed, but the problems continue to defy a solution even now.

Within a decade of Lord Lytton's remarks, the issue of securing India's western frontier acquired urgency for the Government of India. The region's problems became protracted primarily because the Indian government settled for a compromise, refusing to face up to and assume full responsibility of Britain's imperial interests. In the 1880s the Afghan state under Abdur Rahman had begun to take shape and acquire stability. By 1887, the British had resolved and secured their western boundaries with Persia. The southern and eastern frontier, extending 1,200 miles from the Pamirs[134] to the Persian desert where the Afghan boundaries abutted on British Indian territories still needed resolution. All along this frontier, the Amir was making his presence felt. By not asserting on major foreign policy issues, he was proving to be an uncomfortable neighbour to India by encouraging Muslims and fellow Pathans on the Indo-Afghan borders. It was with considerable difficulty, having compromised his independence, that Abdur Rahman became the Amir of Afghanistan. That he would exert his independence was expected. Two letters from the Government of India to the prospective Amir and another conceding the harsh conditions imposed on Abdur Rahman are revealing of the hardened British position. The first letter was from Sir Lepel Griffin,[135] the Government of India's Foreign Secretary, written to Abdur Rahman Khan[136] on 14 June 1880 imposing on him impossible conditions in lieu of British recognition of his Amirship:

> Firstly, with regard to the position of the Ruler of Kabul to foreign powers, since the British Government admit no right of interference by foreign powers in Afghanistan, and since both Russia and Persia are pledged to abstain from all political interference with Afghan affairs, it is plain that the Kabul ruler can have no political relations with any foreign power except the English; and if any such power should attempt to interfere in Afghanistan, and if such interference should lead to unprovoked aggression on the Kabul ruler, then the British Government will be prepared to aid him if necessary to repel it, provided that he follows the advice of the British Government in regard to his external relations.
>
> Secondly, with regard to limits of territory, I am directed to say that the whole province of Kandahar has been placed under a separate ruler, except Pishin and Sibi, which are retained in British possession. Consequently the Government is not able to enter into any negotiations with you on these points, nor in

respect to arrangements with regard to the North Western Frontier, which were concluded with the ex-Amir Muhammad Yakub Khan.[137] With these reservations the British Government are willing that you should establish over Afghanistan—including Herat, the possession of which cannot be guaranteed to you, though Government are not disposed to hinder measures which you may take to obtain possession of it—as complete and extensive authority as has been hitherto exercised by any Amir of your family. The British Government desires...to station, by agreement, a Muhammadan agent of the British Govt at Kabul.[138]

In his reply of 22 June to Griffin, Abdur Rahman had exercised utmost restraint:

> About my friendly relations and communications with foreign powers, you have written that I should not have any without advice and consultation with you [the British]. You should consider well that if I have the friendship of a great Government like yours, how can I communicate with another power without advice and consultations with you? I agree to this also.[139]
>
> You have also kindly written that should any unwarranted (improper) attack be made by any other power on Afghanistan, you will under all circumstances afford me assistance; and you will not permit any other person to take possession of the territory of Afghanistan. This is also my desire, which you have kindly granted.[140]
>
> As to what you have written about Herat. Herat is at present in the possession of my cousin. So long as he does not oppose me and remains friendly with me, it is better that I should leave my cousin in Herat, rather than any other man. Should he oppose me, and not listen to my advice or those of my people, I will afterwards let you know. Everything shall be done as we both deem it expedient and advisable.[141]

Griffin was more than ready now to put his stamp of approval on Abdur Rahman and recognize him as the Amir of Kabul:

> The British Government recognizes Your Highness as Amir of Kabul. The Viceroy and Governor General in Council authorizes

me to declare to you that since the British Government admits no right of interference by Foreign Powers within Afghanistan, it is plain that your Highness can have no political relations with any Foreign Power except with the British Government. If any Foreign Power should attempt to interfere in Afghanistan, and if such interference should lead to unprovoked aggression on the dominions of your Highness, in that event the British Government would be prepared to aid you, to such extent and in such manner as may appear to the British Government necessary in repelling it; provided that your Highness follows unreservedly the advice of the British Government in regard to your external relations.[142]

It was reasonable to expect that Amir Abdur Rahman Khan would not be able to stay for long in such abject surrender.

As Commander of the Faithful, the Amir of Afghanistan was looked upon as the head of Islam, not only in his own country but in north-western India as well. Abdur Rahman, anxious to settle his south-eastern boundaries, was also eager to include under his temporal and spiritual authority as much territory as was occupied by his Islamic followers. And so throughout the 1880s, he watched with displeasure any tendency on the part of the British to advance their boundaries. He was much disturbed when they pushed a railway line into his country after cutting a tunnel through the Khojak hill. In response, he pushed forward his outposts into Waziristan,[143] threatened the Turis of Kurram, assumed virtual sovereignty over the Afridis and strengthened connections with the Mohmands. If unchecked, his dominion could in a few years extend up to the administered borders of India and threaten Peshawar. He also disregarded the Government of India's injunction of not meddling in Bajaur and Dir[144] and seized the district of Asmar. By 1893, tensions between India and Afghanistan were on the rise. The British felt the urgency of checking encroachments by Afghanistan. The outcome was the agreement of 1893, negotiated and signed by Sir Mortimer Durand and Amir Abdur Rahman, a result of hurried discussions. It defined the southern and eastern limits of the Amir's dominions beyond which his authority was not to extend. Each party pledged not to 'exercise interference' in the territories of the other lying beyond the defined limits, professing to regard the agreement as settlement of all differences of opinion regarding the frontier.

The import of this agreement (the Durand Line), went far beyond what was sought. It was perceived then as a symbol of compromise, a manifestation of British policy not carried to its conclusion. Had the Durand Line run along the natural frontiers of India, what would be its long-term effect? Was it not strategically imperative to have the boundary run along the natural frontiers? Britain was to leave many such legacies behind in times to come.

Ethnographically, geographically and strategically, the Durand Line defied reason and logic. It cut across one of the main basins of the Indus watershed, split a nation into two, and divided tribes. Why did Abdur Rahman accept such a boundary? That the Amir failed to comprehend its implications is too simplistic an explanation. He possibly agreed to it under duress, having refused the British on some details, in consequence leaving some portions of the Durand Line undemarcated, with their exact delimitation uncertain. Abdur Rahman and his successor, Habibullah, did not give credence to the non-interference clause in the agreement. To them interference meant armed interference. The agreement did not pose a hindrance in their sending of emissaries across the Durand Line to maintain Afghan influence in the tribal areas, or inviting *jirgas* of tribesmen from the Indian side to come to Kabul. It was an essential part of the Amirs' policy to maintain Afghan influence among the independent tribes all along the border, partly to defend themselves from armed rebellion against the state, and partly as a 'prickly hedge' of defence against possible British aggression.

On the eastern side, the demarcation of the Durand Line spurred the British to adopt a forward policy in the tribal areas, a policy hard to implement without costs in lives and money. In full flow, the policy could destabilize the region and threaten the British Central Asian policy. But the natural impulse of the powerful British to overrun the tribals on their borders was strong. Throughout the 1890s, particularly during Lord Elgin's viceroyalty, the forward tendency along the frontier was clearly discernable, to push outposts up the valleys, to Wana in Waziristan, and up the Tochi valley, the intention being to get nearer the 'independent' tribes.

## With Gallant Young Churchill's Field Force

In 1897, Winston Churchill's mother left no string unpulled, no stone unturned and no cutlet 'uncooked' to ensure that her son was chosen for the Tirah[145] campaign of the NWFP. She lobbied hard for her son, so much so that Lord Roberts was forced to write to her explaining his inability to help:

> I would, with the greatest pleasure, help your son, but it would be no use communicating with General Lockhart,[146] as Sir George White[147] is all powerful and, as he refused to allow Winston to join General Blood's staff, after his having served with that officer in the Malakand Field Force, I feel sure he would not consent to his being sent with the Tirah Field Force... I would telegraph to Sir George White, but I am certain that, under the circumstances, he would resent my doing so.

All Churchill's strenuous efforts to be coopted in the Tirah Field Force came to naught. But the account of his pursuits in the Malakand Field Force earlier, the same year, 1897, makes for fascinating reading.

When young Churchill embarked on his first journey to India, most people who knew him enquired, 'to the Front?', for to that generation, 'going to the east' meant 'going to the seat of war'. The expression 'to the east', had stuck with Churchill. He was commissioned a war correspondent by the *Pioneer* newspaper. His mother also arranged in England for Churchill's reports to be published simultaneously in the *Daily Telegraph*. On his way to the frontier, Churchill broke journey for a day at Rawalpindi. He mentions retiring to the Sergeants' mess after dinner where a 'spirited song' whose 'noble sentiments' he felt much uplifted by was in progress:

> Great White Mother, far across the sea,
> Ruler of the empire may she ever be,
> Long may she reign, glorious and free,
> In the Great White Motherland.

The three brigades of the Malakand Field Force moved in succession. A few political officers who knew the area and people well were also part of the Field Force contingent. Their job was to interact with the tribal chiefs, influential persons and the mullahs. They were there to negotiate and patch things up, wherever possible. This made them not so popular with the army, for it did not think much of their 'shilly-shallying', which in effect meant that matters were not allowed to precipitate. Churchill had with him a brilliant Political Officer, a Major Deane, much disliked, for he always managed deferment of military operations. In Churchill's words:

> Just when we were looking forward to having a splendid fight and all the guns were loaded and everyone keyed up, this Major Deane—and why was he a Major anyhow? So we said—being in truth nothing better than an ordinary politician—would come along and put a stop to it all. Apparently all these savage chiefs were his old friends and almost his blood relations. Nothing disturbed their friendship.In between the fights, they talked as man to man and as pal to pal, just as they talked to our General as robber to robber.

Churchill had observed that it was only the instinct of self-preservation during harvest time that helped preserve peace. This apart, a Pathan tribesman always displayed a propensity for being restive, picking up vendettas and feuds. He soon got a taste of action. After the tribes in Malakand rose in revolt under the mad mullah, Sadullah, Sir Bindon Blood[148] sent orders to retaliate. General Jeffreys, commanding the second brigade, was asked to enter the Mamund valley[149] and punish the assailants. 'If you want to see a fight,' Sir Bindon told young Winston, 'you may ride back and join Jeffreys.'

Churchill, while in India, was drafted in the Regiment of the Fourth Hussars. Largely his mother's contribution, the right connections in army echelons saw him comfortably ensconced as an orderly officer. A fortuitous vacancy had arisen on account of a casualty, which he filled. His was a force of 10,000 men that negotiated the valleys of Dir and Bajaur in September 1897 to take on the Mamunds near Peshawar. The British sustained casualties in their attempt to subjugate them. In a retaliatory offensive, Churchill got attached to a Sikh battalion, one of the three brigade detachments constituted for this mission.

On 16 September, the second brigade, preceded by a squadron of Bengal Lancers, marched into Mamund valley. Gradually they split up into small parties, Winston riding with the cavalry. Around noon, it struck him that there were not many soldiers in the near vicinity, though he could spot a few Lancers who had dismounted. He had suddenly felt vulnerable when he realized how small his own party was. In all, there were five British officers with a small detachment of Sikhs. Churchill, fresh from Sandhurst,[150] recalled the basic lesson on 'dispersion of forces'. 'Like most young fools I was looking for trouble,' wrote Churchill, 'and only hoped that something exciting would happen.' It did!

Suddenly the tribesmen, all armed, appeared along the mountainside and charged towards his party. As they gained ground, the Sikh detachment opened fire. Churchill, in all his foolhardiness, found the target tempting, snatched a Martini rifle from a Sikh soldier, and began taking pot shots. This action lasted perhaps five minutes. Then he found the battalion's adjutant ordering him to back off. When his party rose in retreat, Churchill saw five or six of his men falling; two killed and three wounded. One soldier was shot through the chest and another lay writhing. The British officer behind Churchill had his face covered in blood and one eye cut out.

To avoid hideous mutilation, the soldiers ordinarily would never leave behind their wounded on the Indian frontier. The adjutant had fallen, but the men who were attempting to carry him back to safety abandoned him when they saw a group of Pathans approaching. Churchill became witness to a fatally brutal assault on the adjutant who lay prostrate. Seeing that, Churchill 'forgot everything else except for the desire to kill the attackers. He pulled out his revolver, took, as he thought, a most careful aim, and fired. No result. He fired again. No result. He fired again. Whether he hit them or not he could not tell…he looked around. He was all alone with the enemy. Not a friend was to be seen. He ran as fast as he could. There were bullets everywhere. He got to the first knoll. There were the Sikhs holding the lower one! They made vehement gestures, and in a few moments he was among them.'

Sir Bindon Blood had sent orders that the second brigade was to stay in the Mamund valley and lay it waste. This, it did. So long as the villages were in the plains, it was easy. The tribesmen stayed on the mountains and helplessly watched the destruction of their homes and means of livelihood. But when it came to the villages in the mountains, they resisted fiercely. The brigade lost two or three British officers and fifteen to twenty soldiers per village. However, the British honour stood salvaged in a fortnight.

Churchill dispatched his accounts of the campaign both by telegram and letter to the *Pioneer* and *Daily Telegraph*. The Mamunds claimed great successes. Churchill said, 'They exaggerated the number of our slain… We did the same, but they did not read our newspapers.'[151] By September end, the Afridis of Tirah joined the resistance. The terrain of Tirah was far more difficult than that of Malakand. The Government of India decided to send a separate expedition there. Two divisions of three brigades each, about 35,000 men, with a logistical force and supplies were assembled. But Churchill was not destined to participate in the Tirah campaign. He was not chosen to. Sir George White, the Commander-in-Chief of the Indian army could not be cajoled to do so. Churchill was promptly asked to return to his regiment, which he did. But very soon, in the winter of 1897 itself, he came up with the book *The Malakand Field Force*, which proved to be a 'standard work', a book of reference, and was an immediate success, widely and wisely read, eliciting a lot of praise from the then Prince of Wales.

## Keystone of the Frontier Arch

The North-West Frontier Province, a separate Pathan-dominated province was carved out in 1901. Lord Lytton, fearing the Russians, had long advocated a more centralized control of the frontier. In fact he suggested the creation of one large frontier province, from Peshawar down to the sea. The Second Afghan War put paid to his idea. Right from the time Baluchistan came under effective British control, Quetta was administered centrally. As and when Khyber, Kurram, parts of Waziristan and Malakand became part of British India, the logic of centralized governance over these areas became more obvious.

It was on the king's birthday, 9 November 1901, that the NWFP was created. The four trans-Indus districts of Peshawar, Kohat,[152] Bannu and Dera Ismail Khan,[153] with a fifth, Hazara (Cis-Indus), were separated from the Punjab to form the province proper; adjacent to these and under the same umbrella were the five Political Agencies together with other tribal territory managed by District Officers as far as the Durand Line. Like Baluchistan, the new administration was placed in charge of a Chief Commissioner who combined in his person the administrative charge of the districts with the political control of the tribal belt and was directly subordinate to the central government. The officer selected for the job of Chief Commissioner was Harold Deane,[154] the founder of the Malakand Agency.

In his long career, Curzon had coveted two positions—one, that of the Indian viceroyalty, and second, the prime ministership of Britain. He succeeded to the first on 6 January 1899, but failed to hold the second. With considerable difficulty the government overcame violent tribal risings on its western frontiers when Curzon took office in India, a time of widespread famine and plague. Though he belonged to no particular school of frontier policy, he attached considerable priority to evolving one, pitching forcefully for it in his second budget speech of 27 March 1901: 'Withdrawal of British forces from advanced positions, employment of tribal forces in defense of tribal country, concentration of British forces in British territory behind them as safeguard and a support, improvement of communications in the rear.'

There is not much to show what the Pathans thought of the change, but for the British, the creation of the new province was not easy. After the troubles of 1897, the British government was reluctant to partition Punjab. It was decided that the Commissioners of Peshawar and Derajat,[155] while remaining part of the Punjab government, would be beholden to the central government in dealing with the tribes beyond the administered border. Curzon was doubtful of the wisdom of this compromise. In a series of letters to Whitehall,[156] and finally in the most elaborate minute ever written by a Governor General, he proceeded to rebut all arguments for the maintenance of status quo.

> Curzon developed his case in characteristic style, and as Olaf Caroe would describe, 'First came a sitting shot, followed by sharp single shots on the bull's-eye, culminating in a salvo of concentrated rapid fire.'[157]
>
> 'The Viceroy is responsible for frontier policy,' Curzon wrote on 5 April 1899, [...] Yet he has to conduct it not through the agency of officials directly under him, but through the elaborate machinery of a provincial government, to which the Frontier

and its problems are necessarily something in the nature of sideshows, acting as an intermediary. The result is that in ordinary times the Punjab government does the Frontier work and dictates the policy without any interference from the supreme government at all, but that in extraordinary times, the whole control is taken over by the Government of India acting through agents who are not its own; while the Punjab government, dispossessed and sulky, stands on one side, criticizing everything that is done.[158]

As Curzon developed his case, he met with stiff opposition from Mackworth Young,[159] the Lieutenant Governor of Punjab. In November 1899, Curzon complained that he had told the head of the province exactly what he felt about the frontier problems and believed the matter closed. Yet the Lieutenant Governor continued to argue disputatiously, thus driving him to despair: 'I cannot spare hours in wordy arguments with my lieutenant governors as to the exact meaning, purport, scope, object, character, possible limitations, conceivable result, of each petty aspect of my Frontier policy. If they deliberately refuse to understand it, and haggle and boggle about carrying it out, I must get some fairly intelligent officer who will understand what I mean and do what I say.'[160] And again, 'the Government of India, realizing its own ignorance, but not realizing that it was duplicating the danger, has placed between itself and the Frontier the Punjab government which often knows less and which for twenty years has been an instrument of procrastination and obstruction and weakness.'[161] Then had come the roll of the full battery—the minute of 13 September 1900:

> I venture to affirm, that there is not another country in the world which adopts a system so irrational in theory, so bizarre in practice, as to interpose between its foreign minister and his most important sphere of activity the barrier, not of a subordinate official, but of a subordinate government, on the mere geographical plea that the latter resides in closer proximity to the scene of action—a plea which itself breaks down when it is remembered that for five months in a year the supreme and local governments are both located in the same spot, Simla...

> The system attenuates without diminishing the ultimate responsibility of the Government of India. It protracts without strengthening their action. It interposes between the Foreign Minister of India and his subordinate agents not an Ambassador or a minister or a consul, but the elaborate mechanism of a local government and the necessarily exalted personality of a Lieutenant Governor. Worked as the system has been with unfailing loyalty and with profound devotion to duty, it has yet been the source of friction, of divided counsels, of vacillation, of exaggerated centralization, of interminable delay.[162]

The government in Britain ultimately gave in to Curzon and agreed to the creation of the NWFP. But in submitting proposals for it, Curzon had bypassed the Governor of Punjab. He had not consulted him. Macworth Young was indignant at being ignored, of which he promptly gave expression to Curzon: 'You have not cared to consult me about forming a new Administration out of the territory which I have received as a commission from her Majesty to administer'.[163] There were others too who did not to Curzon's views. One such officer, Herbert Fanshawe,[164] the Commissioner of Delhi, resigned service 'in vicarious vindication of his government's honour'.[165]

During Harold Deane's tenure as the first Chief Commissioner of the NWFP—seven years of the new province's existence—there were no expeditions except against the Mahsuds. In contrast, in the five years from 1894 to 1899, frontier warfare cost the Indian taxpayer 4.5 million pounds; for the first seven years after the NWFP was created, it cost the exchequer only 248,000 pounds to maintain it. Under Roos-Keppel,[166] who succeeded Deane as Chief Commissioner, and for eleven more years, the province remained trouble-free throughout World War I. Perhaps Curzon's policy of creating the NWFP had been well worth it.

### Anglo-Afghan Relations before the Great War

Russia lay defeated at the hands of Asiatic Japan in 1905. This development necessitated a change in the British foreign policy towards Russia. When the British government sought the Indian Viceroy's opinion on this issue, Lord Minto unequivocally suggested that Russia at this juncture be made to publicly recognize Afghanistan as being outside her sphere of influence; undertake to not make any strategic extension of its railway system towards the Indian frontier; recognize the preponderant British interest in Seistan and sovereign Persia; scrupulously respect the integrity of China in Kashgar; and refrain from interference in Tibet. Above all, Afghanistan's external relations were only to be conducted through Britain. Lord Minto would not brook any communication between Russia and Afghan officials, even on purely local matters. He questioned the advisability of a Russo-Afghan Frontier Commission and took the gravest exception to a proposed joint agreement not to extend the Indian railways in the direction of the Afghan border for a period of ten years. He believed the railways to be the true frontier defence of India, a necessary consequence of the frontier military policy. Minto thought it wise to concentrate on the Amir of Afghanistan who was a 'more necessary friend', to be kept on friendly and controlling terms rather than alienating him by entering into a bargain with Russia: 'If we are to enter upon an entente with Russia let us bargain with her elsewhere than in Central Asia…the Government of India should be fully consulted before any agreement is entered into with Russia,'[167] was Minto's contextual response to a query from Lord Morley, the Secretary of State for India.

Morley agreed with Minto on the issue of fostering friendly relations with the Amir of Afghanistan. Lord Curzon had tried to persuade Amir Habibullah to visit India. But the invitation was too much in the nature of a command. Since then a British mission[168] had done much to mollify the Amir. In early 1906, Minto was informed of the Amir's desire to 'make a pleasure trip to the chief Indian cities.'[169] The Viceroy sent a cordial invitation and a ready acceptance followed. It was after a long time, in fact since the days of Lord Dufferin, that a ruler of Afghanistan had consented to an Indian visit.

A great Durbar was held at Agra, where the Amir arrived on 9 January 1907 in a deluge of rain—which he fortunately considered a good omen. The Viceroy and the Commander-in-Chief were there to meet him, and so also a large concourse of guests, English and Indian. It was decided after much anxious discussion to address him as 'His Majesty' and to give him a thirty-one gun salute. There was high comedy too in the visit. The Amir lost his heart to so many ladies of 'diverse types' that it was difficult to say whom he admired most.[170]

Lady Minto, the official hostess to the Amir, described his visit in detail:

> Lord Kitchener entertained the Amir at dinner last night and it seems to have been a great success. He became most hilarious, drank three bottles of soda-water and a tub of plain water, and the effect could not have been more invigorating had the liquid been wine. He led Lord Kitchener to a sofa and said, 'You my friend, I your friend. Now we joke.' Lord Kitchener had the greatest difficulty in getting rid of him towards midnight...He delivered various homilies on total abstinence, and a surprising address at Aligarh College on the need of religious education, but he resolutely declined to mention politics.[171]

Amir Habibullah was soon to make an interesting appearance at the state ball in Calcutta:

> He had never seen dancing in his life, and I [Lady Minto] was terrified that he was going to ask me to teach him. We sat together on the dais in the ballroom discussing old Persian sayings, from which many of our proverbs are derived. There happened to be an eclipse of the moon, and the Amir gallantly said, 'The moon in our country is masculine, and he even hides his face tonight so that your ball may have no rival'. Later at supper I told him that it was our custom to put our knife and fork together if we had finished and wanted our plate removed. He said, 'You tell, I learn!'... he said, 'Please you tell me I been heavy guest or light guest?' Of course I said, 'You've been a light guest,' whereupon he added, 'Then I come and stay with you next year, not official. I come as your friend for a long time.' With a sickly smile I told him that we should look forward to that pleasure, privately praying that the Government will never allow the experiment to be repeated oftener than once in five years.[172]

The Amir purchased enormous quantities of goods while in Calcutta, gave largesse to anyone who took his fancy and tried his best to arrange a marriage for Lord Kitchener, whose celibacy was a constant grief to him. He departed at long last in tears. In his farewell speech the Amir made a promise that he actually kept during the days of the Great War:

> Before I came to India we called ourselves friends; Now I find myself in such a position that our friendship, which was like a plant before, is now like a big tree. I have gained much experience in India, and from that experience I hope to benefit my country in future. Let me say that at no time will Afghanistan pass from the friendship of India. So long as the Indian empire desires to keep her friendship, so long will Afghanistan and Britain remain friends.

Melancholy telegrams and letters were dispatched to the Viceroy from various places on his return journey, and he crossed the frontier in utter dolefulness. 'He drew his escort officer aside, put on his motoring goggles to hide the tears that were coursing down his face, and was too overcome to say one word. He finally jumped on to his horse, spurred him into a gallop, and disappeared through the mountain passes towards his barbaric kingdom.'[173]

The Amir's India visit may not have been personally advantageous to him, but from the British point of view it was an unequivocal triumph.

The cordial relations established with the Amir made it possible for Britain to tide over difficulties of an agreement with Russia. The British government congratulated Minto on the positive outcome of the Amir's visit. I quote two extracts from the correspondence between the Viceroy and the Secretary of State of which one may be taken as an affirmation of Whitehall's appreciation. In a vexatious mood, the Viceroy had written to Lord Morley on 6 February 1907:

> The Amir is still with us. I am afraid these words can hardly convey what they mean to me. Lady Minto and I are at the last stages of exhaustion. He fills up one's every spare moment. He came down to Barrackpore on Sunday for luncheon, after which I hoped for an afternoon to myself, but could not leave him. He then got involved in a game of croquet with my daughters, and finally remained till dark. He dined at the Frasers', and sang a Persian love song to Lady Fraser to his own accompaniment

on the piano, and has shot clay pigeons with me, though for international reasons I thought it wise to divest the amusement of the conditions of a match! The worst of it is he won't go away, and now, though every one was sworn to secrecy, he has discovered that our state Ball is on Friday, and insists on remaining for that. A horrible rumour reached us this evening that he wants to stay for the races on Saturday, but I have told my officers that they absolutely must insist on his leaving, as his Majesty's ships are specially awaiting his arrival at Bombay, and there is a naval programme there which he cannot neglect. He is simply irrepressible, more like a boy out of school than anything else. Not a word of affairs of state…I only pray that the joys of Calcutta may not have entirely unsettled him! The responsibility of another such visit would really be more than I could bear, and I hear with apprehension that his Sirdars say that there is no doubt there will now be an excellent motor-road from Kabul to Peshawar![174] I am in great hopes, however, that the attractions of Western life may suggest a visit to you in London rather than to me![175]

The Secretary of State replied matter-of-factly:

I felt the horrible force of your opening words, 'The Amir is still with us'. Ah, well, *'il faut souffrir pour etre beau,'* and Viceroys cannot have bright feathers in their caps without prodigious doses of boredom. I am glad his Majesty has at last taken himself off, and without one single bit of new engagement on our part. If, as I most confidently expect, he gets knocked on the head some fine morning by his brother or some other near relative, we are not bound to put him back on his shaky gadi, or, rather I should say, to avenge his deposition therefrom. One great spring of mischief in these high politics is to suppose that the situation of to-day is to be the situation of tomorrow. If I were Lord Chesterfield, writing to a son whom I meant to be a statesman, I should say to him, 'remember that in the great high latitudes of policy all is fluid, elastic, mutable; the friend to-day, the foe tomorrow; the ally and confederate against the enemy, suddenly his confederate against you; Russia or France or Germany or

America, one sort of power this year, quite another sort, and in deeply changed relations to you, the year after!' Excuse this preachment.[176]

But the Viceroy failed to induce his government to consult the Amir before concluding negotiations with Russia. Morley felt the difficulty, but his colleagues were obdurate. Candour with the Amir would prevent the speedy execution of a diplomatic coup on which they had set their hearts. On 2 August, Morley wrote to Minto:

> It came to this at last—a choice between accepting the drawbacks and losing the Convention. Of course any one can see that the relations between us and the Amir were never so good as they are at this moment. Nothing can mend them. On the other hand, it is inevitable that the Convention between us and Russia should make him suspicious and uneasy. The notion of his two neighbours 'exchanging views' about annexing and occupying him will naturally have a very ugly look of partition in his eyes. If the Convention goes on—as in spite of all its drawbacks I am bound to hope that it will—I would ask you to encourage yourself in the delicate diplomacy that we shall in that case impose on you with the Amir…Certainly if you do not succeed in managing your Kabul friend, the results of the whole proceeding will be disastrous.[177]

On 31 August, the Secretary of State telegraphed that the Convention had been signed, and on 10 September the part relating to Afghanistan was communicated to the Amir.

The Amir's visit to India had made him far from popular in his own country. In addition, the incidence of plague in Afghanistan added to his difficulties—putting another weapon in the hands of the anti-English faction in Kabul. A general impression got created that the Amir had been bought over by the English. Minto tried his level best to prevent the British cabinet from frittering away their advantages in Afghanistan in their desire to come to an understanding with Russia. Isvolsky, the Russian Foreign Minister proposed, and the British government accepted, the following proviso to be included in the part dealing with Afghanistan: 'Should any change occur in the political status of Afghanistan, the two Governments will enter into a friendly interchange of views on the subject.'[178] This looked innocent enough at first sight but Lord Minto understood its implications—that the British were binding themselves to what they had never done before, namely, to consult Russia whenever a change in the political status of Afghanistan occurred. Such a change could be anything. Lord Minto's protest had its effect and the objectionable clause was dropped.

## ANNEXURE

'Attar Singh' is undoubtedly Mortimer Durand's masterpiece. He came across the details of this poem in a dry office file, which theme he subsequently developed. 'Attar Singh' is a tribute to the Sikh soldiery, a recognition of their support to the British during 1857 and of the fact they had comported themselves well against the Afghans too.

### Attar Singh Looquitur

> I've come to make my salaam, Sahib, my soldiering days are done.
> Your father was ever a friend to me, I'm glad to have seen his son.
> Well, yes, it's hard to be going. I am an old man now I know,
> But I come of a tough old fighting stock, and I find it hard to go...
> I think they are not what we were, who were bred in the wild old time,
> When every Singh was a soldier and Ranjit was in his prime...
> I rode by the side of my father when we scattered the Afghan hordes,
> And I longed for the day when the Khalsa host should roll on the Sutlej fords...
> God's curse on the cowardly traitors who sold the Khalsa to shame,
> My father fell at Sobraon. There was blood on the old man's sword...
> As foot by foot you bore us back to the brink of the flooded ford,
> We never broke, though around us the river was choked with dead...
> I never knew how the end came, for the stream soon forced us apart,
> But he died, as a Sikh Sirdar should die, with the fight still hot in his heart...

*We were all unused to be conquered; you had taught us the lesson at last,*
*But you left us with arms in our hands, Sahib, to brood on the hopes of the past...*
*Full thirty years are gone since then, but still my heart beats high,*
*To think how wild the battle raged against the darkening sky...*
*I led a troop at Chilianwal; they said I led it well,*
*Near half of us were cold and stiff before the darkness fell...*
*But what is the use of boasting now? My lands were taken away.*
*And the Company gave me a pension of just eight annas a day...*
*Ah, Sahib, you were wise to trust us, our fingers itched for the steel,*
*I was first man up to the summons, with a score good Singhs at my heel...*
*I rode to Delhi with Hodson; there were three of my father's sons;*
*Two of them lie at the back of the ridge, in the line of the Moree's guns...*
*I followed him on when the great town fell, he was cruel and cold, they said, The men were sobbing around me the day that I saw him dead...*
*It's not soft words that a soldier wants; we knew what he was in fight, And we love the man who can lead us, aye though his face be white.*

## Notes

1. The Oxus or Amu Darya, 2,580 km long, rises in the Pamir mountains and flows generally north-west, marking much of the northern border of Afghanistan with Tajikistan, Uzbekistan and Turkmenistan.
2. Nadir Shah (c. 1688–1747), King of Persia, perhaps the last great Asiatic conqueror in the tradition of Genghis Khan and Timurlane. He rose through domestic service to high household office and then to state leadership.His light artillery was the best in Asia. During 1738–40, he conducted his Indian campaign.
3. Turkestan is a region in Central Asia, which today is largely inhabited by the Turkic peoples. It has been referenced in many Turkic and Persian sagas and is an integral part of Turan (though Turan dwarfs Turkestan

in the area). Oghuz Turks (also known as Turkmens), Uzbeks, Kazakhs, Khazars, Kyrgyz and Uyghurs are some of the Turkic inhabitants of the region who, as history progressed, have spread further into Eurasia forming such Turkic nations as Turkey and Azerbaijan, and subnational regions like Tatarstan in Russia and Crimea in Ukraine. Tajiks and Russians form sizable non-Turkic minorities. Turkestan is subdivided into Afghan Turkestan, Russian Turkestan and the Xinjiang Uyghur Autonomous region (also known as Chinese Turkestan, East Turkestan or Uyghuristan) in the People's Republic of China. The Tianshan and Pamir ranges form a rough division between the latter two. The Farghana valley is a region in Central Asia spreading across eastern Uzbekistan, Kyrgyzstan and Tajikistan.

4. Kabul is the capital of Afghanistan, located on the Kabul river, in a valley strategically located between mountain passes.
5. Malakand is a region of the NWFP that covers Chitral, Dir, Swat, Buner, Shangla and Agencies like Malakand and Mohmand.
6. M. Foster Farley and Rosali P.Gates, *Journal of Royal Society of Pakistan*, 13(2), 1976, pp.3–4.
7. Alexander (356–323 BC) was a Macedonian who came close to conquering the civilized world. He was a towering figure in ancient Greek history who had Aristotle as his teacher.
8. Peshawar is the capital of the NWFP and the administrative centre for the Federally Administered Tribal Areas of Pakistan. 'Peshawar' literally means 'the high fort' in Persian. The area of the city has been ruled by numerous empires including the Afghan, Persian, Shahi, Greek, Maurya, Scythian, Arab, Turk, Mongol, Mughal, Sikh and the British. In ancient times, a major settlement called 'Pushpapura' was established in the general area of Peshawar by the Central Asian Kushans. It was during the Mughal period that the current city was established by Akbar in the sixteenth century and received the name 'Peshawar'. During much of its history, the city was one of the main trading centres on the ancient silk road and was a major crossroads for various cultures between South and Central Asia and the Middle East.
9. Bajaur is the smallest of the agencies in the Federally Administered Tribal Areas (FATA) of Pakistan.
10. Bactria was situated between the Hindu Kush and Amu Darya in parts of modern Afghanistan, Uzbekistan and Tajikistan. Its capital was the city of

Bactra. From the sixth century BC, it was controlled by the Achaemenian dynasty; conquered by Alexander the Great, the area was ruled after his death (323 BC) by the Seleucid dynasty and for a time (c. 250 BC) formed an independent kingdom. It was long important as a crossroads for overland trade and as a meeting place for various religious and artistic traditions. The area ultimately came under Muslim rule in the seventh century AD.

11. Parthia was an ancient country of south-west Asia corresponding to modern north-east Iran. It was included in the Assyrian and Persian empires, the Macedonian empire of Alexander the Great, and the Syrian empire. The Parthian kingdom lasted from c. 250 BC to AD 226, reaching the height of its influence at the beginning of the first century BC. Parthian soldiers were renowned horsemen and archers.

12. W.K. Fraser-Tytler, *Afghanistan: A Study of Political Developments in Central and Southern Asia*, Oxford University Press, 1950, p.270.

13. The Sakas (Scythians) lived in the eastern part of Central Asia—what is now Kazakhstan, Uzbekistan, Tajikistan, parts of Afghanistan, Pakistan, India and Iran, some of the western portion of China in Khotan, Ukraine, and the Altay Mountains and Siberia in Russia—in the centuries before 300 bc. Saka is a Persian term, while Scythian is Greek.

14. The Kushan Empire (first to third centuries AD) was a state that at its height, about AD 105–250, stretched from what is now Tajikistan to Afghanistan, Pakistan and down into the Ganga river valley in northern India. The empire was created by the Kushan tribal confederation, an Indo-European people. They had diplomatic contacts with Rome, Persia and China, and for several centuries were at the centre of exchange between the East and the West.

15. The dominion of the Huns extended from the border of Persia to Khotan in Central Asia. The Huns entered India when the Guptas were ruling—in the fifth century AD. Consolidating their base in Afghanistan and their capital in Bamiyan, they had a free run when they entered Punjab in AD 458, but had to beat a retreat once they reached the Gangetic valley. But they poured back in once more through the passes of the Hindu Kush and managed to conquer Punjab, Rajputana, Malwa and Kashmir. An indirect effect of the Hun invasion was a general weakening of the Gupta empire, but a more significant effect was a racial admixture. An elaborate racial movement started with their coming in. It threw open the gates of the

north-west for various other tribes. The Huns adopted the Hindu religion and merged with the bulk of Indian population.

16. Herat is both a province in north-western Afghanistan as well as its provincial capital. It is a major city in the country's western region. Close to the Iranian border, the people of the province are largely Persian-speaking. Because of its strategic location, Herat has been a fortified town for several hundred years.
17. Jalalabad is the capital city of Nangarhar province in east Afghanistan, near the Khyber Pass. The city dominates the entrances to the Laghman and Kunar valleys and was a prominent trading centre. During the First Afghan War, British troops in 1842 held Jalalabad against an Afghan siege.
18. Bannu was a town and district of British India in the Derajat division of the NWFP. It formed the base for all punitive expeditions by troops of the British empire to the Tochi valley and Waziristan frontier. A military road led from Bannu town towards Dera Ismail Khan.
19. Lahore is the capital of the Pakistani province of Punjab and is the second largest city in Pakistan after Karachi.
20. S.Q. Fatimi, 'First Muslim Invasion of the North-West Frontier of the Indo-Pakistan Subcontinent', *Journal of Asiatic Society of Pakistan*, 8 (1), 1963, p. 41. Sir Olaf Kirkpatrick Caroe (1892–1981) was an administrator in British India. He was the Governor of the NWFP, from March 1946 till just before the partition of India in 1947. He was accused of being too close to the Muslim League because of which he encountered opposition from Congress politicians. He was replaced in mid-1947 by Rob Lockhart as Governor. He served in the army in Punjab in World War I, and joined the Indian Civil Service in 1919. He subsequently held a number of positions in the Indian Political Service. He was an active administrator in the NWFP. He wrote extensively on the subject after leaving India in 1947.
21. The Yusufzai are a Pakhtun tribe. The majority reside in the NWFP and Federally Administered Tribal Areas of Pakistan, with some tribal Yususfzais settled along the Afghan border. They are predominant in the districts of Swat, Mardan, Malakand, Swabi, Buner and Shangla.
22. Multan is a city in the southern part of the Punjab province of Pakistan. Known as the 'City of Saints', it is a city full of bazaars, mosques, shrines and well-designed tombs.
23. Attock district is in Punjab province of Pakistan.
24. S.Q. Fatimi, 'First Muslim Invasion of the North-West Frontier of the

Indo-Pakistan Subcontinent', *Journal of Asiatic Society of Pakistan*, 8 (1), 1963, p. 41.

25. Ibid. The Sulaiman mountains are a major geological feature of Pakistan and one of the bordering ranges between the Iranian Plateau and the Asian subcontinent. Bordering the Sulaiman range to the north are the arid highlands of the Hindu Kush.
26. The Kurram river drains the southern flanks of the Safed Koh mountain range, and enters the Indus plains north of Bannu.
27. Timur (1336–1405), also Timurlane, was a Turko-Mongol conqueror who created Samarkand. Perhaps a distant relative of Ghenghis Khan, Timur was not a Mongol himself, but from the Turkic Barlas tribe in Transoxania, now Uzbekistan. He invaded India in 1398 and sacked Delhi so comprehensively that it took an interminably long time for the city to recover. He was preparing to invade China when he died.
28. Babur succeeded to the throne of Farghana, a small principality in Central Asia, when his father Umar Sheikh Mirza died. At that time, he was barely eleven years old. His initial years on the throne were marked by continuous wars, battles and treaties. When he lost his state, he had to live in exile. Then fate smiled on him, and he captured the kingdom of present-day Afghanistan. Babur was able to reconquer his home state, Farghana and Samarkand. But he was again driven out. After losing his empire in Central Asia, he turned eastward and invaded India. He was the first king to bring artillery to India. He met the forces of Ibrahim Lodi in the field of Panipat on 21 April 1526 and won this battle known in Indian history as the First Battle of Panipat. This battle marked his conquest over Delhi and changed the course of Indian history. After this he fought another decisive battle with Rana Sanga in 1527, at Khanwa. In this battle, Rana Sanga was defeated and Babur became the unchallenged ruler of northern India. He made himself the ruler of Punjab, Delhi and the Ganga plains as far as Bihar, before his death. He died in 1530 and was succeeded by his son Humayun to the throne of Delhi.
29. Earlier known as Bactra, Balkh was once a major world city but was destroyed by the Mongols. Today it is a small town in the province of Balkh, northern Afghanistan, about 20 km north-west of the provincial capital, Mazar-I-Sharif, and some 74 km south of Amu Darya, the Oxus river of antiquity.
30. A narrow pass, about 53 km long, through mountains on the border

between eastern Afghanistan and northern Pakistan. It has long been a strategic trade and invasion route.
31. A mountain pass of western Pakistan at an altitude of 880 feet. The strategic pass has long been a gateway to India.
32. The Rohillas were Muslim highlanders (Roh means mountains and Rohilla literally means mountaineer) of Pakhtun origin. Roh corresponded to the mountainous region stretching from Swat and Bajaur in the north to Sibi and Bhakkar in the south and Hasan Abdal in the east to Kabul and Kandahar in the west. Most Rohillas belonged to the Yousafzai tribe of Pakhtuns. The term Rohilla was used for all Pakhtuns, except for the Bangashes, who settled in the Rohilkhand region, or men serving under Rohilla chiefs.
33. Mohmands are a Pakhtun tribe, living primarily in south-eastern Afghanistan and in the NWFP of Pakistan.
34. Theodore Leighton Pennell (1867–1912) was a Christian missionary and doctor who lived among the tribes of Afghanistan. He founded a missionary hospital in Bannu in the NWFP of British India. For his work he received the Kaisar-i-Hind Medal for Public Service in India. He published a work on his life under the title *Among the Wild Tribes of the Afghan Frontier* in 1909.
35. Kandahar is one of the largest of the thirty-four provinces of Afghanistan. It is located in southern Afghanistan, between Helmand, Oruzgan and Zabul provinces. Its capital is the city of Kandahar, located on the Arghandab river. It is mainly inhabited by Pakhtuns.
36. Khushal Khan Khattak (1613–1690) was a renowned fighter. The Afghan warrior poet wrote in Pashtu during the time of Aurangzeb.
37. One of two largest groups of Pakhtuns, along with the Durrani tribe, found in Afghanistan and neighbouring Pakistan. They are the most populous Pakhtun tribe in Afghanistan. The Ghaznavids as well as the Lodis were Ghilzais.
38. Ghazni is a city in central Afghanistan; capital of Ghazni province.
39. The Third Battle of Panipat took place on 14 January 1761, 130 km north of Delhi between the Marathas and the Afghans led by Ahmad Shah Durrani. The overriding legacy of the battle was the halting of the Maratha advance in the north.
40. George MacMunn, *The Romance of the Indian Frontiers*, Jonathan Cape, 1933, https://archive.org/stream/in.ernet.dli.2015.52854/2015.52854.

Romance-Of-The-India--Frontiers_djvu.txt

41. Shah Alam (1728–1806) was the Mughal emperor of India in 1759–1806. Driven out of Delhi in 1758, he nonetheless proclaimed himself emperor after the murder of his father, Alamgir II in 1759. He was under the protection of the Nawab of Oudh, and when the Nawab was defeated by the British at Buxar (1764), Shah Alam was forced to become a pensioner of the British East India Company. In 1765 he officially ceded to the company control of Bengal, Bihar and Orissa. With the support of the Marathas, he was able to return to Delhi in 1772, but in 1788 the city was captured by the Rohillas, who blinded and deposed him. The British restored him to the throne in 1803 when they captured Delhi.
42. About 1,448 km long, the Sutlej flows from south-west Tibet through northern India and eastern Pakistan, where it is joined by the Chenab. It is one of the five rivers of Punjab.
42. Mountstuart Elphinstone (1779–1859) was a Scotsman and a civil servant of the British East India Company. In 1808, he was appointed the first British envoy to the court of Kabul, Afghanistan, with the object of securing a friendly alliance with the Afghans against Napoleon's planned advance on India. However, this proved of little value because Shah Shuja was driven from the Amirship of Kabul by his brother before it could be ratified. A valuable result of the visit was the work by him titled *An Account of the Kingdom of Caubul and its Dependencies in Persia, Tartary and India* (Longman Hurst, 1815). Elphinstone was appointed Governor of Bombay in 1819, a post he held till 1827. He returned to England in 1829.
43. Shuja Shah Durrani (also known as Shah Shuja, Shoja Shah, Shuja al-Mulk) (c. 1785–1842) was the ruler of the Durrani empire from 1803 to 1809. He then ruled from 1839 until his death in 1842. Shuja Shah was of the Sadozai line of the Abdali group of Pakhtuns and became the fifth Amir of Afghanistan.
44. General Gaspard-Amédée Gardanne (1758–1807) was a French soldier.
45. Elphinstone, *An Account of the Kingdom of Caubul*, pp.1–2.
46. Tipu Sultan, born in 1750, was the ruler of Mysore who took over the kingdom of Mysore after the death of his father in 1782. He continued fighting the British and breathed his last in 1799.
47. Maharaja Ranjit Singh (1780–1839), also called *Sher-e-Punjab*, was a Sikh ruler of the sovereign state of Punjab. He is credited with uniting various Sikh factions into one state.

48. Elphinstone, *An Account of the Kingdom of Caubul*, p.52.
49. Ibid.
50. Ibid., p.59.
51. Ibid., p.67.
52. A *jirga* is a tribal assembly of elders which takes decisions by consensus, particularly among the Pakhtuns but also in other ethnic groups. *Jirgas* are most common in Afghanistan and among the Pakhtuns of Pakistan.
53. Sita Ram Pandey was a subedar in the Bengal army in 1857. He wrote his autobiography in Awadhi in the 1860s. Impressed with the details his Colonel, James Norgate, translated it into English. Later, the Awadhi version was lost and even the English translation—*From Sepoy to Subedar: Being the Life and Adventures of Subedar Sita Ram* (first English edition, 1873, republished Vikas Publishing House, 1970)—vanished without a trace. Madhukar Upadhyay, working with the BBC Hindi service in London, managed to retrieve an English copy of the only Indian account of 1857 and translated it back into Awadhi.
54. A historical rank in the Indian army below that of commissioned officers.
55. Awadh is a region in the centre of the Indian state of Uttar Pradesh, which before India's independence was known as the United Provinces of Oudh and Agra. Awadhi is an Indo-Aryan language. It is spoken chiefly in the Awadh (Oudh) region of Uttar Pradesh, although its speakers are also found in Bihar, Madhya Pradesh, Delhi and Nepal.
56. The Bengal army was the army of the Presidency of Bengal, one of the three presidencies of British India within the British empire. Although based in Bengal in north-eastern India, the Presidency stretched across northern India and the Himalayas all the way to the NWFP. The Bengal army included some of the most famous units in India: Skinner's Horse from Bengal, the Gurkhas from the Himalayas and the Corps of Guides on the north-west frontier. The Presidency armies, like the Presidencies themselves, belonged to the East India Company until the Indian Mutiny, when the British Crown took over all three Presidencies. Of the 67,000 Hindus in the Bengal army in 1842, 28,000 were identified as Rajputs and 25,000 as Brahmins, a category that included Bhumihar Brahmins. The Brahmin presence in the Bengal army was reduced in the late nineteenth century because they were perceived to have had primary role in the Indian Mutiny, led by Mangal Pandey. In 1903 all three Presidency armies were merged into the Indian army.

57. John Keane (1781–1844) was a British soldier. Lieutenant General Keane served as Commander-in-Chief of the Bombay Presidency in British India from 1833 to 1839 and commanded the combined British and British Indian army (the Army of the Indus) during the opening campaign of the First Afghan War. He commanded the victorious British and Indian army at the Battle of Ghazni on 23 July 1839. For his services, he was elevated to the peerage as Baron Keane of Ghuznee.
58. General Sir Abraham Roberts (11 April 1784 to 28 December 1873) was a British army general who served nearly fifty years in India.
59. The East India Company (also the English East India Company, and sometimes the British East India Company) was an early English joint-stock company that was formed initially for pursuing trade with the East Indies, but ended up trading with India and China. The Company was granted an English Royal Charter by Elizabeth I on 31 December 1600. The Company was colloquially referred to as John Company, and in India as Company Bahadur. 'Bahadur' literally means 'brave'. Its rule in India lasted until 1858, when, following the events of the 1857 Uprising, and under the Government of India Act 1858, the British Crown assumed direct administration of India. The Company itself was finally dissolved on 1 January 1874.
60. Khojak Pass (elevation 7,513 feet) connects Qila Abdullah with Chaman in the province of Baluchistan, Pakistan.
61. Pandey, *From Sepoy to Subedar*.
62. Dost Mohammad Khan (1793–1863) of the Barakzai clan, came in possession of Ghazni and, later, Kabul in 1826. He had to take refuge in the Hindu Kush when Shah Shuja arrived with the British in Kabul in 1839. In 1840 he surrendered to the British but was later released. Upon his return to Kabul, he was received in triumph. He set about re-establishing his authority. During the Indian Mutiny of 1857, Dost Mohammad refrained from assisting the rebels. Sher Ali Khan, his son, succeeded him when he died in 1863.
63. Bala Hissar is an ancient citadel. This magnificent building dates back in parts to the fifth century and has been witness to Kabul's often violent history. The Bala Hissar housed the armoury and the infamous Black Pit, the dungeon of Kabul. From 1839, the British used it as their barracks until the massacre of the British Mission by mutinous Afghan troops in 1879.

64. Pandey, *From Sepoy to Subedar*, p.101, Note 1175.
65. Sir William Hay Macnaghten (1793–1841) was a British interventionist agent in Afghanistan during the First Anglo-Afghan War (1839–42). He was made a baronet in 1840. Macnaghten went to India in 1809, where he served as an administrator and a diplomat in Madras and Bengal, acquired knowledge of Hindu and Muslim law, and became an expert in oriental languages. Made an advisor to India's Governor General Lord Auckland in 1837, he advocated British intervention to counteract Russian influence in neighbouring Afghanistan, which led to the First Anglo-Afghan War. As political agent with the British invasion force in Kabul, he tried (unsuccessfully) to replace Afghan ruler Dost Mohammad Khan with his pro-British rival, Shah Shuja. Macnaghten was captured and killed by Afghans while trying to arrange the withdrawal of British forces in 1841.
66. Pandey, *From Sepoy to Subedar*, pp.103–04.
67. Ibid., p.104.
68. Sir Alexander Burnes (1805–41) was a British traveller and an army officer in India. In 1832 he left Lahore in Afghan dress and travelled by way of Peshawar and Kabul across the Hindu Kush to Balkh and from there by Bukhara, Asterabad and Tehran to Bushire. In 1839 he was appointed Political Resident at Kabul, where he was assassinated two years later.
69. Pandey, *From Sepoy to Subedar*, p.107.
70. Ibid.
71. Major General William George Keith Elphinstone (1782–1842) was an officer of the British army. He took part in the battle for Waterloo in 1815 and for a time served as aide-de-camp to King George IV. He was promoted as Major General in 1837, and in 1841, during the First Anglo-Afghan War, was placed in command of the British garrison in Kabul, numbering around 4,500 troops, of whom 690 were European and the rest Indian. The garrison also included 12,000 civilians, including soldiers' families and camp followers. His troops and civilians were all wiped out during the disastrous retreat from Kabul. He later died a captive in Afghanistan some months later.
72. Pandey, *From Sepoy to Subedar*, p.108.
73. Dr Wiliam Brydon, a British surgeon, was the only European survivor of the Army of the Indus. In January 1842, 16,500 British and Indian

soldiers tried to escape Afghanistan. The Afghan guerrillas intercepted them and proceeded to massacre them during the next seven days. This was probably one of the worst defeats suffered by the British army. Doctor Brydon succeeded in reaching Jalalabad, to be followed by a few other survivors.

74. Edward Law, 1st Baron Ellenborough (1790–1871), was elected to Parliament in 1813 as a Tory. He held the privy seal in Wellington's government from 1828 to 1829; was president of the Board of Control for India, 1828–30 and on three later occasions for short periods; Governor General of India, 1841–4; and First Lord of the Admiralty in 1846. His term of office as Governor General was dominated by the first China War, the winding up of the ill-fated Afghan campaign and the annexation of Sind.

75. Sir George Pollock (1786–1872) was a British Field Marshal. After the disaster of the Army of the Indus, General Pollock was given command of the British army in Peshawar. He advanced through the Khyber Pass to Jalalabad, whose garrison he relieved in April 1842. Pollock reached Kabul on 15 September 1842.

76. Lady Sale, *A Journal of the Disasters in Afghanistan*, John Murray, 1843.
77. Ibid.
78. Ibid., pp. 230-31.
79. Ibid., p. 232.
80. Ibid., p. 233.
81. Ibid., p. 241.
82. Ibid., p. 280.
83. Mohammad Akbar Khan (1813–1845) was the son of Amir Dost Mohammad Khan. He led a revolt in Kabul against the British mission of William McNaughten, Alexander 'Sekundar' Burnes and their garrison of 4,500 men. In November 1841, he besieged Major-General William Elphinstone's force in Kabul. Elphinstone accepted from Mohammad Akbar Khan a safe conduct for his force and 12,000 associated people to flee to India; they were ambushed and massacred. It was claimed in at least one set of British war memoirs that during the retreat, Akbar Khan could be heard alternately commanding his men in Persian to desist from, and in Pushtu to continue, firing. Many believe that Akbar Khan was poisoned by his father, Dost Mohammad, who feared his ambition.
84. Lady Sale, *A Journal of the Disasters in Afghanistan*.

85. Gandamak is 56 km from Jalalabad on the road to Kabul. While the British army was retreating from Kabul in 1842, a hill near Gandamak was the scene of the massacre of the last survivors of the force. Twenty officers and forty-five British soldiers of the 44$^{th}$ East Essex Regiment were killed. The place is also notable for the Treaty of Gandamak, signed on 26 May 1879, between the British government and Yakub Khan, the Amir of Afghanistan.

86. Herbert Edwardes was born in England and went to India in 1840 with the East India Company's first Bengal Fusiliers. He was subsequently sent to Punjab where he became one of Henry Lawrence's loyal supporters. As a young lieutenant, he was chosen by Henry Lawrence to resolve dispute over revenue collection with the Banuchis. He parleyed with them and successfully resolved the issue and, in doing so, evoked reverence and awe rarely seen from the local tribes. When the Uprising of 1857 started, Edwardes thought it to be divine retribution for the lack of force used by the British in bringing their 'God to the people'. Edwardes played a prominent role in quelling the uprising by mustering a large force of Pathans in Punjab. He was later offered the governorship of Punjab but declined because of ill health. Upon his return to England he started work on a biography of Henry Lawrence, a book he never completed. He died on 23 December 1868 after having been knighted for his services to the British crown.

87. John Nicholson (1822–1857) was a Victorian-era British military hero. An officer of the army of the British East India Company, he played a critical role during the 1857 Uprising. He was much feared for his foul temper and authoritarian manner. He inspired the short-lived cult of Nikal Seyn despite the fact that he did not conceal his distaste for Indians and even went so far as to have some of his worshippers imprisoned and whipped. He is best known for his role in the 1857 Uprising, planning and leading the 'Storming of Delhi'. He died on 23 September 1857 in a small bungalow in the cantonments of Delhi as a result of wounds received. He is commemorated on a white marble memorial plaque at the Mutiny Memorial on the Ridge in New Delhi. A tablet in the church of Bannu where Nicholson served as Deputy Commissioner from 1852 to 1854 carries the following inscription: 'Gifted in mind and body, he was as brilliant in government as in arms. The snows of Ghazni attest his youthful fortitude; the songs of Punjab his many deeds; the peace of this

frontier his strong rule. The enemies of his country know how terrible he was in battle, and we his friends have to recall how gentle, generous, and true he was.' He was thirty-four when he died.
88. Field Marshal Sir Neville Chamberlain (1820–1902) was a significant figure in Britain's wars on the Indian subcontinent and the only person to have been appointed to the highest rank in the British army while a member of the Unitarian church. He obtained a commission as an ensign in the East India Company's army through family connections and joined the infantry at Lucknow in 1838. During the next four years he distinguished himself in the invasion of Afghanistan and was wounded six times. His reckless bravery brought him to the attention of senior officers. Although still suffering from a wound, he took part in the battle of Maharajpur in 1843. In 1845 he was ordered to return to England to recover his health. Promotions quickly followed his return to India in 1846. By 1848, at the outset of the second Anglo-Sikh War, he was a cavalry brigade major. By 1854 he was Brigadier. At the commencement of the Indian mutiny in 1857 Chamberlain was appointed Adjutant-General of the Bengal army. At Delhi he led his men in charge at and over a fortified position and was wounded. In 1858 and 1859 he led further actions as commander in Afghanistan. He was wounded again in the arm in fierce fighting against the Wahabis in 1863. He was knighted the same year and in 1864, as soon as he was fit to travel, he returned to England.
89. Quoted in Charles Allen, *Soldier Sahibs*, Abacus, 2001, p.266.
90. Tan Tai Yong, 'Sepoys and the Colonial Punjab and the Military Base of the Indian Army 1845–1900', in *The British Raj and its Indian Armed Forces*, Oxford University Press, 2002, p.16.
91. Ibid.
92. Ibid.
93. Ibid., p.17.
94. Allen, *Soldier Sahibs*, p.266.
95. Hoti Mardan or Mardan was a frontier cantonment of British India in Peshawar district of the NWFP. It is notable as the permanent headquarters of the famous Corps of Guides.
96. Allen, *Soldier Sahibs*, p.276.
97. Lord John Lawrence (1811–1879) was Governor General and Viceroy of India (1864–69). Several of his brothers were in British Indian services and one of them, Sir Henry Lawrence, became President of the Board

of Commissioners constituted for the settlement of Punjab after its annexation in 1849. The three-member board included John Lawrence as well. Later the two brothers quarrelled on the issue of best mode of the Punjab settlement and the Dalhousie administration asked the elder brother, Henry Lawrence, to resign. John Lawrence then assumed responsibility for the Punjab settlement, which he achieved with great credit. He retired from the Indian Civil Services in 1859. After the death of Lord Elgin in 1863, Sir John Lawrence was appointed Governor General of India, a position he held from 12 January 1864 to 12 January 1869. Lord Lawrence's administration was characterized by non-interference in Afghan politics.

98. Amaresh Mishra, *War of Civilisations: India AD 1857*, Rupa Publications, 2008, p.434.
99. Ibid., pp.434–35.
100. Arthur Swinson, *North-West Frontier: People and Events 1839–1947*, Hutchinson & Co., 1967.
101. Ibid.
102. Ibid.
103. Allen, *Soldier Sahibs*, p.282.
104. Rajputs constitute one of the major Hindu Kshatriya groups of India. They belong to many clans and are considered formidable warriors. They were classified as a martial race by the British colonial government and recruited for the military establishment during the subcontinent's colonial period.
105. The British had this to say about him: 'The death of Swat's ruler Syed [sic] Akbar Shah on the 11[th] of May 1857 was a good omen for our Government. This was the day when news of the war of independence had reached our offices in Peshawar. If he were alive by this time, then the political scenario of the Frontier would have been much different.'
106. Gulab Singh (1792–1857) was the founder and first Maharaja of the princely state of Jammu and Kashmir during the British Raj in India. He was made the independent ruler of Kashmir after the British defeated the Sikhs during the First Anglo-Sikh War (1845–46).
107. The Akhund of Swat, Abdul Ghafur (1794–1877), was a Muslim saint who exercised great influence and authority over Muslims in large parts of Central Asia. His residence in the mountainous country of Swat (now part of Pakistan) was a pilgrim destination.

108. Charles Allen, *God's Terrorists*, Little Brown, 2006, pp.142–43.
109. Ibid., p.143.
110. Ibid.
111. Mishra, *War of Civilisations*, p.434.
112. Percy Sykes, *A History of Afghanistan*, Munshiram Manoharlal, 1940, p.94.
113. Sher Ali Khan (1825–1879) was Amir of Afghanistan from 1863 to 1866 and from 1868 until his death in 1879. He was the third son of Dost Mohammed Khan, founder of the Barakzai dynasty in Afghanistan.
114. Sir Frederick John Goldsmid (1818–1908) was a British army officer and a Major General in the British army who, through negotiations with several Asian countries, made possible the Indo-European telegraph, the first rapid communication system linking Europe and Asia. His knowledge of Asian languages enabled him to arbitrate boundary disputes between Iran and Baluchistan in 1871 and between Iran and Afghanistan in 1872. He was knighted in 1871.
115. In the Central Asia of the nineteenth century, half the area covered by present-day Turkmenistan, the whole of modern-day Uzbekistan, almost the whole of present-day Kirghistan and the southern region of what is now Kazakhstan were occupied by the khanates of Khiva, Bokhara and Khokand.
116. Capital of Uzbekistan and also of Tashkent province. In medieval times the town and the province were known as 'Chach'. Later, the town came to be known as Chachkand/Chashkand, meaning Chach city. After the sixteenth century the name changed from Chachkand/Chashkand to Tashkand, or 'stone city'.
117. Lord Northbrook was India's Viceroy from 1872 to 1876.
118. Edward Robert Lytton (1831–1891) served as Viceroy of India during the mid-1870s.
119. Konstantin Petrovich Kaufmann was a Russian General (1811–12). He captured the city of Samarkand in 1868 and was made the Khanate of Bokhara (located on the north of Afghanistan), a Russian protectorate that same year. In 1873 he occupied the Khanate of Khiva (located between Bokhara and the Caspian Sea) and Russia gained all of that Khanate's territory north of the Amu Darya. In 1875, Kaufmann occupied the Khanate of Khokand (north-east of Bokhara) allowing Russia to annex it in 1976. Kaufmann's military successes, however, brought protests from the British government which considered that its interests

in Afghanistan were threatened by Russian expansion.
120. Mazar-i-Sharif is the fourth largest city in Afghanistan. It is the capital of Balkh province and is linked by roads to Kabul in the south-east, Herat in the west and Uzbekistan in the north. Mazar-i-Sharif means 'noble shrine', a reference to the large blue-tiled sanctuary and mosque in the centre of the city known as the Shrine of Hazrat Ali or the Blue Mosque. It is believed by some Muslims to be the site of the tomb of Ali ibn Abi Talib, the cousin and son-in-law of Prophet Mohammad who was the Mazar-i-Sharif. The Twelver Shias, however, believe that the real grave of Ali is within Imam Ali mosque in Najaf, Iraq, as was disclosed by the sixth Twelver Shia Iman, Ja'far as-Sadiq. It is also speculated that underneath the Blue Mosque lies the Prophet Zoroaster's tomb. The dominant language in Mazar-i-Sharif is Persian as well as Uzbek. The city is a major tourist attraction because of its fabulous Muslim and Hellenistic archaeological sites. In July 2006 the discovery of new Hellenistic remains was announced.
121. The Treaty of Gandamak officially ended the first phase of the Second Anglo-Afghan War. Afghanistan ceded various frontier areas to Britain to prevent invasion of further areas of the country. It was signed by Sir Pierre Louis Napoleon Cavagnari for the British and Amir Yakub Khan for the Afghans on 26 May 1879.
122. Pishin is a small town located in Baluchistan, Pakistan.
123. Sibi is a city located in Baluchistan, Pakistan.
124. The Shia sect is one of the popular sects of Islam. The Sunnis in India constitute a major group.
125. The Shia sect is one of the popular sects of Islam.
126. Sir Pierre Louis Napoleon Cavagnari (1841–1879) was a British military administrator. He entered the military service of the East India Company and served through the Oudh campaign against mutineers in 1858 and 1859. In 1861 he was appointed as assistant commissioner in the Punjab region of British India and in 1877 he became the deputy commissioner of Peshawar and took part in several expeditions against the Pakhtun tribes. In September 1878 he was attached to the staff of a British mission to Kabul, Afghanistan, which the Afghans refused to allow to proceed through the Khyber Pass. In May 1879 after the British–Indian forces had invaded Afghanistan and after the death of Afghan Amir Sher Ali Khan, Cavagnari negotiated and signed the Treaty of Gandamak with Sher Ali

Khan's son and successor Mohammad Yaqub Khan. With this treaty the Afghans agreed to admit a British Resident to Kabul and the post was conferred on Cavagnari. He took up his Residency in July 1879 and for a time all seemed to go well. But on 3 September of that year, Cavagnari and the other European members of the mission, along with their guards, were killed by the mutinous Afghan troops.

126. Field Marshal Frederick Sleigh Roberts (1832–1914) was a distinguished Anglo-Irish soldier and one of the most successful commanders of the Victorian era. He played a prominent role in securing British interests during the 1857 Uprising and the Second Anglo-Afghan War.
127. The idea is also reflected in Alastair Lamb, 'A Study of the Frontiers of the British Empire', *Journal of the Royal Central Asian Society,* 3(3), 1966.
128. Lamb, 'A Study of the Frontiers of the British Empire', *Journal of the Royal Central Asian Society,* 3(3).
129. Rose L. Greaves, 'Themes in British Policy towards Afghanistan in its Relations to Indian Frontier Defence', *Journal of the Royal Society of Asian Affairs,* 24(1), 1993.
130. Ibid.
131. Akbar S. Ahmad, 'An Aspect of the Colonial Encounter in the NWFP', *Journal of the Royal Society for Asian Affairs,* 9, 1978, pp.319–27.
132. Akbar S. Ahmad, 'Tribes and States in Central and South Asia', *Journal of the Royal Society for Asian Affairs,* 9(2), 1980.
133. J.G. Elliott, *The Frontier 1839-1947: The Story of the N.W. Frontier of India,* Cassell, 1968, p.53.
134. High mountain region located mostly in Tajikistan, also borders parts of Afghanistan, Pakistan, China and Kyrgyzstan. It is a central mountain knot from which extend several great ranges, including the Karakorams and Hindu Kush.
135. Sir Lepel Griffin (1840–1908), ICS, was the Chief Secretary of Punjab in 1878; AGG Central India in 1881–88; and Chief Political Officer in the Second Afghan War.
136. Abdur Rahman Khan was the Amir of Afghanistan from 1880 to 1901.
137. Muhammad Yakub Khan (1849–1923) was the Amir of Afghanistan between 1879 and 1880. He ruled under British occupation during his reign. His reign ended with his abdication. He was succeeded by Amir Abdur Rahman.
138. Fraser-Tyler, 'Appendix III' in *Afghanistan,* pp.324–25.

139. Ibid., p.326.
140. Ibid.
141. Ibid.
142. Ibid., p.327.
143. Waziristan is a mountainous region in north-west Pakistan bordering Afghanistan and covering some 11,585 sq. km. It is part of the Federally Administered Tribal Areas, outside the country's four provinces. Waziristan comprises the area west and south-west of Peshawar between the Tochi river to the north and the Gomal river to the south. The North-West Frontier Province lies immediately to the east. The region was an independent tribal territory till 1893, remaining outside the British-ruled empire and Afghanistan. Tribal raiding into British-ruled territory from here was a constant problem for the British, eliciting frequent punitive expeditions between 1860 and 1945. The region became part of Pakistan in 1947.
144. Dir is a town in Dir district, NWFP, Pakistan.
145. Tirah is a mountainous tract in Kurram Agency of the Federally Administered Tribal Areas of Pakistan. It was the scene of a campaign that the British launched in 1897. The difficult passes and fierceness of its inhabitants had long preserved its inviolability from invaders.
146. General Sir Rob McGregor MacDonald Lockhart (1893–1981) was a British Indian Army general. He served in India during World War II, including a spell as Military Secretary to the India Office, and later became Commander-in-Chief of the Indian Army in 1947.
147. Sir George Stuart White (1835–1912) was a British Field Marshal. He first achieved distinction in the Second Anglo-Afghan War of 1878–80. He was Commander-in-Chief in India from 1893 to 1898 and was an instrument of Great Britain's 'forward' policy for neutralizing the Russian advance towards India.
148. Major General Sir Bindon Blood (1842–1940) was a British military commander who served in Egypt, Afghanistan, India and Africa. He commanded the Malakand Field Force and the Buner Field Force, relieving the British garrison during the siege of Malakand in 1897.
149. Mamund, a Pathan tribe and a valley on the Peshawar border of the North-West Frontier Province. The Mamunds live partly in Bajour and partly in Afghan territory due north of the Mohmands, a much larger tribe, with whom they must not be confused.

150. Sandhurst is a training college at Camberley, Surrey, south-eastern England, for officers of the British army.
151. From the Malakand Field Force accounts of Churchill.
152. Kohat is a medium-sized town in the North-West Frontier Province. It is the capital of Kohat district. The town centres around a British-era fort, various bazaars and a military cantonment. There are a number of tombs of famous personalities in the area, like that of Sufi saint and teacher Haji Bahadar Ali Abdullah Shah alias Haji Bahadar Sahib and Mian Fateh Shah (Sherkot, Kohat). The town boasts many mosques and schools. To the north of the city lies the Kohat Pass.
153. Dera Ismail Khan is a city in the North-West Frontier Province. The town, the headquarters of Dera Ismail Khan District, is situated on the west bank of the Indus River and lies 200 miles west of Lahore and 120 miles north-west of Multan. It is often referred to as D.I. Khan.
154. Lieutenant Colonel Sir Harold Arthur Deane (1854–1908) was an administrator in British India. Deane served as the first Political Agent of Malakand in 1895 and also as the first Chief Commissioner of the NWFP upon the creation of the province on 9 November 1901. Commissioned in 1874, Deane was promoted as Captain in 1885 and Major in 1894. He became Lieutenant Colonel in 1900. He was knighted in 1906.
155. Derajat is a cultural region in central Pakistan, located in the region where the provinces of Baluchistan, NWFP and Punjab meet. The region consists of three districts—Dera Ghazi Khan (western Punjab), Dera Ismail Khan (southern NWFP) as well as a smaller district, Rajanpur.
156. Whitehall is a road in Westminster in London. It is the centre of the British government. The road is lined with government departments/ministries; 'Whitehall' is also frequently used to denote British governmental administration.
157. Olaf Caroe, *The Pathans 550 B.C.–A.D. 1957*, MacMillan & Co., 1958, p.415.
158. Ibid.
159. Sir William Mackworth Young, Lieutenant Governor of Punjab from 1897 to 1902.
160. Caroe, *The Pathans*, p.415.
161. Ibid.
162. Ibid., pp.415–16.
163. Ibid., p.416.

164. H.C. Fanshawe was Chief Secretary to the Punjab government and Commissioner of the Delhi Division.
165. Caroe, *The Pathans*, p.417.
166. Sir George Olaf Roos-Keppel (1866–1921) served as Political Agent to the Governor General in Kurram and Khyber and later as Chief Commissioner, NWFP from 1908 till 1919. He is also known for his role in the Third Afghan War. In 1913, Roos-Kepppel along with Nawab Sir Sahibzada Abdul Qayyum established Islamia College (Peshawar) which was inaugurated by Haji Sahib Turangzai.
167. John Buchan, *Lord Minto: A Memoir*, Thomas Nelson and Sons, 1924, pp.226-27.
168. Of Sir Louis Dane.
169. Buchan, *Lord Minto*, p.229.
170. Ibid., pp.248-49.
171. Ibid., pp.249-50.
172. Ibid., p.250.
173. Ibid., pp.250-51.
174. Peshawar is the capital of the North-West Frontier Province, Pakistan. It is located west of the Bara River near the Khyber Pass. Once the capital of the ancient Buddhist kingdom of Gandhara, it was a centre of the caravan trade with Afghanistan and Central Asia.
175. Buchan, *Lord Minto*, pp.251-52.
176. Ibid. p.252.
177. Ibid., pp.260-61.
178. Buchan, John. *Lord Minto: A Memoir*. Thomas Nelson and Sons, 1924.

# 3

# Between One Great War and Another

## The Third Afghan War

It never took long for a crisis to precipitate on India's western frontiers. Within months of Sir Alexander Burnes's murder, a whole British army stood decimated in January 1842. Political officer Sir Pierre Louis Napaleon Cavagnari met a similar fate, triggering the Second Anglo-Afghan War. In 1897, just when the Commissioner of Peshawar reported that all was quiet on the 'western front', the Afridis rose in revolt sounding the bugle for others to rise in rebellion. Hardly surprising then for Curzon to remark, 'No man who has read a page of Indian history will ever prophesy about the Frontier.'[1]

The Third Afghan War was ill-timed for the British, coming as it did just a few months after the Great War. The human cost for them in World War I was enormous—a million dead and several million wounded. Many India-based soldiers eagerly awaited passage back home. Territorial army battalions posted locally were a tad too old for active service. About a million troops of the Indian army were equally war-weary when the Third Anglo-Afghan War broke out in May 1919. This war was no skirmish. It involved 7,50,000 British and Indian troops.[2]

Amir Habibullah of Afghanistan had announced his country's neutrality soon after the outbreak of the Great War. In October 1914, Turkey entered the war, incurring, in the bargain, the hostility of both Russia and Great Britain. It was a delicate situation for the Amir of Afghanistan. There had been in existence in Afghanistan, a strong pro-Turkish party supported by religious elements who wanted the Amir to throw in his lot with Turkey. Forced to explain his position, Habibullah told the British agent in Kabul: 'Turkey possessed a great religious attraction on the common mind of the ignorant Muslims of the world in general and on the Afghans in particular.'[3] On the occasion of a Durbar held at Kabul on 24 January 1916, large crowds had assembled outside Amir Habibullah's palace expecting him to proclaim a *jihad* against the British.[4]

In the three decades preceding the Great War, Germany assiduously worked to gain influence in Turkey, Iraq and Persia. In 1883, the Deutsche Bank acquired control of the railway of European Turkey. Very soon, a scheme for the construction of Baghdad Railways across Asia Minor was put on the anvil along with the German demand to secure a port near Kuwait. With the signing of the Potsdam Agreement[5] between Russia and Germany in August 1911, the Russian threat to Baghdad Railways was neutralized. The Russian policy towards Germany weakened the entente created by the Anglo-Russian Convention.[6] Alongside, German influence in Persia grew. The German legation in Persia had, since long, nurtured a close relationship with the Persian revolutionaries. Several *mujtahids* (experts of the sacred law) were won over by the German propaganda that all of Germany had been converted to Islam, Kaiser Wilhelm having already become a Haji after his pilgrimage to Mecca.[7]

It was in the midst of the Great War that Enver Pasha sent a Turko-German mission to Afghanistan. Furnished with credentials from the Khalifa and preaching *jihad*, this mission was aimed at crossing Persia into Afghanistan. The intention was to induce Habibullah to raise the banner of revolt across the Indian border by invoking a holy war. Led by Captain Oscar Niedermayer, the mission had considerable difficulty in getting through the Persian border. Its arrival in Herat on 24 August 1915 was immediately reported by Amir Habibullah to the Indian Viceroy. The position of the Amir in 1915 was unenviable. The declaration of *jihad* by the Sultan of Turkey, who was also the Caliph, had stirred the mullahs and the general Afghan populace. The basis of Afghan policy had long been to balance her two powerful neighbours, Great Britain and Russia, traditionally hostile to one another. But this situation was entirely new. In this instance, both Russia and Britain were on the same side.

Turkey and Germany had never had any direct contact with Afghanistan. In the circumstances, it was fortunate that the Amir had refrained from declaring a *jihad* which would simultaneously attract the ire of Russia and Britain. Attempting to delay matters, the Amir convened an assembly of leading mullahs and sardars to express his firm intention of maintaining neutrality. But to Oscar Niedermayer, he did not commit, forcing the leader of the Turko-German mission to complain in frustration: 'One day the Amir says he is for us, and the next, against us.'[8] Habibullah at the same time refused to let go of the mission, lest circumstances changed and Afghanistan was forced to declare war. Niedermayer was convinced that unless a strong Turkish force arrived in Afghanistan, there was no hope of winning over the astute Amir. When Erzerum capitulated to the Russians in March 1916, the possibility of a Turkish division ever reaching Afghanistan completely receded. On 22 May, the Turko-German mission left Kabul while the Amir continued to reaffirm his loyalty to the British. In the eight months the Turko-German mission stayed in Afghanistan, it concluded a treaty with the Amir that accorded Afghanistan the status of an independent nation, indulging the Amir as they would any head of a sovereign state. It helped strengthen Afghanistan psychologically— to unshackle from the foreign policy bind of Britain. In the spring of 1916, the Amir demanded the presence of an Afghan representative at the Peace Conference, the demand no doubt emanating from the pressure applied by the pro-Turkish party in Afghanistan. The visit of the Turko-German mission had heightened the Amir's confidence.

The defeat of Turkey by the Christian powers in the Great War aroused a feeling in Afghanistan that Britain had failed Islam in the hour of need. On 2 February 1919, more than two months after the armistice, the Amir, worried over the tense situation in Afghanistan, again wrote to the Viceroy, demanding recognition by the Peace Conference of the 'absolute liberty, freedom of action, and perpetual independence' of his kingdom. Before a reply in the negative could reach the Amir, he was dead. In the ensuing battle of succession, his third son Amanullah Khan was declared the Amir. The army at Kabul accepted him. In trying to outbid his uncle Nasrullah Khan to the throne of Kabul, he offered the army a pay of twenty rupees a month against eleven. On 3 March 1919, Amanullah informed the

Viceroy of his accession. Amanullah's condemnation of his uncle Nasrullah Khan as an accomplice in the murder of his father, his subsequent imprisonment, and later his death, did substantial damage to his (Amanullah's) popularity. Nasrullah Khan was a champion of the mullahs. In reinstating the members of the Musahiban[9] family, Amanullah alienated both the mullahs and the army. Discontent spread rapidly. The people refused to read the *Khutba* in the Amir's name in Kandahar on 25 April. Realizing the importance of deflecting attention from himself, Amanullah proclaimed a *jihad*.[10] He was now perceived among his people to be a patriot, attempting to recover the lost territory of Peshawar and Derajat for his country. The thinking went that perhaps even a partial success could force the British to recognize Afghanistan's independence. Taking on the Amir's mantle, Amanullah declared the government of Afghanistan to be 'internally and externally' free. Though his invasion of India failed, Amanullah succeeded in compelling the British to concede that they were no more the sole arbiters of Afghan foreign relations.

The Afghan attack coincided with an outbreak of general disaffection in Punjab. On 13 April 1919, the infamous Jallianwala Bagh incident[11] had taken place in Amritsar. Under orders from Brigadier-General Dyer, the Indian army troops fired upon and killed 379 people, injuring over 1,500, without any provocation.

Amanullah's men were in touch with Indian revolutionaries who called themselves 'the provisional Government of India'. The extent of their contact with the provisional government and its exact nature are not known but there is no doubt that the group had close links with one Qazi Abdul Wadi, the Afghan postmaster in Peshawar, and leader of a joint Hindu–Muslim body, the Peshawar Union Committee. Through the Qazi, the provisional government planned to disseminate revolutionary literature throughout northern India, urging the Muslims to rise. Sample the content of one of their pamphlets: 'A contract has been entered into with the forces of invasion by the Provisional Government. You should therefore use every possible means to kill British, continue to tear up railways and cut down the telegraph.'[12]

The British deliberately sought to establish a link between Indian nationalists active in Punjab and Amanullah's forces. Popular agitation directed against the draconian Rowlatt Act, appeared to them to be part of a grand nefarious design. Brigadier General Dyer's order to fire at the Jallianwala Bagh crowd was considered by most British to be an act of necessity under the circumstances. To construe the brutality as administratively expedient was the only way they could justify this state-sanctioned crime. The British also concluded that the Punjab insurrections had been launched prematurely, the opportunity for a concerted Afghan attack with Indian revolutionaries being lost in the process. Already committed, Amanullah went ahead with his plan of attack. In early May 1919, Sir George Roos-Keppel, Chief Commissioner of the NWFP, noted that the Pathans were getting restive. On 7 May, the Amir's plans for a simultaneous attack on the Khyber, Kurram and the town of Quetta were unknowingly disclosed by the Afghan postmaster to an informer of the British. Upon receiving the information, Sir George Roos-Keppel promptly threw a cordon of British troops around Peshawar and arrested local plotters, including the Afghan postmaster.[13]

In the First and the Second Afghan Wars, it was the British army that invaded Afghanistan. But on this occasion the Afghans intruded into Indian territory. Amanullah raised *lashkars* from both sides of the frontier. The real military strength of Afghanistan lay in its armed population rather than in its army. On the other hand, the inability to ensure supplies limited the number of armed tribesmen who could be kept in the field for a long period. The Afghan army consisted of 38,000 infantry, 8,000 cavalry and 4,000 artillery men, all badly trained and equipped with obsolete guns and rifles, but possessed of remarkable courage and endurance.[14]

The Khyber front saw action from 6 to 25 May. Saleh Mohammad, the Afghan Commander-in-Chief, commenced hostilities prematurely, expecting the Pathan tribesmen to rise in revolt. Arriving at Dakka by April end, the Afghan regulars crossed the frontier on 3 May and occupied Bagh. On 6 May, features above Landi Kotal were taken. The British garrison there consisted of two companies of the Indian infantry and 500 men of Khyber Rifles. The loyalty of the men constituting Khyber Rifles was suspect due to the proclamation of *jihad*. The Afghans let go of a good opportunity when they failed to overpower the weak British force.

Had they done so, there was a good chance of the neighbouring tribes rising in their support. Instead they waited. The situation for the British was saved when reinforcements arrived on 7 and 8 May. On 11 May the Afghan position at Bagh was attacked. The Afghans were driven into flight as the Royal Air Force (RAF) bombed and machine-gunned the area. On the following day, the RAF bombed the Afghan camp at Dakka whereupon the Amir's army was forced to retreat to Jalalabad. Dakka was occupied by the British without opposition.[15] Despite the British victory on 11 May, several disaffected Afridis deserted the Khyber Rifles with their arms and ammunition, forcing the British to disband the force. The British, however, saw to it that they held on to the Khyber Pass. The RAF carried out concentrated bombing raids on Jalalabad, also bombing the Amir's palace and the ammunition factory at Kabul. The demonstration that the capital was within reach of British aircraft produced a profound impression and an immediate desire for peace on the part of the Amir. The effect of the aerial bombing was well described by an Indian eyewitness: 'At 6 a.m. an aeroplane made an appearance at Kabul for the first time… there was a great humming sound in the town after the airship had disappeared, denoting public terror and sensation followed by a death silence after a few minutes. To appease the public from the panic, a band was played and a regiment brought on the parade ground for a few minutes, quite at unusual times.' As the British prepared to advance on Jalababad, unofficial Afghan overtures culminated on 31 May in a formal request from the Amir for an armistice.[16]

On the central front, the forces of Nadir Khan reached Thall on 26 May. The intense appeal of Kabul made it almost a certainty that the Mahsuds and Wazirs would throw in their lot with the Amir. The British forces withdrew from the Tochi valley and Wana through the Zhob[17] and with great difficulty managed to reach Fort Sandeman. During this withdrawal, four British officers were killed and two more seriously wounded. The losses for the British (by death and desertion) were heavy. It was only when reinforcements from Quetta arrived that the British gained an upper hand in this area.[18]

To return to Nadir Khan who was entrenched at Thall—Brigadier-General Dyer of the infamous Jallianwala Bagh episode attacked Nadir Khan's main positions on 2 June and gained victory for the British. The signing of the armistice on 3 June officially ended the war.[19] On 28 May a letter was received from the Amir that ascribed the outbreak of war to a misunderstanding. It stated that the Afghan forces' operations were of a defensive nature. The Amir complained of the air bombardment of Kabul and Jalalabad as unjustifiable acts of aggression but added that he was 'nonetheless prepared to be magnanimous should they issue orders for the cessation of hostilities'.[20] The Viceroy in his reply refuted the Amir's version of the causes of war and laid down the terms for the armistice. The treaty for the restoration of peace was to be followed by a probationary period of six months during which the Amir was to be seen showing signs of friendship and upon fulfilment of these conditions; 'a Treaty of Friendship' was to be concluded. The readiness of the Government of India to accept the Amir's offer was criticized in some quarters. But the British realized that an advance into Kabul would serve no purpose. It would further weaken Afghanistan, the invaluable buffer between India and Soviet Russia. 'After the breakdown of the Russian Empire in 1917, the sole inducement for Afghanistan to remain within the British orbit was removed (at any rate for the time being) and events were to prove that the sudden cessation of the pressure from the north had made a greater impression on the Afghan mind than the victory of Great Britain.'[21]

## Hijrat

Shortly after the Third Anglo-Afghan War, the movement of Hijrat took place. The successors of Mohammad, the Khalifas, had always had their temporal bases, the Khilafat. This was originally set up at Medina and later shifted to Damascus, Baghdad, Egypt and finally to Istanbul. It then fell to the 'Ottomans' to carry the mantle of *imamat*[22] of the Muslims.

The Ottoman empire faced imminent dismemberment after the Great War. Identifying with the larger world order of Islam, Indian Muslims strove to save the Ottoman (Islamic) political power from extinction. Turkish sultans had long claimed Khilafat of the Muslim world. This claim did not hold great appeal for the Muslims of India while the Mughals held sway. With the British replacing the Mughals, Indian Muslims now often looked to the Ottoman sultan as their spiritual sovereign. They also rallied in favour of the Turkish Khilafat, demanding maintenance and unity of the Ottoman empire, displaying remarkable unanimity although separated by thousands of miles from Istanbul. The Khilafat movement was the Indian Muslim way of fighting Istanbul's battles. A tragic offshoot of this movement was 'Hijrat'.

A fatwa was issued by Shah Abdul Aziz[23] and his disciple Abdul Hai, two famous nineteenth-century theologians from Delhi, proclaiming India to be *dar-ul-harb*, a place where Muslim law could not be enforced in matters of worship and protection of the believers. The fatwa was aimed against British rule as the Alims found that it increasingly interfered with the traditions and practices of Islamic law and feared replacement of the Islamic legal system. The fatwa exhorted Muslims to perform Hijrat on the same lines as Mohammad's from Mecca to Medina; retreating from *dar-ul-harb* to another place with an intention to return, reclaim and restore it as *dar-ul-Islam*, the land of the believers. The analogy drawn was with Mohammad's triumphant return to Mecca from Medina. One unfortunate result of the Khilafat agitation was the 'Hijrat' performed by thousands of Indian Muslims during the summer of 1920, having taken a cue from the fatwa of Shah Abdul Aziz. The famous Ali brothers (Maulana Mohammad Ali Jauhar and Maulana Shaukat Ali) and many other prominent Khilafat agitationists encouraged the exodus from India. Amir Amanullah of Afghanistan actively abetted Hijrat, asking India's Muslims to migrate to Afghanistan in the name of Islam. The Amir was in large measure prompted by political considerations. Having lost the Third Afghan War in 1919, he wanted Indian Khilafatists spurred to action in order to cause unease to the British. In Hijrat, the Amir found one such excuse. On the day of the first anniversary of his father's assassination (21 February 1920), the Amir delivered a speech in Kabul vowing to give his own life for the cause of Khilafat. He also welcomed Muslims who intended to migrate to Afghanistan. A delegation lead by the Afghan Foreign Minister that arrived in India in April 1920 professed similar sentiments. These Afghan gestures proved popular and caught the imagination of Indian Khilafatists. Most Khilafat organizations released in the press a summary of what the Amir of Afghanistan had promised, also ensuring that the press reports received wide publicity.[24]

Discontent already prevailed against the British in the NWFP on account of the recent killing of a *mohajir*[25] by a British soldier at Kutcha Garhi near Peshawar. With the arrival of the Khilafatists, there was an immediate popular upsurge in favour of Hijrat in the NWFP. People in Peshawar, Mardan and its rural hinterland took to selling their lands, cattle and property at highly undervalued prices to undertake Hijrat. By the end of July, almost 10,000 Indian Muslims had crossed the Durand Line, this figure rising to 40,000 within a fortnight. The actual numbers were far higher, for many took other routes, via Mohmand country or the Tochi Pass, to cross over. By the second half of August, 7,000 to 8,000 *mohajarin* were pouring into Afghanistan each week.[26]

This enthusiastic response to Hijrat sent the Amir into panic. Poor as it was, his country could hardly support such an influx. In the interim, the Afghan Foreign Minister visiting India had resolved important issues with the British. Politically, it did not suit the Amir any more for the Hijrat to continue. On 9 August 1920, he issued a *firman*[27] declaring that fresh emigrants were to be allowed only after the previous *mohajarin* had been absorbed. The Afghan authorities ensured that fresh emigration from India stopped. Those who had already entered Afghanistan were given such a cold reception that many returned to India. The result of this misadventure (Hijrat) was disastrous. More than 60,000 *mohajarin* had migrated to Afghanistan, out of whom over 75 per cent were forced to return. Some who could not, were forced to migrate to places like Turkey and Russia. Many undertaking Hijrat perished. Some died in Afghanistan or in Russia, while the majority succumbed en route to India via the Khyber.[28]

## The Mollie Ellis Affair[29]

One episode that demanded, and got, major space in print media, both in India and England, was the Mollie Ellis Affair. Perhaps the most talked-about incident reported from the NWFP during the interwar years, it was also illustrative of the kind of relationship that existed between the British and the people of the frontier. Unlike some other occurrences that caused diplomatic rows, the Mollie Ellis affair did not involve Afghanistan or Russia.

It happened on 14 April 1923. In the cantonment town of Kohat was posted a Major Ellis who lived there with his wife and seventeen-year-old daughter. While he was on duty on the night of 14 April, some tribesmen entered his bungalow, murdered his wife, abducted his daughter and escaped into tribal territory before the administration so much as got a whiff of it. It was difficult to fathom the motive; neither could one recall another incident of this kind in the long frontier history where kidnapping accompanied murder.

Sifting through rumours, the Chief Commissioner, Peshawar, decided to follow a possible lead that led to a gang of Afridi tribesmen earlier involved in the murder of a Colonel and his wife and let off for lack of evidence. When caught in a case of stealing rifles, they were all in female attire. Being jeered at by their women while being marched away had so incensed them that Ajab and Shahjada Khan from amongst them decided to execute the kidnapping and murder to avenge the humiliation.

What was the Chief Commissioner to do now? How was he to reach the gang? How was he to prevent the gang from crossing over into Afghanistan? It was almost impossible to follow the lead of the culprits into Tirah. The police could not go in for fear of getting killed by the Afridis. No European had ventured into Tirah after 1897. The job of nabbing the culprits needed to be carried out by carefully selected individuals. The Chief Commissioner set about doing just that. ,Zaman Khan, who was the most prominent Khan of the area, and Bahadur Kuli Khan, the assistant political officer of Kurram valley, were chosen for the job.

The Chief Commissioner chanced upon an Englishwoman, Lillian Starr, a nurse serving at the Peshawar Mission Hospital. It is her daring that stands out most in the whole affair. Married to a doctor of Peshawar Mission Hospital, she was widowed in 1918 when her husband was murdered by tribesmen who entered her house in somewhat similar circumstances. After a two-year gap, Lillian Starr returned to the same hospital to serve the same people from amongst whom a few had murdered her husband. Having nursed many from the area, her name and face were familiar to most. The Chief Commissioner could not have chosen a better person for the rescue mission. Luckily for him, Lillian Starr acceded to his request.

Appreciating the fact that time was of the essence, she left for the mission within a day of saying 'yes'. Leaving on 19 April, she had no definite leads to follow. In her entourage was the son of a famous mullah, a mullah himself, who negotiated with the tribesmen. Lillian Starr was the first white woman to be seen in Tirah. Khan Bahadur Kuli Khan had preceded Lillian Starr's party by a day. By the time Starr arrived at the village of Khanki Bazaar on 21 April, Khan Bahadur Kuli Khan, with the help of the chief mullah of the area, had located the two culprits and arranged to meet them. This meeting took place prior to Starr's arrival in the village. Ajab admitted to the raid at Major Ellis's residence. The abducted daughter of Major Ellis was in their custody. But this last bit information was not readily forthcoming. Initially the kidnappers maintained that the girl had been taken to Afghanistan. Attempting to din some sense into Ajab's head, Kuli Khan said that the girl, if subjected to more travel, could die of exhaustion. Kuli Khan was greatly helped by the mullah of Khanki Bazaar in establishing contact with the girl. The chief mullah forced Ajab and Shahzada Khan to agree to the terms of surrender. Just when the negotiations were nearing fruition, Lillian Starr arrived in Khanki Bazaar. The chief mullah greeted this news with trepidation. An official party with a woman was cause for trouble. Could his (the chief mullah's) friends be thinking that he was in cahoots with the government party? This was bound to raise hackles. Kuli Khan's sane advice saved the day. The chief mullah for a time appeared confused—about the religious propriety of his proposed actions—should he or should he not tolerate the murder of one woman and the abduction of another? How much honour would accrue if he became the leading agent in securing the release of the abducted girl? Letters written by Mollie Ellis were handed over to Lillian Starr when she reached Khanki Bazaar. They contained the terms of her release. Mollie was forced by her captors to write them. 'The girl was in danger but still alive' is the report that went out from Lillian Starr to the Chief Commissioner, Peshawar, on the night of 21 April.

After the evening meal on 21 April, Lillian Starr got the news that the kidnapped girl could be brought to her on the same evening. Sure enough, the chief mullah succeeded in forcing reasonable terms of surrender on Ajab and Shahzada Khan. By 10 p.m., the mullah had despatched the two with his own men to retrieve the girl. At 5 a.m. next morning (22 April), Lillian Starr was informed of the girl's arrival. Two hours later, she was asked to come to the chief mullah's house to meet the girl.

The mullah of Khanki Bazaar had secured the girl's release. The kidnappers succumbed to his charisma and authority. After securing possession of Mollie Ellis and ensuring that the culprits were brought back, Lillian Starr and her entourage commenced their return journey.

The rescue story made headlines, both in Britain and India. Exaggerated reports of Lilian Starr going into Tirah armed to the teeth, leading a wild bunch of faithful tribesmen, appeared in newspapers. Prayer meetings were held across churches in India and England for Lillian Starr and Mollie Ellis. There was widespread anger too in official circles on the issue of the murder and kidnapping, which soon translated into action when two squadrons of the RAF bombed Tirah.

The Chief Commissioner summoned a great council of Afridis—one of the largest *jirgas* that ever met. There was now cause for a feud between the British and the Afridis that involved women—which, by the Afridi custom, had to be paid for in blood. Deliberations over, the mullahs and maliks set their seal on a unique document in the history of the frontier. Here is a translation of some portions:

> We, the chief elders and representatives of the Afridi and Orakzai clans, hereby declare that Azab Khan, Shahzada, Gul Akbar, Sultan Mir, Haida Shah who are the enemies of the British government are likewise our enemies. The five men mentioned above and their families shall from now onwards never enter our country. If they should enter the country or any of our sections, it shall be the duty of the section in question to capture them and hand them over to the British government. If any section or individual of our tribe should give them shelter or passage, it is our prayer that the government shall take such action as it may deem suitable, whether by means of airplanes or otherwise—signed and dated 13 May 1923.

The Chief Commissioner was not finished yet. He ordered the destruction of the country that had given shelter to the gang. He also ordered the burning down of the village where the gang had first stayed after the Kohat murder and abduction. Heavy fines were imposed on the tribes for the 'gang's past acts of omission & commission and for the offense of giving them passage.'

Mollie Ellis returned to Kohat with her father and Lillian Starr went back to the Mission Hospital. Mollie Ellis had been seventeen then. As Mollie Wade, sixty years later, she returned to visit the place where her mother lay buried and planted a lemon tree where her residence had been. There is a place now named after her—Ellis Post, the spot from which she was taken away into Tirah territory. The story of 'Ajab and Ellis' is still a familiar one in Afridi territory. As for the patients of the Mission Hospital, when they found out that Lillian Starr had been to Tirah, they seemed pleased. 'Now you are one of us,' they would say, 'none but Afridis walk abroad in Tirah.'

## The Case of Islam Bibi and the Fakir of Ipi

The force that has always held the Pakhtuns together is Islam—administered by religious leaders. Examples abound of these famous religious men—Mullah Hadda, Mullah Powindah, the Fakir of Ipi and many such others. Their leadership rested on two interacting factors—charisma and militancy. This leadership has prospered since long in Pakhtun society that has normally rejected authority or leadership. It was some decades after Mullah Powindah's death that another famous religious leader emerged in North Waziristan. He was the Fakir of Ipi. Mirza Ali Khan (his real name), born in 1901, belonged to a famous Turi Khel clan of the Wazir tribe of North Waziristan Agency. His father and grandfather were well-regarded religious men of their area. Early in life, Mirza Ali Khan's name became associated with religious leadership. While at Jalalabad, he became the Murid of Naqib Jalalabadi, a prominent Sufi and 'Gadi Nashin' of the Qadariyaa Sufi order in Afghanistan. When he returned from Afghanistan, the inhabitants of Ipi invited him to make that village his permanent abode. Mirza Ali Khan accepted the invitation.

The mosque that Mirza came to occupy gradually gained in prominence. His popularity and influence grew with it. Opposing the British in those days made for instant popularity. The Khudai Khidmatgars and Jamait-i-Ulema were mobilizing public opinion against the British in the NWFP. Mirza Ali Khan readily supported their endeavour. Even at this early stage, he appeared to seek a military rather than political solution. In his fight against the British, he appeared to be on the same side as the Congress.[30]

But at another level, his actions easily qualified as being communal. He consistently sided with his co-religionists if ever a dispute arose between Hindus and Muslims. Despite the non-communal stand taken by Khan Abdul Ghaffar Khan in the Shahid Gunj mosque incident, Mirza Ali Khan openly came out against what he interpreted as the Hindus' hate for Muslims. To him, an Indian Muslim was always an underdog under the economically dominant Hindus. His crusade against the Hindus was second only to that against the British Raj in India. While in favour of the Congress movement despite religious animosity towards the Hindus, he firmly stood behind his co-religionists without supporting the Muslim League. This mutually opposed position of Mirza Ali Khan was difficult to comprehend. Fortunately, this duality did not acquire acute proportions as the Muslims were in an overwhelming majority in the NWFP. Had it been any other province with a large Hindu population, this contradiction would have made Mirza Ali Khan's alliance with the Congress impossible and unworkable.[31]

In March 1936, a young Hindu girl, Ram Kaur, from a village near Bannu converted to Islam and married a Muslim schoolteacher—Sayyid Amir Noor Ali Shah. The change of faith led to change of name. Ram Kaur became Islam Bibi, the name she preferred to be called by in the Muslim community of Bannu district. Possibly she took the cue from another Hindu girl, Chuni Bai of Mianwali, who converted in 1928 and was given the name 'Islam Bibi'.

Ram Kaur's conversion and marriage became news in and around Bannu. Relations between Hindus and Muslims of the area deteriorated. As a community, the Hindus and Sikhs of Bannu city were a prosperous lot. They alleged that Ram Kaur had been kidnapped and forcibly converted to Islam. They demanded that she be immediately restored to her mother. Muslim support built up in favour of Ram Kaur's husband as a reaction. Ram Kaur to them was now Noor Ali Shah's lawfully wedded wife. In the interim, Ram Kaur's mother filed a police complaint against Noor Ali Shah for kidnapping her daughter. The *jirga* of local maliks formed by the district administration tried settling the dispute by effecting a compromise between Ram Kaur's mother and Noor Ali Shah. This temporarily resulted in a withdrawal of the prosecution case. After the compromise, the couple went to live with Noor Ali Shah's cousin.[32]

The *jirga*'s decision was not liked by the Hindu community of Bannu city. It convinced Ram Kaur's mother to institute a civil suit in the court of the Deputy Commissioner, Bannu, demanding her return. But Ram Kaur remained adamant as she found this request repugnant to the principle of 'Pakhtunwali'. The couple therefore decided to escape to Afghanistan when they were informed by a sympathetic Muslim police officer about arrangements for their arrest being made by government authorities. Some in the local Muslim bureaucracy were secretly trying to help the couple to escape.[33]

The attempt to escape failed. The couple was arrested and put in Bannu jail. A *jirga* of Muslim chiefs of Bannu tried to meet the Deputy Commissioner to discuss the case. The Deputy Commissioner declined to meet it. Ram Kaur was presented in the court of the Deputy Commissioner where she explicitly stated that she had converted to Islam of her own free will and was the legally wedded wife of Noor Ali Shah. An altercation with her mother led to charges of contempt of court, as a result of which Ram Kaur was convicted for six months.

This case went through several stages of trial to ultimately come to the judicial commissioner who then had the status of a high court in the province. The judicial commissioner referred the case for medical report to the civil surgeon who, in the medical certificate, certified that Islam Bibi was less than sixteen years at the time of elopement with Noor Ali Shah. She was therefore a minor in the eyes of the law and her consent was not valid. The judicial commissioner ordered Ram Kaur to be released from jail on a fine of ₹200 and to be put in temporary custody of a Sikh honorary magistrate. Noor Ali Shah and his brothers were convicted and sentenced to a three-year term.

The Muslim community was angry and riotous as a consequence of this judgement and attacked the court house, the houses of the Deputy Commissioner and the Sikh honorary magistrate, who had to be rescued by the police. The custody of Ram Kaur was later transferred to a Muslim government official. On 27 September 1936, Ram Kaur (Islam Bibi) was finally handed over to her mother, who, without losing a moment, rushed her to Hoshiarpur in Gurdaspur district and married her off to a Hindu. Her former husband, Noor Ali Shah, was subsequently released from jail after eighteen months. His brothers convinced him to marry again. But within a year of that marriage, Noor Ali Shah left home in search of Islam Bibi, never to return.[34]

The Muslims construed the court's decision in Islam Bibi's case as an interference in their internal social affairs. They grew doubtful of British impartiality. Issues governing Pakhtunwali and *badal* (revenge) surfaced soon. The Muslims of Bannu and Waziristan organized protest meetings in hujras and mosques, demanding 'justice' in the case of Islam Bibi and a guarantee of non-interference in their religious affairs. During the period of the Muslim protest, four Hindu girls were kidnapped by the Wazirs in complicity with local maliks. Mirza Ali Khan, who by now was popular as the Fakir of Ipi, participated in almost all meetings of protest in Waziristan and Bannu. His clan of Wazirs was the first to raise the cry for 'badal' and 'ghaza', which the Fakir of Ipi led. The Fakir of Ipi, being a disciple of the anti-British mullahs, cast away the robe of a Sufi and wore an armour in defence of Islam. The Islam Bibi case was not the only reason why the Fakir of Ipi started a crusade against the British. There were many others, earlier, who carried the crusade and had influenced him. His own father was a diehard anti-British scholar. Then there was the incident of the Shahid Ganj mosque in Lahore, that preceded the Islam Bibi case by a few months.[35]

In 1937, the Government of India was hounding the Fakir: 'They sought him here, they sought him there; those columns sought him everywhere!' The Fakir had become the main adversary of the British on the frontier. Provincial elections were held in the NWFP and a Congress ministry installed. The Fakir's support to his Muslim brethren, in the cause of Islam Bibi and the Shahid Ganj mosque was well known. It was on 16 September that the Fakir wrote to Nehru, addressing him as 'The Leader of liberty-loving people and the distinguished head of the Indian nation.'[36] His letter to Nehru did not have any trace of 'Hindu hate'. Every line was anti-imperialist in tone, the nature and purport of which Nehru could not disagree with:

Sheewal,
(Waziristan),
(September 16, 1937)

...We learn from the various newspapers of India that a great deal of adverse propaganda is being carried on against us throughout the length and breadth of India...We are sincerely and passionately devoted to our people and to our nation. But you, Sir, may rest assured that unless we dislodge these tyrants from our soil at the point of our sword or get exterminated in the struggle, there can be no peace between us and the Government of India. To us one brief moment of freedom is better than thousands and thousands of years of comfortable slavery...cases of robbery and kidnapping that occur from time to time in the vicinity of Bannu and Dera Ismail Khan are entirely manoeuvred by the British agents. We certainly do not approve of these misdeeds. Our religion forbids such actions in unequivocal terms. According to Islam, persons who perpetrate such crimes are 'Zalim' and 'Mardud' and outside the pale...You, Sir, should clearly understand that the war between us and the tyrannical Government is entirely due to their unwarranted attack on our liberties and not because of our proselytizing mania. God has plainly instructed us in the matter of religion and taught us in the holy Book that 'there is no compulsion of religion'. This means that every person is free in the choice of religion. He can choose to be what he likes—Muslim, Hindu or Christian. Hence it follows from the Koran that religion is a matter of temperament, instinct and spiritual outlook ... You should take it from us, revered Sir, that the present situation in Waziristan is a result of [British] excesses and the policy of aggressive conquest adopted by the Government of India and is due to nothing else. Hence as long as there is the breath of life in us it is impossible for us to submit to slavery. With God's help may India emancipate herself from their hands and we free our land at the point of our sword. So be it! Amen!

Sealed
Haji Mirza Ali
[Fakir Sahib Ipi]

Before declaring war against '*firangis*', the Fakir of Ipi put the following demands before the British government in the NWFP: (i) restore Islam Bibi to her husband; (ii) restore the Shahid Ganj mosque of Lahore; and (iii) provide surety of non-interference in their religion. Upon Sir George Cunningham (the then Governor of the NWFP) declaring that Islam was never in danger under British rule, the Fakir of Ipi took to organizing death squads from amongst his Khalifas, generals and war council. He chose the guerilla mode of warfare best suited to the local geography. Having organized his tribal *lashkar*, the Fakir shifted out of Ipi. The British in turn endeavoured to break the allegiance of his supporters—arresting them, demolishing their houses and the mosque of Ipi. But all this was in vain. These reprisals caused his name and fame to spread. His reputation acquired a certain mystique, that of a millenarian personality. The victims of *lashkar* raids by the Fakir were mainly Hindus—kidnappings, killings, sacking and burning of houses. The government used all the resources at its command—tanks, aircraft and ground forces—in its campaign against the Fakir. It also announced a substantial reward on the Fakir's head. The government's attempts proved futile. But in doing so, a whole detachment of South Waziristan scouts was wiped out in the spring of 1938. The British spent more than five million pounds, and at one point deployed 10,000 troops just to keep the channels of communication intact. People who rendered loyal service to the British against the Fakir were generously rewarded, the rewards coming as cash, titles or *sanads*.[37]

The British offered an olive branch to the Fakir when all their efforts to capture him failed. They agreed to restore his mosque. The government was not to ask for compensation on account of losses suffered at the hands of the Fakir's lashkars. The British also promised not to interfere in the religious affairs of the Muslims.

The Fakir's was a personality in contrast, a product of conflicting circumstances. He could be a heroic *ghazi* defying the British might, or a staunch supporter of his Muslim brethren who he thought had to suffer Hindu hate. The Fakir of Ipi, quite simply, was a Muslim fundamentalist the object of whose life was to oppose any movement that was not Islamic, and in that endeavour, he did not mind seeking assistance from any quarter. In his struggle against the British, he was assisted at different times by the Afghans, Germans and Italians.

Nearer the time of India's independence, the Muslim League was always wary of the prospect of the Fakir siding with Khan Abdul Ghaffar Khan. During the run up to the NWFP referendum in July 1946, Sir Feroz Khan Noon, a Punjab Muslim leader, had thought it fit to inform Jinnah of the Fakir's activities. Truckloads of people were taken to the Fakir's hideout and he paid money to those mullahs who signed up to join his jihad. But against whom? That question, the signed document left unanswered. Like an ever-present Hindu bogey, Sir Noon thought that Nehru deliberately facilitated the movement of people to the Fakir of Ipi; Nehru was in charge of tribal areas then. Sir Noon considered the Fakir harboured ambitions of becoming the Amir of Waziristan once the British withdrew from the tribal areas. To realize this ambition, the Fakir was not averse to seeking help from the Hindu Congress.

One of the published documents from the Jinnah Papers is a letter dated 8 July 1947 from one Colonel Shah Pasand Khan to Jinnah. The Colonel once had been an ADC to Amir Amanullah of Afghanistan and was a prominent member of the Muslim League National Guard in 1947. Colonel Shah Pasand Khan wrote to say that Abdul Ghani, the son of Khan Abdul Ghaffar Khan, paid Rs 7 lakh to the Fakir of Ipi and in return sought his support for 'Pathanistan'. Abdul Ghani's movement across the borders to meet the Fakir was facilitated by Dr Khan Saheb's government. Everyone agreed that the Fakir's was the most prominent voice in Waziristan at that time. The Fakir was using local mullahs to propagate Pathanistan and at the same time asking people not to join any political party. He wanted them to rally behind him, for a free state of Waziristan.

Unfortunately for him, the plea did not find fertile ground in Mahsud territory. He had long been wanting to enlist the support of a prominent Mahsud, Shahzada Fazal Din. The Fakir did not meet with much success despite calling for a *jirga* where he invited all prominent Mahsuds. The Afghan government of course sent its representative, Brigadier Shahbaz Khan, before the Mahsud *jirga* could be held. As quid pro quo for supporting the cause of Pathanistan, the Afghan government held out the bait of a free Waziristan state to the Fakir of Ipi. The veracity of Colonel Shah Pasand Khan's letter remains unestablished though Abdul Qayyum Khan, a recent convert to the

Muslim League and soon to succeed Dr Khan Saheb as Chief Minister, corroborated Colonel Shah Pasand Khan's information. According to Abdul Qayyum Khan, the Fakir of Ipi and the Afghan government were inciting the Afridis. Abdul Qayyum Khan advised Jinnah to ask the British authorities to exert pressure upon the Afghan government to stop supporting the Fakir of Ipi. He also informed Jinnah of a gathering that took place at the death of the Fakir of Ipi's brother. The funeral congregation was attended by prominent Congressmen from the Bannu, Khattak and Marwat areas, perhaps the grandest congregation in the history of Waziristan. The Fakir of Ipi's father-in-law, Maulana Zahir Shah, known for his oratorical skills, made a moving speech on this occasion. The Fakir too made an emotional speech condemning the League and the Congress equally. However, he said that nobody was to violate the peace of Hindus for they had consented to pay poll tax to the Fakir.

The Frontier Jamaat-i-Ulama, in alliance with the Fakir of Ipi, was resisting the League and its demand for Pakistan. Afghanistan's Interior Minister, Sardar Mohammad Farooq, called on the tribes to support the cause of Pathanistan and the forces of the Fakir of Ipi and the Khan brothers.

To keep his charisma alive, the Fakir of Ipi frequently disappeared for several months without informing anyone. This helped create an impression of piety among his people. Nearer the date of Id and in the crucial months of 1947, he again played the vanishing trick and disappeared for the month of Ramzan.

After India's partition, the 'Faqueer phenomenon' was no more than a law-and-order problem for the Pakistan government. Instead of dealing with him in an honourable way, the Pakistan government sought to nullify his influence by using the local maliks. The Fakir remained at large, a violater of the law even after Pakistan came into being, and died a free man in 1960.

## Too Little Too Late

Political reforms came late in the NWFP. Except for the limited introduction of elections in the Peshawar municipality, all powers vested with the officials of the government. This was in sharp contrast to the situation in Punjab. Ostensibly, the strategic location of the NWFP proved a hurdle. Both the Minto–Morley and the Montagu–Chelmsford reforms bypassed the Frontier Province. The government of the NWFP continued to rely on its 'Khani' allies. But by the early 1920s, the Khan Bahadurs were fast losing influence. There was some truth in what Olaf Caroe, a junior serving official then in the NWFP said:

> British immobility in conceding a measure of responsible government to the Frontier released other forces...there arose a new political party in the villages, a party which, in the complete absence of the ballot-box or any form of expression by parliamentary means, was necessarily conceived first as a pressure group and subsequently as a mass movement for agitation against the established order.[38]

The Third Afghan War (of 1919) had triggered tribal raids which became endemic, increasing dramatically in the next few years. The victims of these raids were mostly Hindus who considered their Muslim neighbours to be party to it. They feared introduction of representative institutions whereby control of the administration could pass into the hands of the Muslims who had an overwhelming numerical majority in the NWFP. Most Hindus and Sikhs had strongly opposed the province's creation because it cut them off from Punjab's large non-Muslim population. While creating the NWFP, Lord Curzon had called it an experiment that could be altered or abandoned if experience so dictated. Well before the Great War, the Hindu and Sikh leaders started pressing for the province's reabsorption into Punjab. In their endeavour, they failed to win any official sympathy, eliciting outright hostility from Muslim leaders who viewed reunification as an attack on their community's interests.[39]

On 21 July 1921, Sir P.S. Sivaswami Aiyar introduced a resolution in the Indian Legislative Assembly on the judicial merger of Punjab and the NWFP. His speech is revealing, as it set the tone for future 'Hindu' arguments in favour of reunification. While referring obliquely to the Frontier minorities' needs, he focused on the alleged defects in the NWFP administration, insecurity of life and property in order to give his proposal a legitimacy it would lack if he argued on bare communal grounds. Sivaswamy Aiyar's proposal reflected the insecurity of a minority community, much aggravated in the preceding three years.⁴⁰

The minority community of Hindus and Sikhs continued to lobby for amalgamation of the NWFP and Punjab. They also demanded protection from the so-called Muslim legislative tyranny. Their position drew strength even from confirmed nationalists like Amir Chand Bombwal, who had long agitated for Indian self-rule, yet wished to deny it to the Frontier. The province's Muslim leaders resisted the amalgamation proposal because they had no desire to belong to a province dominated by Punjabis.

The government found it convenient to deny reforms, quoting communal antagonism as the main reason for it. Sir H.N. Bolton, the Chief Commissioner, reacted to a Muslim petition for a local body election in much the same fashion:

> I am theoretically entirely in favour of this measure...the communal strife that has resulted from the introduction of communal representation elsewhere and has threatened to develop here, whenever the question of elections to local bodies has been mooted...as long as elections are pressed for on communal grounds only, I am inclined to think that we are better off as we are.⁴¹

The Chief Commissioner's policy encouraged minority intransigence, implying they held a veto over constitutional change.

In April 1922, the Government of India appointed an eight-member committee to go into the affairs of the NWFP. Three, including the president, Denys Bray, were civil officials. From amongst the other five, three were non-official Muslims and the other two elected Hindu members of the Indian Legislative Assembly. Perhaps it was a deliberate ploy of the British to constitute the committee that it divided itself on communal lines. The British already knew that as a community, the Hindus were against the introduction of constitutional reforms in the NWFP, afraid that their positional influence, not commensurate with population, would be lost. Predictably so, the Hindu members—T. Rangachariar and N.M. Samarth—dissented in their note when the Bray Committee report was presented. The other six members of the Bray Committee, the majority, minuted that in allowing for self-determination of the Pathan nationality through a scheme of reforms, the Indian government would be assured of a contented population at India's frontier.[42]

Rao Bahadur T.V. Rangachariar from Madras, having little to do with the affairs of the NWFP, dissenting with the majority report, refused to 'look with equanimity upon the formation of a strong Pathan province when he, the Pathan, considers he can never be Indianized'.[43] N.M. Samarth was convinced that 'from the point of view of all-India interests, external and internal, it would be politically unwise to perpetuate the Pathan province as a separate province—*a fortiori* to allow it to develop into what will ultimately be an autonomous Pathan province by itself...even writers of the school opposed to what is known as the "forward policy" warned against their adjoining kinsmen of Afghanistan.'[44] Within five months of the presentation of the Bray Committee report, the Government of India announced its border policy. Bray by then had become India's Foreign Secretary. This was a 'forward policy' in every sense. Constitutional reforms were not thought expedient; this view receiving immediate endorsement from N.M. Samarth who supported the border policy, the so-called 'peaceful penetration' policy, a euphemism for extending direct British control in the Frontier Province.[45]

Bray later recalled that the committee had 'blazed a communal trail from one end of our Frontier journey to another.'[46] It produced similar results in Punjab where the legislature rejected reunification in 1922 by a vote that saw the legislators divided along communal lines. Alarmed by the controversy's divisiveness, the Government of India took refuge in inaction. It procrastinated for three years before announcing its opposition to any merger in 1925 but simultaneously stated that it had no intention of implementing the Bray Committee recommendations on constitutional reforms.[47]

The dispute refused to fade away. The Muslim League passed a resolution at its May 1924 meeting in Lahore pointing to 'the immediate and paramount necessity of introducing reforms in the NWFP and of placing that province in all respects in a position of equality with other major provinces of India.'[48] Similar resolutions were passed at the Muslim League's next three annual sessions. Maulvi Syed Murtaza, a member both of the Muslim League and the Swaraj Party, reintroduced the controversy by moving a resolution in the Central Assembly in February 1926 urging the government to act on the Bray Committee report. His motion produced no constitutional results except to generate communal hostility. In March 1927, the question resurfaced as part of the Delhi Muslim Proposals which Muhammad Ali Jinnah formulated as a basis for Hindu–Muslim cooperation. He stipulated that Muslims would abandon separate electorates in return for concessions which included elevation of the NWFP to an equal status with other provinces.[49]

Until 1927, the Indian National Congress temporized over the NWFP. Its leadership sympathized with the Frontier minorities, but was constrained from saying so for that would run contrary to their constitutional demands for the rest of India. The appointment of the parliamentary statutory commission (Simon Commission)[50] in November 1927 ended their equivocation, giving them incentive to support self-government in the Frontier. The Congress decided to boycott the Commission over the issue of the next instalment of reforms. In its effort to enlist Muslim support, the Congress offered concessions in the NWFP, an area in which it had no vital interests. The attempt to reach an India-wide consensus floundered over other, irreconcilable differences, but the change in the Congress' attitude on the Frontier was permanent. The Motilal Nehru Committee[51] stated that the NWFP should enjoy the same rights as other Indian provinces.[52]

The Simon Commission visited Peshawar in November 1928, starting a flurry of activities in the province—meetings, deputations, petitions, and processions—all of which were meant to impress the general populace one way or another. A small group of Khilafatists and Congress supporters conducted a brief, ineffectual protest in Peshawar on the day of its arrival. Everyone else wanted to register their opinions and demands. Even Hindu Congressmen, who objected to the Commission in an all-India context, cooperated with it to protect their local interests. Amir Chand Bombwal, in his newspaper *Frontier Advocate*, told the Frontier Hindus:

> Not only should they wholeheartedly welcome the Simon Commission on its arrival in Peshawar, but they should make this

point clear to it, that bearing in mind this province's geographic, economic, and social position, it is extremely inappropriate, and will be dangerous and deadly to government if any kind of democratic arrangement current in various western countries or in other Indian provinces should be started here.[53]

Fearing undiluted democracy could undermine authority too, the prominent Khans asked for a legislature with an appointed two-thirds majority, assuming that the Chief Commissioner would nominate them to those seats. The urban Muslim intelligentsia, with support from some segments of the Khani elite, demanded reforms equal to those of other provinces, citing recommendations of the Bray Committee. Hindus, who saw no means of safeguarding their interests in a system that conceded government by majority, argued against devolution of power. Sikhs, who formed less than 2 per cent of the population, demanded 25 per cent of the seats in any future legislature. The Commission did not respond to these representations before leaving Peshawar as it was only in the fact-finding phase of its mission. Until its report was released in June 1930, people could only speculate about its recommendations, and the government's past resistance to reforms left little hope for substantial change.[54] In its report, the Commission flatly stated that the province's location precluded granting it the same reforms as other provinces: 'The inherent right of a man to smoke a cigarette must necessarily be curtailed if he lives in a powder magazine.'

The British at this time were having to contend at a nationwide level with the civil disobedience movement. In a broader context, both the central and Frontier governments considered suppression of this agitation to be their primary aim. But what was of immediate concern was to detach the NWFP from the Congress agitation. Demands were made to reduce land revenue and suspend the Sarda Act,[55] which had aroused religious antagonism. Suddenly the reforms in the NWFP did not appear unsuitable. Even from an all-India perspective, the government in Delhi considered constitutional reforms a good way of appeasing the Muslim opinion. The home secretary in Delhi wired Sir Stuart Edmond Pearks, Chief Commissioner, NWFP, on 31 May: 'It is clearly in the interest of Muhammadans generally to avoid trouble in the province if reasonable political advance can be secured by constitutional means.' For these reasons Lord Irwin[56] publicly endorsed the reforms in an interview on 4 June:

> I am fully convinced of the importance which the people of the Province attach to constitutional advance and realize the desire of your community in general that a Province which is predominantly Muslim should not be denied the means of self-expression... I can assure you that so far as I and my Government are concerned, when making recommendations on this subject to his Majesty's government, the natural claims of the Province in the constitutional field will be viewed with sympathy.

It was at the third, and final, Round Table Conference that an announcement was made to make the NWFP stand constitutionally at par with the other provinces of India. Instead of the dyarchy[57] that prevailed, there was now to be full 'provincial autonomy'[58] in the NWFP. But before the first elections granting it could be held, the NWFP functioned under a dyarchical form of government for four years. It was decided to treat the Frontier Province and the tribal tracts each on their own merit. The Frontier Province was to become a Governor's province. With the new reforms, the NWFP was to have a government, a legislative council and two ministers—but the council and the ministers were to have no say in the administration of the tribal tracts, that being the Governor's responsibility. Of the two ministers, at least one was to be an elected member. It was open therefore to the Governor to choose an official as the other minister. It was decided that the legislative council be a unicameral[59] body. On the question of administering the provincial departments, bodies like the militia and the Frontier constabulary were not to be under the ministers but remain under central control, under the Governor and the Government of India. The civil police, however, was made over as a provincial subject which meant that the Governor could call on an official to look after this subject as a minister; but did not necessarily have to do so. The dyarchy did not allow for the transfer of the 'law-and-order' portfolio to an elected minister. It remained a preserve of officials, but a minister could, if he so wished, make things difficult for officials dealing with the reserved portfolios. The legislature, could similarly hamper the administrative system. But the NWFP did not have to face such a problem. It had for a minister Nawabzada Sir Abdul Qayyum who was a powerful ally of the governing officials. The legislative council was also pro 'official'. It took some time for it to start opposing the official stance, the opposition coming mainly from the Khudai Khidmatgars.[60]

Speaking of the ministry's prospects with full provincial autonomy, the Governor designate, George Cunningham, was confident of establishing a workable relationship between the Governor and his ministers. He did achieve considerable success. Most of the organized canvassing for the first elections under the 1935 Government of India Act was done by a body called the Parliamentary Board, composed largely of Khudai Khidmatgar sympathizers. But the Board, in policy, did not represent the Khudai Khidmatgar methods. Cunningham was convinced that if they came to power, they would make a creditable government for he was also convinced of the sobering influence of responsibility.[61]

There were other parties in the field too, though not yet clearly defined. There had really not been any scope for the formation of a party with a programme unless it was merely a negative programme of opposing the government. In 1936, much of the canvassing was dependent more on personal ambitions than on any policy lines. But things gradually took shape. In the past, the government had looked to the Khans, the big landowners, for support. The feudal system that still existed to an extent gave them power to call on men and rifles for assistance. It enabled them to control the tenants who lived in their villages. But an elected government now gave others, particularly the educated, opportunities to participate in governance. In Cunningham's opinion, the future of the NWFP greatly depended on the fusion of these two classes—the Khans and the professional class.[62]

## 'Shaitan Sirkar' and the Peshawar Riots

On 23 April 1930, an incident occurred in Peshawar that was forever etched in the NWFP's history; the day thence commemorated as 'Martyr's Day'. The pending grievances of people precipitated in a violent confrontation with state authorities, claiming several lives at the Qissa Khwani Bazaar.

In 1930, there existed two organizations in the NWFP considered subversive by the government. The first, a city movement, older in inception, was a remnant of the Khilafat movement. The other—rural, more nationalistic, and mainly concerned with the Pathans—was the Khudai Khidmatgar movement headed by Khan Abdul Ghaffar Khan. These were the days of the civil disobedience movement in India. In April 1930, the government decided to intern leaders of both organizations to prevent unrest. The Viceroy's visit to Peshawar necessitated postponement of the arrests to 23 April. Peshawar was no different from other places where cultivators were loath to pay land revenue and the Tehsildar,[63] eager for maximum collection. The harvest in 1930 had been good but no market existed for the surplus produce. To a Pathan, the 'government' and 'payment of revenue' were synonymous terms. He believed that if he was rid of one, he could be rid of the other too.[64] This was the nature of the propaganda carried out by Khan Abdul Ghaffar Khan and his Khudai Khidmatgars in the days preceding the Peshawar unrest. The state authorities made the mistake of misreading the law-and-order situation. Insensitive to local grievances and overconfident of their 'Khani' allies, they were sanguine about their ability to keep the towns quiet. Following Independence Day celebrations on 26 January, the Chief Commissioner Sir H.N. Bolton had reported to the Viceroy that he saw no real urgency in prosecuting the Congress leaders, dismissing the Khudai Khidmatgar phenomenon as insignificant. He saw no reason to revise his opinion two months later either. On 19 April, Bolton was confidently proclaiming to Lord Irwin that the 'tranquility prevailing here [NWFP] is largely due to the level-headed loyalty of the people of this province.' On 22 April, arrest warrants were issued for eleven Peshawar politicians. Out of these, nine were arrested from their residences on the morning of 23 April. The other two, who could not be apprehended, were taken into custody from the Congress office.

The 23 April riots have been interpreted differently. One interpretation is based on a government enquiry into the incident while the other, on a report prepared by a committee chaired by Vithalbhai Patel[65] of the Congress party. Two judges, Shah Muhammad Sulaiman and H.R. Panckridge, were appointed by the government to investigate the riots. As per their report, a hostile crowd prevented the police from arresting Ghulam Rabbani Sethi and Allah Bakhsh Barqi from the Congress office. When informed of the crowd's unruly behaviour, H.A.F. Metcalfe, the Deputy Commissioner of Peshawar, entered Qissa Khwani Bazaar with four armoured cars. The vehicles were attacked and a despatch motorcycle rider, who had accompanied the convoy, was killed. Some people were also run over by one of the armoured cars near the *thana*.[66] One car was set fire to, while mechanical failure disabled the second. People found inside these vehicles were assaulted. Metcalfe was knocked unconscious on the steps of the *thana*. On recovering, he gave orders to one of the remaining armoured cars that had come under assault to open fire with its machine gun. A burst of twenty rounds temporarily cleared the streets, but the crowd reassembled. Reinforcements were sent to bring the situation under control. Failing to ward off assailants, firing was again resorted to. Justice Sulaiman and Panckridge estimated crowd casualties to be thirty killed and thirty-three wounded, conceding that the figures could be inaccurate.[67]

The second report, that of Vithalbhai Patel, disputed most of the assertions made by the judges. It contended that the police was not obstructed at the Congress office: that there was no disturbance outside the *thana*, and the non-violent crowd dispersed voluntarily when the armoured cars recklessly rushed into the bazaar without warning, crushing twelve to fourteen people. The motorcyclist, the report claimed, died by coming under the wheels of one of the cars. Allegations that the crowd was responsible was 'an afterthought to serve as a cover for the unjustifiable firing by the authorities.' The report was also critical of Metcalfe's conduct: 'The deputy commissioner had perpetuated a most shocking piece of inhumanity…and he perhaps saw no escape out of it except by giving the happenings of the 23rd April the form of a serious riot and painting the crowd in the blackest possible colour. It seems clear that the deputy commissioner had used this little incident of an injury to himself as an occasion for ordering the armoured car to open fire.'[68]

The second firing was also judged to be unjustified. The Patel Report sought to convey that the crowd, which wanted only to collect its dead and wounded, had agreed to disperse if the armoured cars and troops were removed. When the authorities refused, it stood its ground non-violently while troops shot and bayoneted people for four hours. The report put the figure for the known dead for the day at 125 and confidently stated that the actual figures were undoubtedly higher.[69]

While the riots were limited to one locality of Peshawar on that day, its repercussions were widespread. Bitter anti-British feeling was aroused, uniting people who had been divided over the propriety of civil disobedience. In the surrounding countryside, this fuelled an agitation which paralysed the administration over much of Peshawar district. In other Pakhtun areas, popular reaction was less severe but sufficient to worry the authorities. Throughout the tribal areas the tribesmen came to sympathize with the nationalists. Seeing the apparent collapse of British administration, they were ready to take on the government. Along the Peshawar border, the conflict assumed such proportions that Lord Irwin was forced to wire the Secretary of State in London that 'the whole of Peshawar District as far as Attock must be considered in [a] state of war'.[70]

Troops patrolled the streets of Peshawar on 24 April, but on the same evening, two platoons of the 2/18th Royal Garhwal Rifles refused to enter the city on the grounds that they would have to fire on their people. This put a question mark on the reliability of Indian soldiers. Fearing for British security, Bolton telegraphed Lord Irwin, '...I suggest for consideration of Your Excellency desirability of ensuring considerable reinforcements of British troops in India.'[71] The government withdrew all soldiers from the city on the night of 24 April, while it collected dependable forces. The task of preserving order was left to the influential private citizens of Peshawar. But the strategy misfired. The anti-government feeling aroused by the riots was so intense that the prominent city residents sympathetic to the government could not stop the nationalists from taking over the city. For the next nine days the Congress had de facto control of Peshawar. A parallel administration was created to run the city, using volunteers to patrol streets, man the city gates and apprehend criminals. For the Khudai Khidmatgars, it was an opportune moment to expand their support base in the city and the nearby villages, alongside seeking support from the tribal areas. The police, the sole representative of state authority left in Peshawar, were overwhelmed. The government admitted that 'in so far as they were functioning at all, [they] were doing so on sufferance.'⁷²

Collapse of the administration in Peshawar spawned wild reports about the British abandoning the NWFP and on the verge of being driven out from India. Accepting these rumours at face value, many tribesmen were eager to add to their old adversaries' difficulties in the settled districts. The politicians of the NWFP played upon the tribesmen's sympathies, grievances and avarice, encouraging them to confront the administration.

Ghaffar Khan and some other Khudai Khidmatgar leaders were arrested at Charsadda, just when the city leaders were being rounded up in Peshawar. These arrests provoked a serious reaction, necessitating a recall of troops from Mardan in support of the civil police. They also provoked the immediate arrival of the Haji of Turangzai and his son Badshah Gul on the frontier with a *lashkar* of Mohmands by end April 1930. If there was ever any proof needed of a long-standing rapport between Ghaffar Khan and the Haji Saheb, it is to be found in this swift action of the Haji. The Haji of Turangzai's *lashkar* had grown to about 2,000 men by late May despite air action against it. It remained along the border until mid-June but never actually invaded the valley. Illness, aerial bombing and internal dissension gradually depleted the *lashkar* until the Haji withdrew on 25 June. In the interim, the Fakir of Alingar, another anti-British religious figure, had mobilized a second tribal force in Bajaur with the aid of emissaries from Peshawar. Utman Khel⁷³ tribesmen, numbering over 1,500, filtered into Charsadda tehsil where they established contact with local nationalists in the first week of June. Air action against the tribe's home villages stopped the flow of men, but it would take an army column to drive out those already in the district.⁷⁴

By mid-May the provincial administration was simultaneously confronted with grave challenges on three fronts—Peshawar city, rural Peshawar and the adjoining tribal areas. The intelligence network had collapsed, leaving the administration in the dark about the accelerating agitation. Sir Steuart Pears later wrote that for two weeks after he took office on 10 May, he found it 'very difficult not only to ascertain exactly what the situation was in the Peshawar District and adjacent areas but even to obtain the materials on which to frame an opinion.'⁷⁵ Ignorance added to the sense of being overwhelmed, leading to vacillation, panic, and a tendency to grasp at oversimplified explanations and solutions, such as to hunt for a communist conspiracy, to see Muslim fanaticism as the root cause of the unrest, or to advocate martial law.

H.N. Bolton had suffered a nervous breakdown and left the province on 30 April. Pearks, who was to replace him in September, was instructed to immediately assume office, which he could only do on 10 May. In the interim, Courtney Latimer, the Revenue Commissioner, acted as the Chief Commissioner. He was assisted by Sir Evelyn Howell, the Indian government's Foreign Secretary, whom Lord Irwin sent to the NWFP on 29 April to help manage the grave situation.

By the time Stuart Pearks arrived, Courtney Latimer had restored the government's authority in Peshawar city. The Congress and the Naujawan Bharat Sabha[76] were declared illegal on 3 May. The following morning, troops reoccupied the city and began arresting Congress activists. To prevent a repetition of the April riots, Peshawar was sealed off and severe curbs imposed on activity. Acquiescence before coercive power did not mean that popular attitudes had changed. Resentment flared again on 31 May when an English soldier accidentally killed two Sikh children and wounded their mother. Although he was summarily tried and sentenced to placate public opinion, the children's funeral procession clashed with troops. Fortunately, for the administration, the disaffection this time was immediately contained. Peshawar thereafter remained quiet, even during the Afridi invasion of June and August. By July, authorities had withdrawn soldiers from the city.[77]

As for the Afridis, they had been quick to take advantage of the psychological moment the Peshawar unrest offered, for they saw the government abandon effective control of Peshawar city in April. The Afridi incursions took place in June and August. The British considered the Afridis potentially the most dangerous Pakhtun tribe as they were capable of mobilizing people close to Peshawar city and the Khyber Pass. When they rose in 1897 and 1919, they had seriously threatened the borders in a way no other tribe could. By beginning June, the Afridis had gathered a *lashkar* of 1,200 men on the edge of Peshawar district. Their first incursion into Peshawar district took place on the night of 4 June. They expected support from the Khalils and Mohmands living around Peshawar city, from the Peshawaris themselves and Indian soldiers whose loyalty was questionable. When none of this materialized, they retreated to the tribal area before daylight. After the first attack failed, the Afridis engaged in two months of intra-tribal manoeuvring before trying again. By 7 August, 6,000 men gathered on the Khajuri plain adjoining Peshawar district. In addition, the Orakzais were also exhorted to join. The Haji of Turangzai was again spurred to renew his efforts at raising the Mohmands. On the night of 7 August, units of the *lashkar* evaded troops along the border and slipped into the district. Within two nights, 2,500 tribesmen had infiltrated the settled areas. They brought the administration in Peshawar tehsil to a standstill for twelve days. In a press communiqué of 15 August, the Government of India reported:

> They at one time succeeded in cutting off all communications with Peshawar, and one party forced its way into the Supply Depot where it did considerable damage before being driven out. They have also made several attempts in small parties by night to enter the city and cantonment... Their total strength is now reported to be about 1,200—moving about rapidly in gangs from fifty to two hundred strong among the ravines and walled gardens and villages round Peshawar City. Military action is being taken against them; but decisive action is difficult at the present season, when crops are high...[78]

People in Peshawar tehsil treated the tribesmen as allies and liberators. Villagers fed, sheltered and gave them information, and some even joined their bands.[79] On 16 August, Pearks promulgated martial law which remained in force until the end of the year. But by August end, the threat from the Afridis had considerably diminished.

### The Novelty of Elections[80]

It was in December 1931, that the introduction of the Montford Reforms[81] of 1919 were announced in the NWFP by the provincial Governor at a durbar in Peshawar. In reaction, Ghaffar Khan and the Khudai Khidmatgars declared a boycott of the reforms, in pursuance of the Congress programme. The announcement of the reforms was followed by a wholesale arrest of Khudai Khidmatgar leaders.

It was in some haste that the government decided to introduce the Montford Reforms in the NWFP. An officer, borrowed from Punjab, was tasked with preparing the electoral rolls within just two months of announcement and a timetable was set to hold elections to the legislative council by mid-April 1932. The province was quickly demarcated into various constituencies. The district of Peshawar was divided into seven Muslim rural constituencies; Peshawar city, the cantonments and non-Muslims had their own constituencies.

The province was woefully short of staff—the numbers of election officers and security personnel were highly inadequate. It took a whole week, from 7 to 12 April, to complete the election process. Franchise was conferred on roughly all males above the age of twenty. All those who paid land revenue of ten rupees a year, owned property worth ₹600, or had attained a certain standard of education were eligible to vote. On an average, in a village of a thousand able-bodied men, about a hundred had their names on the electoral roll. The province had never seen an election and almost 90 per cent of the voters had not even heard of such a thing. To them the vote did not convey any intelligible meaning. The contestants and their agents had very little time to explain the meaning of a vote to the electors, and in any case it was impossible for them to reach voters who were scattered in various villages at considerable distances from each other. There was no press worth the name, and the electors being illiterate, pamphlets and posters were of no use. The government had disallowed public meetings, apprehensive of Khudai Khidmatgar activities.

There was only one organized political party in the province—the Khudai Khidmatgars—and they had declared a boycott of the elections. Their prominent leaders were all in jail, but the rank and file and the smaller leaders still remained in the villages. Their organization could not be broken up, and although they gave up the wearing of red shirts in public, they continued to hold secret meetings and to carry on a very active propaganda. Their emissaries went from village to village asking members of their organization to prevent the voters from taking part in the elections.

Religion, as always, played a prominent part in the life of the residents of the province. The Khudai Khidmatgars also had a quasi-religious hold on the uneducated public. It was, therefore, easy for them to proclaim that elections were against religion and any person found voting would be committing a heresy. The Khudai Khidmatgars declared that voting was sinful and was introduced by the 'satanic' government in pursuance of its anti-Islamic policy. Khan Abdul Ghaffar Khan was very popular and was considered a sort of hero by most villagers. Whosoever fixed his thumb impression on the ballot paper or signed the counterfoil was in effect signing the death warrant of Ghaffar Khan. The electors were also told that their signature on the ballot papers would be followed by heavy taxation and other dire consequences. The Khudai Khidmatgars had enough time—more than three months—for this propaganda, and as the elections drew near, their propaganda became more intense.

Care was taken to fix the polling stations at the police stations in the districts, but it was not possible to send police to the villages. Moreover, it was also not found necessary to post police guards on those few roads that existed or for that matter, to arrange flying squads. On election days the voters had to walk several miles, or in some cases, where there were roads, go by lorries or horse-drawn vehicles to the polling stations. The Khudai Khidmatgars had announced picketing of the polling stations and a day or two in advance had arranged to block all roads or paths leading to them. The villagers too, because of the religious colour given to these endeavours, supported them. For safety reasons and due to the propaganda of the Khudai Khidmatgars, a majority of the electors decided not to take part in the elections. No one wanted to confront the Khudai Khidmatgars. Only 10 to 15 per cent of the voters were willing to vote, but no argument could persuade the pickets to allow the voters to pass through, forcing almost all of them to return home.

The Khudai Khidmatgars would first stop the voter and persuade him to go back. If the voter insisted, he was threatened. At times when all efforts to persuade failed, physical force, insults and abuses were used to deter the voters. Most voters who ventured to vote had a story to narrate in the evening. A number of cars and lorries were damaged and at many places, traffic on the roads came to a stop.

The boycott of elections was enforced with a thoroughness that surprised everyone. All this affected the outcome of elections too. Quite a few contests therefore, threw up unexpected results. The first elections in the NWFP did create a feeling of apprehension, both in the minds of willing candidates and of voters, so much so, that in the district board elections that followed a few months later, in nearly all the constituencies no candidate could get nominated, allowing for the elections to go uncontested.

## 'Surkh Posh'—The Red Shirts

In February 1935, a debate took place in the Central Legislative Assembly on the question of the removal of ban on the Khudai Khidmatgars. People like Jinnah and the then Foreign Secretary, H.A.F. Metcalfe, took part in it. Their statements make for fascinating reading and are reflective of the realities that existed in the NWFP in the mid-thirties. Each participant in the debate shared his experience of the days of unrest in Peshawar. Some episodes are also recalled here. Jinnah actively intervened in the debate demanding removal of the ban on the Khudai Khidmatgars. Within a year of course, Jinnah was to change tack. Metcalfe's observations are particularly important for he was the deputy Commissioner of Peshawar in 1930 when the firing took place on 23 April.

B. Das,[82] a member from Orissa, initiated the debate by moving the resolution that 'This Assembly recommends to the Governor General in Council to take immediate and necessary steps to remove or cause to be removed the ban on the Khudai Khidmatgars' organization in the North-West Frontier Province.'[83] In 1930, the NWFP government was still a Chief Commissioner's government. On 10 May the 1930, post the Qissa Khwani Bazaar firing in Peshawar, the Chief Commissioner, frightened of the Khudai Khidmatgar organization and its campaign, addressed a communiqué to his 'Khani' allies. This communiqué shows how the officials viewed the Khudai Khidmatgars:

> Is the Congress going to leave with you your landed property, *jagirs* and *muafis*?[84] Is it going to protect your frontiers? Will it maintain law and order amongst the people? Now it is high time for you to help the Government, which has ever been benevolent to you and has done justice towards you. What help can you render to the Government? You must prevent Congress volunteers, wearing red jackets, from entering your villages.

They call themselves Khudai Khidmatgars (servants of God). But in reality they are the servants of Gandhi. They wear the dress of Bolsheviks,[85] and they are nothing but Bolsheviks. They will create the same atmosphere as you have heard in Bolshevik dominion.[86]

Four days earlier, on 6 May, the Government of India had voiced the same sentiments in another long communiqué:

Agitators belonging to the Congress and the Naujawan Bharat Sabha have been attempting to produce unrest in the North-West Frontier Province...regardless of the fact that the Congress party as a whole were among the most enthusiastic supporters of the Sarda Act in the Legislative Assembly, Congress workers in the North-West Frontier Province have, in their attempts to sow dissension between Government and the people, done their utmost to misrepresent its objects and provisions.[87]

Both the communiques were calculated to undermine the Congress. Concerned, Gandhi too had exchanged letters with the Private Secretary to the Viceroy about the situation in the NWFP. On 31 December 1932 Gandhi received a telegram from the Private Secretary on the activities of Khudai Khidmatgars:

In North-West Frontier Province Abdul Ghaffar Khan and bodies he controls have continuously engaged in activities against [the] Government and in fomenting racial hatred. He and his friends have persistently refused all overtures by the Chief Commissioner to secure their co-operation and rejecting the declaration of the Prime Minister, have declared in favour of complete independence. Abdul Ghaffar Khan has delivered numerous speeches open to no other construction than as incitements to revolution and his adherents have attempted to stir trouble in tribal areas. The Chief Commissioner with the approval of His Excellency's Government has shown utmost forbearance and to the last moment continued his efforts to secure assistance of Abdul Ghaffar Khan in carrying into effect, with the least possible delay, the intentions of his Majesty's Government regarding constitutional reforms in the province... His Excellency understands that Abdul Ghaffar Khan was in August last made responsible for leading Congress movement in province, and that volunteer organizations he controlled were specifically recognized by All-India Congress Committee as Congress organization.[88]

Gandhi promptly responded to this telegram on 1 January 1932: 'If Khan Saheb Abdul Ghaffar asserted the right of complete independence, it was a natural claim and the claim made with impunity by the Congress at Lahore in 1929 and by me with energy put before the British Government in London. Moreover, let me remind the Viceroy that despite knowledge on Government's part that Congress mandate contained such claim, I was invited to attend London Conference as Congress delegate.'[89]

To the Chief Commissioner's accusation that Khan Abdul Ghaffar Khan and Dr Khan Saheb had not attended a durbar, Gandhi reminded the Viceroy that many Congressmen had not attended durbars intentionally. Gandhi believed that the reason why the Montford Reforms could be implemented in the NWFP was because of the work that Ghaffar Khan had done in the province. It was during Norman Bolton's tenure as Chief Commissioner that Peshawar and other areas of the NWFP faced agitation. Bolton had to suddenly resign and leave India. In the year 1931, ordinances were promulgated that resulted in many Khudai Khidmatgars rotting in jail for years. This was provocation enough for even a loyal friend of the British and member of the Legislative Assembly, Sir Zulfiquar Ali Khan, to lament openly:

> Government are riding a tidal wave of repressive policy and have opened the campaign without waiting for Mr Gandhi's decision. I have no doubt that the exasperation caused by this policy of repression *la outrance* will sweep away Mr Gandhi and others and will leave the field in the possession of the desperate youth of the country...The Frontier Province unfortunately is the first to bear the brunt of the fight in which thousands may be shot down and this shedding of the blood may cause resentment among the Moslems in other provinces who have so far abstained from participation in anti-British propaganda.[90]

The Frontier government as well as the Government of India accused the Khudai Khidmatgars of being financed by Russian money (nicknamed Red Shirt—also because the government wanted them associated with the Bolsheviks). These charges of course, remained unsubstantiated.[91]

H.A.F. Metcalfe, India's Foreign Secretary, was also once the Deputy Commissioner of Peshawar. This offered him a first-hand chance of observing the Khudai Khidmatgar movement from close quarters. According to him, when Ghaffar Khan commenced this movement, he had openly and publicly stated that it was intended to promote the social welfare of the Pathan, doing away with blood feuds, reducing wedding expenses and such like measures. All this had initially impressed Metcalfe, the Deputy Commissioner. Through Dr Khan Saheb who at the time was a medical practitioner in Peshawar city, Metcalfe requested Ghaffar Khan to come and meet him. That request was denied. Ghaffar Khan feared the meeting for it could 'ruin his position' in the eyes of his followers. Metcalfe had impatiently then watched the movement grow.

Ghaffar Khan had gone about Peshawar district making speeches, none of which were particularly objectionable at that time.[92]

In the later part of 1929 and early 1930, he also went about setting up his organization in villages. The Khudai Khidmatgars were subjected to complete military training so far as it could be done. There were reports in the early part of 1930 of large bodies of men, with officers in uniforms of their own making, marching about, doing the sort of parades which only soldiers were expected to do.[93]

During the debate, Metcalfe endeavoured to clear the misimpression that the Khudai Khidmatgar movement was non-violent. He was never under any illusion about the 'Red Shirts' being violent unless there was a sufficiently large force to overawe and prevent them from being non-violent. There had been many occasions when the government, in order to avoid confrontation, had taken large forces to a spot where there were chances of the Red Shirts becoming violent. On those occasions the Khudai Khidmatgars merely adopted a defiant and sullen attitude. Metcalfe often wondered about the ordinary peaceful citizen and those small groups of policemen left behind, when those large forces were withdrawn. Speaking against the resolution, Metcalfe went on to narrate three instances of violence in his knowledge which the Khudai Khidmatgars had been responsible for. The first had taken place before Ghaffar Khan was arrested. There was no question then of his arrest and the Khudai Khidmatgars were functioning in their usual way—considered non-violent. One involved an old lumbardar of Metcalfe's acquaintance. He was an estimable old man, a Khan Bahadur known for his loyalty to the government. Defying the diktat of the Khudai Khidmatgars, he sent his son to a government school in Charsadda. He was forced by the Khudai Khidmatgars to crawl on his hands and knees along the streets of Charsadda, sending a message to all those who dared to send their sons to a government school.[94]

The second incident was one when Metcalfe himself had carried out an inquest on the body of the British officer who was the victim and therefore could vouch for its veracity. The officer in question was one Murphy, extremely popular in Mardan sub-division where he had served. In the call of duty he disallowed entry of some Khudai Khidmatgars in Mardan cantonment. He had stopped them at a village three miles outside Mardan. Though troops were present to assist him, he decided to deal with the situation himself, simply to avoid bloodshed. The Khudai Khidmatgars were given a few hours in which to return. A stalemate ensued that lasted for two hours, at the end of which the Khudai Khidmatgars entirely declined to move. Murphy was forced to lead a charge against them to try and push them back. There was no use of violence. As he got into the crowd, Murphy was seized, stoned and belaboured to death, his revolver snatched from his belt and used against him. Though troops were present on the spot, they desisted from retaliating. No shots were fired. His body was recovered later when the crowd dispersed.[95]

The third incident related to an attack upon a government force. Metcalfe had one morning gone to Shabqadar, a Khudai Khidmatgar stronghold, taking with him several press representatives. On the road they encountered a Frontier constabulary lorry that had been attacked the night before. Four of its occupants had been killed and the lorry burnt. Metcalfe was convinced that this had been done entirely with the aid and the guidance of the Khudai Khidmatgar elements of the neighbouring village. Without being directly involved, the Khudai Khidmatgars had fed, helped and guided—as they did constantly along that border—the miscreants who had come to attack.[96] There is no reason to disbelieve the contention of H.A.F. Metcalfe, who in 1930 was the Deputy Commissioner of Peshawar.

Having narrated these incidents, Metcalfe went on to present a report of more recent vintage, of December 1934, in support of his contention that the ban should not be lifted from the Khudai Khidmatgar organization. This report, based on police sources stated:

> On the 6th December, one Amir, a notorious outlaw, said to be wanted for several murders was arrested along with a fully-loaded revolver and dynamite. On the 11th December—in the late afternoon—a gang of outlaws descended on the village of the informant and killed his brother and sister-in-law and caused injuries to a child of two and several other children.[97]

Having quoted extensively, from this report, Metcalfe went on to oppose the resolution for lifting the ban on the Khudai Khidmatgars.

Ghaffar Khan was arrested on 23 April 1930 on the way to Peshawar. He was taken to Naushera and convicted for three years under Section 40 of the Frontier Crimes Regulation, the section specifically meant for dealing with robbers, murderers and notorious outlaws. In May 1930, and in the presence of Metcalfe, a posse of soldiers went to Utmanzai and surrounded the village, occupied the premises that housed the office of the Khudai Khidmatgars, and threw out those people who were on the first storey. Several of them suffered broken arms and legs. Thereafter, the office of the Khudai Khidmatgars was set on fire.[98] Metcalfe was honest enough to admit to this excess committed on the part of his troops. He said during the debate in the legislative assembly:

> I am extremely sorry for all that happened. I immediately went to the spot and stopped any further violence and saw that the people who were injured were properly attended to. It was regrettable. What happened was that insults were hurled at some of the troops who were getting the people out from the house and this led to the regrettable violence on the part of the troops. I very much regret that action, but to say that I encountered violence on the part of the troops is, I venture to say, entirely untrue.[99]

The Home Member, Sir Henry Craik,[100] was of the view that those living in a room full of powder could not afford to smoke, something he felt was eminently true of the NWFP.[101] After the conclusion of the Gandhi–Irwin Pact[102] in March 1931, Khan Abdul Ghaffar Khan had been released and had returned to the NWFP. Sir Henry Craik contended that the Chief Commissioner in 1931 had made every effort to get in touch with Ghaffar Khan, both personally and through his local officers, but all these offers to see the Chief Commissioner were refused. Ghaffar Khan had gone around the NWFP in defiance of orders forbidding public meetings, holding meetings and giving speeches which the British considered seditious. He had proclaimed openly that his object was to turn the British out of India, by force. At Charsadda, the Khudai Khidmatgars were directly responsible for inciting the people to murder the Assistant Commissioner, and shortly thereafter, an attempt to murder another officer, Barnes, was made. Though Ghaffar Khan was absent from the province at the time, the first step he took on his return was to congratulate those who were responsible for this act.[103]

During the debate, Sir Henry Craik also tried to emphasize that the Khudai Khidmatgars were not a non-violent organization, as popularly believed. Their aim was complete independence and forcible ejection of the British. Their activities also included inciting the trans-border tribes against the British, campaigning against payment of taxes, land revenue and such like. The NWFP had remained comparatively calm since a ban was imposed on the organization. The Khudai Khidmatgars had actively campaigned to boycott the elections which were held as a result of introduction of reforms in the NWFP in 1932. But in the three years since 1932, the province had witnessed relative peace. The Home Member felt that if the ban was lifted from the Khudai Khidmatgars, it would be misconstrued as a sign of weakness of the administration by the people of the NWFP as well as by the trans-border tribes, which would give their movement a fillip. This was bound to be taken advantage of.[104]

When it came to Jinnah's turn, he spoke strongly on behalf of the nationalist forces, urging the government to lift the ban. Khan Bahadur Nawab Muzaffar Khan recalled the times when the introduction of reforms had been discussed in the Central Assembly in old Delhi. Expressing his deep sense of gratitude to Jinnah, Syed Murtuza Saheb and Raja Ghazanfar Ali Khan, he said that they had fought valiantly for the Frontier people.[105] Jinnah at that time represented the Muslim urban seat from Bombay city. Speaking for the motion, this is what he said:

> I am not prepared to accept the case of the Government that they were also not guilty of great blunders, and I think my friend, Mr Metcalfe, admitted it, at least in one instance, he very rightly and frankly expressed his regret that such a thing had happened ... But, Sir, when the Honourable the Home Member, after making out a case for the Government, after trying to justify the actions of the Government, came to his conclusion, he lost all my sympathy, because he said it in so emphatic terms, 'We are not going to remove the ban on this organization.'[106] Why? Please do not make too much of these dangers. Do not overdo it. If you have vanquished your enemy, if you are a victor, it becomes you all the more to be generous when he has ceased those activities. And here you have Dr Khan Saheb. He is a member of this house. He has come to this Legislature. Are you not going to help, are you not going to encourage not only one leader of that organization or two leaders of that organization, but the rank and file? Do you want to refuse them, to turn them away and not give them a chance to come on to the path that you desire and I desire? And that is the constitutional path... We are not finding fault with you. We are not apportioning blame. I am not going into that. Do you want to be statesmen, or do you want still to continue this rancour and bitterness. That is the question. I say, if you really want to rise to the occasion, here is an occasion for you. Do restore peace in the North-West Frontier Province, bring them back to constitutional methods, and what is more, respond to the all-India feeling in the house. [Hear, hear]. I tell you, it is not too late for you. Win them back, win them back, and restore real honest peace and goodwill in the North-West Frontier.[107]

The resolution that steps be taken to remove the ban on the Khudai Khidmatgars in the NWFP had then stood recommended to the Governor General in council. It is altogether another matter that the government vetoed it.

## Notes

1. Quoted in Arthur Swinson, *North West Frontier: People and Events 1839–1947*, Hutchinsons & Co., 1967, p.267.
2. Ibid.
3. Percy Sykes, *A History of Afghanistan*, republished by Munshiram Manoharlal, 2000, p.247.
4. Ibid.
5. The Potsdam Agreement was an agreement on the policy for the occupation and reconstruction of Germany and other nations after fighting in the European theatre of World War II had ended with the German surrender on 8 May 1945. It was drafted and adopted by the major victorious powers, the USSR, USA and UK, at the Potsdam Conference (called the 'Berlin Conference' in the text of the Agreement) between 17 July and 2 August 1945.
6. Sykes, *A History of Afghanistan*, p.251.
7. Ibid.
8. Ibid., p.257.
9. When Amanullah's last feeble attempt to regain his throne failed, those next in line were the Musahiban brothers, who were also Muhammadzai Barakzai and whose great-grandfather was an older brother of Dost Mohammad's. The five prominent Musahiban brothers included Nadir Khan, the eldest, who had been Amanullah's former minister of war. They were permitted to cross through the NWFP to enter Afghanistan and take up arms. Once on the other side, however, they were not allowed back and forth across the border to use British territory as a sanctuary, nor were they allowed to gather together a tribal army on the British side of the Durand Line. However, the Musahiban brothers and the tribes successfully ignored these restrictions. After several unsuccessful attempts, Nadir and his brothers finally raised a sufficiently large force— mostly from the British side of the Durand Line—to take Kabul on 10 October 1929. Six days later, Nadir Shah, the eldest of the Musahiban brothers, was proclaimed monarch. Habibullah fled Kabul, was captured in Kohistan and executed on 3 November 1929.
10. Sykes, *A History of Afghanistan*, p.257.
11. The Jallianwala Bagh Massacre or the Amritsar Massacre, took place in the northern Indian city of Amritsar where, on 13 April 1919, while

peacefully demonstrating, an Indian congregration was fired upon by British Indian army soldiers under the command of Brigadier-General Reginald Edward Harry Dyer. The firing lasted about ten minutes and 1,650 rounds were fired, or thirty-three rounds per soldier. Official British sources placed the fatalities at 379. According to private sources there were over 1,000 deaths, with more than 2,000 wounded.

12. Swinson, *North West Frontier*, pp.269–70.
13. Ibid., p.271.
14. Sykes, *A History of Afghanistan,* pp.270, 272.
15. Ibid., pp.273–75.
16. Ibid., pp.276–77.
17. Zhob, the headquarters of Zhob district, is a small city in the Baluchistan province of Pakistan. Zhob is located on the banks of the Zhob river. During the colonial era, it was named Fort Sandeman. It obtained its current name in 30 July 1976 when the then Prime Minister of Pakistan, Zulfikar Ali Bhutto, had the name changed.
18. Sykes, *A History of Afghanistan,* pp.277–79.
19. Ibid., p.280.
20. Ibid., p.283.
21. Arnold Toynbee, 'Survey of International Affairs, 1920–1923', quoted in Sykes, *A History of Afghanistan*, p.283.
22. The position of a divinely appointed leader in the Islamic tradition.
23. Shah Abdul Aziz Dehlavi (1745–1823) was one of the great Sunni Islamic scholars of Hadith in India. He was the eldest son of Shah Waliullah and was only seventeen years old when Shah Waliullah died. He became the leader of the movement started by his father.
24. M. Naeem Qureshi, *The Ulama of British India and the Hijrat of 1920,* Quaid-i-Azam University, 1979.
25. *Muhajir* or *mohajir* is an Arabic word meaning 'emigrant'. The Islamic calendar Hejira starts when Mohammad and his companions left Mecca for Medina in what is known as Hijra. They were called *mohajarin*. The Arabic root word for immigration and emigration is *hijrat*.
26. Qureshi, *The Ulama of British India.*
27. A firman is a royal mandate or decree issued by a sovereign in certain historical Islamic states, including the Ottoman empire, Mughal empire, and Iran under Shah Mohammed Reza Pahlavi. The word firman comes from the Persian 'farman' meaning decree or order.

28. Qureshi, *The Ulama of British India*.
29. Based on the descriptions of Swinson, *North West Frontier*.
30. Fazal-ul-Rahim Marwat and Sayed Wiqar Ali Shah Kakakhel (eds), *Afghanistan and the Frontier*, Emjay Book, 1993, p.239.
31. Ibid., p.240.
32. Ibid., pp.241–42.
33. Ibid., pp.242, 243.
34. Ibid., p.245.
35. Ibid., p.246.
36. Jawaharlal Nehru, *A Bunch of Old Letters*, republished by Viking, 2005, pp. 253–54.
37. Marwat and Kakakhel, *Afghanistan and the Frontier*, pp. 247–55.
38. Sir Olaf Caroe, *The Pathans 550 B.C.–A.D. 1957*, Macmillan & Co., 1958, p. 431.
39. Dewan Chand Obrai, *The Evolution of the North-West Frontier Province*, London Book Company, 1938, p.112.
40. Central Legislative Assembly Debates, 1921, vol. ii, 9/21/21, p.726.
41. Quoted in Central Legislative Assembly Debates, 1926, vol. vii, part ii, 2/16/26, p.1340.
42. A.H. Byrt, Paper read before the Royal Central Asian Society on 14 May 1947, with Sir Hassan Suharawardy in the chair, pp.276–78.
43. Ibid.
44. Ibid.
45. Ibid.
46. Central Legislative Assembly Debates, 1926, p.1326.
47. Central Legislative Assembly Debates, 1926, pp.2767–68.
48. Syed Sharifuddin Pirzada (ed.), *Foundations of Pakistan*, National Publishing House, vol. 1, 1970, pp.578 and 580.
49. Stephan Allen Rittenberg, 'The Independence Movement in India's North-West Frontier Province 1901–1947', PhD thesis, Colombia University, 1977, p. 75.
50. In 1927 the British government wanted a report on political reforms in India and on amending the Government of India Act. So, it appointed a Commission. The Commission consisted of Sir John Simon and six other members. All of them were members of British Parliament. There was not a single Indian member. This Commission aroused great resentment when it visited India.

51. Motilal Nehru chaired the famous Nehru Committee in 1928. The Nehru Report conceived a dominion status for India within the empire, akin to Australia, New Zealand and Canada. It was endorsed by the Congress party, but rejected by more radical Indians who sought complete independence, and by many Muslims who did not feel their interests, concerns and rights were properly represented.
52. Rittenberg, 'The Independence Movement in India's NWFP', p.76.
53. *Frontier Advocate*, 10 October 1928.
54. Rittenberg, 'The Independence Movement in India's NWFP', p.78.
55. The Sarda Act was the only existing law in India that specifically dealt with the issue of child marriage. Its author was Harbilas Sarda. The Act was subsequently amended in 1978, when the age of consent was raised to twenty-one for males and eighteen for females.
56. Edward Frederick Lindley Wood, first Earl of Halifax (1881–1959) was a British Conservative politician. He succeeded Lord Reading as Viceroy of India in April 1926, a post he held until 1931. He subsequently served as British Ambassador in Washington. Irwin's rule was marked by a period of great political turmoil. The exclusion of Indians from the Simon Commission provoked serious violence and Irwin was forced into concessions which were poorly received in London as excessive and in India as half-hearted.
57. A system of double government introduced by the Government of India Act 1919 for the provinces of British India. It marked the first introduction of the democratic principle into the executive branch of the British administration of India. Though much-criticized, it signified a breakthrough in British Indian government and was the forerunner of India's full provincial autonomy (1935) and independence (1947). Dyarchy was introduced as a constitutional reform by E.S. Montagu (Secretary of State for India, 1917–22) and Lord Chelmsford (Viceroy of India, 1916–21).
58. A lecture given by Sir George Cunningham, the then Governor designated to the NWFP in 1936, to the Royal Central Asian Society, pp.90–101.
59. Lecture by Sir George Cunningham, to the Royal Central Asian Society, pp.90–101.
60. Ibid.
61. Ibid.

62. A Tehsildar is a revenue administrative officer in Pakistan and India in charge of a small revenue district.
63. 'Unrest in the Peshawar District, 1930–1932', article in *Journal of Royal Central Asian Society*, 19(4), January 1932, pp.624–42, 10/32 by HRS.
64. Vithalbhai Patel (1871–1933) was an Indian legislator and political leader, who was co-founder of the Swaraj Party.
65. Local police station.
66. Sulaiman–Panckridge Report, p.27.
67. Patel Report, p.17.
68. Rittenberg, 'The Independence Movement in India's NWFP', p.102.
69. Government of India File, 255/V, 1930, Telegram 2665-s, 8/11/30, Viceroy to Secretary of State.
70. HP/24, no. 162, Telegram Cr/16, 4/26/30, Bolton to Viceroy.
71. PJ6/1897, 1930. No 2105. Telegram 1320-S, 5/1/30, Home Department to Secretary of State.
72. The Utman Khels are a Pakhtun tribe who occupy the hills north of Peshawar in the NWFP of Pakistan. The British conducted military campaigns against them in 1852, 1878 and 1898.
73. Rittenberg, 'The Independence Movement in India's NWFP', p.120.
74. Lord Halifax Papers/24, No. 301, Letter 6/12/30 Pears to Viceroy.
75. Naujawan Bharat Sabha was formed in March 1926 and Bhagat Singh was its Secretary and a principal organizer.
76. Rittenberg's, 'The Independence Movement in India's NWFP', pp.115–116.
77. Government of India File, 255/V, 1930, Press Communique, 8/15/30.
78. Ibid., Telegram 12-L, 8/10/30, NWF Peshawar to Foreign Department.
79. As described in the *Journal of the Royal Central Asian Society* (1934).
80. The Indian Reforms Act, also known as the Montford Reforms, was passed in 1919 in Britain. The reforms were aimed at achieving a responsible government in India.
81. A non-Muslim member from Orissa division in the Central Legislative Assembly.
82. Legislative Assembly Debates, 5 February 1935, p.66.
83. *Jagirs* and *muafis* are revenue-free lands.
84. The party founded by Vladimir Lenin, the Russian communist leader.
85. Legislative Assembly Debates, Statement by B. Das, 5 February 1935, pp.367–68.
86. Ibid., p.368.

87. Ibid., p.370, quoted in the debates.
88. Ibid., quoted in the debates.
89. Statement of B. Das, Legislative Assembly Debates, 5 February 1935, p.371.
90. Ibid.
91. Legislative Assembly Debates, 5 February 1935, p.377.
92. Ibid.
93. Ibid.
94. Ibid., p.379.
95. Ibid.
96. Ibid., p.380.
97. Ibid., Statement of Member T.A.K. Sherwani, p.383.
98. Ibid., p.383.
99. Sir Henry Craik (1876-1927), Governor of the Punjab, 1938-41.
100. Legislative Assembly Debates, p.395.
101. Result of the talks between Mahatma Gandhi and Lord Irwin in 1931.
102. Legislative Assembly Debates, pp.398-99.
103. Ibid., pp.399-400.
104. Ibid., p.402.
105. Ibid., p.405.
106. Ibid., pp.405-06.

# 4

# Sometimes Badly Served: Wavell's Viceroyalty

OF MILITARY COUNTENANCE, Field Marshal Archibald Wavell neither visualized nor desired the Indian viceroyalty. He would have preferred to end his career with an active command. No other allied commander could boast of conducting fourteen campaigns in the first few years of World War II. Wavell's successes, of course, were against the Italians and the Vichy French, and his failures, against the Germans and the Japanese. One of his early biographers had sardonically used a quote from W.H. Auden to describe him:

> History to the defeated;
> May say Alas but cannot help or pardon (Lewin 1980: 15).

His was a reserved, stoic exterior, quite in contrast to the personalities of Lord Mountbatten, Field Marshal Bernard Montgomery or General George Patton. Wavell's conception of a General's traits revealed some of his own: 'Does it matter to a General whether he has his men's affection so long as he has their confidence? He must certainly never court popularity. If he has their appreciation and respect it is sufficient. Efficiency in a General his soldiers have a right to expect; geniality they are usually right to suspect' (Connell 1964: 20). Montgomery and Mountbatten had a propensity to court popularity and display calculated geniality.

'On he went up the great, bare staircase of his duty, uncheered and undepressed' (Connell 1964: 23) quite aptly depicts Wavell's persona. Although Churchill appointed him as India's Viceroy, theirs was always a relationship of much unease. For example, during World War II, the

British evacuation of Somaliland had left Churchill indignant. Chafing, he demanded an inquiry. To a 'red-hot cable' from Churchill on the so-called scuttle, Wavell's response was equally acerbic, 'that a big butcher's bill was not necessarily an evidence of good tactics' (Lewin 1980: 25). The obvious reference was to the small number of British casualties suffered during evacuation. Wavell's riposte sent Churchill into a wild rage, not seen before by Sir John Dill, the Chief of Imperial General Staff. Things never did improve thereafter between them. Churchill, like Lincoln during the American Civil War, had not seen very many successes in the initial phase of World War II. He desperately sought triumphs, even minor, and a General who could make that possible. Lincoln changed Generals till he settled for Grant; Churchill likewise tested Wavell, Auchinleck and others to finally settle for Montgomery. Wavell perhaps failed to realize and appreciate Churchill's predicament. Ironically, Generals like Orde Wingate who caught Churchill's attention were discovered by Wavell.

When Wavell returned to England on 22 April 1943, he was not aware of being in the reckoning for India's viceroyalty. His meetings with Churchill had not exactly been cordial. Soon, both of them were on a ship across the Atlantic to discuss future joint operations with the Americans. The frost in their relationship remained well after they returned to London in the first week of June. Wavell was expecting Churchill to entrust him with a responsibility nearer 'home', which, if it did occur, would be a sheer waste of his experience in the east. But his misgivings were soon to be dispelled. Churchill summoned Wavell on 14 June to let him know that he was being considered for the Viceroy's post in India. This was no magnanimity on Churchill's part. Far from being generous he had decided to put Wavell on the 'shelf'.

A book Wavell wrote on Allenby[1] was published in late 1943. On 10 September, Sir Edward Grigg[2] had asked for advance proofs of the book fearing criticism in conservative circles. Wavell had then noted in his diary: 'I don't think I mind if it does, I am not very much in sympathy with the right-wing Conservatives' (Lewin 1980: 232). Churchill, the Colonial Secretary during Allenby's time, had been in Egypt. He was not at all in sympathy with Wavell's book. So anguished was he on seeing Wavell's work that he very nearly cancelled the dinner given by the cabinet in honour of the Viceroy designate. Possibly an earlier publication of the book may have seen Wavell cooling his heels as Governor General of Australia. Instead he took over as India's Viceroy on 20 October 1943.

The India and Burma Committee[3] consisted of Edward Grigg, John Simon, Stafford Cripps, Clemant Attlee and Churchill, who were mostly not well disposed to Wavell. Though at times Stafford Cripps supported Wavell, he did not like him personally. Attlee at best was lukewarm. Wavell, 'fettered hand and foot' (Listowell 1984: 51) by Churchill, could do nothing without the authority of the India and Burma Committee of the cabinet, over which Attlee as Deputy Prime Minister presided. Acting like a 'faint echo of his master's voice' (Listowell 1984), Wavell had to take permission even if he wanted to meet Indian leaders. The unfortunate Viceroy had no friends in the Churchill cabinet apart from Leopold Amery,[4] a well intentioned but 'wholly impotent' (*Indo-British Review* 1984: 51) Secretary of State. Wavell could only wring concessions by threats of resignation. Churchill's main concern whenever Wavell was home on consultations, was how to send him back to New Delhi. On one occasion Wavell was kept waiting in London for three months before he could get Churchill's audience. Churchill's India and Burma Committee far exceeded Attlee's in authority and experience. Several great personalities adorned Churchill's committee. Yet, with all their knowledge and experience, they were in continuous conflict with the Viceroy whose maximum demand was a modest but immediate move towards self-governance. Taking their cue from Attlee, the Labour Party representatives on the committee chose to fall in line with Churchill. No constitutional reforms were to be introduced in India while the war lasted. In the words of Attlee, 'The cabinet had always deferred to the Prime Minister's passionate feelings about India' (Listowell 1984: 52).

Gandhi's release from detention was one of the prominent events of 1944. Wavell had chosen to release him without prior sanction from the British cabinet. Churchill was livid. Mountbatten once narrated an incident to Lord Listowel that took place at Simla in September 1944, which is revealing of how dissimilar Wavell and Mountbatten were.

Wavell had been quite 'put out' by the Secretary of State's refusal to allow him to meet Gandhi. Churchill was furious about Gandhi's release from prison, whereas Wavell found his attitude towards India 'quite impossible'. Mountbatten, as he put it, had to explain to Wavell that 'since Churchill disliked him [Wavell] personally, disliked his policies even more and would do nothing to help him, why did he not simply arrange to get Gandhi sent for while he was on his way from prison to the hospital.' To the upstanding Wavell, this was unacceptable. Mountbatten then asked him what he thought would have happened if he had disregarded this order from Whitehall, met Gandhi and reported details of his meeting to the Secretary of State. Wavell had to admit that Whitehall could possibly have done nothing except send him a rude telegram which he was used to receiving. Mountbatten then urged Wavell to take such steps as he deemed necessary without asking for permission and report what he had done, leaving Whitehall to take the appalling risk of sacking him. Narrating the episode to Listowell, Mountbatten commented: 'I like to think that this effort to put some spunk into his attitude towards Whitehall did some good, and, certainly from my point of view, this incident was uppermost in my mind when I demanded plenipotentiary powers from Attlee' (Listowell 1984).

Shortly after taking over as the Under Secretary of State for India in October 1944, Listowell received a copy of a letter from Wavell to Churchill about his views on India's future, the import of it being the seriousness attached to it while the British fought for survival in Europe and Asia. Listowell considered the letter to be 'an act of imaginative and farsighted statesmanship', not remembered very often because Wavell failed where Mountbatten succeeded in making his policy acceptable to the government in Britain as well as to the Indian leaders. It is worth reproducing some excerpts of that letter:

> To my mind, our strategic security, our name in the world of statesmanship and fair dealing, and much of our economic well being, will depend on the settlement we make in India. If we can secure India as a friendly partner in the British Commonwealth, our predominant influence in countries like Burma, Malaya and China will be assured...political advance [in India] cannot be delayed until after the war...we have reason to dislike Gandhi and Jinnah. But the Congress and League are the dominant parties in Hindu and Muslim India, and will remain so...we cannot bypass them...above all, there is the question of credibility. We have lost the trust and confidence of Indians by promising so much

and doing so little, and we have now to convince them of our sincerity... If we want India as a Dominion after the war, we must begin by treating her much more like a Dominion now (Listowell 1984: 50–51).

It was a pity that this progressive letter by Wavell was promptly pigeon-holed by its recipient, Churchill.

Even with a Labour victory in the elections in 1945, relations between Wavell and the British cabinet did not become amicable. This misfortune can only be explained in terms of personalities, for there was no serious disagreement over policy. In the new India and Burma Committee, Sir Stafford Cripps was the only member with recent first-hand Indian experience, combined with personal acquaintance with Indian political leaders. It was Cripps who dominated the deliberations of the India and Burma Committee. This dominance was fatal to the relationship between Wavell and the Attlee government. Cripps disliked Wavell and wanted to replace him, perhaps since the time of the Cabinet Mission to India in 1946.[5] Listowell felt that Cripps disapproved of soldiers in high places. The perception was that Cripps favoured Congress leaders over the Muslim League, while Wavell believed in holding an even balance. Wavell was handicapped by his lack of diplomatic skills and an inability to nurture personal relationships. In comparison, Mountbatten spent a week getting to know Nehru, Jinnah and their families when he arrived in Delhi (Listowell 1984: 53).

Convinced that an agreed solution was unobtainable, Wavell faced the new British cabinet with a choice of policies that did not depend on an agreement or acquiescence of the Indian leaders. He suggested two options: either enforce British rule for at least fifteen years or have a phased withdrawal from India. The first alternative entailed reinforcement of the Indian army and was therefore, overruled by the India Committee as politically impracticable in the aftermath of World War II. The second choice was a planned withdrawal operation, to be completed by 31 March 1948. Be it noted that Wavell was the first person to suggest a fixed date for the termination of British rule. Far from originating in Whitehall, it was resisted strenuously by Attlee until Mountbatten made it a condition for acceptance of the viceroyalty. The India and Burma Committee decided to put Wavell's second alternative in cold storage (Listowell 1984: 53).

The relationship that Wavell and Mountbatten shared with the India and Burma Committee differed in nature. While Wavell was constrained by the Churchill government, as also by Attlee's, Mountbatten immediately took charge of the policy, the initiative for it coming from Whitehall. The other important difference was in the attitude of ministers. Unfortunately, Wavell had no friends. The distinction was striking when Mountbatten succeeded him. Every minister concerned with India became his good friend, anxious and eager to support him.

Soon after taking over the viceroyalty in October 1943, Wavell made a one-week trip to Punjab and the NWFP. Recalling it, he wrote: 'I have always liked Peshawar, since I was stationed there nearly 40 years ago. All they want at present is a really stout Governor, which they have got at present. They are just beginning to play at politics and I suppose will before long be as political as anyone.' The then Governor, George Cunningham was providing a good apprenticeship to provincial leaders in the art of politics. By the time Wavell joined, a Muslim League ministry was already installed under the Chief Ministership of Sardar Aurangzeb Khan, largely the handiwork of George Cunningham, in which endeavour he received the tacit support of Wavell's predecessor, Lord Linlithgow. Like British civil servants, Wavell too viewed Indian and provincial politics in terms of Hindu–Muslim dialectics. Therefore, when he assumed India's viceroyalty, he had no reason to look at the NWFP Muslim League government with any degree of unease. He allowed Cunningham a free hand to keep it propped for as long as possible. Wavell had more important things to attend to, like India's involvement in World War II and his own battle with the British cabinet.

The opening day of the cabinet delegation's discussions with Indian leaders was 1 April 1946. They began with Dr Khan Saheb, who Wavell thought was 'an attractive personality but very definitely woolly in his ideas'. It appeared to Wavell that Dr Khan Saheb had 'obviously not really thought out the problems of Pakistan and refused to consider its possibility; nor had he considered what Hindu domination at the centre could entail. He had talked entirely from a provincial angle, as if Pathans were a separate nation living in Pathanistan.' According to Wavell, Dr Khan Saheb contributed little of value to the discussions.

Then came Khan Abdul Qayyum Khan, the Muslim League leader. Wavell found him 'a rather unpleasant looking tough, only recently converted from Congress to Muslim League. Like Dr Khan Saheb, Abdul Qayyum was convinced that the provincial administration could manage the tribes much better than the Political Department, and advocated an NWFP made up of additional tribal territories and a part of Baluchistan, which he believed could stand on its own and defend itself' (Moon 1973: 233–34).

It was unreasonable, Wavell believed, for Jinnah to receive both the territory, much of it inhabited by non-Muslims, and the full measure of sovereignty. Wavell felt that if full territories were to be insisted upon, then some element of sovereignty had to be relinquished. If, on the other hand, full sovereignty was desired, then the non-Muslim territories would have to be given up. Cripps too was ready to argue with Jinnah about the inability of the cabinet delegation to press the Congress to accept anything more than a smaller Pakistan—Baluchistan, Sindh, the NWFP and half of Punjab in the west, and eastern Bengal with Sylhet but without Calcutta in the east.[6] By April 1946, Jinnah and the Muslim League felt emboldened to hope that the NWFP may fall into Pakistan's lap. With British acquiescence, it was becoming a bright possibility.[7]

V.P. Menon, the Reforms Commissioner, had helped Wavell and the cabinet delegation outline a plan as to whether there should be one sovereign state in India or two. The broad parameters of the plan were that the Muslim representatives of each of the provinces of Sindh, the NWFP, Punjab, Bengal, plus the district of Sylhet should meet to vote separately for exclusion from the rest of India. In the event of 75 per cent of the Muslim representatives of a provincial assembly voting in favour of exclusion, that province was to be excluded. In the provinces of Sindh, the NWFP, Punjab and Bengal, the distribution of Muslim seats were:

| Province | Muslim League | Other Muslims |
|---|---|---|
| Bengal + Sylhet | 130 | 12 |
| Punjab | 79 | 10 |
| NWFP | 17 | 21 |
| Sindh | 28 | 7 |

Both in Bengal plus Sylhet and in Punjab, 90 per cent of the Muslim League votes would represent more than 75 per cent of the total Muslim votes. In Sindh, however, 90 per cent of the Muslim League votes worked out to only 72 per cent of the total Muslim strength. It would still suffice for the formula to work in case all Muslim League members in Sindh voted for Pakistan. Their representation would cross 75 per cent. But the case of the NWFP was different—a fact recognized by the cabinet delegation as well. If a province stood out in accordance with the procedure, the non-Muslim representatives in the provincial assembly of the Muslim minority districts in that province would then decide by a 75 per cent vote whether such districts should be part of Hindustan.[8]

The cabinet delegation contemplated three rounds of decision-making under this proposal. The first round for Pakistan was to be fought out in the commission (proposed by the cabinet delegation to be created by the interim government at the centre). If in this round Pakistan got more than 25 per cent of the total votes, it qualified for the next round. The next round was to be fought in provincial assemblies of the Muslim majority provinces and was to be confined to Muslim members only to decide which of these provinces would opt for Pakistan. Then came the third round, to be fought amongst the non-Muslim members returned by contiguous Muslim minority districts of the Pakistan provinces to decide which of these areas would be put into Hindustan.[9]

At this stage, the issue of taking the matter back to the commission for final approval arose. Pakistan's final shape would be known only after the conclusion of the third round. It was important, therefore, to take the consent of the commission on the exact contours of Pakistan that would emerge after the third and final round. It was likely that some members who voted for Pakistan initially could take exception to its final outline in which case there was a possibility of that Pakistan being given up.[10]

Although the plan was ingenious, it gave Jinnah very little. In the first round Pakistan was expected to win, but in the second round Jinnah could lose the NWFP. In the third round, Jinnah could also probably lose many non-Muslim districts, including Calcutta. Jinnah could well end up in a situation where the demand for Pakistan itself lay rejected. It would then be left to the Muslim League to refuse participation in the interim government till the demand for Pakistan was conceded. Here Jinnah faced a problem, for there was no aspect of this plan which he could reasonably object to. Nothing much came out of this plan though. This too was pigeon-holed. Knowing well that Jinnah would find it difficult to oppose this scheme, the Congress did not press Jinnah to accept it.[11] This was one way of saving the NWFP and many non-Muslim areas from going over to Pakistan. Since V.P. Menon, Patel's disciple, had helped Wavell formulate this plan, it is hard to understand why the Congress did not insist on its acceptance.

The cabinet delegation proposed the formation of an interim government. Late in May 1946, Weightman,[12] the Foreign Secretary to the Government of India, wrote to the Viceroy's Private Secretary, Sir George Abell, conveying his worries about handing over of the external affairs portfolio to an Indian. Till then, the Viceroy himself had held charge of this department. But with an Indian foreign member and virtual assurance that he and his colleagues in the interim government would shape and implement India's foreign policy, Weightman thought the idea would likely run them into difficulties unless he was clear about the extent to which Her Majesty's Government (HMG) was prepared to abrogate its constitutional responsibility. The Foreign Secretary quoted a few examples where he foresaw difficulties: if as a result of certain pre-existing personal relationships between Indian leaders and the Chiang Kai-sheks[13] the interim government decided to abandon support for Tibetan autonomy or for purely ideological reasons the interim government decided to stop delivery of war materials which the British had agreed to supply to the Afghan government. Weightman also worried about a situation where the Viceroy's advice was disregarded. Was HMG then to stand on the strict constitutional position? Some foreign governments were likely to enquire about who they were dealing with during the interim period.[14]

Wavell agreed to get the matter examined in London in consultation with the foreign office, though his own personal recommendation was that the interim government be allowed to pursue its own foreign policy to a very considerable extent.[15]

Weightman[16] met Wavell with a proposal to take action against the Shabi Khel Mahsuds who had kidnapped a Political Agent, Major

J. Donald, and two of his party near Razmak[17] on 22 June 1946. In order to rescue Donald, the government had to pay ₹110,000 to the Shabi Khels. Weightman proposed to demand this money of the Shabi Khels, plus 250 rifles. Wavell doubted the ethics of this procedure because Frontier regulations would require the area to be proscribed and after due warning, for the villages to be destroyed by bombing in case the Shabi Khel did not comply. Weightman on the other hand was insistent that immediate action be taken. It was only after discussing the efforts involved and its probable effects with the AOC-in-C that Wavell gave his approval to the proposed action. Nehru had enquired about the bombing of the Shabi Khels on 10 September and had wanted to bring this matter before the cabinet. Fortunately, Wavell heard a few hours later on the same day that the Shabi Khel, or rather the Mahsud *jirga* on their behalf had proposed terms which had been accepted. On 13 September the nationalist press headlines claimed that Nehru was responsible for the stoppage of the brutal British bombing in Waziristan, while Jinnah's paper *Dawn* came out with: 'Hands off the Pathan,' implying that the first fruits of a Hindu government had been the bombing of Muslims. Actually the bombing of Shabi Khel villages had started more than a month before the interim government came into power and stopped just when Nehru registered his protest. Such, even then, was the accuracy of the press.

On 28 September, Governor Caroe was informed by the External Affairs Department that Nehru proposed to pay a one-week visit to the frontier in October and that he wished to be accompanied by Khan Abdul Ghaffar Khan and the Chief Minister Dr Khan Saheb. Caroe reacted quite promptly, shooting off an urgent telegram to Wavell on this issue.[18] He felt that the External Affairs Department was demonstrating a partisan attitude to the tribal problem at a most critical juncture. Caroe was convinced that serious tribal reactions would follow in case Nehru insisted on proceeding with his visit to the NWFP, reactions that would wreck any hope of securing a coalition between the League and the Congress at the centre. Caroe believed that if the visit came through, he would not be in a position to maintain tranquillity on the borders of the north-west. Abell found the Governor's view to be overstated, for it was impractical to keep Nehru, the foreign member, away from the Tribal Areas. If Nehru's visit was to have unfortunate consequences, the government would have to put up with it.[19] Wavell's reply to Caroe on 30 September was reasonable. If a coalition government could be cobbled up, Nehru would find it impossible to visit the NWFP according to the scheduled timing. If the coalition did not come through, there was little advantage in Wavell urging Nehru to postpone the visit, for Nehru then would be suspicious of any such attempt. Indeed, if Nehru insisted on going to the Tribal Areas, the government would have to deal with the results of his visit as best as it could.[20]

Wavell advised Nehru to consider taking a Muslim League colleague to balance out the party issue (Moon 1973: 373) in case the Muslim League decided to join the interim government. The advice was received by Nehru without any enthusiasm (Moon 1973). So worried was Caroe that he came to Delhi to meet the Viceroy. Wavell offered whatever comfort he could to Caroe, wishing for a coalition government to be in place before Nehru's visit. He was uncomfortable about Ghaffar Khan accompanying Nehru but told Caroe that he could not stop him from undertaking the visit. Caroe did meet Nehru in Delhi to dissuade him from going ahead with the visit but failed to convince him (Moon 1973: 355–56).

Nehru's tour to the NWFP had disastrous consequences. Its implications have been analyzed in chapters dealing with Nehru and Sir Olaf Caroe. Wavell's impression of this visit, communicated to the Secretary of State, was:

> You will see what a dangerous and foolhardy escapade it was. Nehru himself has written a long note on his experience which shows him at his worst. He seems to be incapable of realizing that the Frontier is something outside his ordinary political experience, that it is dangerous material to handle on doctrinaire lines, and that the Pathan is a very great deal more democratic than the Congress.
>
> The Political Officers were made the scapegoat. It is perfectly clear that the real representatives of the tribes were present in the *jirgas*, that there was no official propaganda except on Nehru's behalf and that had it not been for the efforts of the Political Officers, some of the *jirgas* would not have turned up at all. On

the whole the military and the civil authorities seemed to have done very well and it is due to them and the good fortune that Nehru was not more severely injured. A very mild little Hindu Press photographer who sometimes goes around with me on tour told Abell that during the fracas outside Landi Kotal, a bullet from one of the tribesmen passed within an inch or two of his nose when he was sitting in a car which was part of the convoy. Again, near Malakand, Nehru was undoubtedly lucky to escape… Undoubtedly, Nehru would be well advised to leave the Frontier alone.[21]

On 6 November, Wavell had occasion to discuss with Foreign Secretary Weightman the ramifications of Nehru's disastrous tour and 'his foolish and unrealistic note about it' (Moon 1973: 373) to Wavell. Weightman disclosed to the Viceroy that the Congress was 'gunning for' Olaf Caroe and would have him out if possible. Weightman was also having to face a distressing situation. He saw very little of Nehru, who he felt was trying to do too much and was likely to have a nervous breakdown.

To get a first-hand feel and provide a 'healing touch', Wavell toured the NWFP from 14 to 19 November.[22] During the visit he did not fail to notice that Olaf Caroe and Dr Khan Saheb had fallen out with each other. Caroe was very much on the edge. Wavell found the Chief Minister to be well meaning, though without the necessary force of character or wisdom to run a province. Wavell found the accusations hurled by Dr Khan Saheb at Olaf vague. In fact Dr Khan Saheb was shaken by the results of Nehru's visit to the NWFP and the obvious hostility to the Congress that it had revealed. Wavell reckoned that he was, therefore, making attempts to foist the whole blame on British officials.

The India and Burma Committee was appreciative of Wavell's tour as they had already seen the Governor's report, brought to their notice by Lord Pethick-Lawrence. Wavell's visit had especially been welcomed by the political officers who, the committee felt, had undeservedly been criticized by Nehru and the Congress. In the British Parliament, the Secretary of State had to answer questions on the optional use of troops and the aspersions cast on the political officers. He was also quizzed on why British troops had been employed to escort Nehru during the tour and whether the disturbances were engineered by the Political Department.[23]

On 15 November, Wavell went to Landi Kotal to attend the Afridi *jirga*. He had a tough time convincing them that no one would interfere with their freedom in case the British were to leave soon. The *jirga* demanded that Khyber Pass be returned to the Afridis before the British left. The Afridis had no intention of being ruled by the Hindus and had resented Nehru's visit. Wavell had found the Afridi *jirga* dignified. He had also flown to Wana to meet the *jirga* of the Ahmedzai Wazirs, not quite as impressive as the Afridis, more communal and less composed in their outlook. He pretty much repeated the same thing to the Wazirs and thereafter met the local commanders and officials. His tour also included Naushera (a prominent town in the Punjab province of Pakistan), Dargai,[24] Malakand, Chakdarra[25] and Saidu. At the Malakand Pass, he inspected the scene of assault on Nehru and his party. The Political Agent, Sheikh Mehbub Ali, whose conduct had been called into question by Nehru, met the Viceroy at Dargai. Wavell thought it unlikely that Mehbub Ali could have instigated or been privy to the attack. But he could not condone the fact that Mehbub Ali had gone down the hill leaving Nehru's convoy behind, not having seen them safely past what was obviously a danger point.

Wavell was not happy with the situation in the NWFP. Caroe remained tense as a result of what had transpired during Nehru's visit. The province, which until recently had not been affected by Indian politics, was now getting polarized. This was making the officials resentful. It may have gratified Wavell to receive an endorsed letter by Nehru written to Caroe where he admitted that the Frontier and the tribes had better be left alone for the present.[26]

In a correspondence of 20 November to the Governor of Bengal, Sir Fredrick Bourne, Wavell further elaborated on his tour of the NWFP. To him, the wagers appeared to align themselves with the Muslim League. The morale of the service was low in the province along with a great deal of mistrust between the services and the ministry.[27] To quote Wavell, 'The Political Officers on the Frontier are extremely sour at their treatment by Nehru and the Congress and I fear that a body of men who were as devoted to India as any in the services have been put into a mood to get out as soon as possible, regardless of consequences.'[28] This was a stern observation made by a soldier Viceroy.

In the period between December 1946 and March 1947, serious communal trouble broke out in East Bengal. Bihar followed suit; then Bombay and Punjab. In the midst of all this came HMG's announcement on 20 February 1947 replacing Wavell as India's Viceroy. Thereafter, another telegram arrived from London justifying this decision, critical of the 'inconsistent policies' that Wavell had followed during his viceroyalty.

In early March 1947 Khizr Tiwana, the Chief Minister of Punjab, resigned. Wavell believed that Tiwana had decided to resign with minimum consultation and maximum speed, something which had been markedly absent from other Indian political decisions. He considered the Punjab ministry a rather artificial set-up and thought that its fall would now put an intolerable strain on the Congress ministry in the NWFP, which may not last long. He also observed rather astutely that neither in Punjab nor in the NWFP were the League leaders impressive and therefore, were not likely to be moderate or wise.[29]

Nehru too was troubled by the developments in the NWFP. The Muslim League had gone on a communal overdrive in the province. The issue of the return of the Sikh woman of Hazara[30] to the Muslim fold had come in handy to browbeat Dr Khan Saheb's ministry. The situation created on account of the abduction of the Sikh girl and the march in procession to the Chief Minister's house worried Lord Pethick-Lawrence. He feared a repetition of what the Muslim League was attempting to do in Punjab. The Muslim League was also insistent that the fine imposed on the Nandihar tribes of Hazara be returned, which if agreed to, would end any semblance of administration and authority in that area. Nehru, therefore, thought it prudent to pay a brief visit to Peshawar and take stock of the situation.[31]

While in Lahore, Nehru received a message from Wavell asking him not to proceed to Peshawar (Moon 1973: 428). Perforce he had to cancel his visit. He blamed the Governor for having stymied it. Nehru charged that 'he had been prevented from performing his duty because someone did not approve of his going to the Frontier.'[32] That someone was Olaf Caroe. That Caroe disapproved of Nehru taking charge of the External

Affairs Department had always remained a sore point with him. He was also bitter about the fact that Caroe had approached Wavell to prevent Nehru's appointment. Indignant, he wrote to Wavell on 19 March:

> The incident that happened during my visit made me realize how inefficient and out of date the Frontier administration was. This administration had created a legend about itself and about conditions in the Frontier, and it did not like anyone to interfere with the set up. My experience during the past six months have convinced me that no substantial good can be done to the Frontier areas unless this set up is changed. I cannot continue to shoulder my present responsibilities if I am prevented from doing my work in this way. It is an extraordinary position. Almost anyone can go to Peshawar, but I must not do so, even for a brief and informal visit.[33]

And he closed with, 'I think the matter must be faced squarely and a solution found. That solution should be retirement of the Governor. Sir Olaf Caroe should, therefore, be requested to retire from his present office at an early date.'[34]

Wavell was to hand over charge to Mountbatten within two days of receiving Nehru's letter. He did respond to Nehru but made no mention of his demand for the Governor's retirement. Instead, coming to Caroe's defence, he wrote to him saying that it was not Caroe who had objected to his visit to Peshawar.[35] Caroe had definitely said that the visit at this juncture would be a 'dangerous' proposition because the security forces were fully occupied to allow for special measures of protection, but that he 'will do his best'.[36] Wavell explained to Nehru that he had suggested the cancellation of the visit on his own volition for he was concerned about Nehru's safety and did not wish the police to be diverted from other important duties. In fact, the Governor of Punjab, around the same time, had discouraged the Viceroy from touring Lahore, citing the same reasons.[37] Wavell kept the Secretary of State informed that Nehru had proposed the removal of the Governor. Wavell believed that Nehru was provoked to this because of the completion of the judicial enquiry into the conduct of Shiekh Mehbub Ali,[38] which had exonerated the Political Agent.[39]

In two days' time, Wavell handed over charge and headed home.

## Notes

1. Sir Edmund Henry Hynman Allenby (1861–1936) commanded the cavalry division of the British Expeditionary Force on the Western Front during World War I. In 1917 he was given command of the Egyptian Expeditionary Force. His reputation derives from his command in the Middle East. During his campaign against the Turks in Palestine he captured Gaza in November and Jerusalem in December 1917 and after defeating the enemy on the plain of Megiddo in September 1918, took Damascus and Aleppo. In 1919 he was made a Field Marshal. He served as High Commissioner to Egypt in 1919–25.
2. Edward Grigg was a British politician and member of the India and Burma Committee.
3. The highest decision-making authority on India headed by the British Prime Minister.
4. Leopold (Leo) Amery was born in Gorakhpur, India on 22 November 1873. Educated at Harrow and Balliol College, Oxford, he became a member of the Conservative Party in 1911. In David Lloyd George's government, he served as Under Secretary of State for the Colonies (1919–21). In 1940, Prime Minister Neville Chamberlain appointed Amery as Secretary of State for India and Burma. He held this office also during Churchill's tenure (till 1945).
5. The Cabinet Mission aimed to discuss and finalize plans for the transfer of power from the British Raj to the Indian leadership. Formally an initiative of Clement Attlee, the Prime Minister of the United Kingdom, the mission consisted of Lord Pethick-Lawrence, the Secretary of State for India; Sir Stafford Cripps, President of the Board of Trade; and A.V. Alexander, the First Lord of the Admiralty. It was also supplemented by Lord Wavell, India's Viceroy at the time.
6. L/P&J/10/40: f199, undated, Nicholas Mansergh and Penderel Moon (eds.), *The Transfer of Power 1942–47*, Vol.VII April 1946, p.233.
7. Brief prepared by Wavell for an interview with Jinnah–16 April 1946, L/P&J/10/40: ff191–192, Penderel Moon, *The Transfer of Power*, Vol.VII, p.250.
8. L/P&J/10/40: ff113–117, undated, Moon, *The Transfer of Power*, Vol.VII, April 1946, pp.318–19.
9. Ibid., p.319.

10. Ibid.
11. Ibid., pp.319–20.
12. J.G. Weightman, a British member of the Indian Political Service, who, as Foreign Secretary headed the Foreign and Political Department of the Government of India.
13. During Sun Yat Sen's Kuomintang regime, Chiang Kai-Shek had already attained prominence. After his death in 1925, he emerged to lead the Kuomintang camp (Nationalist) part of China. Madam Chiang Kai-Shek was a politician and a painter. She played a prominent role in the politics of the Republic of China.
14. L/P&s/12/4631: f313 of 27 May 1946, Moon, *The Transfer of Power*, Vol. VII, pp.718–19.
15. L/P&s/12/4631: ff308–309 of 31 May 1946, Moon, *The Transfer of Power*, Vol. VII, 742.
16. Sir Hugh Weightman, ICS, Secretary, External Affairs Department, 1946–47.
17. Razmak: Plateau in North Waziristan, NWFP. The altitude of Razmak varies from 6,000 feet to 11,000 feet.
18. Telegram, r/3/1/92: f7 of 29 September 1946, Moon, *The Transfer of Power*, Vol. VIII, p.626.
19. R/3/1/92: f8, of 30 September 1946, Moon, *The Transfer of Power*, Vol. VIII, p.627.
20. Telegram, r/3/1/92: f10 of 30 September 1946, Moon, *The Transfer of Power*, Vol. VIII, p.627.
21. Moon, *The Transfer of Power* volumes, Vol. IX
22. Described by Wavell in his journal (Penderel Moon (ed.), *Wavell: The Viceroy's Journal*, Oxford University Press, 1973), pp.377–78, as well as in a Report sent by Wavell from Peshawar on 15 November 1946, Moon, *The Transfer of Power*, Vol. IX, pp.72–73.
23. Moon, *the Transfer of Power*, Vol. IX, pp.81–82.
24. Dargai is the name of a mountain peak and a frontier train station in north-west Pakistan. The mountain peak is situated on the Samana range and the Kohat border and is famous for the stand made there by the Afridis and Orakzai in the Tirah campaign of 1897.
25. The historic town of Chakdarra in Dir district lies on the bank of the Swat River. It is about 130 km from Peshawar and 48 km from Saidu Sharif.
26. Described in Wavell's journal (Moon, *Wavell: The Viceroy's Journal*) and

stated in the report which he sent on 15 November 1946 from Peshawar.
27. Wavell to Sir F. Bourne, Governor, Central Provinces, r/3/1/92: f197, 20 November, Moon, *The Transfer of Power*, Vol. IX, p.120.
28. *The Transfer of Power*, Vol. IX, p.142.
29. Wavell to Lord Pethick-Lawrence, L/Po/10/24 of 5 March 1947, *The Transfer of Power*, Vol. IX, p.870.
30. Hazara is Afghanistan's rugged central mountainous core of approximately 50,000 sq. km is known as the Hazarajat, land of the Hazaras.
31. Nehru to Wavell, r/3/1/89: ff111–112 of 13 March 1947, *The Transfer of Power*, Vol. IX, pp.928–29.
32. Nehru to Wavell, l/P&J/8/660: ff181–182 of 19 March 1947, *The Transfer of Power*, Vol. IX, p.988.
33. Nehru to Wavell, l/P&J/8/660: ff181–182 of 19 March 1947, *The Transfer of Power*, Vol. IX, pp.988–89.
34. Nehru to Wavell, l/P&J/8/660: ff181–182 of 19 March 1947, *The Transfer of Power*, Vol. IX, p.989.
35. Wavell to Nehru, L/P&J/8/660: f183 of 19 March 1947, *The Transfer of Power*, Vol. IX, p.989.
36. Wavell to Nehru, L/P&J/8/660: f183 of 19 March 1947, *The Transfer of Power*, Vol. IX, pp.989–90.
37. Ibid.
38. The Political Agent of Malakand. Nehru's convoy had been attacked while on a tour to Malakand in October 1946. An enquiry, thereafter, had been instituted to investigate the incident.
39. Wavell to Lord Pethick-Lawrence, L/Po/10/24 of 19 March 1947, *The Transfer of Power*, Vol. IX, p.991.

# 5

## The 'Not Entirely Accidental' Role of Viceroy Mountbatten

T HE BATTENBERGS, THE FAMILY that Mountbatten belonged to was royal but not royal enough. The last of India's Viceroys, Louis Mountbatten was Queen Victoria's great grandson—she had chosen not to stand in the way of her youngest daughter marrying a Battenberg. Having joined the British navy in 1917, Mountbatten's was an unexpected case of a steady rise in the navy's echelons. When World War II broke out, he was in command of a new destroyer *Kelly* which he almost sank due to his impulsiveness. Mishaps continued to dog him—*Kelly* crashing into another destroyer *Gurkha* and Mountbatten losing a naval ship that accompanied *Kelly*, followed by an incident where *Kelly* rammed into a merchant ship. Finally in April 1941, *Kelly's* luck ran out. It was sunk thick in the middle of the Crete disaster.[1] The captain and some of the crew survived (Tinker 1997: 227–28).

With this kind of a record, any officer sans Mountbatten's royal connections would have lost his command. Though heavily criticized, Mountbatten was saved time and again by Churchill's intervention. He continued to get his promotions. Another failure, the disastrous Dieppe raid[2] under his command, took place on 19 August 1942. Two-thirds of the main Canadian assault force was killed or wounded. Canada never forgave Mountbatten, but Churchill continued to favour him. He was soon appointed Commander of the South East Asia Command (SEAC).

He first set up his headquarters in Delhi but when his team rapidly outgrew its accommodation, he moved to Ceylon (Kandy). Commenting on his command, a senior staff officer, General H.E.

Pyman[3] observed: 'It would be wrong to say that the machinery of command in Kandy is really efficient' (Tinker 1997: 229). At the end of World War II, his Chief Political Advisor was of the view that the SEAC headquarters 'had now attained a standard of inefficiency which makes it a byword' (Tinker 1997). Many referred to it as a 'supreme example of Allied Confusion', an acronym for SEAC, 'a barren bureaucratic waste, rustling with the shuffling and reshuffling of papers by a lot of "brasshats" bent on obstruction' (Murphy 1948: 11). Mountbatten had many nicknames, among them 'Superbo' for 'Supremo' or supreme commander. He was considered a remote and irresponsible master who sat in his luxurious office at Kandy as 'a Zeus[4] on Olympus, coming down once in a while to make sport with the lives of men fighting in a jungle, cool, charming and godlike in his taste for other people's confusions' (Murphy 1948). Kandy Dandy, Kandy Kid and Lord Non-Combatant were some other names he was called by. When asked whether he did not find Mountbatten thoroughly likeable, General 'Vinegar Joe' Stilwell[5] once replied: 'Yes. That's what makes him so dangerous. Even I like him' (Murphy 1948: 12).

At the beginning of World War II when Mountbatten was in command of the fifth destroyer flotilla, the opinion that the army had of him was summed up as: 'There is nobody better to be with in a tight spot than "Dickie" Mountbatten and nobody likely to get you into one sooner.' 'All theory and no practice,' was another verdict. 'He refuses to come down off the chandelier.' 'He reminds me of the type described by Kafka in one of his diaries as "An expert, a specialist, one who knows his role, a knowledge, to be sure, that cannot be communicated, but which fortunately everyone can do without."' When Ray Murphy enquired why Churchill had appointed him (Mountbatten) Chief of the Combined Operations with the acting rank of Vice Admiral and the honorary rank of Lieutenant General and Air Vice Marshal when he had been so ineffective as the Commander of the destroyer flotilla, Murphy was told that Mountbatten and Churchill were both Tories, and that Churchill owed a great debt to Mountbatten's father for giving the order, on his own initiative, to keep the fleet in a state of mobilization just before the outbreak of World War I when Mountbatten's father was the First Sea Lord and Churchill the First Lord of the Admiralty (Murphy 1948: 12).

One naval officer summed up his opinion thus: 'It can never be said of Dickie Mountbatten that he learns from experience, because he never does the same thing twice' (Murphy 1948).

But against all this must be set Mountbatten's insistence on seeing everything for himself. He was at his best in man-to-man encounters with the other ranks and for this reason was actively disliked by many of his seniors. He also possessed a film star-like charisma that came in handy at the time he assumed the viceroyalty of India.

When Mountbatten was in the midst of the Dutch East Indies imbroglio, Nehru visited Malaya in March 1946. Military authorities intended to cold shoulder him but Mountbatten decided otherwise. Nehru too responded in equal measure to Mountbatten's warm welcome, agreeing not to go ahead with engagements that could raise political temperatures. Nehru at once cancelled a visit to lay a wreath on the site of the Indian National Army Memorial, now demolished. During a cabinet crisis on a demand for unconditional pardon to Indian National Army (INA) prisoners, Mountbatten was again successful in persuading Nehru to exert a calm influence on his more extreme colleagues, securing a compromise that the Supreme Court would review their sentences. A rapport of sorts was already beginning to be created. Dorman-Smith, the Governor of Burma was recalled to London in 1946. Attlee is known to have consulted Mountbatten on Dorman-Smith's replacement, ultimately agreeing to Mountbatten's suggestion for a virtual unknown. Mountbatten by then had acquired the title of the Viscount of Burma. Dorman-Smith,[6] in a letter to his friend thus quoted Arthur Henderson, the parliamentary under secretary:

> Henderson in a jocular way said that it was sometimes difficult to know whether Mountbatten was living at the other end of St. James' Park or in King Charles Street [the site of India Office] ... The hand of Dickie is very evident. It stands out a hundred miles that the Viscount of Burma takes his responsibilities towards Burma very seriously. It also would seem that Lord Louis has the PM's ear... it is more than most unlikely that Attlee would have even thought of Rance [Dorman-Smith's replacement]... Dickie must have had a very real say-so in all this...and what

does all that mean? ...is it because Dickie is going to get some monumental appointment in the east and wants to have his own men around him? I just do not know, but I confess that the whole thing smells a bit (Tinker 1997: 232–33).

Dorman-Smith's letter was dated 8 August 1946. Though Smith was an erratic Governor, he had known the world.

Nothing happened for some months. Mountbatten was engaged in preparing a report for the Combined Chiefs of Staff and in the process his research team acquired a London headquarters at 7, Richmond Terrace, Whitehall, right at the heart of decision-making. The second half of 1946 was spent in manoeuvring, lobbying and projecting his personality on a London only too happy to accept him at his own evaluation. He cultivated the King in his special way, giving his Majesty pen portraits of all those who had been his associates. Ostensibly, he could not wait to return to the navy, but the 'navy would be there when he returned' (Tinker 1997: 233).

Mountbatten had the proclivity of taking a dramatic view of things, typically so when it involved him in events of importance. A favourite expression often used by him was 'absolutely staggered' by someone or something which he would describe as a 'bombshell'. He was prone to drop bombshells himself and would be upset if the reaction was anything but favourable. On 18 December 1946, Mountbatten's diary records, 'PM sent for me and staggered me' (Tinker 1997: 234). That was the day Attlee asked him to accept the appointment of India's last Viceroy. The two prominent Indian political personalities he needed to negotiate with were Nehru and Jinnah. Unfortunately, neither of these great patriots—for they *were* patriots—had roots in the soil of India. Nehru was cosmopolitan and international in his outlook and given to secular ideals. Jinnah was completely European, pragmatic and dedicated to the creation of a separate Muslim state. They both accepted communal disturbances as a necessary evil, but with their European outlooks, they firmly believed that they could be controlled, and were stunned when these communal disturbances exploded into unimaginable violence (Ismay 1970: 146–47).

Mountbatten chose Pug Ismay as his Chief of Staff. Ismay had been Churchill's old Chief of Staff. An experienced hand, he often found himself overworked, mainly because of the impossible task of 'getting

Dickie [Mountbatten] to go through the drafts methodically. He is a grand chap in a thousand ways, but clarity of thought and writing is not his strong suit. I have always held that presentation of the case is more than half the battle won and in my conceit, I am convinced that I can present a case better than most people! The result is that I land myself with a terrible lot of detailed drafting.' A few days after his arrival, Ismay set out to visit the Governors of Punjab and the NWFP. In Peshawar he met his old friends, the Caroes, and sought information from Sir Olaf, as Ismay knew nothing of what was happening in the NWFP. To deduce that Ismay returned to brief Mountbatten would be a reasonable assumption then. And what were Ismay's impressions? The glimpses we get from his letter of 2 April written from Peshawar narrates a story akin to the views held by Caroe. But more importantly, the thoughts expressed in the letter are typical of an official attitude: 'In the existing state of intense emotionalism, it is very difficult to say what should be done. There is no good answer to either problem; so the only thing to do is to find the answer that is the least bad' (Ismay 1970: 149). Commenting on the Governor, Ismay said: '... Olaf Caroe himself looks terribly tired and strained' (Ismay 1970). By the time Mountbatten held his eighth staff meeting on 4 April, Ismay had returned from his visit to the NWFP. Ismay's note, based on his interview with Caroe, formed an important agenda for this meeting. Mountbatten was privy to the strained relations between Governor Caroe and Nehru, realizing early the reason for it. Nehru desired a much tighter control than he presently exercised in the NWFP. It was a turf war between Nehru and Caroe. The long-entrenched bureaucracy of the Indian political service was unwilling to surrender to an Indian politician. Ismay voiced this concern succinctly when he talked of the 'unnaturalness of the present situation in NWFP and the tribesmen most unlikely to tolerate it indefinitely',[7] a situation for which Ismay coined the phrase 'bastard situation', for the NWFP was a Muslim majority province with a Congress ministry in office. This was a strong phrase to stress the 'unnaturalness' of the situation. To a British official it was convenient to refer to the Indian National Congress as Hindu—Hindus and Muslims being two distinct communities, and the British officials, umpires appointed in heaven meting out justice.

The proposal for holding fresh elections in the NWFP was formally mooted during the Governors' Conference in mid-April 1947. This was Caroe's idea and was accepted. Based on it, Ismay and Abell carried the recommendations for the NWFP to London for HMG's consideration. Within weeks of Mountbatten's arrival, a decision to split India into two unions was taken.

No suggestion had been offered in the Governors' Conference to advance the date for the transfer of power. Nor had any Governor indicated that the position in his province could not be 'held on to' until June 1948. Even in the meeting of the Defence Committee on 25 April where the issue of the division of the armed forces was discussed in case Pakistan became a reality, the conclusion arrived at was that the transfer of power could not take place earlier than 1 June 1948.

Why then did Mountbatten veer around the view that June 1948 would be too late a date for the transfer of power? On 9 May in his staff conference in Simla, it was for the first time that he gave indications of advancing the date to say, 31 December 1947. A few other dates, nearer 15 August were also discussed before the final decision was arrived at. The reasons for suddenly advancing the date would forever remain disputed. By 13 August, two senior staffers of Mountbatten had returned home. Within seven weeks of Mountbatten's arrival in India, the drama of the abdication of British power in India was over. It took only forty-nine days to obtain the vital cabinet decision to partition India; twenty-one more to announce it and seventy-seven more to hand over responsibility to the two new states, India and Pakistan.

Reverting to the Viceroy's staff meeting of 4 April, Mountbatten was quick to realize how important a factor Nehru was going to be in the 'end game', shortly to be played out. He realized early enough that 'there was nearly no man other than Nehru, if caught at the right moment, to quickly shed all phases of emotionalism.' That he did not err in this judgment was vindicated within weeks. Not surprising then that in the 4 April meeting he was all praise for Nehru's candid and frank ways in which he had asked Caroe to resign (Ismay 1970).

The impressions Ismay carried from Peshawar formed the basis of the report that Mountbatten sent to the Secretary of State on 9 April. Unlike Punjab, the problem in the NWFP was not communal, but rather a result of a conflict between the Congress and Muslims financed by the Muslim League, compounded further by the tribes broadly in sympathy with the Muslim League. Since the Congress ministry had clapped the opposition into jail, feelings were running high in the NWFP. There was real apprehension of a tribal flare up and the Frontier disintegrating.[8] Was this assessment, primarily Caroe's, exaggerated? Subsequent developments proved that Mountbatten erred in his judgment. Communal riots broke out in Dera Ismail Khan and other places. To infer that the problem was essentially a conflict between the Congress and League-financed Muslims was, at best, simplistic. Was Caroe deliberately conveying a doomsday picture of the NWFP—the Frontier disintegrating, a tribal flare-up, and so on? It was Caroe who originally mooted the idea of a general election, the dismissal of the Congress ministry, the dissolution of the legislature and assumption of power by the Governor. Mountbatten well realized the difficulty in following such a procedure, for it would infuriate the Congress.

The situation was never easy. Mountbatten had arrived in India to find a letter from Nehru addressed to his predecessor asking for Caroe's retirement, a letter which Mountbatten largely kept a secret (Ismay 1970). Immediately upon his arrival, Mountbatten faced the problem of taking a decision on the continuance of Governor Caroe. It did not make for sound judgment if he gave in. As advised by Wavell, he asked for time to avoid precipitate action.[9] Eager to know more about the NWFP, he summoned the Chief Secretary, Lieutenant Colonel de la Fargue on 11 April for a meeting. Mountbatten shared with de la Fargue the information that Nehru wanted Caroe removed. When asked for his opinion, de la Fargue was upfront in his reply. In his opinion, Caroe, though knowledgeable about the Frontier, was biased against the provincial Congress government and 'had lost respect of all fair-minded people of the province,' and that 'the Governor in fact was a menace to British prestige.'[10] There appeared no love lost between Governor Caroe and his Chief Secretary. When Caroe arrived in Delhi on 14 April to attend the Governors' Conference, Mountbatten could do no more than forewarn him of strong Congress opposition, and that he could succumb with this opposition getting more determined.

What transpired in the Governors' Conference and in subsequent meetings is discussed in some detail in the chapter on Nehru. It was in the Governors' Conference that the idea of holding fresh elections in the NWFP was formally mooted and accepted; part of the original plan that Abell and Ismay carried to London. The proposal to have a referendum was an afterthought, part of a well considered plan to avoid elections and thus limit options for the people of the NWFP. A referendum it was for the NWFP, when the final declaration on the transfer of power was made on 3 June.

Communal riots raged in the Frontier Province while Governors sat in the conference in Delhi. Appealing for amity, the provincial government on 19 April decided to unconditionally release political prisoners against whom there were no specific charges. But with the League Direct Action campaign already underway, these political prisoners (League supporters) refused amnesty. Abdul Rab Nishtar, the Frontier Muslim League leader and a member of the interim government did not pay heed to Mountbatten's advice. Nishtar felt that unless elections were announced immediately, the Central League leaders would have no handle with which to exert any restraining influence on the Frontier League. Mountbatten then informed Nishtar of his plans to go to the NWFP, to meet leaders of both sides and accordingly take a decision to resolve matters.[11] The announcement of his tour to NWFP followed.

The rebuff by the political detainees of the amnesty put Mountbatten in a bind. He could not meet the Provincial League leaders while their status remained that of prisoners. To escape this embarrassment, he sought Jinnah's help, hoping that the lawyer in Jinnah would appreciate his predicament.[12] He was not disappointed. With Jinnah's intervention, the issue was resolved. The League leaders sought parole to call on the Viceroy in Peshawar.

It suited Mountbatten to visit the NWFP. It provided him a licence to announce early elections. Any prior declaration would have made him vulnerable to the charge of partisanship with fingers pointing at a decision based on second-hand assessment. Having visited the NWFP on 28 April, Mountbatten decided against an immediate proclamation. Nehru and he reached an agreement within ten days of his Peshawar visit to hold a referendum instead, this being decided during their stay together in Simla.

Well before he arrived in Peshawar, Mountbatten knew of the Muslim League's plans to hold a large public meeting in Peshawar on 28

April and then to march towards the Government House in procession. No less a person than Jinnah himself had conveyed this request to him seeking permission.[13] Mountbatten agreed to the League holding a public meeting but did not allow for the march to the Government House. He, however, acceded to a deputation of six Muslim League members to see him after the public meeting concluded.[14] Dr Khan Saheb was justified in complaining that had he known of this permission, his party would have organized a public meeting too. Dr Khan Saheb felt outsmarted as the League scored a point over him. Not many even in the Viceroy's staff knew that Mountbatten had accorded this permission. It came as 'hard news'[15] to them when they arrived in Peshawar. The purpose behind holding the meeting was to impress upon Mountbatten of the support that the League had come to command in a year of the provincial elections. What transpired on 28 April has been captured on camera and described by many. In the words of Alan Campbell-Johnson, Mountbatten's Press Secretary who had accompanied him to Peshawar:

> On arrival at Government house…we found ourselves confronting a situation of crisis bordering on panic. Sir Olaf Caroe, the Governor, in a state of some agitation advised us that there was an immense Moslem [sic] League demonstration less than a mile away…and was ready to risk breaking the law by forming a procession and marching on [sic] Government house. The only alternative, according to Caroe was for the Viceroy to forestall this plan by marching on them and showing himself to the multitude. The demonstrators were estimated at well over 70,000.

Mountbatten agreed to go. When he reached the place of the meeting, 'there was much gesticulation and waving of innumerable but illegal green flags with the white crescent of Pakistan accompanied by a steady chant of "Pakistan Zindabad". Within a few minutes of Mountbatten's arrival, the brooding tension lifted. The slogan changed to "Mountbatten Zindabad". Sullen faces smiled…any sort of speech was out of question.'[16] The show of strength demonstrated by the Muslim League had its desired effect. Mountbatten too started mouthing the same sentiments that his officers in the Frontier had been doing for some time. It was convenient to ascribe the upsurge in communal feeling to the perceived domination by the Hindu Congress. Dr Khan Saheb's government was as Hindu or only marginally less so, just as it had been in his previous two tenures as the premier of the NWFP. The reason for it lay elsewhere. The 20 February announcement by the British Prime Minister set a definite date for the British withdrawal from India. How could the logic of 'a two nation theory' stand if the NWFP opted for India? Jinnah and his League understood the importance of the NWFP joining Pakistan. It had long been the practice of British colonials to view India in dichotomous terms—that of Hindus and Muslims. Mountbatten proved to be no exception when he said 'that the tribal areas were not prepared to contemplate absorption in a state dominated by the Hindus.'[17] As we know, the province was overwhelmingly Muslim and the fear of Hindu domination had, therefore, no basis. It was the news of the communal carnage in Bengal, Bihar, Bombay, Punjab and the Muslim League's aggressive propaganda that put the idea of 'Hindu domination' in the minds of NWFP Muslims.

Astute that he was, Mountbatten knew that the battle cry of Congress since 1942, 'British Quit India', had lost its binding influence as the British had set a definite date to 'quit'. When queried on the rationality of proposing another election when the last elections, held only a year earlier, had been fought on the issue of Pakistan, Mountbatten had a ready reply. For one, things were different now that the British had set a date for their departure from India, and secondly, the Cabinet Mission had not yet come to India when the last provincial elections were held.[18] Dr Khan Saheb and his ministerial colleagues had difficulties countering the Viceroy's explanation.

As an interesting aside, Mountbatten met one Brigadier Nazir Ahmed at Rawalpindi on his return journey to Delhi. The Brigadier was perhaps the third senior-most Muslim officer in the Indian army and had wanted to make Jinnah's acquaintance. Mountbatten went out of his way to ask the Area Commander to give the army officer leave to go to Delhi to call on Jinnah.[19] It appears intriguing that Mountbatten should go to any length of trouble to encourage a soldier of a certain faith to make acquaintance with a politician. The propriety of Mountbatten's action clearly comes into question here.

Soon after his return from the NWFP, Mountbatten began to toy with the idea of holding a referendum instead of an election in the province. Around the same time, he informed Lord Listowel of the possibility of Governor Caroe's removal because of Congress' bitter opposition to him. Quite unsportingly, he indicated that Caroe was showing 'signs of great strain'. This seemingly innocuous remark was bound to raise questions about Caroe's health, insinuating his diminishing capacity to deal with the situation in the NWFP. Mountbatten's comment about Caroe's capacity, or the lack of it, ended Caroe's career within two months of Mountbatten having made it.[20] Reporting to Listowel, Mountbatten also spoke his mind over the wrong choice of Nehru as Member, External Affairs. Mountbatten considered that whosoever was responsible for allotting the tribal affairs and the foreign portfolios to Nehru had caused a most embarrassing situation to arise.[21] Here he was alluding to Wavell's and the India Burma Committee's decision in this matter. Unsparing of his predecessor, Mountbatten thought this to be a matter of elementary precaution to reserve that subject for the Viceroy himself, for he was now forced to make a choice between Nehru and Caroe, an issue not of his own making but one that Nehru precipitated (Ismay 1970). Had the portfolio been with the Viceroy, this piquant situation would not have arisen. Preparing the ground for Caroe's removal, Mountbatten remarked self-righteously that if Caroe did have to resign, it should be with complete honour (Ismay 1970).

When Mountbatten met the League deputationists in Peshawar, he urged them to call off their civil disobedience movement and accept the offer of amnesty for political prisoners. Unless Dr Khan Saheb's ministry was dismissed, the deputationists were not willing to take up this offer. They also wanted the government to announce fresh elections. A word here on the nature of the League's civil disobedience movement. It differed fundamentally from the Congress's. The Congress movement was directed against the British and the League's, against the Congress. Failing to convince the League deputationists, Mountbatten asked Jinnah to bring them around. With this in mind, Mountbatten invited the deputationists to come to Delhi. Provincial League leaders appeared agreeable.

But in the interim, a section of the Hindu press was aggressively calling for Caroe's resignation. An 'anti-Caroe' day was announced.

Though Mountbatten let it be known to Nehru that he would not yield to pressure, he was more or less decided that Caroe would have to go. For his replacement he had General Rob Lockhart in mind. He asked Ismay, who was in London, to get Lockhart's name cleared from the Secretary of State for India and from Auchinleck.[22] Ismay in turn wanted Mountbatten to send the request officially, in writing, giving reasons and the date when Lockhart should join in place of Caroe. Mountbatten was reluctant to broach this proposal officially lest it appear that he had yielded to the 'anti-Caroe' agitation. Ismay was therefore asked to obtain unofficial approval on Caroe's replacement from Lord Listowel. But Mountbatten was yet not clear on the reason to be given while affecting the change. Caroe was to resign, failing which his ill health could be cited as the cause for his replacement. Ismay concurred with the second suggestion.

On 12 May Lord Listowel formally recommended Caroe's removal to the Prime Minister. He did not hesitate in mentioning that 'Mountbatten no longer had confidence in Caroe's ability as a Governor and in his competence to oversee the situation in NWFP.'[23] The issue of Caroe's health cropped up yet again: 'I am told that Sir Olaf, though a man of great intellectual capacity, is highly strung and is prone to suffer these aspersions on his partiality less easily than a man of more equable temperament' (Ismay 1970). Listowel went on to say that Mountbatten should suggest Governor Caroe to ask for the king's permission to lay down office on medical consideration; that he (Caroe) was overstrained and needed relief from his responsibilities.

On 6 June, Mountbatten wrote to Caroe:

> The time has come when I must, for the moment at any rate, replace you as Governor of NWFP…my proposal, therefore, is that you should go on leave as soon as it can be arranged for your temporary successor to arrive, and that you should remain on leave until 15 August, or such date as the two new governments are in a position to select the new provincial governors…if the province goes to Pakistan, it may very well be that the Pakistan Government…would ask for you to be re-appointed… (and) it does not close the door to your future employment.[24]

Mountbatten was not for a moment suggesting that Caroe resign, rather he was all assurance to Caroe of the bright chance of his re-appointment upon completion of the referendum. In all likelihood, the NWFP would join Pakistan, or so he felt. But between Ismay and Listowel, they were clear that there was no second option for Caroe but to resign. Why then would Mountbatten discuss prospects of a re-appointment with Caroe? Was he just sweetening a bitter pill for Caroe to swallow?

Caroe's response to Mountbatten's letter was gracious. He considerably eased Mountbatten's task by suggesting that he was having grave doubts on the propriety of remaining in office when it was openly being said that the Governor identified with one party:

> It is clear you have made up your mind that the charges of partisanship make it wrong to retain me during this critical period, I accept that judgement. It is with deep sorrow that I accept it...the change will be regarded in many quarters as a surrender to unfair attacks. But that is for you and not for me to judge...I wish to go on leave during the next two months... [Caroe was hopeful of Mountbatten's appointment as the Joint Governor General of India and Pakistan.] I don't know whether it would be best to take leave in India or go home—on the whole I think I had better go home, for, if I remained here, it would look as if I were hanging about on an off-chance, and it might keep propaganda on both sides going. [Caroe had remained in Kashmir after taking leave].[25]

Listowel moved the Prime Minister again on 11 June seeking formal instructions on the impending change in the governorship of the NWFP. He was, however, against the assurance that Mountbatten was offering Caroe on his re-employment.[26] Mountbatten's insistence and urgency in this matter forced Listowel to seek the King's informal approval despite his serious reservations (Ismay 1970). But on the manner of affecting this change, Listowel was determined that Mountbatten induce Caroe to lay down office on medical considerations.

On 13 June, Caroe asked Mountbatten for leave. In a letter he suggested that someone else occupy his post till the referendum and the transfer of power took place. He, therefore, asked for two months' leave. Caroe, evidently, did not want to resign; he meant to come back after the referendum, and for the interim period was proposing an officiating Governor. Listowel, of course, was categorical, making explicit his opposition to Caroe's resumption of the governorship on expiry of leave. He made it plain to Mountbatten that on this particular issue, the Prime Minister concurred with him.[27]

On 15 June, approval was received from the King appointing Lockhart to act in place of Caroe. The King granted leave of absence to Caroe and appointed Lockhart to act as Governor in his place. However, this intimation from the Permanent Under Secretary in the India Office unambiguously informed Mountbatten that the issue of Caroe's re-appointment was never to be raised again. Listowel intended to make Caroe's resignation and Lockhart's appointment substantive and forthwith. If the results of the referendum were to go in favour of Pakistan, Caroe's resumption of office was likely to be taken as clear evidence of his being a League's man all along. Since it was too late now, Caroe was to be induced to tender his resignation while on leave and Lockhart's acting appointment confirmed thereafter. But subsequent to Pakistan's creation, were the Government of Pakistan to ask for Caroe, the situation would be different. Responding to Listowel on 16 June, Mountbatten readily agreed not to push for Caroe's re-employment.[28]

The referendum was yet to take place in the NWFP, but its result was a foregone conclusion. By 29 June, Ismay and Mountbatten were both conveying separately how anxious Jinnah was to have Sir George Cunningham as the next Governor of the NWFP. Mountbatten thought it to be a 'grand idea'.[29] All efforts at Caroe's re-appointment were shelved. On 9 July, Mountbatten asked Listowel to use his good offices and persuade Sir George Cunningham to accept the appointment in his place. On 11 July, Sir George Cunningham accepted the offer. Events gathered momentum. Within a week of Mountbatten's personal assurance on his re-appointment, Caroe's fate was sealed. Having reneged, Mountbatten now felt 'it would be grand if Cunningham could join'.[30]

It is unfortunate that Nehru, as the Foreign Minister, allowed the government to solely rely on Jinnah's recommendation while choosing the permanent Governor of the NWFP. The process of the referendum was yet to commence. How could Nehru acquiesce to Jinnah's choice?

Had he reconciled prematurely to the loss of the NWFP to Pakistan? While formally recommending Cunningham, Mountbatten on 9 July asked Listowel to use his 'best endeavours to persuade Sir George Cunningham to accept this appointment as Jinnah feels, in view of the great experience he [Sir George Cunningham] already has, having been a successful Governor for five years, his acceptance would be invaluable.'[31]

Mountbatten and Nehru had already decided on a referendum for the NWFP when they met in Simla in early May. The 3 June plan put an official stamp on this arrangement. Gandhi alone opposed a referendum right till the end. This troubled Mountbatten. He found Gandhi's attitude 'quite unpredictable',[32] and so quickly set about neutralizing him. He sought Gandhi's help, which Gandhi extended, in seeing the referendum peacefully through. Once Mountbatten secured the Khudai Khidmatgars' walkover, his only concern thereafter was to go through the motions of a referendum, as the results were never in doubt. His personal charm ensured that Gandhi did not allow Abdul Ghaffar Khan and his followers to incite violence during the referendum.[33]

The main worry for Rob Lockhart, the new acting Governor, was what action to take once the referendum was over. He personally preferred a coalition government. In separate conversations he explored this option with Dr Khan Saheb and Chundrigar.[34] He found Dr Khan Saheb amenable as he felt that Pakistan was temporarily inevitable. His colleagues could accept portfolios until a new general election was held. But in two separate meetings, on 7 and 8 July, Lockhart failed to convince Chundrigar to agree on the idea of a coalition. Chundrigar wanted the present ministry to be dismissed as he feared it would squander finances and stir up trouble through the Fakir of Ipi. Lockhart believed that Chundrigar was deliberately exaggerating the risk of Ipi's interference. The Fakir of Ipi may have been in touch with the Congress but his influence extended only over certain areas and tribes.[35]

The option of dismissing Dr Khan Saheb's ministry had some obvious disadvantages. Should Governor's rule be invoked on 20 July, it would cease to exist on 14/15 August. Additionally, there would not be a running governmental organization to pass on to the successor government. This was something that Lockhart considered desirable though not vital. Governor's rule had certain advantages. The Congress was more likely to accept Governor's rule than a League ministry. The League too would prefer this arrangement to a coalition or a Congress ministry remaining in office up to the appointed date after which the League certainly expected to take over. But what was debatable and of which Lockhart was not confident was the government's ability to exercise power till such time that the province was under Governor's rule. He was worried about the Congress starting a civil disobedience movement if its government in the NWFP was dismissed. A large proportion of the services had Muslim League sympathizers. How was he, agonized Lockhart, to cope with a situation that demanded imposition of martial law? How he wished that Dr Khan Saheb saw reason and resigned from the Chief Ministership. Since the elections would not be long in coming, Dr Khan Saheb had the option of staking his claim again to the post he currently occupied. The problem could be tided over by inviting the Muslim League to form a government. For this convenient solution Lockhart was prepared to give a 'go by' to constitutional propriety or the 'correctness' of his action. In case Dr Khan Saheb refused to resign, and the government could not be dismissed, Jinnah would have to be requested to rein in the Provincial League to prevent violence. But what if Jinnah and Dr Khan Saheb proved to be intransigent? In that case Lockhart felt that the government should be dismissed and replaced by a coalition. Ideally, he was not for the ministry's dismissal, and would resort to it only if compelled. The formation of a League government was inevitable after 15 August, but Lockhart was not in favour of installing it immediately after the referendum. He therefore wanted Mountbatten's approval to work for a coalition government even if the chances were slim.[36]

Worried, Lockhart sent a seven-page note to Mountbatten seeking instructions. The letter was reflective of Lockhart's dilemma. It was repetitive and demonstrated a lack of clarity. Lockhart was prepared to exercise any option provided he had directives. He did not want to bear the burden of taking a decision. His long note which was suggestive of all options in effect meant recommending none.

Acting safe, Mountbatten decided to go by the advice of an embryo Pakistan government. But an interim Government of Pakistan was yet to be set up. Mountbatten had already had a preliminary discussion with Jinnah on the future course of action in the NWFP.[37] Though not emphatically, Jinnah had favoured a dismissal of the ministry and imposition of Governor's rule. Mountbatten was actively opposed to Jinnah's idea, 'dead set against Governor's rule', which he thought would merely get the British in the wrong during the last four weeks of power.[38] Between them they had discussed the possibility of installing a League ministry by dismissing Dr Khan Saheb. Jinnah, being a lawyer, appreciated the difficulty that the Muslim League would face in such a situation: 'But how can we stay in power if we have not got a majority in the Legislative Assembly?'[39] Having raised the query, Jinnah went on to dismiss Dr Khan Saheb's ministry within ten days of becoming the Governor General of Pakistan.

Mountbatten favoured the idea of the ministry's dismissal after the referendum. He justified it by saying that the Legislative Assembly was yet to be summoned and was not due to be called in the near future. After 15 August, the matter could be referred to the Pakistan Constituent Assembly which would then be the legislature for the Dominion. Mountbatten of course made it clear that he could neither dismiss Dr Khan Saheb's government nor install a League ministry except on the advice of the interim Government of Pakistan. Mountbatten wanted to form just such a body immediately, latest by 18 July, otherwise Jinnah could well find Dr Khan Saheb retaining his government till 15 August.[40] Perhaps Mountbatten was being disingenuous here. Was he exerting pressure on Jinnah to quickly form a Pakistan cabinet which he could then head, hoping to become the Governor General of India and Pakistan? By 14 July the situation had altered. Jinnah himself decided to become the Governor General of Pakistan. Mountbatten broached the topic of the government's reconstitution with Jinnah on 15 July. Jinnah demurred, asking for some time. Mountbatten was not ready to wait now. He made it clear that this was an order from the Viceroy which he proposed to circulate to the cabinet as a matter of courtesy prior to issuing it. Emphasizing urgency, Mountbatten said that the Pakistan cabinet was required for a vital purpose, that of advising the Viceroy in case Dr Khan Saheb's government in the NWFP refused to resign after losing the referendum.[41]

Listowel, in contrast, was not in favour of consulting the Pakistan cabinet before deciding the fate of the NWFP ministry. He had remained unconvinced about the propriety of these consultations. The legal position of the Governor as well as the Governor General was to change soon. With the new India Independence Act coming into operation within weeks, the Governor would cease to have discretionary powers and the Governor General's control would lapse. Constitutionally, appointment of ministries would then be a matter for the Governor to be decided in consultation with leaders of parties in the local legislatures. Listowel found it improper to do anything which gave an impression that the British contemplated appointing provincial ministries through indirect control of the Pakistan government, something that should ideally be decided by the opinion of the local legislature. He preferred consulting Jinnah or Liaquat as Muslim League leaders rather than the Pakistan cabinet.[42] But not being a heavyweight in politics, Listowel was reluctant to press his case. He left it to Mountbatten to decide in case special circumstances justified consultations with the Pakistan cabinet. Listowel could possibly not press his case too much, for Mountbatten had played a substantial role in Listowel's present appointment.

Mountbatten would not allow the question of the NWFP to be settled in Peshawar. Experience of party differences in Punjab and Bengal had shown that these matters were better dealt in consultation with the high command. For him, this practical consideration outweighed any constitutional point that Listowel felt was crucial.[43]

On 20 July Lockhart informed Mountbatten of the referendum's results. The Governor regarded them as a decisive vote in favour of Pakistan and a vote against the present ministry. But he soon found that the present ministry was unlikely to resign. There was little chance for a coalition ministry and the Muslim League was adamant that the present government should not remain in office till 15 August. The local League met the Governor on 20 July to demand that he assume power by dismissing Dr Khan Saheb. Under duress, Lockhart requested Mountbatten to sack him and to dismiss the ministry and assume power. Lockhart also proposed names of some others who could be co-opted as advisors in such an eventuality. He reckoned that both Dr Khan Saheb and Abdul Qayyum Khan were agreeable to Governor's rule. Even Jinnah appeared amenable.[44] Only Mountbatten struck a discordant note. He was set on seeking advice from the Pakistan cabinet on government formation in the NWFP. Some of Mountbatten's advisors like V.P. Menon maintained that constitutionally the decision in the matter was the Viceroy's own responsibility though the Viceroy was bound to act on the advice of the interim government if it was constituted. Mountbatten asked his private secretary, George Abell, to seek time from Liaquat Ali Khan for a meeting of the Pakistan cabinet to discuss the future NWFP government.[45]

Lockhart did not help Mountbatten decide matters. He absolved himself of any responsibility by telling the local League leaders that a decision on the future course of action could only come from the Viceroy. From the time that Lockhart had assumed office, all he had done was to seek instructions from Mountbatten. Perhaps that was his only brief and it suited both—Lockhart, because he was a stopgap arrangement, and Mountbatten, because he considered the NWFP to be far too important to be left to others to decide. To be fair to Lockhart, a reduction of troops in the NWFP had increased his worries. The weakened security situation was exemplified in the latest Afghan demand for Indian territory all along the Durand Line.[46] At times one wonders how Caroe would have tackled the situation.

Lockhart made a crucial observation at this juncture—that the local League leaders did not appear keen on the formation of a League minority ministry. Lockhart thought this was due to bitter factionalism amongst the local Muslim League because of which they could not agree on the choice of ministers.[47]

Mountbatten felt vindicated with the declaration of the referendum results. He found it particularly satisfying that over 50 per cent of the total electorate had voted to join Pakistan and the total votes cast were only 15 per cent less than the last time (the 1946 elections) when the boycott was not in force. He was glad for having 'rightly insisted' on the referendum despite the strongest possible opposition from the Congress till the morning of 3 June. He was also pleased to record the absence of any serious disturbance, as the Congress had prophesied rioting and bloodshed.[48]

Mountbatten had no moral compunctions in exploring the possibility of some Congress legislators shifting their allegiance to the Muslim League. When he enquired, Lockhart could not give any definitive answer to this vital query. Amazingly, Mountbatten made this enquiry at a meeting where Jinnah and Liaquat Ali Khan were present along with Lockhart.[49] How unusual, that on the one hand he would not agree to Governor's rule, and on the other, sit with the leading lights of the Muslim League and consider prospects of defection within the NWFP legislature. Conceivably, rules of ethics and fair play applied to him only when it was convenient. In the meeting Liaquat Ali Khan held the view that non-Muslims would be forced to support the League. This was a time when the League's strident posturing had forced many Hindus and Sikhs to leave the NWFP. They were accused of being 'Kafirs'[50] for not having voted to create a Muslim nation. What Liaquat Ali Khan meant was that this section would be resigned to support the League in case it stayed back. Even Jinnah reminded the meeting of past precedents when, for example in Bombay and Punjab, minority parties had been called to form ministries. Mountbatten shrewdly played along, arguing in favour of not immediately summoning the legislative assembly once the government was dismissed. Alongside, he showed his reluctance to the imposition of Governor's rule.

In this fluid situation where prospects of disbanding Dr Khan Saheb's ministry were bright, Lockhart greatly feared a Khudai Khidmatgar agitation. Mountbatten was insistent that the Congress government should not be cashiered before 15 August. Lockhart was of the view that if the change appeared imminent, it should be made immediately. Liaquat Ali Khan agreed with Lockhart. An immediate installation of the League ministry would give it time to come to grips with the administrative machinery particularly in view of the dangers lurking in the tribal areas.

In a rather curious phrase, Mountbatten expressed a desire to 'legalize the position' as much as possible.[51] He therefore suggested a meeting of the Pakistan cabinet to draw up instructions which the Governor could follow, preferably in the form of an Order-in-Council. Mountbatten also wanted a successor for Maulana Azad, a member representative from NWFP to the Constituent Assembly, to be chosen in the same meeting. It was decided to hold this meeting on 1 August and Liaquat Ali Khan was tasked to arrange it. Mohammad Ali and Sir George Spense were asked to prepare the papers. The

Pakistan Constituent Assembly was duly constituted by the Viceroy's announcement published on 26 July giving the names of the members.[52] Notes were then prepared for a meeting of the Pakistan cabinet on 1 August, as per instructions given by Mountbatten.

In his note Mohammad Ali argued in favour of Pakistan and the Muslim League. For him the referendum's results were a clear demonstration of a majority of the electorate in the NWFP favouring the Muslim League. The obverse conclusion was therefore that the Congress ministry be removed from power. If immediate elections could be held, said Mohammad Ali, the Congress was sure to be defeated. But for the moment Mohammad Ali did not favour immediate elections as he found the situation 'fraught with danger' for these to be held. Instead, since the referendum had been a clear indication of the will of the electorate, Mohammad Ali recommended that the Governor General had full discretion to issue directions to the Governor to ask for the resignation of the ministry and, if it refused, to show it the door. In such an eventuality the Muslim League was to take over the reins of power.[53]

The note which Sir George Spense prepared differed substantially from Mohammad Ali's. In Spense's opinion, the Dominions in which the referendum was a regular feature of the Constitution, a defeat of the government's proposal did not make it constitutionally obligatory on the ministry to resign. It could very well remain in office until its dissolution occurred in the natural course of events. According to Spense, therefore, the referendum had not been held at the behest of the provincial government; neither was the government was party to the issue to which the referendum related. It was not constitutionally obligatory for the government to resign. The ministry was still in a position to command a majority in the provincial assembly. If the old ministry was dismissed, the new ministry would be constrained in its early stage of existence to ask for the dissolution of the assembly. To Spense, the appropriate course of action was for the Governor to offer the present premier the choice between resignation and dissolution. Spense thought dissolution to be a logical and a natural corollary to resignation or dismissal of the ministry. Therefore he felt that any new ministry would be open to accusations when an election process should (rightly) have commenced.[54]

The Pakistan cabinet that met on 1 August was presided over by Mountbatten. Taking a leaf from Spense's note, Mountbatten considered it unconstitutional to remove the NWFP government as he felt guided by the same constitutional principles when dealing with both the NWFP and Bengal.[55] Mountbatten therefore offered to instruct the Governor of NWFP to issue a complete standstill order under which business could only be transacted with the Governor's sanction, which sanction the Governor could only give on the advice of the Muslim League. On 15 August of course, it would be open to the Muslim League to install its own ministry in the province.[56]

Spense had made a reference to the Swiss Constitution which provided for referenda. The government in Switzerland did not fall even if it lost a referendum. During the course of consultations in the Pakistan cabinet, objections were raised on the Swiss analogy; the question here was of the successor authority to whom the power would stand transferred. According to cabinet members, the referendum clearly showed that the successor authority was the Muslim League. The province should therefore have been handed over to the League. To leave the present ministry in power until 15 August would in effect mean that a part of Pakistan territory would pass to the Congress on that date.[57]

The position would have been different if differences between the ministry and the Muslim League were based on party programmes. But in this case the present ministry was opposed to Pakistan itself. There were precedents for removing a ministry which acted detrimental to the interest of the state. The Muslim League felt this to be the case. Constitutionally, it was open to the Governor to dismiss the ministry without assigning reasons if he so thought fit. A 'standstill' arrangement could not meet the requirements of the case because it was likely to be flouted by the ministry and could only be applied in case of those subjects which were the Governor's special responsibility. According to Spense, the action to remove the ministry had to be taken before the appointed date and it would not be open to the Pakistan government to dismiss the ministry on or after 15 August.[58]

Mountbatten assured the Pakistan cabinet that the present ministry would not be allowed to do anything that would injure the Pakistan state. He offered two choices in order of preference. The first was for the

Governor to ask the present ministry to resign and on refusal dismiss it and call on the leader of the opposition from the Muslim League to form a new ministry. The second option was to place the province under Governor's rule with a Muslim League Council of Advisors and with a League ministry to be installed by about 14 August. Whichever course was adopted, Mountbatten wanted it based on the advice of his Pakistan cabinet colleagues and in consultation with his legal advisors and HMG, to ensure the constitutionality of the action.[59]

Lockhart was duly informed of what Mountbatten wanted. On 1 August, the Pakistan government advised the Viceroy to direct the Governor to ask the ministry to resign and, if it refused, to dismiss it. In the last fortnight of his viceroyalty, Mountbatten was reluctant to do anything that could be misconstrued as unconstitutional. Hence the standstill order, so that the Muslim League's interests remained protected. The Pakistan cabinet urged Mountbatten to impose Governor's rule and take a Muslim League team as his advisors in case a League ministry was not installed. The Pakistan cabinet was worried that unless the change in government was effected soon, the Muslim League would inherit chaos on 15 August. Mountbatten decided to accept the advice of the Pakistan cabinet provided he was assured by legal experts that the advice was constitutionally tenable. He told the Pakistan cabinet of his intention to refer the matter to London before taking a final decision. The purpose behind consulting London in Mountbatten's own words was that: 'Jinnah has always stalled on matters he does not want to give me a decision on. He can hardly complain if I follow suit.'[60]

Mountbatten knew all along that the present ministry could either be made to resign or be dismissed before 15 August.[61] But he wanted this action taken as late as possible and invoke Governor's rule for a few days instead of appointing a Muslim League ministry before 15 August. He faced the dilemma of concurrently having to behave constitutionally and also heed to the advice of the Pakistan cabinet. How was he to resolve this conflict? He found the answer in a denial of the problem for it was best, under the given circumstances, to delay the decision by a few days. The Congress was bound to react sharply to the dismissal of the NWFP ministry on the Viceroy's instruction. This was proving irksome to Mountbatten as he perceived the Congress reaction to be only a question of false prestige.⁶²

Even amongst Mountbatten's staff, there existed a difference of opinion. Ismay wanted the matter settled as soon as possible while Abell preferred a dismissal four or five days before 15 August. Menon, of course, believed that a coalition government after 15 August was still a possibility. In the Viceroy's meeting of 2 August it was therefore suggested that the Governor designate Sir George Cunningham, due to arrive in Karachi on 11 August, come to Delhi first to hold discussions with Mountbatten.⁶³ Meanwhile Lockhart had had an informal meeting with Dr Khan Saheb on 2 August. He was certain that Dr Khan Saheb would not resign voluntarily and was in a position to cause serious trouble if dismissed. The League was also expected to court trouble if the ministry remained in office after 15 August. The Governor believed that both the parties, with their Pathan factional character, wanted power. The Congress appeared well organized and disciplined whereas the League, somewhat disunited and mutually suspicious.⁶⁴

Lockhart consulted his Advocate General on the issue of the constitutional propriety of an executive action. The legal opinion did not favour dismissal without dissolution. In Lockhart's assessment, if the ministry was dismissed, the ensuing law and order situation would not ease by 15 August, the day when the oath-taking and the transfer of power was to take place. To confound matters, it was the time of Ramzan,⁶⁵ a bad time for a widespread operation by troops and the police. Such an action would involve the Governor's special powers, the authority for which would have been obscure after 15 August until orders were issued under the India Independence Act. Lockhart therefore veered towards the view that the retention of the present ministry should be made conditional upon its maintaining a constitutional and reasonable attitude towards the Pakistan Dominion so as not to create circumstances that would hamper the administration of the successor government. Lockhart observed: 'Given these conditions, I now feel the less for dismissal and/ or dissolution.' If this was agreed to, he wanted the Viceroy's approval to put these conditions to Dr Khan Saheb for his government continuing in the NWFP.

Mountbatten decided to play for time. Reiterating his earlier stand, he conveyed to Lockhart that he had been formally advised by the provisional Pakistan government to direct the Governor to ask the present ministry to resign, and if it refused, to dismiss it and call on the leader of the opposition, of the Muslim League, to form a new ministry. If this was unconstitutional, it was advisable to place the province under Governor's rule and direct the Governor to appoint Muslim League leaders as advisors with a view to a League ministry being installed by 14 August. Mountbatten had promised to accept the advice of the Pakistan cabinet provided he was satisfied that he could constitutionally do so. He was therefore consulting the Secretary of State for India with regard to the constitutional position.[66] He also informed Lockhart that the Congress maintained that either course of action was constitutionally improper. Lockhart, even at this late stage, was ready to give one last try to persuade Dr Khan Saheb to resign as he did not want the process to look unconstitutional.

Lord Listowel, as earlier and even now, held views at variance with Mountbatten's. As Listowel understood it, the ministry had suffered no defeat in the legislature and still retained the confidence of a majority of its members. Though the Governor may have had good reason to believe that the legislature no longer represented a majority electorate, a general election had been ruled out on security grounds. Dismissal of the ministry with no choice of dissolution of the legislature in these circumstances was unconstitutional, particularly in view of the fact that the Governor would appoint only those as ministers who were best placed to command the confidence of the legislature. It was also clear to Listowel that the government of the province could not possibly maintain law and order if powers were assumed by the Governor. Withdrawal of Governor's discretionary powers after the India Independence Act took effect would prove embarrassing for the viceroy as it would appear that the imposition of Governor's rule had been merely used as a device to install a League ministry in the province. To Listowel, both the options which Mountbatten suggested were unconstitutional, but either of them would be legal in the sense that they could not be challenged in court. To quote Lord Listowel:

> I am not convinced that removal of present ministry by us before 15 August however much desired by the provisional Government of Pakistan would really be wise particularly as it could be done only by an unconstitutional action. Even though

you [Mountbatten] could state that you had acted on the advice of Pakistan provisional government and Mr Jinnah, responsibility, both legal and moral, would be that of the HMG. Governor evidently does not consider that the disappearance of the ministry would necessarily bring about improvement in the local situation on 15 August. Pressure for action to be taken before 15 August appears to come wholly from the Muslim League high command.[67]

Listowel was actually inclined to leave the problem to be resolved after 15 August and without any intervention from the Viceroy and HMG. Resolving the difficulty in a constitutional manner after 15 August might possibly involve urgent action by the Pakistan Constituent Assembly so that under the relevant section of the India Independence Act special powers could then be conferred on the Governor General to deal with the situation. Listowel in fact had no information as to what adaptations, if any, the Viceroy was making or had made or what Jinnah contemplated. Listowel thought that the British were not in a position to judge whether after 15 August any special action described by Jinnah in relation to the NWFP executive could be taken constitutionally without bringing in the Constituent Assembly of Pakistan into the picture.[68]

Listowel pointedly asked Mountbatten if he had any information confirming Liaquat Ali Khan's fears that Dr Khan Saheb's government would try to sabotage the newly created Pakistan state. Listowel thought Liaquat was an interested party. In case Liaquat's unsupported assertion was accepted regarding Dr Khan Saheb's intentions, the Viceroy in India and the Labour government in the British Parliament would have a lot of explaining to do with regard to the knowledge, if any, that they had possessed about Dr Khan Saheb's intentions of declaring an independent Pathanistan. Listowel went a step further to say, 'Even if there appears to be a fairly good ground for believing that Dr Khan Saheb might take such a course, I do not find it wise that any action before 15 August is a wise course to take.' Sir George Cunningham was to take over just before 15 August and if he felt there was a risk of such a step being taken, he could warn Dr Khan Saheb. If Dr Khan Saheb made any attempt to issue any such declaration without the Governor's approval, it would then be followed by instant dismissal of Dr Khan Saheb and his ministry. Listowel suggested that possibly a friendly warning to Dr Khan Saheb from Lockhart on these lines could be useful. But as to the wisdom of that, he left that decision to Mountbatten.[69] Cunningham too concurred with Listowel.[70] Mountbatten met Sir George Cunningham on 12 August who had already had a meeting with Jinnah in Karachi a day earlier. Sir George Cunningham was able to persuade Jinnah 'though not without great difficulty to let him try his hand with Dr Khan Saheb' to obtain a satisfactory settlement without having recourse to drastic means. The matter was thus 'nicely taken out of my [Mountbatten's] hand, and [he] took no further action.' As a consequence, the British Viceroy and the Governor were spared the ignominy of getting rid of Dr Khan Saheb's government, a burden which then fell on the first Governor General of Pakistan, Muhammad Ali Jinnah.

## Notes

1. Tactically, the battle of Crete was a disaster for the British Royal Navy. Three cruisers and six destroyers were sunk and another seventeen ships were damaged; 2,261 men were killed. The battle compared to a major fleet action, yet the only enemy warships sighted were Italian destroyers which had escorted the invasion convoys. It was, however, a battle between a fleet and an air force, a battle which a fleet in 1941 could not win. On 21 May 1941, the fifth destroyer flotilla: *Kelly, Kipling, Kelvin, Jackal* and *Kashmir*, under Captain Lord Louis Mountbatten, was ordered to leave Malta to join the fleet off Crete. Subsequently, Mountbatten, with *Kelly, Kashmir* and *Kipling* was asked to go to Alexandria. While he was rounding the western side of Crete, his three ships came under heavy air attack from 24 Stuka Dive Bombers. *Kashmir* was hit and sank in two minutes and *Kelly* was hit and turned turtle soon after. *Kipling* survived. The Noel Coward film *In Which We Serve* was based on this battle.
2. The raid across the English Channel (Operation Jubilee, 19 August 1942) on Dieppe, a small port on the French coast between Le Havre and Boulogne, was planned as a 'reconnaissance in force' to test the defences of Hitler's continental fortress and the capability of the western allies to launch large-scale amphibious assaults against his *Festung Europa* (Fortress Europe). It was a major disaster; only the battle-hardened

British commandos assigned to subdue the coast artillery batteries near Varengeville and Berneval enjoyed some success. Troops of the second Canadian Infantry Division under Major General J.H. Roberts, landing on the Dieppe esplanade, failed to achieve any of their objectives. The raid lasted only nine hours. Out of nearly 5,000 Canadian soldiers involved, more than 900 were killed and 1,874 taken prisoner—more prisoners than the army lost in the eleven months of the 1944–45 New Europe campaign. The failure was caused by poor planning, inadequate training and insufficient fire support.

3. Sir Harold English Pyman (1908–1971): Served in the North-West Frontier campaign, India, 1937; Deputy Chief of the Imperial General Staff, 1958–1961; General, 1961; Commander-in-Chief, Allied Forces, northern Europe, 1961–63.
4. Zeus in Greek mythology is the king of the gods.
5. General Joseph Warren Stilwell (19 March 1883–12 October 1946) was a United States Army four-star General, best known for his service in China and Burma.
6. Colonel Sir Reginald Hugh Dorman-Smith (1899–1977) was a British diplomat, soldier and politician. He was the Governor General of Burma and was in office when the Japanese invasion took place. The Japanese expelled Dorman-Smith from Burma. Between May 1942 and October 1945 he was in exile in Simla, India. Sir Hubert Rance, a British General, took control of Burma after the liberation of Rangoon, but Dorman-Smith soon returned as Governor in 1946. While Dorman-Smith was back in the UK for medical reasons he was replaced by Rance, who was supported by Lord Mountbatten and fully backed a policy of immediate unconditional independence for Burma.
7. Nicolas Mansergh and Penderel Moon (eds), *The Transfer of Power*, Vol. X, April 1947, pp.115–16.
8. Viceroy's personal report no 2, L/po/6/123: ff23–30 n of 9 April 1947, *The Transfer of Power*, Vol. X, pp.167–68.
9. 'Mountbatten to Nehru, Mountbatten Papers, official Correspondence Files: North West Frontier Province', situation in, Part 1(a) of 10 April 1947, *The Transfer of Power*, 1947, Vol. X, p.182.
10. Mountbatten, Viceroy's Interview No.49, dated 11 April 1947, *The Transfer of Power*, 1947, Vol. X, pp.196–97.
11. Interview between Mountbatten and Abdul Rab Nishtar, Mountbatten

Papers, Viceroy's interview no 80 of 21 April 1947. *The Transfer of Power*, Vol. X, pp.349–51.
12. Mountbatten to Jinnah, Mountbatten Papers, Official Correspondence Files: North West Frontier Province, situation in, Part1(a) of 27 April 1947, *The Transfer of Power*, Vol. X, p.465.
13. Scott to Abell, Telegram, Mountbatten Papers, official Correspondence Files: NWFP, situation in, Part 1 (a), *The Transfer of Power*, April 1947, Vol. X, pp.476–77.
14. Mountbatten to Caroe, Telegram, Mountbatten Papers, official Correspondence Files: NWFP, situation, Part 1 (a), *The Transfer of Power*, 27 April 1947, Vol. X, p.471.
15. *The Transfer of Power*, 1947, Vol. X, April, pp.476–77.
16. Alan Campbell-Johnson (1913–1998): *Mission with Mountbatten* (Hamish Hamilton Ltd., 1951).
17. Mountbatten to Nehru, L/Po/6/119: ff 40–44 of 30 April 1947, *The Transfer of Power*, Vol. X, pp.491–92.
18. Enclosure to 259, Mountbatten's Meeting with Ministers of NWFP and the Governor, 28 April 1947, *The Transfer of Power*, Vol. X, pp.492–95.
19. Mountbatten to Jinnah, Mountbatten Papers, Official Correspondence Files: NWFP, situation in, Part 1 (b) of 1 May 1947, *The Transfer of Power*, Vol. X, p.513.
20. Mountbatten to Lord Listowel, Mountbatten Papers, Letters to and from the Secretary of State, *The Transfer of Power*, 1 May 1947 Vol. X, p.531.
21. Mountbatten staff meeting, *The Transfer of Power*, 3 May 1947, Vol. X pp.579–83.
22. Field Marshal Sir Claude John Eyre Auchinleck (21 June 1884–23 March 1981), nicknamed Auk, was a British army commander during World War II who spent much of his military career in India. He became the Commander-in-Chief of the Indian army when General Wavell was appointed India's Viceroy.
23. Lord Listowel to Clement Attlee, L/Po/8/45: ff 52–54 of 12 May 1947, *The Transfer of Power*, Vol. X, pp.793–94.
24. Mountbatten to Caroe, r/3/1/170: ff 21–22 of 6 June 1947, *The Transfer of Power*, Vol. XI, pp. 172–173.
25. Caroe to Mountbatten, r/3/1/170: ff 26–28 of 11 June 1947, *The Transfer of Power*, Vol. XI, pp.265–66.
26. Earl of Listowel to Clement Attlee, L/Po/8/45: 41–44 of 11 June 1947, *The

*Transfer of Power*, Vol. XI, pp.280–81.
27. Lord Listowel to Mountbatten, Mountbatten Papers, Letters to and from the Secretary of State of 13 June 1947, *The Transfer of Power*, Vol. XI, pp.335–37.
28. Telegram 1463-s of 16 June 1947, Annotation 3, *Transfer of Power*, Vol. XI, p.436.
29. Lord Ismay to Mountbatten, Mountbatten Papers, official Correspondence Files: interviews (2) of 29 June 1947, *The Transfer of Power*, Vol. XI, p.737.
30. *The Transfer of Power*, Vol. XII, p.10
31. Mountbatten to Lord Listowel, Telegram, Mountbatten Papers, official Correspondence Files: Governor General and Governors of Provinces, Appointments of-Part (1) of 9 July 1947, *The Transfer of Power*, Vol. XII, p.28.
32. 506, L/PO/6/123: FF 155-62, *the Transfer of Power*, Vol. XI, 4 July 1947, p.896.
33. 496, R/3/1/151: F 250, *the Transfer of Power*, Vol. XI, 4 July 1947, p.883.
34. Ibrahim Ismail Chundrigar remained President of the Bombay Muslim League from 1940 to 1945. When Jinnah was asked to nominate the members of the Muslim League for the interim government in 1946, he selected I.I. Chundrigar as one of his nominees. After Pakistan's creation, Chundrigar was appointed Minister for Trade and Commerce in the first cabinet of the newly established country. He was later appointed Pakistan's Ambassador to Kabul. He served as the Governor of the NWFP and then of Punjab from November 1951 to May 1953. He also held the post of the Prime Minister of Pakistan for two months. He died in September 1960.
35. Lt. Gen. Rob Lockhart to Mountbatten, r/3/1/165: ff 3–10 of 9 July 1947, *The Transfer of Power*, Vol. XII, pp.52–58.
36. Ibid.
37. *The Transfer of Power*, Vol. XII, p.113.
38. *The Transfer of Power*, Vol. XII, pp.123–24.
39. Ibid.
40. Ibid.
41. Interview between Mountbatten, Jinnah and Liaquat Ali Khan, Mountbatten Papers, Viceroy's Interview no. 165, 15 July 1947, *The Transfer of Power*, Vol. XII, p.163.

42. Lord Listowel to Mountbatten, Telegram, L/P&J/10/82: ff 40–42 of 17 July 1947, *the Transfer of Power*, Vol. XII, p.205.
43. Mountbatten to Listowel, Telegram, r/3/1/160: f 178 of 18 July 1947, *The Transfer of Power*, Vol. XII, p.256.
44. Lockhart to Mountbatten, Telegram, r/3/1/165: f25 of 20 July 1947, *The Transfer of Power*, Vol. XII, p.278.
45. *The Transfer of Power*, p.280; Lockhart to Mountbatten, r/3/1/165: ff28 of 23 July 1947, *The Transfer of Power*, Vol. XII, pp.306–07.
46. *The Transfer of Power*, July 1947, Vol. XII, p.316.
47. *The Transfer of Power*, July 1947, Vol. XII.
48. Viceroy's personal report no 14, L/Po/6/123: ff 196-203 of 25 July 1947, *The Transfer of Power*, Vol. XII, pp.333–34.
49. Viceroy's Miscellaneous Meeting, Mountbatten Papers, 29 July 1947, *The Transfer of Power*, Vol. XII, pp.405–09.
50. Ibid.
51. Ibid.
52. Ibid.
53. 294, r/3/1/165: ff 38-40 of 30 July 1947, *The Transfer of Power*, Vol. XII, pp.432–34.
54. *The Transfer of Power*, Vol. XII, pp.433–34.
55. Meeting of the Pakistan Cabinet, Case no.1/1/47; r/31/1/165: ff 41-45 of 1 August 1947, *The Transfer of Power*, Vol. XII, pp.441–43.
56. Ibid.
57. Ibid.
58. Ibid.
59. Ibid.
60. Viceroy's Personal Report no. 15, L/Po/6/123: ff208-222 of 1 August 1947, *The Transfer of Power*, Vol. XII, pp.446–48.
61. Ibid.
62. Viceroy's Staff Meeting, item 13, Mountbatten Papers, 2 August 1947, *The Transfer of Power*, Vol. XII, pp.485–86.
63. Ibid.
64. Lockhart to Mountbatten, Telegram r/3/1/165: ff 48-49 of 3 August 1947, *The Transfer of Power*, Vol. XII, pp.493–94.
65. Ramzan or Ramadan is a period of fasting for Muslims. The name is derived from the name of the ninth month of the Islamic calendar, considered most holy.

66. Mountbatten to Lockhart, Telegram r/3/1/165: f 55 of 6 August 1947, *The Transfer of Power*, Vol. XII, p.560.
67. Listowel to Mountbatten, Telegram, l/P&J/8/660: ff 12–15 of 8 August 1947, India office, *The Transfer of Power*, Vol. XII, pp.608–10.
68. Ibid.
69. Ibid.
70. Ibid.

# 6

## The Wise Man of the NWFP: Governor Sir George Cunningham

SIR GEORGE CUNNINGHAM was a Governor for whom even his adversaries rarely had a bad word. His style of operation though effective was usually not within norms of strict propriety. He had a rather long first tenure as the Governor of the NWFP from 1937 to 1946, and was recalled later by Jinnah from retirement for a second stint on the eve of the creation of Pakistan. Jinnah thought him seasoned enough to manage the teething problems arising from the dismissal of a constitutionally elected provincial ministry when Pakistan came into being. Cunningham was preferred over Olaf Caroe, a decision that ended Caroe's career—unfairly, as many believed.

Cunningham was suitably acquainted with the NWFP before he assumed its first governorship. All credit to him for managing a popularly elected Congress ministry for the two years preceding World War II. He got on exceedingly well with Dr Khan Saheb, the Congress Chief Minister. After the Congress ministry's resignation, Cunningham steered the province prudently, keeping Britain's war-time interests in mind. He intelligently used the provincial administrative machinery for anti-German, anti-Japanese propaganda, deftly steering the Muslim opinion against the Axis powers. In contrast, the Hindus in the province were deliberately made to appear to harbour pro-Japan sympathies. Familiar with tribal chiefs, Cunningham won them over with open allurements. He used prominent tribesmen, Quli Khan for example, to connive with the local mullahs. Mullah Marwat, a former Khaksar, was recruited by Quli Khan to serve the 'cause of Islam' by raising the slogan of jihad against its enemies. Subsidies (bribes) were regularly bestowed on the mullahs through Mullah Marwat. The mullahs, who had consistently been anti-British, soon began to speak and write against the Russians and Germans. Cunningham reached out to the Fakir of Ipi and successfully convinced him of Britain's righteous engagement in battles against infidels. The response he received from Fakir's deputy, Mohammad Waris, was markedly friendly in tone. So confident was he about the prevailing law and order situation that he remained indifferent to the consequences of the Quit India movement. The Frontier remained quiet for the six years of World War II. Cunningham's was a major contribution in maintaining peace.

Taking exception to the fact that they had not been consulted on India's participation in World War II, the popular Congress ministries all over India resigned in October 1939. For the two years that it was in power, Jinnah's Muslim League had ceaselessly accused the Congress of acting against Muslim interests. With the resignations, Congress scored a self-goal, losing political clout with the British administrators of India. The colonial masters intentionally encouraged the Muslim League, leveraging it against the Congress. This was also Jinnah's phase of consolidation. The Muslim League's Lahore Resolution (1940) changed the nature of the freedom struggle. Actively abetted by the British, Jinnah now sought recognition from the Congress to be the sole arbiter for India's Muslims. British Prime Minister Churchill, was in no mood to commit to India's freedom. To postpone matters, he announced the Cripps Mission to India.

Cunningham and Viceroy Linlithgow regularly corresponded on a gamut of issues concerning India's affairs. The announcement of Cripps Mission, Cunningham wrote to Linlithgow, had raised Muslim expectations, who were now eager to know where they stood vis-à-vis India. Vouching confidently for them, he informed Linlithgow that the Muslims were not in favour of major constitutional reforms during the war period, something the British also desired. He did not stop there. In his letter of 22 March 1942, Cunningham went a step further in suggesting to the Viceroy three ways in which to safeguard Muslim interests: i) equality or very near equality of representation at the centre; ii) something on the lines of Pakistan; and iii) transference of such power to provinces that domination from the centre did not greatly matter.[1] Note needs to be taken here of the fact that it was early

March 1942, and Cunningham was already suggesting the creation of Pakistan. Though in the letter he recommended the first option, Cunningham foresaw practical difficulties in working out the scheme. Some provinces were likely to exercise the option of remaining outside the union. Apart from making enthusiastic suggestions to the Viceroy from a far-flung province, Cunningham was curious to know from him whether the prime ministerial announcement of the Cripps Mission was a forced one, a result of the British reverses in Malaya and Burma, or whether the 'unexpected step'[2] of sending Cripps to India a result of disagreement in government circles over future Indian policy. Well implied in his query was the disfavour with which he looked at this mission to India.

No one of any consequence in the NWFP bothered to publicly comment on the forthcoming visit of Stafford Cripps. It is evident from his correspondence that Cunningham wilfully chose to highlight Hindu–Muslim disagreements at this stage on the issue of constitutional reforms. No practical purpose was to be served in emphasizing Cripps's friendship with Nehru which could facilitate negotiations, but only to the satisfaction of 'Hindus and Congress'. Instead, he chose to play up the concerns of educated Muslims who were solely focused on the issue of sufficient safeguards, 'whatever happens, we must not be under Hindu domination',[3] and who were confident in their belief that His Majesty's Government (HMG) would not come to any decision on constitutional reforms without giving Jinnah full opportunity to represent the Muslim case to Sir Stafford Cripps. The official Muslim League position, stated in one or two unimportant meetings in the NWFP, was that if the government made any declaration favourable to the Hindus and the Congress, the Muslim League would make 'whatever sacrifices necessary to protect the Muslim interests.'[4] Most of Cunningham's assessments came to fruition as British Indian policy.

On 9 April 1942, Cunningham was telling the Viceroy how pleased the Muslims were now that the HMG had at last recognized Pakistan as a feasible proposition. The local Congressmen too seemed gratified that the principle of self-determination stood conceded. Of course, the protracted negotiations between Stafford Cripps and Indian leaders had aroused mixed feelings, with some commenting that they hampered war efforts. But mostly people expected a satisfactory settlement except for the Congress high command making demands for immediate concessions in administration. The government's readiness to negotiate was appreciated. On the question of defence, Cunningham felt that those who held moderate views wanted the government to appoint an acceptable non-official Indian as the defence member to be under the guidance of the Commander-in-Chief. Even here, Cunningham sensed the effect of a communal virus. Some Muslims claimed that a Hindu Defence Minister might favour an increase in the recruitment of Hindus at the expense of Muslims in the army. The industry that Cunningham displayed in fanning anti-Japanese, anti-German propaganda was absent in curbing communally sensitive issues. To him it was nothing more than an administrative problem to be dealt with pragmatically.[5]

On 15 April, the Viceroy sought reactions from his Governors on the failure of the Cripps Mission. Responding to it in detail, Cunningham explained that the majority who took an interest without doubt felt disappointed. But most of the Khans were pleased at the prospect of not having to see the Congress back in power. The provincial services were only too ready to see Governor's rule continuing. The ex-armymen were still loyal and believed in the ultimate victory of Britain. They were not interested in politics. The same applied to the tribes.[6]

Cunningham sought to convey that the people (the population of the province was overwhelmingly Muslim) understood the real reasons behind the failure of the Cripps Mission. Instead of getting swayed by Congress propaganda, they were convinced that the Congress could not agree to the principle of 'Pakistan', nor object to the 'right to self-determination' without facing embarrassment. Therefore, the Congress manoeuvred for a breakdown on other issues. The people believed that the Congress was afraid of assuming responsibility at the present moment and generally refused to concede that the dispute over the defence member was the real reason for the Congress to break off negotiations. According to Cunningham, Dr Khan Saheb regretted the failure of the negotiations because in his 'heart of hearts' he was 'undoubtedly anxious to lead a Ministry again'.[7] He considered Dr Khan Saheb's reluctance to meet Sir Stafford Cripps an act of foolishness. Ali Gul Khan, president of the Provincial Congress Committee, was still hopeful of a settlement, but the rank and file of the Congress appeared ready for an impending civil disobedience movement. Sounding a little worried, Cunningham had a stern warning conveyed to Dr Khan Saheb in case he encouraged these sentiments in the NWFP.[8]

Again, and consciously, Cunningham sought to accentuate the resurgence of the communal divide at the failure of the Cripps Mission. According to him, the Provincial League as well as Jinnah were disappointed at the breakdown of negotiations. Having shared identical aims with the British, they expected the government to come to a separate agreement with the League. The Hindus, who hinted at such a possibility, warned of active opposition if the Muslim Leaguers were given preference and taken on the Viceroy's council. In Cunningham's view, the Hindus were thoroughly alarmed at the 'conditional offer of Pakistan'. The Governor, of late, had heard more talk than usual of the necessity for the Hindus to establish themselves on a strong footing in the army and also that Hindu and Sikh officers were seeking complete independence and a Hindu Raj in India, a sheer misimpression that carried a high potential for mischief.[9]

The Viceroy was always appreciative of Cunningham's 'sagacious' advice.[10] Through usual dexterity and finesse, Cunningham skilfully managed to get out of delicate situations. For example, when Linlithgow sought to appoint a non-official advisor to the Governor to keep the situation 'sweet' after Cripps had returned to England, the reasons offered by Cunningham for not appointing one were several, but it was done so adroitly that Linlithgow could possibly not take exception to it.[11]

In those days the administration intercepted letters as a matter of routine for intelligence gathering. From a correspondence of a leading barrister in Peshawar, Cunningham 'appropriately' inferred that the general feeling was one of relief at the failure of the Cripps Mission as the people in his province were not in favour of a return to a ministerial government. Jinnah was aware of the 'impracticability' of the Pakistan scheme because neither Bengal nor Punjab would follow him, instead preferring to stay with the central government. As for Sindh and the NWFP, it was doubtful whether the necessary majority could be cobbled to 'secure secession'.[12]

Proceedings on 'Martyr's Day' provided a good index of support for the local Congress. It was challenging for speakers to play on public sentiments on that particular day than on other occasions. The crowd seemed to number between 2,000 and 2,500 on 23 April 1942, with about 1,000 Khudai Khidmatgars in uniform. Evidently, there was very little enthusiasm. Neither the Ahrars, a political group, nor the Muslim Leaguers took part. The orators' main anxiety seemed to justify the rejection of Cripps's proposals by the Congress. The only way they did it was by condemning the British government. This was being done, Cunningham said, by Dr Khan Saheb and others only to create a wedge among people. He believed that the Congress' popularity was waning and the only way they could hope to re-establish themselves was by being critical of the government.[13]

Cunningham did not perceive any threat of civil disobedience despite the 'Quit India' call given by Gandhi. Gandhi's threatened campaign, discussed in the political circles of the NWFP, had failed to cause any excitement. Confident in his ability and in the people's reaction, Cunningham still feared Dr Khan Saheb would end up 'saying publicly something foolish'.[14] If Gandhi's utterances could be somehow portrayed as 'anti-Muslim' the British would be saved of much problem, was Cunningham's suggestion to the Viceroy. He reported on 8 July that Gandhi's Quit India campaign, carried into effect would only be supported with 'considerable energy and publicity' by small numbers. Ghaffar Khan's keenness for the campaign had an ulterior motive— he wanted to recover his lost reputation since his niece's marriage to Jaswant Singh, a non-Muslim. To Cunningham, Ghaffar Khan appeared nervous and frightened of losing his influence.[15]

Upon his return from Wardha on 18 July, it became evident that Ghaffar Khan was actively encouraging Congress workers to follow Gandhi's lead, whatever form it took. Cunningham expected the campaign to at best include non-payment of land revenue and picketing of law courts. Reports that he received did not indicate much public sympathy for Ghaffar Khan. But there was anxiety writ large on the faces of most people Cunningham met in Peshawar and elsewhere. Congress workers played on this anxiety. The 'Khani elite' professed support for the government with few exceptions. It was clear to a majority of them that the Congress could become powerful again. They feared jeopardizing their future by coming out too openly against the Congress.[16] On his part, Cunningham did his best to fortify opinion against Gandhi. He held a conference of district officers in Peshawar on 3 August where all agreed on the need to unleash a propaganda, best done by the district officers, exerting the right kind of influence, personally and verbally, on Indian officials and select non-officials, and through them to let it percolate to the people. Cunningham admitted candidly that he had been doing this for some time. To counter picketing, a chosen group of non-officials were placed at courts' entrances to encourage waverers.[17] He reported to the Viceroy on 8 August about the reticence of Congress workers in his province; nobody 'seemed to like to give an opinion on the subject'. The general response to any enquiry was that Ghaffar Khan was awaiting final orders before he divulged his plans. The only explanation for Ghaffar Khan's secrecy was the uncertainty of the methods to be adopted for civil disobedience when the call finally came from Gandhi. In Cunningham's assessment, opinions had strengthened against the Congress. The Mohmands and Afridis proclaimed their objection to any visit to 'their country by Congress agents'.[18]

'Several Maulvis who had been working for us [Cunningham] for a long time now had come out with strong anti-Congress speeches in mosques, mostly on the theme of the anti-Islamic marriage of Dr Khan Saheb's daughter. Government officials too were staunchly supporting the Government. The "Red Shirt Camp" started by Ghaffar Khan in the last week of July had attracted few people. Meetings held during the last two or three weeks had been poorly attended.' But this period of quiescence did not necessarily mean that Gandhi's call would go unanswered.[19]

More than forty-five days had passed since the Congress called for the Quit India movement. Writing to Linlithgow, Cunningham reported that things had gone on extremely well for the government in the NWFP—a great deal better than anticipated. The likelihood of serious disorder was remote. Even if large numbers resorted to picketing, police or military action could be sternly adopted to prevent this without much reaction for there existed little sympathy for Congress at the time. Ghaffar Khan and a few others were being constantly pressed by Congressmen elsewhere in India to show that the Congress in the NWFP was alive. Cunningham made a mention of an intercepted communication from Ghaffar Khan addressed to someone in the United Provinces that was 'pure *apologia*' for the complete lack of success. Ghaffar Khan was therefore 'straining every nerve'[20] to do something. Dr Khan Saheb on the other hand and Ali Gul Khan, the local president of the Congress, were all for peace. Why not then arrest Ghaffar Khan? Cunningham felt it would inevitably force Dr Khan Saheb and Ali Gul Khan into taking a hard position against the government. As Cunningham considered them to be assets, he wanted to avoid such a situation. But in such an eventuality, was it to ever become absolutely necessary, Cunningham proposed to arrest Ghaffar Khan, but only when there was no other option.[21]

Linlithgow wanted Muslims kept out of the present agitation, a tough task in an overwhelmingly Muslim NWFP where many were prepared to follow the Congress. But his deputy, the Governor of NWFP, succeeded to a great extent in arousing anti-Congress sentiments amongst Muslims through effective propaganda. He was happy to report that the effect of the visits by 'Congress agents to the tribal territory had so far been negligible.'[22]

Feroz Khan Noon visited Peshawar as Cunningham's guest. He had come as the Viceroy's emissary to discuss the important question of the formation of a Muslim League ministry. The problem Cunningham faced was the everyday situation of personal jealousy within the Provincial League with increasing prospects of defections. The balance between Congress and non-Congress members in the assembly was so delicate that it would mean a certain defeat for the ministry in case a division took place on any controversial subject. Cunningham, therefore, sought time to make 'more enquiries in the right quarters' before discussing the ministry formation with Feroz Khan Noon.[23]

Cunningham was acutely aware of the anxieties that plagued an Indian official's mind, especially reservations regarding the future. Most of his Deputy Commissioners reported that their Indian officers were staunchly supportive of the government. The police also remained loyal. Cunningham always impressed on his British officials that they must never ask an Indian official to do anything which seemed spiteful to the Congress or any other political party if 'situations that prevailed in 1930–31 were to be avoided'.[24]

On 27 October 1942, Ghaffar Khan was arrested on charges of violating an order forbidding him to go to Mardan and addressing a meeting. Cunningham considered this action necessary as parts of Mardan district were showing signs of disaffection. On 9 November, Cunningham reported the general situation to be calm. With time, Ghaffar Khan, Dr Khan Saheb and other Congress leaders had suffered a loss in prestige, especially since the beginning of August. Though the 'Red Shirt' spirit had revived with its Congress links strengthened, the danger had been avoided. Dr Khan Saheb had undoubtedly proved to be an influence of moderation. Much rather that than the Congressmen indulge in picketing, for 'if they did not do that, they would do something worse,' was what Cunningham thought, correctly.[25] Lately, the Governor had received CID reports of Red Shirts inclined on committing violence.

But by 23 November 1942, Cunningham was revealing that the Congress movement had pretty well died down. Outwardly there were few signs of Congress activity and he doubted if there was much going on below the surface that he did not know about. He had spent five days riding through Peshawar and Mardan and was 'pleasantly surprised by almost a complete lack of interest shown in recent Congress and Red Shirt activities.'[26]

Gandhi undertook a fast in February 1943 to exert pressure on the government. The fast attracted little sympathy in the NWFP. Only one or two diffident Hindus approached Cunningham on this subject. He did not meet even one Muslim who 'had a positive word to say for Gandhi's present attitude' and if Gandhi died as a result of his hunger strike the prevailing sentiment would be that he 'deserved' it. The Congress was finding it impossible to raise its daily quota of four or five men who could offer themselves for arrest. Dr Khan Saheb decided to go to Delhi to meet Gandhi but changed his mind at the last moment. Cunningham sent word to Dr Khan Saheb that he would be running the risk of arrest if he made a 'foolish speech' anywhere.[27]

By 25 February, Gandhi's condition had improved. According to Cunningham, 'Gandhi had once again miscalculated and the government, by sticking to its guns, had scored a victory.'[28] Except for the time when Gandhi was critical, Hindu sentiments remained well under control. In his assessment, Gandhi's death while undertaking the fast, would not have created widespread trouble except for some individual acts of violence.[29]

On 13 May, Cunningham asked Sardar Aurangzeb Khan to form a ministry although his party, the Muslim League, at that time had only a slender majority. Sensing a trend in Aurangzeb Khan's favour amongst the Khans and others of some prominence, Cunningham assumed that once made the Chief Minister, Aurangzeb Khan would manage to bring waverers over to his side. Cunningham was right. The Congress, though it tried to close ranks, was unable to prevent Aurangzeb Khan from forming a ministry. Obliged that he was, Aurangzeb Khan surrendered to the Governor in return for the favour shown to him. He agreed to the authorized budget, publicly declared his wholehearted support for the province's war efforts and promised not to do anything on the issue of general administration that would embarrass the Governor or his officers. For technical advice, Aurangzeb invariably relied on government secretaries. Sardar Aurangzeb Khan's ministry took office on 25 May 1943.[30] For almost two years from then on, Cunningham would continue to rule by proxy.

Cunningham reported on 24 August 1943 that all four by-elections for vacant Muslim seats had gone in favour of the Muslim League. Three of these were expected to go to the League, but the one in Mardan district had been a Congress and a Khudai Khidmatgar stronghold. That Muslim League could wrest this seat from the Congress was significant. The reason was quite straightforwardly put by Cunningham. Had it not been for him and his officials, and the anti-Congress propaganda that they spread on Islamic lines since the inception of the war, the Muslim League would have failed to win the Mardan seat. How effective this campaign was could be gauged from the fact that the Yusufzai mullahs of Mardan, 'traditionally anti-Government, first became anti-Russian and anti-German, then anti-Japanese, and so by natural sequence anti-Hindu and anti-Congress.'[31] Cunningham was content to note that the Muslim League's success in the by-elections was generally perceived as a victory for the British government, made all the more laudable because the Muslim League's election machinery was not as well heeled as that of the Congress. In an open display of bias against the Congress, Cunningham gleefully reported elaborate scenes of jubilation by the people of Peshawar who amused themselves by dressing up a rather aged stork in a dhoti with big spectacles on its beak, leading it through the city in a procession with a placard marked 'Mahatma Gandhi' on it, a truly cruel caricature. The stork died the following day of exhaustion.[32] Linlithgow, in equally bad taste, reacted vicariously to this reportage:

> Very many thanks for your report for the period ending August the 24. I was much interested to get your news of the bye-elections and agree that the success of the Muslim League is significant. I suppose there is a possibility of subsequent embarrassment in the fact that the Muslim League successes are regarded as a victory for the British Government over subversive elements but we can meet such difficulties when we come to them. I was much amused with your story of the aged stork. I wonder who the genius was who thought of it as an electioneering device.[33]

Cunningham would, once in a while, praise the Chief Minister. He thought it prudent of Aurangzeb to have tackled a situation that could potentially cause a rift within his ministry's ranks during the assembly session. When a member of the assembly tried initiating a debate on 'Pakistan', Aurangzeb dealt with it tactfully by refraining from antagonizing the Sikhs. Cunningham worried that the Pakistan question would sooner or later be brought to the fore by enthusiastic Muslim Leaguers. The Peshawar city elements of the Muslim League contemplated holding a conference where they were to invite Jinnah.[34] But this was wisely deferred by Aurangzeb Khan until the Sikh by-elections were over. However, by early February 1944, Cunningham was growing weary of his ministers, particularly the Chief Minister, who was allowing purely party or personal considerations to colour his official action. He often found the ministers trying to 'please their partisans by doing them favours'.[35] Individually, these favours were not of any great importance but the sum total brought great discredit to the ministry. The Chief Minister displayed 'utter weakness'[36] in taking decisions on crucial matters, for example in the case of communal riots in Haripur, where while considering punitive and preventive measures, the Chief Minister was hopelessly swayed by the fear of antagonizing his own party. He also tried to use his powers of clemency for party purposes. Though Cunningham desisted from accusing the Chief Minister of personal dishonesty, his concern emanated from the fact that 'the Muslim League Ministry had shown far less sense of duty to the public than their Congress predecessors'.[37] Fortunately, the attention of local Sikhs shifted from the incident at Haripur to the Sikh by-election that seemed to go in favour of a candidate sponsored by Master Tara Singh, an Akali leader who supported Aurangzeb Khan's ministry.[38]

In the midst of all this, the Muslim League high command sent a committee to assess the party's prospects in the NWFP. This Committee of Actions, as it was called, arrived despite Aurangzeb Khan's opposition. With Aurangzeb Khan's ministry completing an year in office, the committee was clearly disappointed by the functioning of the Provincial League. The committee was given to understand by Aurangzeb that the Muslim League's influence was steadily growing and that it was the predominant party in the province. The committee soon realized that the Muslim League in the NWFP was a misnomer for party factions. Of what the Governor could assess, the Committee of Actions was more interested in strengthening the Provincial League than in bolstering Aurangzeb Khan's ministry.[39]

Efforts gained momentum in early May 1945 for Dr Khan Saheb to take over the reins of the NWFP government. Wavell was away on consultations in London while Sir John Colville deputed for him. How Dr Khan Saheb came to enlist the support of the Congress high command to become Chief Minister is another story. Suffice to say that Wavell cabled Cunningham from London indicating that Dr Khan Saheb's support to India's war efforts be made a precondition to his assuming the Chief Ministership. A misimpression, that Dr Khan Saheb was not in its favour, had been created in the media. Sir John Colville wanted Dr Khan Saheb to clear the air.[40] Not intent on making an issue of it, Cunningham pressed for Dr Khan Saheb's immediate appointment. Defending Dr Khan Saheb he said that a 'great majority of statements attributed to Khan Saheb in the recent press in NWFP were not statements made by him but interpretations or misinterpretations by the pressmen. I am satisfied that he means to cooperate in the War efforts. Let him be judged by his work.'[41] At an all-India level, a Congressman taking over the Chief Ministership of the NWFP was a case of singular exception. The Congress had not yet decided to stake claim to political offices, either in the provinces or at the centre. It was Cunningham, a consummate politician himself, who switched the Chief Ministers like pawns in the chess game he was a master at.

The Simla talks, a Wavell initiative, were held soon. The talks ended the three-year incarceration of prominent Congressmen. In Cunningham's assessment, at least half of the educated opinion in the NWFP did not admit the right of Jinnah or the Muslim League to nominate all Muslims to the Viceroy's executive council. They would rest satisfied if the Viceroy nominated well-known Muslim figures to his council, even if they did not belong to the Muslim League. Cunningham did not think that the Provincial League could do much harm in the NWFP. Aurangzeb lay discredited and with him, for the time being, the local Muslim League.[42] But by this time it had become well established that the British government would not reach a decision on major constitutional reforms without keeping the Muslim League fully on board.

Cunningham had been told that people like Liaquat Ali Khan were likely to desert Jinnah if he insisted on bringing things to an impasse. Cunningham recommended that the Viceroy challenge Jinnah on this point.[43] But by 24 July, Cunningham was reporting a changed situation. The public mood during the last two weeks in the NWFP had been pretty well confined to the outcome of the Simla Conference. Muslim League leaders were elated at Jinnah's success and in the process felt that their own prestige had increased. They appeared determined to oppose any attempt at forming the Viceroy's executive council without the League's sole claim to nominate all the Muslim members.[44]

Educated Muslims who were not keen supporters of the League had more mixed feelings. They found a certain sense of satisfaction in the thought that Muslims had proved too strong for the Hindus, but also regretted the failure of the Simla Conference. The desire for change and constitutional advance appeared greater now with people genuinely wishing to see an end to the present impasse.[45]

At this juncture, Dr Khan Saheb took to 'abusing Jinnah with a good deal of relish'[46] while speaking of the Congress desire to cooperate with the government. He felt that the Congress was now ready to form ministries elsewhere too. Cunningham saw no indication of the Congress returning to civil disobedience despite the rebuff they had received from Jinnah. But the antipathy between Hindus and Muslims in general had increased markedly in the last week or two, and was expected to widen. However, Cunningham was singing a different tune in the Governor's meeting on 1 August 1945. Contradicting his earlier dispatches he said, 'the Simla Conference had resulted in a better feeling all round. The initiative should not be lost. No change should be made in the executive council except on the lines contemplated at the Simla Conference. The Viceroy might of course make individual changes on personal grounds.'[47] He was opposed to any constitutional advance without the Muslim League. The NWFP Muslims did not think Jinnah was justified in rejecting HMG's proposals. But if the Muslim League was now disregarded, the Muslims would rally to Jinnah and the League would be strengthened. He doubted if the NWFP Muslims really believed in Pakistan—they had not considered what it meant. If the Muslim League was seriously antagonized, it could prove troublesome on Islamic questions in the Middle East. The only possible move now was to restore ministries in the Section 93 provinces. If this was done, Muslim League could be more inclined to come into the executive council.[48]

Cunningham wished that the ministries in the 'directly ruled' provinces would become functional early. Dr Khan Saheb was also of the same opinion and expected the Congress party to cooperate. Without popular ministries, it was difficult to deal with problems such as post-war development planning.[49] Cunningham wanted the provincial elections to be held soon, his timetable for it being well within two months. He preferred elections to take place after ministry formation in the 'Governor-ruled' provinces.[50] This would brighten the chances of the Muslim League's participation in the Viceroy's executive council at the centre.[51] Wavell was not very hopeful of a positive outcome as Jinnah was unlikely to agree to the terms acceptable to HMG.[52]

In Cunningham's opinion, the failure of the Simla Conference forced people to think and talk about 'Pakistan': at least there was now an attempt to define, to understand its essence, what it actually meant, the Muslim safeguards at the centre, the nature of the relationship with India and such like. Cunningham had little doubt that the forthcoming elections would largely be fought on the Pakistan issue in its crudest form.[53]

He informed Wavell on 9 October of large defections from the Congress ranks to the Muslim League, symptomatic of the increasing antipathy between educated Muslims and Hindus. The communal situation deteriorated and grew steadily worse than Cunningham had ever known it to be. Muslim senior officials, who had never taken much interest in politics before, turned rabidly anti-Hindu, and therefore pro-Muslim League. Cunningham, however, was still unsure about the extent of electoral mileage drawn from it by the Muslim League. The Congress election machinery, its rank and file, appeared more effective than the Muslim League's. Congress had better organization and more money. Moreover, the League was divided over the nomination of candidates and leadership. Aurangzeb Khan's popularity had waned. A strong section of his party wished to depose him from the leadership. Cunningham was convinced that the League's chances in the elections depended largely on the efforts that its central leadership made to improve the local organization,[54] and of course the help the provincial Muslim League would receive from official quarters.

A letter, somewhat beyond his brief, that Cunningham wrote to Wavell on 27 November 1945, is worth a quote. The INA trials held at this time had caught the people's imagination nationwide. The officers on trial belonged to all three—Hindu, Muslim and Sikh communities. The patriotic fervour that these trials aroused brought the Indians together as a nation. Why allow the Indians a common rallying point? This was exactly Cunningham's anxiety which forced him to write to Wavell. Cunningham recommended an immediate announcement by the Commander-in-Chief that no further proceedings be carried out against any INA prisoner. No one could do this but the Commander-in-Chief himself and that too of his own volition and on his own responsibility. Done by anyone else, even by the King, it would not have the same effect, particularly on the army. Though some senior army officers with whom Cunningham had occasion to discuss this matter held a contrary opinion that leniency at this stage would have a disastrous effect on the army, Cunningham was certain of the action he proposed to the Viceroy. With each passing day this issue was becoming more and more 'purely Indian versus British' and less and less 'ill-disposed Indians versus British-cum-well-disposed Indians'. As time passed, the number of well-disposed Indians defecting to the anti-British camp increased. Whatever the outcome of the trial, an anti-British bias was bound to persist. The only way of stopping the rot was through a clean cut and that too at once. Dr Khan Saheb and some other Congressmen expressed their feelings to Cunningham that 'if only they [the INA prisoners] had been shot in Rangoon or Singapore, everyone would have been pleased.'[55] But that feeling had gone and could not now be revived. Cunningham therefore suggested that the best thing at the moment for the British was to cut their losses. Cunningham's letter had a salutary effect on the Viceroy who thanked him for sharing his views. On 30 November, Wavell informed Cunningham that no future trials were to take place except if there were allegations of gross brutality against the accused, a policy that the executive council also approved.[56]

Provincial elections in the NWFP concluded in February 1946. In a missive of 27 February 1946 to the Viceroy, Cunningham conveyed the results. The Congress had won thirty seats on its own in a house of fifty, certain to be joined by one of the two independent Muslims, or both. It now had a safe majority, having secured more than 50 per cent of the Muslim seats: nineteen on Congress tickets plus two probable independents, to seventeen Muslim Leaguers. Cunningham concluded that ever since the canvassing commenced in October 1945, the Muslim League had remained unduly optimistic about the election results.[57]

His expectations belied, Cunningham was at pains to spell out the reasons for the Muslim League's failure. The League accused the Congress of the unfair advantage of being in office when the elections took place. The logic here was that the Congress government pleased people by doling out largesse. Cunningham considered this to be an excuse rather than an explanation, and even if that was partially true, it was neutralized because most of the Muslim officials at the senior level favoured the Muslim League. Cunningham ascribed bad organization and factionalism as two main reasons for the poor performance of the Muslim League. The Congress appeal was more intelligible to the people. In addition, the Congress projected the Muslim League as friends of the British government. Congress attention was focused on the less well-to-do over whom the bigger Khans (League supporters) were losing hold. It was only in the district of Hazara that the big landholders still wielded some authority over their tenants. The Muslim League won eight of the nine Muslim seats that it contested in that district.[58]

During elections, the Muslim League talked of little else except 'Pakistan'. This was not really an intelligible war cry to almost 90 per cent of 'their hearers'. To an average Pathan villager, the suggestion that there could be such a thing as Hindu domination was laughable.[59]

In March 1946, soon after elections, Sir Olaf Caroe replaced Cunningham as the Governor of the NWFP. Cunningham, coincidentally was reappointed to the governorship again in August 1947. Nearer the date of the final transfer of power, Jinnah was anxious to have Cunningham back in the same post. Cunningham, who had retired by then, was cajoled and made to agree by Lord Ismay at Mountbatten's insistence. Strangely, all this transpired within a week of Caroe being forced to go on leave, on an assurance from Mountbatten that he would rejoin the post after his leave got over.

On 9 July 1947, Mountbatten formally received nominations for the Governors of Pakistan provinces. Jinnah had recommended Sir George Cunningham's name for appointment as the Governor of the NWFP. The Secretary of State for India, Lord Listowel, was requested to persuade Cunningham to accept the appointment as Jinnah thought his past experience to be of immense value. No doubt, Jinnah was anxious to have Cunningham as the Governor of the NWFP, but he did not want special treatment meted out to just one Governor. If Cunningham was appointed on concessional terms, it would hardly remain a secret for long. There were other Governors to be appointed too. Cunningham had asked for a tax-free salary as compensation for the expenses he would incur in maintaining a home in the United Kingdom, also for being deprived of the director's fee. He also tried negotiating a single lump sum payment of 2,500 pounds on account of losses suffered. Jinnah refused to grant these concessions. Cunningham eventually accepted the governorship on Jinnah's terms.

Things had changed drastically by the time Cunningham rejoined. A referendum, boycotted by the Khudai Khidmatgars, had been held in the NWFP, the verdict going in favour of the NWFP joining Pakistan. Caroe never returned from his leave. He was asked to retire. The referendum's results were announced on 20 July. The Muslim League now wanted the NWFP Congress ministry dismissed. Mountbatten opposed the idea of 'Governor's rule' so near the appointed date of the transfer of power. While confabulations continued, Cunningham took oath as the Governor in the second week of August 1947. He met Dr Khan Saheb over long discussions on 13 and 15 August and secured the Chief Minister's loyalty for Pakistan as long as he worked as a minister. He then promptly and formally conveyed to Jinnah that he trusted Dr Khan Saheb's words. If Jinnah had no serious objections, Cunningham wanted Dr Khan Saheb to continue in power till the next general elections were held under a new Constitution, but left it to Jinnah to decide Dr Khan Saheb's fate. If Jinnah directed him to dismiss the ministry, Cunningham would 'understand'. He also conveyed to him that Abdul Qayyum, the Chief Minister designate 'appeared to be in the know of the situation and that by this time next week, they all shall be in smooth waters'.[60]

On the day of Pakistan's independence, a late decision by the NWFP ministers not to attend the flag hoisting ceremony considerably weakened Dr Khan Saheb's case. Dr Khan Saheb genuinely feared for his ministers having to suffer indignity from the crowds if they participated in the function celebrating independence. Kazi Ataullah, a minister, 'inspired by Ghaffar Khan seemed to think that their attendance would be derogatory to the ministry'.[61]

Cunningham suggested that in case the ministry was to be dismissed, it should not be done before 19 August. Movement of troops, to be placed at vantage points, would be easier after Id was over.[62] However, on 22 August 1947, Cunningham sent a telegram to Jinnah stating, 'I dismissed Dr Khan Saheb's Ministry at 1 p.m. today and have invited Abdul Qayyum to form a ministry'.[63] Abdul Qayyum took over as Chief Minister along with Khan Muhammad Abbas Khan as a member of his cabinet. The new ministry took oath on 23 August. Cunningham's second stint was not very long. In October 1947, infiltrators from the tribal areas of the NWFP descended on Kashmir, precipitating a warlike situation between India and Pakistan. Cunningham claimed no knowledge of these raids, something which was hard to believe.

## Notes

1. Nicholas Mansergh and Penderel Moon (eds), *The Transfer of Power*, Vol. I, 22 March 1942, p.456.
2. Governor's Report No-6 of 22 March 1942, *The Transfer of Power* Vol. I, p.457.
3. 364, MSS. EUR.F.125/77, *The Transfer of Power* Vol. I, Pg. 457.
4. Ibid, p.458.
5. 573, MSS. EUR.F.125/77, Governor's Report No-7, 9 April 1942, *The Transfer of Power* Vol. I, p.712.
6. Governor's Report No-8, 23 April 1942, *The Transfer of Power* Vol. I, pp.831–32.
7. Ibid, p.832.
8. Ibid, pp.832–33.
9. Ibid, p.833.
10. 713 Mss. EUR.F 125/77 dated, 30 April 1942, *The Transfer of Power* Vol. I, p.875.
11. I4 Mss. EUR.F. 125/110 dated, 4 May 1942, *The Transfer of Power*, Vol. II, p.20.
12. I4 Mss. EUR.F. 125/110, Governor's Report No-9, 9 May, 1942, *The Transfer of Power*, Vol. II, p.59.
13. Ibid.
14. 135, MSS. EUR.F.125/77, Governor's Report No-11, 9 June 1942, *The Transfer of Power* Vol. II, p.194.
15. 237, MSS EUR.F 125/77, Governor's Report No-13, 8 July 1942, *The Transfer of Power* Vol. II, p.353.
16. MSS EUR.F 125/77, Governor's Report No-14, 23 July 1942, *The Transfer of Power* Vol. II, p.444.
17. 419, Telegram Mss. EUR.F. 125/110, August 1942, *The Transfer of Power* Vol. II, p.572.
18. 625, MSS.EUR.F. 125/77, Governor's Report No-15, 8 August 1942, *The Transfer of Power* Vol. II, pp.625–26.
19. Ibid.
20. 625, MSS.EUR.F.125/77, 28 September, 1942, *The Transfer of Power* Vol. III, p.55.
21. Ibid.
22. Ibid., p.56.

23. Ibid.
24. Ibid.
25. MSS.EUR.f.125/77, 9 November 1942; *The Transfer of Power*, Vol. III, p.222.
26. MSS.EUR.F.125/77, 23 November 1942; *The Transfer of Power*, Vol. III, p. 293.
27. MSS.EUR.F.125/78, 24 February 1943; *The Transfer of Power*, Vol. III, p.728.
28. MSS.EUR.F.125/78, 8 March 1943; *The Transfer of Power*, Vol. III, p.772.
29. Ibid.
30. MSS.EUR.F.125/78, 24 May 1943; *The Transfer of Power*, Vol. III, p.1006.
31. MSS.EUR.F.125/78, 24 August 1943; *The Transfer of Power*, Vol. IV, pp. 186–87.
32. Ibid., p.187.
33. MSS.EUR.F.125/78, 3–6 September 1943; *The Transfer of Power*, Vol. IV, p.207.
34. MSS.EUR.F.125/78, 13 September 1943; *The Transfer of Power*, Vol. IV, pp. 245–46.
35. L/P&J/5/2211f119, 9 February 1944; *The Transfer of Power*, Vol. IV, p. 708.
36. Ibid.
37. Ibid.
38. Ibid.
39. L/P&J/5/221: f 72, 24 June 1944; *The Transfer of Power*, Vol. IV, p.1046.
40. Telegram, L/P&J/8?659: f 31, 30 April 1945; *The Transfer of Power*, Vol. V, p.989.
41. Telegram, L/P&J/8/659: f 29, 2 May 1945; *The Transfer of Power*, Vol. V, p.1000.
42. Telegram, Wavell Papers, Political series, April 1944–July 1945, Pt. II, p.71, dated 2 July 1945; *The Transfer of Power*, Vol. V, p.1190.
43. Ibid.
44. L/P&J/5/222: f 53, 24 July 1945; *The Transfer of Power*, Vol. V, p.1293.
45. Ibid.
46. Ibid.
47. Second Meeting, 1 August 1945, *The Transfer of Power*, Vol. V, p.10.
48. *The Transfer of Power*, 1 August 1945, Vol. VI, p.11.
49. *The Transfer of Power*, 1 August 1945, Vol. VI, p.13.

50. *The Transfer of Power*, 1 August 1945, Vol. VI, p.14.
51. *The Transfer of Power*, Third meeting, August 1945, Vol. VI, p.19.
52. Ibid.
53. L/P&J/5/222: f 48, 9 August, 1945—Letter to Wavell, *The Transfer of Power*, Vol. VI, pp.42–43.
54. L/P&J/5/222: f 29, 9 October, 1945, *The Transfer of Power* Vol. VI, pp.318–19.
55. Cunningham to Wavell, Wavell Papers, Official Correspondence: India, January–December 1945, pp.383–84, reproduced in *The Transfer of Power*, 27 November 1945, Vol. VI, p.546.
56. Wavell Papers, Official Correspondence: India, January–December 1945, p.385, a letter from Wavell to Cunningham dated 30 November 1945, published in *The Transfer of Power* Vol. VI, p.573.
57. L/P&J/5/223: ff 152–3, dated 27 February 1946; *The Transfer of Power*, Vol. VI, p.1085.
58. Ibid.
59. Ibid., pp.1085–86.
    Cunningham to Jinnah 253, F.46-GG/5–6, Peshawar, dated 14 August 1947, pp.358; Telegram F.46–GG/7, Peshawar, 15 August 1947, pp.12–13, Jinnah Papers.
60. Ibid.
61. Ibid.
62. Cunningham to Jinnah, Telegram F.46-GG/14, pp.82–83, Jinnah Papers, Vol. V, First Series, dated 22 August 1947.

# 7

# A Paladin Himself: Governor Sir Olaf Caroe

THE PATHANS BY Sir Olaf Caroe, a vastly popular book even now, has a chapter on the Paladins of the NWFP. Caroe does not figure in the list of knights simply because he is the author of the book. A greatly experienced hand at the NWFP, he played a critical role on India's western frontiers just when the British stood to withdraw from India. In March 1946, after his taking over as Governor of the NWFP, there arrived a cabinet delegation from England to decide upon the transfer of power. Within sixteen months of that, the NWFP had been co-opted by the newly created state of Pakistan.

Before he took over as Governor, Olaf Caroe was Foreign Secretary to the Government of India. The external affairs portfolio had traditionally been with the Viceroy. It was for the first time in September 1946 that an Indian, Jawaharlal Nehru, came to hold this charge. It is a well-known fact that Caroe had objected to Nehru's appointment. Though the reasons were not personal, Caroe believed that a Hindu and a 'Pandit' to boot would be completely unacceptable to the Frontier tribesmen, whose welfare Nehru would come to oversee as Minister in charge of external affairs. Tribal affairs had always been part of this responsibility.

The beginning of the Great War saw the Oxford-educated Caroe training for the territorial army. He rejoiced when it was decided that his battalion would be headed for India instead of France, for his chances of survival in France would have been slim. Authors like Rudyard Kipling and Flora Annie Steele[1] and parental guidance had imbued Caroe with a colonial concept of Britain's mission in the East—

he was glad to be going to India.[2] Tasked with the responsibility of guarding the residency of Hyderabad upon his arrival in India, it was here that the young Caroe got his first glimpse of power, vested in the Indian Political Service, which he would soon join: 'I remember thinking of myself, if we are going to live in this sort of way there must be something to be said about the Indian Civil Service. It is the sort of thing that a socialist must feel when he gets into the house of Lords!' (Singer 1984: 191). He was next to serve in Punjab and for some time in Peshawar, a stay he found very pleasant. To effect his return to the NWFP, it was necessary that he join the Civil Service. It was not a hard decision, as Caroe admitted to not being much of a military man. He cleared the Civil Service examination and returned to Punjab as a magistrate. But in order to exchange Punjab for Peshawar, Caroe needed to move from the Indian Civil Service to the Viceroy's Diplomatic Corps—the Indian Political Service. The selection process involved an interview by a board that comprised the Foreign Secretary, the Political Secretary and a few others. The candidate had to personally appear before the Viceroy for assessment. Caroe was approved and thus began his tryst with the NWFP.

In 1930, Caroe was posted as Secretary to the Commissioner of the NWFP, Sir Norman Bolton (Singer 1984: 193). This was a time of unprecedented unrest in the NWFP, which till then had remained politically immune. For Caroe as a District Officer, a sixteen-hour day was nothing unusual and he brought this habit of hard unremitting work into the secretariat. A man with a mission, 'he would not let sleeping dogs lie. Indeed, he thought that the dogs in the North-West Frontier never slept; they only pretended to sleep; and if the rulers were easygoing or lethargic, the dogs would pounce on them. 'Eternal vigilance' was Caroe's watchword. He was devoted to the Frontier and sedulously prepared himself for the highest post in the province' (Menon 1965: 93).

Serious riots broke out in Peshawar in 1930.[3] The government lost control of the city for a considerable time. As a consequence of his actions, Sir Norman Bolton had to leave Peshawar ignominiously. As for Caroe's intervention in those riots, this is how he describes it:

One morning in April 1930, I was doing my work in the secretariat when the Governor [Chief Commissioner Sir Norman Bolton] rang up and said there was a riot that had started in the city and said would I please go down. I said, 'Well, I'm not a district officer at all, I'm only in the secretariat. I'm your secretary, why should I go down to deal with the riot?' He said, 'You understand these people and anyway you're on the spot, so will you please obey my orders and go down to the city.' So I went down to find that the police were fighting in the main street of the city called the *kissa khani*, which means 'the place where story-tellers are.' There were about fifty policemen, the Deputy Commissioner had been hit on the head with a brick, and there were already about ten corpses lying about. I walked down and got the corpses collected. By this time we'd got a small body of troops who had arrived to help. I said I didn't want to open fire if we could avoid it...We marched through the narrow streets of Peshawar with me at the back. We got to a narrow street when we met a funeral procession. We were about thirty or forty but coming along the road was a mob of about 2,000 to 3,000 men. I told the men that they would have to fire. They fired about seven or eight rounds in all, killing around thirteen people. Everyone disappeared at once. We were then able to occupy the city. The Chief Commissioner's nerve broke and he had to be removed and I became Deputy Commissioner, therefore responsible for all the laws in the city (Singer 1984: 198–99).

In the government's assessment, Caroe had dealt adroitly with the riots and was therefore promoted. Caroe's career in the NWFP was a successful one. He suffered no such setback as Metcalfe[4] in 1930. The very crisis that had tarnished Metcalfe's reputation enhanced Caroe's, for he was perceived to have handled the Khudai Khidmatgars in Peshawar with a firm resolve. He was not only considered a good District Officer; his efficiency as a secretariat man also equalled his reputation for executive ability. His distinguishing feature was that he 'would take nothing for granted, not even the Himalayas. Once in every few centuries, even the Himalayas had let the Indians down' (Menon 1965: 133).

After his stint as Deputy Commissioner, Peshawar, Caroe was deputed as Chief Secretary to the Frontier Government in 1933-34. He was later summoned to Delhi and appointed Deputy Secretary, Foreign and Political Department of the Government of India. He also officiated for some time as the political representative for the Persian Gulf. The Political Department then sent him as an agent to the Governor General in Baluchistan. Between 1937-38 Olaf Caroe was posted as Resident in Waziristan. This was the time when the Fakir of Ipi raised the banner of revolt against the government. The Fakir was still at large when Caroe left Waziristan. Caroe also worked for some time as the Revenue Commissioner in 1938-39 in Baluchistan. In appreciation of his meritorious service, he was appointed Secretary in the Indian External Affairs Department in 1939 and continued in this capacity till he was made the Governor and Agent to the Governor General in the NWFP.

A detailed note on the Frontier prepared by Caroe as India's Foreign Secretary provides an interesting insight both into the psyche of the Pathans and Caroe himself. Here are some of Caroe's observations about the tribes of NWFP from that note:

> The Pathan tribesman is unstable and anarchic by nature; intolerant of and resistant to control in any form by outside authority—Asiatic no less than European; on his own ground probably the finest minor tactician in the world; careless of his own and other people's lives and prone to fanaticism. From our end of the Frontier to the other the Pathan tribes could probably muster nearly 500,000 rifles and some LMGs.

Caroe's note did not preclude the possibility of chaos resulting from a communal conflagration in India, which could be an open invitation for tribal unrest, both because of its Islamic appeal as also for the 'purely barbaric motives of loot and destruction'.[5] The anarchic Pathan was quick to sense indecision or weakening of authority. Most Indian political leaders failed to realize the destructive vitality of a purely Muslim tribal belt that could emerge as a major factor in the constitutional settlement in India. On future prospects, Caroe's assessment indicated that the problem of the tribal areas could only be kept at bay if the Muslim community in India remained satisfied.

On 28 March 1946, Caroe met the cabinet delegation which was in India to suggest options for the transfer of power. Caroe was opposed to a loose federation in which the Indian provinces could coexist. Who would then finance the disbursal of subsidies? The disbursal itself would pose a problem. All this was unachievable without a strong central authority. Caroe argued in favour of an independent Pathanistan. As an archetypical British civil servant, he firmly believed that a member of the Muslim majority party should be given charge of the External Affairs Department in the Viceroy's executive council.[6] But when it actually came to that, Wavell chose Nehru, much to Caroe's chagrin.

A Frontier officer of long standing, Caroe did not consider the NWFP legislature a proper body to deal with tribal matters. It was impossible, he felt, for each of the tribes to sit individually with the legislature. Instead, leading members of the *jirga* of each tribe could instead confer with the ministry, leaving the Governor to preside over discussions on tribal affairs. The Chief Minister could attend tribal *jirgas* only when tribal affairs affecting the entire province was under consideration. The Chief Minister's role could at best be marginal.[7]

Impending changes concerning transfer of power in the tribal areas was a serious cause of worry for Caroe. He was certain that any announcement of British withdrawal would make the tribes restive. The situation, he feared, could worsen if the tribes gained an impression that they were to be brought under Hindu rule. He favoured some form of regional autonomy, not to be called Pakistan, rather a realignment of provincial boundaries for the Muslims of northwestern India within a unit where they were preponderant and, therefore, given less to communal appeal. Despite factionalism, Pathan patriotism was very much a living thing. An autonomous Pathan province, inclusive of some northern portions of Baluchistan, would be agreeable to the Congress Muslims of the NWFP.[8] Caroe knew that the Congress's hold on the Muslims of the NWFP was fast becoming tenuous, largely dependent as it was on the personality of the two Khan brothers. It was a matter of some urgency for him that both the Congress and the Muslim League reconcile their political differences at the provincial level, that reconciliation happening through a petition to the Congress Frontier Party in the name of Pakhtunistan and to those in sympathy with the Muslim League along the lines that the Frontier could never pay for itself.[9] This could pave the way for the NWFP's amalgamation into a regional federation for the Muslims of western India.

Appreciative of the unique situation of Congress Muslims of the NWFP where fear of Hindu domination did not exist, he well realized how important it was for peace to prevail for constitutional parleys to take place. His fears were not unfounded. Communal riots broke out in Punjab. How could the NWFP remain unscathed?

How should the tribes be made politically conscious of the impending changes? This too considerably disturbed Caroe. Some form of commission had already been suggested to ascertain the views of the tribes. If a commission was to be constituted at all, it was to be done with utmost care and by involving both the Governor and the Chief Minister. Caroe was against co-opting outsiders, as he felt that they would render themselves to pressure from political parties. It would be a daunting prospect for a newcomer to sit through tribal *jirgas* without knowing the language. It was probable that the presence of an outsider would upset the tribes, thus affecting constitutional parleys.[10]

Voicing his concerns at a meeting of Governors in August 1946, Caroe said that any attempt to proceed with the Constituent Assembly and the formation of an interim government at the centre minus the Muslim League would prove infructuous. If the Constituent Assembly met without the League and thence set up an Advisory Committee to settle tribal affairs, there were chances of trouble, so also in the NWFP. The Frontier had to be held firmly while Constitution-making went on. Caroe did not want an Advisory Committee until it had the Muslim League on it. He was also against Constitution-making in the Section B[11] provinces (of the Cabinet Mission plan) in the absence of the Muslim League.[12]

On 2 September Nehru took over as Member, External Affairs and Tribal Areas, in the interim government. Soon he wanted to visit the tribal areas of the NWFP and accordingly informed Caroe. Caroe vehemently objected to Nehru's visit, which he immediately made known to the Viceroy: 'This is deliberate partisan approach to tribal problems at [a] most critical juncture. If this plan is carried out at this moment and before [the] League comes to terms I am convinced that serious tribal reaction must be expected and that any hope of securing coalition [in the interim government] is likely to be wrecked.

Nor should I be in [a] position to discharge my responsibility for maintaining tranquillity of border.'[13] All of the Viceroy's staff and the Viceroy himself found this response 'quite impossibly out of date' to keep the foreign member (Nehru) away from the tribal areas.[14] Caroe was left with no other choice but to reconcile to Nehru's visit.

Nehru's tour of the NWFP had consequences that have been discussed in some detail in the chapter on Nehru. On the conclusion of that tour, Caroe wrote to Wavell from Parachinar[15] that Nehru's week-long tour had been 'one of great anxiety and no less difficult'[16] than what he had anticipated. As the tour progressed, Caroe had an 'odd sense of watching the unfolding of a new act in a Greek tragedy on the old theme of hubris followed by nemesis.'[17]

'I have never met Nehru before our meeting last week in Delhi, but had always heard of his attractions. But in the eyes of many one feels that his charm must be overlaid by his intellectual arrogance, and I could not help noticing how like he is to his friend Madame Chiange Kai Shek [sic] [the First Lady of the Republic of China, the wife of former President Chiang Kai-shek] in a sense during his visit here he showed courage, but it was courage better described as bravado, with something feminine in its composition,'[18] is how Caroe described Nehru's persona.

Till the autumn of 1946, League leaders had been persuaded directly and indirectly to desist from entering tribal territories and appealing on communal lines. Implied was a fear that the Congress too would follow the League into this area with moneybags. Until the political parties came together in the Constituent Assembly, Caroe did not want the tribes to entertain them; sane advice, no doubt. The implication of Nehru's appointment as Foreign Member, that carried with it the responsibility of tribal affairs, was not understood by the tribes at first. But it did not take long for the Muslim League to exploit the situation. The League sent its emissaries, particularly the Pir of Manki Sharif, into the tribal territory.[19] Caroe initially did consider the idea of restraining the mullah by arresting him but then shied away from risking an open challenge. The League intensified its propaganda among the tribes as soon as it became known that Nehru was coming to the Frontier. At their express behest, the Pir of Manki Sharif toured the tribal areas, his tour preceding that of Nehru. Caroe admitted to a good deal of fanaticism being stirred as a consequence of Manki's tour. Some concerned Political Agents and a few level-headed tribesmen had striven to persuade the mullah against entering tribal territory but had failed. Given the fact that Nehru's tour was intended to push the Congress cause, Caroe thought it wrong to put active restraints against the League's propagandists entering tribal territory.[20]

Knowing that Nehru might face a hostile reception in the NWFP, Caroe wanted Chief Minister Dr Khan Saheb to go to Miran Shah and oversee arrangements. He even arranged for special air transport to facilitate the trip, but Dr Khan Saheb, for reasons known only to him, remained indifferent to this idea. In Caroe's opinion, an advance visit by Dr Khan Saheb to Miran Shah would have definitely helped. Caroe had pointed out to Wavell that he was anxious to give Dr Khan Saheb and his people a fair run in the field.[21]

When Nehru arrived at Peshawar airport, he was greeted by a large unfriendly crowd of League demonstrators. The situation turned ugly, obliging him to slip out through a rear exit. The Political Department was publicly accused by Ghaffar Khan—an accusation subsequently endorsed by Meher Chand Khanna, Caroe's Hindu minister—of having staged the demonstration. This prompted the Governor to observe: 'I cannot imagine that even Congressmen in their hearts believed the charge. What they want is to pass on the blame for the hostile reception from themselves, and to find an excuse to sweep away the present methods of control on the Frontier. Nobody of any other persuasion does more than laugh at the assertion...British and foreign pressmen saw through these tactics from the beginning.'[22]

The next day Nehru visited Waziristan, Miranshah (a town in north Waziristan) and Razmak, where he received a generally cold reception from tribal leaders. These chiefs were not part of any *jirga* but had been selected on the basis of tradition and family. It did not help that Ghaffar Khan kept reminding them that they had been slaves soon to be set free. Nehru lost his temper once or twice, further enraging the Pathans. He and his party did not understand that a 'steady quiet bearing turning off to a smile or joke when tempers got frayed' was the proper way to deal with them. Caroe felt that the tribesmen were greatly upset to see a Hindu coming down to talk to them from a position of authority. They curtly told Nehru that 'they regarded Hindus as *hamsayas* (their tenants or serfs), and would have no dealings with them'. Enough cause for provocation was given by Nehru who called the tribesmen 'pitiful pensioners' to their faces, something which the allowance holders considered an abuse and a slight. A rumour that the Congress might stop allowances embittered the tribesmen further.[23]

Nehru's decision to journey north by road caused Caroe great anxiety. The situation in the Khyber was alarming. The strongest amongst the Khyber tribes, the Afridis, refused to meet Nehru. The Political Agent of Khyber spent an entire day segregating a large number of armed tribesmen at Jamrud to avoid an untoward incident. It was by sheer luck that Nehru's party got through the pass. But on the way back from the Afghan frontier, near Landi Kotal, Nehru's convoy was stoned by crowds; a collection of Afridis, Shinwaris and Ningraharis who were provoked enough by Manki Mullah's visit preceding Nehru's. Caroe was in no doubt that the Muslim League had a hand in this. Had it not been for the Khyber Rifles, who intervened by opening fire, the situation could have turned ugly for Nehru.[24]

Next on Nehru's itinerary was Malakand. He had wisely given up on the idea of visiting Shabquadar where the situation was not peaceful. Caroe depended on the Indian Political Agent to manage the situation at Malakand but he failed him. Nehru had to face angry demonstrations at two points on this visit at Malakand and Dargai. At Dargai, Nehru, Dr Khan Saheb and Ghaffar Khan could only escape after firing was resorted to, to avoid disaster. The party would normally have returned via Mardan and Naushera. But the Deputy Commissioner, Mardan, who had gone ahead to find the road blocked by angry crowds, with great difficulty and overriding Dr Khan Saheb's bravado, managed to persuade Nehru to return via Charsada instead. There was no doubt that these protests were organized by the Muslim League, but the protestors were unarmed and carried only black flags. However, their stone-throwing certainly made the crowd dangerous.[25]

The Frontier Congress prepared a fine show for Nehru when he visited Ghaffar Khan's ashram at Sardaryab (20 km north of Peshawar on Charsadda road). Khudai Khidmatgars from all over gathered to line up Nehru's route. The League intended holding a counter-demonstration, a dangerous prospect, for Caroe then expected a pitched battle between rival armies. Luckily, the League called off the demonstration at the last moment, perhaps because of numerical weakness or Caroe's pleas conveyed to Jinnah through Wavell.[26]

Police, constabulary guards and troops had been pressed into service during Nehru's tour in the north of the province. The situation became so precarious at the end of the tour that Nehru could not venture outside the cantonment of Peshawar without strong police and troop escort. The situation for Frontier ministers was no different. This was in stark contrast to the journeys Caroe made, entirely without escort. Caroe was objective in his assertion that without the help of the police and the troops, Nehru's visit might well have been a complete disaster.[27]

The Congress's relations with Caroe and the Political Department were not cordial. Congress leaders blamed the officials for all that had gone wrong during Nehru's tour. In the absence of any such acrimony with the League, the officials were accused of using the League's organization to make the Congress' position in the province untenable. Caroe found these charges malicious and vehemently refuted them. It was not long ago, he said, when the Pir of Manki Sharif, a League supporter, had threatened to shoot the Governor if he was only allowed by Jinnah to do so.[28]

On Caroe's request Nehru met him on the last day of his NWFP tour. Caroe observed that Nehru had bruises on his ear and chin, though he was not badly hurt. Nehru made no general charges against the Political Agents but accused the subordinate Indian officials of machinations against him. He specifically picked on the Political Agents of Khyber and Malakand (both Indians) and the Deputy Commissioners of Peshawar and Mardan, indicting them for their inefficiency and inability to prevent demonstrations. Caroe curtly told Nehru that he resented attacks on officers who had been subjected to immense strain by his untimely tour.

He also informed him that the party approach to the tribal problem was bound to fail, and that the visit could not have come at a worse time. If Nehru had gone around quietly without losing his temper and making the tribes feel that he was their guest, he would certainly have been received politely. But taking politicians like Abdul Ghaffar Khan with him had proved fatal. He should have taken care to include representatives from other parties in his entourage.[29] Nehru responded with a tirade against the League, strongly asserting that it was not his wont to desert old friends. Caroe then received a lecture on 'the authoritarian habits of the ICS'.[30] He reacted by stating that 'in his experience both League and the Congress were far more authoritarian than any ICS officer had ever been for they [the political parties] had a tendency to override law when in power.'[31] He candidly observed that Nehru's visit had put paid to any hopes of bringing the tribes peacefully into the new India. The visit, he felt, had unfortunately heightened communal feelings and strengthened a party approach to the Frontier, also weakening the ministry's position.

A colonial civil servant, Caroe favoured status quo while Nehru leaned towards an enlightened style and a far greater role for the popular ministry. The current system of governance for Nehru was more that of 'romancing the Frontier'.[32] Caroe had remonstrated with Wavell 'that this politician of world wide [sic] repute [Nehru] was entirely without any element of statesmanship, and that matters such as timing, adjustment, a quiet approach and a decision after weighing a great issue were beyond his ken.'[33] Nehru's visit considerably diluted Wavell's efforts at getting a coalition government in place in Delhi. Retention of Nehru or any other Hindu in charge of tribal affairs portended trouble. Caroe and his officials had been told by the tribes that they would have none of him (Nehru).[34]

Nehru was bitter about the conduct of the Malakand Political Agent and wanted him enquired against. Caroe, however, favoured a 'full dress' enquiry[35] by an independent tribunal. Since the charges were grave, Caroe ensured that the officer, in public interest, was given every chance to defend himself. In January 1947, Justice R. Clark, a Judge of the Madras High Court, was appointed by the Government of India to conduct a judicial enquiry. In his report of 28 February, Justice Clark exonerated Sheikh Mehbub Ali, the Political Agent of Malakand.[36] This incensed Nehru no end.

Caroe had consistently advised Nehru to discourage the tendency of the Pathan tribes seeking political alignments. He believed that a policy aiming to stir up class or economic rivalry could rebound. To Caroe, the real genius of the Pathan lay in a nationalism of his own and if that nationalism got aligned to India without the tribal body politic being tampered with, much could be done to achieve a stable equilibrium. He thought it equally dangerous to appeal to religious intolerance. Another piece of prudent advice that he gave Nehru was to dissociate from the general criticism of Political Officers.[37]

An Advisory Committee of the Constituent Assembly on tribal and excluded areas was to tour the NWFP. Caroe did not favour this idea. He implored Wavell to dissuade Nehru from sending the committee. He feared this would provoke Jinnah into sending one of his own. He wanted this deferred till an all-party committee was set up.[38] Weightman, the Foreign Secretary, broadly in agreement with Caroe, well realized that flat opposition to the committee's visit would only harden Nehru's resolve. He suggested, therefore, that Nehru be dispassionately explained the consequences of the committee's visit and if he saw reason in it, the visit could be postponed.[39]

Caroe considered demoralization in police ranks as an inevitable process associated with all Congress governments. But in the case of the NWFP, the real rot, according to him, had set in with Nehru's visit. Most Muslim government servants increasingly came to perceive Dr Khan Saheb's ministry to be dominated by Hindus. The action taken against Malakand's Political Agent Mehbub Ali and a few others worsened matters. 'The continual diatribes of that idiot Ghaffar Khan'[40] exasperated Caroe.

As a result of the Muslim League's Direct Action campaign, most of the opposition was in jail. This was the situation that existed on the eve of the assembly session commencing 10 March 1947. Caroe at this juncture wanted the provincial government to seek a fresh mandate. He believed that the numerical position in the assembly was not reflective of the correct situation. The minorities (non-Muslims) in the NWFP had a 25 per cent share in the legislature, though their population percentage was less than 8 per cent.[41] Caroe wanted Dr Khan Saheb to ascertain afresh whether a majority of the Pathans still backed him. In March 1947, there appeared to be a shift away from the Congress when it lost the Mardan by-election. The Direct Action campaign had since rejuvenated the Frontier League. The communal atmosphere too had deteriorated in Hazara and Punjab. A recent case of the conversion of a Sikh girl had done much to polarize the Hindus and Muslims in the province. League processions, picketing of courts and public buildings and defying ban orders under Section 144 CrPC had become daily occurrences. Though most of the League leaders were in jail under bailable offences when the assembly began on 10 March, they refused to obtain freedom by offering security.[42]

The Muslim League organized a procession towards the assembly house on 10 March. In the melee and the police firing that ensued, fifteen of the League's supporters sustained injuries, two of them succumbing to them. In the resultant backlash, seventeen Hindus were stabbed in Peshawar on the same day and curfew was imposed. Instead of the government being targeted, the ire of the people fell on Hindus. The reason for this was the people's perception of the government, which they felt was controlled by Hindus. Gurudwaras were burnt in Hazara, Sikhs murdered, and people forced to convert. Large demonstrations took place in Mardan, Bannu, Kohat and Dera Ismail Khan. Caroe became weary of the deteriorating situation, more so if the 'Congress acted foolish enough to send the Advisory Committee of the Constituent Assembly to enquire into the tribal problems or interfere in other ways.'[43]

The letter that Mountbatten received immediately upon his arrival in India helps us to understand Caroe's attitude. Caroe considered it unnatural for the Congress to be in power in the NWFP: 'Here are we between the storm-ridden Punjab on one side and the tribes on the other and in the strange position of having a Congress Government which has, or had, a considerable Muslim backing. But the influence of the North Western Punjab to the east and the tribes to the West all declaiming against Hindu Sikh domination, I think is certain to squeeze the Congress out before long, for Congress is not natural here.'[44] A shift in balance would have long taken place had the League leaders been comparable in stature to the Khan brothers. The attitude of the tribes was beginning to crystallize under the leadership of the Afridis. Any attempt to send an Advisory Committee was sure to be boycotted by the tribes.[45] They were unlikely to submit to any local control that remotely appeared dominated by Hindus. With the situation worsening, Caroe curtailed the budget session.[46]

Nehru wanted to visit the NWFP again in March 1947. On being advised against it by Wavell, he held Caroe indirectly responsible for scuttling his tour. In his last letter of 19 March to the outgoing Viceroy,

Nehru asked for Caroe's retirement. He was also forthright enough to share this letter with Caroe. That Nehru had asked for Caroe's retirement was generally kept a secret. Without hurriedly conceding to Nehru's request, Mountbatten, the new Viceroy, asked for time to consider the matter.

Immediately after taking over as India's Viceroy, Mountbatten sent Lord Ismay to the NWFP to assess the situation. It was a short visit. Any assessment could at best be based only on the inputs provided by Caroe. Mountbatten's suggestion to HMG for holding a fresh election in the NWFP was a result of Caroe's briefing to Ismay.

Caroe had not only found it difficult to get along with Nehru and Dr Khan Saheb, even his own Chief Secretary, Lieutenant Colonel de la Fargue, was not favourably disposed towards him. When Mountbatten met de la Fargue on 11 April and broached the subject of Nehru's request for Caroe's retirement, the Chief Secretary did not mince his words: 'Although the Governor was a man with great knowledge of the Frontier, he was in fact biased against his Congress Government and had lost the confidence of all fair minded people in the province... the Governor's continuation in office was in fact a menace to British prestige.'[47] All was not well between the Chief Secretary and the Governor—that de la Fargue had proceeded on leave when important decisions regarding the NWFP were yet to be taken was no mere coincidence. He only rejoined on 31 July, by which time the referendum in the NWFP had been held and the results announced.

The India and Burma Committee gave due diligence to a letter from Caroe that provided an analysis of the situation in tribal areas. This letter was taken up for discussion in London on 11 April. Referring mainly to the Afridis of Khyber, Caroe had tried to emphasize that they considered any interference by Nehru as 'Hindu' and regarded the Muslim League to be a representative of Muslim India. The letter inferred that the Afridis, who felt much closer to Afghanistan, could easily tilt away from India if ever a need arose. The old adage, 'what Afridis said today, the rest of the tribes would say tomorrow'[48] troubled Caroe so much that he immediately brought this to the notice of HMG. The Afridis were not prepared to deal with any Advisory Committee, be it of the Congress or the League. They wanted it understood that the Muslim League was representative only of Muslim India. If it ever came

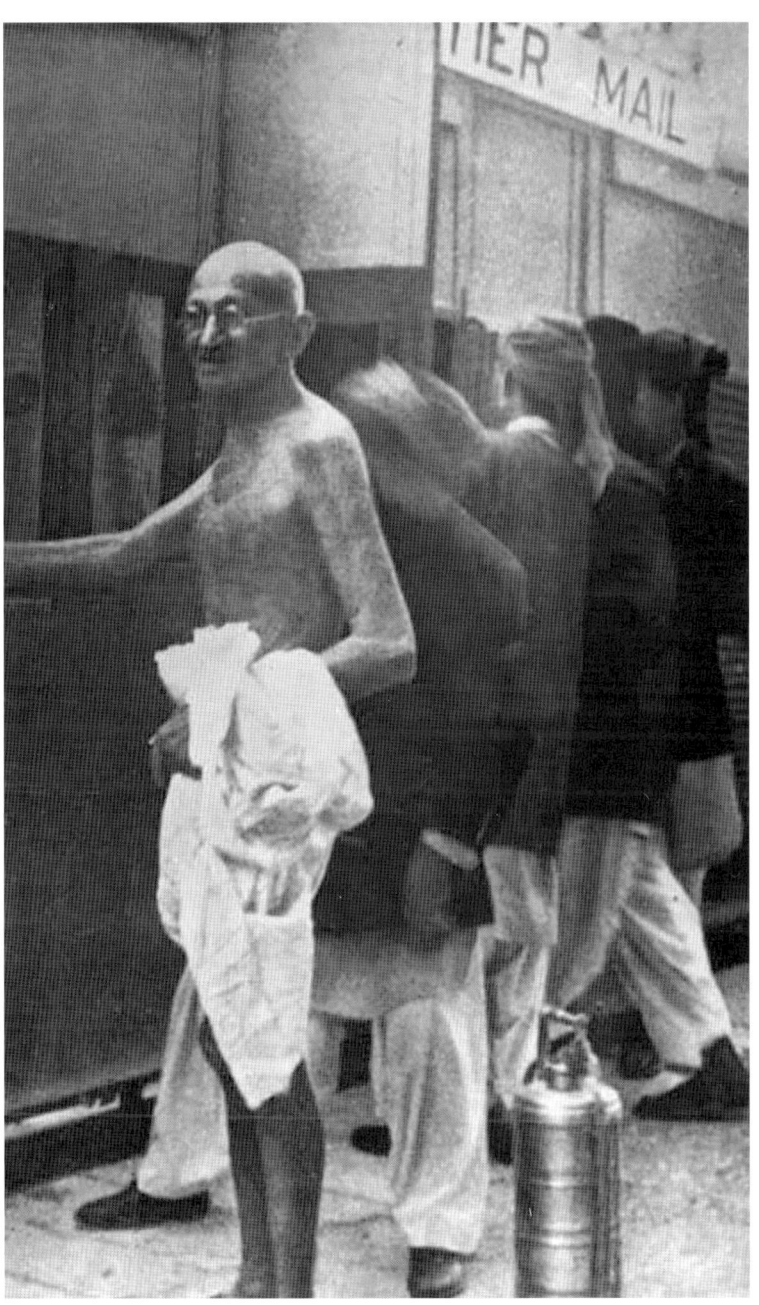
*Gandhi on a train journey to the NWFP on the Frontier Mail.*

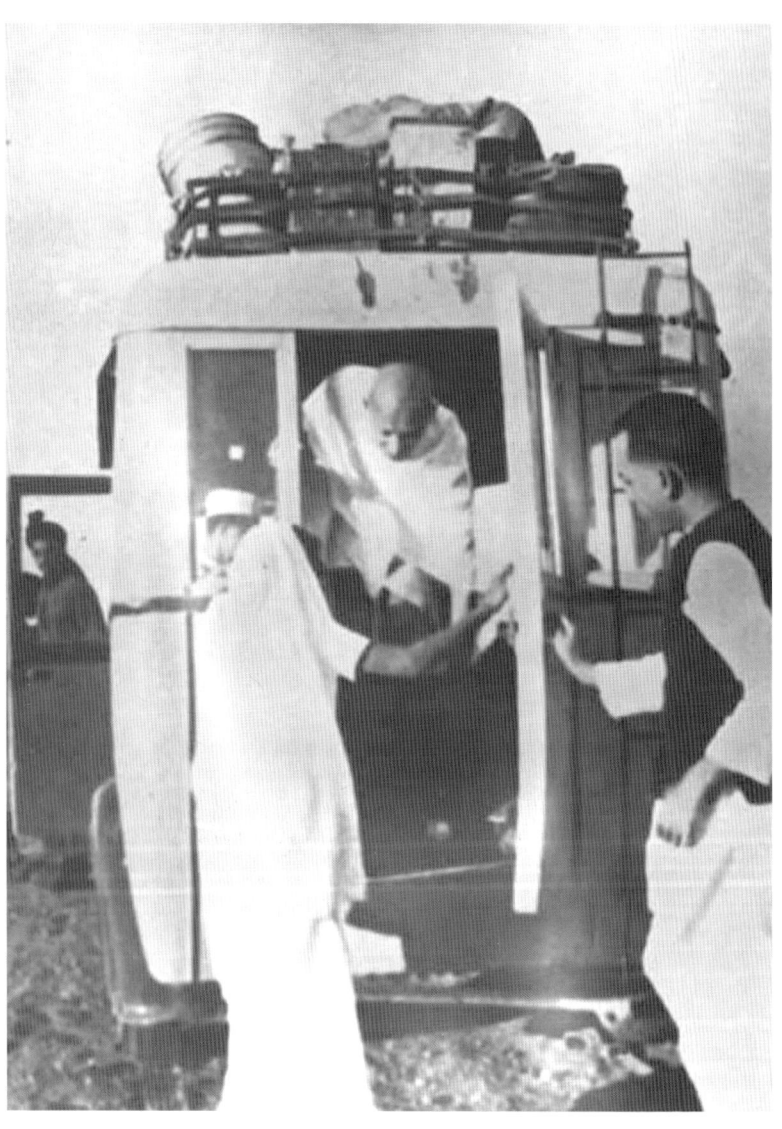

*Gandhi alighting from the vehicle given to the Frontier Congress for propaganda work in the NWFP.*

*Mahatma Gandhi with Dr Khan Saheb on his way to a meeting at the Governor's house, Peshawar, May 1938.*

*Mahatma Gandhi addressing a public meeting in the presence of Khan Abdul Ghaffar Khan in Peshawar, May 1938.*

*Mahatma Gandhi with Khan Abdul Ghaffar Khan during his visit to the North West Frontier Province, October 1938.*

*Mahatma Gandhi with the Nawab of Dera Ismail Khan, during his visit to the North West Frontier Province, 29 October, 1938.*

*Gandhi with the Red Shirts, 1938.*

*Secretary of State for India, Lord Pethick-Lawrence, who headed the three-member Cabinet Delegation to India, welcoming Badshah Khan at the Viceregal Lodge, Shimla, 1946.*

*Dr Khan Saheb, Chief Minister of NWFP, with members of the British Parliamentary delegation visiting Peshawar in early 1946.*

*Dr Khan Saheb with his Finance Minister, Mehar Chand Khanna, standing with an umbrella.*

*At the start of his NWFP visit in October 1946, Nehru was greeted by a large unfriendly crowd at Peshawar airport. Nehru had, perforce, to be whisked away.*

*Nehru in a Chitrali cap during his October 1946 visit to the NWFP.*

*Badshah Khan, the Frontier Gandhi.*

*Nehru's convoy was heckled, his aircraft sniped at and his car stoned while in the NWFP in October 1946. He needed constant escorting by the army and uniformed personnel during his visit.*

At Wana, NWFP, during his October 1946 visit, where Nehru was to meet the Wazir tribesmen who had lined up to wave black flags. Waiting for Nehru to arrive, they grew restive. An infantry company was deployed, which annoyed them. They refused to participate in the jirga that Nehru was to attend. Nehru had to leave Wana without meeting the tribesmen.

Nehru and Dr Khan Saheb look disturbed in this photograph taken during Nehru's NWFP visit of October 1946.

*During a fracas outside Landi Kotal, a bullet fired by an NWFP tribesman passed within an inch or two of Nehru while he was sitting in the car. Notice the broken windshield of Nehru's car.*

*Sir Olaf Caroe, second from the left. He had no love lost for Dr Khan Saheb, Nehru and Badshah Khan, standing with him.*

*Badshah Khan with Subhas Chandra Bose, who does not look in the best of health.*

*Nehru and his daughter, Indira, with Jinnah's sister, Fatima.*

*Badshah Khan in discussion with Madan Mohan Malviya.*

*Dr Khan Saheb and his English wife, Mary Khan Saheb, with Nehru. Dr Khan Saheb and his wife were both socially very close to Governor Sir George Cunningham and his family. They often dined and played bridge together. The cordiality between Mrs Mary Khan Saheb and Lady Cunningham was considerably commented upon in the local press.*

*Pensive-looking members of the Congress Working Committee which took the decision on the partition of the Punjab in 1947.*

*Lord Mountbatten, India's last British Viceroy.*

*Badshah Khan, taking oath in the Pakistan Constituent Assembly in Karachi in 1948.*

*Badshah Khan, Nehru, his daughter, Indira, and Sheikh Abdullah. Notice the closed left fist of Ghaffar Khan as he keeps his hands consciously away from the lady.*

*Khan Abdul Ghaffar Khan with his son, Abdul Ghani, at Dar-ul-Aman, Kabul, May 1955.*

to a choice, they would much rather align with Afghanistan.[49] They had expressed surprise at the British Prime Minister's announcement of 20 February 1947 which made no mention of the tribes. They expected the British to hand over Khyber Pass to them, and not to the Hindu Congress or the Muslim League. They preferred to negotiate the use of Khyber Pass with others on their own terms.[50] Caroe's letter was an unambiguous recommendation to the British cabinet to consider a third option for the NWFP and not to see it merge with India or Pakistan. He did not leave matters hanging at his end. He wanted the tribes to be given a chance to decide their own fate. The British cabinet considered Caroe's letter important enough for discussion while deciding on the NWFP's fate.

In mid-April, Governors were called by the Viceroy for a conference in Delhi. Here again Caroe reiterated how precarious the Punjab situation was and that it could further worsen if the Frontier became restive. He thought the situation akin to 1897 when, in a rare display of tribal unity, the whole of the Frontier had rebelled against the British.[51] Both Ismay and Caroe considered fresh elections an imminent necessity. For them a Congress government in the NWFP was more of an anachronism. To Ismay, who had coined a rather curious phrase, a 'bastard situation' needed correction. Sir Evan Jenkins, the Punjab Governor, went a step further in suggesting that the NWFP legislature be dissolved without dismissing the provincial ministry.[52]

During deliberations in Delhi, Caroe kept the Viceroy informed of Afghanistan's interests in negotiating directly with the tribes on the Indian side of the Durand Line: 'This was welcomed by the tribes, and was a further sign of disintegration on the Frontier.'[53] Caroe's views on the issue of 'Tribal Areas' were at variance with Weightman's. India's Foreign Secretary did not favour a policy of status quo till the transfer of power was effected in June 1948.[54] Leaving the tribes to negotiate later with the future dispensation would only make matters difficult for the new governments. The Foreign Secretary's views were more in sync with Nehru's, not Caroe's.

Strangely, in a one-to-one meeting with the Viceroy, Caroe was full of assurances on the issue of tribes—expecting little trouble from them for some time, as they were busy preparing for a situation when the British left. The League's propaganda and Direct Action campaign were proving a headache for Dr Khan Saheb and the Congress. As long as the trouble caused by the tribes was directed towards the Congress, there was no cause for worry. Caroe was confident of the control he exerted over the prominent tribes.

Mountbatten personally got a chance during the Delhi meeting to forewarn Caroe about the grudge that Congress members of the interim government bore towards him. If they were to make his position completely untenable, Mountbatten would be left with no option but to replace him. If it ever came to that, Mountbatten promised to do it in as friendly a spirit as possible. Though he sympathized with Caroe's predicament, the writing on the wall was clear. Mountbatten was ready to buckle under Congress pressure.[55]

The NWFP had a higher ratio of British officials compared to other provinces. That he could not count on the presence of any military officer staying in the NWFP later than 1 January 1948 worried Caroe. He, therefore, asked for the dates of the withdrawal of the uniformed officials to be adjusted accordingly. Little did he know then that the final date for the British transfer of power would be advanced by ten months. Notwithstanding the situation in the NWFP, Caroe wanted the arms of the British administration to be in place in full strength till they finally withdrew.[56]

The Governors' conference recommended a general election in the NWFP as soon as it was feasible for the British to make an announcement on their withdrawal plan. The Viceroy hoped to make such an announcement within a month. Caroe wanted to use the prevailing situation in the tribal areas as a lever to extract a compromise on the lines of the Cabinet Mission plan. It frustrated him to see that the 'powers that be' failed to appreciate the strategic importance of the tribal areas while deciding the fate of the NWFP. The Prime Minister's announcement had made absolutely no mention of the Frontier. Caroe wanted recognition of subventions that helped the province exist.[57] It would bolster his position if the government paid heed to his recommendations in the shortly-to-be-made announcement by HMG. Caroe favoured dissolution of the provincial assembly but retention of the ministry to oversee elections. Appearing neutral, he professed that the Congress position would be strengthened if it came back to power in the NWFP. On the other hand, if the League won, it would be more moderate and less inclined to push for a partition plan.⁵⁸

A mere public announcement of elections, Caroe believed, would greatly ease the tension. It would bring to the fore the pan-Indian importance of the Frontier. The opposition leaders would also stand released. Caroe preferred to deal with the resultant disturbances of an election rather than risk large emotional processions organized by the Muslim League. A compromise, on the lines of the Cabinet Mission plan, was far more attainable. If the Muslim League won the elections, they would be less inclined to push for a partition plan. In hindsight, an early announcement could still retrieve prospects for a Congress win, despite the worsening communal situation. The Viceroy differed over the issue of 'immediate announcement of election'.⁵⁹ He believed it would fog the main issue of policy announcement by HMG on British withdrawal from India. The announcement would definitely annoy the Congress too.⁶⁰

Caroe did not like the idea of the Afghan government negotiating directly with the tribes. Heeding to Caroe, the Viceroy directed George Abell, his Private Secretary, to ensure that any answer sent by the Government of India on Afghan requests was to have the Viceroy's prior approval.⁶¹

Around mid-April riots broke out in Dera Ismail Khan, the wealthiest town in the Frontier with a roughly fifty-fifty Hindu-Muslim population.

The situation being communally sensitive, it was easy for the Muslim League to precipitate it. Caroe was asked to stay in Delhi, though he had intended to meet General Frank Messervy at Rawalpindi on his way back to discuss the worsening situation in Dera Ismail Khan.⁶² While the riots raged, even the Chief Minister was summoned from Peshawar, leaving the province completely at the mercy of the officials.

In Caroe's opinion there had been a substantial swing in people's sentiments against the present government in the last one year. The tribes who had remained quiet were now busy organizing themselves, something hitherto not seen by Caroe in all his years in the Frontier.⁶³ The parallel that he drew from Punjab seemed to support his contention. The Unionist Party, for long in power, had been swept out of existence during the 1946 Punjab elections. And within a year, in March 1947, the

Unionist Chief Minister of Punjab, Khizar Hayat Tiwana,[64] was forced to resign. Though Punjab was put under Governor's rule, Caroe did not favour it, instead preferring fresh elections and a popular government thereafter.[65] He was also against arresting the Pir of Manki Sharif, as he believed him to be more of a nuisance behind bars than outside. The Pir's arrest had the effect of uniting the tribes against Dr Khan Saheb's government. Though the Governor wrongly maintained that the Pir had not been stirring up trouble, after his arrest the Pir's followers were undoubtedly responsible for causing disturbances. Nehru did not concur with Caroe on the Pir's issue for there was enough evidence of the Manki Pir openly advocating methods other than peaceful. It was wishful thinking on Caroe's part to hope that once released, the Pir of Manki could be brought to bear influence on the side of communal harmony.[66]

With important decisions still pending, Mountbatten did not allow Caroe to return after the Governors' Conference. Instead he sent for Dr Khan Saheb to come to Delhi. The meeting on 18 April, which Dr Khan Saheb, Caroe, Nehru and Mountbatten attended, has been dealt with in considerable detail in the chapter on Nehru. The confabulations were followed by a trip by Mountbatten to the NWFP on 28 April, described adequately in the chapter on India's last Viceroy. Upon his return from the NWFP, Mountbatten wrote to the Secretary of State, Lord Listowel, that it was not in their interest to retain Caroe in the face of bitter opposition from the Congress. Mountbatten was now preparing the ground to ease Caroe out. In passing reference, he also mentioned to Listowel that Caroe was showing signs of great strain 'under which any man in his position must suffer'.[67] On 3 May Mountbatten announced in his staff meeting that 'if Caroe did have to resign, it would be with complete honour.'[68] Ismay, who was then in London, was asked to follow up on Caroe's replacement with Listowel.[69] In the interim, an agitation had broken out in the 'Hindu press' calling for Caroe's resignation. Things reached such a pass that a call for an 'anti-Caroe day' was given, and observed, in Delhi.[70] Personal attacks against Caroe did not cease despite Mountbatten's protestations to Nehru. Rather, on Nehru's behest, two senior Congress leaders, the General Secretary of the party, Acharya Jugal Kishore, and Diwan Chaman Lal, issued a lengthy statement on the NWFP that appeared in all prominent Delhi newspapers under headlines such as 'NWFP Governor must be recalled'.[71] Pressure against Caroe was thus building up. Mountbatten asked Ismay to get Lockhart's name as Caroe's replacement cleared from Listowel.[72] Ismay was reluctant to do Mountbatten's bidding until a formal official intimation to Listowel was sent from the Viceroy giving details of the date of relief, reasons, etc. Only then would Ismay follow this up at his end.[73] Mountbatten hesitated in sending an official telegram, especially at a time when the 'anti-Caroe' agitation was at its peak. But his mind was made up. He asked Ismay to forewarn Listowel of his impending request and unofficially obtain agreement on Lockhart's appointment. Mountbatten was yet to decide on the possible excuse he would proffer as a reason for Caroe's removal.[74]

Through May, Peshawar, Dera Ismail Khan and Bannu continued to be seriously disturbed. The government had announced a general amnesty but the imprisoned League leaders in the NWFP were refusing to take advantage of this. Caroe wanted them forced out of jail but Mountbatten would not accede. Having consulted Nehru, Mountbatten asked for a clear warning to be issued that anyone found not taking advantage of the amnesty within a certain time limit was liable to be re-imprisoned. Special facilities extended to political prisoners would stand withdrawn and those uncooperative would be transferred to other provinces. Reporting to Mountbatten, Caroe had mentioned that political prisoners in Peshawar jail, while accepting deprivation in default of going out under amnesty, had demurred on withdrawal of their 'charpoys' (from the Punjabi word '*charpai*').

Caroe took the issue of private armies in the NWFP seriously. The Khudai Khidmatgars openly flaunted weapons while serving as armed escorts for some Congress leaders. Abdul Ghani, one of Ghaffar Khan's sons, organized a new armed outfit called Zalme Pakhtun. The League also set up its own armed organization. To Caroe, the situation that existed was strange, as the government of the day had two armed organizations: one, a sort of 'corps de chite' (its SS) which was acknowledged to be armed, and another, the Red Shirts (its SA) also known to be widely armed. In some cases, the weapons were licensed, but Caroe believed that Dr Khan Saheb issued licences without discretion. For Caroe this was ample cause for worry: 'How are we to hold any form of referendum or election with the Private Armies going up and down the country?' The logical course, no doubt, was to declare Zalme Pakhtun unlawful but that would have to be done by the provincial government.[75]

Caroe had even suggested forming a coalition government in the NWFP.But this drew a furious response from his ministry and from Ghaffar Khan. The coalition, Caroe said, would be based on the notion of a Pathan National Province. Appealing to the people on these lines could be more constructive than the communal cry of 'Islam in danger'. The Pathans till yet had been too divided to set up a stable state. Caroe did not consider Afghanistan a true Pathan state. His open support and preference for a Pathan National Province did not endear him either to Nehru or Mountbatten, as both were against granting the NWFP an independent status.[76] But locally in the province, efforts were on to form a coalition government. The proposal was to co-opt Frontier League leaders like Abdul Qayyum Khan and Samin Jan into the provincial government. Both had been Congressmen at one time. To scuttle this plan, another faction of the Provincial League sent representatives to convince Jinnah against such a prospect.[77] Caroe's urgings for a 'coalition' proved ineffective.[78] The British withdrawal plan was soon announced on 3 June. As part of that, the NWFP was to hold a referendum on the subject of joining India or Pakistan. There was no third choice of an autonomous state for the Pathans. The absence of a third option forced the Khudai Khidmatgars to boycott the referendum. After speaking to members of the NWFP ministry—Qazi Ataullah and Meher Chand Khanna—Caroe informed Mountbatten on 4 June that they had decided against joining Hindustan.[79] For them the issue was to either join an independent Pathanistan or the new Constituent Assembly of Pakistan. If the option of an independent Pathanistan was not given, the Khudai Khidmatgars (they did not refer to themselves as the Congress anymore) would decline to take part in the referendum. The Khudai Khidmatgars envisaged a separate Constituent Assembly for the NWFP.[80] Caroe had intimated to the members of his ministry that the issue of whether the NWFP could stand alone had been considered in detail before the 3 June announcement. It was impossible to review the decision. Presuming Dr Khan Saheb did not differ with his ministers, Caroe was certain that

Mountbatten would not be able to carry through the referendum in the absence of ministerial collaboration.[81] On 5 June Caroe recommended the inclusion of the third option of Pathanistan in the referendum, as the Chief Secretary and other senior officials of the province were convinced that it would help in holding a peaceful referendum.[82] The third option would also secure ministerial cooperation. Caroe referred to a press interview of 4 June by Mountbatten wherein he appeared willing to consider the Pathanistan issue if all political parties agreed to it. But he knew well that there was little chance of the League agreeing to a separate Pathanistan. Further, a decision in favour of a third option on Pathanistan was bound to upset a large measure of agreements already secured between political parties on an all-India basis. Even then Caroe wanted that those in favour of Pathanistan should oppose the referendum, for therein lay the rationale for a rethink on this issue. Caroe believed that there were numerous sincere supporters of Pathanistan and many among Jinnah's local supporters were also sympathetic to this idea.[83]

Instead, Caroe was summarily informed by Mountbatten on 6 June that 'for the moment at any rate he would be replaced as the Governor of NWFP, but while taking this grave step no possible injury would be caused to him and doors to his further employment in India would not be closed if Caroe was to so desire.'[84] Mountbatten proposed that Caroe should go on leave as soon as a temporary successor for him was arranged and should remain on leave until 15 August or till such a date as the two new governments were in a position to select new provincial Governors. If the NWFP opted for Pakistan then there was likelihood of Caroe getting reappointed. If Caroe agreed to the proposed course, it would strengthen Mountbatten vis-à-vis the Congress. In case Caroe remained the Governor and the Congress lost the referendum, accusations would be hurled at him for facilitating the League to win. Caroe's relinquishing charge did not foreclose the option of future employment.[85]

About a month earlier, on 9 May, Ismay and Sir David Monteath[86] had discussed the possibility of replacing Caroe with General Lockhart. Monteath was unable to provide a firm answer to Ismay on whether the Secretary of State for India would agree to it. Ismay shortly thereafter had left London. This issue now assumed urgency.

The Viceroy wanted to replace Caroe immediately. He was in no mood to wait till a future Government of Pakistan asked Caroe to resume governorship before he went on leave.[87] Somewhere in all this was a presumption that the Muslim League would win the referendum. Mountbatten moved to obtain the King's unofficial approval for Caroe's removal. Ismay wanted Jinnah informed of this impending change lest he react strongly. It was best to cite Caroe's failing health and nerves as a reason for his removal.

Caroe was gracious in response to Mountbatten's letter of 6 June. Agreeing on the issue of propriety of not continuing in his post lest accused of partisanship, Caroe contemplated writing to Mountbatten on this subject. He could not resist commenting about 'authoritarianism and maliciousness in high places' which he had always opposed.[88] This not-so-veiled-reference was to Nehru. As for the League assuming power in the NWFP, he felt it to be 'more in the tradition of things'.[89] It was not hidden from anyone that Caroe considered a Congress government in the NWFP unnatural. He was quite hurt because of the decision to replace him. He took leave but remained in India.

Caroe chose to remain in Kashmir during the initial period of leave. Liaquat Ali Khan protested strongly. He found the replacement of a prominent Governor 'an extraordinary and a dangerous step'.[90] He doubted whether in the absence of Caroe, the ministers would find it easy to abuse power. Liaquat therefore wanted the ministry also removed, now that the Governor had been replaced.[91]

Lord Listowel informed the Prime Minister of the likelihood of Caroe's removal as early as 12 May. A month later, he received a telegram from Ismay on 11 June which stated that 'the situation had become so urgent' that the Viceroy had decided to replace Caroe immediately.[92] Personally, Listowel was strongly opposed to the idea of Caroe resuming the governorship once he had relinquished it. Listowel moved to obtain the King's formal approval to allow the Viceroy to take immediate action regarding Caroe's replacement. Listowel also asked the Viceroy to induce Caroe to lay down office on medical grounds.[93]

To expedite matters, Mountbatten sent two drafts to Caroe—the first was the letter he expected Caroe to write to him and the second was to be his reply in response to Caroe's letter. Both the letters would then be published; they were rather like letters between ministers and the Prime Minister at home (Britain) when a change was made in the cabinet. The publication would be followed by an announcement that the King had appointed Lockhart to act.[94] Mountbatten wanted Lockhart to reach Peshawar by 24 June.[95] Caroe wrote to the Viceroy on the lines suggested. This communication was passed through as a telegram to Mountbatten on 13 June. Privately Mountbatten conceded that 'neither Ismay nor I [Mountbatten] feel his [Caroe's] nerves are in a fit state to stay under such conditions.'[96] Caroe suggested only some minor changes in the draft letter Mountbatten would write in response to his. He also informed Mountbatten about his plans to go to Kashmir briefly before leaving for Britain by mid-July.[97] Caroe wanted to be in India for a while, just to ascertain whether he finally needed to pack his bags or not.

Caroe asked for a two-month leave, suggesting an officiating Governor during his absence.[98] In view of the wider implications of the referendum—his presence would cause suspicion about its conduct—he preferred taking leave and letting someone else hold the post. Caroe clearly did not lay down the office of the Governor. He meant to return after the referendum. Ironically, it was on the same day, 13 June, when Caroe wrote to Mountbatten asking for leave, that Lord Listowel informed the Viceroy about the unsuitability of Caroe later resuming the post. Listowel believed that such an action would imply that the British themselves believed Caroe to be prejudiced in favour of the Muslim League and had therefore replaced him for the period of the referendum.[99] Ismay also received a letter from Sir David Monteath reflecting much the same sentiments. The King had given an informal approval for Lockhart to act in place of Caroe. The King had also granted Caroe a leave of absence. However, Monteath made it clear that henceforth no reference to the possibility of Caroe resuming the governorship after the referendum was to be made in their exchange of letters.[100] Both the Secretary of State and the Prime Minister were of the firm view that Caroe should resign and Lockhart's appointment be made substantive.[101] But it was too late for that. Caroe was to be induced to tender his resignation while on leave, after which Lockhart's acting appointment could be confirmed. Subsequent to the creation of Pakistan, if the Pakistan government was to ask Caroe to resume or be reappointed, then that situation would be entirely different.[102]

While replying to these communications on 16 June, Mountbatten readily concurred that 'there was no question of Caroe taking over again as Governor unless a recommendation in his favour was made by the Pakistan Government.'[103] To Caroe's letter of 13 June asking for two months' leave, Mountbatten responded after four days stating that he was recommending to HMG that Lockhart should be the acting Governor in the interim period. This letter, along with Caroe's, was published on 19 June.

The last letter that Caroe wrote to his Viceroy was on 23 June; he was to hand over charge in two days. Reflecting on times gone by, Caroe could not stop remarking: 'Most of our troubles started when Nehru took tribal affairs under his wings. Before that time the province was going along very nicely, all things considered, but it was an impossible thing to do to bring these tribes under a Pandit. Practically all our frictions and tensions date from that time.'[104] He made another oblique remark about the External Affairs Department in his final telegram of 25 June before demitting office. In it he referred to Afghan incursion in the Frontier's affairs. He believed that this was to some extent inspired by the provincial Congress leaders. He mentioned Ghaffar Khan's visit to Qashan, a small town in the USSR, north of the Afghan border. Moreover, Caroe believed that Gandhi too was wedded to the idea of Pathanistan, which would make it difficult for the External Affairs Department to approach the issue objectively. Caroe was mindful of the disturbing effects the arrival of an Afghan mission could have on the tribes.[105]

Caroe found it difficult to reconcile to British rule in the NWFP finally coming to an end. Aware of how strategically important the NWFP was, he was certain that the British government would not entirely break connections with 'this most delicate and difficult land frontier'. He also put up a stout defence for his junior colleague, the Political Agent of Malakand, in his last letter to the Viceroy:

> I must put in a final word about Mahbub Ali's case, I told Khan Saheb that we should have to show Mahbub Ali a copy of Clark's finding, and he did not demur. It is very unjust to leave an officer who has been exonerated after suspension and a departmental inquiry without an opportunity of seeing the findings exonerating

him. I could have given him the copy which I have here, but I did not think it right to do so without Nehru's authority. I must ask that, whether Nehru agrees or not, Mahbub Ali should be shown this document. It can be made clear to him that it is for his personal information only.[106]

The idea that a referendum should be held in the NWFP was not Caroe's. Mountbatten, having seriously toyed with the idea of holding fresh elections in the NWFP, eventually decided to hold a referendum after consulting Nehru. Mountbatten was to oversee its logistics. This he could do only with the help of the Indian Civil Service and army officials. Caroe by now had served his purpose in the NWFP and could clearly see his career in the Frontier coming to an end:

> You see, the price that had to be paid by Mountbatten for getting this referendum through was getting rid of me. Nehru thought I had thwarted him and that so long as I was in Peshawar, his Congress had no chance and that I was not giving sufficient support to Khan Saheb. His price for agreeing to Mountbatten's proposals for a referendum was that I must go. Well, in June, Mountbatten wrote to me and said, 'I am very sorry because I think you have done a marvellous job but the only way in which I can resolve this enigma is to ask you to take leave.'

How to sack a Governor on political grounds was the dilemma Mountbatten faced. That Nehru favoured the sacking made his task more difficult. The best Mountbatten could do was to extract an assurance from Nehru that Congress leaders would not publicly attack Caroe. Having got the assurance, he wrote to Caroe: 'The only thing I can ask you to do is to take leave. If as a result of the referendum the League gets back, I suppose you will be able to go back as Governor, but otherwise I do not know what will happen.' Caroe went on to explain:

> He [Mountbatten] was playing politics for very large stakes—the future of India if he could get Nehru to agree to the voice of the people being heard then it is arguable that it was worthwhile sacrificing one man. But it was a shock he said, 'in this particular case the whole future of India is at stake and I can do nothing else.' So we agreed that some military officers would be put in to run

the machinery of government while I went on leave, and I went on leave to Kashmir for a month waiting to see what would happen.

Caroe waited for a recall but in vain. With the Congress defeated and the Muslim League back in power, Caroe had contributed enormously to the founding of Pakistan, but Jinnah preferred to have the last days of British rule supervised not by Caroe but by his predecessor Cunningham. A disappointed Caroe retired to watch the final transition of power from his home in Sussex. He accepted his retirement gracefully.

Sir Norval Mitchell of the Indian Civil Service, and later of the Indian Political Service, has noted in his memoirs that Caroe, under whom he had served as Chief Secretary of the NWFP, was treated 'very casually' in the matter of his retirement. In a letter he wrote to Caroe on 23 September 1968, more than two decades after the drama of India's partition was over, he observed: 'I did not in fact know how badly you had been treated in 1947 until I read Sir George's Cunningham, Governor of the NWFP in 1937–46 and diaries, I...but distinctly remember a mention of the fact that Mountbatten's conduct in this respect was unpardonable. In all the circumstances, however, I thought it better to say nothing at all.'

A separate letter that Caroe received from Iskander Mirza of the Indian Political Service—who was also the first President of Pakistan (1956–58)—on 26 September 1968 expressed somewhat similar sentiments:

> The unhappy and dishonourable circumstances in 1946 and early 1947 in connection with your tenure as Governor of the NWFP bring back some very unhappy memories. There was no doubt in my mind that Lord Mountbatten was no friend of yours and he was guided more by Nehru than by anybody else. Lord Mountbatten wanted to keep Nehru happy and even before you went to Kashmir stories were going round that you had a nervous breakdown and required rest. But believe me there was no honour then or later. No other reason but health was given to sabotage you and I was quite helpless. Lord Mountbatten must have told Lord Ismay that you won't go back. Sir George Cunningham's return was a great surprise. I learnt later that he

was not at all willing to come back as Governor and pressure was put on him by no less a person than His Majesty King George VI.[107] But what did the politicians do to Sir George. Behind his back they pushed tribesmen into Kashmir. Sir George was about to resign in late 1947 and I had to beg of him not to do so. They got rid of a good friend like Mudie and installed that fanatic Nishtar as Governor. I don't think you should feel sorry. Knowing as I do you could not have stuck all those dishonourable intrigues so very rampant since the very inception of Pakistan.

It was on 15 July 1947 that Caroe received a communication from the Viceroy saying that his reappointment was not to be considered.

## Notes

1. Flora Annie Steel (1847–1929) was an English writer. She married a member of the Indian Civil Service in 1867. For the next twenty-two years she lived in India, mainly in Punjab. Most of her books are connected with Punjab. Some of her works are *From the Five Rivers*, *Tales of the Punjab* and *On the Face of the Waters*.
2. Interview, Sir Olaf Caroe, The Imperial War Museum, Department of Sound Records.
3. On 23 April 1930 the Indian army under British officers attempted to suppress a general strike in the city of Peshawar that a non-violent organization formed in the late 1920s had organized. For six hours between 11 a.m. and 5 p.m., Indian soldiers fired at unarmed civilians killing, as some estimates have it, 400 citizens. During this, at least one platoon of the Garhwal Rifles refused to fire. They were later all disarmed and court-martialled later.
4. H.A. Metcalfe, predecessor of Olaf Coroe. Caroe succeeded him as Deputy Commissioner of Peshawar.
5. L/P&J/5/337: pp.23–26, Penderel Moon (ed.) 28 March 1946, *The Transfer of Power* Vol. VII p.36.
6. Ibid.
7. Ibid., p.37.
8. Ibid.
9. Ibid.

10. Ibid.
11. Provinces with Muslim predominance.
12. *The Transfer of Power*, August 1946, Vol. VIII, pp.207–08.
13. Caroe to Viceroy Wavell, Telegram R/3/1/92: f 7, 29 September 1946 *The Transfer of Power* Vol. VIII, p.626.
14. Minutes by George Abell and Viceroy Wavell, R/3/1/92: f8 of 30 September 1946, *The Transfer of Power* Vol. VIII p.627.
15. At 5,600 feet, this is the headquarters of Kurram Agency, the Federally Administered Tribal Areas (FATA) of Pakistan. It is about 290 km west of the capital, Islamabad. It is situated on a neck of Pakistani territory south of Peshawar that juts into Paktia province in Afghanistan and is the closest point in Pakistan to Kabul and borders on the Tora Bora region in Afghanistan.
16. Caroe to Wavell, R/3/1/92: ff 48–54 of 23 October 1946, *The Transfer of Power*, Vol. VIII, p.786.
17. Ibid.
18. Ibid.
19. Ibid.
20. Ibid., p.787.
21. Ibid.
22. Ibid., pp.787–88.
23. Ibid., p.788.
24. Ibid., p.789.
25. Ibid.
26. Ibid., p.790.
27. Ibid.
28. Ibid.
29. Ibid., pp.790–91.
30. Ibid.
31. Ibid.
32. Ibid.
33. Ibid.
34. Ibid., p.792.
35. Caroe to Nehru, R/3/1/92: ff 147–50, 7 November 1946, *The Transfer of Power*, Vol. IX, p.21.
36. Ibid.
37. Ibid., p.22.

38. Caroe to Wavell, R/3/1/131: f 165, 8 February 1947, *The Transfer of Power*, Vol. IX, pp.651–52.
39. Weightman to Abell, R/3/1/131 ff 167–68, 15 February 1947, *The Transfer of Power*, Vol. IX, pp.723–24.
40. Caroe to Wavell, l/P&J/5/224: ff 79–80, Peshawar, 22 February 1947, *The Transfer of Power*, Vol. IX, pp.788–89.
41. Caroe to Wavell, L/P&J/5/224: ff 73–75, 8 March 1947, *The Transfer of Power*, Vol. IX, p.896.
42. Caroe to Wavell, Telegram, L/P&J/8/660: f 217, 13 March 1947, *The Transfer of Power*, Vol. IX, p.930.
43. Ibid., pp.930–31.
44. Caroe to Mountbatten, L/P&J/5/224: ff 68–69, 22 March 1947, *The Transfer of Power*, Vol. X, p.1.
45. Ibid.
46. Ibid., p.2.
47. Record of interview between Mountbatten and Lt. Col. De la Fargue, Mountbatten Papers, Viceroy's interview no 49, *The Transfer of Power*, March 1947, Vol. X, p.197.
48. Caroe to George Abell, 17 March 1947, *The Transfer of Power*, Vol. X, p.204.
49. *The Transfer of Power*, March 1947, Vol. X, p.206.
50. Ibid., p.206.
51. Record of Meeting between Lord Ismay, Sir Olaf Caroe, Sir Evan Jenkins, Sir Eric Mieville, Weightman (the Foreign Secretary of India) and George Abell on 14 April 1947, *The Transfer of Power*, Vol. X, p.233.
52. Ibid.
53. Ibid.
54. Ibid.
55. Record of interview between Sir Olaf Caroe and Mountbatten, Mountbatten Papers, Viceroy's interview No. 60, 14 April 1947, *The Transfer of Power*, Vol. X, pp.234–35.
56. *The Transfer of Power*, April 1947, Vol. X, p.249.
57. Ibid., p.252.
58. Ibid.
59. Ibid., p.253.
60. Ibid.
61. Ibid.

62. Minutes of Viceroy's Third Miscellaneous Meeting held in New Delhi on 16 April 1947, *The Transfer of Power*, Vol. X, p.286.
63. Ibid., p.287.
64. Nawab Sir Malik Khizar Hayat Tiwana (1900–1975) came from a family which had been prominent among the landed aristocracy of Punjab since the fifteenth century. He was elected to the Punjab Legislative Assembly in 1937 and joined the Unionist cabinet of Sir Sikander Hyat Khan. He later succeeded him as the Chief Minister of Punjab and remained in that post till March 1947.
65. *The Transfer of Power*, April 1947, Vol. X, p.289.
66. Ibid., p.290.
67. Mountbatten to the Earl of Listowel, Mountbatten Papers, Letters to and from the Secretary of State, 1 May 1947, *The Transfer of Power*, Vol. X, pp.530–31.
68. Minutes of Viceroy's Twenty Fifth Staff meeting, Item 3, Mountbatten Papers, May 1947, Vol. X, p.581.
69. Mountbatten to Lord Ismay, Telegram R/3/1/170: ff 3–4 of 3 May 1947, *The Transfer of Power*, Vol. X, p.600.
70. Mountbatten to Lord Ismay, Telegram R/3/1/170: f 10 of 6 May 1947, *The Transfer of Power*, Vol. X, p.635.
71. Telegram, R/3/1/170:F 13, *The Transfer of Power*, 7 May 1947, Vol. X, p.663, note 1.
72. Transfer of Power, May 1947, p.636.
73. Lord Ismay to Mountbatten, Telegram R/3/1/170: f 9 of 6 May 1947, *The Transfer of Power*, Vol. X, p.636.
74. Mountbatten to Lord Ismay, Telegram R/3/1/170: f 12 of 7 May 1947, *The Transfer of Power*, Vol. X, p.662.
75. Caroe to Mountbatten, Mountbatten Papers, official Correspondence Files: Private Armies, Formation of a Territorial Army in India, Letter dated 17 May 1947, *The Transfer of Power*, Vol. X, pp.874–75.
76. Caroe to Sir John Colville, extract, L/P&J/5/224: f 45, dated 22 May 1947, *The Transfer of Power*, Vol. X, p.944.
77. Caroe to Mountbatten, Telegram, R/3/1/151: f 91 of 31 May 1947, *The Transfer of Power*, Vol. XI, p.28-29.
78. Ibid.
79. Caroe to Mountbatten, Telegram R/3/1/151: ff 110–11 of 4 June 1947, *The Transfer of Power*, Vol. XI, p.126-127.

80. Ibid.
81. Ibid.
82. Caroe to Mountbatten, Telegram, R/3/1/151: f 115 of 5 June 1947, *The Transfer of Power*, Vol. XI, pp.151–52.
83. Ibid.
84. Mountbatten to Caroe, R/3/1/170: ff 21–22 of 6 June 1947, *The Transfer of Power*, Vol. XI, p.172-173.
85. Ibid.
86. Sir David Taylor Monteath (1887–1961) was a civil servant, working at the India Office in London, and was the last Permanent Under Secretary of State for India and Burma. In 1927, he became Private Secretary to the then Secretary of State for India, F.E. Smith, Lord Birkenhead, a great friend of Sir Winston Churchill's. He continued to act in this capacity till 1931, when he was promoted as Assistant Under Secretary of State to look after the Indian and Burmese Round Table conferences, especially the Burmese, where he was secretary to the Conference. In 1937, he was given independent charge of Burmese Affairs as Under Secretary of State till 1941, whereafter he became Under Secretary for both India and Burma. He remained there till the independence of India and Pakistan made his post unnecessary.
87. Lord Ismay to Sir D. Monteath, Telegram, R/3/1/170: f 23 of 8 June 1947, *The Transfer of Power*, Vol. XI, p.195.
88. Caroe to Mountbatten, R/3/1/170: ff 26–28 of 11 June 1947, *The Transfer of Power*, Vol. XI, pp.265–66.
89. Ibid.
90. Liaquat Ali Khan to Mountbatten, R/3/1/170: ff 31–32 of 11 June 1947, *The Transfer of Power*, Vol. XI, pp.267–68.
91. Ibid.
92. Earl of Listowel to Clement Attlee, L/po/8/45: ff 41–44 of 11 June 1947, *The Transfer of Power*, Vol. XI, pp.280–81.
93. Ibid.
94. Mountbatten to Caroe, R/3/1/170: f 34 of 12 June 1947, *The Transfer of Power*, Vol. XI, p.285.
95. Ibid.
96. Viceroy's Personal Report No-9, June 1947, Vol. XI, p.308.
97. Caroe to Mountbatten, R/3/1/170: ff 46–47 of 13 June 1947, *The Transfer of Power*, Vol. XI, pp.334–35.

98. Ibid.
99. Lord Listowel to Mountbatten, Mountbatten Papers, Letters to and from the Secretary of State of 13 June 1947, *The Transfer of Power*, Vol. XI, pp.335–37.
100. Sir David Monteath to Lord Ismay, Telegram, L/Po/8/45: ff 25–28, India office, 15 June 1947, *The Transfer of Power*, Vol. XI, pp.414–15.
101. Ibid.
102. Ibid.
103. Mountbatten to Caroe, R/3/1/170: f 65 of 17 June 1947, *The Transfer of Power*, Vol. XI, pp.439–40.
104. Caroe to Mountbatten (Extracts), L/P&J/5/224: ff 29–30 of 23 June 1947, *The Transfer of Power*, Vol. XI, pp.578–80.
105. Caroe to Mountbatten, Telegram, Mountbatten Papers, Official Correspondence Files: NWFP situation in, Part ii of 25 June 1947, *The Transfer of Power*, Vol. XI, p.633.
106. Caroe to Mountbatten (Extracts), L/P&J/5/224: ff 29–30 of 23 June 1947, *The Transfer of Power*, Vol. XI, pp.578–80.
107. George VI (1895–1952) was King of the United Kingdom and the British Dominions from 11 December 1936 until his death. He was the last Emperor of India (until January 1950) and the last King of Ireland (until 1949). King George's reign saw the acceleration of the break-up of the British empire and its transition into the Commonwealth of Nations.

# 8
# Nehru's Kamerad

ANSWERING PROPHETICALLY WHEN interviewed by a French journalist in 1946, Nehru[1] said three things in his closing remarks—India would never agree to be a Dominion; there would never be a Pakistan; and when the British finally departed, there would be no communal trouble in India. He was proved wrong on all three counts. He admitted to this in his next meeting with the same French journalist, Jacques Marcuse, after a two-year gap. 'Wasn't I wrong?', was all Nehru exclaimed, recalling the earlier interview (Hughes 1972). Was it an owning up to the responsibility of India's partition marked by bloodshed or was he, like so many others, convinced that all of India's ills were attributable to the presence of the British colonials?

In Nehru's scheme of things, achieving India's independence took priority over other important matters like communalism. Educated in England, Nehru had a European outlook on most issues, including communalism, which he saw as an offshoot of problems that afflicted colonial India. Till the late 1920s, Nehru did not have to seriously contend with communalism, and therefore, he did not even make an attempt to define or understand it. To him it was just an issue of riots, causes of which were religious. Factors compounding the problem were ignorance and bigotry which the British were ever ready to exploit. In Nehru's opinion, communalism was confined only to the upper and middle classes of India, both amongst Hindus and Muslims, a set that came to squabble over spoils of office. A separate electorate only helped broaden cleavages. However, political representation based on economic criteria could provide cover for this problem. A 'socialist republic' model of India appeared to him to be a panacea for this ill. Nehru was also convinced that mass participation in India's political process could overcome the middle-class phenomenon of communalism. But as it came to be, important provinces like the NWFP and Baluchistan defied Nehru's theoretical solution. The two provinces that opted for Pakistan really had no middle class to boast of. The upper classes in the NWFP were conservative and therefore pro-League (for the League was considered pro-government). The others gradually fell under the powerful spell of communalism and therefore became League supporters. Nehru's belief that communalism, especially Hindu communalism, could easily be mistaken for nationalism came true but in a converse way. There was of course no mistaking the fact that Muslim communalism in the NWFP, an overwhelmingly Muslim province, got converted into Pakistani nationalism (Gopal: 172 and 183). Suffice to say here that it was Islamic unity that provided the organizing power in this province in 1947.

'It is after all a side issue,' wrote Nehru in April 1936, 'and it can have no real importance in the larger scheme of things' (Gopal: 190). The absence of unity on the Muslim communal front in 1936, Jinnah's professed willingness to forget the Communal Award[2] and to 'apply our mind to larger questions affecting India' (Singh) may have seemed to justify Nehru's belief. The results of the provincial elections of 1937[3] did not discourage Nehru's optimism about the future of communal politics. Nehru could derive much comfort from the fact that communal organizations had not fared well in the elections—the Hindu Mahasabha[4] had been routed, and of greater significance for the Congress was the fact that, the Muslim League secured only 4.8 per cent of the total Muslim votes in India in an electoral system based on separate electorates. Its decision to accept office highlighted the fact that the League had been the least successful in the Muslim majority provinces. It won only two out of eighty-four Muslim seats in Punjab, and in the NWFP it was the Congress that formed the government (Singh).

But things changed as time passed. The two years that the Congress was in power saw increasingly strident propaganda by the Muslim League to make the Congress appear more like a sectarian party. The Quit India movement (9 August 1942) had the top-level Congress leadership cooling their heels in jails for almost three years while the League consolidated. When it came to the crux, Nehru had difficulty accepting that opinion in the NWFP had swung away from the Khudai Khidmatgars towards the Muslim League. He claimed that the League's success was solely due to violence and intimidation. He rejected the notion that Frontier tribes were different and required special treatment. 'People exactly similar to the Frontier tribes had been dealt with successfully elsewhere,' he declared (Yapp 1968: 66). He rejected Caroe's opposing views of the Frontier people as being out of date. Nehru continued to be closely involved in the affairs of the NWFP, not only because the province had its own romance as the historic frontier of India but also because he believed that it was its future frontier. In the British claim to the distinctiveness of this province lay a negation of Nehru's concept of Indian nationalism. Perhaps this was also one of the reasons why he constantly endeavoured to vindicate himself in the province through his various acts of omission and commission.

Nehru had visited the NWFP thrice, the first time in October 1937. His last visit, commencing on 18 October 1946, came exactly nine years later. Addressing the people of Peshawar in 1937, he had proudly declared that 'the frontier was not only a historic but a living part of India.'[5] But in less than a decade the NWFP stood severed from India. In a chance meeting in England in 1935 with a 'gentleman unfriendly to India' he was asked what would befall India if the British army suddenly withdrew from the Indian frontier. Nehru's spontaneous response was that there would be general rejoicing and illumination on both sides of the border. Left to Badshah Khan, Nehru felt that the Frontier issue could solve itself in no time. 'As a matter of fact,' he said, 'any person could solve it, for it was not such a complicated problem.'[6] Clearly, Nehru had misjudged the situation. His role amongst the Congress leaders was to prove critical in shaping the destiny of the NWFP. It was only a matter of time before the Muslim League moved in with its bold communal offensive.

On his return from the October 1937 visit, Nehru was sufficiently impressed by the 'courage, brave endurance, splendid discipline, virile enthusiasm and simple nature of the people of the NWFP.'[7] His gushing response before leaving the province was, 'I go back with living and throbbing pictures in my mind and tens of thousands of voices ringing in my ears. These voices pull me back, and even as I go away, the call of the Frontier comes to me.'[8] That call, prophetically, came nine years later in October 1946, when Nehru embarked on his last tour of NWFP, much against the advice of his Congress peers.

Ram Manohar Lohia, the great Indian socialist and Nehru's contemporary, was to interview Nehru soon after his first visit. Excerpts of it appeared in the *Congress Socialist* of 6 November 1937. To a question about whether the Frontier people were a distinct cultural unit, separate from the rest of India, Nehru enthusiastically retorted by emphasizing their 'Indianness':

> They were continually referring both in their public addresses and in their private talks to the freedom of India and not to any local freedom of their own… It is true that they have a strong feeling of kinship with the people across the border…because of language and cultural relations, but politically speaking, they look very definitely to India. It is obvious that the tightening of the political bonds between the Frontier Province and the rest of India has been due to common sacrifices for a common cause.

The Khudai Khidmatgars' contribution to India's civil disobedience movement notwithstanding, Nehru's last sentence was an overstatement. Historically, this entire region, since the break-up of the Mughal empire, was transformed into a sort of a corridor for the Durrani and Sikh armies to pass through. The situation remained unstable even when the British took control in 1849 as the people of the Frontier continued to live on the margins of Punjab. The creation of the new province of the NWFP in 1901 only helped to draw together the settled districts and the tribal territory. Since the tribal areas were governed from Calcutta (and later from Delhi), the Pathans perceived that their concerns and ambitions received primacy over provincial interest, which revived a tendency, dating from the days of the Mughals, to look to the East rather than to the West. Once more the Pathans had a familiar centre in Peshawar; they no longer needed to travel to Lahore except for pleasure.[10] Was it, therefore, a bond based only on common sacrifice that made the Pathans look towards India? Perhaps not.

Nehru followed up his first visit to the NWFP with a second one, not entirely fortuitous, in January 1938. Some glimpses of it are provided in his letter to Abdul Ghaffar Khan:

I need hardly tell you that I am greatly distressed at many things that are happening in the Frontier Province [It was reported that due to differences, the Khudai Khidmatgars had threatened to disassociate themselves from the Frontier Provincial Congress Committee]... But in the Frontier Province there is the additional obstacle of complete want of contacts...It is absolutely necessary therefore for all of us to meet frequently... I am sailing for England... As I am going away for some time I would particularly like to meet you and Khan Saheb before I go. This is why I repeat my request that both of you should come to Bombay for the Minister's meeting. [11]

Clearly, all was not well with the Frontier Congress and its ministry in the NWFP within less than a year of government formation.

It was not in Nehru's ken to approach the Frontier exclusively from a strategic angle. Issues that impelled him were of 'development' and of 'human' interest. Nehru could never quite believe that a tribal Pathan lived in a 'rigid, semi-theocratic, fear-governed feudal society, in an age of science, mechanics and interdependence.' Nehru was also not familiar with a Pathan's 'extreme clannishness and the thick overlay of Islamic doctrine on his psyche, of the Old Testament kind of tribal law.'

Between the two provincial elections in the NWFP in 1937 and 1946, the Pathans increasingly became the target of high-pressure political campaigns. From 1937 onwards, but more particularly after the Lahore Resolution[12] of 1940, Muslim League politicians had started stimulating Muslim clannishness, to which the communal riots provided an effective fillip. Deaths of Pathan moneylenders and labourers in Bombay and stories of Muslim victims in Bengal had already agitated the Pathan community. Very soon, news of large Muslim casualties would trickle in from Bihar. Pro-Pakistan arguments were freely proffered by professionals and bureaucrats of both superior and inferior ranks, as well as by sub-district revenue assistants, subordinate inspectors, secretarial clerks and others who before World War II had been outside the mainstream of Indian politics. Partisan feelings ran both high and deep.

Besides lawyers, landlords and the professional bureaucratic set, a third element that helped infuse strength into the Frontier Muslim League was the 'Sajda Nashins', religious men. The most prominent of this group in the Frontier was a young mullah, the Pir of Manki Sharif, a man still in his twenties. His cry was simple and direct: 'Islam is in danger'. He stated that 'Muslims will be slaves in the Hindu raj', and that Muslims must 'organize before you are crushed.' It was in this backdrop that an interim government prepared to take office for the first time in Delhi.

In September 1946, Nehru effortlessly donned the mantle of a Minister in charge of External Affairs in the interim Government of India. The NWFP tribal areas were part of his parish. The Minister, the Governor, the department, as also the officers, were for the first time learning to work together at the 'centre'. Teething problems therefore were bound to arise.

Nehru's external affairs portfolio was also responsible for the Frontier and tribal areas, quite distinct from the Political Department that was controlled by the Political Advisor to the Crown's representative (the Viceroy), and to the Governor in the provinces. Both departments were serviced by the same cadre of officers, from the Indian Political Service (IPS). Unfortunately for Nehru, his department had no control over this cadre of officers. The IPS was traditionally controlled by the Political Advisor. The only constitutional link that existed between the Political and the External Affairs Departments was provided by the Viceroy in his dual capacity as the Governor General and the Crown representative. That Nehru would face resistance from his officers, who belonged to a joint cadre and were controlled by a different department, was very much expected. These officers too were facing a new situation—coming face-to-face for the first time with the popular aspirations of an Indian political leader who headed their department. Nehru, perhaps a man in hurry, was left frustrated by this fact.

Trouble was brewing in the Frontier well before Nehru took office. The Political Agent of south Waziristan, Major Jos Donald, and two of his party were kidnapped near Razmak[13] on 22 June 1946 by the Mahsuds.

The kidnappers demanded a one-sixth share in the government allowance given to some other Mahsud tribesmen. Without the knowledge of the rest of the clan, a section of Mahsuds had decided to kidnap a British official to press forth their demand. The official they had decided upon was a garrison engineer based at Razmak. But by mistake they ended up kidnapping the Political Agent who happened to pass by the place where the Mahsud gang lay in ambush. It was only after ten days, on 2 July, and after a payment of over a lakh and a half rupees, that the release of Donald and his party was secured. British reprisals followed thereafter. The government decided to proscribe six villages by 'aerial bombardment'. This began on 1 August 1946 but the news of it was deliberately suppressed. Nehru did not know of it till he took office in the interim government. He did intervene, asking for the matter to be raised in the cabinet though the matter resolved itself just then and the bombing operations stopped.[14] But the larger implication of the aerial operation cast a shadow, on Nehru personally and generally on the Frontier Congress. In the fast-changing political climate of the province, the blame for the air force action got pinned on the Congress, more so on Nehru since he headed the External Affairs Department—the Muslim League propaganda ensured this. This was most unfortunate and also ironical, because Nehru had consistently, and quite resolutely, taken up the issue with the British authorities. Right from 1937, he had consistently protested against aerial bombardment, and was in fact, instrumental in getting the Congress to condemn this barbarous method of assault in its annual session at Faizpur.

## The Portentous Visit

Through a telegram sent on 28 September 1946, the Foreign Department, New Delhi, first informed the Governor, Sir Olaf Caroe, of Nehru's proposed one-week visit to the Frontier in October. Nehru wanted Khan Abdul Ghaffar Khan to accompany him and also enquired if Dr Khan Saheb could join. Two officers from the External Affairs Department, including the Secretary, formed part of his entourage as well. Caroe's reaction to the 28 September telegram was uncharacteristically strong. He lost no time in making his objection immediately known to the Viceroy. George Abell, Private Secretary to the Viceroy, found Caroe's reaction a trifle exaggerated.[15]

Caroe met Nehru nearer the date of his visit (9 October) to dissuade him but could not succeed. Caroe was perturbed and did not approve of the timing of Nehru's visit. To an extent, Nehru did agree that the tour should neither have political overtones nor be along party lines, but nonetheless, he insisted on going with it. The Governor was particularly apprehensive and said that if the visit was undertaken it could lead to adverse tribal reactions and any hope of securing the League's cooperation in the interim government would be wrecked.[16] Caroe could now at best only hope for some positive news coming in from Delhi on the outcome of fresh negotiations on the formation of a coalition government at the centre. Whatever be the outcome, Caroe wanted Jinnah to generously instruct his Frontier League supporters to treat Nehru as a guest of the people of the Frontier and tell them that there were to be no counter-demonstrations staged on his arrival or during his tour. The Congress would behave likewise if the tour was to be in 'double harness'.

Wavell heeded Caroe's advice and immediately sent a letter to Jinnah, saying he hoped to announce the formation of a coalition government the same night and that Nehru, during his tour, would make a point of welcoming the formation of a coalition government. Wavell thought that Jinnah would recognize the undesirability of hostile demonstrations against a member of a government of which the League was also to be a part. Wavell wanted Jinnah to ask his Frontier League leaders to restrain their supporters. Jinnah was prompt in his reply. It arrived the same day. After consulting the League Working Committee Jinnah advised deferment of Nehru's visit. He felt that people in the Frontier looked upon Nehru's visit with disfavour. He, however, reassured Wavell that no instructions to stage demonstrations had been issued from his side to the Frontier League.

Though the Muslim League gave, in principle, its consensus on the date of 13 October to join the interim government, it was only after thirteen days that they took office. Nehru's visit transpired in between. Most of his prominent Congress colleagues like Maulana Azad and Sardar Vallabhbhai Patel unsuccessfully tried to dissuade him but he insisted on going ahead with the visit, with the Khan brothers in tow. No one from the Muslim League accompanied them. This provided excellent fodder to the Muslim League for anti-Congress, anti-Nehru propaganda.

Nehru commenced his tour on 16 October, arriving by an official plane at the Peshawar aerodrome. The start itself was not propitious.

A hostile reception awaited him at Peshawar. The multitude present at the Peshawar airport comprised people dressed in the green uniforms of the Muslim National Guards. Though the airport was contiguous to the cantonment, the authorities there failed to stop the demonstrators from forcing their way through the airport premises. Nehru perforce had to be whisked away, quite literally, through the back door. The ruling party's plan for his reception fell through for an assembly of Congress supporters within the airport premises would certainly have led to a clash.[18] The demonstrators who turned violent at the Peshawar aerodrome were led by Abdul Qayyum Khan, leader of the Muslim League Party in the Frontier Assembly. This was an extraordinary incident, occurring as it did in an area where no such incident had happened before, and where normally the entry of people was regulated. Without doubt it was either a case of gross mismanagement or of passive acquiescence. The authorities were forewarned of the possibility of a demonstration; that they could not avert violence had they so wished was difficult to imagine.

The next day, on 17 October, Nehru flew to Miranshah in north Waziristan. Khan Abdul Ghaffar Khan unfortunately gotten involved in a heated argument with some of the members of a *jirga* that met Nehru, calling them mere pawns in the hands of their Political Agent and accusing them of only repeating the lines they had been asked to say. Riled by the accusation, *jirga* members left en masse without bothering to hear Nehru. Nehru's next stop was Razmak in southern Waziristan. Even before he arrived, the venue of his meeting was sniped at. The aircraft in which he flew was also not spared. The reception was equally hostile. To Nehru's dismay, the *jirgas* at Miranshah and Razmak refused to utter a single word of protest against the recent aerial bombing in Waziristan, something that had affected their very being. Instead, they protested against what had happened in Calcutta. A tribal Malik[19] accused Nehru's government of treating the Muslims harshly in the Indian provinces. The Mahsud Maliks quite rudely, and without mincing words, told Nehru that they preferred Jinnah to him. At Razmak it was now Nehru's turn to get embroiled in a verbal duel with the tribal Maliks. He enquired from the Maliks the reason for their non-cooperation, considering they received such liberal allowances. Getting a little carried away, he accused them of being slaves of the British. Nehru's statement provoked a volley of angry retorts from several prominent Maliks. They haughtily declared they had never been dominated by anyone in the past and likewise, would not be in the future. The Maliks thought that the allowances they received were in lieu of their roads and lands which the government used.

While at Razmak, Nehru had received an invitation from some prominent 'religious men'—one of them being Mullah Fazal Din, the son of the famous Mullah Powindah [20]—which Nehru declined. Gulab Khan, a senior and influential Mahsud Malik of Waziristan, who subsequently led a Mahsud *lashkar* in Kashmir, was decorated, and was also a senator in the Pakistan Parliament in 1970s, recounted what transpired at Razmak:

> He [Gulab Khan] had paid some men Rs 200 to snipe at Nehru's plane when it landed at Razmak. The receiving party of some sixty odd Mahsud Maliks at Razmak had been invited by the Resident of Waziristan, Colonel Packman. Much against Dr Khan Saheb's advise, Nehru walked towards the Maliks to meet them. As was the tradition, the Maliks were expected to get up and greet Nehru, something that they did not do. Malik Khaisor did reluctantly rise to greet Nehru but not the others. On being questioned by the province's premier about their rude behaviour, Malik Khaisor replied that he did not want to shake hands with Dr Khan Saheb because he had given his daughter in marriage to a Sikh. There followed an uproar forcing the British officers to intervene. In the melee that ensued, Colonel Packman ended up facing Nehru's ire whereupon he ordered his men to move away from the scene of confusion. Nehru's threats to the Mahsud Maliks only confounded the situation. Fortunately, there were no weapons at hand; the Maliks had not been allowed to carry any as the meeting was to be held in the cantonment area. Nehru is alleged to have told the Mahsud Maliks that the British were just about to be thrown out and when that happened, he would squeeze those Maliks, to which Gulab Khan was provoked to dare him for 'even the British had not been able to do so'.

Another Mahsud told Nehru that his job was to measure cloth, that he was a shopkeeper and not a warrior. Yet another wanted to hit Nehru, but was prevented.

The next stop in Nehru's itinerary was Wana[21] where he met the Wazirs. Most of them had lined up on the road to wave black flags when Nehru passed by. Waiting for Nehru to arrive, they grew restive. An infantry company was then brought in to control them. This action annoyed the tribesmen so much that they refused to participate in the *jirga* which Nehru was to attend. Nehru had to leave Wana without meeting them. At Tank, it was a similar story—a hostile reception; supporters of the Muslim League threw stones at his convoy and in the fracas sixteen Congressmen and four supporters of the League were injured. At an impromptu stop that Nehru made at Jandola[22] (Waziristan) on 19 October, he was pleasantly surprised when he was received by a small but friendly Bhittani[23] *jirga*. This surprise reception prompted Nehru to say that the crowds at the fixed destinations had been tutored. The Bhittanis, according to Governor Caroe, were a tame little tribe, mostly from Dera Ismail Khan, and therefore not real tribesmen. They had been brought by a dismissed naib-tehsildar[24] who was made to leave government service during the League ministry's tenure. The naib-tehsildar had also been an unsuccessful Congress candidate for the provincial assembly elections in 1946. Some others like G.C.S. Curtis maintained that the Bhittani *jirga*, which consisted mainly of 'Kundis', a small pro-Congress tribe settled in Dera Ismail Khan, was brought together by a Hindu Assistant Commissioner.[25]

On 20 October, Nehru proceeded to the Khyber Agency by road, to be sniped at again by the tribesmen. Firing had to be resorted to when his party faced a belligerent stone-pelting crowd. The Afridis refused to meet him and some who were willing were prevailed over. Undaunted, Nehru went to Malakand the same day to make an overnight halt. There too the tribal *jirga* refused to come to his reception. The road to Malakand also had demonstrators waving black flags at him. The next day, as he was leaving, the infamous Malakand incident occurred, Nehru and his party fortunately getting away with only minor injuries. To avoid further trouble, his entourage was forced to take a different route to Mardan. There was relief, finally, when his tour concluded with a meeting at Sardaryab where he was warmly received by the Khudai Khidmatgars.

Nehru's romantic notions did find expression in his address to the Khudai Khidmatgars at Sardaryab on 21 October 1946: 'If drops of our blood fell on Pathan soil today, I regard them as seeds which will bring good to all of us—to Pathans and to India... A few drops of my blood and the blood of our leader, Khan Abdul Ghaffar Khan, were shed today outside the Malakand Fort' (*Selected Works of Jawaharlal Nehru*, Second Series, Vol. 1, p.316).

Erland Jansson, whose account of the Frontier of this period is well-researched, had met up with one Faridullah Shah, the then assistant political officer of Khyber Agency. Faridullah Shah's version was that he, along with some others, had primarily been responsible for stoking anti-Hindu feelings among the Afridis, especially after the Congress formed the interim government. This is how Faridullah Shah recounted the incident to Janson:

> At that time Colonel Khurshid was the Political Agent of the Khyber Agency. Two or three days before Nehru's arrival Khurshid sent for me and told me [that] Nehru was coming to Khyber. He said that if the tribals received him in a docile way, all Mussalmans of this part of the country will go under the suzerainty of the Hindus; as a Mussalman I should do something, but at the same time he warned me not to tell him of the action I would take. Do you know why? He was a religious man and if he was asked anything, he could say he did not know... I went straight to Jamrud.[26] I contacted a certain Kuki Khel Malik called Swatai Khan. The question he asked was as to what would be the reaction of the Political Agent. And I told him: 'Don't worry.' I very strongly told him that nobody was to be killed. They would resort to heavy sniping. On return from Jamrud I contacted Mullah Sahib of Manki Sharif. He had then a lot of disciples among the Shinwaris[27] and Mullagoris.[28] So he also went on tour to Landi Kotal[29] and the Mullagori area (Jansson 1981: 186).

In all fairness to Governor Caroe, he had steadfastly advised Nehru against converting his visit into a political tour. Nehru had been convinced that he, as a representative of the government, could not completely divest himself of his responsibility as a leader of the

Congress party. Nehru's Foreign Secretary, though, differed from him on this issue. After his return from the tour, Weightman had formally recorded that 'Sir Olaf Caroe and all of us have at all times stressed the overriding necessity of a non-party approach to the problems of the Frontier and the H.M. (Nehru) himself had endorsed that view; yet H.M. on his tour was accompanied by the leader of the Congress party in the Frontier and by the Premier of the Congress government of the Province.' Being from the plains it was difficult for Nehru to appreciate references to a non-party approach to the problems of the Frontier. A little annoyed, he had counter-questioned: 'Does a non-party approach mean that every problem should be considered by a mixed crowd representing various viewpoints?' And why, in order to ensure this non-party approach, was it necessary to keep aloof from his own colleagues simply because some people did not approve of it? To Nehru this business had nothing to do with a party or a non-party approach; it meant just giving in to threats. No government, according to him, could function this way.

Nehru had committed a serious error in leaving it entirely to the Governor and the officials to draw up his tour programme. As a result, he was to meet only those whom the Political Agents wanted him to. Surrendering to official discretion, he informed Dr Khan Saheb to obtain the tour programme from the Governor, thus undermining the Chief Minister's position too. The job of structuring Nehru's tour was left completely to the officials of the province. Dr Khan Saheb had no say in it. Had the trip been totally political or official, the fallout would not have been so negative. With his flexibility curtailed by an exclusively official programme, Nehru ended up drawing flak from all quarters. He was accused of following a political agenda, which he did not because of the nature of the itinerary. Unable to extract political mileage, he in fact ended up carrying the blame for it.

It was not as if Nehru was oblivious to the negative fallout of the canard the Muslim League was spreading—that he and the Congress were responsible for the aerial bombing in Waziristan. He was forced to defend himself in his addresses while on tour. Speaking at Peshawar on 19 October he said: 'Soon after I took charge I learnt there had been a bombardment in Waziristan. It is worthy of your noting that I first came to know of it through Badshah Khan's statement. When I tried to understand this question, intricate and baffling problems stood up before me and assumed formidable proportions.'[30] Both the Congress and Nehru were cornered by the communal onslaught unleashed by the League's propaganda. In such circumstances the disinformation inevitably stuck.

A day before the unfortunate incident, Governor Caroe had met Nehru at Malakand. Referring to the conversation he had had with Nehru, Caroe reported to Wavell: 'He [Nehru] accused our Indian subordinates of machination. He also charged the Political Agents in the Khyber and Malakand (both happen to be Indians). I told him, a party approach to the tribal problem was bound to fail...it was fatal to take a party politician like Abdul Ghaffar Khan. He said... "the romance of the frontier must come to an end."' [31]

The trip to the NWFP impacted Nehru and left him shaken. Within a day of his return, he wrote a long note on it to the Governor and the Viceroy. Nehru knew that officers of the Political Department did not welcome his visit but had not fathomed such active hostility as he witnessed on arrival in the NWFP. From then on, he was reminded at each and every step that he was there much against their wishes (*Selected Works of Jawaharlal Nehru*, Second Series, Vol. 1, p.323). Nehru had hoped that an immediate announcement of a coalition government at the centre would make a difference but in vain.

Nehru found it odd that the tribal Maliks should behave the way they did unless they had been tutored. In some places, he himself had been told of some minor officials asking people what they would say or do, deliberately inviting only those who fell in with their wishes. Nehru at times received information of this mischief even before an ugly incident occurred.

The warm reception that he got during an impromptu visit to Jandola stood in prominent contrast to the receptions where his visits were prearranged. At Khyber, Nehru's party had prior information of some miscreants who had gathered en route to Landi Kotal. Despite the advance notice, no steps were taken to avoid the incident. Foresight shown by officials in this case would certainly have led to an incident being avoided (*Selected Works of Jawaharlal Nehru*, Second Series, Vol. 1, p.324).

The conduct of the Political Agent of Malakand came in for

serious criticism by Nehru. To him, Sheikh Mahbub Ali was either incompetent or he approved of what had taken place and therefore, did not intervene. He did not appear to be a person lacking in intelligence, so his behaviour could not possibly be ascribed to sheer incompetence. Whether it was something worse was not important. Sheikh Mahbub Ali showed himself to be completely unfit for any responsible charge (*Selected Works of Jawaharlal Nehru*, Second Series, Vol. 1, p.325). Nehru demanded an enquiry into his conduct. He also wrote to Governor Caroe demanding his removal. The issue snowballed enough to be raised in the central legislative assembly on 29 October 1946.

Sheikh Mahbub Ali was perceived as a strong supporter of the Muslim League. He was also under investigation by an Anti-Corruption Committee of the provincial government. As he blamed the NWFP government for his predicament, there was no love lost between him and the government. A High Court judge from Madras was appointed to conduct an enquiry into Sheikh Mahbub Ali's conduct. Caroe had successfully prevailed upon the NWFP Chief Minister to confine the enquiry only to charges of negligence and not to include the charge of instigation within the enquiry's ambit. Sheikh Mahbub Ali was subsequently exonerated of the charge by Justice Clark.[32] Wavell, unconvinced of Justice Clark's report, commented: 'I must also say that the report is most unsatisfactory for it is strongly biased against Khan Abdul Ghaffar Khan and other Congress witnesses, while witnesses favourable towards the Political Agent are taken at their word without question. The three who arranged the demonstration were not questioned at all' (Jansson 1981: 186). On Wavell's suggestion, Sheikh Mahbub Ali was retired. He was promptly reinstated by the Pakistan government after India's partition.

Colonel Mohammad Sharif Khan, Sheikh Mahbub Ali's successor, had conducted his own private investigation into this affair. If he is to be believed, Sheikh Mahbub Ali had told members of the local *jirga* that Nehru was an important person and should be welcomed in a friendly manner, emphasizing simultaneously that Nehru was a Hindu. This left the Khans of the *jirga* confused. Colonel Sharif Khan's personal view was that Sheikh Mahbub Ali did not want a friendly welcome for Nehru, but at the same time wanted to avoid his direct involvement in the affair (Jansson 1981: 186–87).

Erland Jansson had occasion to interview two of those three men directly responsible for the demonstration at Malakand—Fazal Sattar, Majidullah Khan and Mohammad Nawaz Khan. Their leader Fazal Sattar, an engineering diploma holder from Lucknow and a League supporter, was well acquainted with Indian political sentiments. Till Nehru's visit, the Malakand Agency had remained quite untouched by Indian politics. The people there had never taken part in any political activity. It was only when Fazal Sattar and Majidullah Khan heard over the wireless of the reception that Nehru had received in Waziristan and Khyber that they also decided to stage a demonstration. The idea was their own, coming to them as a result of what had happened with Nehru in Waziristan and Khyber. Had Nehru commenced his visit of the Frontier from Malakand, possibly nothing untoward would have happened. In a meeting convened locally on the morning of 20 October 'the group of three' had decided to march to the Dir airfield, as Nehru was expected to land there. While on the way, the leaders were informed that Nehru had already arrived at Malakand by road. The three leaders in the car, and the rest in trucks, drove to the Agency gates where they managed to stage a demonstration. Unfortunately, things got out of hand. Majidullah Khan recounted having slapped Khan Abdul Ghaffar Khan (Jansson 1981: 187).

It appears from Fazal Sattar and Majidullah Khan's version that Sheikh Mahbub Ali was not responsible for the demonstration, though Majidullah Khan did concede that the Political Agent did not protect Nehru and his party, which he could have done. If Sheikh Mahbub Ali wanted to, he could have prevented the incident by use of force (Jansson 1981: 188).

After that episode, the three leaders formed a Muslim League branch in the Malakand Agency. Fazal Sattar became its President, Majidullah Khan its Vice President and Mohammad Nawaz Khan its General Secretary. Though their organization lacked a firm institutional structure, they still mobilized a 1,500-strong contingent that participated in the League's show of strength on 28 April 1947 in the presence of the Viceroy.[33]

An unintended consequence of Nehru's visit was the swift drawing of the tribal areas into the orbit of Indian politics. From then on, the religious sentiments of the tribes, fanned by officials, students and regular Muslim leaders, weighed heavily in favour of the Muslim League and Pakistan. Those who were inclined towards the Congress found their position weakening. As a consequence, many among the Frontier Congress started to stress the Afghan connection or talk in terms of independence (Jansson 1981: 188).

The issue of Nehru's visit was also raised in the British Parliament as allegations surfaced that disturbances during the tour had been deliberately engineered by the Political Department. Unnerved by the tour, Nehru shelved an earlier plan of his to bring about basic changes in the Frontier policy. This visit made Nehru even more critical of the officials. To him:

> The higher services in India had functioned in a special kind of environment for some generations. This environment had led to authoritarian methods of government and a great deal of complacency and belief in one's own rectitude. This belief inevitably led to dislike and condemnation of any person who challenged it or came in the way. There was something almost religious about it in the sense that the maintenance of the group and its method of functioning became an article of faith.

To Nehru, these officers appeared wedded to a system completely out of date and therefore it was not so much these officers but the system that was at fault. Nehru also observed a complete lack of harmony between the popular NWFP government and its officials, as also between the officials and the party in power, the Congress. This permanent official group of members thought themselves more as experts in the mould of statesmen, rather than as members of a service. Nehru had also sensed the officials' bitter dislike and hostility towards Khan Abdul Ghaffar Khan, a leader of eminence and head of the political organization that controlled the government. This in itself was reflective of the extreme lack of appreciation of the democratic process and of the present government in the province, for to Nehru, 'snobbery was not a virtue at any time, much less in democracy' (*Selected Works of Jawaharlal Nehru,* Second Series, Vol. 1, p.328).

Nehru was wary of some of these officers. The Congress was yet to join the interim government, and the responsibility of external and tribal affairs was yet to be bestowed upon Nehru. In July 1946,

Nehru wrote to Dr Khan Saheb demanding action against partisan civil servants. The letter was intercepted. In response, Wavell, in end July, circulated this letter to all his governors. I reproduce excerpts of Nehru's letter, little appreciated by the British Indian officialdom:

There has been considerable feeling in Congress circles in regard to events that took place in August 1942 and subsequently and the official repression that followed. There has been and is a strong popular demand for enquiry and punishment of officials.... have now had occasion to have another talk with the Viceroy on this subject... you [Dr Khan Saheb] might approach this question in the following manner. There need not be any large scale public enquiry, but your government might enquire into specific and flagrant cases which are well known. Such an enquiry can be private. Where your government is satisfied, you might take up this case with the Governor and arrange for the retirement from service of such person...I need not go into any greater detail, as you will, no doubt, know best how to proceed. I think that there should be no delay about this.[34]

While circulating this note, Wavell appended a note saying that the cases which Nehru referred to were never discussed with him. Wavell also denied ever discussing with Nehru cases against officers connected with the incidents of 1942.[35] There is no reason to disbelieve that Governor

Caroe in this case must have shared the contents of Nehru's letter with senior officials of the NWFP and that too at a time when Nehru, in a few months, would take over charge of the NWFP's tribal affairs. How propitious was his start going to be? The pitch was already getting queered.

Nehru's relations with Sir Olaf Caroe, the NWFP Governor, had never been cordial. Alluding to an incident that had occurred some months back, Nehru insinuated that Sir Caroe, as a former Foreign Secretary and then as the Governor of NWFP, had serious objections to his taking over the external affairs portfolio:

> Long before the Interim Government was formed, when it was privately suggested that I should become Member for External Affairs, which included Tribal Areas, I was told that this would be unwelcome to the tribal people. Hardly anyone even in the

innermost circles of the government knew about this proposal, and it was obvious that the tribal people could not have heard of it. Obviously, the objections, at that time were voiced by the officials and not the tribal people. Much later I heard of some meetings or Jirgas of the tribal people who had expressed their disapproval also. At that time too no public announcement of my appointment had been made. It was curious that the tribal people should agitate themselves about a fact which was not publicly known and indeed which had not been fully decided upon. The inference was obvious that a broad hint had been given to them and they reacted to it. Of course they only reacted to it because the background was favourable for it (*Selected Works of Jawaharlal Nehru,* Second Series, vol. 1, p.340).

## The Unpleasant Memories

The incident at Malakand occurred just when Nehru's party left the place. His entourage had prior information that a group of persons waiting outside the gates of the Agency were going to create trouble. The Political Agent was also privy to this information. His car had preceded Nehru's convoy. Immediately after emerging from the gate of the Agency, Nehru's party was faced with a crowd of people blocking the road. Nehru's car was stoned and the glass smashed. In all this confusion, the Political Agent's car had gone ahead, leaving Nehru and his party completely isolated. Nehru was fortunate to escape with Dr Khan Saheb's help who cavalierly brandished his security guard's revolver. Abdul Ghaffar Khan sustained injuries. Nehru felt decidedly lucky to have escaped for they could have been grievously hurt or even murdered. His impressions of the officer (Sheikh Mahbub Ali) therefore were none too charitable: 'His past record is not an inspiring one...his behaviour at the time was disgraceful. His car was only a few feet away... As soon as we came out we saw a small crowd and a bus-load of people... Mahbub Ali's car just passed the bus when we were held up by the bus itself. Immediately, of course, the distance between his car and our car increased rapidly... For him to go forward then and not even to look back is inexplicable' (*Selected Works of Jawaharlal Nehru*, Second Series, Vol. 1, p.342).

The exchange of letters after Nehru returned from his tour of the NWFP indicates a definite downturn in his relationship with the Governor. The fallout and experience of the visit had left Nehru disturbed. He had honestly remonstrated:

> You will have realized that there is a big hiatus between you as a Governor and the Agent to the Governor General and the Provincial Government and those whom they represent. There can be no cooperation when there is this lack of confidence in each other and a desire to pull in different directions... This larger question cannot be ignored... This was so obvious [Nawab Sheikh Mahbub Ali's involvement] and patent that the question of enquiry even hardly arises...it seems to me impossible that Sheikh Mahbub Ali should continue in his present post and this matter should be taken in hand immediately...it has been decided that Dr Dring, the Deputy Commissioner of Peshawar should be transferred. The main reason for this was that he did not have the confidence of the Provincial government. It seems the sooner he leaves the district, the better... I greatly regret that events should have happened which have brought a certain personal element in the consideration of public problems (*Selected Works of Jawaharlal Nehru*, Second Series, Vol. 1, p.331).

The crux of the problem lay in the 'personal element' that coloured Nehru's public response. Unintentionally and subconsciously, it may have affected objectivity, impelling him to respond passionately when not required. Their relationship was now pegged on this 'personal' perception of each other, leading to some unfortunate consequences. Indicative of the relationship was a note that Nehru wrote to the Foreign Secretary, Sir Hugh Weightman, on 14 November 1946, wherein he repeatedly harped on the Malakand incident, complaining of delay in acting against the Political Agent:

> It was not made clear in the note [Sir Olaf Caroe's] whether the Political Agent of Malakand has been suspended or not pending such an inquiry. In one of my earlier letters to Sir Olaf Caroe I

had suggested that in any event the first step to be taken should be the suspension of the Political Agent pending further enquiry and action. I should like to know whether this was done or not... Another important consideration to be borne in mind is the necessity for speed in dealing with any such matter (*Selected Works of Jawaharlal Nehru*, Second Series, Vol. 1, p.347).

Things between Nehru and Caroe spiralled, going from bad to worse. In mid-March 1947, when yet another opportunity arose for Nehru to go to Peshawar, Wavell advised against it. Nehru thought it was Caroe who was indirectly responsible for scuttling his visit. It was right on the eve of Wavell's departure that Nehru served the government with an ultimatum:

> Someone does not like me or does not approve of my going to the Frontier. That someone presumably is Sir Olaf Caroe, the Governor. It is patent that he disapproves of my being in charge of the External Affairs Department. Long before I took charge of this, he tried to prevent my doing so by approaching you on the subject... My experience during the last six months has convinced me that no substantial good can be done to the Frontier areas unless this set-up is changed... I think the time has come when this matter must be faced squarely and a solution found. That solution should be the retirement of the Governor. Sir Olaf Caroe should, therefore, be requested to retire from his present office at an early date (*Selected Works of Jawaharlal Nehru*, Second Series, Vol. 1, p.315–17).

To be fair to Sir Olaf Caroe, it was Wavell who on his own initiative had suggested that Nehru cancel his Peshawar visit. But these were times when even Wavell was not getting along well with Nehru. The die was cast. Nehru followed this up by directly asking Sir Olaf Caroe to resign. On the new Viceroy's arrival, copies of the two letters—to Wavell and to Caroe—were both sent to him.

With Mountbatten's arrival on 22 March 1947, the end game of the British Indian empire had truly begun. How was the transfer of power to be achieved? Though the British Prime Minister's announcement of 20 February 1947[36] had set a definite date for the British withdrawal—of June 1948—it was deliberately not made clear to whom the British would demit power. Mountbatten immediately applied himself to the situation, initiating negotiations with the leaders of the Congress and Muslim League.

Within a matter of a few meetings with Mountbatten and as early as 8 April 1947, Nehru was saying that elections could be held afresh in the NWFP if the British government was ready to make a statement on the final arrangements for the transfer of power. Nehru's acquiescence was indicative of two things; one, that Partition would not be late in coming along with Independence; second, that Nehru was ready to concede elections a second time in the NWFP within an year of the earlier one and on the same issue of Pakistan. The idea of holding fresh elections, of course, was not his. It originated from Governor Caroe and was being examined by the British government as one of the possible options for the NWFP.

Mountbatten was agreeable to Caroe's idea of holding fresh elections. To a direct query from Maulana Azad as to why he considered it expedient, Mountbatten had reasoned with him on 12 April that in all other provinces the separate electorate enabled one to forecast with considerable accuracy the results of the election as between the League and the Congress since all Muslims had voted for the League. In the NWFP, the elections were largely an issue between the Congress Muslims and the League Muslims and of course, in the case of the NWFP, no separate electorate existed. Mountbatten, therefore, thought that the results of a fresh election would be a clear indication whether the NWFP wanted to stay with the Congress or the Muslim League.[37] The logic of holding a referendum could still stand technically—but to hold another election within a year of an earlier one, that too on the same issue—that of Pakistan, smacked of the Viceroy's partisanship. He definitely wanted to give the pro-Pakistan elements in the NWFP another chance at the hustings.

Lord Ismay[38] had visited the NWFP for a first-hand assessment of the situation. Since that was a short visit, Ismay, going only by Caroe's recommendation briefed Mountbatten on the desirability of holding another election in the NWFP. Predictably, the Governors' Conference convened thereafter in mid-April also gave the same recommendation—a general election in the NWFP as soon as possible after HMG had made the policy announcement on the transfer of power—and the Viceroy felt that HMG's announcement could come in a month's time.

Caroe, of course, wanted the Viceroy to make an immediate announcement about the general elections, whereas Mountbatten thought it best to defer till HMG had made its statement. At a meeting held on 16 April 1947, Nehru agreed with the Viceroy, Caroe and others that it would be desirable to hold the elections before the British demitted power, but immediate elections could cause some disturbances.[39] The minutes of the 16 April meeting suggest that Nehru's reaction to the suggestion for holding elections did not stem from annoyance. On the contrary, Nehru, with some amount of cajoling, came around to Mountbatten's view. As member in charge of the external affairs department, he had information on the prevailing situation in the NWFP. But had he at this stage consulted his NWFP colleagues on the proposal of holding fresh elections? If not, then how could he agree to this proposal on 16 April? These are some questions that still beg answers.

In the meeting of 16 April, Nehru even went on to discuss the modalities of holding the elections. He was apprehensive of the impartiality of these elections if the permanent officials were given complete charge of holding them. He, therefore, did not want the NWFP government dismissed as a precondition to holding fresh elections. Mountbatten, on the other hand, was attempting to hustle Nehru into agreeing that Caroe be allowed to make an immediate announcement after returning to Peshawar about holding fresh elections with a caveat that this would only be after HMG had made the statement. This, Nehru would not agree to. He felt that the Governor's announcement would make it appear as if the Muslim League agitation had forced the government's hand.[40] Caroe was not allowed to return to Peshawar and instead it was decided to call Dr Khan Saheb to Delhi for further discussions. Nehru agreed to this. Dr Khan Saheb's presence in Delhi meant that the Viceroy and the Governor could now jointly exert pressure on the NWFP Chief Minister for an early announcement of elections. Why force the Chief Minister of the NWFP into taking a fixed position, for which tactically there was no immediate need? Nehru agreeing to Dr Khan Saheb's instant summons to Delhi meant he was still undecided about the early announcement for holding elections in the NWFP. Plus, he had not consulted Dr Khan Saheb and was reluctant to carry the sole burden of a decision. Dr Khan Saheb's presence in Delhi would give an impression that decisions were arrived at only after holding joint consultations, something that was not quite correct.

An important meeting that Dr Khan Saheb was made to attend took place on 18 April. A lot has been said about the heat this meeting generated and also about open accusations and charges that the Chief Minister and the Governor traded. But in reality, all this was marginal to the purpose of the meeting, which was to come to a decision on the immediacy of the announcement for holding elections. The Governor and Mountbatten showed a singleness of purpose and as soon as the steam was vented, they set about pushing their agenda. It would be pertinent to mention that both the Chief Minister and the Governor had been called to Delhi at a time when serious communal rioting was on in Dera Ismail Khan. In the meeting Mountbatten shared a draft announcement that Caroe would make about impending elections upon his return to Peshawar. Dr Khan Saheb in his usual expansive style proclaimed that he was prepared for an election 'at any time'. A secondary issue pertaining to the release of political prisoners was also clinched.[41] The 18 April meeting had achieved its objective. The Chief Minister had been successfully brought into the loop of consultative democratic decision-making, squarely and gamely, by Nehru. Though a draft statement was prepared by Ismay on Mountbatten's instructions, surprisingly the announcement on the holding of elections was withheld.

The personal report[42] of the 18 April meeting that Mountbatten sent to the Secretary of State for India differed quite substantially in content from its 'minutes'. It was incumbent that the minutes be shared with the members attending the meeting but that was not the necessary protocol for the personal report. Mountbatten's personal report clearly stated that it was Nehru who had asked Dr Khan Saheb to come to Delhi, something on which Nehru and Mountbatten may have mutually decided. That, however, was not the main point of divergence. The minutes give one the feeling that an agreement had been reached: 'Subsequently the Viceroy handed over a draft statement which was to be issued by Caroe upon return, announcing that elections would be held in NWFP in due course. Dr Khan Saheb said that he would be prepared for election at any time...The Viceroy then invited Lord Ismay to prepare a draft statement to be issued by the Government of NWFP...'

And now sample the relevant lines of Mountbatten's personal report that he sent on 24 April: 'The elections would be necessary in due course but the province must settle down before the elections are held...' Why then was a misimpression conveyed through the 18 April 'minutes'? Were the 'minutes' glossing over disagreements? The decision to leave out those portions pertaining to holding of elections from the draft announcement were far too important to be left out. Securing Dr Khan Saheb's consent on an announcement for the elections was the only reason why he had been summoned from the NWFP by Nehru, and that too, when communal riots raged in Dera Ismail Khan.

In late April, Mountbatten paid a visit to the NWFP. Upon his return he sent two separate but important communications to Lord Listowel on 1 May. Mountbatten was now beginning to suggest important changes in arrangements for demission of power. Till the end of April 1947, he had maintained that elections would be held in the NWFP and the newly elected representatives would also have the option of declaring themselves as an independent Constituent Assembly.[43] But on 1 May he introduced a new proposal of holding a referendum in the NWFP. Referring to Nehru, Mountbatten said that he would accept the new proposal provided the referendum held out only two choices—that of the NWFP joining either Hindustan or Pakistan.[44] After consultations within his party, Nehru reverted to Mountbatten, making clear the Congress's inability to take part in the elections if they were forced upon them as a result of Muslim League pressure. The NWFP ministry had also appeared to be 'violently opposed' to the Viceroy ordering fresh elections. A referendum offered the best solution under the circumstances—elections could then be avoided. There would arise no need for the Governor to assume the reins of government. Since there would then be no newly elected legislature, the possibility of its coming together as a Constituent Assembly would stand pre-empted. In effective terms Mountbatten was now indicating that HMG would bring in changes to the very terms of the demission of power. The reason for Mountbatten's changed stance was Nehru. It was Nehru who had earlier agreed to the possibility of holding elections in the NWFP and then shown a preference for a referendum. But had he (Nehru) consulted the NWFP government or more importantly, Khan Abdul Ghaffar Khan, before suggesting such momentous changes?

The original plan for transfer of power that Ismay carried to London on 2 May proposed elections in the NWFP. Jinnah knew this plan. However, the *Hindustan Times* of 3 May leaked the plan. Mountbatten suspected Patel's role in this for he felt that Nehru had never really contested the 'justice' of the argument for holding elections in the NWFP the way Patel had done. Patel had in fact openly disagreed with the proposal of the dissolution of the government in the NWFP. From the records it is clear that both Nehru and Mountbatten were trying to find a solution that encountered the least possible resistance. Nehru's qualified acceptance of a referendum was a step in that direction. Both Nehru and Mountbatten knew that the Congress high command and the Frontier Congress would also oppose the idea of a referendum and perhaps react in the same vein as they had on the issue of holding fresh elections.

The second plan (the V.P. Menon[45] plan) which landed in London two weeks later contained the proposal for holding a referendum in the NWFP instead of elections. That Nehru had played a major role in Mountbatten effecting this change was obvious. Also obvious was the extremely short time frame in which this change was effected. The Menon plan was formalized in Simla during the early part of the second week of May in the presence of Nehru and Mountbatten. Sadly, the change effected was not agreeable to those most likely to be hit by this decision—Khan Abdul Ghaffar Khan and Dr Khan Saheb. Gandhi too was opposed to this idea. In Nehru's absence, for he was then in Simla, a meeting on Frontier affairs was held in Delhi, which the Khan brothers and other Congress leaders along with Gandhi attended. Proceedings of this meeting had disturbed Nehru, but more on that later. What assumed significance was the finalization process of the second plan that sealed the fate of Khudai Khidmatgars and their leader, Khan Abdul Ghaffar Khan, for was that process not extraneous to them? The explanation that Nehru proffered for having chosen a referendum with only two options—of Hindustan and Pakistan—had been 'post-facto'.

The whole business of taking a decision on the referendum does not end here. The draft that the Cabinet Committee in London considered on 7 May relating to the transfer of power contained both options—that of elections as well as a referendum. In the case of elections, a newly elected legislature and creation of a new Constituent Assembly of twelve members was envisaged. The twelve, instead of the original three, could then decide whether the province wanted to be with Pakistan, Hindustan or remain independent.[46] The Cabinet Committee was inclined to decide in favour of the third option in the case of the NWFP, Baluchistan and Sylhet.[47] The Congress definitely had enough clout then to prevail upon HMG for those regions to remain independent. But Nehru was set against the idea of a third option, of the NWFP's independence. On 7 May, therefore, the Cabinet Committee approved of the referendum and informed the Viceroy accordingly.

Then came the crucial meeting of 8 May at Simla which Nehru attended. Nehru was of the view that 'it was essential to know definitely which way the NWFP wanted to go…possibly there would be new elections soon after the new constitution[48] had been decided.'[49] Nehru was insistent that whatever was done in the NWFP should be in an 'all-India' context. While the Cabinet Committee had agreed to a referendum on 7 May, the prospect of holding subsequent elections and possible options for a referendum had still been left open. Nehru felt this would bring in 'enormous' complications. He wanted that no province be given the right to secede. There were to be only two Constitutions—one for the old union and one for the new. Not wanting new members from NWFP for the Constituent Assembly and therefore also not wanting a new legislature, the existing members from the NWFP were to continue in the Constituent Assembly so that their position remained unaltered. Nehru also wanted that until the Constitution was framed, provinces were not to be given the right to secede. But the delay on account of Constitution-making was not acceptable to either Mountbatten or V.P. Menon.[50]

Why was Nehru insistent on wanting to wait till the Constituent Assembly had drafted the essentials of a Constitution? Mountbatten, in a letter to Ismay, gives the reason for this. Nehru had been very disturbed by the meeting on Frontier affairs held in Delhi where the NWFP government representatives, Abdul Ghaffar Khan, Congress leaders and Gandhi had met. The provincial government's view was that 'even a referendum held now would be yielding to force and would upset the equilibrium in NWFP leading to grave disorder'. Mountbatten therefore wanted Ismay to impress upon HMG to approve the proposal of a referendum in the NWFP and a statement made on these lines in the approved plan on the transfer of power.

In the Simla meeting of 8 May, Nehru gradually came around to Mountbatten's view when he (Nehru) stated that 'intellectually he was in favour of a referendum' and agreed that the referendum would settle matters.[51] At this meeting, he did not appear to be opposed to a referendum. His only disagreement now was *when* to hold it. Mountbatten wanted Nehru to suggest the date for holding the referendum, as the process was linked to the issue of the date on which the transfer of power would take place. Mountbatten hinted quite crucially at this point to Nehru that he wanted the date of the transfer of power advanced and would suggest to HMG likewise. But for HMG to agree, a decision on the NWFP was an obvious precondition.[52] Nehru could not resist the bait that Mountbatten so brazenly dangled. Events transpired at great speed while Nehru was in Simla, at a location where he possibly was unable to properly consult the Khan brothers.

What had disturbed Nehru so much about that Delhi meeting was his inability to attend it.[53] Nehru long considered the affairs of the NWFP as part of his parish. He could have attended this crucial meeting and then come up to Simla to be with the Mountbattens. A clear answer as to why he could not attend this meeting is yet to be found.

As the day of 8 May progressed, Mountbatten, with some personal satisfaction, was able to inform his Chief of Staff Lord Ismay in London that Nehru had agreed to the proposal of a referendum. The letter that Nehru personally dictated to V.P. Menon was a handy piece of evidence. The rationale provided for holding a referendum was that a piquant situation was likely to arise if West Punjab opted for partition and joined Pakistan. In that event, the NWFP had to be given a chance to exercise its option of either joining India or Pakistan. The only precondition was Nehru's insistence that the referendum be held with the concurrence of the provincial government and under the supervision of the Viceroy.[54] How convincing was the explanation for holding a referendum? As events played out, the NWFP government was never consulted, neither on the choice for a referendum, nor on the questions of options and dates. The provincial government also had no say in the selection of officers who would oversee the elections. Even the clause that the referendum would be held with the 'concurrence of the provincial government' was removed at Ismay's insistence, for it was felt that it would raise the hackles of Jinnah and his League. In the 3 June announcement, this particular clause was missing.

Nehru and Patel had both acquiesced to the referendum. Many in the Congress who had initially opposed it also eventually fell in line. The question of the Frontier Congress boycotting a referendum was an entirely separate issue, different from the Congress's acceptance of the referendum.

On his return from Simla, Nehru sought Patel's help in convening a meeting of the Congress Working Committee for which Gandhi and Abdul Ghaffar Khan were also to be invited. To help him form a consensus, and to take Gandhi and Abdul Ghaffar Khan along with him, Nehru expected Patel to do his bit. Nehru had all along known how difficult it would be to carry along Gandhi and Khan Abdul Ghaffar Khan on the subject of a referendum. Nehru openly admitted to Mountbatten that 'he found his mind not at all clear about the various possible developments'.[55] He also confessed 'not seeing much light and that many things troubled him', finally saying, 'I find from one of your letters that you have asked Caroe to tell Khan Saheb that I am in general agreement with the procedure suggested, namely a referendum. Now this is one thing on which there is very strong opinion among my colleagues not only in the Congress Working Committee but also of the Khan Saheb's government.'[56]

Mountbatten spent the latter part of May in London, consulting and helping the Cabinet Committee draft the Partition Plan. HMG, on 3 June 1947, announced the arrangements as well as the date of the demission of power. The NWFP was to undergo a referendum and the options given were only to be two—to either join India or Pakistan.

The Frontier Congress was not agreeable to this arrangement. Even Gandhi was not. This perhaps forced Nehru to spell out his case as well as HMG's on the arrangement. In a lengthy explanatory note of 8 June meant for the Khan brothers and other Frontier Congress leaders, he provided the defence.

Did Nehru well appreciate the consequence of the 3 June announcement for the NWFP? Perhaps not, as he used a curious sentence in his explanatory note: 'It must be remembered that the future of NWFP for some considerable period, is going to be decided' (*Selected Works of Jawaharlal Nehru*, Second Series, Vol. 3, p.277) conveying that the future arrangement for the NWFP was to be rather provisional and that the province was not to be permanently lost to India. Another example perhaps are two letters that Nehru wrote to Krishna Menon[57] and Gandhi on 23 and 24 May 1947 respectively. In those letters he argued that since Bengal and Punjab would be partitioned, what would be left of Pakistan may not be worth having, inferring therefore that the Pakistan project would collapse. A possibility exists of course that Nehru's apparent optimism was intended merely to sugarcoat this pill for Gandhi, though it seems more likely that Nehru genuinely believed that the result would be the end of the Pakistan demand. What the partition really meant in Nehru's opinion still remains uncertain. He did not seem to think that Pakistan would have full sovereignty. In his interview of 24 May 1947, he stated that Pakistan would be unable to allow any foreign power to use its bases. Nehru seems to have found it as difficult to conceive of a truly independent Pakistan as Britain found it hard to contemplate a truly independent India. Such was the force of inherited patterns of thought. The proclivity of Nehru to view the pivotal events of 1947 as temporary and interim, for example, the ad hocism shown while dealing with the Radcliffe Boundary Commission,[58] had fateful consequences for India.

Building his defence, in the note of 8 June Nehru expatiated on the way the 3 June plan had developed and how it then became necessary to give certain provinces or their parts a choice to opt out of the Indian Union. Nehru alluded to the possibility of west Punjab seceding from the Indian Union, which meant that the NWFP would be physically cut off. In view of this new situation he felt it advisable to hold a referendum. Arrangements were not only to be made in the case of the NWFP; it was now part of a larger plan that would provide for a referendum in the NWFP, Baluchistan and Sylhet (*Selected Works of Jawaharlal Nehru*, Second Series, Vol. 3, p.316).

Faced with a referendum, the Frontier Congress demanded a third choice, the choice of opting out to stand independently as a free Constituent Assembly. What is ironical is that the NWFP had had the choice of standing out independently even in the original plan that Ismay had taken to London on 2 May. The Cabinet Committee was also of the view that the choice to remain free should be included in the scheme if it was to be consistent and defensible in Parliament. The Cabinet Committee also wanted Baluchistan and Sylhet to be given that choice. Theoretically, even the two Bengals and the two Punjabs had that choice earlier. The Cabinet Committee on 12 May had not shied away from making its views known: 'But now because of the amendment suggested by the Viceroy, that of the option to remain independent being withdrawn from NWFP, it ought also to be withdrawn from Baluchistan and Sylhet. The Cabinet Committee was therefore deferring to the Viceroy's strong views at the cost of illogicality.'[59] These were strong views!

For Nehru, the question of having a referendum in the NWFP depended on decisions yet to be taken in the case of Punjab and Bengal. In his 8 May note he admitted to this: 'If those decisions [for secession] were not taken in Punjab and Bengal, then there would be no question of referendum in the NWFP.'[60] Therefore, for him the issue was still open. The Khan brothers were of course not convinced by this explanation. Even if they were ignorant of the views of the Cabinet Committee on the stipulation of free choice in the scheme, could they not see that East Pakistan,[61] if created, would suffer a similar predicament as the NWFP, of being separated from West Pakistan[62] by over a thousand miles?

Nehru conceded that not everyone in the Congress was committed to a referendum, though he and some others 'more or less' were. The Congress had taken cognizance of the growing demand in the province for independence and the subsequent decision about its relations with the rest of India. It wanted the referendum to make provisions for that. But for Nehru, the 3 June announcement had settled the issue of a referendum. He could not get out of it now. For the Viceroy to get out of it was even more difficult (*Selected Works of Jawaharlal Nehru*, Second Series, Vol. 3, p.275). Nehru therefore wanted the Congress Frontier leaders to reconcile to the fact of a referendum and in the absence of a third option of independence.

Based on British official estimates, Nehru concluded that the Frontier Congress had a 50-50 chance of victory in the referendum, a guess not based on his consultations with the Khan brothers or other leaders of the Frontier Congress. Unsure of 'what developments may take place during the month of June' (*Selected Works of Jawaharlal Nehru*, Second Series, Vol. 3, p.277) (the referendum took place in July), he was curiously optimistic about the developing situation working out to their advantage. As to the 'why and how' of it, he neither questioned nor elaborated upon it. It became difficult, therefore, for the Khan brothers to derive solace just from Nehru's wishful thinking and his pious intentions.

Nehru wanted the Frontier Congress to fight democratically in the referendum. Even if they lost, they would not be weakened for long. To him, giving up without a struggle meant a certain lack of integrity, for it symbolized a fear of the consequences, something that could lead to the collapse of the organization. Subjects like 'development' and 'freedom' were close to Nehru's heart. He insisted that the Frontier Congress participate in the referendum on these very issues in the face of a situation made impossible by communal strife. As he understood it, the NWFP would neither get freedom nor independence if it aligned with Punjab, for the latter would dominate over the Frontier. And even if the Congress lost the referendum, it would still be a blow to Pakistan (*Selected Works of Jawaharlal Nehru*, Second Series, Vol. 3, pp.277-78).

The 3 June announcement left just eleven weeks in hand for Partition to take formal effect. Events therefore acquired a dynamic of their own. The Frontier Congress would have to sever connections with the parent party in case they lost the referendum. The NWFP was the only province where the Muslim League had not been able to cash in on 'Pakistan' in the 1946 provincial elections. A good performance by the Congress on the same issue now could not score the same point twice over. Communal riots had already taken place in Bengal, Bihar, the United Provinces and Punjab. The NWFP too had not been spared.

With the atmosphere so inflamed and vitiated, Nehru's suggestions can at best be explained as a lack of appreciation of that highly emotive issue—communalism.

Nehru unsuccessfully tried to impress upon the Khan brothers that in future Mountbatten was going to play an important role in the developments taking place and that he had no doubt about Mountbatten's sincerity and his desire to do the right thing. Nehru was convinced that Mountbatten realized the difficulties the Frontier faced and would do everything in his power to settle them. He felt that Mountbatten's predicament of having committed himself to a referendum should be sympathetically considered as it was now impossible to get out of it without grave injury to his own prestige and impartiality. Mountbatten would rather resign than face a situation where he had to retract from his decision (*Selected Works of Jawaharlal Nehru,* Second Series, Vol. 3, p.278). Nehru was not one to fight shy of defending his friend. But in doing so he lost the NWFP for India.

Nehru had taken much care to reiterate the important aspect of 'fullest consultation and thought' (*Selected Works of Jawaharlal Nehru,* Second Series, vol. 3, p.279) in disposing of as vital a matter as that of the referendum in the NWFP. Was he entirely correct in saying so? To the note of 8 June he forwarded to Gandhi was attached a simple remark of his: 'You will deal with it as you think best' (*Selected Works of Jawaharlal Nehru,* Second Series, Vol. 3, p.279).

Nehru persevered with his efforts to convince the Frontier Congress leaders. He followed up on this with another note of 13 June: 'We have, willingly or unwillingly accepted the referendum and this is going to take place. Even the British officers selected to supervise the referendum have been approved by Dr Khan Saheb' (*Selected Works of Jawaharlal Nehru,* Second Series, Vol. 3, p.280). What Nehru contended was not actually true. The list of the officers was shown to Dr Khan Saheb only on the condition that the Viceroy could overrule his objections. What choice did Dr Khan Saheb then have? Really none. But Nehru was not going to raise this 'minor' point with the Viceroy in view of the 'major' issues involved. That Dr Khan Saheb was decent enough to approve the list of officers even when he really had no choice was not appreciated as it should have been.

A joint meeting of the Frontier Provincial Congress Committee, the Congress Parliamentary Party and the Khudai Khidmatgar commanders convened in Peshawar on 12 June, resolved to authorize Khan Abdul Ghaffar Khan to take whatever action he thought best on the question of participation in the referendum. In an effort to bring Abdul Ghaffar Khan around, Nehru was now using all his persuasive powers: 'With western Punjab seceding there will be a barrier between India and the NWFP. Even if NWFP joined the Union, it will at best be a buffer state deserving of a special treatment which meant fullest autonomy.' Nehru wanted that the Congress Working Committee adopt a resolution that in case west Punjab opted out of the Union, the NWFP would enjoy fullest freedom. A vote for the Union meant a vote for self-determination and freedom. He wanted people to vote on this basis, for to Nehru, the Congress resolution would then have also recognized the urge for Pathanistan and yet afforded an opportunity to vote in the referendum. Nehru, therefore, wanted propaganda to be spread by the Frontier Congress along these lines. But the Khan brothers and Gandhi stood unconvinced.

Finally giving up on his efforts to convince the Khan brothers, Nehru wrote to Dr Khan Saheb on 30 June, asking him what he intended doing after the 'one-sided' referendum, mentioning alongside that as things stood, he could not do very much. On the same date he also wrote to Khan Abdul Ghaffar Khan, albeit with a sense of resignation: 'I wish I could meet you and discuss all these matters with you. But I fear that is not possible now or in the near future.' Nehru had thrown Abdul Ghaffar Khan 'to the wolves'.

Despite his best efforts, Nehru could not persuade the Khan brothers to participate in the July referendum. In a statement issued on 24 June 1947, Abdul Ghaffar Khan appealed to all Pathans who believed in a free Pathan state to not participate in the referendum. The results of the referendum were declared in the third week of July. The decision was overwhelmingly in favour of Pakistan for the Frontier Congress had boycotted it. The blame game on who lost the Frontier for India has long since gone on. On 14 August 1947, the day when the NWFP formally became an integral part of Pakistan, it still had a Congress ministry. The first undemocratic act of the Pakistan government was to dismiss it on 22 August.

## Notes

1. Jawaharlal Nehru was born in Allahabad (in the United Provinces) in British India in 1889 to an influential political family. He was educated at Cambridge, after which he joined Inner Temple, London. His political career began in 1920 in the United Provinces.
2. When the Indian leadership failed to resolve the constitutional issue of the communal problem, British Prime Minister Ramsay MacDonald announced his own formula. After the failure of the Second Round Table Conference, MacDonald announced the 'Communal Award' on 16 August 1932. According to the award, the right of a separate electorate was given not only to the Muslims of India but also to all minority communities. The award declared 'Harijans' as a minority and thus the Hindu depressed classes were given special seats to be filled from special depressed class electorates in the areas where their voters were concentrated. Under the Communal Award, the principle of weightage was also maintained with some modifications in the Muslim-minority provinces. The principle of weightage was also applied for Europeans in Bengal and Assam, Sikhs in Punjab and the NWFP, and Hindus in Sindh and the NWFP. The award was not popular with any Indian party. Gandhi protested against the declaration of 'Harijans' as a minority and undertook a fast unto death. He managed to sign the Poona Pact with Dr B.R. Ambedkar, the leader of the depressed classes, in which the Congress met many of their demands.
3. In the winter months of 1936 to 1937, in elections for seats in the new provincial legislative assemblies, 54 per cent of the eligible voters participated. The Congress Party won 711 of the 1,585 seats on the campaign of opposing the Government of India Act of 1935 with the express intention of wrecking it. The Congress won control of the provincial legislative assemblies in the Central Provinces, the United Provinces, Assam, Bihar, Orissa, Bombay and Madras. Later in 1937, Congress ministries were formed in the NWFP and in March 1938 in Assam. The Muslim League won 105 of the 489 seats won by Muslims. Throughout the period of March to June 1937, the Indian Viceroy, Lord Linlithgow, expressed an unwillingness for the provincial Governors to annul their special or reserved powers as a form of assurance to elicit Congress entry into the provincial ministries. On 22 June his reassuring

statements, when combined with those of British Prime Minister Neville Chamberlain in the House of Commons, won Congress acceptance and entrance on 7 July into the provincial government.
4. The Akhil Bhartiya Hindu Mahasabha, a Hindu nationalist organization, was originally founded in 1915.
5. Speech at Peshawar, 16 October 1937, from *The Hindu*, 17 October 1937.
6. A quote from Nehru's speech of 16 October 1937, reported in *The Hindu*, 18 October 1937.
7. Statement to the press, Peshawar, 18 October 1937, the *Hindustan Times*, 19 October 1937.
8. Ibid.
9. Primarily the views of Sir Olaf Caroe as expressed in his book *The Pathans*, Macmillan & Co., 1958.
10. All India Congress Committee File No. p.16/1938–1939, p.71
11. From 22 March to 24 March 1940, the All India Muslim League held its annual session at Minto Park, Lahore. This session proved to be historic. The resolution passed during this session read, 'No constitutional plan would be workable or acceptable to the Muslims unless geographical contiguous units are demarcated into regions which should be so constituted with such territorial readjustments as may be necessary. That the areas in which the Muslims are numerically in majority as in the north-western and eastern zones of India should be grouped to constitute independent states in which the constituent units shall be autonomous and sovereign.' The resolution repudiated the concept of a united India and recommended the creation of an independent Muslim state consisting of Punjab, the NWFP, Sindh and Baluchistan in the northwest, and Bengal and Assam in the northeast.
13. Razmak is one of the three subdivisions of North Waziristan Agency, the other two being Miranshah and Mirali. It is home to the Uthmanzai Wazirs.
14. File No. 201-Ps/46-PMs, *Selected Works of Jawaharlal Nehru*, Second Series, Vol.1, p.302.
15. Sir George Edmond Brackenbury Abell (1904–89) was an English civil servant. He held an important place in the Indian Civil Service in the years prior to independence, serving as private secretary to the last two Viceroys, Lord Wavell and Lord Mountbatten. He later returned to the United Kingdom and became the first Civil Service Commissioner, and later still was a Director of the Bank of England.

16. Caroe's telegram to Wavell on 29 September 1946, *Selected Works of Jawaharlal Nehru*, Second Series, Vol. I, p.306.
17. Governor's Report of 23 October 1946 and Weekly Intelligence Summary, India Office Library, London (IOL) L/P&s/12/3200.
18. The term 'Malik' is used in Afghanistan and the tribal areas of Pakistan, especially among Pakhtuns, for a tribal leader or a chieftain. Maliks serve as de facto arbiters in local conflicts, interlocutors in state policymaking, tax collectors, heads of villages and town councils and delegates to provincial and national *jirgas* as well as to Parliament.
19. Born Mohiuddin Mahsud (died 1913), Mullah Powindah was a religious leader of the Pakhtun tribe of the Mahsuds. Mullah Powindah led a long-standing guerrilla insurgency against the British forces in the late nineteenth century.
21. Wana is the most important town of South Waziristan Agency in Pakistan's Federally Administrated Tribal Areas (FATA). It is the summer headquarters for the Agency's administration, Tank, located in neighbouring Tank district being the winter headquarters. During the period of the British empire, beginning in the late nineteenth century, the British established a cantonment on the Wana plain, which was used as headquarters by the British forces in South Waziristan until they departed in 1947. During their rule, the ferocious Pakhtun tribes of Waziristan (a part of the Karlanri Tribal Confederation) gave the British much headache. At one time during the 1930s, the British had up to 18,000 troops in and around Waziristan, with Wana being used as the forward headquarters and air base.
22. Jandola is a town in South Waziristan, FATA, Pakistan.
23. The Bhittanis are a Pathan tribe located in the FATA of Pakistan. The Bhittanis' area is a buffer zone separating the Tank area from the Mahsud tribe of the South Waziristan region.
24. Naib-tehsildar is a position of some authority in the revenue administration.
25. Intelligence Summary 26/10/46, P&s/12/3200/IOL, and the Prime Minister of India's visit to NWFP, Curtis Papers, p.8, IOL.
26. Jamrud is a town located in Khyber Agency in the FATA of Pakistan. The town is the doorway to Khyber Pass, part of the Hindu Kush range. Jamrud, lying in proximity to the Khyber Pass, has remained a location on the trade route between Central Asia and South Asia and a strategic military location.

27. The Shinwaris are an ethnic Pakhtun tribe of Afghanistan and of FATA of Pakistan. Among the greatest poets of the Pashto language in the twentieth century was the late Ameer Hamza Shinwari, also known as 'Hamza Baba' and 'Father of the Ghazal'.
28. The Mullagoris are a Pakhtun tribe that inhabit the Khyber Agency, one of the FATAs of Pakistan. The Mullagoris are believed to be one of the tribes descended from Muhammad of Ghor. They settled just north of the Khyber Pass during the times when Islam was brought to South Asia.
29. Landi Kotal or Landikotal is a town in FATA, Pakistan. It lies on the Khyber Pass in Khyber Agency. At 1,072 m above sea level, it is the highest point on the Khyber Pass and is the route across the mountains to the city of Peshawar.
30. Speech at Peshawar, 19 October 1946, from *Hindustan Times*, 21 October 1946.
31. Malakand incident (Caroe had a meeting with Nehru on 20 October 1946 about which he wrote to Wavell on 23 October, R/3/1/92, IOL).
32. Justice Clark's Report of 28 February 1947 in R/3/1/92 IOL.
33. Weekly Intelligence Summary 3/5/47 L/P&s/12/3200 IOL.
34. Wavell to all Governors, L/P&J/8/659: FF3-5, 30 July 1946, p.146, Vol. VIII.
35. Ibid.
36. The British Prime Minister made a formal announcement in the House of Commons on 20 February 1947, that the whole responsibility for the government and administration of India would be transferred to Indian hands and that if no settlement was arrived at between the political parties in India, the responsibility would be transferred to a central government and to provinces and other authorities in such a manner as may appear to His Majesty's Government to be in the best interest of India.
37. Interview between Mountbatten and Maulana Azad, Mountbatten Papers, Viceroy's Interview No. 56 of 12 April 1947, *The Transfer of Power*, 1947, Vol. X, pp.215–17.
38. General Hastings Lionel Ismay (1887–1965) was a reputed British soldier and a diplomat. Commissioned in the army in 1905 he joined the Indian army in the Twenty-first Cavalry and served on the North-West Frontier. In 1931, Ismay became the Military Secretary to Lord Willingdon, then Viceroy of India. In 1940 he was selected by Winston Churchill as Chief of his Personal Staff in the Ministry of Defence, with the duty of

liaising between the War Cabinet and Chiefs of Staff. He was promoted to Lieutenant General in 1942 and to General in 1944, retiring from the British army in 1946. In January 1947 he was raised to the peerage as Baron Ismay. Lord Ismay served as Chief of Staff to Lord Mountbatten in Burma, then Viceroy of India from March to November 1947. He was nicknamed 'Pug', which is the name by which both Mountbatten and Churchill knew him.

39. Viceroy's Third Miscellaneous Meeting, Mountbatten Papers, *The Transfer of Power*, 16 April 1947, Vol. X, p.286-292.
40. Ibid.
41. Minutes of Viceroy's Fourth Miscellaneous Meeting, Mountbatten Papers, 18 April 1947, *The Transfer of Power*, Vol. X, pp.315-19.
42. Viceroy's Personal Report No. 4, l/Po/6/123: ff 51-59 of 24 April 1947, *The Transfer of Power*, Vol. X, pp.404-05.
43. The Constituent Assembly of India was elected to write the Constitution of India, and served as its first Parliament in an independent nation. The Constituent Assembly of India was set up as a result of negotiations between Indian leaders and members of the British Cabinet Mission. The Constituent Assembly was elected indirectly by the members of the Provincial Legislative Assemblies. The Congress secured an overwhelming majority in the general seats while the Muslim League managed to sweep almost all the seats reserved for Muslims. It first met on 9 December 1946 in Delhi, while India was still under British rule. It originally included the provinces that now compose Pakistan and Bangladesh, and the representation of the princely states of India. In June 1947, delegations from the provinces of Sindh, East Bengal, Baluchistan, West Punjab and the NWFP formed the Constituent Assembly of Pakistan in Karachi. On 15 August 1947, India became an independent nation, and the Constituent Assembly became India's Parliament.
44. Mountbatten to Lord Listowel, Mountbatten Papers—Letters to and from Secretary of State, 1 May 1947, *The Transfer of Power*, 1947, Vol. X, p.531.
45. V.P. Menon was an Indian civil servant who played a vital role during the partition of India and the integration of independent India. In 1946, he was appointed Political Reforms Commissioner to the British Viceroy. Menon was the political advisor to the last Viceroy of India, Lord Louis Mountbatten.

46. India and Burma Committee Papers, I B (47) 56, L/P&J/10/79: ff 375–76 of 6 May 1947, *The Transfer of Power*, 1947, pp.378–84, 386, 637, Vol. X.
47. Sylhet is a major city of northeastern Bangladesh. It is the headquarters of Sylhet division and Sylhet district.
48. Constitution and elections: The Constituent Assembly of India approved the Constitution on 26 January 1949, making it official. On 26 January 1950, the Constitution took effect, a day now commemorated as Republic Day in India. At this point, the Constituent Assembly became the Provisional Parliament of India, until the first elections under the new Constitution took place in 1952.
49. Viceroy's Tenth Miscellaneous Meeting, Mountbatten Papers, Simla, 8 May 1947, *The Transfer of Power*, Vol. X, pp.670–73.
50. Ibid.
51. Ibid.
52. Ibid.
53. Mountbatten to Lord Ismay, Telegram R/3/1/153: ff 1–2, Simla, 8 May 1947, *The Transfer of Power*, Vol. X, p.697.
54. Mountbatten to Lord Ismay, Telegram, Mountbatten Papers, Official Correspondence Files, Provinces and their Futures, Part 1(a), 8 May 1947, *The Transfer of Power*, Vol. X, p.698.
55. Nehru to Mountbatten, R/3/1/151: ff 50–51, Simla, 10 May 1947, *The Transfer of Power*, Vol. X, pp.739–40.
56. Ibid.
57. V.K. Krishna Menon (1897–1974) was a prominent Indian political figure. He was an ardent socialist and served as a Labour member of the St Pancras Borough Council from 1934 to 1947. His primary political interest in England centred in the struggle for freedom in India. He strove tirelessly for this cause as Secretary of the India League from 1929. His long and close relationship with Jawaharlal Nehru began during that period. With the coming of Indian independence in 1947, Krishna Menon was appointed High Commissioner (Ambassador) of India in London. He returned to India in 1952 after twenty-seven years of residence in England, becoming a Member of the Indian Parliament in 1953, Minister without portfolio in 1956, and Minister for Defence in 1957. The military reverses suffered by India at the hands of the Chinese in the Himalayas in 1962 were attributed to some to his policies. Overwhelming opposition forced him to relinquish the Ministry of Defence in October 1962.

58. Two boundary commissions were set up by Viceroy Mountbatten. One of them was to deal with the partition of Bengal and separation of Sylhet from Assam and the other to deal with the partition of Punjab. Each of the commissions had a Chairman and four members, two appointed by the Congress and two by the Muslim League. Sir Cyril Radcliffe, a leading member of the English bar, was appointed the Chairman of both the commissions. Radcliffe had never visited India before and there is no indication that he had any worthwhile knowledge of Indian affairs. He arrived in Delhi on 8 July 1947. Mountbatten disclosed the awards to Indian leaders on 17 August. The awards satisfied no one. The Congress criticism of the award relating to Bengal mainly related to the allotment of Chittagong Hill Tracts to Pakistan. The major Pakistani criticism was the allotment of Calcutta to India. With regard to Ferozepore district, Pakistan pointed out that Muslim-majority tehsils of Ferozepore and Zira, contiguous to Pakistan, were first allotted by Radcliffe to Pakistan and later on, as a result of a last-minute intervention by Mountbatten, they were allotted to India.
59. India and Burma Committee, Cabinet, L/P&J/10/79: ff 197–200 of 12 May 1947, *The Transfer of Power*, Vol. X, pp.783–84.
60. Mountbatten to Ismay, 8 May 1947, *The Transfer of Power*, Vol. X, p.698, and S. Gopal, ed., *Selected Works of Jawaharlal Nehru*, Second Series, Vol. 3, p.275.
61. East Pakistan was a former province of Pakistan that existed between 1955 and 1971 and is now the country of Bangladesh. Bengal was divided into east and west parts in 1947 when British India was separated into Pakistan and India. The eastern parts become East Bengal, one of the five provinces of Pakistan (the others being West Punjab, Sindh, Baluchistan and the Afghania Provincial Region).
62. West Pakistan was the official western wing of Pakistan until 1971, when the eastern wing became independent as Bangladesh. The politically dominant western wing was composed of three Governors' provinces (the NWFP, Punjab and Sindh), one Chief Commissioner's province (Baluchistan), the Baluchistan States Union, several other princely states (notably Bahawalpur, Chitral, Dir, Hunza, Khairpur and Swat), the Federal Capital Territory (around Karachi) and the tribal areas.

# 9

# The Muslim League Punch

IT TOOK JUST three and a half months, from 20 February to 3 June 1947, for the Muslim League in the NWFP to transform itself into an enterprising organization, such that years of work done by Ghaffar Khan and his Khudai Khidmatgars was swept away by the popular communal upsurge, upholding for the time the 'two-nation' theory of Jinnah. The NWFP voted for Pakistan in the July referendum at a time when the duly elected Congress government of little more than a year was still very much in office.

The civil disobedience movement of the provincial Muslim League was launched as soon as the British Prime Minister proclaimed a final date of withdrawal from India. The Muslim League had secured nearly 50 per cent of the Muslim seats in the general elections of February 1946. In the intervening period of one year, before they launched the civil disobedience movement, the Muslim League received a shot in its arm with Nehru's visit to the Frontier and the subsequent toppling of Khizar Tiwana's government in Punjab. March 1946 saw the appointment of a friendly Governor in Sir Olaf Caroe. A palpable sense of urgency imbued the central and provincial Muslim League ranks, for they had limited time to overturn popular sentiments. On what basis would they claim Pakistan if they failed to capture a Muslim province like the NWFP? It was incumbent that they did so, something plainly apparent to the British. Did the Congress fail to foresee what was coming? HMG announced India's partition, and the decision alongside to hold a referendum in the NWFP, offering just two choices, to either opt for Pakistan or India. The campaign against Dr Khan Saheb's ministry had gathered sufficient steam by February 1947, what with the leading Pirs of Punjab and the NWFP touring the region to whip up support for the

Muslim League. Pir Sahib of Zakori and prominent Afridi, Mohmand and Waziri tribal leaders visited the communally ravaged areas of Bihar post-haste, to return with wildly exaggerated accounts of what they had seen. Pir Sahib of Manki Sharif was a special invitee to the provincial Muslim League's marathon eight-hour deliberations in Peshawar on 20 February. The meeting was convened to assess political temperatures in Punjab and the NWFP. A communally sensitive resolution was adopted, demanding prompt return of Basanti (a Sikh girl from Hazara) to the Muslim community, for allegedly, she had converted to Islam. Critical of Dr Khan Saheb's ministry, the resolution stated that, 'the ministry in enforcing apostasy on a Muslim convert under duress had led to a province wide resentment amongst the Muslims of NWFP and Tribal areas.'[1] The resolution was not widely off the mark. The incident provided a timely opportunity to the Muslim League to exploit the situation. The government too did not help improve matters, for on the same day it arrested Abdul Qayyum Khan, the leader of the opposition, while he was addressing a small crowd near the Hoti Mardan police station. A Muslim League procession had gone to the Deputy Commissioner's residence in Mardan demanding Basanti's release, and the arrest took place when Abdul Qayyum Khan was returning from the Deputy Commissioner's quarters. He asked for permission to address the crowd so that he could tell them to disperse. But he did the opposite, exhorting the crowd to defy the Deputy Commissioner's order. On 14 March, Abdul Qayyum Khan, Samim Jan Khan and Mohammad Ali Khan, the last two, president and secretary of the Provincial Muslim League, and forty-eight others, were sentenced to three months' imprisonment.

The situation in Peshawar deteriorated immediately. The military now came to guard Dr Khan Saheb's residence and was entrusted with the responsibility of securing the periphery of Peshawar city. For reasons of safety, the city's exit that led to Kohat was given over to the combined forces of the army and police. An order under Section 144 of the Criminal Procedure Code prohibiting public meetings and processions was promulgated within Peshawar's city limits. With the onset of the civil disobedience movement, the arrests of prominent Muslim Leaguers in the Frontier districts started. As the movement grew, so did the arrests.[2] Though some leaders managed to go underground, the arrests by and large proved counter-productive, bestowing popularity to the movement as people's sympathy veered towards the Muslim League. On 1 March, arrests, especially of the leading Muslim divine of Waziristan, Pir Abdul Latif Sahib of Zakori who had lakhs of *murids* (followers) in Derajat and Waziristan, came as a shock to the people of Dera Ismail Khan. Thousands came out to court arrest. Collectively, all this led to an exponential increase in the numbers participating in the movement. Within days of Pir Abdul Sahib's arrest, a procession of 20,000 Muslims paraded the bazaars of Dera Ismail Khan. With each passing day, the processions became numerous, gaining in strength.[3]

Within ten days of its announcement, the movement was in full swing. Having addressed twenty-four meetings in Peshawar itself, the Pir of Manki Sharif was covering Bannu extensively. Wherever he went, he took pains to explain the current position of Muslim demands, especially in view of the latest announcement made by the British government. Referring to Dr Khan Saheb, he said: 'If the traitors didn't give up the part they were playing, or if the nation did not get rid of them, the future prospect of Muslims in India would be gloomy indeed.'[4] He appealed to non-League Muslims to think of the interest of the 'Millat'.[5] In Kohat, he held a meeting of 20,000 Muslims that had a fair sprinkling of women processionists. The Pir vehemently condemned the Frontier ministry as anti-Islamic. He characterized the government's action of handing Basanti back to her Sikh parents against 'her will' and 'snatching' her away from her lawful husband after she had embraced Islam 'of her own accord' as 'direct interference with the religion of Muslims'.[6] As a result of Manki Pir's 'spirited speeches' two prominent Ahrar leaders, Hafiz Pir Mir Alam Shah and Pir Ayub Shah immediately switched sides to join the Muslim League, pledging to 'sacrifice their lives for the cause of Pakistan'.[7] Emotions had begun to run high. The tide was turning fast.

The chief organizers of the movement were designated as 'dictators' by the Muslim League. A Provincial Muslim League War Council was also constituted which decided to observe a complete *hartal* throughout the Frontier on 10 March, at a time when the Legislative Assembly would be in session at Peshawar. There was to be complete cessation of all activities on that day except mass meetings and rallies.[8]

The movement was poised to continue unabated. The *ulema* now openly professed support for the movement, declaring in the Juma prayers that Dr Khan Saheb's ministry was a ministry of infidels, for 'the Congress was cutting at the roots of Islam by prohibiting conversion'.[9] The agitation was coming 'full swing' in 'strongly fortified and predominantly Hindu towns'.[10]

What was proving to be a popular weapon in the Muslim League's hand was causing considerable unease to Dr Khan Saheb. He was forced to issue a statement on 10 March, the day of the *hartal*, that:

> It was incumbent on the majority community to see that minorities were able to live safely in the Province, but dissemination, in certain quarters, of communal doctrines had led to a number of unfortunate occurrences in the Hazara district, which caused grave loss of life. Consequently the Provincial Government were obliged to take proper measures…It was necessary for the Governor to promulgate the special ordinance. The Government had at first thought of replacing it with a Bill…but unfortunate happenings in Punjab had rendered it necessary to retain the ordinance for some time.[11]

Such statements certainly did not add to the government's popularity.

The movement did wonders for the confidence of the Muslim League. On 18 March, Nawab Qutub-ud-Din, deputy leader of the Muslim League Assembly Party, referring to a recent statement by Dr Khan Saheb that the majority of Pathans were with him, haughtily challenged him, 'to choose one Muslim constituency in each district, and have six by-elections…we are ready to vacate six seats in the Assembly. Let him do the same. I am confident that the Muslim League will win all the seats, and the Congress candidates will forfeit their securities… If Dr Khan Saheb has the courage, let him come forward and contest the election on the straight Pakistan issue.'[12]

Pitted against this newly acquired arrogance of the Muslim League came a forced repartee from Dr Khan Saheb. Addressing a Khudai Khidmatgar gathering in Mardan on the same day, he compared the civil disobedience movement of the Congress with the present agitation of the Muslim League in the NWFP. Defensively, he said that 'the Congress civil disobedience movement was launched against the bureaucratic rule of an irresponsible and irremovable foreign Government while the Muslim League's present movement was an unconstitutional agitation against the popular Government of the Frontier people,'[13] and that they were not going to yield to the League's unconstitutional methods. But within three months, Dr Khan Saheb had to yield when the League won the referendum. Dr Khan Saheb and his ministerial colleagues fully understood the nature and purpose of the League movement but had no effective answer for it. 'The Frontier Province will be always with the Congress,'[14] Qazi Atta Ullah Khan, the Frontier Revenue Minister declared in an interview. In reply to a question whether the trouble in the Frontier was economic, not communal, he claimed: 'This is absolutely false. The trouble in the Frontier is communal',[15] reiterating his resolve that the NWFP shall always remain with the Congress. He was soon to be proved wrong.

The situation, communally, had indeed become sensitive. On 19 March, 2,000 Khudai Khidmatgars arrived in Peshawar city from Charsadda tehsil (eighteen miles north of Peshawar) to resist the violence 'non-violently' and restore confidence among the 30,000 Hindu and Sikh residents. The Khudai Khidmatgars were accommodated in the southern part of Peshawar town.[16] Education Minister Yahya Khan's claim that they did not have weapons was found to be incorrect as a large number of them were seen to be carrying arms, some unlicensed. Their effort to get Hindu and Sikh shops to open did not bear fruit. The minority community was too scared to resume business unless it had the assurance of the Muslim League National Guards. The Khudai Khidmatgars, therefore, 'generally made a nuisance of themselves roaming around the streets after curfew hours and consequently embarrassing the police authorities.'[17] Khan Mohammad Abbas Khan, a former minister in Dr Khan Saheb's cabinet strongly condemned the tactics of the Frontier Premier for having 'invited an invasion' of the capital by the Red Shirt volunteers. This, he said, was a 'sinister move on part of Dr Khan Saheb to precipitate a fratricidal bloody war between the Red Shirts and the Green Shirts.'[18]

Dr Khan Saheb's ministry was also accused of being 'under the thumb of a selfish clique that looked to Wardha for guidance'.[19] Khan Bahadur Allah Nawaz Khan, Speaker of the Frontier Assembly was heckled at a public meeting and stones were hurled at him when he sounded pro-Congress in his speech. Dr Khan Saheb's party was coming increasingly under pressure. Stories, true and false, started appearing in newspapers. It was once reported that a large number of people had gathered on all roads leading to Kohat city shouting anti-Congress slogans as the news of Dr Khan Saheb's arrival was received. When the Chief Minister, who was travelling in a car, found that all roads to Kohat were 'resounding' with anti-Congress slogans, he 'climbed in to a lorry, which took him incognito to his destination'.[20] Pro-League newspapers were now boldly publishing exaggerated accounts of events in the Muslim League's favour.

On the last day of the assembly session, a procession went to the assembly building and succeeded in hoisting the Muslim League flag. A large number of Khudai Khidmatgars shifted allegiance, discarding their red uniforms for the green shirts of League volunteers.[21] Some top-ranking League leaders took to a hunger strike, their welfare causing great anxiety among people. The government was being pushed to the wall. The president of the Peshawar city Muslim League, Mian Burhanuddin's arrest further queered the pitch on 21 March. Before being incarcerated, he had stated that Dr Khan Saheb was 'trying to create a schism between two sections of the Muslim community by claiming that the present political agitation was in the hands of fanatic Shias'.[22] The Khudai Khidmatgars now took to joining the Muslim League and burning their red uniforms in the presence of enthusiastic crowds, an indication of the way the wind was blowing. The law and order situation had deteriorated, especially in Hazara where the civil administration stood paralyzed since mid-March. The courts in Hazara, Dera Ismail Khan and Kohat were not allowed to function. 'Pakistan Day' was observed throughout the province on 25 March. A mile-long procession was taken out in Dera Ismail Khan, unprecedented in that town's history, in which 60,000 people participated. News that greatly affected the popular sentiments was the commencement of the trial, on the same day, of Pir Sahib of Zakori. Ahrar volunteers had helped the Muslim League National Guards to organize a *hartal* that followed the sentencing of the Pir Sahib of Zakori.[23] The strike was a complete success in Dera Ismail Khan. Not a single shop opened in the town. A procession was also taken out in protest that culminated in a public meeting. The Mahsuds and Wazirs held a joint *jirga* declaring themselves in favour of Pakistan. Alongside, the *jirga* also sent a protest note to the Afghan government about some of its employees who were playing into the hands of the 'Hindus'.[24]

Sir Olaf Caroe, the Frontier Governor, was on a tour of Dera Ismail Khan when the strike, procession and the meeting took place. A large number of Pathans carrying the crescent-spangled League flag lined up along the road from Abbotabad to Manshera to let the Governor know of their feelings against the 'Khan-Khanna' ministry. If pro-League papers are to be believed, this demonstration had a tremendous impact on the Governor, and affected his assessment about the import and extent of the League's movement.[25] At a provincial cabinet meeting which he attended on 28 March in Peshawar, Sir Olaf Caroe reportedly discussed with Dr Khan Saheb the advisability of the Congress ministry's resignation because of the rising unrest and discontent among the Pathans. It was being said that the League civil disobedience movement was costing the government ₹5 lakh a day for maintaining law and order.[26]

The city of Peshawar observed a complete strike on 30 March, which was celebrated as Martyrs' Day. The shops remained closed and there was a large police and Khudai Khidmatgar presence in the city. Government clerks in most offices did not attend work. On that day, Pir Sahib of Manki Sharif was also to lay the foundation stone of the Martyrs' Memorial at the same spot where Muslim League supporters were killed in the 10 March police firing. But before he could go to the function, he was arrested. The Deputy Commissioner of Peshawar called on him early enough to serve the warrant of arrest. The 'Sahib-i-Mubarak', as Pir Sahib was addressed by lakhs of his *murids*, expressed his desire to be arrested at the Muslim League's office. While he walked to the office, the news of his impending arrest spread. The students of Edward College, situated nearby, took to the streets immediately in large numbers. They, too, were arrested by the police which had fanned out in good strength.[27] Pir Sahib of Manki Sharif was considered one of the most influential personalities in the NWFP and his arrest no doubt exacerbated the situation. The conflict so far had been confined to towns and villages of the settled districts. It was now affecting the crags and gorges of the tribal belt.[28] The Deputy Commissioner of Peshawar was forced to extend curfew hours in the city, and he also forbade the assembly of more than five persons, even on rooftops. Persons who went out after dark were ordered to carry lights, the new restrictions being a direct consequence of extreme tension prevailing in the city following Manki Pir's arrest.[29]

Clashes took place between the Khudai Khidmatgars and the Muslim League National Guards. As an act of caution, the provincial administration withdrew the Khudai Khidmatgars from towns. The 'Pir of Manki Sharif Day' was observed throughout the NWFP on 5 April.[30] During a twenty-four-hour curfew imposed in Peshawar, army troops were called to assist the civil forces in enforcing it. Despite the curfew and in defiance of it, about 25,000 Muslim League supporters took out a procession and were severely lathi-charged.[31] Subsequently, another procession of a mock funeral of Dr Khan Saheb was organized in the city of Peshawar. A son of Manki Pir, defying curfew orders, also led a big procession at Naushera.[32] On 6 April, a *jirga* of Mahsuds held a meeting at Tank in Dera Ismail Khan to protest against the arrest of Pir Sahib. The *jirga* decided to send its men to the Tribal Agencies for fixing a date for a combined *jirga* to decide on support for the League movement.[33] A resolution demanding immediate release of the Pir of Manki Sharif was also passed at a joint *jirga* of the South Waziristan and Kurram Agencies. The resolution said: 'We deeply regret that the Frontier Governor should have allowed this arrest, knowing that it would provoke Tribesmen. The Governor General-in-Council as well as the Frontier Governor should have known that this arrest would provoke Tribesmen. We urge the Governor General-in-Council as well as the Frontier Government to release him forthwith. In case he is not released, the Government will be responsible for the consequences.'[34] Another resolution of the same *jirga* asked for the resignation of the Khan ministry and warned against the visit of the Patel Committee to the tribal areas. The salutary effects of the League's movement in the tribal areas were now being ably demonstrated.[35]

Aid to the movement was readily forthcoming from the neighbouring province. Syed Amir Hussain Shah, Salar-i-Ala of the Muslim League National Guards made a public statement that the National Guards of Punjab were 'ready to go to the help of their brothers in the Frontier Province at a moment's notice'. Muslim women from Punjab journeyed to Peshawar to participate in the League movement. Begum Fatima, acting president of the Punjab Muslim Women's League, after returning to Lahore following a fortnight's tour of the Frontier, made strong allegations of maltreatment of Muslim League volunteers in Frontier jails. She had led deputations to the Governor and the Premier while in NWFP. The Governor, she said, had given a sympathetic hearing to the deputation, but Dr Khan Saheb had refused point blank to go into the matter, saying that 'jail was not forced on the Muslim League volunteers—as it was their own choice, let them have a taste of it.' Begum Fatima had also exhorted the students of the Islamia College, Peshawar, to quit their books at that time and actively join the struggle for Pakistan.

Dr Khan Saheb's government faced the odds with a growing sense of stoicism. Qazi Atta Ullah Khan, the ministry's Education Minister, made his government's position clear to the press in Delhi, saying that they would not resign even if the Governor asked them to do so. He also stated that had 'the Pir of Manki Sharif been arrested in the early stages of the movement, there would not have been too much of trouble.' The ministry as well as Ghaffar Khan were all in agreement that as long as the conditions were disturbed, it was not advisable for the sub-committee of the Constituent Assembly on the North Western Tribal Areas to visit the province (On 24 January 1947, the Constituent Assembly set up an Advisory Committee, popularly known as the Patel Committee, to deal with fundamental rights, minorities' rights and questions relating to settled areas).

Sahibzada Ahmad Gul Sahib, the younger brother of Manki Pir was arrested on 15 April after a 'dramatic hold-up' by Dr Khan Saheb near the radio station in Peshawar. Pir Sahib's brother, returning from a public meeting was stopped by Dr Khan Saheb himself who was escorted then by British and Gorkha troops. The Premier, at pistol point, ordered the younger Pir and his companion Maulvi Shakir Ullah to get out of the car and had the car searched. Though nothing incriminating was found, Dr Khan Saheb had the two of them arrested. Events took a 'dramatic turn' when a procession of nearly 50,000 tribal Pathans of the Khalil Mohmand tribe appeared on the scene. Apprehending trouble, the Premier, 'fled with his escort'.[36] This story appeared in *Pakistan Times*, a newspaper whose reports were usually biased in favour of the Muslim League and therefore prone to exaggeration. Sahibzada

Ahmad Gul Sahib was sentenced to one year's rigorous imprisonment in default of furnishing security. The Muslim League observed the annual Martrys' Day in Peshawar on 23 April in memory of those killed in the Kissa Khawani Bazaar firing of 1930. Public meetings and processions were organized in Peshawar city. What, of course, was of significance was a complete absence of Khudai Khidmatgars in these events. Earlier, these were occasions that acted as barometers of support that the Khudai Khidmatgars commanded. Depending on the people's participation then, one could assess their popularity.

On 24 April, Sir Feroz Khan Noon, a former member of the Governor General's Executive Council made a startling declaration, for at that time no one either in the Congress or the government or in Muslim League circles had talked of holding a referendum in the NWFP. He said: 'The Frontier Congress Ministry is in office only for a week or two and a referendum is imminent.'[37] He, along with Sardar Abdur Rab Nishtar, had extensively toured the NWFP and felt that the Provincial League had provided tremendous fillip to the civil disobedience movement. In the week preceding 6 May, while stirring up people's emotions in favour of the League movement, he had steadfastly insisted that 'referendum alone could bring peace to the disturbed province…and a free and independent verdict [could] only be attained if the general election or referendum [was] held under the direct rule of the Governor for no referendum was ever held while one of the contesting parties was running it.'[38]

Mountbatten was to visit Peshawar on 28 April. Abdul Qayyum Khan, Pir Abdul Latif of Zakori, Khan Mohammad Ali Khan (secretary of the Provincial Muslim League) and Khan Ghulam Mohammad Khan (a prominent Muslim League member) were brought to the Peshawar central prison from Dera Ismail Khan to enable them to confer with other Muslim League leaders on the eve of the Viceroy's arrival. Their meeting took place in Peshawar jail on 25 April. A deputation of Muslim League leaders thereafter met the Viceroy, Lord Mountbatten, when he arrived in Peshawar on 28 April. Two days later, the Provincial League met to consider the Frontier government's announcement about the release of some political prisoners. It was decided in the meeting that steps taken by the Frontier government in no way met the demands of the Muslim League and were not acceptable. The movement, therefore, was not to be called off (the Provincial Muslim League had demanded settlement of the dispute of the Sikh girl Basanti, withdrawal of the Hazara Public Safety Ordinance, Section 144 of the CrPC, the Frontier Crimes Regulations and refund of fines. The provincial government had released the political prisoners though, unconditionally).

A Muslim League deputation arrived in Delhi from the NWFP on 2 May. The deputation consisted of the Pir of Manki Sharif, Abdul Qayyum Khan, Khan Samin Jan Khan (president of the Frontier Muslim League), Mian Abdullah Shah (vice president) and Arbab Noor Mohammad Khan to meet Jinnah. With the exception of Mian Abdullah Shah, the rest of the delegation had been released on parole by the Frontier government to enable them to come to Delhi. These leaders met Jinnah thrice. Khan Abdul Qayyum Khan found the Congress' decision to oppose fresh elections in the Frontier most unfortunate. Upon their return to Peshawar jail on 7 May, the League leaders were received amidst enthusiastic slogan shouting. A warrant of arrest for Mian Abdullah Shah had already been issued.

Desertions in the ranks of the Khudai Khidmatgars that had started some time back were now set to increase. A large number of Khudai Khidmatgar leaders along with their followers were calling on the Muslim League offices (at the provincial headquarters and in the districts) in full red shirt uniforms, ready to declare their resignations from the Congress and join the Muslim League. On 23 May, a prominent leader, Khan Muhammad Jafar Khan, who had been seriously affected by the tear-gassing of prisoners in Peshawar central jail, died. A complete *hartal* was observed in Peshawar in his memory—and the movement continued to gain in popularity. The communal ploy of the Muslim League had worked. It was only after HMG announced a plan to partition India on 3 June that the League called off this movement. An interesting description of those days by a British civil servant, Fraser Noble, who was serving in Peshawar, makes for fascinating reading.

Fraser Noble worked under Major Aga Syed Badshah Shah, the Deputy Commissioner, who had joined Peshawar just three months earlier in January after finishing his stint as a Counsellor in the Embassy of Kabul. Shah belonged to a well-known Peshawari family and was partisan to the cause of the Muslim League. Fraser Noble was forced at times to turn to the superintendent of police when he was baffled by the actions and thoughts of the Deputy Commissioner. Sir Feroz Khan Noon, a prominent Muslim League politician from Punjab, counselled Jinnah on 28 June 1947 that 'though Major Shah was badly needed in Peshawar, he felt and with "reason" that he (Major A.S.B. Shah) could be of immense use to Jinnah in Delhi.' That the Deputy Commissioner, Peshawar, had approached Sir Noon (a politician) twice and was asked to run up to Delhi, meet Jinnah and place his case and then leave it to Jinnah to decide where he wanted him, speaks volumes for his conduct. Deputy Commissioner Major A.S.B. Shah, therefore, could not be expected to be fair in discharging official responsibilities. It was under such a Deputy Commissioner that Fraser Noble had to serve when Mountbatten decided to visit Peshawar on 28 April.

On the Saturday before the Viceroy's visit, that is, on 26 April, the Deputy Commissioner held a meeting of his staff to coordinate arrangements. Mountbatten's plane was to arrive before 9 a.m., necessitating early positioning of the police and troops. The administration was worried about the law and order situation near the aerodrome where a large crowd was expected to congregate. The area around the assembly building, the government house and the cantonment along the railway line, had already been given over to a Sikh regiment. Fraser Noble was uneasy about this arrangement. He had wanted the Sikhs tucked away less provocatively from the front line.[39]

After a quiet day's reflection over the weekend, Fraser Noble's uneasiness steadily grew. His main worry was the possibility of a confrontation with Muslim League supporters who, in a show of strength, were to gather for a public meeting on 28 April. The government in Peshawar was a Congress one whereas local support was for the Muslim League. The Muslim League was expected to do everything to impress the Viceroy. As Fraser Noble reminisced:

> At about seven in the evening I was so restless that I decided to call on the Deputy Commissioner. Although I arrived without warning, his orderly took me straight to him. He was sitting in his dining room with Sir Feroz Khan Noon. That was the first

surprise of many that evening. Shah asked me quietly what I wanted; embarrassed by the presence of Feroz Khan Noon (a former member of the Viceroy's Executive Council, and a very prominent Punjab politician who was rather on the sidelines of the Muslim League at the time). I stammered out my anxieties about the next day. Calmly, Shah said that this was exactly what they were discussing and did not know what to do. After some discussion, Feroz said that some effort must be made to prevent the crowd from assembling at the aerodrome; he seemed to be sure that a demonstration there was intended by the League. But he opted out of any part in pursuing his suggestion, implying that his own influence with the Provincial Muslim League War Council (so it was designated) was so negligible that representation by him would be counterproductive.[40]

To Fraser Noble's surprise, Major A.S.B. Shah rang up the headquarters of the League War Council and then proceeded in his transport along with Sir Feroz Khan Noon and Fraser Noble to meet them. Fraser Noble was under the impression that most of the effective League leaders were in prison. Though he had known of the existence of the War Council of the League, Noble had no idea of its effective functioning. To his utter surprise he found Sardar Abdur Rab Nishtar at this meeting, whom Noble knew as a minister in Aurangzeb Khan's government in 1943. Abdur Rab Nishtar was now a Muslim League nominee in the Viceroy's interim government. Noble was absolutely shaken to 'find him in this cabal which was clearly responsible for arrangements that might threaten the Viceroy's whole mission to India'.[41]

Abdur Rab Nishtar took charge of the discussions at once. Major Shah explained his anxiety about the demonstration at the aerodrome which could become uncontrollable. Abdur Rab Nishtar agreed but wanted to know what the alternative was since the people were already informed of the assembly point. Muslim League leaders wanted an assurance given to the gathering that the Viceroy had seen them in the assembly, and assessed their numbers. Noble suggested that this might best be achieved in a confined space like Cunningham Garden which had an added advantage of being neither in the cantonment area nor in the military environment of the aerodrome but was conveniently situated near the city. Some members of the War Council emphasized how difficult it would be at such a late hour to change instructions that had already gone to various units or groups of Muslim League volunteers. No change could possibly be made unless they had an assurance that the Viceroy would review the gathering in Cunningham Garden. That the Viceroy would see assemblage from the air when his plane landed was not acceptable. The Deputy Commissioner said he had no means of providing such an assurance that night; Abdur Rab Nishtar at once intervened to say that all that was required was a telephone message to Delhi. Nishtar knew the Viceroy's working habits and was sure that if the Governor rang up Delhi at any time before midnight he would be put through to Mountbatten.[42]

There appeared no alternative. It was already after 10 p.m. Shah undertook to ring up the *hujra* with the answer before midnight, to give them time to put out new instructions for their followers. When the party left, Noble noticed that the Deputy Commissioner was very depressed and hesitant about approaching the Governor. Noble then suggested they call on Brigadier C.H. Smith first and request him to approach the Governor (Sir Caroe) on their behalf since the matter had important implications for the army's arrangements too. The Brigadier was quick to appreciate the brewing situation and agreed that this was their best chance of averting a clash of arms. He appeared perturbed though by the prospect of having to deal with a large crowd at or near the aerodrome. But the matter was one 'for the civil power' not the army at his stage, and so he declined to accompany the Deputy Commissioner's party to the government house.[43]

Encouraged by the Brigadier's reaction, the Deputy Commissioner went to the government house. The Governor had gone to bed, and his ADC (David Bivar) was understandably unwilling to disturb him. When Major Shah insisted, a hesitant David Bivar disappeared, to return five minutes later with a dishevelled and sleepy-looking Governor in his pyjamas, 'his normally immaculate grey hair tousled and his eyes heavy and tired'. He sat on a settee in the hall outside the drawing room, and listened patiently to what the Deputy Commissioner had to say. He showed no sign of surprise, and scarcely interrupted Major Shah with a question. He sat with his head bowed, resting on his hands, and Noble wondered if he was going to fall asleep. Suddenly, the Governor got up, and saying, 'You can tell Nishtar to go to hell,' left the room.[44]

David Bivar too bade the Deputy Commissioner's party an embarrassed goodnight and went out. Major Shah then looked for a telephone, found one meant for use by the Governor's orderlies and the military guard. He gave the operator the *hujra* number which he clearly remembered. The conversation he had with Abdul Rab Nishtar was part Persian, part some form of Peshawari dialect which Noble could not follow, though he did try to listen intently. When the Deputy Commissioner put the phone down, Noble enquired as to why he had told Abdur Rab Nishtar that things at the government house had gone on right. 'What will he do now?' Fraser Noble had pressed on further. 'That is up to him, isn't it?' was the Deputy Commissioner's reply. Major Shah was despondent and exhausted, and they all drove back to the Deputy Commissioner's residence without another word.[45]

Riding back home that night on his motorcycle, Noble was revived by the rush of cool air, and lay for a long time in bed pondering over what would happen. At dawn, he went down to the city gates on his motorcycle and was surprised by the number of people already on the move. He rode through Cunningham Garden, and saw that large numbers had spent the night there and on the open spaces beyond. He also spotted Gilbert Grace, the Inspector General of Police, and rode over to greet him. Like Noble, the Inspector General was also on an expedition, anxious to know what was going on. Noble briefed him about the Muslim League's apparent plan, and enquired if he would be prepared to advise the Governor to request the Viceroy to visit the scene if all went well with his arrival. The Inspector General not only agreed, but suggested that Noble go straight to the Chief Secretary, and request him to approach the Army Commander, General Ross MaCay. Norval Mitchell had recently replaced Colonel de la Fargue as Chief Secretary who had gone on long leave. Noble found the Chief Secretary at breakfast and told him his story and got his immediate response—he would speak to the Governor while Fraser Noble was to go to the general headquarters to see the General. When Ross MaCay was informed, he took Noble with him to inspect the grounds. From the ramparts of Bala Hissar, they could see Cunningham Garden and observe the crowds moving out of the city across the Grand Trunk Road. Away in the distance, they could also see people coming in from the villages, perhaps some having been recalled from the aerodrome. Already the numbers appeared impressive. What struck Noble was the apparent calm and relative quiet of the scene. As yet there was none of the angry buzz associated with a hostile procession. 'From the fort, it all looked like a crowd assembling in anticipation of an exciting football match.'[46]

Noble learnt later that nothing about the demonstration had been said to Lord Mountbatten during the formalities of his arrival, but that in the car on the way to the government house the Governor had told him about the crowd, making it clear that he had been advised by all the senior officers and by the military commanders, to recommend that the Viceroy should agree to see the crowd himself. As Noble was given to understand, the Governor himself declined to make such a positive recommendation, possibly on the grounds that it smacked too much of playing the Muslim League's game. But the Governor did explain the fears, which everyone shared, that if the Viceroy did not go to see the crowd, they would try to force their way through to the government house to see him.[47]

When the Viceroy arrived at the government house, Mountbatten and Sir Olaf Caroe were still discussing the situation and stood within earshot of Noble at the door. Suddenly the Viceroy said, 'I must go, but not unless I have the Chief Minister's agreement. What is his view on the matter?' Everybody had forgotten to think about that. Noble was dispatched to fetch Dr Khan Saheb. Pretending that he knew nothing of the reasons for this hasty summons so soon after the Chief Minister had greeted the Viceroy at the aerodrome and left him in the Governor's care, Noble ushered the Chief Minister into their presence. The Viceroy said very briskly that he had been advised to see this Muslim League crowd to avoid a serious risk of a violent disturbance. Provided the Chief Minister had no objection, he proposed to go. It seemed to Noble that Dr Khan Saheb was completely taken aback. He was never particularly quick in oral repartees, and spluttered, 'Your Excellency must just do whatever you please.' Without hesitation Mountbatten said, 'Very well, thank you.'[48]

Nothing more was said at this stage, but later in the day when the Viceroy met the ministers officially, Dr Khan Saheb remarked that it was the Governor who had arranged for this Muslim League demonstration, and that he himself had cancelled a similar demonstration of Congress supporters in order to avoid the risk of a clash.[49]

It took a few minutes to escort the Chief Minister back to his house. When Noble returned, the party at the government house was almost ready to leave. When she heard about the plan, Lady Mountbatten insisted on going along. The cars were left near the assembly building, where they were still out of sight of the crowd in Cunningham Garden, screened by the railway embankment. There was a line of policemen across the road on the other side of the bridge, and a considerable party of police around the cars. The troops were in position well back from the bridge and, of course, out of sight of the demonstration. The Viceroy's party scrambled up the rough, steep bank and walked along the line to the bridge over the road, which was clear of onlookers. The crowd in the park was impressive, much more densely packed than when Noble had last seen them. They had spilled over to the railway, in the direction of the city station. Although the vast majority were below the level of the Viceroy's party and in the park, several thousands had spilled on to the embankment level and at their level, the nearest no more than 20 yards away. The party was standing only a few yards from where shots had been fired on the advancing crowd on 10 March, and from the scene of the railway accident involving a women's demonstration on 14 April.[50]

The early morning silence had been replaced by considerable noise, which was hard to interpret. It was not the angry sound of a mob about to riot, but was not reassuring either. The Viceroy moved forward to the parapet—a low wall hardly more than a foot high— then stood erect on it. Noble suddenly felt that the noise was dying away; seconds ticked past in a strange silence, then perceptibly, the sound increased—a gigantic murmur swelling almost to a roar. But Noble immediately sensed that this was not a note of anger, but of amazed approval. The Viceroy must have known at once that he had won the day. Turning to face the crowd on the line nearest to him, he called out, 'Get the people nearest to sit down so that others behind can see better.' A senior police officer and Noble entered their ranks, calling out in Pushtu that the 'Lat Sahib' wanted them to sit so that more could see better. Some of them did; the feeling Noble got from them was one of amazement and bewilderment. They were not noisy and elated, but respectful and a little over-awed. While in the crowd, Noble stopped in astonishment as he came face-to-face with a Tori Khel Malik, Sanobar Khan, whom he had known well while in Waziristan three years back. They greeted each other warmly, as Pathans do, but when Noble asked him what he was up to, he was uncharacteristically reticent. Perhaps he did not want to admit that he was now on the Muslim League side. Men had certainly come long distances to join this demonstration.[51]

If Noble's account is objective, it adds to the significance of the events of the morning of 28 April. He was convinced that if something had gone wrong that morning, the effect on Mountbatten's negotiations might have been irretrievable. That nothing did go wrong was partly an enormous fluke, partly the product of the Viceroy's peculiar genius and flair. Late on Sunday evening (27 April) in Delhi, Jinnah had told the Viceroy that there would be a procession to the government house in Peshawar, a show of the Muslim League's strength to impress the Viceroy. The Viceroy had telegraphed the Governor immediately (at 10.35 p.m.) saying that he had made it plain to Jinnah that any procession would be 'completely contrary to assurance he had given to Dr Khan Saheb'. He would have no objection to a meeting or gathering from which not more than six delegates would be allowed to go to the government house to see him. It can therefore be assumed that Abdur Rab Nishtar had been in touch with Jinnah on Sunday evening, probably before Major Shah and Noble saw him, though quite possibly immediately after A.S.B. Shah went to see the Brigadier and the Governor. It is not clear when the telegram reached Sir Olaf Caroe. If he had it before he saw the Deputy Commissioner, it is strange that he did not tell them about the telegram. In any case, it is clear that Mountbatten was not altogether taken by surprise by the Governor's news that a crowd had gathered and wanted to see him.[52]

## Notes

1. Appendix VIII. 4, p.329, *Jinnah Papers*, First Series, Vol. I, part II, 1993.
2. Appendix VIII. 6, p.331, *Jinnah Papers*, First Series, Vol. I, part II, 1993.
3. Appendix VIII. 14, p.339, *Jinnah Papers*, First Series, Vol. I, Part II.
4. Appendix VIII. 15, p.340, *Jinnah Papers* First Series, Vol. I, Part II.

5. Ibid.
6. Appendix VIII. 20, p.345, *Jinnah Papers*, First Series, Vol. I, part II, 1993.
7. Appendix VIII. 24. p.347, *Jinnah Papers*, First Series, Vol. I, part II, 1993.
8. Appendix VIII. 18, p.343, *Jinnah Papers*, First Series, Vol. I, part II, 1993.
9. Appendix VIII. 20, p.344, *Jinnah Papers*, First Series, Vol. I, part II, 1993.
10. Ibid.
11. Appendix VIII. 22, p.346, *Jinnah Papers*, First Series, Vol. I, part II, 1993.
12. Appendix VIII. 27, pp.348–49, *Jinnah Papers*, First Series, Vol. I, part II, 1993.
13. Appendix VIII. 28, p.349, *Jinnah Papers*, First Series, Vol. I, part II, 1993.
14. Appendix VIII. 30, p.350, *Jinnah Papers*, First Series, Vol. I, part II, 1993.
15. Ibid.
16. Appendix VIII. 32, p.351, *Jinnah Papers*, First Series, Vol. I, part II, 1993.
17. Appendix VIII. 36, pp.353–54, *Jinnah Papers*, First Series, Vol. I, part II.
18. Appendix VIII. 42, p.358, *Jinnah Papers*, First Series, Vol. I, part II, 1993.
19. Appendix VIII. 46, p.361, *Jinnah Papers*, First Series, Vol. I, part II, 1993.
20. Appendix VIII. 60, p.370, *Jinnah Papers*, First Series, Vol. I, part II.
21. Appendix VIII. 36, p.354, *Jinnah Papers*, First Series, Vol. I, part II.
22. Appendix VIII. 35, p.352, *Jinnah Papers*, First Series, Vol. I, part II.
23. Appendix VIII. 39, p.356, *Jinnah Papers*, First Series, Vol. I, part II.
24. Appendix VIII. 39, p.356, *Jinnah Papers*, First Series, Vol. I, part II, 1993.
25. Appendix VIII. 40, p.357, *Jinnah Papers*, First Series, Vol. I, part II, 1993.
26. Appendix VIII. 52, p.364, *Jinnah Papers*, First Series, Vol. I, part II, 1993.
27. Appendix VIII. 44, pp.359–60, *Jinnah Papers*, First Series, Vol. I, part II, 1993.
28. Appendix VIII. 53, p.366, *Jinnah Papers*, First Series, Vol. I, part II, 1993.
29. Appendix VIII. 65, pp.373–74, *Jinnah Papers*, First Series, Vol. I, part II, 1993.
30. Appendix VIII. 71, p.377, *Jinnah Papers*, First Series, Vol. I, part II, 1993.
31. Appendix VIII. 74, p.379, *Jinnah Papers*, First Series, Vol. I, part II, 1993.
32. Ibid, p.380.
33. Appendix VIII. 76, p.381, *Jinnah Papers*, First Series, Vol. I, part II, 1993.
34. Appendix VIII. 89, pp.388–89, *Jinnah Papers*, First Series, Vol. I, part II, 1993.
35. Ibid.
36. Appendix VIII. 90, p.389, *Jinnah Papers*, First Series, Vol. I, part II, 1993.

37. Appendix VIII. 105, p.398, *Jinnah Papers*, First Series s, Vol. I, part II, 1993.
38. Appendix VIII. 123, p.415, *Jinnah Papers*, First Series, Vol. I, part II, 1993.
39. Sir Fraser Noble, 'Recollections of Civil Disobedience Movement: NWFP 1947', *Indo-British Review—A Journal of History*, 19(1), p.45.
40. Ibid., pp.45-46.
41. Ibid.
42. Ibid.
43. Ibid.
44. Ibid., pp.46-47.
45. Ibid.
46. Ibid.
47. Ibid.
48. Ibid., pp.47-48.
49. Ibid.
50. Ibid.
51. Ibid.
52. Ibid., p.49.

# 10

# Malang[1] Baba's Abounding Optimism: Gandhi

How IMPORTANT IT was for the Muslim League to win over the NWFP for Pakistan could hardly have escaped the Congress' notice. Time was of crucial significance, especially after HMG had set a date—June 1948—for British withdrawal from India. If the Muslim League failed to clinch the issue, there was imminent danger that their edifice of Pakistan would crumble. What started with the Great Calcutta Killings[2] of August 1946 acquired a dynamic of its own—Noakhali, Bihar, Bombay and Punjab witnessed terrible carnage that sharply polarized India along communal lines. As a result, the Muslim League came to represent the Indian Muslims' interest and Jinnah became their sole spokesman.

Mountbatten arrived in India on 20 March 1947, vested with the responsibility of overseeing the British withdrawal, a task he set about immediately. The following analysis is the story of those four and a half critical months—April to mid-August—that shaped the destiny of the NWFP. Within seven weeks of his arrival, Mountbatten had foisted a referendum on the NWFP, which in effect ensured that the Frontier Province join Pakistan. Surprisingly, all prominent Congressmen agreed with Mountbatten—Gandhi and Khan Abdul Ghaffar Khan being the only two exceptions.

There is enough evidence to show that during Mountbatten's viceroyalty, the NWFP had taken up Gandhi's attention considerably. It was he alone who fought to save the NWFP for India, striving till the end to achieve victory in a losing battle. He battled alone and failed. This chapter is a portrayal of Gandhi's struggle for the NWFP and for India on behalf of the Congress and a struggle soon to be lost to Pakistan and also to the Frontier Gandhi—Khan Abdul Ghaffar Khan. Gandhi's role in this struggle features prominently in the last few months before India stood partitioned. These were Gandhi's finest hours too, touring the villages of East Bengal and Bihar with Khan Abdul Ghaffar Khan, providing succour to victims of communal violence. Right from the time of the Lahore Congress of 1929,[3] Khan Abdul Ghaffar Khan had established a personal rapport with Gandhi. Gandhi in turn always defended Khan Abdul Ghaffar Khan in action, deed and words. Notwithstanding his trips to the NWFP, it was Gandhi who allowed the second Khan Saheb's ministry to be formed in March 1945. We pick up the threads of Gandhi's story with Mountbatten's arrival, for the history of the NWFP was soon to be written afresh.

Recently arrived in India, Mountbatten quickly met important political leaders—Gandhi, Jinnah, Nehru, et al. Gandhi arrived in Delhi for his first meeting with the new Viceroy on 31 March. In a series of confabulations, Gandhi was quick to raise the issue of the NWFP. In a complaining mood, he brought up the topic on 3 April. His ire was directed largely against the British bureaucracy. He was particularly severe on Governor Olaf Caroe, accusing him of demonstrating excessive partiality towards the Muslim League and asking for Dr Khan Saheb's resignation. Caroe's conduct had unduly influenced both the Muslims and the British. Gandhi found the Governor of Sindh to be equally inclined in favour of the Muslim League. He wished that the Governors were not biased, one way or the other, allowing for their friendliness with their government to remain impartial. It suited the British officialdom when the Muslim League publicly pleaded for the British to prolong their stay in India, as if in their absence, India would be plunged into civil war. In some ways, Mountbatten's meetings with prominent Congress leaders had been much the same. Nehru, Maulana Azad and Patel had all complained in unison against British civil officials, which hardly endeared them to the British bureaucracy. Rather, it provoked Lord Ismay to remark in the Viceroy's staff meeting of 5 April: 'Mr Gandhi, the previous day, had accused Sir Evan Jenkins[4] of responsibility for the present situation in Punjab, Sir Olaf Caroe of responsibility for the present North West Frontier troubles, Sir Francis Mudie of excessive support of the Muslim League Government in

Sindh and the whole Civil Service and Indian Political service of all manner of sins, including corruption.'

Gandhi came from Bihar to Delhi to meet the new Viceroy. But his presence this time round had not been sought by Congress leaders with whom he now increasingly felt out of sync. No other member of the Congress Working Committee except Khan Abdul Ghaffar Khan, appeared to be in tune with him on important policy issues. Some, in fact, had been brusque. Pained by the attitude of most of those he had closely worked with, Gandhi lamented: 'I have not met Sardar [Patel] for more than a few minutes. Sometimes I feel that perhaps I am the only one here in the whole company with spare time on hand.' How effective was Gandhi in influencing decisions on the NWFP when the main flock of Congress leaders was not at one with him on the issue of partition?

Mountbatten was in no mood to seek a consensus on the modalities of the transfer of power. Wavell's experience had convinced him that the British would have to make an award of it once the date of their withdrawal from India was decided. Within three weeks of his arrival, by mid-April, he was ready with the broad outlines of this award. He convened a Governors' Conference on 15 April to seek reactions from the men on the spot on his partition plan. An important agenda of this meeting was the holding of fresh elections in the NWFP, this agenda being firmed up after consultations with Governor Olaf Caroe. Nehru's support became crucial in carrying this decision through. He obliged Mountbatten on this issue when he forced Dr Khan Saheb to agree to this proposal.

Gandhi came to Delhi again but this time at the request of the Congress Working Committee members to attend its meeting on 1 May. That Gandhi's views were at variance with the majority opinion in the Working Committee was now clearly evident. He was, unfortunately, becoming increasingly redundant at a time when his active and effective intervention was critically required. The Congress Working Committee took a momentous decision during the meeting, an operative part of which was the acceptance of the principle of partition. The decision greatly disappointed Khan Abdul Ghaffar Khan. He and his followers, who had cast their lot with the Congress, now faced the bleak prospect of being deprived of belonging to India. They well realized that they would have no place in Pakistan. Disillusioned and shattered, Khan Abdul Ghaffar Khan said: 'Before long we shall become aliens in Hindustan. The end of our long fight will be to pass under the domination of Pakistan—away from Bapu, away from India, away from all of you. Who knows what the future holds for us?' When Gandhi heard of this from his niece Manu, he said: 'Verily Badshah Khan is a *Fakir*. Independence will come, but the brave Pathan will lose his. They are faced with a grim prospect. But Badshah is a man of God.' What else could Gandhi say? When Gandhi was leaving for Calcutta on 7 May, Khan Abdul Ghaffar Khan's parting words to him at the railway station were: 'Mahatmaji, I am your soldier. Your word is law to me. I have full faith in you. I look for no other support.' Ceaselessly worried about him, Gandhi sent Rs 36,000 from Calcutta to help Badshah Khan construct a school in Utmanzai.[5] The more Gandhi worried over Khan Abdul Ghaffar Khan, the more he felt that a grave wrong was being done to him. With an intent to save the situation, Gandhi wrote a personal letter to Mountbatten on 8 May, while on a train journey, forewarning him that a referendum at this stage in the Frontier or any other province would be a dangerous proposition. Gandhi was of the firm view that nothing should be done going over Dr Khan Saheb's head. But that was not to be.

Gandhi endeavoured to keep Khan Abdul Ghaffar Khan's spirits alive. Not a man given to melancholia, he impatiently waited for the 3 June announcement of a death warrant on him and the Khudai Khidmatgars. A sense of despair can be discerned in the exchange of dialogue between Khan Abdul Ghaffar Khan and Gandhi on 31 May 1947: 'So, Mahatmaji, you will now regard us as Pakistanis? ...A terrible situation faces the Frontier Province and Baluchistan. We do not know what to do.'[6] To which Gandhi's response was:

> Have you read what I have been saying during the past two or three days? One who has faith in non-violence should not yield to despair in this manner. You and your Khudai Khidmatgars are going to be tested now. You can say that you do not accept Pakistan and then submit to whatever is inflicted on you. We have, as you know, adopted the motto of 'do or die'. It does not befit one who professes such a motto to give way to despair. And

whatever happens I am going to visit the Frontier Province, for I don't believe in these divisions of the country. I am not going to ask anybody's permission. If they kill me for my defiance, I will embrace death with a smiling face. That is, if Pakistan comes into existence, I intend to tour it, live there and see what they do to me.

Gandhi was not destined to tour NWFP again.[7]

In his prayer meeting on the same day, Gandhi recounted an incident of years gone by, that of a man from Khan Abdul Ghaffar Khan's country, drawing an analogy of a lesson from it:

> There was a man called Mir Alam. He belonged to the Frontier, Badshah Khan's land. He was my friend at one time. Somebody told this man, Mir Alam, that Gandhi had taken Rs. 15,000 from General Smuts[8] and had betrayed the Indian community. That was enough. One day Mir Alam confronted me as an enemy. He carried with him a heavy-headed stick. He hit me with it right on my neck. I fell down on the pavement and broke my teeth. I survived because God willed it. Mir Alam was caught by a few Englishmen who were passing. But I had him released. He became a close friend. God willing, Jinnah Sahib too will come and sit here one day and say that he is not, and never has been, our enemy (*The Collected Works of Mahatma Gandhi*: 44–45).

2 June was a day of silence for Gandhi. Since he could not talk to Mountbatten when he met him that day, he passed on written requests to the Viceroy for the removal of the Governor of the NWFP: 'Badshah Khan is with me in the Bhangi Colony.[9] He said, "Do ask the Viceroy to remove the Governor. We won't have peace till he is gone." I don't know whether he is right or wrong. He is truthful. If it can be done decorously, you should do it' (*The Collected Works of Mahatma Gandhi*: 60). Both Gandhi and Khan Abdul Ghaffar Khan were sure that Governor Olaf Caroe would add to the trouble. In a day's time, the country was to know of the partition plan. It was decided that the NWFP would hold a referendum with only two options, whether to join India or Pakistan. In the absence of the third option, that of 'Pathanistan', Gandhi knew that Khan Abdul Ghaffar Khan's future was dark. Though he did not want to stand in the way of the Congress

Working Committee, Gandhi made his dissent with the committee's decision regarding division of India quite clear on 2 June (*The Collected Works of Mahatma Gandhi*: 61).

On 3 June, the final plan for dividing India was made public. The referendum to be held in the NWFP allowed just two options to the province of either aligning with Pakistan or remaining with the old Union. No alteration in its terms could now be made without the Muslim League's concurrence. The Congress too was not prepared to make an issue of it at this stage. The Congress high command wanted the Pathans to participate in the referendum with all their might. What the Congress leaders failed to appreciate was that the Pathans did not possess Gandhi's 'fourth-dimensional' way of satyagraha in which one stooped to conquer and won even through defeat. In political parlance, the battle for the Frontier Province was already lost. It never had been Gandhi's intention to hold the Frontier Province for India. He just wanted to save it for the Pathans and for the ideal of non-violence, for that is what had kept him united with the Khan brothers. The NWFP, some day, could even serve as a golden bridge between India and Pakistan. Gandhi had all along known what was coming as he had knowledge of it while the partition plan was being redrafted. Gandhi woke up on the morning of 1 June earlier than usual musing to himself in a low voice:

> Today I find myself all alone. Even the Sardar and Jawaharlal think that my reading is wrong and peace is sure to return if the partition is agreed upon. They did not like my telling the Viceroy that even if there was to be a partition, it should not be through the British intervention or under the British rule. They wonder if I have not deteriorated with age. Nevertheless, I must speak as I feel, if I am to prove a true and loyal friend to the Congress and the British people, as I claim to be. I cannot bear to see Badshah Khan's grief. His inner agony wrings my heart. But, if I gave way to tears, it would be cowardly, and the stalwart Pathan as he is, he would break down. So I go about my business unmoved. That is no small thing.

The decision to partition India and hold a referendum in the NWFP was taken by the Congress high command without consulting Khan

Abdul Ghaffar Khan. Sardar Patel and C. Rajagopalachari[10] too were in favour of holding the referendum in the NWFP. Only he and Gandhi had opposed this decision. 'Mahatmaji, you have thrown us to the wolves,' Khan Abdul Ghaffar Khan had bitterly complained to Gandhi after the Congress Working Committee's decision approving partition and referendum on 3 June. Gandhi on his part assured him that if the Frontier Province was not given a square deal or if the Khudai Khidmatgars were oppressed, India would feel honour-bound to come to their rescue. When Khan Abdul Ghani Khan, Ghaffar Khan's son, asked Gandhi about what would happen to his non-violence in that event, Gandhi had told him not to worry: 'I am non-violent, the Government is not.'

Just before Nehru and Jinnah were to go on air on 3 June, Gandhi in his prayer speech remonstrated that the leaders were 'not above or beyond criticism'. Referring to Nehru as 'our king', he continued: 'We should not be impressed by everything the king does or does not do. If he has devised something good, we should praise him. If he has not, then we shall say so.' The obvious reference here was to the numerous differences that Gandhi had with Nehru and the Congress high command, of which the NWFP formed a major subject of dispute.

Nehru's response to Gandhi was a strong note rationalizing the surrender of the NWFP. Defending the referendum, Nehru contended that it was necessary after it became part of a larger plan that also provided for a similar solution in Baluchistan and Sylhet. He frankly admitted that the Viceroy and the British government were now committed to the referendum and so were most of the Congress leaders. And that Gandhi too should take it as a settled fact. Gandhi was naturally peeved. He had also had an hour-long meeting with Patel and was at pains to point out to Nehru that:

The oftener we meet the more convinced I am becoming that the gulf between us in the thought world is deeper than I had feared.

He [the Sardar] says that you are largely responsible for the present situation. He is of the opinion that Badshah Khan's…influence is on the wane. Badshah Khan has not left any such impression on me. I also feel that Dr Khan Saheb and his colleagues would be nowhere without the Badshah. He alone counts in so far as the Congress influence is concerned. If the Qaid-e-Azam does not go to the Frontier and does not woo the Badshah, his brother and his other colleagues, the Frontier Ministry should resign on the sole ground that a referendum at this moment must lead to bloodshed. Amrit [Rajkumari Amrit Kaur][11] tells me that you think to the contrary. You think the referendum should take place now... I do not share this view. I had told the Badshah that if I do not carry you with me, I shall retire at least from the Frontier consultation and let you guide him. (Pyarelal 1956: 268–69).

Exasperated, Gandhi wanted to wash his hands off this affair. He forwarded the note 'of surrender' from Nehru to Badshah Khan stating that:

> It is the result of a difference of opinion between him [Nehru] and me. In the circumstances I must not guide you. He has put forth his argument as usual in his very able manner. Now you have to act as you think best. His suggestion that you should come to Delhi and discuss the situation before taking any final decision is worthy of consideration. I am planning to go away to Bihar, if I can, before the meeting of the A.I.C.C.

To Nehru he wrote:

> If I shared your premises, I should wholeheartedly agree with you. I am sending your note by a messenger to the Badshah. The more I contemplate the difference in outlook and opinion between the members of the Working Committee and me, I feel that my presence in Delhi is unnecessary, even if it is not detrimental to the cause we all have at heart. May I not go back to Bihar in two or three days? Would it be wrong if you insisted that referendum would be wrong without the presentation of the picture of Pakistan? (Pyarelal 1956: 289).

In the interim, Khan Abdul Ghaffar Khan had returned to Peshawar to consult his party and the Khudai Khidmatgars. He informed Gandhi on 8 June that they could not agree to the holding of a referendum. He felt that the conditions prevailing in the province could lead to serious violence if a referendum was held. His party and followers were also against Pakistan and wanted a free Pathan state within India. He responded to Gandhi on 11 June after receiving from him Nehru's note of surrender:

> This evening a joint meeting of the members of the Frontier Provincial Congress Committee, Congress Parliamentary Party and the Salars (chiefs) of the Khudai Khidmatgars was held for about four hours. Representatives from all over the Province took part in the meeting. The consensus of the opinion was that we should not take part in the referendum. On the issue in para 4(a) of the announcement, they all desired that the issues should be amended on the basis of Pakistan and free Pathan state.

The all-important question of a referendum worried Gandhi immensely. He wanted to avoid it at any cost. But he also knew the weakness of his position, especially the fact that Nehru was not with him on this issue. The decisions on the NWFP, now part of the unalterable 3 June plan, had been taken by Mountbatten in consultation with Nehru. What was Gandhi to do now, if not just to sit quietly and watch events unfold in the NWFP? Gandhi pleaded with Lord Ismay and Mountbatten that Jinnah be made to see reason, as there was every likelihood of a referendum causing bloodshed. Gandhi fervently wanted Jinnah to go to the NWFP, thereby providing Khan Abdul Ghaffar Khan a chance to resolve matters. In case the attempt failed, Khan Abdul Ghaffar Khan could then advise Dr Khan Saheb to resign. Since Gandhi was yet to discuss this with his Congress colleagues, he did not want Mountbatten to share this assurance with anyone at this stage. Mountbatten, of course, knew that Gandhi's ideas would not commend to Nehru and his colleagues. Realizing how handicapped he was, Gandhi still wanted Mountbatten to put pressure on Jinnah to go to the NWFP where the ministers, Khan Abdul Ghaffar Khan and his Khudai Khidmatgar followers would be offered an opportunity to meet him. Gandhi was ready to assure Jinnah of a courteous hearing from Khudai Khidmatgar leaders. He was aware of the fate that awaited Khan Abdul Ghaffar Khan and his Khudai Khidmatgars and was pragmatic enough to realize that their only hope lay in the installation of a homogenous ministry, a mechanism of joint responsibility both of the Congress and of the Muslim League in case Jinnah's visit proved successful. Unfortunately for Gandhi, Jinnah did not take his suggestion seriously. But Gandhi persevered. He sincerely wanted to prevent a situation where the Khan brothers and their party found themselves completely isolated. The fact that the NWFP would merge with Pakistan was staring in his face.

The All India Congress Committee met in Delhi on 14 and 15 June to ratify the decision of its working committee, that of India's partition. Gandhi, who attended the meeting could now only strike a despondent note. His efforts had not borne any fruit:

> You will no doubt agree that no one could be as much hurt by the division of the country as I am. And I don't think that anyone can be as unhappy today as I am... Why was the Congress Working Committee formed? When a government has to be run, even if it is a government of the people, a cabinet of ministers has to be appointed. Our Working Committee performs a similar function. It acts in your name. You have the power to keep it going or to dismiss it. The Working Committee has on your behalf accepted partition... If you want to throw out the resolution you can do so. But you cannot make any changes in it... The decision has not been mine to take and the Working Committee has accepted it because there was no other way. They now see it clearly that the country is already divided into two camps... But I have not come here to plead for them. Who will listen to my pleading? But the President said that I should atleast show my face here. Hence I have come to show my face and to speak a few words.[12]

How worried and anxious Gandhi was about Khan Abdul Ghaffar Khan's welfare, finds reflection in a personal letter he wrote to a friend on 15 June:

> Today Badshah Khan, who has been so brave, is not able to show bravery. For years he has been instructing the Pathans in ahimsa. But today he says he cannot declare allegiance to India. If he did that there would be a carnage ten times as bad as in Bihar. What is he to do? Ahimsa is not a commodity which can be bought in the market. If we could display true ahimsa, the Frontier Province alone could save the whole of India.[13]

Gandhi was guilt-ridden and confused on account of Khan Abdul Ghaffar Khan, his internal turmoil finding expression in a prayer meeting:

> Today my tongue, my words, have lost their power. But he [Jinnah] still has that power. He is the ruler of Pakistan and

nobody can deny it. So I ask the ruler of Pakistan, what he intends doing. He should make his intentions public. Let me now go a little further. Badshah Khan is a friend. Badshah Khan can go somewhere else...

He is a *fakir*. Dr Khan Saheb is his brother. Dr Khan Saheb can do nothing without Badshah Khan's help. Badshah Khan is a *fakir*. That is why he is 'Badshah' or king... When I go there I never hear him called by any other name. It is here that he is called the Frontier Gandhi. There they do not even know Gandhi, to say nothing of Frontier Gandhi... Tempers have not yet cooled, for Pathans are hot-blooded. What will be gained by a referendum?...there will be division among the Pathans. I should like to ask the leader of Pakistan if he wants a division among the Pathans. And will he compel one of the parts? Would it not be better for him instead to explain what Pakistan is?

Tirelessly and no doubt with a sense of stubborn doggedness, Gandhi struggled to prevent the isolation of the Khan brothers. He met Jinnah in the Viceroy's presence on 17 June. Recalling the meeting, Mountbatten revealed that Gandhi and Jinnah spoke to each other in such low voices that he could barely make out what was being said. Even then it was apparent that there was 'a good deal of mutual recrimination over their previous correspondence', that necessitated Mountbatten's intervention. Mountbatten counselled that Jinnah take advantage of Khan Abdul Ghaffar Khan's presence in Delhi and meet him. How anxious Gandhi was about a positive outcome of this meeting can be gauged by his utterances of the same day in his prayer meeting:

The Viceroy has left Delhi today but he would have been happy if we could have met. We therefore went to Lord Ismay at 4:30 in the afternoon. Badshah Khan has now gone to see Mr Jinnah at his residence and he is still with him. Do not please build any great hopes on this... The result is in the hands of God. What would be a happy result in this instance? This, that the Pathans in the Frontier Province may all be united. Pathans are a sword-happy people...

From generation to generation vendetta rules their lives but Badshah Khan saw that they could defend themselves better by dying than by killing. He wanted the Pathans to develop this lofty courage and render service. But before this dream could be realized this question of referendum came up. Some will now say that they want to be with Pakistan... And the Congress of course has come to be regarded by some as an organization of the Hindus. This will create a schism among the Pathans... Badshah Khan wants that by some means it may be made possible for the Pathans to remain free without having to submit to a referendum. They should make their own laws and remain united. It would not then matter whether they chose Pakistan or India... They do not want to be an independent nation.

But they would decide which country to join after they have got over the present quarrels. Then it also irks Dr Khan Saheb that some Hindus found it necessary to take refuge in Hardwar.[14] Therefore Badshah Khan wants these Hindus to return to NWFP. There are still numerous Hindus in the NWFP who are too poor to be able to leave. They can feel secure only after this question of the referendum is settled. It is for this that Badshah Khan has gone to see the Qaid-e-Azam. What he brings from there remains to be seen.[15]

In the meeting with Jinnah, Khan Abdul Ghaffar Khan gave an assurance of their willingness to join Pakistan provided it was on honourable terms, terms that gave them an option to opt out and form a separate state. All matters concerning tribal areas were also to be settled by the Pathans themselves without interference from non-Pathans. But these were impossible terms for Jinnah to agree to. Perhaps they were offered as a basis for further bargaining. But with Jinnah proving his usual intransigent self, the meeting proved a failure. This troubled Gandhi greatly. It kept him awake till 12.30 that night. The thoughts that he penned before his usual 3 a.m. wake-up time were:

> I cannot cease thinking of Badshah Khan even when I have ceased desire to live up to 125 years. Badshah Khan is a prodigy. I am seeing more and more of his deeply spiritual nature everyday. He has patience, faith, and non-violence joined to true humility. Countless Pathans have enshrined him in their hearts as their uncrowned King. For such a person there can be no defeat. I am

sure he will not shrink from any sacrifice or suffering, but will die serving the Pathans with his last breath. He lives only for that. He is a man of penance, also of illumination, with love for all and hatred towards none.

Gandhi then lay down and tried to doze off but was unable to sleep, the thought of Khan Abdul Ghaffar Khan had robbed him of his sleep. He echoed his disappointment again at the next day's prayer meeting:

I had said yesterday that Badshah Khan was seeing Mr Jinnah and that we should pray for the success of the meeting. It may be asked what fruit our prayer has yielded. I cannot tell you more than what Mr Jinnah has stated in the newspapers. He says that the talks were cordial. That is good. But what has been the issue? He says the issue will be known when Badshah Khan sends word from the NWFP. This means that there is no issue.... In the NWFP today it has been made clear to the people that they are to cast their ballot for either India or Pakistan. India is being represented as Hindu Raj and people are reminded of Bihar. In this atmosphere hardly any Muslim would want to give up Pakistan for India. Under the circumstances Badshah Khan wants that for the time being NWFP should be a free province, i.e., without joining either Pakistan or India, the Pathans should be allowed to formulate their own laws and frame their own constitution. The Congress should tell the Pathans to make their own constitution and assure them that the Congress will not interfere in it in any way. We shall have such control as the centre exercises in other provinces, but in internal matters they can carry on their affairs according to the *Shariat*. The League should similarly declare that the provinces to be included in Pakistan will have freedom in internal matters and the centre will be responsible only for certain given subjects. That is to say, we shall be having two centres with the provinces enjoying the maximum autonomy. If this is conceded there will no longer be any need for a referendum. I will also then advise the Pathans that since they are nearer to Pakistan geographically they should join Pakistan... If in this confused situation a referendum is still considered necessary it may be held but the choice should not be between

Pakistan and India but between Pakistan and Pathanistan. Let both [Congress and the Muslim League] honour the Pathan sentiment and let the Pathans have their own constitution for internal affairs and administration... Any premature referendum would be a leap in the dark.[16]

Khan Abdul Ghaffar Khan had Gandhi's unequivocal approval to move for a free Pathanistan to have its own local constitution and, when the Pakistan and Union constitutions were out, to decide either to belong to one state or the other. But in this move, Khan Abdul Ghaffar Khan had failed. Therefore, the referendum was to go on without any interference from Khan Abdul Ghaffar Khan and his followers. They were to abstain from voting, realizing fully that by doing so, they would allow the NWFP to go to Pakistan. Khan Abdul Ghaffar Khan wanted Gandhi to draw the Viceroy's attention to the influx of Punjab Muslims into the NWFP along with notable non-Frontier Muslims. This was bound to affect not only the referendum but also increase chances of violence. The non-Muslim population of the Frontier Province was threatened with dire consequences should they dare exercise their franchise. It sounded amoral and contradictory to Gandhi that Jinnah was contending that Pathan abstention from voting was a breach of the terms of the referendum. The contention didn't carry force as a majority of the non-Muslims, also the Pakhtuns who were Khudai Khidmatgars, were threatened with violence.

Gandhi's good intentions and efforts to stall the process of referendum came to nought. By end June, he was resigned to the referendum, which was due to commence from 6 July. Realizing how little in actual terms was the worth of his moral support to Khan Abdul Ghaffar Khan, he still continued to defend his actions:

> People are today watching the referendum that is about to be held in the Frontier Province because legally the Frontier Province has been and still is a Congress province. Badshah Khan and his co-workers are being asked to choose between Pakistan and India. The word Hindustan is being misunderstood as if Hindustan is Hindu and Pakistan is Muslim. The problem before Badshah Khan is how to get out of this difficulty... The Khudai Khidmatgars will not participate in the referendum.

This will result in a clear victory for the Muslim League and the Khudai Khidmatgars will also not have acted in defiance of their inner voice, granting that they have one. How does this violate any conditions of the referendum?... Badshah Khan is chided for raising a new demand for Pakhtoonistan... Badshah Khan does not want to set up a separate state. If he is only free to make his own constitution he will gladly join one of the two federations. I can see no ground for objection to this demand of Pakhtoonistan. Of course if the idea is to teach the Pathans a lesson and to humble them anyhow it is a different matter. A serious charge leveled against Badshah Khan is that he is playing into the hands of Afghanistan. I am quite sure that Badshah Khan cannot practise deceit against anyone. He will never allow the Frontier Province to be absorbed into Afghanistan.[17]

The Khudai Khidmatgars campaigned for some time for a boycott of the referendum. The possibility that this would bring them into direct conflict with Muslim League worried Mountbatten. He, therefore, wanted Gandhi to persuade Khan Abdul Ghaffar Khan to discontinue this campaign. That the Khudai Khidmatgars had given a walkover to the League in the referendum did not bother Mountbatten's conscience. The realist in Mountbatten would on the one side persuade Gandhi ever so politely if the situation so demanded, and on the other not hesitate to brand him an 'inveterate and a dangerous Trotskyist', if Gandhi posed hurdles. Cajoled into it by Mountbatten, Gandhi wrote to Khan Abdul Ghaffar Khan to refrain from organizing demonstrations against the Muslim League. Gandhi perhaps was the only important Congress leader who endorsed the proposed actions of Khan Abdul Ghaffar Khan. Gandhi agreed with him that in the present state of tension and misrepresentation, a Khudai Khidmatgar should not vote at all, one way or another. They were also entitled in their internal affairs to claim and to have complete autonomy without any interference from Pakistan or the Union; they could come to a decision on their choice between the Union or Pakistan when the constitutions of the two states were being promulgated and when the NWFP had fashioned its own autonomous constitution (*Collected Works of Mahatma Gandhi*, Gandhiji's correspondence with the government).

The referendum lasted for two weeks—from 6 July to 20 July. Gandhi had advised Ghaffar Khan and his ministers 'not to cast their votes either way'.[18] He had offered similar advice to the Muslim League. The result, because of the boycott by the Khudai Khidmatgars, was a foregone conclusion, declared in favour of Pakistan. The NWFP was lost to India—though a Congress-run NWFP ministry was still in place on 15 August. Gandhi alone in the Congress had supported the Khudai Khidmatgars. Everyone else failed Khan Abdul Ghaffar Khan and as he himself said, 'had thrown him to the wolves'; by doing so, they had so easily allowed the NWFP to become a part of Pakistan. In their sentiment, they were no different from Lord Ismay, who had called it a 'bastard situation'.

On 30 July, Gandhi left Delhi for Kashmir and Khan Abdul Ghaffar Khan returned to the NWFP. Gandhi's final advice to him was 'to make Pakistan really "paak" (pure).' They never met again. After partition, the Khan brothers seldom wrote to Gandhi or to their Indian colleagues. A campaign of vilification and persecution continued against them. When disquieting reports of it reached Gandhi, he wrote to Khan Abdul Ghaffar Khan in November 1947, suggesting openly that he should leave the Frontier and develop his non-violent techniques from India: 'This you can do here with me or otherwise. What that otherwise can be, I do not know. I do not believe as some do that non-violence can only be offered in a civilized or partially civilized society. Non-violence admits of no such limit.' Unfortunately, Gandhi was soon to die a violent death.

## Notes

1. *Malang* is an Urdu word which is usually used with the word 'mast' as a prefix. It is a Punjabi Sufi word that conveys a carefree and, therefore, happy person. Why was Gandhi referred to as 'Malang' Baba by the Pakhtuns? Perhaps because the tribes had a hidden degree of respect and love for his non-violent politics, something they could not easily accept, understand or conceive of as being practicable.
2. The Calcutta riots of 1946, also known as the 'Great Calcutta Killings', were four days of Hindu–Muslim riots in the capital of Bengal, resulting in 5,000 to 10,000 dead, and 15,000 wounded. The riots took place

between 16 and 19 August 1946. These riots are probably the most notorious single massacre of the 1946–47 period, during which large-scale communal violence occurred in many parts of India.
3. It was at the Lahore Session of the Indian National Congress from 31 December 1929 to 1 January 1930 that the Indian tricolour was unfurled by nationalists, and a pledge taken that every year on 26 January 'Independence Day' would be celebrated and that the Indian people would strive for the establishment of a sovereign democratic republic of India.
4. Sir Evan Meredith Jenkins was the last Governor of Punjab before partition.
5. Utmanzai is a town in Charsadda district in the NWFP of Pakistan. It is the birthplace of Khan Abdul Ghaffar Khan.
6. *Bihar Pachhi Dilhi* (in Gujarati), pp.45–46.
7. Ibid.
8. Field Marshal Jan Christiaan Smuts (1870–1950) served as a British Field Marshal in World War II.
9. A colony where scavengers resided. *Bhangi* is an Indian term for people who were engaged in removing night soil.
10. Popularly known as 'Rajaji', C. Rajagopalachari was the first Indian Governor General of India. Rajaji became the Prime Minister of Madras Presidency in 1937 but gave up office in 1939 following the Congress's decision against cooperating with the British for unilaterally involving India in World War II. He became a member of the interim government formed in 1946 in Delhi. On independence, he became the Governor of West Bengal. In 1948, he became the first Indian Governor General. In 1952, he became the Chief Minister of Madras as a challenge to fight the communists in the Madras state legislature. He relinquished office in 1954. He was given the Bharat Ratna, the highest national award, in 1954.
11. Rajkumari Amrit Kaur (1889–1964) was the Health Minister in the Indian cabinet for ten years after India's independence from the British in 1947. She was an eminent Gandhian, a freedom fighter and a social activist.
12. Speech at AICC meeting, New Delhi, 14 June 1947, pp.153–55, *The Collected Works of Mahatma Gandhi; Bihar Pachhi Dilhi* (in Hindi), pp.142–46.
13. Letter to Prema Kantak, New Delhi, 15 June 1947, *The Collected Works of*

*Mahatma Gandhi*, p.164; *Prarthana Pravachan-1* (in Hindi), pp.166–70; *The Hindu*, 17 June 1947.
14. Hardwar or Haridwar, is one of the holy places for Hindus in India.
15. Speech at Prayer Meeting, New Delhi, 18 June 1947, *Prarthana Pravachan-1* (in Hindi), pp.173–77.
16. *Prarthana Pravachan-I* (in Hindi), pp.178–82; *The Hindu*, 29 June 1947.
17. *Prarthana Pravachan-I* (in Hindi), pp.209–10.
18. Ibid., pp.224–26.

# 11

# The Pathan Jeremiad: Khan Abdul Ghaffar Khan[1]

KHAN ABDUL GHAFFAR Khan, Fakhr-e-Afghan, Frontier Gandhi, Badshah Khan, Bacha Khan—call him by any name—was perhaps the only statesman who came close to Gandhi in matters of creed and faith. A key political figure of the NWFP, he passed away in Peshawar on 28 January 1988. Within hours of his death, the then Indian Prime Minister Rajiv Gandhi flew into Peshawar and both Afghanistan and India declared a state of mourning. Sadly, his own country, Pakistan, where the National Assembly and the senate were in session, made no reference to his demise. What is most regrettable is the unusual number of years Ghaffar Khan so ungrudgingly spent in jail as a political prisoner. Born in 1890, he got his first taste of detention immediately after the Jallianwala Bagh massacre in April 1919. Thereafter, it was just a case of one incarceration after another, more so when the freedom struggle was over in 1947.

Pyarelal, one of Gandhi's secretaries, had the good fortune of meeting Khan Abdul Ghaffar Khan again in 1965. But the doughty fighter was loath to recount experiences of yore: 'Let that be…the past is dead and buried.' Pyarelal had insisted: 'I entirely agree with you… but the past is neither dead nor buried. It is always with you. Why else should you and I be meeting here today in such strange circumstances.' With a 'distant and faraway look in his eyes' Khan Abdul Ghaffar Khan reminisced, 'neither the issue of partition nor of referendum in NWFP[2] was discussed with us… Sardar Patel and Rajaji pressed for it…we were stunned to find that the decision on both the issues had already been taken by the Congress High Command.'

'After the Working Committee's meeting (3 June 1947) I said to Gandhiji, "You have thrown us to the wolves." Gandhiji asked us to have no fear. He would spare no effort to see that justice was done to us and India would stand by us if we were oppressed.' Asked what would happen to his non-violence in that event, Gandhi's amused response was: 'Don't you worry about my non-violence. I know how to take care of it.'

'That promise had not been kept. Gandhiji would never have let this happen if he had lived. India owed it to them and to Gandhiji to make Kaffara (expiation) for it.' With head bowed in humiliation, Pyarelal admitted to Khan Abdul Ghaffar Khan that Indians could 'not be exculpated from what Vinoba Bhave called in the language of the Bhagvad Gita "the heinous sin of betrayal of one's friends and comrades" and Maulana Abdul Kalam Azad who sat near Khan Abdul Ghaffar Khan in the Working Committee that approved partition, noticing his dejection said to him, "you should now join the Muslim League."'

Khan Abdul Ghaffar Khan was pained to find how little his comrades understood what they had fought for all those years. 'How could they imagine we would compromise our principles for the sake of power?'[3]

With a twinge of sorrow, Khan Abdul Ghaffar Khan recalled those days when he could have asked the Muslim League for anything if only he had severed his connections with the Congress. But he had refused. While in Gujarat jail (Punjab) in 1931, the British had indicated that in case he agreed to dissociate with the Congress, he would be allowed a far greater measure of political reforms for his province. In a chance meeting with Sir Feroz Khan Noon,[4] a prominent member of the Punjab cabinet, Khan Abdul Ghaffar Khan was accused of betraying Indian Muslims by joining the Congress. He promptly rebutted this, pointing out that it was impossible to face the British alone in the NWFP as they were bent upon crushing his movement. He joined with the Congress only after the Muslim League spurned his overtures for a tie-up: 'If the Muslim League leaders were prepared to join the freedom struggle, the Khudai Khidmatgars were ready to break away from Mahatma Gandhi and resign from the Congress. But in that event, Sir Feroz Khan Noon would have had to surrender his sinecures'

(Pyarelal 1966: 138–39). When Khan Abdul Ghaffar Khan had another run-in with Sir Feroz at Patna in 1946, he asked Khan Abdul Ghaffar Khan once again what his feelings were, especially after the communal riots in Bihar. Khan Abdul Ghaffar Khan's response was much the same.

Ghaffar Khan felt grievously let down by Congress leaders who had assured him that they would never accept partition. The Khudai Khidmatgars were not even given any advance notice; instead they were asked to fend for themselves, leaving them completely in the lurch: 'I was in Delhi at that time,' said Khan Abdul Ghaffar Khan, 'yet nobody whispered a word to me...and now see the result... The Congress leaders thought that by accepting Partition they would have peace, the hatchet would be buried for good. But how can you expect love to sprout from the seeds of hatred? What has been founded on hatred can be sustained also by hate' (Pyarelal 1966: 128).

Khan Abdul Ghaffar Khan's son Wali Khan informs us that his father was not allowed to go to England to pursue his studies. The ostensible reason was Dr Khan Saheb, his elder brother, who had ended up marrying a white girl and Ghaffar Khan's mother had 'absolutely no intention of exposing her only other son to the danger of becoming a Farangi'. A chance witness to an incident where his friend was insulted by a white army officer put paid to his ambitions of seeking an appointment in the Indian army. While attending the all-India session of the Muslim League in 1913 in Agra he had occasion to hear Maulana Azad, Sir Ibrahim Rahimtoola and Sir Aga Khan. Hailing from a conservative Pakhtun environment, Khan Abdul Ghaffar Khan also thought it proper to visit the Deoband seminary and interact with its not so stereotypical devout holy men in 1914. These Deoband ulemas were nationalists and Ghaffar Khan's early propensity to resist British rule was a result of this influence. Leading by example, Khan Abdul Ghaffar Khan started his first vernacular 'Azad school' at Utmanzai, his home, and had 'the honour of becoming its first student'. It was in fact from his early days that Khan Abdul Ghaffar Khan took to 'furrowing untread paths', wearing *khaddar*, practising non-violence and maintaining a frugal life, long before he came in contact with Gandhi. Upon his return home, he also opened a small centre at Bajaur with the express aim of sensitizing his men to struggle against

British rule. The centre had to shut down because the Political Agent of Malakand would not let it run.

Gandhi was soon to appear on the Indian political firmament. Against the patently unjust Rowlatt Acts, enforcing indefinite preventive detention and imprisonment without a trial or judicial review, Gandhi called for a nationwide strike on 6 April 1919. On 13 April, the Jallianwala Bagh massacre took place. Martial law was imposed in Peshawar district. When Khan Abdul Ghaffar Khan convened a meeting of protest against the Rowlatt Acts at Utmanzai, the authorities arrested his father and threatened to execute him. Ghaffar Khan, who had escaped the official dragnet, surrendered. After his release, he joined the Khilafat movement and soon took over the presidency of the Frontier Khilafat Committee. His was a stellar role in the agitation that led to the Hijrat movement when some ulema urged Muslims to migrate from their homeland to neighbouring Afghanistan to escape British rule. He went with a large party of *muhajareens* to Afghanistan where he met Amir Amanullah. But the Hijrat movement failed and the would-be migrants had to return.

In the Azad High School that Khan Abdul Ghaffar Khan had established at Utmanzai, tenets of Islam, the history of Pakhtuns and weaving were taught. Pashtu was the medium of instruction. He had also set up an association, the 'Anjuman Islah-ul-Afghania' for spreading education. Khan Abdul Ghaffar Khan's activities alarmed the Chief Commissioner of the province who asked him to close down the school. When Khan Abdul Ghaffar Khan refused, he was arrested and jailed for three years and kept in solitary confinement. During this term he got a chance to read the Bhagvad Gita, Guru Granth Sahib and the Bible. By the time he was released in 1924, his mother had passed away, of which he got to know only through the newspapers. His father died in 1926 where after, he along with his wife and sister, embarked upon Haj. He took long tours of his province on foot after he returned from the pilgrimage. In May 1928, he started *Pakhtun*, the first journal in Pashtu that was nationalist in orientation. It was banned by the British in April 1930. It was published with breaks and was finally ordered to shut shop by the Pakistan government soon after independence.

In 1928, Khan Abdul Ghaffar Khan went to Calcutta to attend the Khilafat Conference. Mohammad Ali's presidential address left him unimpressed as the speech castigated Hindus and their culture. Concurrently in Calcutta, the Congress was holding its session of the subject committee where Khan Abdul Ghaffar Khan got a chance to listen to Gandhi. Between the two leaders he preferred Gandhi and when he left Calcutta, he also left the Khilafat movement.

In January 1929, Amir Amanullah of Afghanistan was forced to abdicate. The new claimant to the Amirship was the son of a water carrier, popularly called Baccha-i-Saqao. By October of the same year, the Pakhtuns had come together to remove him. Mohammad Nadir Khan was installed on the throne of Afghanistan. Khan Abdul Ghaffar Khan had organized a meeting of Pakhtun leaders in Utmanzai to celebrate Nadir Khan's victory in Kabul and also to show his solidarity with the Pakhtun nation. It was at this meeting that he announced the founding of a pan-Pakhtun organization, calling it the Khudai Khidmatgars. The organization was declared strictly socio-religious. The Khudai Khidmatgars were organized on military lines, though non-violence was to be their article of faith. The rifle, the revolver and the sword, so dear to a Pathan, were rejected. But this socio-religious and expressly non-political movement was launched in direct consequence of a violent politico-military event, culminating in the overthrow of one and the installation of another regime in Kabul that bore a distinctly ethnic label. Thus a violent event in Kabul was celebrated in a non-violent setting in Utmanzai, giving birth to a non-violent movement. The political kinship between the ruling family in Kabul and the non-political prime movers of the new movement had repercussions on both sides of the Khyber for a long time.

The Khudai Khidmatgar movement rested on three tenets—unity of Pakhtuns, the spirit of Islam and the creed of non-violence. In the Lahore session of the Congress in 1929, the Khudai Khidmatgars, whose participation in their colourful Red Shirt uniforms was conspicuous and overwhelming, were overjoyed to see Nehru, the new president, wearing a Pathan turban while presiding over Congress deliberations. The transformation of the socio-religious movement into a political organization occurred immediately after the movement was born. The annual session of the Congress was held barely a month after the birth of the Khudai Khidmatgars. A Pathan turban was chosen as the new president's headgear, although Punjabi headgear in Lahore would have been more apt. This was a landmark gesture. The call for complete independence appealed to the psyche of Pathans. Till April 1930 there were only 500 Khudai Khidmatgars, but inspired by the Lahore Resolution of 1929, the recruits swelled to 50,000 within six months. Incessant touring by Khan Abdul Ghaffar Khan in the Frontier led to the swelling of ranks. The Chief Commissioner of the NWFP asked Khan Abdul Ghaffar Khan to rein in his movement, which he refused. On 23 April 1930, he addressed a gathering in Utmanzai exhorting people to join the call for civil disobedience (Gandhi's Salt March of 12 March and Nehru's arrest on 14 April). While proceeding to Peshawar, he was arrested along with his followers. In the resultant commotion at Qissa Khwani Bazaar[5] (Peshawar), hundreds were killed in firing by government forces, but the crackdown by authorities had the effect of further raising the membership of the 'Surkh Posh'.[6]

Khan Abdul Ghaffar Khan was confined to the Gujarat (Punjab) jail. His associates, Mia Jaffar Shah and Abdullah Shah, met him then and were asked to visit Lahore, Delhi and Simla to seek help from the Muslim League. Finding that the Muslim League was not keen to join hands because of the Khudai Khidmatgars' nationalist stance, his associates returned to inform him about this. The Congress, which was then approached, readily agreed to help. Khan Abdul Ghaffar Khan, the undisputed leader of Pakhtuns joined the Congress from a position of strength. He did not need the Congress, rather the Congress needed him. He provided the Congress a link to Kabul and a springboard to the Hindu Kush. In 1931, Devdas Gandhi visited the NWFP and was vastly impressed by Khan Abdul Ghaffar Khan's popularity. He encountered spinning wheels, an unlikely object, in most NWFP villages that he visited. In the all-India Congress Committee meeting held in Bombay on 6 August 1931, the Khudai Khidmatgars were formally inducted as a Congress volunteer organization. Their black flag was replaced by the Congress tricolour. On 9 August 1931, Khan Abdul Ghaffar Khan made an agreement with the Congress that the Frontier Afghan *jirga* would be renamed as the Frontier Congress Committee. As Congress volunteers, the Khudai Khidmatgars dominated the political scene in the Frontier.

In the 1932 elections in the NWFP, the British felt the effects of their boycott quite acutely.

Khan Abdul Ghaffar Khan languished in a solitary cell in Hazaribagh jail till his release on 27 August 1934, but a ban was put on his entry into the NWFP and Punjab. On 19 October, he reached Bombay to attend the annual session of the Congress which was being held after three and a half years. Khan Abdul Ghaffar Khan was offered presidentship of the Congress, which he declined. While in Bombay on 27 October, he was invited to speak at the Nagpada Neighbourhood House by the Indian Christian Association. The government arrested him on 7 December for the speech he gave at this venue, which the government considered seditious. On earlier occasions, Khan Abdul Ghaffar Khan had refused to offer a defence, but this time, under Gandhi's instructions, Bhulabhai Desai, the famous Bombay lawyer, defended him. During the trial, Khan Abdul Ghaffar Khan pleaded guilty. In a written statement that he submitted he said:

> I admit the correctness of the main statement of my speech, which, my lawyer friends advise me, are capable of bringing it within the clauses of the section under which I am charged. I am a loyal Congressman and have accepted its policy of not seeking arrest and imprisonment at the present moment. [In 1934, the Congress leadership had decided to refrain from breaking the law.] I had, therefore, no desire to utter words of sedition. I am, therefore, sorry that I made the statement in the speech, however unwittingly, which are open to exception from the prosecution point of view.

Khan Abdul Ghaffar Khan was awarded a two-year jail term. His apology had not only hurt his dignity, pride and stature, but also caused dismay among Congress ranks. Sardar Patel made a futile appeal to the home member, Sir Henry Craik, for his release, adding insult to the already injured pride of the Pathan. After being sentenced, Khan Abdul Ghaffar Khan had observed: 'I was not guilty of any sedition, because how could I indulge in any sedition in a meeting of Christians who were of the same faith as the Englishmen! My real sedition was that in my heart lay sympathy for the downtrodden Bengal Muslims...the Government knew that I was to reach Bengal by about 8 December. It could not tolerate the idea of my work among the Muslims of Bengal' (Anand 2003: 20). He was kept in Sabarmati central prison and was released in end July 1936. The British ban on the Khudai Kidmatgar movement continued. Nehru was re-elected as Congress president at the Faizpur session of the Congress, where Khan Abdul Ghaffar Khan was handed a government order extending his ban on entry in the NWFP till 29 December 1937.

Immediately after the Congress ministries had taken office in 1937, the Muslim League started levelling charges that the Congress was conducting itself as a Hindu body. The Muslim League brought out well-drafted documents like the Sharif and Pirpur reports about Congress governments' and Hindu actions against Muslims to substantiate these charges. When Britain unilaterally decided to involve India in World War II, the Congress ministries resigned. The Lahore Resolution of 22 March 1940 changed the entire politics of India's freedom struggle. Prominent Muslims nationalists like Syed Mahmood and Asif Ali openly criticized Congress policies and its inability to carry along India's Muslims. Within two years of the ministry being formed in 1937, Jinnah had started claiming the 'sole representative' status for India's Muslims. The worrying fact was that it put the Congress leaders on the defensive.

The British knew, and so did the Congress, of the strategic importance of the NWFP. They realized how crucial it was to sustain its ministry during those years. Recognizing the significance, Gandhi toured the Frontier twice with the sole purpose of resolving factional disputes in the provincial Congress. The stature of Khan Abdul Ghaffar Khan, both within and outside the NWFP, was such that had he supported people like Asif Ali and Syed Mahmood, the Congress leaders would have been forced to sit up and take notice. But Khan Abdul Ghaffar Khan's reaction on pronouncements of people like Syed Mahmood and Asif Ali were either absent or at best ambiguous (Korejo 1994: 132–34).

Khan Abdul Ghaffar Khan, forever a staunch follower of Gandhi, resigned from the Congress Working Committee in 1940 entirely on Gandhi's bidding. Gandhi justified its necessity because of the 'peculiar position [Ghaffar Khan held] in his province':

> People followed Ghaffar Khan without questioning him and like Ceasar's wife, Ghaffar Khan had to be above suspicion that he was not turning over to violence. Some recent resolutions

of the Congress Working Committee indicated that they are restricting the use of non-violence to fight for India's freedom... it is difficult for me [Gandhi] to continue in the Congress Working Committee and I am resigning from it... Non-violence has added greatly to the courage of the Pathans... He [Ghaffar Khan] is a Pathan and a Pathan may be said to be born with a rifle or a sword in his hand. But Khan Saheb [Ghaffar Khan] deliberately asked his Khudai Khidmatgars to shed all weapons when he asked them to join the satyagraha... He saw that his deliberate giving up of the weapons of violence had a magical effect... They took up his message and put into practice what with them became non-violence of the brave... Being so clear about his own faith and that of the Khudai Khidmatgars, there was for him no escape from resignation of his membership of the Congress Working Committee. His continuing on it would have been anomalous and might have meant an end of his life's work.

But Gandhi withdrew his resignation soon, when through an AICC resolution passed by 192 votes to seven, he was requested to resume leadership of the Congress party.

Gandhi's decision to thrust India into the Quit India agitation saw Khan Abdul Ghaffar Khan faithfully following suit. Though he was detained later, Khan Abdul Ghaffar Khan escaped arrest when Gandhi and other prominent Congress leaders were rounded up in Bombay following the famous call of 'British Quit India'. In 1942, many Congress leaders harboured sympathetic feelings towards Japan. Subsequently, when the Allied victory was in sight Gandhi and his non-violent group was forced to offer an olive branch to the British, something the British did not then need. The Congress offer was therefore ignored.

Khan Abdul Ghaffar Khan's Khudai Khidmatgars was the only Muslim mass-based group which consistently fought against the yoke of British rule. His role was more that of an organizer—he left administration to his brother, Dr Khan Saheb. Khan Abdul Ghaffar Khan regarded constitutional politics as a futile exercise, had opposed the formation of the second Congress ministry in the Frontier in March 1945, and had not shown any enthusiasm for the 1946 elections. In early December 1945, he attended the Congress Working Committee meeting in Calcutta and made it clear that he had no intention of taking part in the elections. At the time of the 1946 elections, he was lukewarm to the idea of participating in them. He felt that the Khudai Khidmatgars had lost their zeal for social work and strayed in their path, thereby reducing their movement to the status of an 'election board'.

This was naturally an ominous development for the Congress's election prospects in the NWFP. In the past, during the elections of 1937 and at the time Dr Khan Saheb assumed office for the second time, Khan Abdul Ghaffar Khan was in prison. However indifferent he might have been in his attitude towards parliamentary activities, it had not then affected the Congress rank and file and the public. But between September and December 1945, his stance regarding the elections, particularly when he was free and moving about, was bound to influence the public mind adversely.

Electoral prospects for the Congress in the initial stages were not encouraging. Although the party wielded considerable clout among the Hindu electors generally, there was unhealthy rivalry between Congressmen over the candidature for Hindu seats. The Congress' position in the three Sikh seats was far from certain and the Panthic Akali Party nominees were equally powerful competitors. Fortunately for the Congress, the election for the central legislative assembly seat raised its morale and Khan Abdul Ghani, the Congress nominee, defeated his League-supported independent opponent early in December 1945. Again in December, Abdul Ghaffar Khan changed his mind and decided to take part in the Congress election campaign. He must have realized the importance of the elections by now, as well as the main issue—India or Pakistan.

A true Gandhian, Khan Abdul Ghaffar Khan plodded along, engaging in civil disobedience and offering succour to victims of communal carnage. But on political issues, he perhaps erred, most grievously when the Cabinet Mission visited India in 1946. He had been nominated by the Congress to negotiate on its behalf. Just when it appeared that a consensus could be reached between the Muslim League and the Congress, Nehru's famous press interview of 10 July queered the pitch. Nehru recklessly announced that the Congress would enter the Constituent Assembly without any conditionality. The Cabinet Mission offer was tied to a scheme whereby India was to be divided into three groups of provinces—A, B and C. The NWFP was to be clubbed with Punjab and Sindh in one of the groups.

Khan Abdul Ghaffar Khan was fiercely opposed to the 'grouping' scheme for he feared the overbearing influence of Punjab during the framing of the group's constitution. It was his bitter opposition that found expression in Nehru's press interview of 10 July. The resultant effect was Jinnah's refusal to accept the Cabinet Mission plan; he instead opted for a Direct Action Day that culminated in the Great Calcutta Killings (August 1946). The communal violence then spiralled out of control, making any effort at unity impossible.

The Cabinet delegation's offer or rather the agreement reached between the Congress and the Muslim League in no way precluded the right of a province to secede from the 'group'. But to make this precondition a prime consideration, citing inability to work with Punjab within the group, was a cardinal error committed by Khan Abdul Ghaffar Khan. Within months, communal riots broke out all over India, making the partition inevitable. Much against Khan Abdul Ghaffar Khan's wishes a referendum was imposed on the NWFP, and to confound matters, the province was given the choice to either join India or Pakistan. That the NWFP would opt for Pakistan by then was a foregone conclusion. Khan Abdul Ghaffar Khan became prey to the circumstances of history. It is ironical that despite being the most important leader of the Congress in the NWFP, he was entirely ignored by his party when it came to shaping the province's destiny. Gandhi too was ignored as Patel and Nehru by then had claimed independence from him. As for Khan Abdul Ghaffar Khan, he did not seem to figure greatly in the urgent calculations of Nehru and Patel, who had emerged as the Congress' decision makers.

The reason why Nehru opposed the Cabinet Mission plan was different. He preferred a unitary structure, which in essence meant that the federal government would be centralized. Built into this scheme (plan) were options whereby a province could opt out of its 'group', and if the situation so demanded, opt out of India's federal set-up altogether if the provincial legislature so voted. It is unfortunate that Khan Abdul Ghaffar Khan could not foresee implications of the Cabinet Mission plan, which under the given circumstances was perhaps most advantageous to Dr Khan Saheb's government. Had he exerted pressure in 1946 for accepting this plan, who knows, the geography of the Indian subcontinent would have been different. In the mid-1940s, his stature was that of a national leader beyond the narrow confines of a provincial leader whose popularity is based on regional or ethnic considerations. After the Calcutta riots of August 1946, he was found touring different parts of India offering succour to the riot-affected people. If he was lukewarm to the idea of participating in the 1946 provincial elections, which he initially was, he should have boycotted all political activities which the British constitutional reforms provided. This would have taken the sting out of the Muslim League's propaganda that soon gathered momentum. Ghaffar Khan was in a position, theoretically at least, to force the Congress party to accept the Cabinet Mission plan for a united India in 1946 itself, much before the communal feelings in the country touched a crescendo. His was a case of a missed opportunity. In the absence of a strong Muslim lobby in the Congress, the party could not be forced to negotiate for a united India from a position of strength. Jinnah's Muslim League had appropriated for itself the 'sole spokesmanship' of the Muslims. People like Khan Abdul Ghaffar Khan and Maulana Azad, who could provide strength to the pan-Indian Muslim nationalist cause, failed to take up the cause. They, or for that matter any other element within the Congress, did not criticize the party's failure to resolve the dispute with the Muslim League.

With the formation of an interim government in September 1946, Nehru came to hold the external affairs portfolio. For the first time the tribal areas of the NWFP were in the charge of someone other than the Viceroy himself. The British had long held this area as 'sacred', disallowing any kind of political activity there. Taking advantage of Nehru's position, Khan Abdul Ghaffar Khan along with his brother, Chief Minister Dr Khan Saheb, planned a week-long trip for Nehru in these areas. They too accompanied him, much to the chagrin of the provincial Governor. The trip, as we know, proved to be a political disaster for the Khan brothers—and it signalled the decline of the Congress party in the NWFP.

Between December 1946 and May 1947, Khan Abdul Ghaffar Khan spent a major part of his time outside the NWFP, touring the riot-affected areas with Gandhi. On 8 March 1947, the Congress Working

Committee passed a resolution agreeing to partition Punjab, much around the same time as when the unionist ministry of Khizar Hayat Tiwana in Punjab had been made to resign.

As the final hour of India's independence approached, the Congress lagged in its support for the cause that Khan Abdul Ghaffar Khan had propounded all along. The Congress Working Committee had stood steadfast in its support for the Assam Chief Minister, Gopinath Bardoloi, when he demanded the right to opt out of the 'Eastern Grouping' of Muslim provinces, as also for the cause of Gurdaspur for Indian Punjab. But when it came to the NWFP, a case which was vastly different in magnitude and importance for at stake was a far greater issue on which rested the mantle of Jinnah's two-nation theory, Ghaffar Khan was let down by the Congress.

In Gandhi's absence, the Congress Working Committee approved the partition of Punjab on 8 March 1947. This step was a virtual acceptance of India's partition and the creation of Pakistan. And all this when Mountbatten had yet not arrived in India. Khan Abdul Ghaffar Khan, as we know, was mostly absent from the NWFP in those initial critical months of 1947. Gandhi and he felt increasingly marginalized in the actual decision-making process of the Congress Working Committee. Khan Abdul Ghaffar Khan came to Delhi with Gandhi on 31 March and had his first audience with Mountbatten on 4 April. In the light of what had already transpired in the Congress Working Committee on 8 March, his protestations against the British bureaucracy in the NWFP appeared abysmally irrelevant. He constantly harped on the issue of Sir Olaf Caroe's removal. Of what use was this objection? It was certainly not to endear him to the British officials in the NWFP.But he persisted with this request. As late as 2 June, Gandhi, on behalf of Khan Abdul Ghaffar Khan, conveyed to Mountbatten that 'we won't have peace till he [Caroe] is gone... I do not know whether he [Ghaffar Khan] is right or wrong. He is truthful. If it can be done decorously, you should do it.'[7] Through April, HMG continued to maintain that the newly elected representatives of the provincial legislature of the NWFP would have the option of declaring themselves an independent Constituent Assembly. Built into this was a proviso that the legislature too would be freshly elected. But the freshly introduced idea of a referendum circumvented the necessity for a new legislature. Alongside, and more importantly, it foreclosed the option of a newly elected Constituent Assembly, and with it, the possibility of an independent Constituent Assembly.

Mountbatten informed Lord Listowel that Nehru would only accept a referendum if the NWFP had the limited choice of joining either Pakistan or Hindustan. What in fact was being suggested now was a change in the terms of arrangement for demission of power. Such momentous decisions—for agreeing to hold elections afresh and subsequently to go in for a referendum were taken by Nehru without pretty much consulting the NWFP government, Gandhi or the man who really mattered, Khan Abdul Ghaffar Khan.[8]

Nehru sought Patel's help in convening a Congress Working Committee meeting on 16–17 May for which he wanted Gandhi and Ghaffar Khan to be present. Patel was privy to all decisions on the NWFP that Nehru made. V.P. Menon, the Reforms Commissioner, and a Patel acolyte, was closely assisting Mountbatten on these vital negotiations. Nehru expected Patel to use his influence with Khan Abdul Ghaffar Khan and Gandhi to smoothen things out for him in the forthcoming Congress Working Committee meeting.[9]

In May 1947, Khan Abdul Ghaffar Khan had taken a clear position on the formation of a Pathan National Province, if possible under a coalition and with suitable alliances. When Caroe had originally mooted this idea though, it was greeted with what amounted 'to fury' at its mere suggestion. Caroe believed that the idea of a Pathan nation had far greater appeal and was more constructive than the one of 'Islam in danger'.[10] But the shift in Khan Abdul Ghaffar Khan's thinking perhaps came a bit too late. Caroe's support for the idea must have surely put Mountbatten and Nehru to certain unease, especially Nehru who was not in favour of an independent Pakhtunistan.

On 30 May, both Khan Abdul Ghaffar Khan and Dr Khan Saheb flew to Delhi from Peshawar. Accompanying them were the two famous Provincial League leaders Abdul Qayyum and Sameen Jaan, especially released on parole to go with the Khan brothers. Both leaders had sought Jinnah's permission to hold discussions with the Khan brothers in Delhi. They had been in negotiations with Khan Abdul Ghaffar Khan and Dr Khan Saheb, exploring possibilities for a coalition to hold office together. Abdul Qayyum and Sameen Jaan had at one time been

Congressmen. Faction-ridden that the Provincial League was, many distrusted this development and sent representatives from Peshawar to Delhi by train to dissuade Jinnah from approving any agreement. Even Sir Olaf Caroe advocated a NWFP coalition ministry, but feared that matters could get complicated if the issue of Pakhtunistan was introduced as a consequence of the 3 June announcement.[11] Caroe was also certain that securing the cooperation of the NWFP ministry was going to be a difficult task for the Viceroy. Chief Secretary Dudley de la Fargue and other officials also believed that a peaceful referendum could only be held if the electors were given the three options of Hindustan, Pakhtunistan and Pakistan. Caroe had come across far too many sincere advocates of Pakhtunistan of which several of them were local Jinnah supporters.[12]

While Dr Khan Saheb was in Delhi on 5 June, Mountbatten met him to explain that the 'third choice' for all provinces stood permanently excluded on the express request of the Congress. But when this issue came up for discussion once again between Mountbatten and Nehru later in the day, the external affairs member appeared convinced that the Frontier, with a population of three million, could not stand alone. Dr Khan Saheb, of course, categorically stated that the NWFP would never join Pakistan and also told the Viceroy that he considered it absolutely necessary that Caroe be replaced before the referendum.[13]

Gandhi was the lone man in the Congress who, to the very end, remained extremely worried about Khan Abdul Ghaffar Khan's future. To save the situation for the Frontier Gandhi, he strove relentlessly for a Khudai Khidmatgar–Muslim League rapprochement, for he foresaw the hopeless predicament Khan Abdul Ghaffar Khan and his followers would find themselves in once the NWFP joined Jinnah's Pakistan. On 13 June, he fervently asked Mountbatten to request Jinnah to undertake a visit to the Frontier to 'woo the Ministers including Badshah Khan and the Khudai Khidmatgars'. Gandhi guaranteed Jinnah a 'courteous hearing from them'. Once in the NWFP, Jinnah could freely explain his 'Pakistan scheme' to the people. Gandhi's sole purpose was to open channels of engagement between Jinnah and Khan Abdul Ghaffar Khan so that a 'homogeneous ministry' could be formed in the NWFP.[14]

Earlier, on 2 June, Acharya Kripalani, the Congress president, wrote to the Viceroy saying that 'the proposed referendum should provide for the people voting for independence and subsequent decision as to their relation with the rest of India.' Raising the issue once again with Mountbatten, Kripalani wrote to him on 17 June: 'I understand that you have been unable to agree to this unless the Muslim League also agreed. This has added to our difficulties and we have been giving anxious thought to the matter.'[15] Kripalani assured Mountbatten that the Congress, having accepted the 3 June plan, would not do anything that went against the scheme. But the Congress was facing difficulties while it sought to impose 'a certain course of action to which the leaders and people of NWFP were opposed to'.[16] Khan Abdul Ghaffar Khan, who had the authority to negotiate on behalf of the NWFP Congress leaders, had refused to participate in the referendum. Kripalani, of course, had no objection to the referendum taking place as that was his party line too. Rather relieved and casual, he said that Khan Abdul Ghaffar Khan and his followers' boycott of the referendum would only 'ease the situation' though 'the Province may be lost to the Congress, at least for the time being'.[17] This was a display of utter callousness, reflective of the Congress top brass' thinking on a very serious issue. To further put Mountbatten at ease, Kripalani informed him that the Congress had 'no intention of sending anyone from outside the province to influence voters there for this referendum'.[18] The Congress chief also advised Khan Abdul Ghaffar Khan to avoid electioneering speeches. Clearly for reasons best known to them, the Congress leadership had decided to let the province go to Pakistan. Kripalani concluded his letter to Mountbatten with a promise that the Congress was 'very anxious that whatever might be done in the Frontier Province, it should in no way be in opposition to the working out of the Plan we have agreed to. We have impressed this upon our colleagues of the Frontier. On behalf of the Congress I hope to make a public statement explaining the Congress position in regard to Province [sic].'[19] The Congress was doing its utmost to accommodate the Viceroy.

Responding to Kripalani, Mountbatten endorsed a copy of his reply to Nehru. In the postscript he added: 'I have not of course made the point in this reply that it was at your written request that the option for Provinces to vote for independence was taken out.'[20] In his letter of 11 May, Nehru had violently disagreed with the Viceroy's draft proposals, which he thought presented 'a picture of fragmentation and conflict and disorder', and likely to 'invite the Balkanisation of India'.[21] This resulted in Mountbatten altering the original HMG proposal wherein an option to opt for independence to the provinces was provided. Jinnah, who was supportive of an independent Bengal, knew that Mountbatten had rejected this proposal on Nehru's insistence. Mountbatten, on the other hand, felt that both his and Nehru's position would become completely untenable if either of them were to go back on the 3 June arrangement. Now that Sir Olaf Caroe had been forced to go on leave, Khan Abdul Ghaffar Khan could be prevailed upon, Mountbatten hoped, to accept the referendum.[22]

Gandhi, in the interim, met Mountbatten to discuss this very issue. He urged a meeting between Khan Abdul Ghaffar Khan and Jinnah which he believed could still resolve matters. Accordingly, Mountbatten invited Jinnah to come early for a preliminary discussion with Gandhi before they met. Having talked for an hour, the three agreed to meet later the same evening (17 June) along with Khan Abdul Ghaffar Khan to find a solution to the impasse. Mountbatten was quite hopeful of its outcome but was sorely disappointed to find Khan Abdul Ghaffar Khan missing from Delhi—he was then in Deoband some hundred miles away. Those were days of limited communication. It was impossible to get Khan Abdul Ghaffar Khan in time for this important meeting. On behalf of Gandhi, Rajkumari Amrit Kaur rang up the Viceroy to inform him that Khan Abdul Ghaffar Khan could not be found. Mountbatten then requested Jinnah to defer the meeting by a day, to 18 June, over which Lord Ismay would preside. Rajkumari Amrit Kaur personally assured the Viceroy that Khan Abdul Ghaffar Khan would be present in the meeting along with Gandhi. Mountbatten was optimistic about the outcome of this meeting and he recorded this in a letter he wrote to Nehru on 17 June.[23]

The meeting took place in the Viceroy's chamber, though in his absence, at 4.30 in the evening of 18 June. Gandhi was anxious that the discussions take place there and then, to which Jinnah did not agree. As Jinnah understood it, he was there to extend a verbal invite to Khan Abdul Ghaffar Khan for a subsequent meeting. He was adamant that we would not discuss matters with Khan Abdul Ghaffar Khan even if the two were left alone. So the exclusive meeting was fixed for 7.30

the same evening at Jinnah's residence. 'They all went away in the best of tempers!'[24] The meeting at Jinnah's residence sadly failed to achieve any results.

Having returned to the NWFP on 20 June, Khan Abdul Ghaffar Khan convened a meeting of the Khudai Khidmatgars, the Zalme Pakhtoon, the Frontier Provincial Congress Committee and the Congress Parliamentary Party at Bannu on the next day where he addressed a gathering of approximately 1,200 people. This congregation adopted the following resolution: 'That a free Pathanistan of all the Pakhtoons be established. The constitution of the state will be framed on the basis of Islamic conception, democracy, equality and social justice. This meeting appeals to all Pathans to unite for the attainment of this cherished goal and not to submit to any non-Pakhtoon domination.'[25] The Muslim League, too, on the same evening, held a meeting at Bannu which over 8,000 people, many of whom were armed, attended. Gun shots were fired in the air and considerable tension prevailed. A night curfew had to be imposed to prevent violence in Bannu.[26]

When Khan Abdul Ghaffar Khan arrived in Peshawar, he again issued a lengthy statement boycotting the referendum except on the issue of Pakhtunistan and Pakistan. He declared:

> Great changes that are taking place in India, resulting in the ending of the British domination, not only affect the whole of India, but the Frontier Province especially…I have given the greatest thought to these changes and have also consulted my co-workers. For more than a generation we have struggled for freedom in the Frontier. In the course of this struggle, we Pathans have suffered great hardships, but have never given up the struggle…I would appeal to all Khudai Khidmatgars and others, who believe in a free Pathan state, not to participate in the referendum…but this does not mean that we should sit still. A new struggle has been forced on us. After bringing to a successful conclusion our eighteen years' struggle for freedom against the British domination, we are now faced with a new danger. Not only the liberty of the Pakhtoons but their very existence is at stake.[27]

Jinnah reacted furiously to this statement, which hardly helped improve matters. Expressing his regret on 28 June that Ghaffar Khan had so far not communicated directly the decision of the Frontier Congress organization, he said that he had been forced to respond to what had appeared in the press as the text of the resolution adopted by Khan Abdul Ghaffar Khan. Jinnah considered the Bannu resolution a 'direct breach of the acceptance by the Congress of HMG's plan of 3 June'.[28] Since the Congress had accepted the 3 June plan at its AICC meeting of 15 June with Gandhi urging the 'AICC to do so', Jinnah felt that the Frontier Congress was 'honour-bound' to accept the plan. The Frontier representatives of the Congress were present, both in the Congress Working Committee as well as in the AICC, where a decision to accept the plan had finally been taken. Jinnah rightly contended that Gandhi was now wrong in expressing views at his prayer meetings that were 'calculated to encourage the Khan Brothers to sabotage the Plan'.[29] Jinnah found portions of the Bannu resolution disingenuous wherein it was said that the 'Constitution of the proposed Pathanistan will be framed on the basis of Islamic conceptions of democracy, equality and social justice' thereby insinuating that the 'Pakistan Constituent Assembly composed of an overwhelming majority of Muslims, will disregard the Islamic concepts of democracy'. This provoked Jinnah into a long diatribe:

> There is no truth in it; nor is there any ground or reason for it… The Khan Brothers, especially Abdul Ghaffar Khan who is proud to call himself Frontier Gandhi, have not the monopoly of true Islamic conceptions of democracy…and till yesterday, they were wedded to nationalism, the theory of one Indian nation and the Congress demand for a strong federal Government for all India!… This sudden and new volte face is a piece of pure political chicanery and a monoeuvre intended to prop up the Khan clique in power and it pains me that it has received the apostolic blessings of Mr Gandhi who has declared himself most anxious to see that the fratricidal fight amongst the Pathans is avoided at all costs…the Pakistan Constituent Assembly…can only frame a Constitution in which the Frontier Province will be an autonomous unit, and, as such, the people of the Frontier will be their own masters… But the Khan Brothers have raised another poisonous cry that the Pakistan Constituent Assembly

will disregard the fundamental principles of the Shariah[30] and Quranic laws. This, again, is absolutely untrue. More than thirteen centuries have gone by and inspite of bad weather and fair that the Mussalmans had to pass through, we have not only been proud of our great and Holy Book, the Quran, but we have adhered to all the fundamentals of these pages... What would have happened to the Khan Brothers, who have now suddenly started out Heroding Herod in their championship of Islam and Quranic laws, in the Hindu Constituent Assembly with a brute majority of the Hindus which they willingly joined without demur? I want the Muslims of the Frontier Province to clearly understand that they are Muslims first and Pathan afterwards; and that the Province will meet a disastrous fate if it does not join the Pakistan Constituent Assembly... The Khan Brothers are the last ditchers and we want to expose thoroughly the fraud that they have practiced upon the Muslims of NWFP for nearly a decade. They have succeeded in the past in bamboozling and misleading the Pathans at the bidding of the outside authority of the Congress. Let us hope that they will not succeed in deceiving the Pathans for all time and that you will give your clear and thumping verdict in favour of the Province joining the Pakistan Constituent Assembly.[31]

In an article in the *Indian News Chronicle* of 23 June, Nehru was reported to have made the following statement at Haridwar: 'That in the event of a one-sided referendum, the present NWFP ministry will resign and fight elections afresh on the issue of Pakistan versus free Pathanistan and that whatever may me the immediate future of the Province, the freedom loving Pathans will continue their struggle for an independent Pathan state.'[32] Jinnah protested against this statement. Nehru denied making such a statement. The statement, he said, 'appeared to have been extracted by a reporter from refugees with whom he had been in a conversation, and did not represent either what he said or his views.'[33]

Khan Abdul Ghaffar Khan was now resigned to the idea that the NWFP would fall under the Pakistan umbrella. His efforts for a free Pathanistan (third option) with 'its own local Constitution' had come to a naught. He was coerced into the referendum with a promise that he would not interfere with it. The Muslim League meanwhile focused on facilitating the Muslim influx from Punjab into the NWFP affecting the referendum results. The Pirs and other prominent League politicians were roped in to garner support for Pakistan. Khan Abdul Ghaffar Khan helplessly watched the exodus of non-Muslims from the NWFP. Several thousands of them could not vote, threatened as they were with dire consequences by League supporters. Jinnah appealed to the Pathans to vote for Pakistan contending that their abstention would constitute a breach of the terms of the referendum. Gandhi questioned this contention, asking Jinnah why he had not advocated this in the context of non-Muslims. Addressing those who had assembled for his prayer meeting on 30 June, Gandhi said: 'The Khudai Khidmatgars will not exercise their vote thus providing a walkover for the Muslim League and at the same time doing no violence to their conscience. Is there in this procedure any breach of the terms of referendum? The Khudai Khidmatgars, who bravely fought the British, are not men who shirk defeat at polls.'[34] Who could dispute the moral force of this argument?

In the last week of June, Lieutenant General Rob Lockhart[35] replaced Sir Olaf Caroe as the new Governor of the NWFP. Informing Lockhart of his failure to secure Jinnah's agreement, Khan Abdul Ghaffar Khan reiterated his desire to resolve the impasse. If at all possible, he was willing to air dash to Delhi to meet Jinnah. Lockhart on his part sincerely believed that Ghaffar Khan was serious on a compromise. Reports had also reached him that in a desperate bid to salvage the situation, Ghaffar Khan was trying his best to meet the Pir of Manki Sharif so that he could ask him to mediate. Finding the request worthwhile, Lockhart contacted Mieville in Mountbatten's office to approach Jinnah. But by this time the referendum process was already complete and the results were a mere formality. Predictably, Mieville reverted with the news that Jinnah was not too enthusiastic on meeting Khan Abdul Ghaffar Khan again. On 25 July, Jinnah wrote to Mieville regretting his inability to meet Khan Abdul Ghaffar Khan. In his letter Jinnah explained that at this late a stage only the Constituent Assembly of Pakistan could take decisions on the matters likely to be raised by Khan Abdul Ghaffar Khan to resolve matters before 15 August. It was with some considerable satisfaction that Jinnah informed Mieville that, 'It is obvious that I cannot negotiate with any section or party over the head of the Constituent Assembly. Besides, I have no power to commit the Constituent Assembly in advance or anticipate their final decisions.'[36] Mountbatten conveyed the gist of Jinnah's reply to Lockhart who in turn passed it on to Khan Abdul Ghaffar Khan on 25 July. Even on the day before Jinnah finally flew out of Delhi for Karachi on 7 August, Lockhart was still pleading with Mountbatten that, 'It might help towards a solution if Liaquat Ali Khan[37] or Lord Ismay or Abell could fly across to Peshawar and discuss things over with him (the Governor) and Dr Khan Saheb.'[38] But as we all know, things did not work out for Ghaffar Khan. Within a fortnight, his brother was removed by Jinnah from the Chief Ministership of the NWFP. Then started a process, initiated by the Provincial Muslim League government, to crush the Khudai Khidmatgars.

## Notes

1. Khan Abdul Ghaffar Khan (1890–1988) was a pioneer of the Indian independence movement and a Pakistani politician. He was born in village Utmanzai near Charsadda in the NWFP. Dr Khan Saheb's younger brother, Khan Abdul Ghaffar Khan (Badshah Khan) and his Red Shirt movement stayed away from electoral politics. Khan Abdul Ghaffar Khan actively opposed the One Unit and Dr Khan Saheb's government. No major Red Shirt leader or worker ever joined the Republican Party founded by Dr Khan Saheb. The Red Shirts or Khudai Khidmatgars (Servants of God) joined hands with nationalist and progressive workers and leaders from both the then East Pakistan and West Pakistan to form the National Awami Party (National People's Party) in 1957.
2. Created in 1901, the North-West Frontier Province of British India became a province of Pakistan on 15 August 1947.
3. Excerpts of conversation narrated by Pyarelal in his book *Thrown to the Wolves: Abdul Ghaffar,* Eastlight Book House, 1966, pp.96–97, 108, 112.
4. Malik Sir Feroz Khan Noon (1893–1970) belonged to an influential landowning family in Punjab. He held many posts in the government both before and after India's partition and was an important figure in the Pakistan movement. He was India's High Commissioner to the United Kingdom from 1936 to 1941, and in 1947 he was sent as Jinnah's special envoy to some countries of the Muslim world. This one-man delegation

was the first official mission sent abroad by the Pakistani government. Noon was Chief Minister of Punjab (Pakistan) from 1953 to 1956, after which he became Foreign Minister of Pakistan until 1957. On 16 December 1957 he was elected as the seventh Prime Minister of Pakistan. He held this post till 7 October 1958, when martial law was enforced for the first time in Pakistan's history by Iskander Mirza.

5. The massacre at Qissa Khwani Bazaar (the storytellers' market) in Peshawar, British India (modern-day Pakistan) on 23 April 1930 was a defining moment in the non-violent struggle to drive the British out of India. It was the first major confrontation between British troops and non-violent demonstrators in the then peaceful city. Some estimates at the time put the death toll from the shooting at nearly 400. The gunning down of unarmed people triggered protests across the subcontinent and catapulted the newly formed Khudai Khidmatgar movement on to the national scene.
6. Another name for the Khudai Khidmatgars on account of the red shirts that they wore.
7. Interview between Mountbatten and Gandhi, Mountbatten Papers, Viceroy's Interview No. 142, dated 2 June 1947, *The Transfer of Power*, Vol. XI, p.48.
8. Mountbatten Papers, Viceroy's Interview No. 30, *The Transfer of Power*, Vol. X, pp.120–21.
9. 206, dated 23 April 1947, *The Transfer of Power*, Vol. X, p.385.
10. Caroe to Sir John Colville, Extract, L/P and J/5/224: f 45; 22 May 1947, *The Transfer of Power*, Vol. X, p.944.
11. Caroe to Mountbatten; Telegram, R/3/1/151: f 91, 31 May 1947, *The Transfer of Power*, Vol. XI, p.28.
12. Caroe to Mountbatten, Telegram, R/3/1/151: f 115; 5 June 1947, *The Transfer of Power*, Vol. XI, pp.151–52.
13. Interview 1.1 Mountbatten and Dr Khan Saheb, Mountbatten Papers, Viceroy's Interview No. 144, 5 June 1947, *The Transfer of Power*, Vol. XI, p.150.
14. 176, Mr Gandhi to Mountbatten, R/3/1/151: f161-62, p.329, *The Transfer of Power*, Vol. XI.
15. Appendix V.9, First Series, Vol. II, p.866, 1994, Jinnah Papers
16. Ibid.
17. Ibid.

18. Ibid.
19. Ibid., pp.866–67.
20. Appendix V.10, First Series, Vol. II, p.867–68, dated 17 June 1947, 1994.
21. Ibid., note 7, p.868
22. Ibid., p.868.
23. Viceroy's Interview No. 148, 17 June 1947, *The Transfer of Power*, Vol. XI, pp.448–49.
24. Sir Eric Mieville to Mountbatten, R/3/1/159; f 6, 18 June 1947, *The Transfer of Power*, Vol. XI, pp.494–95.
25. Annexure II to No. 299, Bannu Resolution, Jinnah Papers, First Series, Vol. II, pp.566–67,1994
26. Jinnah Papers, Appendix V, V.17, First Series, Vol. II, p.873,1994
27. Annexure III to No. 299, Jinnah Papers, First Series, Vol. II, pp.567–69, 1994.
28. F–142/26–9, Jinnah Papers, First Series, Vol. II, p.563, 1994.
29. Ibid., p.564.
30. The Sharia is the body of Islamic religious law. It is the legal framework within which the public and private aspects of life are regulated for those living in a legal system based on Islamic principles of jurisprudence and for Muslims living outside the domain. The Sharia deals with many aspects of day-to-day life including politics, economics, banking, business, contracts, family, sexuality, hygiene and social issues. There is no strictly static set of laws of the Sharia. Islamic law is now the most widely used religious law, and one of the three most common legal systems of the world alongside common law and civil law.
31. F–142/26–9, Jinnah Papers, First Series, Vol. II, pp.564–66, 1994.
32. Appendix V.19, Jinnah Papers, First Series, Vol. II, p.874, 1994.
33. Ibid.
34. '442', *The Transfer of Power*, Vol. XI, p.810.
35. General Sir Rob McGregor MacDonald Lockhart (1893–1981) was a British Indian Army General of World War II. General Lockhart served in India throughout World War II, including a spell as Military Secretary to the India Office; he later became Commander-in-Chief of the Indian army in 1947.
36. Jinnah to Mieville, R/3/1/165: f30, 25 July 1947, *The Transfer of Power*, Vol. XII, p.340.
37. Nawabzada Liaquat Ali Khan (1896–1951) was a Pakistani politician

who became the first Prime Minister of Pakistan. Liaquat rose to political prominence as a member of the All India Muslim League. He played a vital role in the partition of India and the creation of Pakistan. In 1947, he became the Prime Minister of Pakistan, a position that he held until his assassination in October 1951. He was regarded as the right-hand man of Muhammad Ali Jinnah, the leader of the Muslim League and first Governor General of Pakistan.

38. Governor Lockhart to Mountbatten Telegram, R/3/1/165; f 56; 6 August 1947, *The Transfer of Power*, Vol. XII, pp.561–62.

# 12

# The Kafir King: Dr Khan Saheb

AGITATIONAL POLITICS CAME easy to Khan Abdul Ghaffar Khan. He would much rather leave constitutional politics to Dr Khan Saheb, his eldest brother, who was different in temperament to him. Anglicized and with a degree from England, Dr Khan Saheb practised medicine in London before the Great War. He then came to hold a commission in the Indian Medical Service and served in France during the war, after which he returned to Peshawar with his English wife to set up a medical practice. The early 1930s saw him getting involved in his brother's political activities. Politically, Dr Khan Saheb was more moderate and cautious than his brother. He was the lone representative of the Congress in the central legislative assembly from the NWFP before provisions of provincial autonomy came into force. Subsequently, he headed three Congress ministries and was the Chief Minister of the NWFP when Pakistan came into being. It was left to Jinnah to dismiss his Congress ministry within eight days of partition.

Dr Khan Saheb was elected to the central legislative assembly in December 1934. This was the first election in which his party, the Congress, participated. A sufficiently long ban on the Khudai Khidmatgars prevented the Khan brothers from entering the NWFP. Despite his absence, Dr Khan Saheb won the elections. It was only later, in November 1936, that he was allowed entry into the NWFP, barely months before the first provincial elections under the 1935 Government of India Act took place. In those elections the Congress could only win nineteen of the fifty seats in the NWFP. The Muslim League did not exist in the province then. An independent group of twenty-five was cobbled up by Nawabzada Sir Abdul Qayyum who became the Chief Minister but only for a brief period, from April to

September 1937. This happened with overt and covert official help. On 3 September, Nawabzada Sir Abdul Qayyum's ministry was voted out and a Congress-led coalition came to power under the leadership of Dr Khan Saheb for the first time.

Governor Cunningham, unable to save Sir Abdul Qayyum's ministry, was quick to mend fences with Dr Khan Saheb. Socially amenable, Dr Khan Saheb was soon attending dinner parties at the Governor's house, taking care not to dress in 'khaddar' and a Gandhi cap on such occasions. His family's intimacy with the Governor's family grew. That Dr Khan Saheb had an English wife helped. The cordiality between Mrs Mary Khan Saheb and Lady Cunningham was considerably commented upon in the local press and it was not uncommon to see Mrs Khan Saheb and her son, John Khan Saheb, spend a weekend at the Governor's residence. In deference to the wishes of his Congress supporters, Dr Khan Saheb once had to miss out on a grand ball at Government House. His wife attended the party, but Dr Khan Saheb was sorely disappointed at having to miss it. For the Frontier Congress rank and file, this social connection with the Governor was a handicap to the nationalist cause.[1]

Till 1937, the Congress had traditionally been hostile to the law-enforcing agencies in the NWFP, the administration reciprocating in equal measure. This attitude of the Congress changed once it came to power. Dr Khan Saheb frequently sided with the administration when its role came up for criticism in the provincial assembly. He also allowed police intelligence sources to attend public meetings to monitor people's sentiments. The Chief Minister's inclination to support moderate forces made him defend several conservative actions of the provincial administration. A Repeal and Amending Bill to abolish 'repressive' laws was introduced in the provincial legislature in its autumn session of 1937. Abdul Rab Nishtar,[2] an independent allied with the Congress, introduced the bill. The Governor decided to withhold assent to the bill after it was passed by the provincial legislature. Dr Khan Saheb readily acquiesced to the Governor's decision; it caused him no embarrassment though his own party clamoured for the resignation of the ministry. The unfortunate result of Dr Khan Saheb's action was that Abdul Rab Nishtar completely severed his connections with the Congress.

In February 1938, Govind Ballabh Pant[3] and Sri Krishna Singh,[4] two Congress Chief Ministers from United Provinces and Bihar respectively resigned over the contentious issue of the release of political prisoners. At one stage it appeared that the matter would snowball, leading to the resignation of all Congress ministries. The crisis was averted when Viceroy Linlithgow yielded and the resignations were withdrawn (Mehra: 84). At that time, Dr Khan Saheb appeared loath to resign even if the other Congress Chief Ministers followed suit. Subsequently, in September 1939, when the Congress decided that all its provincial ministries would resign as they had not been consulted on the issue of India's participation in World War II, Sir Arthur Parson,[5] the acting Governor of the NWFP could not stop remarking on Dr Khan Saheb's absolute reluctance to resign. He had hoped, right till the end, that an exception would perhaps be made in his case, in view of the special conditions in the NWFP. When no such thing happened, he was forced to resign on 7 November 1939. Cunningham was on home leave (August–December 1939) when Dr Khan Saheb's ministry quit office.

When Dr Khan Saheb quit office, the NWFP legislature was left in a state of suspended animation, with the Governor assuming powers of administration. But this did not affect Dr Khan Saheb's relations with the Governor. They continued to meet and so did their families. Dr Khan Saheb was rather relieved as he did not have to carry the burden of governance at the time. By and large, he was ready to extend all help to the Governor during war time. He did not support the idea of the Congress starting a non-cooperation campaign in the NWFP. He very much wanted to join the Governor's Defence Committee, but the Congress high command directed him not to do so.

During the days of individual satyagraha (October 1940–December 1941), the future President of Pakistan and the then Deputy Commissioner of Peshawar, Iskander Mirza,[6] indulged Dr Khan Saheb by depositing him with his wife in the name of arresting him. Despite the Viceroy's directions to apprehend Dr Khan Saheb, Cunningham resisted taking such an action.

Cunningham was not unduly worried about the effects of the Quit India movement in the NWFP. In no small measure, this was due to Dr Khan Saheb's reassuring presence. Cunningham's diary entry of 19

August 1942 demonstrates how lightly he took the threat: 'I sent Khan Saheb a message a few days ago that if he meant to start on the slogan "English, leave India," he must come and say it to me first, in which case I would take him at his word and go off to England, taking Mrs Khan Saheb with me.' Dr Khan Saheb continued to play bridge with the Governor, notwithstanding the Quit India movement. So confident was Cunningham about the situation that he did not alter his prearranged fishing holiday to Kashmir which he undertook from 19 August till 10 September, just when the Quit India movement was launched. How much of this confidence emanated from his friendship with Dr Khan Saheb is seen from his diary entry of 13 September 1942: 'Congress had a meeting today in which they are said to have decided to picket courts intensively and by force if necessary. As Khan Saheb, however, has promised to come and dine and play bridge with me tomorrow it is difficult to believe they really mean business' (Mehra 1998: 41–42).

Dr Khan Saheb, himself not much for Congress action, was pushed by Khan Abdul Ghaffar Khan and other Congress leaders to adopt a strident position against the government. Cunningham, in fact, preferred Dr Khan Saheb to remain in the forefront of the Congress agitation as that would prevent extreme action on Congress's part. Dr Khan Saheb believed that it was not long before his party would resume its constitutional ways, allowing him to reclaim the chief ministership. During the days of the Quit India movement, when messengers or deputations representing extreme Congress groups arrived from outside trying to persuade the Khudai Khidmatgars to blow up bridges, Dr Khan Saheb invariably refused to encourage them.

In the chapter on Governor Cunningham, I have described how he ran the affairs of the NWFP during the war years in detail. After more than three years of Governor's rule, he propped up a Muslim League ministry, very much a pro-British outfit. Aurangzeb Khan, a provincial Muslim Leaguer, was made the Chief Minister. It was only in March 1945 that Dr Khan Saheb succeeded in toppling that ministry and forming his own. The formation of Dr Khan Saheb's government had not been a foregone conclusion, preceded as it was by several behind-the-scene political machinations.

As 1945 commenced, it became clear that four Muslim League MLAs would be joining hands with the Congress to pull down

Aurangzeb Khan's minority ministry. It was now only a question of the Governor summoning the assembly to session, which he did by calling for the budget session in February 1945. A section of the Congress that foresaw a stake in forming the ministry immediately set about seeking permission for forming the ministry from a competent authority within the Congress. The All India Congress Committee and the Congress Parliamentary Board had stood in abeyance as most of their members were in jail. Gandhi was the only one left to be approached—and his word would carry weight. A three-member Frontier Congress deputation (Ali Gul Khan, Arbab Abdur Rahman and Meher Chand Khanna) met Gandhi at Wardha on 16 February 1945 to plead the case of forming the ministry. The ostensible reason was the release of political prisoners of the NWFP once the Congress took office. Gandhi favoured 'leaving things to local initiative'. He wrote a letter to Dr Khan Saheb without making its contents public. Gandhi did not oppose ministry formation, leaving it to the 'reason' and 'instinct' of the concerned people on the spot. But the deputationists encountered unexpected resistance from Khan Abdul Ghaffar Khan when they visited him in Haripur jail. He was against forming the ministry and would not relent. It would have been impossible to ignore Ghaffar Khan, but confined within the four walls of a prison, he could not exert much influence. The deputationists succeeded in having their way.

The no-confidence motion against the Aurangzeb Khan ministry was passed on 12 March and on 16 March 1945, Dr Khan Saheb's second ministry assumed office in the NWFP. This was a startling development. The Congress had yet not officially revoked its decision to renounce office. Nowhere else in India had the Congress thought of forming provincial ministries. Even at a later date, in July 1945, following the release of Congress leaders and improvements in Congress-government relations, Jawaharlal Nehru and Abul Kalam Azad could still not find a 'suitable circumstance' for forming provincial Congress ministries. When a League member in the NWFP legislative assembly congratulated the Frontier Congress for its courage in accepting office by defying the All India Congress Committee, Bhanju Ram Gandhi, Congress leader of the NWFP asserted that the Congress ministry was formed 'according to the wishes of the High Command'. However, he never repeated nor elaborated upon this 'indiscreet assertion'. Dr Khan Saheb, on his part, pointed out that the people of the province were 'hanging between life and death' and the Congress was interested only in 'serving the people'.

Being a moderate, Dr Khan Saheb always erred on the conservative side. A story, similar to that of his first tenure, deserves a mention. Having appointed a committee to investigate charges of corruption against officials, Dr Khan Saheb encountered an immediate hurdle in the Governor who refused to allow any 'promiscuous vilification of the services'. As a compromise, the committee submitted an interim report before starting enquiries. In deference to the Governor's wishes, Dr Khan Saheb did not initiate any action. Any further action was shelved.

Pro-government political observers were delighted to see Dr Khan Saheb give 'an undertaking in support of war efforts' without jeopardizing Congress membership or caring for their detained compatriots in the rest of India. Ordinary Congressmen and the Khudai Khidmatgars were taken aback and resented 'the haste' with which the Congress ministry was installed. The Congress rank and file became rather hostile to the newly formed ministry, and signs of a breach within the Frontier Congress became apparent. While the provincial Congress leaders justified 'the re-formation of the Congress ministry', the Khudai Khidmatgars were in favour of 'continuing the deadlock'. Even some of the pro-ministry Congress leaders like Ali Gul Khan and Hakim Ali Nadvi, were said to have turned critics of the ministry's activities. The difference of opinion was never fully reconciled and the attitude of the Khudai Khidmatgars towards the ministry remained lukewarm throughout 1945. The Congress was back in power for the second time in the NWFP but this time, it was without its former standing in public esteem and devoid of much of its traditional Khudai Khidmatgar image.

Dr Khan Saheb's second ministry did not bring legislative measures to secure tenant rights, nor did it take steps to improve the lot of landless labourers. Not only the Congress ministry, but the entire legislature in the NWFP was found wanting in radical temper. Dissident League members, who sided with the Congress, remained devoted to their feudal cause, pleading for the restoration of *inams* (a gift of land or land revenue). The ministry's record contained nothing characteristic of Congress rule. Neither any Gandhian ideal nor the social democratic views of the Congress were reflected in its activities. The second Dr Khan Saheb ministry aroused no great public enthusiasm.

Apart from the strongly entrenched bureaucracy, the only other organized opposition to the Congress in the NWFP was the Muslim League. Throughout 1945, the Muslim League carefully nursed its anti-Congress forces of reaction, loyalism and vested feudal and commercial interests. The Muslim League prepared for the inevitable trial of strength with the Congress, not in the familiar way of winning over MLAs, but by challenging its adversary's hold over the province. In June 1945, the British authorities released Congress Working Committee members and convened a conference of Indian political leaders in Simla. On 21 August 1945, the Viceroy announced that elections in India would be held in early 1946.

A new Congress ministry in the Frontier could no longer be installed by ignoring Khan Abdul Ghaffar Khan, the architect of the Congress victory in the 1946 elections. He did not object to ministry-making as long as the ministry worked under the guidance of a Central Board of the Frontier Congress and functioned like 'a people's government in the real sense of the term'. Dr Khan Saheb's third ministry, sworn in on 9 March 1946 was largely a family affair for Khan Abdul Ghaffar Khan. Dr Khan Saheb was his elder brother; the Revenue Minister Qazi Ataullah's daughter was married to one of Khan Abdul Ghaffar Khan's sons. Yahya Jan, the Education Minister was his son-in-law. Ghani Khan, Khan Abdul Ghaffar Khan's eldest son, replaced Abdul Qayyum in the central assembly. The solitary outsider in the ministry was Meher Chand Khanna from the erstwhile Hindu–Sikh Nationalist Party who took over the finance portfolio in Dr Khan Saheb's government. Around the same time, George Cunningham superannuated and was replaced by Sir Olaf Caroe as the new Governor of the NWFP.

Despite the Muslim League's insistence on revoking the decision taken in 1938 to have a system of joint electorate for elections to local bodies, the Congress ministry refused to give in. It took two notable socialist measures—abolition of the lambardari system[7] and the prohibition of the recovery of Haq-i-Tora. The Haq-i-Tora was a feudal levy exacted by big landlords from their tenants, in cash or kind, at the time of betrothal, marriage or other social functions. But these measures were not followed up by the popular government. Not much was done to further the interests of the rural poor. No serious attempt at tenancy reforms nor at reducing the burden of agricultural debt was made. Dr Khan Saheb's third ministry proved as politically modest as his second one, staying away from confrontation with the British authorities.

Dr Khan Saheb met the Cabinet Mission delegation on 1 April 1946. He did not avoid it as he had done with the Cripps Mission. In his view, it was plain that 'Pakistan' could not succeed. No one knew its actual meaning and its physical boundaries were yet to be defined. He ascribed the popularity of the 'two-nation' theory to vicious communal propaganda by the Muslim League in urban areas. In rural areas, the Muslim League 'played upon the ignorance of the villagers'. Dr Khan Saheb did not recognize the Muslim League to be the true representative of Muslim India though he admitted that in the NWFP the League had won almost as many Muslim seats as the Congress, seventeen against nineteen, but the success of the Muslim League was mainly due to the influence of vested interests.

In Dr Khan Saheb's view, the people of the NWFP were different from their neighbours in Punjab and would never join Pakistan. If they could not stay in a united India, they would like the province to become entirely independent. When asked how the province would provide for its defence and get on without subsidies from the centre, he countered the question by stating that Pakistan would face the same problems in case it came into being. On the issue of a future constitution, he preferred a regime where the people of the NWFP enjoyed provincial autonomy with an all-India centre which exercised control on foreign affairs, defence, communications and, possibly, customs. He was not afraid of domination by a Hindu centre and did not admit to a political distinction between Hindus and Muslims. He wanted the tribal areas to remain free of central control. He was also not in favour of disarming the tribes by force. He believed that the constitution-making body should be composed of people elected by provincial assemblies, and that elections should be held by proportional representation so that the minorities got representation corresponding to their strength in the provincial legislatures. He was not in favour of a large constitution-making body.

There were three small states bordering the NWFP—Dir, Swat and Chitral. He wanted these states to join the province through friendly agreements when independence came. He was convinced that a large hinterland was necessary for the adequate defence of the NWFP. Going by that logic, Pakistan would be unable to defend itself even if there was a satisfactory agreement for mutual defence between Pakistan and Hindustan. He had no objection to the retention of British troops to protect India against external aggression. In return, India could offer services that could include sending Indian troops abroad subject to certain conditions. Dr Khan Saheb did not foresee the Congress and Muslim League coming to any broad agreement in the immediate future. Nevertheless, he wanted Britain to leave India soon. Dr Khan Saheb had honestly shared his views with the cabinet delegation. At no stage did he attempt to obfuscate issues, his belief largely in consonance with that of the Congress. Surprisingly, Wavell was less than fair to him in the comments penned down in his journal of the same day:

The opening day of our discussions with the Indian leaders…we began with Dr Khan Saheb of NWFP, who is an attractive personality but very definitely wooly in his ideas. He had obviously not really thought out the problems of Pakistan and refused to consider its possibility. Nor have we considered what Hindu domination at the center might entail. He talked in fact entirely from the Provincial angle, as if the Pathans were a separate nation staying in Pathanistan. He contributed little of value… In the afternoon came Bardoloi, the Congress Premier of Assam, a more forcible and [of] quicker intelligence than Khan Saheb, but not a very pleasant personality.

One reason why Wavell continued to be critical of Dr Khan Saheb was the less than cordial terms that existed between the Governor and the Chief Minister of the NWFP. Wavell found Dr Khan Saheb's accusations about Sir Olaf Caroe vague. The only specific complaint he received from Dr Khan Saheb was about Caroe's attitude towards the lambardari system. In a note of 15 November Wavell remarked: 'He [Dr Khan Saheb] does not get on with the Governor, who is a different type to George Cunningham; he has been shaken by the results of Nehru's visit and the obvious hostility to Congress that it has revealed;

and he therefore attempts to throw the whole blame on the British officials.' Wavell found Dr Khan Saheb ineffective. To him, Dr Khan Saheb was a pleasant, well-meaning person, without the 'necessary force of character or wisdom' to run a province.

Dr Khan Saheb's ministry was reluctant to implement radical measures for fear of running into conflict with British authorities. The Muslim League on the other hand was increasingly adopting a strident posture while the Cabinet Mission was on a visit to India. The Muslim League in the NWFP did not favour the Cabinet Mission scheme, particularly the 'grouping' arrangement. The Frontier Congress Committee and its parliamentary party also found the proposed 'grouping' of provinces totally unacceptable. The Pathans feared Punjabi domination and were, therefore, against the 'grouping' arrangement. Dr Khan Saheb gave vent to this popular feeling in a public address: 'No one can force the Frontier people to join any group.' Seeing all this, the Muslim League preferred concentrating its energies on communal propaganda. Nehru's visit had already inflamed the communal atmosphere in the tribal areas of the NWFP.

Caroe arrived in Peshawar on 1 March 1946, to take over as the new Governor simultaneously with Dr Khan Saheb's swearing in on 10 March as the Chief Minister. But almost immediately on his joining, Caroe was expressing his discomfiture to Delhi about Dr Khan Saheb's government. Dr Khan Saheb's style of functioning, which Cunningham easily adjusted to, was now to be a constant source of friction with the new Governor. Caroe would find countless faults—interference in court affairs, misuse of the Frontier Crimes Regulation, abolition of the post of *lambardar*s and many such others. Things came to such a pass that Dr Khan Saheb threatened to resign. The crisis blew over, but not without leaving its impact.

Nehru took charge of the external and tribal affairs portfolio after joining the interim government on 2 September 1946. The portfolio put the tribal areas of the NWFP directly under him. Much against the advice of his senior Congress colleagues, Nehru went ahead with an ill-timed visit to the tribal areas of the NWFP, and Dr Khan Saheb accompanied him on his week-long trip in October. The Muslim League had laboured enough to vitiate the communal atmosphere in those areas. Nehru's visit created the impression that Dr Khan Saheb's ministry was being remote-controlled by the Hindu Congress. The Muslim League propaganda was so effective that Nehru and his so-called Hindu Congress were apportioned all blame for the bombing raids in Waziristan. Nehru had nowhere been in the picture when the decision to selectively bomb some places in the NWFP was taken. Dr Khan Saheb's ministry was forced to go on the defensive, explaining to the people that neither Nehru nor Dr Khan Saheb's government were responsible for the bombings. In fact, Dr Khan Saheb and Nehru had for long protested against such indiscriminate retaliatory measures. But who cared to ascertain facts? The impression that Dr Khan Saheb hobnobbed with Nehru, whose Hindu co-religionists were busy perpetrating atrocities on Muslims in Bihar and elsewhere, harmed the image of the NWFP ministry.

The Muslim League was successful in breaking the Congress stranglehold on the predominantly Muslim-majority province. It emerged less as an organization but more as a movement fed on religious and political passions. Communal riots broke out in Hazara and Peshawar in December 1946. In their wake started the exodus of Hindus and Sikhs from the Frontier. The *sajdanashins* and tribal mullahs threw their weight behind the Muslim League. A Direct Action Campaign was launched by the Muslim League in the NWFP (February–March 1947), directed not against the British but against Dr Khan Saheb's Congress government.

The situation was further compounded for Dr Khan Saheb by an acute shortage of food in the NWFP. As the food situation worsened, communal riots broke out in Hazara district from the night of 7–8 December, resulting in deaths and forced conversions of Hindus and Sikhs. Dr Khan Saheb came under severe criticism, both from the Hindus and the Sikhs, for his weakness and inability to provide protection and from the Muslim League for repression of Muslim 'patriots'. As a knee-jerk reaction, Dr Khan Saheb banned public processions and speeches in Hazara district and also promulgated the Public Safety ordinance. The case of a Hazara Sikh girl acquired prominence, providing the Muslim League with material for propaganda. On 24 February, a mob assembled at Peshawar to free the Sikh girl alleged to be in Dr Khan Saheb's custody and some 5,000 League supporters marched towards Dr Khan Saheb's residence, breaking the police cordon and entering the gardens of his house. Dr Khan Saheb withstood the attack bravely, refusing to relent. The revocation of the Sikh girl's conversion was exploited by the Muslim League to the hilt. The Direct Action campaign of the Muslim League resulted in virtually the entire League leadership being put behind bars for which Dr Khan Saheb's government earned the sobriquet of the 'Vichy government'. All this came at a time when Nehru's visit had left Dr Khan Saheb shaken.

March and April 1947 saw a running battle and a growing rift between Caroe and Dr Khan Saheb. Caroe was increasingly viewed as a man in collusion with the Muslim League. Though he was fast losing popularity and support, Dr Khan Saheb perhaps failed to realize how far public opinion had fallen away from him. As Caroe remarked, 'He [Dr. Khan Saheb] entirely fails to appreciate the strength that lies behind the League movement based as it is on the traditional Islamic and Pathan culture determined to shake free, if it can, from any regime that can be represented as financed or dominated by Hinduism.'

In March 1947, A.S.B. Shah, the Deputy Commissioner of Peshawar drew up a six-page memorandum to re-establish the authority of the government and prevent political bodies from resorting to lawlessness. He advised Dr Khan Saheb to be reconciliatory towards the opposition and allow them to vent their grievances. Sadly enough, Dr Khan Saheb did not heed A.S.B. Shah's advise.

Soon Caroe started advocating a coalition led by Dr Khan Saheb—a Pathan outfit that had no connections with the Congress. By implication, Caroe wanted Dr Khan Saheb to shed all his extra-Pathan linkages. The provincial Muslim League was also to delink itself from the parent body. Dr Khan Saheb welcomed this possibility, but tied to his brother Khan Abdul Ghaffar Khan, and through him to Nehru, found it impossible to act upon it. Sir Olaf Caroe was inclined to think, as was Sir Fraser Noble,[8] that had Dr Khan Saheb taken the course of delinking himself from the Congress in 1947, the whole history of the transfer of power would have been different. By himself, Dr Khan Saheb counted for little. Unlike his brother Khan Abdul Ghaffar Khan, he lacked an independent mass base of his own.

Two meetings, one on 18 April in Delhi and the other at Peshawar on 28 April, show how widely divergent the views of Sir Olaf Caroe and Dr Khan Saheb were. Mountbatten was present for both the meetings while Nehru attended the first, which was a regular screaming match. The necessity for the meeting arose when the question of fresh elections in the NWFP came up. Nehru wanted Dr Khan Saheb to be present in Delhi when discussions took place. The actual purpose of the 18 April meeting was to make the Chief Minister of the NWFP party to a decision for holding fresh elections, in which aim Nehru and Mountbatten succeeded. Dr Khan Saheb agreed in the meeting, as did Nehru, to test public opinion afresh. Within ten days of this meeting, Mountbatten visited the NWFP. His visit to Peshawar was for others to note that the Viceroy was sincere in making a personal assessment of the situation in the NWFP. The Muslim League arranged a large demonstration in Peshawar on 28 April to impress the Viceroy and at some personal risk, Mountbatten went to the venue to pacify the assembled crowd. The Chief Minister had no option but to go along with the Viceroy.

Dr Khan Saheb's gullibility was exploited time and again by Mountbatten. During the mid-April consultations in Delhi, decisions had mostly gone against Dr Khan Saheb. To assuage his feelings, Mountbatten indulged in gimmicks like seating Dr Khan Saheb on a high table, more prominently than his Governor and next to Lady Mountbatten. The trick produced the desired result. Another instance of Dr Khan Saheb's simple-mindedness relates to the process of the referendum. After he was forced to accept the referendum, he informed Mountbatten of the absolute necessity of replacing Sir Olaf Caroe. Playing along and in deference to Dr Khan Saheb's distrust of Indian Civil Service officials, Mountbatten arranged for nine British officers of the Indian army to conduct the referendum. Dr Khan Saheb was very pleased and observed that he 'preferred military people'. On a recorded copy of this conversation between Mountbatten and Dr Khan Saheb, Lieutenant Colonel Erskine Crum noted: 'For the edification of PSV, DPSV and APSV'; 'Wise men,' George Abel rejoined: 'I wonder he did not ask for sailors'! Of course, the army officers too, were all old Frontier hands, and it was a case of the 'one-eyed deer being sensitive about danger coming from a particular direction only.'

Mountbatten spent a week in Delhi after returning from Peshawar before proceeding to Simla where Nehru joined him. It was in Simla that Mountbatten decided in favour of the referendum as against fresh elections—Nehru was certain to have been party to this decision. It was henceforth Nehru's brief to justify and rationalize the decision to his colleagues in the Congress. Nehru had been kept in the loop to force the decision of a referendum on Dr Khan Saheb. In a telegram of 10 May to Nehru, the Viceroy acquainted him with the future course of action—that Sir Olaf Caroe would inform Dr Khan Saheb of the decision for a referendum. There was no need now for 'Governor's rule' in the NWFP before the elections. Sir Olaf Caroe was also to inform Dr Khan Saheb, mainly for effect, that Nehru was in general agreement with this proposal. When the news of a referendum in the NWFP came to Dr Khan Saheb, it was as a *fait accompli*. It would really have been in the fitness of things for Nehru himself to have conveyed this information first to Dr Khan Saheb, but was Nehru hesitant in communicating this decision to Dr Khan Saheb? While Nehru was away in Simla, Dr Khan Saheb and his NWFP ministerial colleagues had held a meeting with Gandhi and other Congress leaders in Delhi, which had left Nehru considerably disturbed.

As he came to know of the referendum, Gandhi, during the course of a train journey to Patna on 8 May wrote to Mountbatten making his objections clear. To him, a referendum in the Frontier amounted to a dangerous proposition. Gandhi said that 'nothing should and could' be done over Dr Khan Saheb's head as a premier. Nehru, too, was willing to reconsider the decision because of the strong opinions expressed in the Congress Working Committee against the referendum. Lord Ismay, who carried the first transfer plan to London on 2 May, proposed the dismissal of the Congress ministry in the Frontier prior to fresh polls.

But that plan underwent a revision. The second plan, the Menon plan, which Mountbatten himself carried to London on 19 May, suggested a referendum in the NWFP. On 3 June the partition plan was finally announced. It offered only two options in the referendum—the NWFP either aligning with Pakistan or India.

While Dr Khan Saheb insisted on replacing the Governor before the referendum, his ministers Qazi Ataullah and Meher Chand Khanna threatened to form an independent Pathanistan or join the new Constituent Assembly of Pakistan, deciding not to tie up with Hindustan. Conflicting signals were being sent out from within the NWFP government. Alongside, the provincial Congress now demanded that if the option of independent Pathanistan was not given, the Khudai Khidmatgars (they had now stopped referring to themselves as Congress members) would decline to participate in the referendum. Mountbatten again used the stick of Nehru to browbeat Dr Khan Saheb. He was forced to agree that a province of three million could not stand alone with a reasonable chance of success and, therefore, needed to fuse with one Constituent Assembly or the other. The message sent out was that the 3 June announcement was final and no changes to the partition plan could now be made.

When the question of referring the names of army officers to the Chief Minister for his comments came up, Mountbatten's staff was wary of taking such a step for fear of rejection, arguing instead that no time would be left for finding suitable replacements in case some names were turned down. But Lord Ismay thought it best (and safe) to run the list past the Chief Minister. In case of any objection, it was always open to the Viceroy to over-rule Dr Khan Saheb. A decision was taken to follow this procedure but the opportunity did not present itself. Lord Ismay suggested a list of fifteen army officers to which Dr Khan Saheb gave his ready concurrence. There was always a hint of contradiction in what Dr Khan Saheb professed and what he actually did. Was he really hopeful of the British government's offer for a third option of an independent Pathanistan in the referendum? Or did he consider it a solemn duty, as premier of the NWFP, to go through the correct motions of preparing the province for a referendum? If Dr Khan Saheb claimed to boycott the referendum, his actions certainly seemed to belie that resolve.

Mountbatten was ready to make minor concessions to the Congress, both at the Centre and in the NWFP. He replaced Sir Olaf Caroe with Major General Sir Rob Lockhart. As the process of the referendum neared completion, it became increasingly certain that Dr Khan Saheb had no intentions of resigning. On 19 July, he indicated that he would only resign if assured of a general election, to be held in the reasonably near future. Lockhart began to worry over the possibility of the Frontier Congress starting a violent movement, Dr Khan Saheb personally admitting to the Governor on 21 July of such a possibility. He also reiterated that the general election be held early under a new Pakistan constitution and only after fresh electoral rolls were prepared. By implication it meant that Dr Khan Saheb did not expect the elections to take place soon. He was now agreeable even to the idea of a coalition government. What worried him most, of course, was a dismissal of his ministry by the Pakistan government and rule through an Ordinance Raj.

Results of the referendum were announced on 20 July, and as expected, they went overwhelmingly in favour of Pakistan. Because of the abstention of Khudai Khidmatgars, hardly any votes were cast in favour of India. It was now formally declared that the NWFP would merge with Pakistan. But sticking to his guns, Dr Khan Saheb refused to resign. However, he agreed to the dissolution of the assembly and was ready to wait for three or four months till the elections, but only on the condition that his ministry would function as a caretaker government. He was agreeable to any standstill agreement on the administration that the government would order as long as the government of the day allowed him to work in a constitutional way for Pathanistan. He continued to bargain, as if from a position of strength, which certainly was not the case now. He also threatened a campaign against any move to dismiss his government. Lockhart, too, believed that Dr Khan Saheb was in a position to cause serious trouble if his government was dismissed. On the other hand, the Muslim League could also be counted upon to precipitate a law and order situation if Dr Khan Saheb's ministry continued in office after 15 August.

Khan Abdul Ghaffar Khan and Qazi Ataullah were back in Peshawar after a meeting with Liaquat Ali Khan in Delhi; Liaquat Ali Khan appeared conciliatory. Jinnah's 30 July statement of letting 'bygones be bygones' also raised hopes of reconciliation between the Muslim League and the Khudai Khidmatgars. But all this came to naught when it was learnt that Dr Khan Saheb's ministry could be dismissed before 15 August. In a party meeting on 5 August at Khan Abdul Ghaffar Khan's house which Dr Khan Saheb attended, it was decided that the Khudai Khidmatgars would keep away from the 15 August celebrations, a wrong decision taken in the heat of the moment which the Khudai Khidmatgars would rue for a long time to come.

Lockhart met Dr Khan Saheb on 6 August to discuss arrangements for the 15 August celebrations. Lockhart wanted the ministers to attend the official ceremony, but found it exasperating to decide details of celebratory arrangements without knowing which party would be in power on that day. Matters evolved at great speed thereafter. Dr Khan Saheb still reiterated his impossible demands on which may hinge his party's cooperation and acceptance of Pakistan. Why, at such a late stage, would the Muslim League agree to his demand of provincial autonomy in all matters except external affairs, defence and communications? Why would the Pakistan government make allowances for Dr Khan Saheb to carry on his party programme for an independent Pathanistan? Inadvertently, Dr Khan Saheb may have forced the new Government of Pakistan to dismiss his government. His actions in the fortnight preceding 15 August could only gain him a moral high ground and at best some sympathy.

Members of Dr Khan Saheb's party continued to make threatening, sometimes provocative, speeches. Vigorously advocated, 'Pathanistan' appeared to be catching the imagination of numerous Pathans. Rumours about the Fakir of Ipi's activities were afloat and Lockhart was convinced that the Congress was encouraging him to precipitate trouble after Eid.

With the approaching date of 15 August, Dr Khan Saheb's intransigence softened. He was inclined now to cooperate with the Pakistan government. There was no alternative to a clear dismissal but to accept the prospect of a coalition government. A politician of some experience, he must have known that even this option of a coalition government would not be forthcoming from Jinnah. On the other hand, Lockhart feared that others in his party, people like Qazi Attaullah or Khan Abdul Ghaffar Khan could still resist the Muslim League's attempt at wresting power. But the Khudai Khidmatgars' plans of fomenting trouble, if at all they had one, did not fructify.

The Muslim League was insistent that Dr Khan Saheb's ministry be dismissed before 15 August. But following Mountbatten's instructions, Lockhart resisted, realizing and appreciating the fact that one reason why Dr Khan Saheb had refused to resign was because the Muslim League had steadfastly refused to dissolve the provincial legislature. There was serious dissension, too, amongst the provincial Muslim League leaders. Many among them disapproved of the appointment of a British Governor. Some were disappointed with Jinnah's choice of ministers for the League ministry, and several were annoyed because

Jinnah had refused the establishment of 'Shariat' law in the new country. What worried Lockhart was the already hardened attitude of the Muslim League to deal firmly with the opposition when it assumed power. The personal safety of the present ministers once they were divested of their ministership, and how to prevent their maltreatment by the Muslim League once it formed the government, also concerned Lockhart.

There were rumours floating thick and fast that Dr Khan Saheb would proclaim the founding of 'Pathanistan'. People tended to give credence to these for Dr Khan Saheb could resort to it as an act of desperation and as a last resort. It was four days to 15 August when Lockhart saw Dr Khan Saheb again. He was reassuring, rubbishing the rumours, as according to him, 'there was no question of this or any other unconstitutional action'. To Lockhart he said that though his party would not participate in the 15 August celebrations, they would not interfere with them either. However, ministers, if still in power, would attend. In view of Dr Khan Saheb's assurance, Lockhart did not refer to the issue of his resignation again.

Closer to 15 August, another changeover was effected. Jinnah's nominee, George Cunningham, took over from Lockhart on 13 August. Cunningham met Jinnah in Karachi on 11 August and Mountbatten on 12 August in Delhi. He, thus, arrived in Peshawar to tackle his old friend Dr Khan Saheb with the full knowledge of what his masters wanted him to do. Cunningham met Dr Khan Saheb on the same day he took charge.

Cunningham was prepared to dismiss Dr Khan Saheb's ministry upon Jinnah's orders, of which he made a mention in his last report to the Indian Viceroy: 'but I am not particularly gloomy as to the course of events thereafter.' He had also taken an assurance from Jinnah that no such orders of dismissal would be issued until he (Cunningham) had assessed the situation himself. Cunningham told Dr Khan Saheb that he had conveyed to Jinnah that as a Governor he was, of course, bound to loyally carry out such directions as Jinnah gave him as Governor General but he also wanted to satisfy his own conscience as to any action he took and, therefore, asked for some time to talk to local leaders and to judge for himself what their attitude was. Cunningham repeated to Dr Khan Saheb what he had told Jinnah, that the only grounds on which Cunningham would consider justified in dismissing Khan Saheb would be:

> If he insisted on declaring that Pathanistan was to be an independent unit, or if he was not satisfied that Khan Saheb meant genuinely to co-operate with the Pakistan Constitution.

Jinnah agreed to wait till 15 August before Cunningham sent him his final views. Dr Khan Saheb, on his part, assured Cunningham that as long as he remained a minister, he would do nothing injurious to the Pakistan Constitution, and that, if the final Constitution decided by the Constituent Assembly was one that he felt he could not support, he would give up the ministry; also that he had no intention of making any declaration about an independent Pathanistan. If Jinnah dismissed his ministry, he would stoically accept that decision without creating any trouble, though he had reservations on the installation of a Muslim League ministry. Dr Khan Saheb was still hoping for the imposition of Governor's rule until the next general elections were held.

Cunningham kept Dr Khan Saheb informed of his intentions of meeting Abdul Qayyum, the Muslim League contender for the Chief Ministership. Dr Khan Saheb, being in a friendly frame of mind, for he had met his old friend Cunningham after a long gap, promised that he and his ministers would go to the flag-hoisting ceremony on 15 August.

On being asked about the kind of flag he would fly on his house from 15 August onwards, he said he would pull down his present Congress flag and probably fly nothing in its place. Dr Khan Saheb had obviously not given serious thought to what was so plainly staring in his face.

Cunningham met the Chief Minister-designate Abdul Qayyum on 14 August. Making him privy to the information that Jinnah's mind was made up and that he was only waiting for Cunningham's report before issuing dismissal orders for the present ministry, he cautioned Abdul Qayyum to say nothing of this to his friends. Astute as he was, Cunningham was trying to establish a rapport with Abdul Qayyum. He was also able to convince the prospective Chief Minister that Jinnah had no intention of trusting or cooperating with Dr Khan Saheb.

Dr Khan Saheb's ministry could only last for one more week after Pakistan's creation. It was dismissed and a Muslim League ministry took over on 23 August 1947. This ministry did not have a majority in the provincial legislature. It met in March 1948 for the first time—and by then, seven Congress members had shifted allegiance to the Muslim League. Abdul Qayyum's party now had a majority and Dr Khan Saheb became the Leader of the Opposition.

## Notes

1. Based on impressions contained in George Cunningham's diary. This diary is unpublished. However, a copy is available at the British Library, London.
2. Sardar Abdur Rab Nishtar (1899–1958) was a Muslim League stalwart, Pakistan movement activist and later a Pakistani politician.
3. Govind Ballabh Pant (1887–1961) was an Indian independence activist and a prominent political leader from the United Provinces (now Uttar Pradesh).
4. Sri Krishna Sinha (1887–1961) was the first Chief Minister of the Indian state of Bihar. He is considered to be among the architects of modern Bihar.
5. Sir Arthur Edward Broadbent Parsons was an administrator in British India. He served as Governor of the NWFP in 1939.
6. Major General Sahibzada Sayyid Iskander Ali Mirza (1899–1969) was the last Governor General of the Dominion of Pakistan (1955–56) and the first President of the Islamic Republic of Pakistan (1956–58). In 1926, he left the Indian army to join the Indian Political Service and was posted as Assistant Commissioner in the NWFP. He was promoted to District Officer in 1931. Much of his career as a District Officer was spent in the tribal areas. Before the creation of Pakistan, he served in the Ministry of Defence, Government of India as a Joint Secretary. At the time of partition, he was appointed as a member of the team that was to divide personnel and assets between the Indian and Pakistan armies.
7. A *lambardar* was an unofficial link between the landowner in his village and government officials. He represented landowners and not the government. While he was appointed by the Revenue Department, he did not hold any formal office.
8. Until 1947, Sir Fraser Noble was a member of the Indian Civil Service. He later settled in university life in Britain, becoming Vice Chancellor of Leicester and Aberdeen universities. In 1940 he was transferred to the

Indian Political Service from the Royal Highland Regiment. In 1941 he was posted to NWFP, where he remained throughout the War and until the British left India. After a spell as Assistant Commissioner Hazara, he was appointed Assistant Political Agent, North Waziristan, and then Controller of Rationing, Peshawar. The last two posts Noble held in India were those of Joint Deputy Commissioner Peshawar and Civil Aide to the Referendum Commissioner. Half a century later, he published an autobiography titled *Something in India* (1997).

# 13
# Kestrel of Kashmir: Abdul Qayyum Khan

For two years before India's partition, Khan Abdul Qayyum Khan was a prominent Congressman holding fort as Deputy Speaker in the central legislative assembly. In 1945 he defected to the Muslim League, positioning himself as a prospective leader of the Frontier League once Aurangzeb Khan had fallen out of Jinnah's favour. In less than ten days after he became the Governor General of Pakistan, Jinnah had installed Abdul Qayyum Khan as the Chief Minister of the NWFP, a post he occupied till 1953. Thereafter, Abdul Qayyum Khan continued as a federal minister of Pakistan before he was removed and jailed by Ayub Khan, the second President of Pakistan. Subsequently, he also held a ministerial position in Zulfikar Ali Bhutto's[1] government in the 1970s.

For a person who came up in politics as a Congressman, to suddenly change tack and join the Muslim League, his statements and penned down thoughts before and after he joined Jinnah's party make for interesting reading in contrast. As a Congressman, Abdul Qayyum Khan's pronouncements were predominantly anti-British. He was censorious of the so-called 'peaceful penetration' of the British into the NWFP, which to him was a polite euphemism for wanton aggression. He was a fierce critic of the British strategy of bombing tribal areas. He ascribed 'tribal lawlessness' to British apathy towards the plight of tribesmen. Sympathetic to the demand for a Pathan homeland in the NWFP and to a Pathan's right to decide his fate, Abdul Qayyum Khan was averse to the idea of the NWFP joining Pakistan. He wanted all controls exercised by the British government in the tribal area to end, and was in favour of freely elected tribal *jirgas* or councils, with each *jirga* responsible for its internal affairs. The tribal *jirgas*, in turn, could send their elected representatives to a bigger *jirga* of the tribal belt. The duty of the *loya jirga*,[2] the all-tribal council, would be to settle internal tribal disputes and negotiate matters of common interest between the tribal belt and the province. He regretted Pathan factionalism and wanted those in the NWFP, the tribal belt and Baluchistan to be brought into one unit. The analogy he drew was of British attempts at maiming and mutilating Bengal, Assam and Punjab (Qaiyum 1945: 71).

On a visit to Bombay in 1942 for private medical consultations and also to meet Bhulabhai Desai, Abdul Qayyum Khan had a chance encounter with a young man called Mushtaq Ahmad. The conversation they struck up is engaging. Abdul Qayyum Khan was the Deputy Speaker in the central legislative assembly then. When asked about Jinnah, Abdul Qayyum Khan was forthright, describing him as a vain person, holding his vanity responsible as a principal hurdle to Hindu–Muslim unity. He found Jinnah's dream of Pakistan unrealistic; all provinces that Jinnah thought would form Pakistan were deficit provinces, living on central subsidy and subvention. To Abdul Qayyum Khan, the idea of Pakistan was a consequence of an anxiety that the Muslims suffered as a minority community. He was confident in his declaration to Mushtaq Ahmad: 'We in the majority provinces suffer from no such inhibitions particularly in the frontier where I come from.' The Deputy Speaker was proud to be a 'Red Shirt'. How ironic that later as a Chief Minister of the NWFP, he relentlessly persecuted the Khudai Khidmatgars (the Red Shirts). Of course, in 1942 he believed that Hindus were ready to make sacrifices for India's unity even at the expense of their majority position being compromised at the centre. He was confident that the Congress would agree to give a 50 per cent representation to the Muslims in the central legislature of a free India.[3]

But a complete turnaround had taken place by August 1945. In a letter of 16 August, Abdul Qayyum Khan from Lucknow informed Jinnah of his 'most momentous decision'—a result of 'anxious heart searching and hard thinking for days on end.' 'Any Muslim who opposes you [Jinnah] is betraying the cause of Islam in India,' he said. This was soon after the failed Simla Conference convened by Wavell. In his reply of 20 August, Jinnah stated that there was 'no room or place for any honest Muslim in the Congress, or support to it, at any rate, after the

Simla Conference.' Jinnah exhorted him to 'serve selflessly, the national cause of Muslim India and all that Islam stands for.'[4]

Soon Abdul Qayyum had an occasion to meet the British Cabinet delegation visiting India. In a meeting of 2 April 1946, where Wavell was present, Abdul Qayyum Khan made his dissatisfaction apparent with the External Affairs Department's approach to managing affairs of the tribes in the NWFP. He also reiterated his long-standing demand for amalgamating the tribal areas with the settled districts of the NWFP. He believed that the people of the Frontier were one by race and language and it was unnatural to separate them. Amalgamation would also give the local government greater control over the officers.

Having become a spokesperson for the Frontier Muslim League, Abdul Qayyum's position on issues like 'Pakistan' and a unitary form of government changed. He now wanted the basis for 'Pakistan' recognized. In case of a Hindu administration at the centre, the Muslims were bound to revolt along communal lines. But in the event of a unitary Indian government coming into being, he now preferred the NWFP to be an autonomous unit in the Pakistan cluster of provinces. Accusing the Congress of manipulating the 1946 elections, Abdul Qayyum insisted that an independent referendum, held at once in the NWFP, would see a large majority voting for Pakistan. He maintained that Pathans had no love lost for the Hindus and only supported the Congress because of its anti-British stance. Deprecating Abdul Ghaffar Khan's role in the Indian national movement, he said that Ghaffar Khan had joined the Congress simply on grounds of expediency as he had always restrained himself from publicly repudiating Pakistan. Abdul Qayyum Khan was comfortable with the idea of an eastern and western unit of Pakistan and believed that nothing could prevent them from coming together. He now strongly objected to a predominantly Hindu centre which to him meant an extinction of Muslim rights.

The cabinet delegation was unable to offer a mutually acceptable solution on the transfer of power to the Congress and the Muslim League and returned to Britain in June 1946. Dr Khan Saheb's third ministry continued to administer in the NWFP. By February 1947, the Governor and the Chief Minister were completely at odds with one another. On 20 February the British Prime Minister unilaterally announced British withdrawal plans from India, setting a time frame of June 1948. It became imperative that the NWFP opt for Pakistan. Otherwise Jinnah's two-nation theory would not stand vindicated. The only quick way for the Muslim League to wrest the NWFP from the Congress was to portray the provincial ministry as Hindu-controlled. In this effort, the Muslim League welcomed support from all quarters. Announcement by the Frontier League of a civil disobedience movement and a Direct Action campaign were primarily aimed at garnering support along communal lines.

As Nehru concluded his NWFP visit in October 1946, news of the Bihar carnage arrived. This gave the Muslim League an opportunity to intensify its campaign against the Khudai Khidmatgars and non-Muslims. The exaggerated versions of League representatives who had visited Bihar helped the 'Pakistan' cause. The Frontier League organized processions shouting slogans like *'Bihar ka badla sarhad mein leynge'* (We will avenge Bihar in the Frontier) and *'Khoon ka badla khoon'* (Blood will be avenged by blood). Some processionists marching through Hazara exhibited a number of skulls, which they said were the remains of Muslims murdered in Bihar. They showed photographs of atrocities committed in Bihar, blood-stained clothes of children and torn and mutilated leaves of the Quran. Despite a question mark on whether what was displayed was genuine or not, its exhibition had the desired effect of arousing bitter communal feelings. A *'khooni mushaira'* (blood recital) was held in a hall, the entrance of which was decorated with human skulls and bones. A picture of Khan Abdul Ghaffar Khan attending a meeting with Gandhi portrayed him as a Muslim worshipping a Hindu Bania. It was also said that Abdul Ghaffar Khan had committed a sin against God in allowing his son Ghani to marry a Parsi woman who was a fire-worshipper. People were reminded that Dr Khan Saheb's daughter Mariam had married an Indian Christian. Bricks, said to belong to a mosque in Bihar allegedly desecrated and demolished by Hindu rioters, were carried about and shown around. Pathans, forever excitable, did not take kindly to what was being shown and said about the Hindus in the NWFP.

The Muslim League propaganda soon began to show results. Rioting started in December in 1946 in a number of villages in Hazara district. The small Hindu population in these villages was unable to defend itself. Hindu and Sikh shops were looted and set on fire. A few non-Muslims were murdered. There were instances of desecration of gurudwaras and temples, but the energy of the Muslim mob was concentrated chiefly on looting and burning. The disturbances spread to the hilly tracts of the district to Nathia Galli and continued through January 1947.

Hazara and Dera Ismail Khan districts were non-Pushto-speaking areas with Punjabi influence predominating. The other districts of the NWFP, mainly Pushto-speaking, were largely Congress-controlled. The rioting in Hazara and Dera Ismail Khan had been widespread and violent. The civil disobedience movement, started in February 1947, was largely responsible for poisoning the communal atmosphere in the NWFP. Beginning in March, a number of stabbing and shooting incidents took place in Peshawar city and its cantonment. Persecution and forced conversions were leading to an exodus of non-Muslims from the NWFP. The budget session of the provincial assembly was also being held in March. Dr Khan Saheb felt that any drastic action on their part may result in the Governor dissolving the Assembly. But in April 1947, Dera Ismail Khan was in flames. On 14 and 15 April, villages around Dera Ismail Khan and the town itself were under attack. To escape mob fury, the entire non-Muslim population withdrew and entrenched itself in a distant quarter of the town. The assault continued for three days. This attack reduced the city to a smouldering ruin. Attacks on other villages in the district followed and in some cases the entire non-Muslim population was killed or forcibly converted.

On 14 August 1947, Pakistan was established, and soon Abdul Qayyum Khan replaced Dr Khan Saheb as the Chief Minister of the NWFP. Immediately, the new Chief Minister began a virulent propaganda against non-Muslims. Inflated account of events in East Punjab and atrocities that the Muslims had been subjected to, spread in the province to arouse passions. A Muslim League deputation sent to East Punjab, on its return gave such a description of its visit that the situation got further aggravated. Haripur witnessed turmoil during the last week of August. The ire of the rioters was directed against the Hindus, three hundred of whom were killed. Several temples and gurudwaras were ransacked and set on fire. On 27 August, villages around Hazara were attacked. Trouble spread to other districts and to Waziristan. Since Bannu, Mardan and Charsadda had a strong

Khudai Khidmatgar presence, the rampage could not assume a serious proportion. But arson, looting and killings started in Peshawar city in early September. The attack this time was far more determined. It began with the usual stories spread by the Muslim League that a mob of Sikhs had assembled to assault the Muslims. In order to ward the attack off, the Muslims were asked to arm and collect in large numbers. The Muslim mob then proceeded against the imaginary Sikh assailants and positioned themselves in the suburbs of Peshawar. They invaded the city and went about looting, burning and killing; some of the rioters were seen going about in jeeps and cars. Khan Abdul Qayyum Khan, the Premier, had to go to Rawalpindi to meet his West Punjab counterpart and the mayhem began soon after he left Peshawar on 7 September. The following is an account given by an official of the Government of India posted at Peshawar at the time:

Khan Abdul Qaiyum Khan could hardly have left Peshawar when Leaguers went about in a car in Peshawar City proclaiming that a Sikh regiment was going to attack Muslims... The myth of a Sikh attack has invariably been the signal for the butchery of minorities in the Frontier... The Deputy Commissioner and the Inspector-General of Police could not be contacted on the telephone.

Thus the field was left open for the *goondas* to start murder and arson. Curfew was not even formally imposed till 5.30 p.m. For nearly twelve hours the non-Muslims fought the ruffians heroically while flames enveloped them and bullets were being showered on them. Some brave women committed suicide.

In spite of the curfew, till Khan Abdul Qayyum Khan arrived at 5 p.m. on Monday the 8th, loot, arson and murder went on unchecked.

Incumbency fast caught up with Abdul Qayyum Khan. In less than two years of his Chief Ministership, the editor of *Pakistan Times* commented:

This Frontier leader seems to be laboring under the delusion that a manoeuvered majority in the Legislature and the support of a gerrymandered League organization give him the licence to ride roughshod over people's rights and contravene every rule of decent, democratic government... he has managed to convince Mr Liaquat Ali Khan that as Frontier Premier he is indispensable

and irreplaceable. But we hope this is not true, for unless
Mr Qayyum can learn to change his ways he is probably a far
more serious danger to the Frontier's stability than many of those
whom he has so light-heartedly jailed. The Central Government
must seriously think of cleaning up the mess in the Frontier, and
if no other solution is possible, new elections on the basis of adult
franchise should be ordered (Khan 1996: 314–15).

In April 1953, Khan Abdul Qayyum Khan got co-opted in the Pakistan central cabinet. But the manner in which the post of the NWFP Chief Minister was filled brought little credit to the Frontier Muslim League Assembly party. The NWFP Inspector General of Police, Sardar Abdur Rashid Khan[5] was nominated to head the ministry, a novel political experiment. The announcement of this appointment was made at a police parade. This was also perhaps indicative of the fact that no one in the Muslim League Assembly party was considered fit to inherit Abdul Qayyum Khan's mantle or that the imposition of a senior police officer on the party was the only way to control personal and group rivalries. It was Abdul Qayyum Khan who had secured the appointment of Sardar Abdur Rashid Khan, his personal nominee. It was apparent to everyone that Khan Abdul Qayyum Khan would continue to guide the destiny of the NWFP. He had also chosen to retain the presidentship of the Frontier Muslim League as well as the membership of the provincial assembly. This meant that the new ministry would remain wedded to the policies of Abdul Qayyum Khan who was to be the de facto Chief Minister of the province (Khan 1996: 321–22).

Predictably enough, Khan Abdul Qayyum Khan continued to devote a great deal of his time in maintaining his hold over the NWFP Muslim League. For the first few months all went well and the central Food Minister (Khan Abdul Qayyum Khan) continued to pay frequent visits to the NWFP to ensure that his word was still law in his own political 'khanate'. But as time passed, his remote control of the NWFP became a matter of serious contention. Dismissal of some ministers in the province, instead of frightening the anti-Qayyum Muslim Leaguers into quiescence, only added fuel to the fire. Even the Frontier Chief Minister realized how suicidal it was to continue holding fort for Abdul Qayyum Khan. Gradually, Abdul Qayyum Khan's position got undermined and his political khanate crumbled. He gave up the presidency of the Frontier Muslim League, pretending to make a gift of what had virtually been snatched away from him. Thus occurred Khan Abdul Qayyum Khan's exit from the Frontier's political stage (Khan 1996: 323–24).

## Notes

1. Zulfikar Ali Bhutto (1928–1979) was a Pakistani politician who served as the President of Pakistan from 1971 to 1973 and as Prime Minister from 1973 to 1977. He was the founder of the Pakistan People's Party (PPP). His daughter Benazir Bhutto also served twice as Prime Minister; she was assassinated on 27 December 2007.
2. A *loya jirga* is a 'grand assembly'; a Pashto phrase meaning 'grand council'. It is a political meeting usually used to choose new kings, adopt constitutions, or decide important political matters and disputes. In Afghanistan, the *loya jirga* was originally attended only by Pakhtun groups, but later included other ethnic groups. It is a forum unique to Afghanistan in which, traditionally, tribal elders meet together.
3. The dialogue published in Mustaq Ahmed, *Jinnah & After—A Profile of Leadership*, Royal Book Company, 1994. Available in the Parliament Library, New Delhi.
4. Both the letters are published in Syed Sharifuddin Pirzada (ed.), *Quaid-e-Azam Jinnah's Correspondence*, East and West Publishing Company, 1977, pp.300–01.
5. Sardar Abdur Rashid Khan (1906–1995) was a senior police officer from the NWFP and a cabinet minister in Pakistan. He was serving as the Deputy Superintendent of Police in Peshawar city when Pakistan became independent. Sardar Rashid rose to become the Inspector General of the NWFP police, but resigned from the police service on 23 April 1953 when appointed as the eighth Chief Minister of the NWFP. His nomination was controversial in that he was handpicked by his predecessor, Abdul Qayyum Khan. However, he proved to be a popular choice, and in November 1953 he was elected as the provincial president of the Muslim League despite the efforts of Abdul Qayyum Khan to retain the post for himself following his elevation to the central government. He remained Chief Minister until 18 July 1955, when he was forced to resign because of his opposition to

the 'one unit scheme'. He was succeeded by Sardar Bahadur Khan (older brother of General Ayub Khan) who secured approval from the provincial assembly for the controversial scheme. After the fall of the Ayub Khan government, Sardar Abdur Rashid served as Minister for Home Affairs (Interior), Kashmir Affairs, States and Frontier Regions in the presidential cabinet of President and Chief Martial Law Administrator General Yahya Khan from 4 August 1969 to 22 February 1971.

# 14

## Difficult under Difficult Conditions: Muhammad Ali Jinnah

MANY CONSIDER JINNAH to have single-handedly created Pakistan. Jinnah himself had no violent disagreement with this contention. A contemporary of Gandhi, he appeared on India's political firmament much earlier, preceding Gandhi by almost ten years. In politics, he always considered Gandhi his equal and Nehru his junior. Never in awe of Gandhi, his associations with Nehru were decidedly recondite.

Marginalized by Gandhi during the Non-Cooperation and Khilafat movements,[1] Jinnah left the Congress. For almost fifteen years thereafter, he continued to look for political relevance in India. He spent some years in England in the early 1930s trying to secure a berth in the British Parliament. When he finally returned to India in 1934, the Muslim League was still a party largely on paper. Gradually he consolidated the Muslim League, more so during the war years (1939–45), giving a call for Pakistan in 1940. Within seven years of that call, he had attained his objective.

Jinnah had all along been a strong votary of reforms in the NWFP. His famous fourteen points, made public in 1928, included this long-pending demand, a major precondition for settlement with Congress. Why this settlement with Congress, for what objection could Congress have to these reforms? Jinnah personally intervened twice in the Indian Legislative Assembly debates, arguing vociferously in favour of constitutional reforms for the NWFP, the debates taking place in 1926 and 1928. Conscious of its sensitivity, Jinnah in his interventions, was at times deferential to the senior Hindu Mahasabha leaders who disagreed with him. He took recourse to humour in delicate situations just to defuse matters.

In the first debate commencing on 16 February 1926, the Hindu members were disinclined to concede elementary constitutional rights to the Muslims of the NWFP. Syed Murtaza Sahib, a member from Madras (South), moved a resolution for extension of the Government of India Act[2] in the NWFP, especially sections that concerned the Legislative Council, appointment of ministers and protection of minorities.[3] The NWFP till then had been bereft of the benefits of the 1919 reforms. This was one curious case in which the British and the Congress, each for their own reasons, were united in opposition to the extension of reforms to a Muslim majority area.

Syed Murtaza Sahib was both a member of the Congress party as well as of the Muslim League. In the Legislative Assembly, he represented the Swaraj Party[4] led by Motilal Nehru (he had moved the resolution not as a member of Swaraj Party but as a member of the All India Muslim League).[5] Many from the Congress party opposed him when he rose to move the resolution for introduction of political reforms of 1919 to the NWFP. Leaders like Madan Mohan Malviya[6] were outspoken in their opposition. When the debate began, the Swaraj Party suddenly decided to boycott the assembly session. Syed Murtaza Sahib was refused permission to attend the session by Motilal Nehru. For his refusal to accept the party diktat, Syed Murtaza Sahib was expelled from the Swaraj Party.

When discussions resumed, Jinnah, leader of the Independent Party then, decided to make an active intervention. At the very outset, he made it clear that his intention was not to adopt a communal approach to the issue. He was cautious, lest the debate engender bitter feelings between the Hindus and Muslims. Speaking on the resolution on 18 March 1926, Jinnah said:

> Sir, the question before the house is one which requires a great deal of restraint...I do not wish to deal with this question from the communal point of view at all. I have had the honour of working with my honourable friend Pandit Madan Mohan Malviya since 1906. If I remember it rightly, when I first stepped on the platform of Indian National Congress, it was my friend before whom I stood as a junior who introduced me and

persuaded me to make my first speech on the platform of the Indian National Congress. Ever since then I have worked with him and I have always looked upon him with greatest admiration and respect. I have a feeling that my honourable friend Pandit Madan Mohan Malviya is as much a nationalist as any living Indian today in India.

But Sir, we are sometimes likely honestly to be prejudiced. I cannot agree with the language of my honourable friend as to what he feels. And I can also equally enter into the spirit of my Mohammedan friends as to what they feel when they think of horrible incidents which have taken place not only at Kohat but in other parts of India as well. Sir, it is common ground; it is our misfortune. But I appeal to my honourable friend: are we going to lose heart?[7]

Jinnah asked for the NWFP to be treated in the 'same spirit' as one would treat other provinces. He was against the demand for amalgamating the NWFP with Punjab, for to him, 'the people of NWFP linguistically, geographically and in every other sense were different from the Punjab people.'[8] 'Amalgamation or no amalgamation,' he wanted reforms to be 'given to NWFP.'[9] He was convinced that no harm would come to the Hindus on account of it. On the contrary, if the reforms were delayed, the Muslims would hold the Hindus responsible, and the Hindus on the other hand would be encouraged to feel that their agitation forced the government to withdraw the reforms, 'an impression fraught with danger.' The culmination of Jinnah's cogent and eloquent pleading was the adoption of Syed Murtaza Sahib's resolution in the assembly. But opposition from Hindu sections and the government did not allow for its implementation in the NWFP for many more years to come.

True to his wont, Jinnah again persevered and pleaded in 1928 for introducing the same reforms. The government had deliberately stalled the action to be taken on the Bray Committee report on reforms in the NWFP. Speaking in the assembly on 14 March 1928, Jinnah criticized the policy of the government with respect to the Bray Committee report while castigating it for playing one party against the other: 'Suddenly, Sir, the Government develops a particular kind of affection or love for the Hindus and their feelings and their sentiments.[10] My Hindu friends have realized and my Muhammadan friends have realized now that this is the old game which is continued with a certain amount of success. But, Sir, do not play this game ... what is your answer? Still under consideration...'[11]

After the grant of provincial autonomy under the Government of India Act 1935, provincial elections in the NWFP were to be held for the first time in early 1937. To explore the possibility of a tie-up for the Muslim League in these provincial elections, Jinnah undertook a visit to the NWFP in October 1936. Jinnah observed of this first visit: 'When I came to the Frontier in 1936, I was deeply disappointed. At that time there were only two distinct camps, one, the bureaucratic camp and the other, the Congress. Opportunists went to the first camp while the careerists put on the Gandhi cap and joined the Congress.' But he himself could hardly escape the accusation of being a part of the bureaucratic camp when he arrived in Peshawar on 18 October 1936. As a part of the officialdom, Nawabzada Sir Abdul Qayyum had obvious difficulties in issuing a formal invitation to Jinnah. Instead, he asked a prominent member of the Muslim Independent Party to perform the courtesy. Nawabzada Sir Abdul Qayyum, of course, provided the hospitality which Jinnah gladly accepted. Jinnah was the Nawabzada's guest during his first visit to the NWFP.

The situation in the NWFP was yet to polarize communally. Just a few months had elapsed since Jinnah effectively intervened in an assembly debate to lift a ban on the Khudai Khidmatgars. Though he did have meetings with prominent Congressmen in Peshawar, Jinnah was unwilling to make positive overtures towards the Khudai Khidmatgars or try to establish contact with Khan Abdul Ghaffar Khan as he had been advised by some members of his entourage to do. Instead, he concentrated his energies in getting the conservative elements on his side—the Khan Bahadurs and supporters of the British. That Jinnah was allowed to move freely within the province was not liked by many. It gave an impression that his visit had the seal of official approval, something that was in utter contrast to the treatment meted out to two Congress leaders, Sardar Vallabhbhai Patel and Bhulabhai Desai[12] who visited the NWFP to assist their local organization in the forthcoming elections. This was a time when the official ban on the Khudai Khidmatgars and the Congress was still in operation. The two Congress leaders were not allowed to move out of Peshawar, their engagements were checked and sometimes curtailed. The Pathans saw through the discrimination in the treatment meted out to Jinnah who was allowed to visit places that had forever remained out of bounds to Khan Abdul Ghaffar Khan. In consequence, the Pathans refused to deal with Jinnah over the head of their exiled leader (Yunus 1980: 21).

Mohammad Yunus,[13] a Nehru acolyte, spent ten days with Jinnah while he was in the NWFP. Queried once by Mohammad Yunus on the rationale of organizing the provincial League with the help of reactionary elements, Jinnah's response was: 'Look at the rascals and the scoundrels following me. Have I got a Nehru, or a Patel or a Rajendra Prasad? Yet I am putting up a fight against Gandhi' (Yunus 1980: 74). Mohammad Yunus felt that Jinnah had not tried enough to attract the right kind of people. Those who were not with the provincial Congress and the Khudai Khidmatgars were racked by bitter infighting. Jinnah held private meetings with local politicians, assessing for himself the prospects of forming a provincial Muslim League in the NWFP. But his effort did not bear any result, rather it proved to be still-born. The candidates who opposed the Congress in the 1937 elections either contested on their own or on Nawabzada Abdul Qayyum's party tickets. Interest in the Muslim League's communal ideology was still lacking in 1937. Jinnah's first mission to the NWFP was a failure.

The Lahore Resolution demanding Pakistan came much later. Many who met Jinnah during his first visit to the NWFP asked him to bring the Muslims of the province on one single platform. But this was not palatable to the British. The Khudai Khidmatgars and the Congress largely followed an anti-government policy; it was also the reason for their popularity. A single platform could not have fructified. The Muslim League as an organization was nascent, in need of British official support to grow. It was not possible for Jinnah to deal with the Khan brothers on equal terms, and he would have no truck with the followers of Gandhi. The British would also not allow this to happen. Most of the Khan Bahadurs of the NWFP were staunch supporters of the government, a group the British wilfully encouraged as a bulwark against the Khudai Khidmatgars and the Congress. Many who saw no career prospects in the Congress ranks joined the Muslim League. The irony of the situation lay in the fact that in February 1936, Jinnah had put his entire weight behind removing the ban on the Khudai Khidmatgars.

The provincial elections of February 1937 were not a bitter electoral battle between the Congress and the Muslim League. At many places it remained merely a friendly fight. Both parties sought each other's goodwill lest they require support from them after the elections. The Congress won the Hindu majority provinces, while the Muslim League did well only in places like the United Province and the Bombay Presidency. Many, even now, consider attempts at popular ministry formation in 1937 to be the turning point in the relationship between the Congress and the Muslim League. Having fared well in the elections, the Congress did not want to share power with the Muslim League in the United Province and in Bombay. Congress leaders wanted the Muslim League to merge with the Congress. The two years subsequent to the formation of the ministry in 1937 provided ample opportunity to the Muslim League to criticize the Congress and portray it as a Hindu political body. This was also a period of the consolidation phase of the Muslim League, its membership rising in geometric progression. Jinnah now wanted the Muslim League treated at par with the Congress. He claimed for his party the sole spokesmanship of the Muslim community. The Lahore Resolution of March 1940 raised the level of his demand to an altogether different plane—creation of a separate state for the Muslims of India.

During the war years, the British were reluctant to negotiate with the Congress on the question of India's freedom. To rein the Congress in, they decided not to grant further reforms without the consent of the Muslim League. Instead of fighting the British, the Muslim League now fought the Congress to attain the objective of Pakistan.

The popular Congress ministries resigned in October 1939 over Britain's unilateral decision to involve India in World War II. It was only very reluctantly that Dr Khan Saheb gave up the post of the Congress Chief Minister of the NWFP. Jinnah at that time was desperate to install a Muslim League ministry in its place. He was sorely disappointed when the provincial Muslim League failed to form a ministry. In a telegram he sent to the provincial Muslim League leaders, he said: 'Form ministry at any cost, even interim ministry, waverers and others will come afterwards' and when he was informed that it was impossible to form even a League coalition ministry, he wrote: 'Your telegram. Great mistake, missing opportunity, form coalition ministry, make every sacrifice, let others be ministers.'[14] Factionalism at the local level prevented the formation of a Muslim League government. The struggle for leadership between Khan Bahadur Saadullah Khan and Sardar Aurangzeb Khan was the main cause for the Muslim League's inability to form a government.

Provincial League and Congress leaders took more interest in local politics than in 'all-India' issues. Dr Khan Saheb, who had literally been forced to resign, was strongly opposed to any form of a civil disobedience movement against the administration. Gandhi had to concede that the 'Frontier possessed no one fit enough to carry the civil disobedience in a non-violent manner.'[15] Governor Cunningham believed that the Pathans were 'simply not interested in the Congress'[16] implying that because of their provincialism, they would also not pay heed to Jinnah. Enlisting for the war and issues locally pertaining to agriculture were far more important. Viceroy Linlithgow was inclined to see a League ministry installed in the NWFP. He urged the Governor to explore this possibility, but the internal squabbles in the local Muslim League had taken such centre stage by now that the Viceroy had to admit that 'local jealousies'[17] had become a serious obstacle to any real political progress. The League leaders continued to busy themselves with waging family feuds under the Muslim League's banner.

Jinnah applied himself to unifying the Muslim League. But even after two years of the passing of the Lahore Resolution, he remained singularly unsuccessful in installing a single government of his choice in the Muslim majority provinces. Fazlul Haq[18] in Bengal, Sikandar Hayat Khan in Punjab and Allah Bux[19] in Sindh were not under his control. Factionalism continued to plague the provincial Leagues—the Mamdot–Daulatana faction in Punjab, the Nazimuddin–Suhrawardy faction in Bengal and the Khuro, Syed and Allah Bux factions in Sindh. Aurangzeb Khan of the NWFP remained more interested in joining the National Defence Council, much against the wishes of Jinnah.[20] Muslim League leaders in Sindh were ready to join ranks with Allah Bux if he rid himself of the Congress.[21]

During the war years, the Governor chose to enlist the support of the Khan Bahadurs and mullahs in maintaining a strong bulwark against the so-called disaffected elements like the Khudai Khidmatgars and the Congress. He constantly endeavoured to build a tempo of 'anti-Congress' propaganda. Some Khudai Khidmatgars who were not sympathetic to the Hindus supported the Governor in his efforts.[22]

Sardar Aurangzeb Khan could finally be installed as the Chief Minister in August 1943. It was not Jinnah but Governor Cunningham who played a stellar role in installing the first Muslim League ministry in the NWFP. The four by-elections that the League won prompted Jinnah to eagerly but falsely claim people's support in the NWFP. The victory for the Muslim League had largely come due to British official support. Even when the Muslim League ministry finally came to be installed in 1943, Jinnah remained peripheral to it. To sustain himself, the Muslim League Chief Minister, Sardar Aurangzeb Khan, had to look more towards Cunningham than towards Jinnah. Since support to his government was always in doubt, Cunningham warned Aurangzeb Khan not to get seriously involved with Jinnah and his demand for Pakistan.[23] Aurangzeb Khan, therefore, studiously avoided taking a firm stand for fear of losing the non-Muslim members of the provincial legislature. But the provincial Muslim League continued to be beleaguered with factionalism. Aurangzeb Khan and Khan Bahadur Saadullah Khan sparred unceasingly. Jinnah, therefore, was reluctant to intervene on anyone's behalf. What else could he possibly do? His inability to remote-control the situation would become immediately known in case he threw his weight behind someone. His usual advice to anyone found complaining was to keep his own house in order (Mirza 1999: 151–52). Jinnah became increasingly strident in his public statements prior to the formation of the Muslim League ministry in May 1943. He strove hard to communalize the situation in the NWFP, though success came much later. In his message of 4 April 1943 to the NWFP Muslim Students' Federation, Jinnah sought to impress upon them that the province 'by virtue of its unique position, is a very important province...strengthening yourselves (the students) is, really speaking, strengthening the borders of Pakistan.' He also said that the 'Musalmans of India have great faith and hopes in you and believe that you will be unconquerable soldiers of Islam like your unconquerable rocks and through you Islam in India will be able to revive its glorious past.'[24] The reference here was to passes like the Khyber which had traditionally been invasion routes into India.

Well before the Simla talks began in June 1945, the Muslim League ministry in the NWFP had been replaced (12 March 1945) and Dr Khan Saheb was back holding the fort. In late 1945, provincial elections were announced. Things were now polarizing in the name of Pakistan. Abdul Qayyum Khan, an important Congress leader from the NWFP defected, helping the Muslim League prospects. As Khan Bahadur Saadullah Khan and Aurangzeb Khan continued to bicker, Jinnah appointed Sardar Abdur Rab Nishtar as his point man in the NWFP. Though Jinnah kept Aurangzeb Khan out of the parliamentary board, he was not successful in keeping his men out of it. Soon Abdul Qayyum and Abdur Rab Nishtar also came to lock horns. Jinnah saw to it that Aurangzeb Khan did not get to contest the elections. The disagreements within cost the Muslim League dear, resulting in a Congress win in the NWFP. The Muslim League had fought the election on the plank of 'Pakistan'; this was now to be their clarion call. But the Muslim League's decision to allocate seats was taken behind closed doors, allowing for little transparency. Reactionary elements, title-holders and ministry mongers managed to secure nominations. That Congress emerged victorious in the NWFP was indicative of the fact that the Pathans had largely remained unaffected by the fear of Hindu domination. Governor Cunningham, on the other hand, did not think that the Pathans would long be content to remain in an undivided India without safeguards or guarantees. Had the Muslim League substituted its demand of Pakistan for Pathanistan, Cunningham believed they would have fared better.

Jinnah arrived in Peshawar for the second and the last time on 19 November 1945 to provide an impetus to the Muslim League election campaign. Invariably, he raised the topic of Pakistan in his public speeches. To him, the forthcoming elections were the first step towards achieving that aim. Cunningham felt that Jinnah's visit had strengthened the Muslim League's cause in NWFP and provided it with a 'fairly effective propaganda.'[25] At a conference in Peshawar on 21 November, Jinnah especially chose to stress on the changed position of the 'Sarhad Musalmans'[26] since 1936, and how proud he was to see that they had woken up and were 'no more under the snare of the fraud Hindu Congress.'[27] Jinnah tirelessly repeated in his public addresses that the fight for the 1946 provincial elections was not to form ministries, but to get a verdict from the Muslims on Pakistan. He would thunder dramatically: 'If we fail to realize our duty today, you will be reduced to the status of *shudras* and Islam will be vanquished from India.'[28] He often reminded the Muslims of their history too: 'Remember, Muslims can never be crushed. They have not been crushed during the last 1000 years by any power.'[29] When asked about the sacrifices he and the Muslim League had made, his answer was: 'It is true that I have not been to jail. Never mind I am a bad person. But I ask you, who made sacrifices in 1920-21? Mr Gandhi ascends the gaddi of leadership on our skulls. But what happened? Ali brothers[30] who were the devoted servants of Islam were kicked out after they had been used by the Congress.'[31] Referring to the unrest that took place in NWFP in 1930-31 during the Civil Disobedience Movement, Jinnah queried in Peshawar:

> You sacrificed here in 1930-31 and what did Muslims get out of it? In 1924 when the Muslim League was fighting for reforms in your province the Congress opposed the League in the Central Assembly on this issue. Again the Congress attitude towards League demand for reforms in your province was of hostility.... I do not believe in starting a movement for the sake of jail going. Believe me it will not be difficult for me to go to jail for 6 months or so. After all nothing happened to Mr Gandhi. He was safely lodged in the Agha Khan's palace. He had his Private Secretary. In fact his whole family was with him, but who will face the bullets? It will be my brethren.[32]

Iskander Mirza, an Indian Political Service Officer and the future President of Pakistan, met Jinnah for the first time in March 1943. Jinnah then had been extremely keen on a Muslim League government being installed in office in the NWFP. Iskander Mirza was an important official functionary, working as the Deputy Commissioner of Peshawar. He had called on Jinnah to share his assessment about the Muslim League's prospects in the NWFP, and to brief him about provincial leaders. The local Muslim League politics of the NWFP was never in Jinnah's control. Iskander Mirza would prove beneficial if kept on the right side. If Humayun Mirza, Iskander Mirza's son, is to be believed, his father's assessment helped Jinnah decide on the choice of the Chief Ministership. Iskander Mirza had perhaps recommended the induction of Abdur Rab Nishtar in the Muslim League. Nishtar was a former Ahrar leader, who till then had been making vitriolic public statements against Jinnah. Of course, the installation of the Muslim League government in May 1943 was largely Governor Cunningham's handiwork.

After leaving Peshawar, Iskander Mirza joined the Ministry of Defence in Delhi as a joint secretary. Humayun Mirza, in his book *From Plassey to Pakistan—The Family History of Iskander Mirza*, makes a startling revelation, though it is not backed by any documentary evidence. He claims that Iskander Mirza had met Jinnah in Delhi in February 1947 in the immediate aftermath of Clement Attlee's announcement on a fixed date for the British withdrawal from India. The impending but unpalatable prospect of the NWFP, ruled then by a Congress government aligning with India had dawned on the Muslim League. According to Humayun Mirza, Jinnah asked Iskander Mirza to resign from the service and go to the NWFP to organize a jihad in support of Pakistan. Jinnah also promised to 'take care' of Iskander Mirza's family in the event of any harm coming to him in the line of duty. The Nawab of Bhopal was to provide money for Iskander Mirza's secret venture into the NWFP. The ostensible reason for his disappearance was to be shown as Iskander Mirza's posting to the state of Kalat. For out of pocket expenses, Iskander Mirza was given Rs 20,000 by the Nawab of Bhopal, no small sum then by any account.[33]

There is evidence to prove that Iskander Mirza met Jinnah in the last week of February to discuss important strategic matters. In a secret undated personal note of February 1947 that finds place in the Jinnah papers, Iskander Mirza called for an Islamic confederation or the formation of an Islamic bloc. Excerpted here are relevant lines from that note:

> The announcement [Feb 20 1947] makes it incumbent on the Muslim nation to start preparations immediately to meet all eventualities. Our position is specially precarious in the Armed Forces... Our fighting strength is in the North West. We should take practical steps in this area. I suggest an Islamic confederation

of the North West... If we succeed, we will have a fighting strength of 300,000 men at the disposal of the Confederacy with another 150,000 men from the Afghan tribes...We should work secretly and try and get the sympathy of the British administrators of the areas concerned. We can obtain rifles, machine guns and ammunitions through Kalat state by doing a little 'gun running' up the Persian Gulf.[34]

What better example of Iskander Mirza's collusion with Jinnah—a high functionary of the Government of India, that too from the Ministry of Defence—than this letter: a letter to a politician which went clearly beyond his brief? Jinnah's encouragement, no doubt, must have prompted Iskander Mirza to write to him.

Jinnah regularly received anonymous reports about the NWFP from people Iskander Mirza was in touch with. One such report of April 1947 said:

Our aim should be...to attack from Kalat to Nandihar (a mountain range) in NWFP. Nothing much has been done yet towards the formation of an Islamic Confederation of the North West...A factor which must be tackled as early as possible is the pro-Congress attitude of the Afghan allowance holders amongst the Mahsuds. Colonel Zehruddin, Colonel Musa Khan Abdullai and Parmana Khan Shammi Khel, these three leading Maliks (all Afghan allowance holders) have been reported to be working in the Congress interest. We should [therefore] build up an organization which can contact authorities in Kabul quickly. Afghan authorities have also been putting pressure on Badshah Gul, son of the Late Haji of Turangzai,[35] to restrain the Mohmands from taking sides in the Indian quarrel. The attitude of the Mahsud Maliks, holding Afghan allowance is not accidental but that the Afghan Government is following a policy inimical to Muslim interests. I suggest a Goodwill or a Trade Mission to Afghanistan at an early date. The Afghans want an outlet to the sea. We might be able to come to some terms on this issue.[36]

The report also analysed the allegiance of Maliks in different tribal areas. With the date set for the British withdrawal from India, the pace of political activity quickened. On 20 February, the British formally announced the appointment of their last Viceroy to India, Lord Mountbatten, who joined on 22 March. He was mandated to devise a suitable blueprint for transferring power to the Indians. Mountbatten immediately began confabulations with prominent Indian political leaders to put together a formula. By mid-April, he had readied a rough plan for India's partition. The Governor of the NWFP recommended fresh elections in the province to decide whether the Congress ministry still held the people's endorsement. The Direct Action campaign of the Muslim League had created a communally volatile situation in the NWFP and the fragile and explosive condition in other parts of India, especially Punjab, was of little help. The Viceroy, on advice from his Governor, wanted to test the political waters of the NWFP.

Jinnah attended a meeting that Mountbatten convened on 23 April to decide on fresh elections in the NWFP. To cool political temperatures, Mountbatten wanted Jinnah to visit the NWFP to rein in his supporters. To facilitate the visit, Mountbatten readily offered his aircraft, only to find Jinnah unwilling. Jinnah could at best appeal to his supporters through the press and radio to maintain peace and calm.[37]

At the time when Mountbatten decided to visit the NWFP, most provincial Muslim League leaders were interned. The only possible way of meeting then was to have them released on parole. These Muslim League leaders had refused to seek the amnesty offered by Dr Khan Saheb's government, as also parole. Mountbatten then appealed to Jinnah's sense of legal propriety as a way out of this dilemma to which he obliged.[38] The local leaders did call on Mountbatten in Peshawar on 28 April. On Jinnah's bidding, they had all sought parole and were granted permission. Just before leaving for the NWFP, Mountbatten received a request from Jinnah for allowing the provincial Muslim League to hold a public meeting and take out a procession in Peshawar on 28 April. While Mountbatten had no objection to a public meeting on the day of his arrival in Peshawar, he was not very comfortable with the idea of allowing a procession thereafter to march towards the government house and did not grant permission for the latter. However, he agreed to meet a delegation of six members of the provincial Muslim League at the end of the public meeting. He accordingly informed the provincial Governor. Fearing violence, Chief

Minister Dr Khan Saheb desisted from a similar show of strength by the Congress and the Khudai Khidmatgars. But it remains a puzzle still why so many in Mountbatten's entourage did not know of the Viceroy's consent. To Scott, one of Viceroy's staff, this came as 'hard news' when he arrived in Peshawar. Dr Khan Saheb too was disappointed when he was informed though he graciously agreed to the Viceroy's suggestion of a personal appearance at the venue of the meeting.

On his return from the NWFP, Mountbatten sent Lord Ismay to London to get the first partition plan approved by the British cabinet. Ismay left for London on 2 May. Jinnah had the foreknowledge of the plan which allowed for holding elections in the NWFP but on the condition that the Muslim League withdraw its Direct Action campaign.[39] Otherwise it was impossible for Mountbatten to obtain the Congress' acquiescence for the proposal. With this in mind, Mountbatten invited the provincial League leaders to come to Delhi for another round of discussions. In Mountbatten's scheme of things, provincial League leaders were to be prevailed upon to withdraw the Direct Action campaign if Jinnah was made to see reason.

Jinnah had the impression that announcement of elections in the NWFP would not be withheld until the partition plan was made public. Waiting for it meant a definite delay in holding elections. The declaration on the 'transfer of power' was not to be expected before end May. Cabinet approval for it was not expected any sooner. Jinnah impressed upon the Viceroy his constraints; he could do only so much and no more. Regarding Mountbatten's visit to the NWFP, Jinnah reminded him of the fulfilled promises—no procession, a peaceful meeting and parole for the provincial League leaders. He faced a tight situation now. He was not in a position to ask the Frontier League to stop the agitation. Neither was he confident of his directive being carried out unless he offered something substantial in lieu of the withdrawal of the Direct Action campaign. Jinnah's position was quite untenable, liable to be 'reduced to dust'[40] in the eyes of his followers. That fresh elections would only be announced after the partition plan was made public, did not help matters. Jinnah wanted Dr Khan Saheb's ministry dismissed, but Mountbatten would not oblige. Jinnah was somehow convinced that the continuance of a Congress ministry in the NWFP was a perfect recipe for violence. Even if he urged his followers to carry on the Direct Action campaign peacefully, he was certain of his instructions being flouted.

To obviate problems, Mountbatten for the first time broached the idea of a referendum in his staff meeting of 3 May,[41] within twenty-four hours of Lord Ismay leaving for London with the partition plan. He took care, of course, to immediately inform Ismay of this new idea. Jinnah too acquiesced. The Cabinet Committee in Britain took up the suggestion of a referendum on the assumption that Mountbatten would secure Congress support. But this option also carried with it the possibility of a delay in case the referendum's results went in favour of Pakistan. A fresh election in the NWFP would become inevitable, for only then could the new legislature send its representatives to the Constituent Assembly.

Jinnah was in favour of elections to be held after the referendum. He reckoned that people would not be satisfied unless elections, subsequent to a referendum, were announced. He flatly turned down the two drafts that Mountbatten wanted to send to London for the cabinet's consideration, the reason being that there was no mention of an election in them. He decided to issue a statement, the gist of which he sent to Mountbatten: 'He [Jinnah] had reasons to believe that the Viceroy had recommended to HMG a referendum in NWFP. This could only be done by the Viceroy through his own agency and that he hoped that the HMG would accept the recommendations. If the results of the referendum went in favour of Pakistan, in his judgement, elections were then inevitable and must be held. He would not advise the people to call off the movement, but that they should remain peaceful.' Jinnah had it conveyed to the Viceroy through Mieville[42] that under no circumstances would he agree to the Cabinet Mission plan.

Mountbatten was left with no alternative but to inform Ismay of Jinnah's refusal to acquiesce to the draft announcement on the NWFP because of the absence of the provision for general elections. His attempt to convince Jinnah that any reference to elections in the draft announcement would make it impossible to obtain Nehru's consent, failed. Mountbatten was anxious to obtain Nehru's approval. He persisted with Jinnah, impressing upon him the great embarrassment it would cause in case Jinnah chose to issue his *suo moto* statement.

HMG was bound not to take kindly to it, in which case Mountbatten would be forced to explain the full facts of the case to HMG. And as for the Cabinet Mission plan, it had not formally been abandoned and 'presently still held the field in London.' The partition plan could only be announced after Ismay returned from Britain with amendments that were also acceptable to the Indian leaders. In the interim, Mountbatten pleaded, Jinnah could issue a statement on maintaining peace in the province, explaining his position on 'Direct Action' without touching upon the issues of a referendum and elections. But all this did not cut much ice. Jinnah was set on issuing the statement. Attempting to play safe, Mountbatten forewarned Nehru of what to expect from Jinnah. Mountbatten's press attaché, Alan Campbell was also alerted of this possibility so that when it did occur, he should let the press know that the final decision was yet to be taken in London. Jinnah issued the statement on 7 May, but did not directly implicate the Viceroy. There were good reasons, according to him, to believe that a referendum would be followed by an election in case the results went in favour of Pakistan. Jinnah was gracious enough to inform the Viceroy in advance that he would say nothing that embarrassed either the Viceroy or HMG. And he stood true to his word.

In the first week of May, Mountbatten went to Simla followed by Nehru for a short sojourn. Their days together, away from Delhi, were critical to India's future, for important decisions were taken in Simla. On 8 May, after meeting the Viceroy, Nehru proposed a referendum for the NWFP if the provincial government agreed. Ismay, who received this communication in London, immediately realized that Jinnah, already suspicious of Dr Khan Saheb, would never agree to Nehru's conditional offer of obtaining the provincial government's concurrence on the referendum. Ismay, therefore, immediately advised Mountbatten to do away with the 'conditional' clause. Instead, a compromise was suggested: substitution of the word 'concurrence' by 'consultation.' This would still offer a possibility of acceptance by the Congress. Nehru was refusing to relent from his earlier position of holding a referendum only with full concurrence of the Frontier government. He was also not in favour of giving discretion to the tribes to re-negotiate treaties. In case the NWFP remained with India, an alliance between the people of the tribal areas and another state could create grave difficulties. The two amendments that Mountbatten suggested, and the British cabinet considered were:

i) referendum to be held in consultation with the provincial government;
ii) the electorate to choose between two unions, India and Pakistan.

> How could Jinnah ever be in favour of the 'consultation' clause? He was already worried over the uncertain position of the provincial government in case the NWFP gave its verdict in favour of Pakistan. He suffered considerable unease too over the vague announcement about the tribal areas, which said that 'the appropriate successor authority would negotiate with the tribes of NWFP.' He wanted no anomaly to exist—in his opinion, the successor authority could only be the Pakistan Constituent Assembly.

Unlike Nehru, who made no reference to the NWFP in his 3 June broadcast to the nation, Jinnah devoted almost half his speech to it, his references to the NWFP being markedly political in tone and inappropriate for the occasion. Amongst other things, he said:

> Now that the Plan makes it clear...that a referendum will be made to the electorate... I call upon all the leaders of the Muslim League and the Mussalmans to generally organize our people to face this referendum... I feel confident that the people of the Frontier will give their verdict by a solid vote to join the Pakistan Constituent Assembly. I cannot but express my appreciation of the sufferings and the sacrifices made by all classes of Mussalmans, and particularly the great part the women of the Frontier played in the fight for our civil liberties. Without a personal bias, and this is hardly the moment to do so, I deeply sympathise with all those who died and whose properties were subjected to destruction, and I fervently hope that the Frontier will go through this referendum...

Patel, also in-charge of the Ministry of Information and Broadcasting, was deeply distressed by Jinnah's breach of the rules of the broadcast. He made his displeasure clear about 'Jinnah departing from the script and thereby committing a sacrilege by making a political, partisan and propagandist broadcast.'

'Had I known it in time, I would have certainly prevented him from turning the All India Radio into a Muslim League platform by appealing to Frontier voters to vote according to League persuasion,' he said while reacting to Jinnah's 3 June broadcast. Patel also, and rightly so, thought that this was grossly unfair to the Frontier ministry.

The scheme to partition India was announced on 3 June. On the same day, the Congress Working Committee gave its approval to it. The All India Congress Committee ratified the plan on 14 and 15 June. Chances that anything would now change appeared slim. Sensitive to the fate that awaited the Khan brothers, Gandhi, on 6 June, conveyed to Mountbatten that he wanted Jinnah to visit the NWFP to explain to the people there across party lines what Pakistan actually meant. If Jinnah succeeded in 'wooing' the people, a referendum could still be avoided. If Jinnah did not succeed in evolving a consensus during his visit to NWFP, Gandhi still had a chance to reconsider the situation. He therefore also had it conveyed through Ismay how anxious Khan Abdul Ghaffar Khan was to avoid permanent blood feuds, so easily created if the referendum took place. Khan Abdul Ghaffar Khan was ready to go to the extent of even asking his brother to resign.

Jinnah did not take Gandhi's suggestion of a visit to the NWFP seriously. Why would he? He foresaw a situation where the NWFP's umbilical cords with the Congress were soon to be cut. In the already ionized communal atmosphere of the NWFP, the Khudai Khidmatgars were considered pro-Hindu and anti-Pakistan. The position of Dr Khan Saheb's party had grown steadily worse and everyone realized it. Rather, Jinnah's response to Gandhi's request was patronizing. He wanted the Congress to stop interfering in NWFP's affairs—an impossible precondition.

On 17 June Gandhi met Jinnah in the presence of the Viceroy. The minutes of the 17 June meeting, especially the exchanges between Gandhi and Jinnah, make for a disappointing read, falling far short of what was expected from leaders of such stature. Both concurred with Mountbatten's suggestion. Gandhi's response, though, upped Jinnah's ante. Gandhi wanted Jinnah to formally invite Khan Abdul Ghaffar Khan and that too in writing, as the Pathan leader was 'most distrustful of Jinnah.' Jinnah retorted that he had no intention of sending a written invitation to Khan Abdul Ghaffar Khan; at best a verbal invitation could be extended. After this quarrel had gone on long, Mountbatten himself offered to invite all concerned the same evening. To this, they agreed. Unfortunately, Khan Abdul Ghaffar Khan, who had an engagement a hundred miles outside Delhi, could not make it on time for the meeting. The meeting was postponed for the next day and took place at the Viceroy's house. Ismay presided over the meeting in the absence of Mountbatten.

Ismay, Mieville, Gandhi, Jinnah and Khan Abdul Ghaffar Khan met at the Viceroy's residence at 4.30 p.m. on 18 June 1947. Nothing much came out of this meeting too, what with Gandhi and Jinnah standing on formalities and sparring as usual. Jinnah opened the discussion by extending a verbal invitation to Khan Abdul Ghaffar Khan to come to his residence. Gandhi intervened, trying to hustle Jinnah into having a meeting there and then. Not one to be pushed, Jinnah reminded Gandhi of what they had decided earlier. Gandhi continued to insist on an immediate dialogue between Khan Abdul Ghaffar Khan and Jinnah, suggesting that he and the others withdraw to another room leaving Jinnah and Khan Abdul Ghaffar Khan alone. But Jinnah did not concede. It was finally agreed that Khan Abdul Ghaffar Khan call on Jinnah at his residence later in the day, at 7.30 p.m. The minutes of the meeting dishearten and exasperate a little: 'having agreed…they all went away in the best of tempers!' Gandhi clearly displayed desperation and anxiety in trying for a rapprochement between Jinnah and Khan Abdul Ghaffar Khan. Even at the best of times it was impossible to coerce Jinnah. Why would Jinnah care much about this meeting? The partition plan of 3 June had virtually ensured that the NWFP would opt for Pakistan. As it turned out, the evening meeting between Jinnah and Khan Abdul Ghaffar Khan was not successful. Since the referendum did not provide a separate option for Pathanistan, Khan Abdul Ghaffar Khan and the Khudai Khidmatgars decided to boycott it. Mountbatten was relieved that the Congress (that is, Nehru) had agreed not to revisit the issue of a referendum.

Reconciliation efforts between the Khan brothers and Jinnah continued till the end of July. Governor Rob Lockhart also mediated, communicating to Jinnah the amended terms of the agreement that

Khan Abdul Ghaffar Khan offered. The referendum's results had been one-sided, in favour of Pakistan. As expected, on 25 July Jinnah disclosed to Lockhart his inability to meet Khan Abdul Ghaffar Khan to discuss the offer. He conveniently revealed that only the Constituent Assembly of Pakistan, which was to frame the Constitution for the Pakistan Federation could deal with it later. And that no purpose would be served in meeting Khan Abdul Ghaffar Khan at this late stage. As he contended, 'It was obvious that he could not discuss with any section or party over the head of the Constituent Assembly.' Besides, he thought, he had no power to commit the Constituent Assembly in advance or anticipate its final decisions.

A decision by the Khudai Khidmatgars to boycott the referendum meant a walkover for the Muslim League in the NWFP. Jinnah kept exhorting the Pathans that their abstention from the referendum would constitute a breach of its terms. On the other hand, non-Muslims were threatened with dire consequences if they voted. That Jinnah's advocacy did not apply in the case of the non-Muslims of the province was a matter of politics. Jinnah was opposed to the idea of a free Pathan state and, therefore, had not agreed to a third option in the referendum. If a separate Constituent Assembly for the NWFP came into being, it would place the province in a strong bargaining position vis-à-vis Pakistan. There were bright prospects of the new Pathan Constituent Assembly independently coming to terms with India. The much-touted argument that West Punjab would come between Pathanistan and India could not hinder the process. If East and West Pakistan were to form one unit, why not Pathanistan and India? Some Muslim League leaders of the NWFP were none too unwilling to work out a coalition ministry with the Frontier Congress on the basis of 'Independent Pathanistan.' According to the Governor of the NWFP, 'Too many advocates of Pathanistan were sincere and some of Jinnah's local supporters were not without sympathy for this idea.' Jinnah's hold over the NWFP was at best precarious. It was crucial therefore that the Government of Pakistan quickly stamp out the 'Pathan' issue. As the Governor General, Jinnah could amend the 1935 Act relating to the provincial legislature, abolish the large weightage given to the minorities and ensure the Muslim League's majority. The position of the Governor Generalship of Pakistan would provide Jinnah with just such needed power at this juncture. As president of the All India Muslim League, that power would always elude him.

On 2 July, Jinnah finally informed Mountbatten of his intention to become Pakistan's first Governor General. Mountbatten stood opposed to the Government of Pakistan being invested with the power to order the provincial Governor to dismiss his ministry. But he could not prevent it from happening. This was Section 93 coming into force with a vengeance. It was intended as a means of ousting the Congress ministry in the NWFP. That it was put into immediate effect is part of history now.

Within a week of making his intention clear on the Governor Generalship, Jinnah sent his nominations for the Governors of Pakistan to the Viceroy. He formally asked Mountbatten to nominate Sir George Cunningham as the Governor of the NWFP. Mountbatten immediately recommended Cunningham's name to the Secretary of State for India. What needs to be noted here is the process of referendum that got initiated in the NWFP on 6 July. Why were Jinnah's recommendations for the Governors on the Viceroy's table so soon, by 9 July, losing no time in forwarding Cunningham's name to London? Propriety demanded that Jinnah wait till the process of the referendum was complete before nominating Cunningham. That the NWFP would join Pakistan had become a foregone conclusion for the British and to the Muslim League. The Congress had surrendered. Its leaders did not object to this much obvious and brazen breach of protocol.

To Weightman, Foreign Secretary, Government of India, Jinnah offered the governorship of Baluchistan. When asked by the Secretary of State for India to accept this position, Weightman was none too complimentary in his remarks about Jinnah while declining the offer:

> I know Jinnah fairly well and I know Baluchistan and its people intimately. I know too that these people have little regard for Jinnah and the League and that they would look upon me as an old friend whom they would expect to 'protect' them from Jinnah and his henchmen. I dare say it would be easy enough to steer a middle course but it would be vastly unpleasant and a possibility of a real bad misunderstanding would be always present. That however is not the main difficulty. If I had to serve in India I

would frankly prefer to serve Nehru rather than Jinnah...
I feel that he [Nehru] would regard my acceptance of a post in
Pakistan as a crude piece of chicanery and, unimportant as
that may be in the larger issues which the Viceroy visualizes, it
would quite certainly offset any advantage that there might be
in my accepting Jinnah's offer.

Weightman was India's Foreign Secretary while Nehru officiated as member, external affairs, in the interim government. Some amount of loyalty towards Nehru was, therefore, expected from Weightman. But for Jinnah to offer the post of governorship of Baluchistan to Weightman, already knowing of Weightman's cordial relations with Nehru, speaks well of Jinnah's generosity too.

The referendum's results were to be formally announced on 21 July. Mountbatten was curious to know what was on Jinnah's mind. Jinnah on his part, favoured dismissal of the ministry and assumption of power by the Governor. But Mountbatten did not want the Governor to assume power at such a late stage, expecting accusing fingers to be raised if it happened. Surprisingly though, both Jinnah and Mountbatten had reservations about installing a Muslim League ministry after dismissing Dr Khan Saheb's. In the absence of a Muslim League majority in the provincial legislature, Jinnah well understood the difficulty in appointing a Muslim League Chief Minister. To put Jinnah's mind at rest, Mountbatten quite cleverly suggested a way out of this dilemma—the legislature was yet to be called to session, and not due for long in the near future. And after 15 August 1947, instruction if needed, could be sought from the Pakistan Constituent Assembly, the legislature of Pakistan (Dominion). The way events during those crucial days took place give the impression of being somewhat contrived. Jinnah was not naïve. He was a lawyer and a politician with a lifetime of experience. He well realized the consequences of installing a Muslim League ministry that lacked majority support in the provincial legislature. He was also well aware that no likelihood existed of the legislature being called to session in the near future. Jinnah was not any better informed even after Mountbatten explained the implications to him.

Mountbatten decided not to dismiss Dr Khan Saheb's ministry even if he refused to resign, and would only do so on the advice of the Pakistan cabinet. Usually not averse to patting his own back, Mountbatten commented: 'How fortunate it was for Jinnah that he [Mountbatten] intended to form such a body [the Pakistan Cabinet] on 18 July, since otherwise Jinnah may well find Dr Khan Saheb's ministry remaining in power until the 15 August, 1947.' Instead, it was Mountbatten who appeared willing to dismiss the Congress ministry if the interim Government of Pakistan said so.

It was 15 July and Jinnah, according to Mountbatten, was still demurring on the issue of constituting an interim Government of Pakistan. When asked to consider forming the cabinet as an executive order from the Viceroy, Jinnah relented. Mountbatten wanted the Pakistan cabinet to convene for a special purpose. A fall-back option was necessary in case Dr Khan Saheb's government refused to resign after having lost the referendum to Muslim League. The onus of taking any decision in this regard could then lie with the Pakistan cabinet.

Mountbatten held a meeting with Jinnah to decide on the future course of action. The results of the referendum had been declared by then. In the meeting Jinnah referred to some past precedents when, for example, in Bombay and Punjab minority parties had been called to form ministries. In the eventuality of the minority League ministry taking office, he did not want the legislative assembly to be summoned. He also wanted to avoid the assumption of power under Section 93 by the Governor. The only feasible step was to again ask Dr Khan Saheb to resign, and if he refused, to dismiss him and form an interim ministry of the next largest party (the Muslim League). He suggested that a ministry of three could be formed to begin with. Possibly later, the fourth place could be offered to a Hindu. In Jinnah's opinion, the Hindus would be the first to support such a new ministry.

Jinnah was neither in favour of dissolving the legislative assembly nor calling it to session until the budget session of March 1948. He believed there was no need to convene the legislature for choosing a successor to Maulana Abul Kalam Azad, who had resigned from the membership of the Constituent Assembly. He also did not want any election. He was in fact confident that the soon-to-be-installed Muslim League ministry, given sufficient time, would be able to cobble up a majority in the legislature. That is precisely what happened. In his meeting of 29 July with Mountbatten, what Jinnah was suggesting was clearly not in accordance with constitutional propriety. And Mountbatten, unfortunately, had decided to concur with Jinnah.

Sardar Vallabhbhai Patel was not in favour of any drastic action against the present NWFP ministry till the date of partition. He told Mountbatten on 2 August to postpone action till 15 August. Jinnah, on the other hand, was extremely keen that immediate action be taken, preferably before the arrival of Sir George Cunningham. Jinnah feared that the present ministry, in a desperate act, could sabotage the position of the NWFP vis-à-vis Pakistan.

Before leaving for Pakistan on the Viceroy's aircraft on 7 August, Jinnah and Liaquat Ali Khan asked Mountbatten what he proposed to do in the NWFP. Both the Pakistan leaders sounded worried about the impending rumours that Dr Khan Saheb intended to declare the NWFP as 'Pathanistan' on the morning of 15 August if he was still in power. Mountbatten continued to maintain that he had referred the matter to London and was waiting to hear from the Secretary of State for India, and that he did not wish to act in any unconstitutional manner till he heard from him. Mountbatten also told Jinnah that he had no supporting evidence to believe that Dr Khan Saheb was planning to declare the NWFP as 'Pathanistan.' To quote Mountbatten:

> I told them [Jinnah and Liaquat Ali Khan] that I had it in mind to tell Lockhart to call on the ministry to resign on the 11 August and that if they failed to do so to dismiss them on the 12 August. The new Governor, Cunningham (who was of course Governor up to 1945) is seeing Jinnah in Karachi on 11 August, and Mountbatten in Delhi on the 12 August, and arrives in Peshawar on the evening of the 12 August. He will be sworn in on the morning of the 13 August and his first act can be to form a new Ministry in accordance with Jinnah's instructions in anticipation of the transfer of power on August 15. This proposal had been telegraphed to the Secretary of State for approval. Jinnah did not like this delay, but finally shrugged his shoulders and said 'I am in your hands in this matter.'

Dr Khan Saheb's government, as we all know, lasted for a week after Jinnah became the Governor General of Pakistan. It was dismissed by Jinnah on 22 August 1947.

## Notes

1. The Khilafat movement (1919-24) was a political campaign launched mainly by Muslims in South Asia to influence the British government and to protect the Ottoman empire during the aftermath of World War I.
2. The Government of India Act, 1935, was the last pre-independence regulation of the British Raj which granted Indian provinces autonomy and ended the dyarchy introduced by the Government of India Act 1919. It also provided for the establishment of an Indian Federation. Direct elections were introduced for the first time and the right to vote was increased from 7 million people to 35 million people. But Governors retained discretionary powers regarding summoning of legislatures, giving assent to bills and administering certain special regions (mostly tribal). The federal part of the act was never introduced due to strong opposition from rulers of princely states. In 1937, the first set of elections under this act was held.
3. The Legislative Assembly Debates, 16 February 1926, pp.1296-1344 and 18 March 1926, pp.2713-45. Available in the Parliament Library, New Delhi.
4. The Swaraj Party was a political party in India which was formed by Indian politicians and members of the Indian National Congress who had opposed Mahatma Gandhi's suspension of all civil resistance in 1922 in response to the Chauri Chaura tragedy where policemen were killed by a mob of protestors. In December 1922, Chittaranjan Das, N.C. Kelker and Motilal Nehru formed the Congress-Khilafat Swarajaya Party with Das as the president and Nehru as one of the secretaries. Other prominent leaders included Huseyn Shaheed Suhrawardy of Bengal, Vithalbhai Patel and other Congress leaders who were becoming dissatisfied with the Congress. The other group was the 'No-Changers' who had accepted Gandhi's decision to withdraw the movement. With the death of Chittaranjan Das in 1925, and with Motilal Nehru's return to the Congress the following year, the Swaraj Party was greatly weakened.
5. The Legislative Assembly Debates, 16 February 1926, p.1297. Available in the Parliament Library, New Delhi.
6. Madan Mohan Malaviya (1861-1946) was an Indian politician, notable for his role in the freedom struggle and his espousal of Hindu nationalism. He later established the Banaras Hindu University.

7. The Legislative Assembly Debates, 16 February 1926, p.2740. Available in the Parliament Library, New Delhi.
8. Ibid., p.2741.
9. Ibid., p.2742.
10. Legislative Assembly Debates, 14 March 1928, General Budget, List of Demands, p.1461. Available in the Parliament Library, New Delhi.
11. Ibid., p.1462.
12. Bhulabhai Desai (1877–1946) was an Indian freedom fighter and acclaimed lawyer. He is well remembered for his defence of the three Indian National Army soldiers accused of treason during World War II and for attempting to negotiate a secret power-sharing agreement with Liaquat Ali Khan of the Muslim League.
13. Mohammad Yunus worked with Khan Abdul Ghaffar Khan from 1936 to August 1947. He was imprisoned during the Quit India movement and again in Kashmir in 1946. Unlike his fellow Pakhtun colleagues in the Congress party, he elected to stay on in the new post-partition Indian union rather than relocate to the NWFP in the new nation of Pakistan.
14. Cunningham to Linlithgow, 12 November 1939, L/P&J/5/215, India Office Library, London (IOL).
15. Cunningham to Linlithgow, 9 April 1941, L/P&J/5/218, p.107, IOL.
16. Ibid.
17. Linlithgow to Cunningham, 16 March 1940, Mss.eur.F.125/75, pp.7–8, IOL.
18. A.K. Fazlul Haq, Huseyn Shaheed Suhrawardy and Khwaja Nazimuddin constituted a trio that occupied a central place in shaping Bengali politics in the first half of the twentieth century. Very different from each other, they contested each other and fought fierce political battles against each other.

In 1927, Fazlul Haq established the Krishak Proja Party, a rural-based political organization. Acknowledging his place in Bengali politics, Haq was invited to the Round Table Conference held in London between 1930 and 1932. In 1935–36, Fazlul Haq served as the mayor of Calcutta.

Khwaja Nazimuddin was an ardent and loyal supporter of Jinnah's. When Jinnah came to Calcutta in 1936 he entrusted Khwaja Nazimuddin with the responsibility of organizing the Muslim League by bringing together the different groups and individuals under one banner. Khwaja Nazimuddin was the Home Minister in the cabinet of A.K. Fazlul Haq's coalition government from 1937 to 1941 and the Chief Minister of undivided Bengal from 1943 to 1945. He was made a member of the working committee of the Muslim League, and his influence within the League grew in the following years.

Suhrawardy started his career as an ally of the famous Swarajist leader C.R. Das. He served as a member of the Bengal legislative council after 1924. The Khilafat movement provided him a wider platform to reach out to the masses. On the national stage, he made his debut when he served as the chairman of the reception committee of the All Parties Conference. In 1936, he established the United Muslim Party (UMP). The party was later merged with the Muslim League on Jinnah's proposition and on the understanding that the UMP would in fact become the Muslim League party of Bengal. Suhrawardy was elected the secretary of the Bengal Muslim League. Post-1935 Bengal increased the political stakes of each of the three leaders.

Though in the 1937 elections, Congress emerged as the single largest party, it was not in a position to form a ministry on its own or even to strike alliances with other groups to achieve that end. The Muslim League and Fazlul Haq's Krishak Proja Party struck a deal with the result that Haq got an opportunity to lead a coalition ministry. But as the Muslim League had more members in the assembly as compared to the Krishak Proja Party, Fazlul Haq depended on the League's support.

19. Khan Bahadur Allah Bux Soomro was a politician from Sindh, Pakistan. He was Chief Minister of Sindh for two separate terms: from 23 March 1938 to 18 April 1940 and from 7 March 1941 to 14 October 1942.
20. Cunningham to Linlithgow, 8/24 August 1941, L/P&J/5/218, pp.69/63, IOL.
21. Dow to Linlithgow, 12 December 1941, L/P&J/5/257, and 29 January 1942, L/P&J/5/258, IOL.
22. Cunningham to Linlithgow, 23 September 1942, L/P&J/5/219, IOL.
23. Cunningham to Linlithgow, 9 August 1943, L/P&J/5/220, p.59, IOL.
24. Special message conveyed through Nawab Mohammad Ismail Khan Saheb to the Muslims of the NWFP on the eve of the bye-elections to the provincial assembly, 20 July 1943.
25. GR, 8 December 1945, MSS.EUR, D 670/16, IOL.
26. 'Sarhad' in Urdu means 'frontier'; so 'Sarhad Musalmans' means 'Frontier Muslims'.

27. Speech at the Frontier Muslim League Conference, Peshawar, 21 November 1945.
28. Ibid., 21 November 1945.
29. Ibid.
30. The Ali brothers were Maulana Mohammad Ali and Maulana Shaukat Ali who were at the helm of affairs during the Khilafat movement in India.
31. Speech at the Frontier Muslil League Conference, Peshawar, 21 November 1945.
32. Ibid.
33. Humayun Mirza, *From Plassey to Pakistan—The Family History of Iskander Mirza, The First President of Pakistan*, University Press of America Inc., 1999, pp.151–52.
34. First Series, Vol. I, Part I, Jinnah Papers, undated, February 1947, pp.143–44, F.895/242–44.
35. Haji Sahib Turangzai led a successful battle against the British from the area presently known as the Mohmand Tribal Area (Mohmand Agency).
36. First Series, Vol. I, Part I, Jinnah Papers, pp.651–52, F.917/149–51.
37. Viceroy's Seventh Miscellaneous Meeting, Mountbatten Papers, 23 April 1947, 203, p.378-379, *The Transfer of Power*, Vol. X.
38. *The Transfer of Power*, April 1947, Vol. X, p.465.
39. Interview, Mountbatten, Jinnah and Liaquat Ali Khan, Mountbatten Papers, Viceroy's Interview No 112 of 2 May 1947, *The Transfer of Power*, 1947, Vol. X, pp.566–69.
40. Ibid.
41. Viceroy's Twenty Fifth Staff Meeting, 3 May 1947, *The Transfer of Power*, Vol. X, pp.579–83.
42. Sir Eric Charles Mieville (1896–1943), assistant private secretary to the King and a colonial civil servant.

## 15

# An Epoch, an Episode and an Epitaph: Britain, Afghanistan and the NWFP

HAVING PERSEVERED IN maintaining relations with Persia, Germany was soon to become involved in the affairs of Afghanistan. Despite the failure of the Turko-German mission of 1915 to Afghanistan, Germany continued promoting commercial interests and arms supplies to Afghanistan. Germany was well set geo-politically before World War II to participate as an additional power in the great game. Afghanistan was now to contend with the Soviet Union and Germany on one side and Great Britain on the other. As for Great Britain, Germany was an added threat to an already existing one—the Soviet Union.

During the inter-war years, the Government of India developed several plans to deal with the Soviet peril—the Blue plan of 1927 (which centred on traditional British advances to Kabul from the two railheads on the India–Afghanistan border), replaced in 1931 by a Pink plan, less ambitious and only limited to advances up to Jalalabad and Kandahar in case the Afghans sided with the Soviet Union, and finally, an interim plan, developed in 1939 just before the war in Europe broke out—the Nazi–Soviet (Molotov–Ribbentrop) Pact.[1] This reduced the burden of the Soviets' plan to attack north Afghanistan, as plans were made to restore the former Amir, Amanullah, through German assistance. Soon after this pact, Britain went to war with Germany.

The threat of a Soviet invasion of Afghanistan increased drastically after 17 September 1939, when the Red Army joined the Wehrmacht[2] in the liquidation of the Polish state. At this stage, the Germans claimed that their allies would receive portions of the British empire as a reward in the event of their victory. In the case of Afghanistan, this was to include large parts of north-west India along the Indus river and the port of Karachi. As the British rightly assessed, India lay completely at the mercy of an air attack from Russia. They just had one anti-aircraft battery and no fighter planes, whereas the Afghan defence consisted of just forty anti-aircraft guns. In the absence of trained personnel, their defensive value could not be rated high. It was entirely within the realm of possibility that the Russians could mount an air attack on Turkestan and assemble 400 aircrafts, of which two-thirds would be modern bombers at aerodromes close to the Afghan border. Prospects of reinforcement from the German Luftwaffe[3] were feasible.

In the midst of all this, Soviet Union invaded Finland on 30 November. Fraser-Tytler,[4] the British minister in Kabul, repeatedly warned how the Soviet invasion of Afghanistan could seriously prejudice the British position in the eyes of the Muslims in the Middle East and India in case Britain refused to intervene. George Cunningham, the Governor of the NWFP, on his part expected the 'pro-British' tribes to participate in the war with the 'godless' Russians. But the Viceroy was hesitant, as he feared a coup d'état in Afghanistan, a far more imminent prospect than the Soviet invasion. It was very likely then that the tribal forces would march to Kabul, not in support, but against the present government and in favour of the deposed Amir Amanullah. The news of German successes against Norway and Holland continued to cause much trepidation among British Indian officials. Then France fell to the Germans. By the end of June 1940, the Afghans came to realize that the war had reached their doorstep and chances of the British empire disintegrating were high. For the moment the Soviet threat faded, replaced by an impending German invasion. The temptation to jump on the Axis bandwagon was strong for the weak Afghan government. It was a public secret that the Afghan government would be rewarded by the Germans with a large slice of India's frontier if they stirred up trouble for India. The German minister in Kabul had confidently announced that 'by the middle of August 1940, Hitler would be in London'. The Afghans recognized that if the British empire went, Afghanistan with its present political system would go with it. As 1940 progressed, the Russian threat to Afghanistan diminished.

The Soviets were now increasingly being drawn into European affairs. Their bargaining power vis-à-vis Germany had fast declined after the fall of France.

A plan to restore Amanullah to the Amirship of Afghanistan had been hatched in Berlin immediately after Britain declared war on Germany, the plan originating in the German foreign office. This represented a double threat to British India since the restoration of the former Amir was conceived as a joint Nazi–Soviet venture coupled with a political coup in Afghanistan to remove the pro-British Afghan government. Widespread rumours circulated in the NWFP of Amanullah's expected return to Afghanistan by air from the Soviet Union. In lieu of the Soviet guarantee of Afghan annexation of the NWFP, Afghan Turkestan was to be ceded to the Soviets. Olaf Caroe, Foreign Secretary to the Government of India, summed up the situation thus:

> There can be little doubt that the Germans will seize any opportunity that may present itself of upsetting the present regime in Afghanistan. There is, moreover, much to be said for the view that the Middle East, and particularly Afghanistan, is probably the field on which German and Russian interests at the present time must nearly coincide. And in spite of the preoccupation in Finland and elsewhere where they are engaged, it would not be difficult to stage a Russian coup in Afghan Turkestan under cover of an Amanist pretender or a puppet government.

Luckily for Britain, Hitler decided to abort the Amanullah plan in the last days of 1939. Fortunately, Afghanistan, unlike Poland and Finland, was saved from proving to be yet another test case of the British guarantee. Afghanistan, which had a common frontier with British India, was regarded as an integral part of India's defence. There could be no possible British excuse for failing to come to Afghanistan's rescue for geographical reasons as Britain had so often pleaded in the cases of Poland, Czechoslovakia and Finland.

Thanks to George Cunningham's astute policy, the NWFP remained peaceful. Even when the Soviet, and then the German threat was real, the Afghan government had not departed from its policy of friendship with Britain. But soon enough another threat, that of a Japanese invasion of India, began materializing along with a realization that Britain alone may not be able to withhold the invasion. Hence the United States should intervene by extending lease and lend facilities to Afghanistan. The Afghan government was impatient to convey its concerns to Washington. To the British, the situation in Afghanistan was revealing itself to be fluid, with its southern and eastern provinces susceptible to intrigues as a result of Axis propaganda. Governor downwards, British officials in the NWFP unleashed local religious elements on the populace, an effective propaganda tool, that on the one hand brought pecuniary gains to the mullahs and on the other, engendered anti-German, anti-Japanese (and therefore pro-British) sentiments. British officials also encouraged the feeling that the provincial government ruled by the Congress was Hindu-dominated, in the hope that the Afghan government would reorient policies once it found that the future Indian government was unable to maintain a balance of power between Russia, India and Afghanistan, the way the British had been able to do. They also drew comfort from Afghan concerns that the tribes on the Indian side of the Durand Line were soon to come under the control of the so-called 'Hindu-dominated' Government of India.

Like the Soviet and the German, the Japanese threat of invasion receded too. The British policy on India's NWF proved remarkably successful during the war years. The Afghan government held on while the tribes on both sides of the Durand Line remained generally at peace. But during the war, the British frequently and quite deliberately chose to mention Afghan concerns about their treaty obligations. They wanted it reviewed once it became clear that the transfer of power would take place soon.[5] In this eventuality, the Afghan government wanted to lay claim to those parts of India which earlier belonged to Afghanistan and whose inhabitants were of Afghan origin—the Pushtu-speaking areas of the NWFP (west of the Indus), including the Agencies and tribal areas and parts of Baluchistan ceded to the British by the Treaty of Gandmak,[6] 1879 (Aitchison 1933: 240–42).

It suited the British to interpret the claim as an Afghan wish to not allow the Afghan territories acquired by the British to go to a country dominated by a Hindu government. The pretext was that the Afghan government considered the Indians incapable of preventing the descent of the NWFP into chaos once the British left. Its logical corollary was that unless Britain intended to retain these territories, they should give the local people the option of self-determination before incorporating them in an independent India. Afghanistan, for its part, had suggested two alternatives—either the areas voluntarily join Afghanistan, or they be constituted as a separate and independent Pathan state. The Afghan government thought the second option more workable.

On 22 March 1947, when Mountbatten took over the Indian viceroyalty, the British cabinet (the India and Burma Committee) circulated a memorandum on the possible course of action to be taken with respect to the tribal areas of the NWFP. The implication of the British Prime Minister's announcement on 20 February 1947 that Britain shall withdraw from India not later than June 1948, needed to be explained to the countries bordering India. Plus, there were treaty obligations that had since long governed relations between British India and Afghanistan. To whom would these obligations devolve was a question on which Britain had as yet remained evasive. Then there was the business of the future of the tribal areas which Afghanistan was now claiming for itself. These matters had suddenly assumed urgency in the aftermath of the Prime Minister's declaration. Earlier, Wavell had thought of resolving the issues in consultation with the interim government, but he intentionally decided to keep them pending until HMG resolved whom to transfer the power to. Was it to be to India— one country—or to India and Pakistan?[7]

Sir Giles Squire, in-charge of the British Legation at Kabul, had already written to the Foreign Secretary in Delhi about the anxiety caused within the Afghan government on the issue of tribal territory. Having met the Afghan Foreign Minister and the Prime Minister, he was prompt in conveying their views to the Foreign Secretary that the tribes should either be given the option of complete independence or joining Afghanistan. Sir Giles Squire believed that the Afghan government was constrained in approaching the Pathans living east of the Durand Line because it was a separate country. The fact that the Congress and the Muslim League were already visiting the tribal areas to secure adherence was also objectionable to the Afghan government.

Considerable confusion prevailed at this stage. Instead of unambiguously asking the Afghan government not to meddle in India's affairs, Sir Giles Squire chose to cloud matters by telling the Afghans that his government did not wish to put obstacles in the way of a reasonable presentation of the Afghan case. He felt that the Afghan authorities were under considerable pressure from their own people, with several tribes complaining that their government was giving them no lead or advice in matters of their political future. Afghan authorities, therefore, could no longer afford to keep aloof. Under pressure, they could be forced to privately invite the tribal leaders to Kabul or send secret emissaries to the tribes east of the Durand Line to advise them on 'the Afghan point of view'. The Prime Minister of Afghanistan was, however, reluctant to take action behind the Indian government's back. Sir Giles Squire preferred and therefore suggested that the Afghan emissaries be invited by the Government of India. To this end, he encouraged Afghan authorities to send a formal proposal to the Indian government.

Delhi found it inconvenient to accept the Afghan point of view. It responded by explaining that ever since the Durand Agreement of 1893, all territory including the tribal areas on the Indian side of the Durand Line had formed part of British India. The fact that there was an interim government in India did not alter that position. This matter had had a long history and Afghan attempts to interfere in India's tribal areas had always been strenuously resisted. This position, Delhi considered, was to be maintained so long as the Afghans continued to recognize the Durand Line as the boundary between India and Afghanistan. Delhi took it that there was no intention on their part to denounce it. It was irrelevant for Delhi whether or not the Afghan government was under pressure from its own subjects. The Indian government remained sceptical of the Afghan Prime Minister's statement that their tribes were looking to the Afghan government for a lead. Delhi's information indicated that the tribes were indifferent to Afghan interest in the problem of their future and intended to rely more on themselves when it came to deciding on their association with an independent Indian government. This issue, the Afghan government well knew, was one for negotiations between the tribes and the Constituent Assembly. Nehru had made it amply clear in his public declarations that there was no intention of depriving the tribes of their existing freedom or of attempting to impose any scheme on them against their will. Afghan anxiety, Delhi felt, was therefore misplaced.

Sir Giles Squire was asked to speak to the Foreign Minister or the Prime Minister of Afghanistan on these lines if the subject was brought up again. It was to be made clear that the Government of India could not possibly countenance any interference in the tribal areas by emissaries of the Afghan government. But that did not imply that the Government of India[8] refused to recognize the Afghan government's 'lively interest' in seeing a satisfactory arrangement emerge from the discussions with the tribes and the Government of India. Giles conveyed these views to the Afghan Foreign Minister who received them with considerable disappointment.[9]

HMG's 3 June partition plan, when deciding on a referendum in the NWFP, offered only two choices—to either join the old Union of India or Pakistan. The option of an independent Pathanistan was refused. The Afghan media, audio-visual and print, uniformly expressed dissatisfaction over this British refusal. It called for the matter to be referred to the United Nations. More with an idea to humour the Afghan authorities, Sir Giles Squire made efforts to explain that the Pathans of the tribal areas were 'entirely free to negotiate a new agreement with India and that freedom included the freedom not to negotiate'. At the same time he also pleaded the Afghan case with the Secretary of State for India for allowing the Afghan government to declare that the NWFP should not be coerced into joining Pakistan or Hindustan. 'Perhaps I could at least say that his Majesty's Government will not use compulsion', was how he ended his letter of 11 June to the Secretary. On the same day, the Afghan Foreign Minister called on the Secretary at the India Office in London. The purpose was to reiterate the Afghan position of either allowing the territory to rejoin Afghanistan or forming a separate state. The claim, argued the Afghan Foreign Minister, was based on ethnological considerations. Strangely, the Afghan request was not refused as unequivocally as the Government of India had earlier indicated to Sir Giles Squire in Kabul. Instead, the Afghan minister was asked to submit a note setting out in detail his government's proposals. He was assured that due consideration would be given by HMG to Afghanistan's request.[10]

The proposal detailing the Afghan position on the future of the NWFP was delivered to the Secretary of State on 13 June. It listed out all previous discussions that the Afghan Foreign Minister had

had with HMG between 1944–46 on the Frontier question. To the Afghans, British annexation of their territory had been an act of arbitrary dismemberment of their country. The note claimed that connections between the Afghans of the NWFP and India were at best artificial and that for the last ten years, it had always been their stated position that in the event of any change in India's status, the future of Afghans within the Indian boundary was not to be neglected and the obligations created by the Anglo-Afghan treaties with respect to these territories were no longer to be binding in the future. Now that the future of India was being settled, it was imminent that the future of the NWFP be discussed as it could not be left in the hands of the new governments shortly to come into being. The decision to hold a referendum, therefore, was not compatible with justice, as it debarred the NWFP from either opting for independence or rejoining its motherland, Afghanistan. The Afghan government could not be indifferent to any decision contrary to justice and to the freedom of the Afghans in the NWFP.

The Secretary of State asked for the note to be examined before responding to it. He also wanted the Government of India to apprise him of its views. Meanwhile, Sir Giles Squire was summoned by the Afghan Foreign Minister on 23 June. Informing Sir Giles that it was not proper to consult the Russian embassy or the American Legation as the 'matter was purely one for friendly settlement with HMG and the Government of India', the Foreign Minister stated his government's wish to send an urgent mission to India to 'inform themselves of the feelings' that prevailed in the NWFP. The mission intended meeting Indian political leaders, both in Delhi and in Peshawar. The Afghan Foreign Minister hoped that the Viceroy would also meet the Afghan mission. Convenience was to be obtained immediately from the Government of India about the dates as well as to ascertain whether the visit was to be official, semi-official or purely private. He impressed upon Sir Giles Squire the urgency of formalizing this visit as he wanted it to happen within a week of this request.[11]

The Afghan government realized that its only chance lay in getting HMG to change its decision on the issue of a referendum in the NWFP; hence the request for an immediate announcement on its part that the Pathans should be free to choose independence. The Afghans hoped for an early British response, well before the referendum took place. Sir Giles Squire was worried about 'unpredictable' developments in case the Afghan request was refused. According to him, the 'Afghan government's instigation' had already caused such publicity and excitement, that if their representation failed, it would be difficult to placate heightened public opinion. Sir Giles Squire hoped that his government would agree to refer the case to the United Nations and give an assurance for it. The tribes on the Indian side could at the same time be asked to remain aloof or be left free to act as the Government of India thought fit. The Afghan Foreign Minister was anxious and ready to leave for India on urgent immediate consultations.[12]

The media campaign that raged in Afghanistan had been officially inspired. The Afghan government was openly asserting its claim over the NWFP. In a meeting on 19 June with the Indian Ambassador at Nanking, the Afghan Minister made it clear that his country expected recompense for 'all the wrongs done to her in the last century' now that the British were finally going to withdraw from India. Though the minister did not explain the nature of 'recompense', he thought that the Afghanistan government could insist on an outlet to the sea. In earlier consultations, Afghan authorities had remained vague on the territorial scope of Afghan interest. That vagueness was now gone. They specifically stated that the whole area between the Durand Line and the Indus should become Afghan territory.

The British responded by threatening Afghanistan with the cessation of aid if the Afghans persisted with their claims on the NWFP. The Afghans were reminded of the danger that still lurked on their northern boundaries. Alongside, the Americans were asked to send an informal warning to Afghan authorities against their policy of 'adventure'. The Government of India counter-argued that the historical basis on which Kabul claimed a special interest in India, if stretched, could also justify India's claim on Afghanistan. Things had to be dealt with 'as they were' and not 'as they were in some less or more distant past'. Delhi, therefore, recommended to the India Office in London that it should categorically reject the idea of receiving a mission from Kabul. A free state could also not be conceded to the people of this territory (tribal areas). The fact that two sovereign states were being created out of one could not dilute the strategic importance of the territory. Changes in India's political status could not alter geographical factors of strategic significance.[13]

After receiving the report from Delhi on 1 July, the Secretary of State reverted directly to Sir Giles Squire to say that nothing much could be done now that the partition plan of 3 June had been endorsed by all major political parties in India. Despite the blood ties and religious affinity that the Afghans shared with the people of tribal areas, the Afghan government's right to intervene in India's internal matters could not be admitted as it was not in consonance with an article of the Treaty of 1921 concluded between Britain and Afghanistan.[14] The Afghan Minister in London was also told not to press claims on territories that formed an integral part of India. In India too, Nehru, the external affairs member in the Viceroy's council, refuted the Afghan claim.[15] On 5 July, the Foreign Office in London accordingly handed over to the Afghan chargés d'affaires, an aide-memoire in reply to the Afghan representation. Sir Giles Squire in Kabul also received instructions to communicate with the Afghan government on similar lines. The basis of British response was the Anglo-Afghan Treaty of 1921.[16]

As instructed by the Foreign Office, Sir Giles Squire called on the Afghan Foreign Minister to convey the HMG's position on Afghan claims over the NWFP. The response it evoked from the Afghan Foreign Minister was predictable. Violently disagreeing, the Foreign Minister referred to the three Afghan wars, disputing that it was not the Indian government but the British who had seized Afghan territories and the transfer of those territories to India now was an arbitrary act. The referendum, under present limitations, was bound to lead to 'absorption of Afghans of NWFP under alien rule' which was not acceptable, something that would inevitably leave a legacy of disagreement between the Afghans and whichever government came to be responsible for the area. In reply, Sir Giles Squire reiterated that 'any further appeal to the HMG to change its course would be treated as an act of stubbornness and would not be viewed in positive light by the HMG'.[17]

Sir Giles Squire also met the Afghan Prime Minister to impress upon him the harm being caused by the press and radio campaign which the British and Indian governments believed had been encouraged by Afghan authorities. Not denying the charges, the Afghan

Prime Minister explained that circumstances compelled him to allow young Afghan elements certain latitude. But he was ready to heed to the British minister's advice and would immediately discontinue this propaganda and bring in moderation in the press campaign.[18]

Assuming that the NWFP referendum went in favour of Pakistan, Sir Giles Squire advised the Afghan Prime Minister to meet Jinnah rather than insist on current claims of Afghanistan to find a mutually agreeable solution.

The Afghan Prime Minister expressed his disappointment at the refusal of the Indian government to receive his proposed mission. To mollify him, Sir Giles Squire said that the Prime Minister could certainly visit Delhi provided his attitude was reasonable. He recommended this visit to the Government of India as it would provide for the withdrawal of Afghan claims without much loss of face for the Afghan authorities. He thought it beneficial too if Jinnah and the Viceroy could meet the Afghan Prime Minister, in case his visit to Delhi materialized.[19]

What had worried Sir Giles Squire was the reluctance of the American minister and his state department to intervene or tender any advice to the Afghan government on this issue. Instead they appeared to suggest that an Afghan emissary be sent to Delhi to discuss the matter with the Viceroy. In a fortnight's time, the Afghan Prime Minister was expected to leave for America. It would suit the Afghan Prime Minister to break his journey in Delhi to meet Jinnah and the Viceroy. This was also what Sir Giles Squire had suggested. The British Foreign Secretary was also not against the visit, preferring it to be one in transit rather than being a formal one. The Government of India agreed to facilitate the visit and accordingly sent an intimation to Sir Giles Squire: 'In view of Shah Mahmud's[20] more reasonable attitude and on the understanding that he will not in any sense be regarded or treated as an official emissary of Afghan Government, Government of India agree that there might be an advantage in establishing informal personal contacts with him at Delhi and are prepared to facilitate these.' The Afghan Prime Minister passed through Delhi on 24 July but did not break journey. The meeting with Jinnah and the Viceroy, therefore, did not fructify.

Lord Listowel wanted the provisional Pakistan government to make early overtures to the tribes now that the NWFP had opted for

Pakistan. This was to be on similar lines as with the Indian states. The idea was to make provisional arrangements pending a formal settlement on future relations. Anything that implied continuity of policy, in Listowel's view, would have a stabilizing effect.

According to Rob Lockhart's information, the tribes were getting restive about the future policy governing them now that the NWFP formed part of a new Dominion. Lord Listowel was keen that Pakistan settle its policy and make a timely announcement (before 15 August for the tribal agreements would otherwise lapse) of allowances and how it proposed to administer the tribal areas.

The contentious issue of a referendum and to which union the NWFP would cede now resolved, the British government was anxious to find a role for itself in the strategy and geography of the NWFP and Afghanistan. Aware of the delicate nature of the task, it wanted the initiative for a joint arrangement for the NWFP's security to come from Pakistan. With this in mind, a concept note was prepared by Lord Listowel with the concurrence of the British Foreign Office as well as with inputs from George Cunningham.[21] Speaking in the debate of 14 July on the India Bill in the House of Commons, the British Prime Minister had already indicated that issues concerning the NWFP's defence would come under the purview of a Joint Defence Council, provided Indian leaders (both Congress and the Muslim League) consented. Of course, there was a need to keep the tribes on both sides of the Durand Line at peace, but their welfare was not the only reason why the British evinced interest in the Joint Defence Council. At a broader level, they realized the urgency for a strong and independent buffer state between the Commonwealth and the Soviet Union. HMG, time permitting, wanted Pakistan to quickly resolve the problems of allowances, political control of agency areas and organization of its forces for the Frontier's defence. In the interim, a 'standstill agreement' could be reached with the tribal *jirgas*.

The note circulated by the India Office contained a crucial point that gave away British intentions: 'That in view of the all-India character of the problem of frontier defence, if the Pakistan Government thought of involving the Government of India for consultations and if there was a further desire to extend the consultation to include HMG, a proposal to this effect could be sympathetically considered. All this, for it was consonant with the Commonwealth policy designed to secure independence and stability of Afghanistan as a buffer state between the Commonwealth and the U.S.S.R.' The areas that formed part of the policy consultations were transit facilities, customs exemptions and the supply of military equipment (including aircraft) at concessional rates and the provision of instructors and training facilities for Afghan forces. Having worked out a common policy, the concept note finally proposed a joint approach to be made in Kabul to the Afghan government. Both Jinnah and Nehru agreed to the idea of a Joint Defence Council that would hold discussions with representatives of chiefs of staff on Commonwealth defence problems. The security concerns of the NWFP would fall well within its ambit.

After a brief lull, the Afghan press had resumed its campaign on the problems of the Frontier. The writers continued to criticize the so-called forced referendum and urged the Pakistan government not to allow disunity among Muslims, but the tone of the general press campaign remained mild. On his way to the United States, the Prime Minister of Afghanistan made a brief stopover in London. Records of discussions which the British Foreign Secretary, Ernst Bevin,[22] had with the Afghan Prime Minister on 31 July were sent to Sir Giles Squire in Kabul for information. The Afghan Prime Minister had again raised the same vexed issue of a referendum, whereby the people of the NWFP had merely been called upon to decide on a religious question— whether they wished to be associated with Muslims or Hindus. To the Afghan Prime Minister it was natural that the overwhelming Muslim population of the NWFP chose to be with Pakistan. Ernst Bevin was quite relieved though, for the Afghan Prime Minister had not pressed forth Afghan claims over the NWFP. But on the issue of the Anglo-Afghan Treaty of 1921, the Afghan Prime Minister felt that it had been concluded with HMG and that the Afghan government was not going to regard it as valid after the HMG had withdrawn from India. The Afghan government was, however, prepared to abide by any treaty subsequently negotiated with Pakistan. Would Pakistan negotiate treaties with Afghanistan, and why? There lay the problem.

Ernst Bevin stressed the strategic need of avoiding disturbances in the frontier and the rationale behind non-interference with her vital trade routes through India. HMG intended to continue exercising influence over India (India and Pakistan henceforth) and, therefore, it concerned the British how Afghanistan chose to act on the borders of Pakistan. Bevin assured the Afghan Prime Minister that Britain would retain its presence in this area and be available if required to mediate with India or Pakistan. Surprisingly, Bevin was ready to examine once again the expression that HMG had used about the NWFP being an 'integral part of India'. When the talks were about to conclude, Bevin referred to the contretemps that prevented the Afghan Prime Minister from meeting Mountbatten on his way to Britain. Bevin expressed the hope that he would be able to see Mountbatten on his return, and was sure that the meeting would be of 'the greatest value'.

The legal view, however, was that after the India Independence Act came into effect on 15 August 1947, all treaties and engagements with the tribes except those that related to customs, transit, communications and posts and telegraph would stand terminated. The Government of India was reluctant to share this information with the Government of Afghanistan. Sir Giles Squire was specifically asked on 8 August not to inform the Afghan government, even informally, of this important piece of information. Perhaps the provisional Government of Pakistan, privy to this information and its implications, had requested the Government of India to pass such instructions to Sir Giles Squire in Kabul.

### The Validity of the Durand Agreement

Earlier Britain's and subsequently, Pakistan's stated position had been that the plebiscite held in the NWFP in 1947 foreclosed the issue of Pathan self-determination. The tribal areas too had expressed their assent through the special *jirgas* (Wilber 1962: 184). But for the Afghans, the Treaty of 1893, known famously as the Durand Agreement, had been forced upon them under duress and was, therefore, invalid. They claimed that the British, too, recognized a special Afghan interest and influence among the Pakhtun tribes east of the Durand Line even before or after the treaty had been signed. They had never conceived of the Durand Line as an international boundary, but rather saw it as a line demarcating British and Afghan zones of influence. The Afghans claimed the right of self-determination for the Pakhtuns on the basis of ties of kinship, history, religion, races and language. The 1947 plebiscite, they argued, did not satisfy this requirement. It was primarily a unilateral act, undertaken without Afghan consultations or consent and was boycotted by a substantial number of Pakhtuns. Approval of the tribal *jirgas* was also obtained by offering a limited choice of either ratifying the plebiscite decision to join Pakistan or not. For the Afghans, Pakistan was not a successor state to Britain but an entirely new creation. Whatever treaty rights existed, therefore, were extinguished after the creation of a new state.[23]

The primary legal issue involved here was whether the 1893 treaty was valid or not. In international law, a treaty is considered similar to an agreement between individuals. It is recognized in international law that 'duress' can invalidate an agreement. But the law at the same time also recognizes the degrees of coercion. It is not enough to merely show that negotiations were conducted under pressure. What needs to be adduced as evidence is also the quantity and quality of compulsion exerted to substitute the will of one with another, thus destroying the element of free consent, a prerequisite for a valid agreement.[24] Sufficient evidence exists to show that Abdur Rahman, the Afghan Amir, was operating under severe pressure before concluding the treaty of 1893. The British had already been in control of his country's foreign policy and the Russians were nibbling at his western borders. Rebellions were seething within his country. The British controlled commerce and the transit of arms and ammunition into Afghanistan and there were veiled threats of embargo. Plus, there was the added pressure of the British forward policy. As Collin Davies puts it: 'One is led to the conclusion that Abdur Rahman Khan turned out to be a ram caught in a thicket… in the light of subsequent events it is difficult to understand the reasons which permitted the Amir to sign this agreement. Perhaps his consent was purchased by the increase of his subsidy…and by the recognition of his right to import munitions of war' (Davies 1932: 162, 184). The British wanted the demarcation and put strong pressure on the Amir, including a letter from the Viceroy of India which the Amir interpreted as an ultimatum (Rahman 1900). This would support the thesis that the treaty was concluded under duress. But on the other hand, there is also substantial evidence to show that the agreement served many of the Amir's own interests as well. It can reasonably be inferred that even though the Amir negotiated reluctantly, his perceived advantages could not be construed as suppression of his will (Poullada 1979).

Was there a meeting of minds, if at all, between the contracting parties? Key negotiations were conducted in private between the Amir and Sir Mortimer Durand. Since the Amir knew no English, the conversations took place in Persian. The Amir thought that he had negotiated about zones of influence. The British negotiator also viewed it as a demarcation of the 'frontier' in the sense of a zone rather than a 'boundary' marking an abrupt transition of sovereignty. There may have been a meeting of minds at this stage but subsequently, the administrators in Whitehall, conditioned by European notions, found it convenient to construe the Durand Agreement as an international territorial settlement (Poullada 1979: 137).

From the subsequent behaviour of the British and Afghans, it appeared that both sides regarded their respective areas on either side of the Durand Line as zones of primary influence rather than an integral part of their territorial sovereignty. The British part made it clear at first that they had no intention of 'annexing' the territory in tribal areas up to the Durand Line but rather hoped for an orderly administration of those regions, a position more consistent with 'hegemony' than 'sovereignty'. The 'meeting of minds' argument can be made at two levels: either the parties negotiated about two different things—the British about an international boundary and the Afghans about the zones of influence or that they negotiated about the zones of influence which the British later interpreted differently. Either argument tends to support Afghan claims questioning the validity of the 1893 treaty (Poullada 1979: 139).

Till 1947, the British recognized legitimate Afghan interests in the tribal people on their side of the Durand Line. But 1950 saw a change in that position. Noel Baker, the Secretary of State for Commonwealth relations, stated in the House of Commons that: 'In his Majesty's Government's view, Pakistan is in international law the inheritor of the rights and deeds of the old Government of India and his Majesty's Government in the United Kingdom in these territories and that the Durand Line is the international frontier.' Of course, the statement was made three years after the British left India. It would perhaps be fair to infer that the statement was made at Pakistan's request as a gesture of political support for this new member of the Commonwealth.

There are three historical documents—the Anglo-Afghan Pact of 1905, the Treaty of Rawalpindi of 1919 and the Anglo-Afghan Treaty of 1921 in which the Afghans appear to ratify or at least accept the 1893 Durand Line Agreement. Let us take them up one by one. The 1905 pact was rather vague and couched in general language and on personal terms by Amir Habibullah to the effect that 'he will continue to act towards all agreements entered into by his father in the same manner as his father had done'. The hard practical fact was that his father Amir Abdur Rahman had, to a large extent, disregarded the Durand Line in his dealings with the tribes. Amir Habibullah on his part made no mention of any specific commitment, maintaining silence on the issue of the Durand Line. Further, the 1905 pact was signed when his newly acquired throne was still somewhat shaky. At best, the Amir's reiteration could only be considered an expression of goodwill. The Treaty of Rawalpindi of 1919 was comparatively more explicit: 'The Afghan Government accepts the Indo-Afghan frontier accepted by Amir Habibullah.' The 1919 Agreement was signed as a temporary armistice agreement at the end of the Third Anglo-Afghan War. Both the parties intended to negotiate a prominent treaty later, which they did in 1921, superseding it in 1921 by a much more complete and formal engagement. There are two interesting points to ponder over in the formulation of the 1919 treaty. The first is that it merely relates to the 1905 commitments by Amir Habibullah which were extremely vague, and second that the use of the word 'frontier' suggests that both the parties were still thinking of the Durand Line as a demarcating zone of influence in a 'frontier area' rather than an international boundary. The Anglo-Afghan Treaty of 1921 was a good deal more explicit. In the relevant extracts of Article II:

> The two high contracting parties mutually accept the Indo-Afghan frontier as accepted by the Afghan Government on 8 August, 1919…being mutually satisfied themselves, each regarding the goodwill of the other and specifically regarding their benevolent intentions towards the tribes residing close to their respective boundaries, hereby undertake each to inform the other in future of any military operations…among the frontier tribes residing within their respective spheres.

This treaty interestingly also referred to the Afghan acceptance of the 'frontier', this time without a capital 'F'. It reiterated its commitment to the treaty of 1919 and referred to the word 'boundaries'. The treaty of 1921 recognized the reality of the situation regarding the tribal areas which neither the British nor the Afghans controlled (Poullada 1979: 139–41).

To this treaty should be added another important document, a letter from the British representative to the Afghan Foreign Minister. This letter was intended as an integral part of the agreement. It was well known that without this letter, the king would have refused to sign the 1921 treaty. The letter stated that 'the conditions of the frontier tribes of the two governments, are of interest to the government of Afghanistan'. From this it seemed fair to conclude that by 1921 the British government was prepared to admit Afghanistan's 'interest' in the tribal people east and south of the Durand Line, something which was inconsistent with later British and Pakistani pronouncements of complete sovereignty, as also with the claim that Afghans accepted such sovereignty. Taken together with the annexed letter of the British representative, the treaty of 1921 at least recognized residual Afghan rights. The precise nature and extent of these rights was vague. But should they not be entitled to at least some standing in international law by virtue of being recognized in a formal treaty and its annex (Poullada 1979: 142)?

If the 1893 treaty was originally valid, it required no further ratification by the Afghan government. A subsequent clear-cut Afghan approval of the 1893 Durand Line as an international boundary should have been obtained. It is difficult to find any Afghan words, actions or intent to relinquish its interest in the Pakhtun tribes east of the border, so much so that in 1949 the Afghan government took the extraordinary step of convoking the Parliament to repudiate all treaties with Britain affecting the status of the Pakhtuns, a dramatic gesture emphasizing that they had no intention of allowing their rights to lapse by default (Poullada 1979: 142–43).

## India's Western Neighbourhood

Even after the creation of Pakistan, Afghanistan continued to stake territorial claims across the Durand Line. The creation of Pakistan presented a new geo-political situation, for strategically, a physical gulf had been created between Delhi and Kabul; there was also the absence of a direct land or sea route between India and the landlocked Afghanistan. With the creation of Pakistan arose the Kashmir dispute as well as differences between Afghanistan and Pakistan over the legality of the Durand Line (Khaled 1989: 12).

Political reasons for a British presence in the Gulf now no longer existed; 1947 had ended British power in India. It was at this stage of a weakened British influence in the Afghan region, that the Soviet Union moved in. By 1953, Afghanistan was closer to the Soviet Union than to any other power. Nikolay Bulganin[25] and Nikita Khrushchev both visited Kabul in 1955 and with it came the first large loan for Afghanistan. In 1956, Afghanistan concluded another first—an arms agreement with the Soviet Union. The period between 1955–70 witnessed numerous state visits being exchanged between the Soviet Union and Afghanistan (Foot 1980).

The coup,[26] perhaps with Soviet complicity, established a republic in Afghanistan in 1973. After the coup, Afghanistan raised the level of propaganda regarding 'Pakhtunistan' and referred to the NWF and Baluchistan as the 'northern' and 'southern' occupied areas. They also launched an attack on Pakistan at the Non-Aligned Conference in Algeria in 1973 and the Afghan Ambassador to the UN in a speech to the General Assembly referred to Baluchistan and 'Pastunistan' as 'usurped land' (*Asian Recorder,* 1974). In view of the increased propaganda regarding the Baluchis, Tehran's relations with Kabul became strained after July 1973.

The Afghan regime was never really secure after 1973 and had to face several counter-coup attempts between 1973 and 1978. The one that succeeded in April 1978 established the Democratic Republic of Afghanistan. As in 1973, the Soviet Union was again the first country to give it official recognition, closely followed by India. Shortly, Afghanistan declared a foreign policy which sounded all too familiar—taking up with Pakistan the Pakhtun and Baluch right to self-determination. Kabul continued to raise this issue in the Non-Aligned Conferences and at the United Nations (Foot 1980).

The Shah had been ousted in Iran and with the regime change, it increasingly viewed Afghanistan as a place where Islam was in danger.

A large number of refugees from Afghanistan were beginning to cross over into Pakistan. As discontent grew, Afghanistan's reliance on the Soviet Union increased (Foot 1980).

What was the Indian foreign policy perspective then? Prior to the arrival of Soviet troops in Afghanistan, New Delhi had more than once expressed the 'hope for a return to stability in Afghanistan and an end to the interference of outside powers'. Morarji Desai,[27] the then Prime Minister of India, never fully accepted the Soviet explanation. Even his successor, Charan Singh,[28] could not refrain from expressing his anxiety over the Soviet intervention in Afghanistan. Charan Singh's views coincided wholly with India's expressed principles, at least on the non-aligned issue, yet his detractors and 'hawks' dubbed him as a man who was 'as familiar with the intricacies of international politics as a buffalo with the philosophy of Kant' (Khaled 1989: 14). Contrary to Moscow's expectations, following Soviet military intervention in Afghanistan, the Charan Singh government made it clear to the Soviet Ambassador that in India's view, 'the sending of military troops would have far-reaching and adverse consequences' for the entire region. The Soviets should withdraw their troops and return the situation to 'normal'. Later, when the government changed and a new dispensation took over in New Delhi, India's Afghan regional policy changed too. The then Prime Minister of India instructed the Indian envoy Brajesh Mishra[29] at the United Nations to make a statement on the following lines:

- The USSR sent troops to Afghanistan on 26 December 1979 at the request of Kabul's Babrak Karmal regime.
- While India was against the foreign troops and bases in any country, it had no reason to disbelieve a friendly country like the Soviet Union when it said that it would withdraw troops from Afghanistan when asked to do so by the government in Kabul.
- India hoped that the Soviet Union would not violate the independence of Afghanistan and would not keep troops in that country a day longer than necessary.
- India was gravely concerned about the response of the United States, China, Pakistan and others to the Soviet

action because the arming and training of Afghan rebels and the encouragement of subversive activities in Afghanistan amounted to interference in Afghan affairs (Khaled 1989: 14).

When the UN General Assembly passed a resolution on 14 January 1980 calling for the immediate, unconditional and total withdrawal of foreign troops from Afghanistan, India chose to side with the non-voting nations (Khaled 1989).

With Rajeev Gandhi, the new Prime Minister, India underscored its special relationship with Moscow when he visited the Soviet Union in May 1985. In a joint communique which was issued on this occasion, Afghanistan did not find a place. Soviet military assistance to India continued. Alongside, Rajeev Gandhi did try to crisis-manage the Afghanistan issue when he invited President Zia-ul-Haq[30] of Pakistan to visit new Delhi for consultations, but was unsuccessful in his efforts with the western neighbour (Khaled 1989: 16).

There were more than visible signs now of fundamentalism raising its ugly head in Afghanistan. This worried India too. Resistance had grown when the Afghan Marxists forcibly tried to transform society, something which the Taliban also tried and then faced the consequences.

Gulbuddin Hekmatyar[31] of the Hizb-i-Islami had long arrived in Peshawar in 1974–75 with some fifty Muslim fundamentalists from Kabul University after failing in a plot against Daud Khan.[32] These fifty people eventually split into four groups with Gulbuddin enjoying the backing of the Pakistan Prime Minister. Gulbuddin found help for his brand of Islamic fundamentalism not because of its intrinsic qualities, but because it served as a useful response to the 'Pakhtunistan' idea purveyed from Kabul at that time (Hyman 1980).

Jamaat-i-Islami,[33] another fundamentalist party, was led by Professor Burhanuddin Rabbani.[34] This party was mainly non-Pakhtun in its membership, and was largely Tajik (of Badkashan). The leaders of these parties were based in Peshawar and linked up closely with the tribes of south and south-east Afghanistan. They claimed to be leading and directing a jihad against communism and Russian domination but in truth, they were less guided by the ideology of strict Islamic practices than by the delivery of arms. The party militants in Peshawar, as across the border, were often educated young Afghans from Kabul University. Offices of these parties were decorated with Iranian posters of Ayatollah Khomeini as well as Maulana Maududi. But in private conversations, militants would often admit to problems in converting the Afghan population to their version of Islam; they admitted that Afghans, after all, knew little about Islam. These parties had one serious defect. They had limited appeal and were concentrated only towards one ethnic grouping, the Pakhtuns, and to one region or group of tribes, rather than to the Afghan people as a whole. An initiative, that of a great assembly or Parliament (*loya jirga*) ended in disunity, something which could be ascribed to infiltration of Soviet-trained agents. But this endemic disunity is also deeply rooted in Afghan culture. Even among the Marxists of Afghanistan there was disunity. Afghanistan is a much divided culture, with tribe pitted against tribe, ethnic group against ethnic group. History, geography and politics combine to reinforce strong traits of individualism (Hyman 1980).

Afghan society at this juncture also saw a profusion of arms. The regular Afghan army had disintegrated, a process which began in March 1979 with the mutiny in the Herat garrison followed by mutinies and mass desertions of units all over the country. The 100,000-strong Afghan army, supported by the Soviet Union, diminished to perhaps one-third with many crossing over to guerrilla groups (Hyman 1980).

In Quetta the prominent Hazara leader, a former Member of Parliament, Wali Beg, set up base and it was from here that assistance was provided to the cause of resistance. Hazaras joined forces with other ethnic groups, the Uzbeks, Turkoman, Taziks and Chahar Aimak tribes, all Sunni Muslims, yet fighting alongside Shia Hazaras (Hyman 1980).

Soviet air raids led to an exodus of Afghan refugees to the NWFP and Baluchistan camps. The links and ties between families, clans and tribes on both sides of the Durand Line had helped settle thousands of refugees from Pakhtun areas without any serious friction. This factor also accounted for sympathy for the entire border region for refugees and guerrillas among ordinary Pathans (Hyman 1980).

Much has been written about the period when the Taliban controlled Afghanistan. I would therefore refrain from discussing it here. But the country would face instability despite the Taliban having lost Afghanistan. History seemed to be repeating itself. The surviving members of the Taliban moved out of Afghanistan; some moved into Pakistan. The NWFP tribal areas became their refuge, just as was the case earlier during the Soviet occupation. The tribal population of the Special Areas too was overwhelmingly sympathetic to the Taliban. All had not been lost even after Taliban had lost the war on terror against America. The 13 December 2001 attack on the Indian Parliament[35] was clearly suggestive of the fact that Pakistan-based terror groups were receiving fresh recruits from across the Afghan border (Ayoob 2002: 51).

Various Afghan groups came together at Bonn (27 November 2001) to form a transitional regime under Hameed Karzai. But even there, internal squabbling was visible. Also visible was a division within the Northern Alliance and the absence of major contenders for power at the Bonn Conference. Ismail Khan,[36] a warlord from western Afghanistan, was not happy with the constitution of the interior government for he felt that the western provinces were under-represented. Similarly, the Uzbek chief from northern Afghanistan, General Rashid Dostum[37], had strong reservations about the distribution of offices. The fact that the Tajik component of the Northern Alliance had retained control of the defence, interior and the foreign ministries had upset Dostum greatly. These mutual bickerings, at the very outset, did not augur well for the anti-Taliban coalition (Ayoob 2002: 52).

Stability has also eluded Afghanistan because the strategic interests of its neighbours have always been at odds. Its neighbours would much rather have Afghanistan divided into fiefdoms in order to dominate those areas which are important to them strategically as well as politically. The over three-decade-long internecine conflict within Afghanistan has deepened ethnic and tribal animosity. This situation has also spawned its own vested interests who thrive on unsettled conditions. These 'conflict entrepreneurs' sustain themselves on poppy cultivation, drug trafficking, gun running, protection money and control of scarce resources. The illicit economic activities have also benefited external partners, especially the Pakistan Inter Services Intelligence and other international drug mafia by generating cash that can be spent on weapons and manpower (Ayoob 2002: 53).

The Taliban went through a phase of consolidation specially in south and eastern Afghanistan. The Federally Administered Tribal

Areas (FATA)[38] became a mini Taliban state where the federal writ of Pakistan did not run.[39] In 2002, President Musharraf of Pakistan manipulated elections in such a way that Islamic parties came to power in the NWFP and Baluchistan. When the Northern Alliance took Kabul, elements of Taliban under the leadership of Mullah Dadullah escaped into the NWFP. Most of the Kandahar-based Taliban leadership crossed over from Chaman to Pakistan. Pakistan then selectively provided members of the second-rung Taliban leadership to the Americans. Until the end of 2006, not a single Taliban leader had been killed or captured.

In 2002, the Pakistan administration also reached an understanding with the local militants in Waziristan. There was then an unwritten deal between the two and a written one the following year. Finally in August 2006, the administration in north Waziristan signed a peace agreement with the local Taliban militants. But problems with this agreement surfaced soon enough, a major one being that of foreigners not only in north Waziristan but all over FATA.[40] The 2004 and 2005 deals had mainly floundered over this issue. The administration on its part neither registered the foreigners nor did anything to evacuate them. Quite a few of them who have there for long had earlier fought the Russians and subsequently the Americans on Taliban and al-Qaeda dictates. These foreigners had local support and given their anti-Americanism, found acceptability.

The agreement of August 2006 had also aimed at preventing cross-border infiltration, an aim highly ambitious for the administration was fully aware of either governments' inability to seal the border along the Durand Line.[41] Given the reality of the situation, for the Government of Pakistan to withdraw the checkposts from the Special Areas only confounded an already fragile situation. Pakistan's proposal to fence the border, already disputed, was most impractical.

Pakistan's writ did not run in FATA and the NWFP. The government's control was always limited in these areas and got increasingly challenged by the Taliban locally. Even the Interior Minister of Pakistan, Aftab Ahmad Khan Sherpao, admitted to this.[42] There were attempts to impose religious customs over tribal traditions, pro-government tribal elders were systematically being targeted and eliminated and the punishment meted out was in typically Taliban style. The administration also decided to lift the ban on display of weapons and at the same time handed over AK 47s to many of the militants.[43] The local Taliban patrolled main towns in the tribal areas. Suicide bombings and rocket attacks also took place. The Pakistan government had taken all these steps with the full knowledge of its consequences. The government just wanted to buy peace. But at what cost? The government was ready to let FATA get Talibanized. For the government it was a lesser threat than an FATA with extreme Pakhtun consciousness and anti-Pakistan sentiments.

March 2007 witnessed Taliban attacks in Tank, a town in the NWFP,[44] where the Taliban engaged the security forces as they attempted to take over the town. Eventually, the army had to be called in to deal with the issue. The government had clearly failed in anticipating the situation, not paying attention to the creeping Talibanization in the district. Perhaps the government believed that once the Taliban got control of Waziristan they would rest content. One can in fact discern a direct link between the August 2006 agreement that the government signed with Taliban supporters in Waziristan and the growing Taliban influence in the settled districts adjoining Waziristan. The Taliban thereafter arose to influence administration outside Waziristan in areas of Bannu, Darra Adam Khel and Kohat.

Now to reflect a little on the cause of violence in Tank. It started with Taliban supporters attempting to forcefully recruit students from local schools. With Taliban announcing a spring offensive to counter Allied forces in Afghanistan, it was essential to have new recruits. When they went to the local school in Tank, the school principal instead of conceding to their request called the police. A gun battle ensued in which the station house officer and two militants were killed. The same evening, militants came again and attacked the Frontier Constabulary Fort. They abducted the school principal and blocked the Tank–Bannu road. Then with rockets and mortars they targeted the local police station, the paramilitary fort and five banks in the area and left with around Rs 3 million in loot. Clearly there was a pattern in the Taliban initiative outside the tribal regions. With north and south Waziristan under their control besides Bajaur, they were now attempting to expand into the settled districts of the NWFP, especially Bannu, Tank and Dera Ismail Khan.[45] The agreements signed between the government and local Taliban had only allowed them to consolidate their position inside the tribal region. The Taliban was looking eastwards now.

Reports[46] of local tribesmen fighting foreigners then started to surface. But their implications did not appear to be serious. The fight was between a section of the local Waziri tribesmen and Uzbek fighters under the leadership of Tahir Yuldashev[47] settled in south Waziristan. It was not a fight against all the foreigners and was limited to three villages of south Waziristan.

Pakistan at that moment appeared to be lacking options. There was pressure on it to close the refugee camps.[48] Since 2002, more than 2.8 million Afghans had returned but almost an equal number remained. The fate of the Afghan refugee community was an important piece in the puzzle of regional militancy.[49] Simply shifting them across the border could inflame tension. Many of the refugees apprehended reprisals if they were sent back.

States live by geography and geography is not a matter of choice or preference. Efforts at map-making have become ever so difficult. In hindsight, the boundaries of the NWF were always fluid. Even the Durand Line is not accorded a historical (customary and traditional) sanction. The Pakhtun dispute will persist. It surfaced in the Pakistani army when its Pakhtun officers refused to fight in the NWFP and faced a court martial.[50] But the army's reluctance to fight forced President Musharraf of Pakistan to broker a deal with Taliban. In the NWFP many districts got Talibanized, the phenomenon having spread across Naushera to Islamabad, resulting in the Lal Masjid incident.[51]

The repercussions of the attack on Lal Masjid were serious. On 15 July 2007, the Taliban revoked the August 2006 agreement that they had concluded with the Pakistani government. Over the weekend of 15 July 2007, a spate of suicide attacks in the NWFP directly targeted Pakistani security forces in Swat, Dera Ismail Khan and Miranshah with casualty figures of over one hundred.

Whatever the issues that plagued the border, it was unlikely that the historical backdrop of the Durand Line was going to stop being a hindrance in conflict resolution. Afghanistan will lay claim to much of the NWFP on the grounds that it is a Pakhtun-dominated area. But Pakistan can hardly be expected to give up this territory that forms more than 20 per cent of its total territory. In the face of growing militancy, warlordism and narcotics right across its borders, Pakistan is caught between a rock and a hard place.[52]

## Notes

1. The Molotov–Ribbentrop Pact, 1939, was a Nazi–Soviet Non-Aggression Pact.
2. 'Wehrmacht' was the name of the unified armed forces of Germany from 1935 to 1945.
3. 'Luftwaffe' is a generic German term for an air force.
4. William Kerr Fraser-Tytler (1886–1963) was a former British minister in Kabul. When he left that post in 1941, he had spent his last thirty-one years on or just beyond the NWFP in the Indian army or in the Political Department of the British Indian government.
5. Anglo-Afghan Relations; 256; Sir F. Wylie (Kabul) to the Marquess of Linlithgow; Telegram, L/Po/6/106b: f128; Most immediate, Kabul, 6 March 1942, 3.30 p.m.
6. The Treaty of Gandamak (1879) was concluded between the British government and Muhammad Yakub Khan, Amir of Afghanistan, at Gandamak on 26 May 1879.
7. Anglo-Afghan Relations; Folder II; cabinet; India and Burma Committee; Future Relations between India and Adjacent Countries; Memorandum by the Secretary of State for India; India Office, 22 March 1947, India Office Library (IOL). Also see, Sir G. Squire to Mr Weightman; British Legation, Kabul; 5 April 1947.
8. In his letter D.O. No. F706/44/N.G.O. of 9 May, Sir G. Squire reported that he had conveyed to the Afghan Foreign Minister the views of the Government of India as contained in No. 213. Ali Muhammad was 'disappointed and said so frankly. He admitted that the government of India's contention was unanswerable but reiterated what he had often said before that as long as the British Government remained responsible for the control of the frontier, the Afghans had nothing to say. He thought it however somewhat hard that when we had announced that the British Government would be relinquishing that control in June next year we should still expect the Afghan government to refrain from all attempts to clarify a potentially dangerous situation until the British had actually left India. He expressed the fear that the new Indian government would

attempt to coerce the tribes to come under Indian administration and that this would lead to conflagration in which Afghanistan would inevitably be involved, with results that no-one could foresee.'
9. Anglo-Afghan Relations; 213 Major Crichton to Sir G. Squire; New Delhi, 24 April 1947; SECRET; D.O. No. D.3140-NWA/47.
10. H.M. Minister at Kabul to Secretary of State; Kabul, 11 June 1947, 10 a.m.; received: 11 June, 1.30 p.m.
11. H.M. Minister at Kabul to Government of India, External Affairs and Commonwealth Relations Department; immediate; Kabul, 23 June 1947, 5 p.m.; received in India Office: 23 June, 8.25 p.m.
12. H.M. Minister at Kabul to Government of India, External Affairs and Commonwealth; immediate; Kabul, 27 June 1947, 4.30 p.m.; received in India Office: 27 June, 8 p.m.
13. Government of India, External Affairs and Commonwealth Relations Department, to Secretary of State; Most immediate; New Delhi, 30 June 1947, 5.15 p.m.; Top Secret; received: 30 June, 7 p.m.
14. Secretary of State to H.M. Minister at Kabul; immediate; India office, 1 July 1947, 11.15 p.m.
15. Minute 4; Relations with Afghanistan.
16. The Earl of Listowel to Rear Admiral Viscount Mountbatten of Burma; important; India Office, 5 July 1947, 7.15 a.m.; Secret; received: 5 July, 2 p.m.
17. H.M. Minister at Kabul to Secretary of State; Kabul, 11 July 1947, 6 p.m.; received: 12 July, 9.40 p.m. important.
18. In his telegram No. 68 of 20 July, Sir G. Squire reported that the Afghan Prime Minister had kept his promise and stopped all radio propaganda since 15 July. Only one article had since appeared in the Afghan press which explained the difference between Pathans and Indians and demanded a reference to the UNO.
19. H.M. Minister Kabul to Government of India, External Affairs and Commonwealth Relations Department; immediate; Kabul, 16 July 1947, 3.40 p.m.; received: 17 July, 10.45 p.m.
20. Mohammed Zahir Shah (1914–2007) was the last king of Afghanistan, reigning for four decades from 1933 until he was ousted by a coup in 1973. Following his return from exile he was given the title 'Father of the Nation' in 2002, which he held till his death. He was the son of Mohammed Nadir Shah, a senior member of the Barakzai royal family

and Commander-in-Chief of the Afghan army under former King Amanullah Khan. Nadir Shah assumed the throne after the execution of Habibullah Ghazi on 10 October 1929.
21. Government of India, External Affairs and Commonwealth Relations Department to Secretary of State; Immediate; New Delhi, 16 July 1947, 11.55 p.m.; received: 16 July, 11.40 p.m.
22. Ernest Bevin was the Labour Party's Foreign Secretary, appointed by Clement Attlee after the Labour Party's victory in the 1945 general elections. Bevin had no love for communism and believed that Stalin's Russia was a threat, despite the wartime alliance. He played an important part in the establishment of the North Atlantic Treaty Organization (NATO) and Britain's development of nuclear weapons. Bevin, as Foreign Secretary, also had to play a part in issues involving the empire such as withdrawal from India. He also had to deal with the Middle East where Britain had a mandate in Palestine. He initially opposed moves for the creation of Israel but gave in to American pressure. Israel came into being in 1948 with United Nations' support. Bevin retired from Attlee's government in March 1951 as he was in poor health. He died on 14 April 1951.
23. A. Rahman Pazhwak, *An Article on Pakhtunistan: A New State in Central Asia*, Afghanistan Information Bureau, 1960, p.147.
24. Wilson-International Law, St. Paul, Minnesota, West Publishing Company, 1939.
25. During World War II, Bulganin served under Joseph Stalin in the War Cabinet. He was also Chairman of the State Defence Committee. In 1947 Bulganin became Minister of the Armed Forces. Granted the rank of Marshal of the Soviet Union, he also became a full member of the Politburo of the Central Committee. After the death of Joseph Stalin, Bulganin served as Deputy Premier and Minister of Defence under Georgy Malenkov. However, he supported Nikita Khrushchev against Malenkov and in February 1955 was rewarded with the post of Chairman of the Council of Ministers of the Soviet Union.
26. The Afghan king had gone to Britain for medical treatment in the summer of 1973 when the events leading to Daoud Khan's coup began unfolding. By 17 July 1973, while Zahir Shah and his family were on a reported stopover visit to Italy, the then army commander Lieutenant General Mohammad Daoud Khan seized control in Kabul. Daoud

Khan declared Afghanistan a republic, calling the coup a 'national and progressive revolution' and then declared himself president. Daoud Khan's coup marked the end of the last relatively peaceful and prosperous period in Afghanistan. For the remainder of the twentieth century, Afghanistan suffered through unstable governments, bloody coups, and after the Soviet invasion in late 1979, more than two decades of war. Daoud Khan had been the Afghan Prime Minister during the 1950s and early 1960s. But his views on the so-called 'Pakhtunistan' issue seriously damaged Kabul's relations with neighbouring Pakistan. Daoud Khan saw all of the Pakhtun tribal regions straddling the two countries' borders as part of historical Afghanistan. Pakistan, for its part, felt threatened by this claim. Whatever the causes behind Afghanistan's 1973 coup, the years that followed saw the opposite of Daoud Khan's announced desire to better the economic and spiritual conditions of Afghans. Daoud Khan was killed, along with his wife and children, in the Saur Revolution of 1978 that brought Afghanistan's communists to power. And after the Soviet invasion of 1979, millions of Afghans were either killed or they fled to refugee camps in Pakistan, Iran or neighbouring Central Asian republics. When Moscow finally withdrew its troops from Afghanistan in 1989, the mujahidin commanders who had fought against the Soviet forces began fighting among themselves, creating the desperate conditions that gave rise to the Taliban regime.

27. Morarji Desai (1896–1995) was an ardent Gandhian and served as a minister in the cabinets of Jawaharlal Nehru and Indira Gandhi. Desai's personal rectitude and fastidiousness on matters of diet and health are famous for contributing to his longevity. He was Prime Minister in the Janata Party government in 1977–79.
28. Charan Singh (1902–87) was the Prime Minister of India from July 1979 to January 1980. When Prime Minister Morarji Desai resigned in July 1979, Charan Singh was asked to lead the government until the general elections in January 1980 returned Mrs Indira Gandhi and the Congress (I) to power.
29. Brajesh Chandra Mishra was the first National Security Advisor and Principal Secretary to the Prime Minister of India, Atal Bihari Vajpayee. Brajesh Mishra's father, the late Dwarka Prasad Mishra, was a staunch and ambitious Congressman, very close to Indira Gandhi.
30. General Muhammad Zia-ul-Haq (1924–88) was the President and

military ruler of Pakistan from July 1977 till his death in August 1988. Appointed Chief of Army Staff in 1976, General Zia-ul-Haq came to power after he overthrew ruling Prime Minister Zulfikar Ali Bhutto in a military coup on 5 July 1977 and became the state's third ruler to impose martial law. The coup itself was largely bloodless; however, he later had Bhutto executed. Zia initially ruled for a year as Chief Martial Law Administrator and later assumed the post of President of Pakistan in September 1978. During his tenure, he advanced Islamization and radicalization of Pakistan. To shore up the increasingly tenuous control of the central government over the tribal provinces, he appointed martial law administrators as governors of Baluchistan and the tribal areas with wide powers, including the abridgement of civil liberties. Zia was killed along with several of his top Generals and the then United States Ambassador to Pakistan, Arnold Lewis Raphel, in a mysterious aircraft crash near Bahawalpur (Punjab) on 17 August 1988, the circumstances of which remain unclear. His death with the American Ambassador gave rise to many conspiracy theories.

31. Gulbuddin Hekmatyar (born 1947) is a mujahidin leader and former Prime Minister of Afghanistan. He is the founder and leader of the Hizb-i-Islami political party and paramilitary group.He was a rebel military commander during the 1980s Soviet War in Afghanistan and fought in the Civil War that followed Soviet withdrawal. He held the office of Prime Minister of Afghanistan from 1993 to 1994 and again in 1996. One of the most controversial of the mujahidin leaders, he has been accused of spending 'more time fighting other Mujahidin than killing Soviets' and wantonly killing civilians. He is currently wanted by the United States for participating in terrorist actions with al-Qaeda and the Taliban, and on 19 February 2003, the United States Department of State declared him a 'Specially Designated Global Terrorist'.

32. Sardar Muhammad Daud Khan (1909–78) was Afghan's Prime Minister in 1953–63 and President in 1973–78. He was a cousin of King Muhammad Zahir Shah (ruled 1933–73). Opposition to his authoritarian rule forced his resignation from the premiership in 1963. With support from Pathan tribes in the north-west and Soviet backing, he overthrew the monarchy in July 1973 and declared the country a republic. He was assassinated in a military coup.

33. Jamaat-i-Islami (JI) is an Islamist political party in Pakistan. It was

founded in Lahore, India, by Sayyid Abul Ala Maududi on 26 August 1941, and is the oldest religious party in Pakistan. JI envisions an Islamic government in Pakistan governed by Islamic law. It is opposed to westernization, including capitalism, socialism or such practices as bank interest and liberalist social mores. JI advocates the use of the Pakistani army in separating the predominantly Muslim province of Kashmir from India, its president calling Pakistan-administered Kashmir the base-camp for the jihad in Indian-administered Kashmir. Insinuations of links between JI and al-Qaeda have also been made.

34. An ethnic Tajik, Burhanuddin Rabbani was born in 1940 in Badakhshan, a province of Afghanistan. In 1992 he became President of the Islamic Council of Afghanistan (effectively ruler of the country), until Kabul was captured by the Taliban in 1996. He set up headquarters in the northern Afghan town of Faizabad and led, with support from Iran and Russia, one of the five anti-Taliban factions, the Northern Alliance. He was still recognized as ruler of Afghanistan by the United Nations and most other countries until he formally handed over power to an interim government headed by Hamid Karzai on 22 December 2001. He was not given a cabinet post, and was an outspoken critic of the Karzai government.

35. Terrorists attacked the Parliament of India on 13 December 2001, resulting in a forty-five-minute gun battle in which nine policemen and Parliament staffers were killed. All the five terrorists were also killed by security forces and were identified as Pakistani nationals.

36. General Mohammad Ismail Khan (born 1946) is a warlord of Tajik origin, and is known as the 'Lion of Herat'. He was from time to time the Governor of Herat province, Afghanistan. During the Soviet invasion of Afghanistan in 1979, Khan was an officer in the Afghanistan army, reaching the rank of mujahidin commander. After becoming Governor of Herat for the first time, he was forced to flee after the Taliban took over authority in 1995. While organizing opposition against the Taliban, he was handed over to them by his old adversary General Pahlawan after a deal in 1997. Two years later in March 2000, he escaped and worked as a low-profile member of the Northern Alliance. Along with General Mohammed Fahim and ethnic Uzbek warlord General Abdul Rashid Dostam, Ismail Khan was one of the three factional leaders that comprised the Northern Alliance. Ismail Khan is known for his reluctant support for Afghanistan's central government.

37. Abdul Rashid Dostum (born 1954) was a pro-Soviet fighter during the Soviet War in Afghanistan and is considered by many to be the leader of Afghanistan's Uzbek community. He joined the Afghan military in 1978, fighting with the Soviets and against the mujahidin throughout the 1980s before switching sides and joining the mujahidin. Dostum again switched sides and has become infamous for switching allegiances. Most recently he was a General and Chief of Staff to the Commander-in-Chief of the Afghan National Army, a role often viewed as ceremonial. In early 2008 he was removed from his army role because of the Akbar Bai kidnapping incident.
38. FATA consists of areas outside the four provinces bordering Afghanistan, comprising a region of some 27,220 sq. km. The other areas of Pakistan also outside the provinces are Azad Kashmir, Islamabad Capital Territory and the Northern Areas. FATA is bordered by Afghanistan to the west with the border marked by the Durand Line, NWFP and Punjab to the east and Baluchistan to the south. In 2000, the total population of FATA was estimated to be about 3,341,070 people, or roughly 2 per cent of Pakistan's population. Only 3.1 per cent of the population resides in established townships. It is the most rural administrative unit in Pakistan. The tribal areas comprise seven agencies: Khyber, Kurram, Bajaur, Mohmand, Orakzai, north and south Waziristan and six frontier regions, namely FR Peshawar, FR Kohat, FR Tank, FR Bannu, FR Lakki and FR Dera Ismail Khan. The main towns include Miranshah, Razmak, Bajaur, Darra Bazaar, Ghalanai as headquarters of the Mohmand Agency and Wana. The seven tribal areas lie in a north-to-south strip that is adjacent to the west side of the six frontier regions, which also lie in a north-to-south strip. The geographical arrangement of the seven tribal areas in order from north to south is Bajaur, Mohmand, Khyber, Orakzai, Kurram, north Waziristan and south Waziristan. The geographical arrangement of the six frontier regions in order from north to south is Peshawar, Kohat, Bannu, Lakki Marwat, Tank, Dera Ismail Khan. There are twenty legislators from FATA in the National Assembly and Senate of Pakistan (twelve MNAs and eight senators).
39. 'Pakistan: The Way Ahead', report of the Panel Discussion held at the IPCs on 25 June 2007; prefaced by Priyadarshee Andley and Swapna Kona, p.1.
40. IPCs issue Brief 37, September 2006, Peace Agreement in Waziristan, D. Subachandran, p.2.

41. Ibid., p.3.
42. Ibid.
43. Ibid., p.4.
44. Article No. 2252, 3 April 2007, IPCs-Pakistan, D. Subachandran.
45. Ibid.
46. Article No. 2253, 3 April 2007, IPCs Pakistan, D. Subachandran.
47. Tahir Yuldashev is the leader of the Islamic Movement of Uzbekistan and the Islamic Movement of Central Asia.
48. Article no. 2218; 23 February 2007, IPCs Pak, Srinjoy Bose.
49. Ibid.
50. 'Pakistan: The Way Ahead'; report of the Panel Discussion held at the IPCs on 25 June 2007, prefaced by Priyashree Andley and Swapna Kona.
51. Ibid., p.2.
52. Quoted from Article No. 2224, 28 February 2007, Swapna Kona, IPCs Pakistan.

# 16

## The Danger of Little Knowledge

IT STRIKES ONE AS a fine example of British understatement, coming as it does from a famous civil servant who served long years in Afghanistan and the NWFP: 'The British are extremely efficient administrators and rulers, not only of their own, but also of other peoples' countries.'[1] The why, and the explanation for it, finds an apt expression in Lord Asquith's eulogy of his fellow students at Balliol College, Oxford: 'There is nothing in this world so exasperating to the inefficient as the supreme consciousness of effortless superiority displayed by the efficient, and in proportion as the former developed and in due course became less inefficient, so do they seek with increasing vehemence to rid themselves of a yoke which inspite of its security, carries with it the humiliating stigma of inferiority. Such has been the inevitable consequence of British rule over alien people.'[2] How and what are we to argue, faced with a statement such as this!

To retain their hold over India, the British, cognizant of the historical role of the Hindu Kush, maintained its sanctity as the outer bulwark of India's defence. Strategically, the Hindu Kush formed the basis of India's security. The British Indian civil servants ensured this by prevailing upon the Afghans. India's frontier was gradually extended. Amir Abdur Rehman was forced to forsake an independent Afghan foreign policy, where after, the British created an artificial boundary (the Durand Line) in 1893 and subsequently bound the Afghan government by an Anglo-Russian convention of 1907. Whenever mechanisms regulating relations between India and Afghanistan came under strain, Britain entered into a treaty alliance with the buffer state (Afghanistan), or with Russia (Soviet Union), coaxing Afghanistan to behave. At times, Britain also facilitated a claimant to the amirship of Kabul to come to power. The armistice following the third Anglo-Afghan war was a case in example of just such a treaty alliance.

That Britain may one day withdraw from India was already being mentioned in some quarters in the mid-1930s. What was then to become of Afghanistan (the buffer state) and the Hindu Kush? This question posed equally to the British, the Pathans and the Afghans. The clarification offered are revelatory of the prevailing attitude. To the British civil servants there was nothing strange about India being ruled by foreigners. The Afghans had ruled substantial parts of it and the British already displayed a knack for maintaining a delicate balance between the great warring creeds of Hindus and Muslims. These civil servants could find no plausible explanation for the British withdrawal. But if they were at all to leave, the only possible solution to India's problem was a division of sovereignty between the Hindus and Muslims. Resolution based on a union of India was anathema. This British approach was encouraged in Kabul long before the validity of division had even been admitted in Britain or India. The British justified it by saying that it was not based on any ill-will towards Hindus, with whom the Afghans were prepared to live in harmony. The simple fact was one of history, of fundamental difference of creed—how could the great Muslim community of northern India submit to the rule of Hindu majority, no matter what form it took. It was steadfastly impressed upon everyone that the Afghans understood this clearly, and any attempt to impose unity on India would be disastrous. It came somewhat as a relief when the British Indian officials learnt of HMG's decision to partition India in 1947.

Sir Olaf Caroe, the last and the most controversial of the NWFP governors, whose book, *The Pathans*, is considered an authoritative source, propagated the same stereotypical argument about India's division, suggesting reasons 'why the important elements among the Pathans in the 1920–40 period were prepared to accept an alliance with the Indian Congress'.[3] According to him, it was 'hard to see how the Pathan tradition could reconcile itself for long to Hindu leadership, by so many regarded as smooth-faced, pharisaical and double dealing. The Pathan never regarded himself as an Indian; he still spoke daily of going to, or coming from Hindustan, a country that began vaguely somewhere on the other side of the Margalla Pass. How then could he have associated himself with a party under Indian, even Brahmin, inspiration? ... Not even the frontier Congress leaders could conceive future conditions in which it would ever be possible for a Hindu dominated Government to tell the Pathans what to do or how to do it.'[4] In defence of his argument, Sir Olaf quoted two lines from the famous Pathan warrior poet Khushal Khan Khattak:

> I hear the story of Bahlol and Sher Shah;
> That in days gone by, Pathans were kings in Hind.[5]

Concluding that 'in good time, when the British had gone, that predominance would come again; what was the harm in using Congress money and Congress brains? so thought many and lulled conscience to sleep... Only when the British move to bring their authority to an end acquired a momentum so unmistakable that even the unbelieving were compelled to read the signs often against their will, only then was the two nation theory translated into practical politics'.[6] Acceptance of the two nation theory was actively abetted by the British civil servants in the NWFP. The preceding lines from Olaf Caroe's book are evidence enough. Caroe was rightly and vociferously accused by the then Congress leadership as he had for long years served in the NWFP, eventually becoming its Governor.

Caroe firmly believed that Nehru's visit to the NWFP in 1946 as India's Foreign Minister proved 'fatal to those who thought in terms of a united India'.[7] To a majority of the Pathans, it was a submission 'to the direction and homily by a Brahmin, another Birbal, vastly arrogant'.[8] They would have none of it in the plains or the hills. Simplistically though, Caroe argued that the flags of Islam were unfurled after Nehru's visit; Jinnah had his way and Dr Khan Saheb and his brother were swept away from power.[9] The tribal influence, 'such as it was, was cast on the side of Jinnah's forthright appeal to Islam in peril',[10] but the 'paranoia of Islam in danger' was zealously encouraged by the British bureaucracy headed by Governors Cunningham and Olaf Caroe who urged its propagation by the sajdanashins and the mullahs of the NWFP.

The triumph of the two-nation theory, seemingly settled the contentious issue of who would control the frontiers. But in reality, the question has remained long unresolved. Both the Mughals and the British could not find an answer to it. Even as long back as when Alexander's armies passed through what is now Afghanistan and its adjoining eastern highlands, he found the Pakhtun tribes inhabiting this area. From the Kushans, Huns, Mongols, Arabs, Turks to the Mughals and finally the British, the Pakhtuns have had a history of successfully resisting all; a difficult record to match. The strategic position of Pakhtuns in their mountainous 'land of insolence'[11] has always provided them with control of the military and trade routes, thus enabling them to exact tributes and political concessions from the empires that surrounded them. The expansion of the Russian and British empires in the nineteenth and twentieth centuries allowed for this area to become even more strategically important.

It was the Battle of Plassey (1757) that turned the East India Company of Britain into virtual rulers of the eastern part of India. Coincidentally, around the same time, Russia developed Orenburg in the Urals as a base for their conquest of the central Asian Khanates.[12] The expanding interests and areas of both these empires in the intervening territories of central south Asia was bound to bring them into conflict. The warlike Pakhtun tribesmen became an important pawn in the Great Game as they lay directly in the path of these expanding empires. If a line is drawn from Calcutta to Orenburg, it will be seen that Kabul is approximately midway. Britain used Afghanistan as a buffer state to halt the Russian advance at the great barrier of the Hindu Kush.[13]

The Pakhtun tribes were a prickly hedge, a buffer, between Russia and British India. This prickly hedge of Pakhtun tribal resistance, well before the times of the Great Game, had made the Pakhtuns accustomed to a way of life that placed a premium on a disregard for organized processes of government. Their nuisance value was held in esteem and delinquencies encouraged by subsidies or bribes by the Mughals and British. They were also punished as a consequence and in excessive measure, which turned them into social outlaws. As a result, these tribes developed their own ingrown society with their own code of honour (Pakhtunwali), as well as internal tribal government. The Pakhtun tribes thus defied any form of institutionalized authority like the British, the Afghan, or the Pakistani with relative impunity. The British could never succeed in completely pacifying or winning over the loyalty of Pakhtun tribes, often wrestling with alternating policies, of either masterly inactivity or attempting to push through the tribal areas by force.[14]

The enforced separation of tribes, largely a consequence of British map-making, almost equally divided the tribes between Afghanistan and Pakistan. Their tradition has frequently created situations that have led to tensions, mutual enmity and incidents, exactly what the imperialists needed to divide and rule.

William Kerr Fraser-Tytler, a veteran official from the Frontier and author of a definitive account on political developments in Central and South Asia, narrates an incident that could be a pithy analogy of what may be in store for the future. Many years back, he once sat with a squadron of his regiment on a ridge overlooking a ravine in the hills of the NWFP, a mile or two from the Durand Line. Where the ravine joined the main valley, there was a pool of water. On its far side waited a party of tribesmen, and in between them grazed a large flock of sheep, property of the tribesmen. Fraser-Tytler and his men sat all day, patiently watching the sheep. From the opposite side came shouts and curses, and occasionally great lumps of lead, fired from jezail. But Fraser-Tytler continued to sit there, biding his time, for he knew as in the words of Captain Bindon Blood:

> Whatever happens we have got
> A maxim gun, and they have not.[15]

Fraser-Tytler was aware that the tribesmen could do little harm, so long as he stayed on the ridge. He also knew well what the end must be. With the evening, the shadows would lengthen and the sheep would move to Fraser-Tytler's side for a drink at the pool. And at that point, Tytler and his party mounted their horses, rode down and took possession of them.[16] The telling comparison he drew then was of the same lengthening shadows over the subcontinent of India, and the country of the Hindu Kush.

A simple lesson derived from the region's history south of the Hindu Kush is the ample opportunities it has provided to Britain, the erstwhile Soviet Union and the United States to meddle actively in the area's internal affairs. Another contrasting but an equally important inference is drawn by the famous thirteenth-century Persian poet, Saadi:

You can swallow a rough bone;
but once it is embedded in your bowels, it will cut it open.

[Caroe, 1958: *Epilogue on Russia*, p.526.]

The lines apply directly to those who sought to subdue the Pathans/Afghans. The United States, which till recently was engaged in this territory, also withdrew. If history is anything to go by, this landmass may again be transgressed by those powerful enough to cross the Hindu Kush.

In the high uplands of the Pamirs that divide Central from South Asia, the Chinese have long enforced their claim, venturing three times into Turkestan. Their first foray was in the second century BC during the Han period. The second westward initiative came under the Tangs in the seventh century. In AD 751, the advancing Islamic armies of the Arabs defeated the Chinese, forcing a retreat. Another thousand years, and the Chinese had again walked into Turkestan. This huge swathe of territory, about 700,000 square miles in size called Xinjiang, if it were a country, would be the sixteenth largest in the world, bigger than Britain, France, Germany and Spain put together. Not only did the frontiers of Mongolia and Tibet meet here, but also those of the erstwhile USSR, China and India. Until the eighteenth century, China stretched only up to the last fort of the Great Wall. Whoever lived beyond it was considered barbarian. The Chinese character 'hui' pronounced as 'hway', has, as one of its constituent characters radicals denoting 'dog'. The barbarians were no better than 'dogs'. This attitude towards non-Chinese not only extended to the Muslims of Xinjiang but also to the 'ocean people'.[17] With the annexation of Xinjiang in 1760 by the Qing emperor, a buffer state was created for the first time against anyone wanting to invade China.

Since the takeover of Xinjiang was strategic, the Qing emperor allowed religious freedom to the local Muslims. Xinjiang's annexation became largely possible because the Qing rulers were Manchus.[18] It was the Manchu trait that set them apart as empire builders. Had the Qing rulers of China (AD 1644 to AD 1912) been ethnic Chinese, they may not perhaps have expanded into Turkestan and Tibet. The ethnic Chinese Ming dynasty (AD 1368 to AD 1644) burnt every ship in their navy, hardly indicative of a mentality given to expansion. But once the

Manchu empire was created, subsequent Chinese rulers endeavoured to maintain it, well after the Manchus were overthrown.[19]

In the mid-1870s, the Manchus regained Xinjiang which they had lost to a self-styled Amir of Kashgar who ruled the area for a little over ten years. But in the interim the Russians found an opportunity to advance up to Khokand and were soon knocking on the doors of China west of Kashgar. By 1891, they had moved across the eastern end of the Afghan border beyond which lay an undemarcated gap and the Chinese frontier. Any further move by Russia would bring it to the Indian border, outflanking the buffer state (Afghanistan). The British hastened to stop this move by persuading Amir Abdur Rahman to take control of the Wakhan corridor. Concurrently, they took up the matter of boundary demarcation, eastwards, towards the Chinese frontier, with Russia and China. If Britain could succeed in this aim, direct Russian access to India's border would safely stand denied.

Several attempts were made by Britain to include China in the negotiations, but to no avail. Confusion prevailed in London and Saint Petersburg about the alignment of the Chinese border in the Pamirs. Despite an agreement reached between Britain and Russia in 1895, the boundary alignment remained imprecise. Britain desired an eastward extension of the Russo-Afghan border till it culminated on the Chinese frontier. The Russians preferred a shorter line, and a stalemate ensued. The British continued with their effort east across the Bayik Pass until they reached the first Chinese post (Fraser-Tytler 1950: 330). An agreement with the Chinese was reached, the intention being to keep the Russians away from the Indian frontier. Between the last Russian point and the Chinese post lay a territory that was no man's land. Britain hoped that the Chinese would soon fill the gap left by the commissioners. This situation carried on right uptil the middle of twentieth century. But in 1950, describes Fraser-Tytler, when two American travellers passed through the Wakhan corridor of Afghanistan, resolved to cross over into Chinese Turkestan, they were stopped by a patrol of Chinese soldiers about a mile from the Wakhjir pass and refused entry. The Chinese by then had taken effective control of the area. The British by then had withdrawn from India.[20] The reason for narrating this story in some detail is to emphasize the

Chinese persistence in taking control of the territory where the Russo-Afghan boundary ended.

In 1911 there took place a tripartite conference between Great Britain, China and Tibet to define the frontier between India, China and Tibet and the famous McMahon line came into existence. The Chinese, however, refused to ratify this agreement. Thereafter, for over 30 years, the Government of India simply took the McMahon line for granted; they could afford to do so because China, torn by civil wars, was in no position to assert itself and Tibet, under a strong Dalai Lama, was firmly wedded to its independence. Sir Olaf Caroe, however, with a prescience which, in the light of later events, must be regarded as remarkable, realized that the north-east frontier might one day become as live as the north-west, and pressed for the extension of administration, civil and military into the areas abutting the McMahon line. But for his foresight, independent India might have found herself in an even more difficult position to resist China's aggressive designs.[21]

India had a political officer based in Sikkim who would frequently visit Lhasa. The consulate in Kashgar in Xinjiang was the remotest post of the British Indian empire. The Government of India's policy in Xinjiang was not consistent with its policy towards Tibet. In Tibet, India did all that it could to repudiate Chinese sovereignty; in Xinjiang, it did everything to affirm it.[22] The reason was simple, to prevent Xinjiang from falling prey to the Russian menace.

India's support of Chinese sovereignty in Xinjiang alongside their repudiation of Chinese sovereignty in Tibet sprung from the same basic geo-political compulsion—Chinese sovereignty over Xinjiang was shadowy, whereas the Russian authority over it could have been formidable. As for Tibet, the Government of India strove hard to keep China as well as Russia out of it. India's relations with Xinjiang and Tibet in British days were based on a mistrust of her neighbours (China and Russia), and a recognition of the play of power politics.[23] Independent India began by following a different policy, somewhat naïve, seeking to establish fraternal relations with China, despite its rigid ideology. But China's subsequent conduct towards Tibet and her aggression on the Indian frontier came as a rude shock to India.

A Manchu official had continued to rule Xinjiang since 1911. He was assassinated in 1928, having displeased the Soviets. His murder, people believed, was committed with the active connivance of the Soviet consul general in Urumchi. Five confused and bloody years of civil war followed, turning Xinjiang into a battleground of warring Chinese and Tungan warlords, fanatical mullahs and wild tribal chiefs. Chinese were massacred in large numbers. Independent governments were periodically set up, some calling themselves republics, and others, kingdoms under Amirs. By 1932, Xinjiang was reaching an anarchic state.[24]

In the early 1930s, the Japanese had occupied Manchuria and were in control of the five north-eastern provinces of China, having also penetrated as far south and west as Kansu. These developments worried the Soviets. Fearing that the Japanese or British may encourage rebellion across their Asiatic republics, the Soviets decided to intervene in Xinjiang in 1933. They propped up a local Chinese general and helped him suppress the Muslim revolt. By 1934, the Muslim rebellion stood quelled and the Chinese influence eliminated as Xinjiang gradually came to settle under Soviet guidance.[25]

The Soviets however could sustain their influence in Xinjiang for only a decade. During the period of occupation, they tried to silence the reactionary Muslim and the nationalist voice, closing down mosques and ridiculing the mullahs. The policy aroused strong local hostility. As the Soviets came under increasing pressure from the Germans in 1942, their influence in Xinjiang waned and their authority was completely erased by 1944.[26]

K.P.S. Menon, an Indian Political Service officer, in 1944 had journeyed overland in these areas, taking the northern Silk Road on which Hsuan Tsang once travelled to India.[27] During the times of the ancient traveller, Xinjiang was culturally quite akin to India, dotted as it was with Buddhist kingdoms, the most famous being Khotan. With Islam's advent in the tenth century, the past was blotted out, not altogether though, because remains of the civilization that preceded Islam survived to be unearthed later by Sir Aurel Stein. The rock-cut temples that Menon saw during his journey had reminded him, in detail and design of Ajanta and Ellora.

Thirteen years after that journey, Menon had an occasion to revisit Xinjiang. He was then India's Ambassador to the USSR. He described himself as feeling like a Rip Van Winkle. Urumchi had changed beyond recognition, touched by the magic wand of communism; beggars had disappeared and women were no longer in purdah. Agriculture was collectivized and mechanized. The institution mainly responsible for the agrarian revolution was the Army Production Corps, consisting of 240,000 former soldiers of the People's Liberation Army.

Xinjiang's isolation lay destroyed. Roads and railway lines were being built at a frenetic pace. Menon had observed in 1957 that a road connecting southern Xinjiang to the borders of Tibet, via Aksai Chin, had just been completed and that another surface route from Yangihissar to the Chinese Pamirs was in the process of completion. To Menon, the Chinese appeared determined to prevent any intrusion into Xinjiang. The historical pilgrim and caravan route from India to China was closed. India's consulate at Kashgar and the British and American consulates in Urumchi were withdrawn. Even the Soviet consulate in Kashgar was shut down. The only consulate left in Xinjiang was the Soviet one in Urumchi, and even that seemed to be existing on sufferance.

What surprised Menon most was that Urumchi had become a predominately Chinese town. In 1944 he had hardly seen a Chinese face in the bazaar. In 1944, when Chiang Kai-shek wanted to settle some refugees in Xinjiang, it nearly caused a revolt locally. But thirteen years later, the same people watched the Chinese influx helplessly.

Menon wondered if a similar fate would overcome Tibet. Would Tibet, too, be opened up like Xinjiang? Would the landmarks of Tibet be similarly destroyed? Within five years of Menon's second visit, the social and political institutions of Tibet were set aside and the Dalai Lama was forced to flee India. The Chinese launched an Indian invasion soon thereafter and Nehru, who had been accorded a hero's welcome in China, became the 'Enemy of Peace No. 1' and Khrushchev was proclaimed 'Enemy of Peace No. 2'.

China shares a short 90 km border with Afghanistan along Xinjiang, the only Chinese province with a Sunni majority population. The area lies across the path of the silk route from Rome to China and has always shown high resistance to the Chinese authorities. China's earlier lack of strategic concern with this area was mirrored by the weak lines of communication. Moreover, to the Chinese, the strategic importance of Afghanistan was never significant. Beijing did not regard Afghanistan as a serious threat, preoccupied as it was with its northern border and north China Sea issues. But the coup against King Zahir Shah in 1973 had the Chinese growing weary of the increasing Soviet influence in Afghanistan. China had reason to be perturbed because of the location of its nuclear arsenal in Xinjiang, near the Afghan border. After the Soviet invasion of Afghanistan, China became gravely concerned about Soviet military activity in Badakshan and the Wakhan corridor that bordered China. Afghanistan adjoins Iran and Pakistan, and is only 400 km from the Indian Ocean. The Chinese also became concerned about the security of Pakistan. They feared Baluchistan becoming a target of the Soviet drive to the warm waters of the Indian Ocean.[28] To the Chinese, Pakistan stood out as being most menaced. From Afghanistan, Soviet military aircraft were within striking distance of the strategic strait of Hormuz at the entry point of the Persian Gulf, the world's chief oil-producing centre.

Throughout the Cold War, Afghanistan remained an important cross-roads of confrontation, involving not only the USA, the Soviet Union and China, but also Pakistan. Afghanistan acquired primacy in the Chinese foreign policy under the changed circumstances as China endeavoured to bring back Afghanistan under its sphere of influence. Afghanistan not only served as a critical land bridge between south-west and south-east Asia, it was also the gateway to the plains of South Asia and the shores of the Indian Ocean.[29]

The Chinese reacted strongly when the Soviet Union annexed the Wakhan corridor and altered the border without consulting China. According to Western intelligence reports, the Soviets had built all-weather roads in the corridor, enabling rapid deployment of Soviet troops to either side of the Pakistani or Chinese border. Their purpose in gaining control of the Wakhan corridor was to penetrate into Pakistan's northern border areas. China's worst fears were confirmed when the Soviet Union concluded a border agreement with Afghanistan on 16 June 1981, pertaining to the Wakhan corridor. The Chinese declared the treaty 'illegal and invalid'.[30] Soviet troops began to occupy the Wakhan corridor in May 1980, and took full administrative control of the area, though never publicly admitting to the fact.

With the collapse of the Soviet Union in December 1991, the Soviet threat to China subsided. But soon enough, China's west witnessed the rise of strong ethno-nationalist sentiments in Xinjiang that precipitated in riots, inspired as the leaders of the movement were by the ideals of a 'holy war', borrowed from the Afghan mujahidins. The Chinese government came down heavily to supress the uprisings which they considered separatist.

China has been sensitive to any attempt by outside forces to foster separatism in Xinjiang, often accusing the West of trying to foment trouble through Uyghur exiles, considered 'outsiders' and 'separatists'. Although they share commonalities with Tibetan exiles, the Uyghurs suffer certain major disadvantages. The most important is the lack of leadership.There is nobody with an image remotely similar to that of the Dalai Lama, an icon of spirituality in the West. Islam's negative image and its lack of emphasis on non-violence does not carry much popular appeal in the West.[31]

For Uyghurs, Islam and ethnic consciousness are closely linked—'they are Muslims because they are Uyghurs'.[32] The Chinese authorities find themselves in a piquant situation—if they allow Islam to flourish, it alienates Uyghurs from Chinese society, and if they attempt to suppress it, it causes resentment among the Uyghurs. It is a no-win situation. What always worries China is a sudden and strong resurgence of Islam in Xinjiang.

The ethnic tension in Xinjiang is not just religious. The Uyghurs perceive the Chinese as oppressors, with Chinese immigrants having taken over the natural resources and land of Xinjiang, which ought to belong to the Uyghurs by right. On the subject of employment, the Uyghurs feel that it is the Han Chinese who have cornered all the jobs in Xinjiang and that the Han employers generally look down upon Uyghurs as less 'civilized' and less educated. Most modern cities like Urumchi appear dominated by Han Chinese.

Earlier, the military threat of the Soviet Union had forced China to station its forces in Xinjiang. The Chinese also had to place their troops along the Mongolian border to balance out the Soviet forces. But the historical rivalry with Russia over Mongolia got resolved in 1991, just around the time the Soviet Union broke up—a double military gain for China which greatly reduced its defence burden.

In close geographical proximity, the Central Asian states are not in a position to resist the dominance of China, the USA or a resurgent

Russia. This region too is of high strategic significance as it links Europe with Asia. Control over this territory also means containment of Europe. China knows the real purpose of US involvement in this region, which is to weaken Russian influence and curtail Chinese presence. China, for its part, plays an active role in promoting the Shanghai Cooperation initiative, largely in self-interest. The region is vital as it borders China's old enemy Russia, also for the fact that the US is gradually establishing its influence in this area. In geo-political terms, this is one of the key sites of great power competition. Sovereign states in the region are weak and unlikely to resist intervention by powerful countries.

In the almost unipolar world of today, China has fast emerged as an alternative to the United States. It is now intent on reviving the old Silk Road. This route came into existence some 2,000 years ago to subsequently fall into disuse when the region of modern Xinjiang and principalities of Central Asia became Islamized. The old Silk Road was a consequence of an attempt by early Chinese emperors to extend their influence westwards, over land, to the Mediterranean and thence to Rome. Some such similar effort is under way now. China is heavily dependent on sea trade for its import of crude oil. The routes pass through areas of American influence. China, by increasing the prospects of overland trade, wants to nullify this strategic vulnerability.

China has consistently striven to augment its influence across regions. A recent and clear example is the 2015 White Paper on military strategy, eighth in the series since 1998, which self-acknowledges China's national strength. The paper is reflective of an ambition to rejuvenate the Chinese nation by 2049, the year of the centenary celebrations of the People's Republic of China. The paper focuses on the role of China's navy, in line with the strategic requirement for oil, denoting a shift from 'offshore water defence' to 'open seas protection'. A crucial assertion is 'preparation for military struggle', an implicit reference to ethnic, religious, border and territorial disputes and conflicts that are recurrent. What China wants recognized is that its armed forces have come a long way from being a rustic and bucolic 'Red Army' that waged a 'People's War' more than six decades ago. Another important aspect is the Chinese armed forces which seek to deter adversaries by the sheer military might at their command. China's 'peaceful rise' definitely appears 'belligerent'.

International concern exists on the issue of China reclaiming lands from coral reefs in the South China Sea. China lays claim to 90 per cent of these waters, which is disputed by countries like Vietnam and Malaysia. The President of the Philippines, while in Tokyo in June 2015, drew an analogy between Nazi Germany's annexation of Czechoslovakia and China's activities in the South China Sea. On Fiery Cross Reef in Spratly Islands, China has built military facilities that includes a 3-km runway capable of handling fighter jets. The next logical step for China would be to claim the air space over South China Sea by declaring an air defence identification zone. Is China presenting this region with a *fait accompli*?

Pakistan is an old and trusted ally of China's. Pakistan, time and again, has reiterated that the two countries are 'true iron brothers'. With China ready to invest more than 45 billion dollars in Pakistan, its clout there is bound to increase. Mainstream political parties of Pakistan are all praise for China's decision to invest in their country. No debate has taken place on China's expanding role and agenda in South Asia.

China is run by an all-pervasive communist party whose ideology is different from that of Pakistan's leadership. The clergy and political leadership in Pakistan feel hardly discomfited by this fact. To them, Islam and 'Pakistaniyat' can safely coexist with the contradictory communist ideology. The benefits that accrue from China's patronage far outweigh those from Washington's, for the 'development' footprint of the USA in Pakistan is limited. However, China's investment in Pakistan's infrastructure is not only for development purposes. It most certainly has strategic implications.

China's engagement in the Af-Pak region has become intensive. Before the new Afghan President, Ashraf Ghani, could visit Delhi in April 2015, he had already visited China, his first overseas outing. China has invested heavily in Afghanistan's copper reserves and its oil fields. It has also been involved in the reconciliation process initiated by the Afghan President with the Taliban. In May 2015, China facilitated an informal meeting in the Xinjiang capital Urumchi between the Taliban and Afghan officials. China would like to control the radical Muslim Uyghurs in Xinjiang and is interested therefore in the affairs of Afghanistan. The trilateral strategic dialogue between

China, Pakistan and Afghanistan was held in Kabul in February 2015. China has committed to financing the construction of a new dam in Kunnar, a motorway connecting Peshawar with Kabul and a railway linking Quetta with Kandhar. Pakistan and China have become prominent players in Afghanistan at the expense of the Delhi–Kabul special relationship. India is hard put to be part of the solution to the Taliban problem in the Af-Pak region.

It is in China's interest to intervene in Afghanistan and contain Islamic radicalism of the Taliban and Islamic State. It is in a position to coerce Pakistan to cooperate with Afghanistan on this issue. Pakistan, on the other hand, is equally keen to get out of the economic quagmire it finds itself in and is quite solicitous of China's help to contain the restive situation that exists in Baluchistan and Sindh. Pakistan has a 900-km-long border with Iran. Once China takes up the work of infrastructure development along the economic corridor in earnest, the problems, Pakistan hopes, in Sindh and Baluchistan shall die out. The same may also be true of Gilgit-Baltistan, where considerable disaffection brews among the Shia Muslims. Much of the newly announced China–Pakistan economic corridor passes through Gilgit-Baltistan, an area six times that of Azad Kashmir. The Siachen Glacier lies in this region. Gilgit-Baltistan is also the only land connection Pakistan has with China. This adjoins the 225-km-long Wakhan corridor of Afghanistan. China has a substantial military presence in this area which will further get consolidated with the construction of this corridor. The territory of Xinjiang provides China with a base to intervene in Tibet and Kashmir. In fact Gilgit-Baltistan, where it already has a strong presence, is part of the erstwhile princely state of Kashmir.

**The Hindu Kush: History Recounted**

The present impasse in the NWFP and Afghanistan is a cause for deep concern for India. As we know, the region of the Hindu Kush, though formidable, is neither inhospitable nor impassable. It comprises many fertile valleys, for example the valley of Bamian. Several passes— Anjuman, Khawak, Salang or Shibar—have long provided access from the north and west into India. The territories of the Hindu Kush are key to India as political crystallization has always tended to centre around it. The Greco-Bactrians, the Kushans, the Ghaznavids, the Ghorids and the Durranis, were all holders of the Kabul–Ghazni area. By the beginning of 19th century Russia emerged as an heir to the nomadic empires of Central Asia, and in India the British replaced the Marathas as effective rulers. But the Hindu Kush continued to be the key. Britain was vitally interested that the 'key'[33] did not fall into unfriendly hands, and hence the Anglo-Afghan wars. When Britain lost control of Afghan foreign policy after the Treaty of Rawalpindi (1921), it hurried to establish a mission at Kabul so that 'the key' did not go too far astray. With the British withdrawal in 1947, India stood divided. The old Indian Army disappeared. Afghanistan, also the country of the Hindu Kush, accustomed to nearly a century of a counterpoise provided by Britain to Russia, faced a new situation. In a vastly changed scenario, the importance of the 'key' increased.

The territory of the Hindu Kush has always been a migrating human highway for expanding civilizations and religions and a 'key-point in the structure of empires'.[34] People from Central Asia en route the Indian subcontinent have long since passed through it. The Aryans, in the second half of the second millennium BC, came down to supplant the pre-Aryan Indus Valley culture.

It was the expanding Achaemenid Persian empire across Afghanistan into the Indus valley (in and after the sixth century BC), that brought with it the Aramaic script, the alphabets of which were taken from the Phoenicians. From Afghanistan, the use of Aramaic script spread to the Indian subcontinent and across Asia.[36] The second surge of Iranian-speaking people was that of the Sakas who came in the second century BC, some of them settling in the delta of Helmand river, Seistan, then known as Sarangia. Yuechis, another nomadic group of Central Asians who followed close on the heels of the Sakas, put down their roots in Bactria, the country between the Oxus and the Hindu Kush. In the first century AD, one of the Yuechi tribes, the Kushans, built an empire that straddled the Hindu Kush and stretched from the southern banks of the Oxus to the western banks of the Yamuna. In the course of the last nineteen centuries, the Kushan empire has had more than one avatar. Approximately the same area was ruled subsequently by Mahmud of Ghazni and Ahmad Shah Abdali.

In the fifth century AD, the Huns invaded India across the Hindu Kush, but the Mongols surpassed them in destruction and ferocity when they overran this swathe and most of continental Eurasia in the thirteenth century. On the mainland, only India and Western Europe escaped. In the early sixteenth century, the Turkish-speaking people from western Siberia, the Uzbegs, had come to occupy northern Afghanistan and Uzbekistan on the opposite side of the Oxus river. Though they never crossed the Hindu Kush, the Uzbegs pushed the Timurids (previous Turkish rulers of Central Asia) out by conquering their territory. It was these Timurids who founded India's Mughal empire.

Why is it that the direction of migration has almost always been from the west to the east on the 'Hindu Kush' highway? The period of ancient India notwithstanding, the Arabs, the Turkish rulers of Ghazni, and the Ghoris who supplanted them followed this route. The Lodis, the Mughals, the Rohillas, all of them moved in the same direction—east into India.

Except for the spread of Buddhism, which was a migration in the westerly direction, all movements in India's long history followed the opposite direction. The Kushan empire was the thoroughfare along which Buddhism made its way from India, through Central Asia and Xinjiang. From there it spread to the rest of China, into Korea, Japan, and Vietnam. The role of the Hindu Kush as a 'roundabout' has never been played to greater effect. This route from India to China via the Afghan/Pathan territory looks strangely circuitous on the map (Toynbee 1961:11).

There is a message, a warning, here for India. History should caution us of an impending threat from the north-west, through the valleys and passes of the Hindu Kush. The migration highway of the Hindu Kush till now has only facilitated one-way traffic—west to east—an important enough reason for India to be sensitive to the critical strategic importance of this thoroughfare, which if ignored, can seriously imperil its security.

For some 150 years, the Afghans have done a fine balancing act, first between the Russians and the British and later the Soviet Union and the US. But the benefactors of Afghanistan have been no 'disinterested philanthropists'. Though the USSR was Afghanistan's next-door neighbour, it is difficult to say which of the competing parties was less dangerous. Great Britain and the USA, geographically sundered from Afghanistan by oceans, have aggressively meddled in this region. Even if their ambitions were not near territorial, their active interference severely affected Afghanistan's sovereignty.

Long ago, Arnold Toynbee drew a not-so-light-hearted analogy between India and Europe, calling Kashmir a subcontinental Vilna and the region of the Pathans the subcontinental Sudetenland. He also went on to explain how the Durand Line became sacrosanct to Pakistanis, the McMahon Line to Indians, Gibraltar to Englishmen and West Berlin to the Germans. To use his phrase, 'lines arbitrarily drawn by Britain ended up getting retrospectively consecrated as precious national assets of the British Indian empire's non-British successor-states'.[37] When these lines were drawn, 'the exercise produced no great stir among the Hindus and Muslims'.[38] Durand and McMahon had only contributed to the 'immoral game of power-politics that the British imperialists played'. Arnold Toynbee, himself a Briton, offered an apologia when he stated that the consecration of these 'British-made lines as heirlooms in the successor-states national heritage was an unexpected result'.[39] It was also unfortunate, to say the least.

When India was undivided, the government had just one frontier to hold: the north-west frontier facing Afghanistan, and beyond Afghanistan, Russia. The Indo-Chinese frontier had not yet lit up. For purposes of military defence, it could still be ignored. Yet the cost of holding the single frontier imposed severe financial strain. Today, India has a frontier in Bengal and one in Punjab and a third against China. As for Afghanistan, her entente with the Soviet Union ended perilously. All the three countries have been subjected to strains that were best avoided by resolving disputes and standing together for their common defence. The possibility of future aggression by a powerful country always exists. Neither India, nor Afghanistan, nor Pakistan has been spared. The resolution of Kashmir and the Durand Line conflict therefore is a big imperative, as time and again, nationalism in these countries has triumphed over statesmanship.[40]

Certain patterns and themes in history—usually referred to as cul-de-sacs and roundabouts—help to better comprehend the lay of the land that is India's neighbourhood. It was not until the fifteenth century that the Portuguese came to command sailing ships which kept them long enough on sea to cross the Atlantic. Before this happened, the European continent had remained a virtual cul-de-sac. But not long thereafter, Western Europe was transformed into the world's central 'roundabout', 'from which all sea-routes radiated and converged'. Unfortunately, for the expanse of territory south of the Hindu Kush, it resulted in the drying up of overland traffic, the single most important factor for the region's fortunes. Temporarily the land of the Afghans/Pathans ceased to be what it was, a historical 'roundabout'.[41]

After India's independence, Britain's influence gradually diminished in the Indian subcontinent. The Russians moved in quickly to fill the vacuum. It is inherent in history that power dynamics should change, and it does change. The nuclear weapon states have desisted from going to war, but this has not stopped the international power game that must always go on. The rivalries among powerful nations mostly play out inconclusively in different hemispheres of the world, usually as a race for establishing influence—economic, strategic and political. In Afghanistan's case, the US and the USSR vied for influence by providing aid, constructing roads or developing irrigation systems. But the economic bonus, valuable though it was, came with an accompanying risk for Afghanistan, for its 'roundabouts', the strategic assets, were to become tempting political prizes.[42] Instead of Afghanistan gaining from this cooperation, it was subjected to an invasion and takeover by the Soviet Union. This situation lasted for a decade in the 1980s. The 1990s saw the rise of the Taliban in Afghanistan—subsequently driven out by NATO forces in 2001. America's war on terror resulted in a virtual US takeover of Afghanistan.

It is mainly the Pakhtuns on both sides of the Durand Line who provide sustenance to the Taliban. Clannish in their social mores, they display traits of broad commonality of race, religion, language and history. The tribes in this belt have governed a fairly well-defined territory and have successfully excluded other claimants of authority. They display a substantial degree of ethnic and linguistic unity, share the same religion, follow the same customs and have a somewhat uniform family structure. In short, they display the homogeneity of social and political institutions which through time developed into a political cohesion giving rise to Pakhtun nationalism. The ideological content of Pakhtun nationalism has been kept alive in the writings and speeches of the Pakhtun people—their philosophers, poets and politicians.

The Pakhtuns have always resisted conquest and integration within a larger nation. At the same time they themselves have been in a perpetual state of internal conflict and disunity.[43] The internal authority within the Pakhtuns is a sum total of relations between the individual and the leaders of the tribe, the khans and the mullahs. The individual Pakhtun respects both, but at best can only be influenced by them and not controlled. The authority structure therefore becomes tenuous, making the Pakhtuns volatile and difficult to harness. Their leadership is dependent on personal qualities rather than obedience or loyalty to a hierarchy or ideology. As a result, no mystique is attached to kingship. The kings (and now the presidents) have been viewed merely as first among equals who command loyalty only by virtue of superior force, wealth or personal qualities admired by tribal standards. The element of legitimacy plays a minor role in tribal loyalty to the central authority. For this reason, it has not been difficult to change dynasties, depose kings, or abolish the monarchy altogether and establish a republic. The resultant history of Afghan polity has been one of periodical fusion and fission, passing through cycles during which a strong charismatic leader captures the throne and unites the disparate tribal elements, thus enhancing the power of the central authority only to be followed by a period of fission when the charismatic leader weakens or dies and the centrifugal forces of tribal separatism reassert themselves.[44]

Historically, the tribes have been king breakers and makers, and any government that wants to rule in Kabul has to make peace with the tribes, usually on their terms. Attempts at building a strong army loyal to the central government have faced strong tribal and religious opposition, and have been made possible only by justifying them on grounds of 'Pakhtunistan', which everyone knows the mullahs and tribes would support.[45]

Pakhtun nationalism has also bridged cleavages and provided a platform for politicians to create their own popular base. The other two unifying factors have been monarchy and Islam. But as I have said, the legitimacy of kingship as an institution is at best quite weak in Pakhtun tribal society.

If tribal cleavages are an obstacle to a strong centralist government, why would the Afghan leaders want to incorporate transborder tribesmen into Afghanistan? Would it not increase their problems? The Afghan leaders, aware of the problem, cannot disown the transborder Pakhtuns. To most Afghans, Pakhtunistan is a symbol of a glorious past, a formula for the political present and a harbinger of a more powerful future.[46]

People of this tract are bound by a strong sense of kinship, a sub-tribal structure, that substitutes for political and economic institutions. The Pathan/Afghan society is largely semi-literate. The brand of Islam practised is of a village variety, operating at an 'inward-looking' level to meet the needs of the people. The people here are born into a set of 'answers', with their marriages and vocations predetermined. Kinship plays a major role in a man's political status. To the question 'why', everyone knows the answer, quite in contrast to most other societies where an individual is born to a set of questions instead.[47] In this society, where rights and obligations centre on the village, tribe or group and not on the central government, dissension cannot be allowed to brew.[48]

Most daily activity revolves around basic subsistence—survival; whereas in a successful society, a far smaller percentage of population is involved in food production. What about the majority of the people? In an evolved community, there exists a 'great waste potential',[49] or potential for production outside the economic subsistence sphere. The factor contributing most to the growth of civilizations has been their 'waste potential', where one can afford to waste twenty-three or twenty-four years (or more) in educating children. In the Pathan/Afghan fraternity, young children are forced to begin work early. They learn about their reciprocal rights in the village. There is not much chance in this society for waste potential to develop. At one time, this neighbourhood, together with much of the Middle East, had a civilization based on 'waste potential'. During the Ghaznavid period, more than nine hundred poets lived in the capital city at Ghazni under the patronage of Shah Mahmud, an indication of the waste potential enjoyed by this society. But nothing of the kind now exists.[50]

## Two Nations or Two States!

The Hindu Kush is of paramount importance to India. The last twenty years are a witness to the effect it has had on Pakistan which saw the rise of the Taliban and other Islamist forces. This development has impinged on the integrity and structure of the Pakistani state. The Pakhtuns make up a disproportionate percentage of the Pakistani army, around 20 per cent, though they are only 12 per cent of the population. The Pakistani army is a Punjabi/Pakhtun army with Punjabis in large majority. The Pakhtuns come second. The Baluchs and Sindhis are almost absent.[51] The Punjabis, who constitute the rank and file, are mostly from a relatively limited number of districts in northern Punjab, some of which though Punjabi speaking are heavily coloured by Pakhtun traditions. It is the Pakhtun area which is of concern because it is this region which has seen incidents where the Pakhtun units of the army sent in to fight against the Taliban and its local allies in the tribal areas have refused to fight. The state of Pakistan on the other hand cannot rely on nationalism because it is not a nation, much rather a federation. There is no such thing as Urdu nationalism because for an overwhelming majority of Pakistanis, Urdu is a second language, a learned language, not as alien as English, but still not native. The Baluchs, the Sindis and the Mohajirs quite resent the overbearing Punjabi sub-nationalism.

There is another serious problem that the Indian subcontinent has to contend with. This one is intrinsic, the arithmetic of which needs internal resolution. While over sixty years old, India and Pakistan are still very young. The experience encountered in their shared path to freedom is still relevant to draw lessons from, though the common baggage of ancestry continues to confound efforts at conflict resolution. The past is constantly lamented—Jinnah's and Congress's intransigence and British chicanery, leading to India's fractured freedom. Those who experienced the trauma of partition still relive it. The usual refrain is to blame the then Indian leadership for having misread the situation. Had the consequence of vivisection and human suffering been known to Nehru, Jinnah or Mountbatten, India may have remained united. But this implied argument in hindsight does not hold good. Why? Perhaps the answer lies in the all-important question of our 'identity', in the nationhood of communities that transformed into two and then three states. The idea of 'population transfer' on the lines of religion, race and language was not alien and certainly did not surprise the Indian political leadership when it faced the imminent prospect of partition in 1947.

South Asia's contemporary history is that of fractured identity. We still contend with the problem of 'national identity'. Is it to be defined in terms of territory in which people live regardless of their ethnic, racial or religious origins or in terms of shared heritage—of a common ethnic ancestry? This second definition of national identity, where the subjective belief in the reality of a common 'we' has a high emotive value, is broadly presented as 'ethno-nationalist'. Central to it is the theme that nations exist, that each nation ought to have its own state, and that each state should be made up of members of a single nation. Extend this argument and you have a troubling theoretical construct of 'making the state and the nations commensurate with each other and practically reducing to a subject condition all other nationalities that may lie within the boundary'.[52] This statement of Lord Acton, made in 1862, is unfortunately borne out by the historical experience of modern Europe: from voluntary exodus to population transfers to ethnic cleansing—much of its history is in fact a process of ethnic disaggregation. The newly created states always tended to protect and promote dominant ethnic populations, whether it was the Balkans when the Ottoman empire disintegrated or the break-up of the Hapsburgs and Romanovs. An extreme case in example was the Nazi attempt to reorder the ethnic map of Europe by force.[53] While the map making after the Great War became an exercise at drawing borders that homogenized with the dominant ethnic groups, the post World War II period saw populations move out of borders in large numbers. Leaders like Churchill, Roosevelt and Stalin were all in agreement with the expulsion of ethnic Germans from non-German countries for they believed that such a movement would provide stability to the post War order. In a speech to the British Parliament in December 1944, Churchill said: 'Expulsion is a method which, so far as we have been able to see, will be the most satisfactory and lasting. There will be no mixture of population to cause endless trouble. A clean sweep will be made. I am not alarmed of the prospects of the disentanglement of population. Nor am I alarmed by these large transferences.' It was with the tacit approval of these world leaders that the largest forced population movement in Europe's history took place. Hundreds of thousands died as a result.[54]

This historical process is common as countries like Czechoslovakia, the Soviet Union and Yugoslavia have amply demonstrated. Czechoslovakia split into the Czech and Slovak republics; the Soviet Union into a variety of national units. After Croatia and Slovenia had seceded, Yugoslavia descended into a war over Bosnia and Kosovo.

That Britain would transfer power to India was never in doubt after World War II. With just a few weeks left before they withdrew from India, the British hurriedly decided to draw a line of partition, a partition that saw the bloodiest transfer of population in Asia's history. Fifteen million people became refugees. Soon thereafter, a Jewish state was created in 1948 out of the former British Mandate for Palestine. The resultant wars saw Arabs forced out from the areas under Jewish control and vice versa. In 1962, after the French control in Algeria ended, most Algerians of European origin emigrated to France. The Asian minorities were similarly forced out of the African continent. Pakistan was divided on the issue of language. Language as we know is a strong basis of ethno-nationalism. What is being seen now is that groups best positioned to take advantage of globalization are the ethnically national dominant groups, a development that is sure to deepen social cleavages in multi-ethnic societies.

Jinnah, the principal player of India's partition episode, well appreciated the emotive power of a common 'we', of a nation state based on common faith. A case in point is his call for a 'Direct Action' day on 16 August 1946. On this day erupted a communal Vesuvius in India which completely polarized the Hindus and Muslims. Once ethno-nationalistic antagonism crossed a certain threshold, maintaining the rival groups within a single polity became impossible. Lord Listowel was a minister who served on the India Committee of both the Churchill and Attlee governments of Britain and was also the last Secretary of State for India. Giving for the first time his version of the events that led to the creation of India and Pakistan, he said, 'We failed to foresee the mass migrations and the horrific massacres...we relied on Mountbatten for advice, and he told us subsequently that he himself was totally unaware of the scale of violence.' But going by Lord Acton's premise, India had to be partitioned, for how could Jinnah's nation of Muslims then coexist with Hindus in a united India under conditions of perpetual numerical minority? The problem remains far from being solved. India still has 154 million Muslims and we are not twentieth-century Europe.

## Notes

1. Quoted in W.K. Fraser-Tytler, *Afghanistan: A Study of Political Developments in Central and Southern Asia* (second edition), Oxford University Press, 1950, p.193.
2. A phrase used by Lord Asquith in praising his fellow students of Balliol College, Oxford, Ibid.
3. Olaf Caroe, *The Pathans, 550 B.C. to A.D. 1957*, Macmillan & Co, 1958, p.433.
4. Ibid., p.433.
5. Ibid., p.434.
6. Ibid., p.434.
7. Ibid., pp.434–35.
8. Ibid., p.435.
9. Ibid.
10. Ibid.
11. A term aptly coined by Carlton Coon in his book *Caravan: The Story of the Middle-East*, Holt, 1961.
12. Olaf Caroe, *Soviet Empire*, Macmillan & Co., 1953.
13. An article by Leon B. Poullada 'Pakhtunistan: Afghan Domestic Politics and Relations with Pakistan', in Ainslee T. Embree (ed.), *Pakistan's Western Borderlands: The Transformation of a Political Order*, Vikas Publishing house Pvt. Limited, 1977, p.130.
14. Ibid., pp.131–32.
15. Hilaire Belloc, *The Modern Traveller*, Edward Arnold, 1898.
16. Fraser-Tytler, *Afghanistan*, Oxford University Press, 1950, pp.314–15.
17. Rob Gifford, *China Road*, Bloomsbury, 2008, p.252.
18. The Manchus invaded China from Manchuria (now north-east China) in 1644. To rule the vast empire, they adopted many Chinese ways, but retained the Manchu traits as well. Earlier, the Manchus had been hunters

and horsemen, with a pan-Asian view more similar to the Mongols than to the Han Chinese.
19. Gifford, *China Road,* p.254.
20. Inquiry into the Proceedings of Pamir Boundry Commission by W.K. Fraser-Tytler, Appendix 4, in his book *Afghanistan,* p.330.
21. Ibid., p.331.
22. K.P.S. Menon, *Many Worlds-An Autobiography,* Oxford University Press, 1965, pp.139–40.
23. Ibid., p.141.
24. Ibid., p.142.
25. N.L.D. McLean, 'Sinking Today', *International Affairs,* 8 May 1948, p.379.
26. Ibid., pp.379–80.
27. K.P.S. Menon describes this visit in the chapter on Central Asia in his autobiography, *Many Worlds,* pp.193–210.
28. A.Z. Hilali, 'China's Response to the Soviet Invasion of Afghanistan', *Central Asian Survey* (2001), 20(3), pp.323–25.
29. Shen Yu Dai, 'China and Afghanistan', *China Quarterly,* 5(2), January–March 1966, p.107.
30. Gargi Dutt, 'China and the Development in Afghanistan', in K.P. Mishra (ed.), *Afghanistan in Crisis,* Advent, 1981 p.41.
31. *Beijing Review,* no 5, 4 February 1980, p.4.
32. *The New York Times,* 30 December 1979.
33. 'Russia versus China: Struggle for Asia', *U.S. News & World Report,* 5 February 1979, and *New York Times,* 10 January 1980.
34. *People's Daily,* 10 March 1980.
35. A.Z. Hilali, China's Response to the Soviet Invasion of Afghanistan, pp.328–29.
36. C. G. Jacobsen, *Sino-Soviet Relations since Mao: The Chairman's Legacy,* Praeger, 1981, pp.92–105.
37. Beijing Domestic Service, 1 February 1980; FBIS–SAS Report no. 80, 4 February 1980, PFI.
38. J. Bruce Amstutz, *Afghanistan: The First Five Years of Societ Occupation,* Washington, National Defence University Press, 1986, p.296.
39. Colin Mackerras, 'Xinjiang at the Turn of the Century : The Causes of Separatism', *Central Asian Survey,* 20(3), 2001, p.294.
40. Ibid., p.296.
41. Ibid., p.299.

42. Russell Ong, 'China's Security Interests in Central Asia', *Central Asian Survey*, 24(4), December 2005, p.427.
43. Ibid., p.428.
44. Ibid., p.435
45. Ibid., p.437.
46. Phrase used by Sir Michael Gillet during his address on Afghanistan given to the Royal Central Asian Society on 19 April 1966.
47. Arnold J. Toynbee, *Between Oxus and Jumna*, Oxford University Press, 1961, p.4.
48. Ibid., pp.4–5.
49. Ibid., pp.6-7.
50. Ibid., p.11.
51. Arnold J. Toynbee, 'The Roundabout in Retrospect', in *Between Oxus and Jumna*, p.190.
52. Ibid.
53. Ibid.
54. Ibid., pp.190–91.
55. Ibid., p.2.
56. Address given by Louis Dupree on 'Afghanistan in the Twentieth Century' to the Royal Central Asian Society on 8 July 1964, published in the *Journal of the Royal Central Asian Society*, 1965, p.27.
57. Toynbee, *Between Oxus and Jumna*, p.4.
58. Poullada, 'Pakhtunistan', p.145.
59. Ibid., pp.145–46.
60. Ibid., pp.146–47.
61. Ibid., p.151.
62. Dupree, 'Afghanistan in the Twentieth Century', p.21.
63. Ibid.
64. Ibid.
65. Ibid., p.22.
66. Ibid.
67. Ashraf Ghani, 'Isam and State-Building in a Tribal Society Afghanistan: 1880-1901' *Modern Asian Studies*, 12 (2), 1978, pp.269–84.
68. Gazetteer of Afghanistan, II, 197–215.
69. Ghani, 'Islam and State building in a Tribal Society Afghanistan', pp.269–84.
70. Address given by Anatol Lieven of King's College, London to The Royal

Society for Asian Affairs on 30 October 2007; Asian Affairs, 39(1), March 2008, p.58.
71. Ibid., p.64.
72. Ibid., p.58.
73. Ibid., pp.58-59.
74. Ibid., pp.59-60.
75. Ibid., pp.65-66.
76. Ibid., p.67.
77. Ibid., pp.67-68.
78. Jerry Z. Muller, 'Us and Them', *Foreign Affairs*, March/April 2008, p.20.
79. Ibid., p.23.
80. Ibid., p.26.
81. Ibid., p.27.

# References

**Prefatory Note**

Ahmad, Akbar S. (1983), *Religion and Politics in Muslim Society*. Cambridge University Press.
Chaudhuri, Nirad C. (1964), *The Autobiography of an Unknown Indian*. Jaico Publishing House.
Harris, John (1975), *Much Sounding of Bugles—The Seize of Chitral*. Hutchinson.
Jain, Girilal (1994), *The Hindu Phenomenon*. UBS Publishers.
Lewis, Bernard (1986), 'State, Nation and Religion in Islam', in Joseph Alpher (ed.), *Nationalism and Modernity—A Mediterranean Perspective*. Praeger.
Moorhouse, Geoffrey (1986), *To the Frontier*. Coronet Books, pp.254-55.

**Chapter 1: India's Partition: A Strategic Necessity for Britain**

Afroz, Sultana (1988), 'Pakistan and the 1951 Middle East Defence Plan—The US and the UK Positions', *Journal for the Royal Society of Asian Affairs*, 19.
Blyth, Robert J. (2000), 'Britain versus India in the Persian Gulf: The struggle for political control—1928-48', *Journal of Imperial and Commonwealth History*, 28 (1).
Campbell-Johnson, Alan (1951), *Mission with Mountbatten*. Hamish Hamilton Ltd.
Caroe, Olaf (1952), *Wells of Power*. Macmillan & Co.
Gilbert, Martin (1988), *Never Despair: Winston S Churchill, 1945-1965*. Heinemann.
Hansard, 6 March 1947.
Kothekar, Shanta (1998), 'Winston Churchill and the Partition of India', in Ramakant and Rajan Mahan (eds), *India's Partition*. Rawat Publications.

*Manchester Guardian*, 7 March 1947.
Ziegler, Philip (1985), *Mountbatten*. Collins, p.366.

## Chapter 2: Convoyed through the Land of Insolence

Ahmad, Akbar S. (1978), 'An Aspect of the Colonial Encounter in the NWFP', *Journal of the Royal Society of Asian Affairs*, 9, pp.319–27.
———. (1980), 'Tribes and States in Central and South Asia', *Journal of the Royal Society of Asian Affairs*, 11 (2).
Allen, Charles (2001), *Soldier Sahibs*. Abacus.
———. (2006), *God's Terrorists*. Little Brown.
Buchan, John (1924), *Lord Minto, A Memoir*. Thomas Nelson and Sons.
Caroe, Olaf (1958), *The Pathans 550 B.C.–A.D. 1957*, Macmillan & Co.
Elliot, J.G. (1968), *The Frontier 1839–1947: The Story of the N.W. Frontier of India*. Cassel.
Elphinstone, Mounstuart (1815), *An Account of the Kingdom of Caubul and its Dependencies in Persia, Tartary and India*. Longman Hurst.
Farley, M. Foster and Rosali P. Gates (1976), *Journal of Royal Society of Pakistan*, 13(2).
Fatimi, S.Q. (1963), 'First Muslim Invasion of the North-West Frontier of the Indo-Pakistan Subcontinent', *Journal of Asiatic Society of Pakistan*, 41.
Fraser-Tytler, W. K. (1950), *Afghanistan: A Study of Political Developments in Central Asia* (second edition). Oxford University Press.
Greaves, Rose L. (1993), 'Themes in British Policy towards Afghanistan in its Relations to Indian Frontier Defense, 1798–1947', *Journal of the Royal Society of Asian Affairs*, 24 (1).
Lady Sale (1843), *A Journal of the Disasters in Afghanistan*. John Murrray.
Lamb, Alastaire (1966), 'A Study of the Frontiers of the British Empire', *Journal of the Royal Central Asian Society*, 3(3).
Mishra, Amaresh (2008), *War of Civilisations: India AD 1857*. Rupa Publications.
Pandey, Sitaram (First edition 1873), *From Sepoy to Subedar: Being the Life and Adventures of Subedar Sita Ram*, Lieutenant Colonel James Thomas Norgate, Bengal Staff Corps (trans). Republished by Vikas Publishing House, 1970.
Swinson, Arthur (1967), *North-West Frontier: People and Events 1839–1947*. Hutchinson & Co.
Sykes, Percy (1940) (2002), *A History of Afghanistan*. Macmillan & Co., republished by Munshiram Manoharlal.

Yong, Tan Tai (2002), 'Sepoys and the Colonial Punjab and the Military Base of the Indian Army 1845–1900', in *The British Raj and its Indian Armed Forces*. Oxford University Press.

## Chapter 3: Between One Great War and Another

Caroe, Olaf (1958), *The Pathans 550 B.C.–A.D. 1957*. Macmillan & Co.
Marwat, Fazal-ul-Rahim and Sayed Wiqar Ali Shah Kakakhel (1993), *Afghanistan, and the Frontier*. Emjay Books.
Nehru, Jawaharlal (1958) (2005), *A Bunch of Old Letters*. Republished by Viking. Obrai, Dewan Chand (1938), *The Evolution of NWFP, Peshawar*. London Book Company.
Pirzada, Syed Sharifuddin (ed.) (1970), *Foundations of Pakistan*, vol. 1. National Publishing House.
Qureshi, M. Naeem (1979), *The Ulama of British India and the Hijrat of 1920*. Quaid-i-Azam University.
Rittenberg, Stephan Allen (1977), 'The Independence Movement in India's North-West Frontier Province, 1901–1947', PhD thesis, Columbia University.
Swinson, Arthur (1967), *North West Frontier: People and Events 1839–1947*. Hutchinson & Co.
Sykes, Percy (1940) (2002), *A History of Afghanistan*. Macmillan & Co. Republished by Munshiram Manoharlal.
Toynbee, Arnold (1940) (2002), 'Survey of International Affairs, 1920–1923', in Percy Sykes (ed.), *History of Afghanistan*. Munshiram Manoharlal Publishers.

## Chapter 4: Sometimes Badly Served: Wavell's Viceroyalty

Connell, John (1964), *Wavell, Soldier and Scholar*. Collins.
Wovell, A.P.(1941), *Generals and Generalship*.Macmillan & Co.
Listowell (1984), 'Further Reflection on Transfer of Power, *Indo-British Review*, 2 (1).
Lewin, Ronald (1980), *The Chief Field Marshal Lord Wavell, Commander in Chief and Viceroy*. Hutchinson and Company.
Moon, Penderel (ed.) (1973), *Wavell: The Viceroy's Journal*. Oxford University Press.

## Chapter 5: The 'Not Entirely Accidental' Role of Viceroy Mountbatten

Murphy, Ray (1948), *Last Viceroy.* Jarrolds Publishers.
Tinker, Hugh (1997), *Viceroy: Curzon to Mountbatten.* Oxford University Press.
Wingate, Ronald (1970), *Lord Ismay: A Biography.* Hutchinson of London.

## Chapter 7: A Paladin Himself: Governor Sir Olaf Caroe

Caroe, Sir Olaf (1958), *The Pathans 550 B.C.-A.D. 1957.* Macmillan & Co.
Menon, K.P.S. (1965), *Many Worlds: An Autobiography.* Oxford University Press.
Singer, Andre (1984), *Lords of the Khyber.* Faber & Faber.

## Chapter 8: Nehru's Kamerad

Caroe, Sir Olaf (1958), *The Pathans 550 B.C.-A.D. 1957.* Macmillan & Co.
Hughes, Richard (1972) *The Foreign Devil.* Andre Deutsch Ltd.
Jansson, Erland (1981), *India, Pakistan or Pakhtunistan.* Uppsala University.
  Yapp, Malcolm (1986), 'Nearing His Tryst with Destiny: Nehru and the Interim
Government, A Review Article', *Journal of Royal Society for Asian Affairs*, 17.

## Chapter 9: The Muslim League Punch

Noble, Fraser, 'Recollections of Civil Disobedience Movement: NWFP 1947', *Indo-British Review—A Journal of History,* 19 (1), pp.41–50.

## Chapter 10: Malang Baba's Abounding Optimism: Gandhi

Pyarelal (1956), *Mahatma Gandhi: The Last Phase.* Navajivan Publishing.
*The Collected Works of Mahatma Gandhi* (1956), 31 May 1947. Publications Division, Government of India.
*Gandhiji's Correspondence with the Government, 1944–47* (1959). Navjivan Publishing.

## Chapter 11: The Pathan Jeremiad: Khan Abdul Ghaffar Khan

Pyarelal (1966), *Thrown to the Wolves: Abdul Ghaffar*. Eastlight Book House.

Khan, Khan Abdul Wali (1995), 'Life and Thought of Badshah Khan', in, *Khan Abdul Ghaffar Khan—A Centennial Tribute*. Nehru Memorial Museum and Library. Har-Anand Publications.

Anand, Y.P. (2003), *Life of Abdul Ghaffar Khan: The Non-violent Revolutionary*. National Gandhi Museum.

Korejo, M.K. (1994), *The Frontier Gandhi—His Place in History*. Oxford University Press.

## Chapter 12: The Kaffir King: Dr Khan Saheb

Mehra, Parshotam (1998), *The North-West Frontier Drama: 1945–1947*. Manohar.

## Chapter 13: Kestrel of Kashmir: Adbul Qayyum Khan

Ahmad, Mushtaq (1994), *'Jinnah & After'—A Profile of Leadership*.Royal Book Company.

Khan, Mazhar Ali (1996), *Pakistan—The First Twelve Years*. Oxford University Press.

Pirzada, Syed Sharifuddin (ed.) (1977), *Quaid-e-Azam Jinnah's Correspondence*. East and West Publishing Company.

Qaiyum, Abdul (1945), *Gold and Guns on Pathan Frontier*. Hind Kitabs.

## Chapter 14: Difficult under Difficult Conditions: Muhammad Ali Jinnah

Mirza, Humayun (1999), *From Plassey to Pakistan—The Family History of Iskander Mirza, The First President of Pakistan*. University Press of America Inc.

Yunus, Mohammad (1980), *Persons, Passions and Politics*. Vikas Publishing House.

## Chapter 15: An Epoch, Episode and Epitaph: Britain, Afghanistan and NWFP

Aitchison, C.U. (1933), *A Collection of Treaties, Engagements and Sanads*, vol. 13.
*The Asian Age*, 17 July 2007.
*Asian Recorder*, (1974), No. 46.
Ayoob, Mohammad (2002), 'South-West Asia after the Taliban', *Survival*, 44(1): 51.
Davies, Collin C. (1932), *The Problem of the North-West Frontier, 1890–1908*. The University Press.
Foot, Rosemary (1980), 'The Changing Pattern of Afghanistan's Relations with its Neighbours', *Journal of the Royal Society of Asian Affairs*, 11 (1).
Hyman, Anthony (1980), 'Afghanistan-Pakistan Border Disputes by Anthony Hyman, Asian Affairs', *Journal for Royal Society for Asian Affairs*, 11 (3).
Khaled, Zulfikar A. (1989), 'The Afghan Crisis 1979–89, Indian Interests and Choices', *Pakistan Journal of History and Culture*, 10 (2).
Poullada, Leon B. (1979), 'Pakhtunistan: Afghan Domestic Politics and Relations with Pakistan', in Ainslie T. Embree (ed.), *Pakistan's Western Borderlands: The Transformation of a Political Order*. Vikas Publishing House Pvt. Limited.
Rahman, Abdur (1900). *The Life of Abdur Rahman, Amir of Afghanistan*. Murray.
Shukla, Ajai (2007), in *Business Standard*, 17 July.
Wilber, Donald (1962), *Afghanistan—its People, its Society, its Culture*. HRAF Press.

## Chapter 16: Danger of Little Knowledge

Amstutz, J. Bruce (1986), *Afghanistan: The First Five Years of Soviet Occupation*. National Defence University Press.
*Beijing Review* (1980), No. 5, 4 February.
Belloc, Hilaire (1898). *The Modern Traveller*. Edward Arnold.
Caroe, Olaf (1953), *Soviet Empire*. Macmillan & Co.
———. (1958), *The Pathans*. Macmillan & Co.
Dupree, Louis (1965), 'Afghanistan in the Twentieth Century', *Journal of the Royal Central Asian Society*.

Dutt, Gargi (1981), 'China and the Development in Afghanistan', in K.P.Mishra (ed.), *Afghanistan in Crisis*. Advent.

*Gazetteer of Afghanistan*, II, 197–215.

Ghani, Ashraf (1978), 'Islam and State-Building in a Tribal Society Afghanistan: 1880–1901', *Modern Asian Studies* 12 (2): 269–84.

Gifford, Rob (2008), *China Road*. Bloomsbury.

Hilali, A.Z. (2001), 'China's Response to the Soviet Invasion of Afghanistan', *Central Asian Survey*, 20(3).

Jacobsen, C.G. (1981), *Sino-Soviet Relations Since Mao: The Chairman's Legacy*. Praeger, pp.92–105.

Lieven, Anatol (2008), 'Address to The Royal Society for Asian Affairs on 30 October 2007', *Asian Affairs*, 39 (1).

Mackerras, Colin (2001), 'Xinjiang at the Turn of the Century: The Causes of Separatism', *Central Asian Survey*, 20 (3).

McLean, N.L.D. (1948), 'Sinkiang Today', *International Affairs*, 8 May.

Menon, K.P.S. (1965), *Many Worlds—An Autobiography*. Oxford University Press.

Muller, Jerry Z. (2008), 'US and them', *Foreign Affairs*, March/April.

Ong, Russell (2005), 'China's Security Interests in Central Asia', *Central Asian Survey*, 24 (4): 427.

*People's Daily* (1980), 10 March.

Poullada, Leon B. (1977), 'Pakhtunistan: Afghan Domestic Politics and Relations with Pakistan', in Ainslie T. Embree (ed.), *Pakistan's Western Borderlands: The Transformation of a Political Order*. Vikas Publishing House Pvt. Limited.

Shen Yu Dai (1966), 'China and Afghanistan', *China Quarterly*, 5 (2).

*The New York Times* (1979), 30 December. Toynbee, Arnold J. (1961), *Between Oxus and Jumna*. Oxford University Press. Fraser-Tytler, W.K. Fraser (1950), *Afghanistan: A Study of Political Developments in Central and Southern Asia*. Oxford University Press.

# Index

*Note*: The letter 'n' following locators refers to notes.

Abell, George, 152, 180, 231, 253, 281n
Aden Protectorate, 1, 17n
'Aerial bombardment', 253, 255, 259
Afghan aggression, 4
Afghan mission, 238, 416
Afghan supremacy, 56
Afridi invasion, 126
Afridi *jirga*, 156
Afridis of Khyber, 32, 228
Ahmad, Mushtaq, 373
Aiyar, Sivaswami, 115–16
Akhil Bhartiya Hindu Mahasabha, 281n
Akhund of Swat, 48, 50
Al-Qaeda, 432, 439n, 440
Alexander, A.V., 3, 17n, 76n
Ali brothers, 102, 390, 405n
Ali, Amir Sher, 51–53
Ali, Mehbub, 156, 158, 226
Ali, Mohammad, 102, 181–82, 289, 297, 329
Ali, Sheikh Mahbub, 156, 225, 261–62, 265–66
Ali, Vazir, 36
All India Congress Committee, 317, 355, 398
All India Muslim League, 382, 401
Allenby, Sir Edmund, 159n
Ambedker, B.R., 281n
Ambeyla campaign of 1863, 57
America's war on terror, 461
Amir Amanullah, 69–70, 95–96, 102, 113, 329–30, 410, 425

Amu Darya, 76n
*The Anabasis of Alexander*, 24
Anderson, John, 14, 20n
Anglo-Afghan defence of India, 35
Anglo-Afghan Pact of 1905, 425
Anglo-Afghan relations, 68–74
Anglo-Afghan Treaty, 416, 418, 421, 425
Anglo-Russian convention, 443
Anglo-Soviet engagement in Iran, 2
Anti-British feeling, 124
'Anti-Caroe day', 172–73, 232–33
Anti-Congress propaganda, 203, 388
Anti-Corruption Committee, 261
Anti-German propaganda, 194, 197
Anti-government feeling, 124
Anti-Islamic policy, 129
Anti-Japanese propaganda, 194, 197
Anti-Taliban coalition, 431
Arab Islamic armies, 26
Arabian Sea, 19n
Army of the Indus, 38–42
Army Production Corps, 452
Ataullah, Kazi, 211
Attack on Indian Parliament (13 Dec. 2001), 431
Attlee, Clement, 10, 19n, 245, 391, 437
Attock, 28, 32, 78n, 124
Auchinleck, Claude John Eyre, 190n
Auden, W.H., 144
Authoritarianism, 236
Awadh, 82n
Azad Kashmir, 441, 457
Azad, Abul Kalam, 181, 254, 268, 309, 327–28, 355, 403, 337
Aziz, Shah Abdul, 102

Ba'ath Party, 16n
Babur, 28, 30, 56, 79n
Baccha-i-Saqao, 330
Bactra, 79n
Badshah Khan. *See* Khan Abdul Ghaffar Khan, 326
Baghdad Pact, 9
Bajaur, 23, 60, 63, 76n, 125, 328, 433, 441
Baker, Noel, 424
Bala Hissar, 40, 83n, 302
Bangladesh, 281n
Bannu, 27–29, 65, 78n, 108–11, 114, 227, 233, 290, 343–44, 376, 433, 441
Barqi, Allah Bakhsh, 123
Bengal army, 38, 45–46, 82n
Bengal Native Infantry (BNI), 46–47
Berlin Conference, 138n
Bevin, Ernest, 421, 437n
*Bhangi*, 324n
Bhave, Vinoba, 327
Bhittanis, 281n
Bhutto, Zulfikar Ali, 372, 379n, 439
Bihar, communal riots in, 328
Bivar, David, 301–2
Blood, Sir Bindon, 63–64, 92n
Bokhara, 51
Bolan Pass, 29, 38, 53
Bolton, Sir H.N., 116, 122, 126
Bolton, Sir Norman, 216–17
Bonn Conference, 431
Bourne, Sir Fredrick, 156
Bray Committee, 116–19, 383
Bray, Denys, 116
British bureaucracy, 47–48, 309, 338, 445
British Commonwealth, 6, 19n, 147
British empire, 1, 15n, 55, 246, 409–10, 446
British Indian Army, 20n
British mandate in Iraq, 1
British policy, manifestation of, 61
British Quit India, 171, 334
Brydon, William, 41–42, 44, 84n
Buchan, John, 94n
Buddhism, spread of, 459

Buffer zone, 56
Bulganin, Nikolay, 427
Bulganint, 437n
Burnes, Sir Alexander, 40, 84n, 95
Bux, Allah, 387

Cabinet Committee, 273, 275, 277, 395
Cabinet delegation, 149–52, 215, 219, 359, 374
Cabinet Mission, 148, 159n, 171, 220, 230–31, 335–37, 358, 360, 395–96
Caliphate of Muawiyah, 27, 30
Campbell-Johnson, Alan, 15, 21n, 170
Caretaker government, 366
Caroe, Olaf, 8, 28–29, 66, 115, 154–55, 157–58, 166, 170, 194, 210, 215, 217–18, 223, 227, 231, 235, 237, 245, 253, 259, 264, 266–67, 288, 294, 303, 305, 309–10, 312, 338, 340, 342, 346, 357, 359, 362–65, 411, 444–45, 450
Cavagnari, Sir Louis, 53
Chakdarra, 160n
Chaman Lal, Diwan, 232
Chamberlain, Neville, 45, 52, 87n
Chandragupta Maurya, 25
Chauri Chaura tragedy, 405n
China–Pakistan economic corridor, 457
Chinese activities in the South China Sea, 456
Chinese interest to intervene in Afghanistan, 457
Chinese Turkestan, 76n
Chundrigar, Ibrahim Ismail, 191n
Churchill, Sir Winston, 9–15, 56, 62–65, 144–49, 162–63, 195, 245, 465–66
City of Saints', 78n
Civil disobedience movement, 119, 122, 172, 177, 198, 288–89, 291, 294, 297, 375–76, 387, 390
Civil war, 11–13, 35, 309, 450–51
Coalition government, 154, 176–77, 185, 225, 234, 254, 260, 367
Coalition government, idea of, 366
Coalition government, prospect of, 367
Cold War era, 7

Collapse of the administration in Peshawar, 125
*The Collected Works of Mahatma Gandhi*, 312–13
Colville, Sir John, 205, 244
Commercial rivalries, 2
Commonwealth policy, 421
Communal antagonism, 116
'Communal Award', 248, 281n
Communal riots, 168–69, 220, 278, 361
Communal upsurge, 288
Communalism, 247–48, 279
    middle-class phenomenon, 248
Communist conspiracy, 126
'Conflict entrepreneurs', 431
*Congress Socialist*, 250
Conservative and Labour politicians, 14
Conservative Party, 15
Constitutional principles, 183
Constitutional propriety, 177, 185, 404
Constitutional reforms, 116–17, 119, 131, 146, 195–96, 206, 337, 381
Cotton, Sydney, 45
Craik, Sir Henry, 135–36, 332
Crete, battle of, 188n
Cripps Mission, 10, 195–96, 358
    communal divide, 198
    failure of, 197–98
Cripps, Stafford, 3, 13, 17n, 146, 148, 196–97
Crum, Erskine, 363
Cunningham, George, 3, 18n, 112, 121, 149, 175–76, 185, 187–88, 194–211, 240, 300–304, 352–54, 357, 359–60, 368–69, 387–89, 401, 404, 410–11, 420, 445
Curtis, G.C.S., 257

*Daily Telegraph*, 62, 65
Dalai Lama, 450, 452, 454
Dargai, 156, 160n, 223
Das, B., 130
Davies, Collin, 423
Davy, A.E.G., 8–9
*Dawn*, 153

Deane, Harold, 66, 68, 93n
Dehlavi, Shah Abdul Aziz, 139n
Dera Ismail Khan, 65, 93n, 111, 168, 227, 231, 233, 257, 290, 293–95, 297, 376, 433–34, 441
Dera Ismail Khan, communal riots in, 231, 270–71
Derajat, 66, 93n, 98, 290
Desai, Bhulabhai, 332, 373, 384, 405n
Desai, Morarji, 428, 438n
Dill, Sir John, 145
Din, Mullah Fazal, 256
Dir, 63, 92n, 262, 359
Direct Action, 169, 226, 229, 336, 361–62, 375, 393–96, 466
'Dispersion of forces', 64
Dogra Rajput Kashmiri troops, 48
Dominion status, 13
Donald, Major J., 153
Dorman-Smith, 164–65, 189n
Dost Mohammad, 39–42, 48, 83n
Dostum, Rashid, 431, 441n
Double government system, 141n
Drug mafia, 431
Drug trafficking, 431
Durand Agreement, 414, 422, 424–25
    validity of, 422–26
Durand Line, 22, 27, 30, 54–61, 66, 103, 180, 229, 412–14, 417, 420, 422, 424–27, 430, 432, 434, 441, 443, 447, 460–61
    compromise solution, 55
    conflict, 460
    demarcation of, 61
    elaborated boundary system, 55
    northward or westward extension, 56
    rigidity of international frontiers, 57
Durand, Sir Mortimer, 38
Durrani, Shuja Shah, 81n
Dyer, Brigadier-General, 98–99, 100. *See also* Jallianwala Bagh massacre
East India Company, 39, 46, 446
East Pakistan, 4–5, 18n, 277
Eden, Anthony, 14

Eden, Robert Anthony, 20n
Edwardes, Herbert, 45–48, 86n
Electoral prospects, 335
Ellis, Major, 103, 105
Elphinstone, Mountstuart, 35–37, 41–42, 81n, 84n
Emotionalism, phases of, 167
Eyre, Lt Vincent, 43

Factionalism, 180, 209, 219, 373, 387–88
Fakhr-e-Afghan. *See* Khan Abdul Ghaffar Khan
Fakir of Ipi, 107–14, 176, 195, 218, 367
Fanaticism, 31, 218, 222
Fanshawe, H.C., 68, 94n
'Faqueer phenomenon', 114
Farooq, Sardar Mohammad, 114
Fatima, Begum, 296
Fatimi, S.Q., 78n
Fazal Din, Shahzada, 113
Federally Administered Tribal Areas (FATA), 281n, 242n, 431–33, 441n
*Firman*, 139n
First Anglo-Afghan War, 45, 51
'Forward policy', 61, 117, 423
Fraser-Tytler, William Kerr, 410, 435n, 447, 449
French alliance, 35
French and Indian War, 15n
*From Plassey to Pakistan*, 391
*Frontier Advocate*, 118
Frontier Arch, Keystone of, 65–68
Frontier Congress, 223, 251, 253, 263, 272, 275–80, 297, 331, 344, 352, 355–57, 360, 400
Frontier Government, 218, 295
Frontier Jamaat-i-Ulama, 114
Frontier League, 169, 226, 234, 254, 372, 375, 394
Frontier minorities, 115, 118
Frontier Muslim League, 169, 251, 298, 374, 378–79
Frontier warfare cost, 68
'Full dress' enquiry, 225

Gandamak, 86n
Gandhi, Bhanju Ram, 355
Frontier Gandhi. *See* Khan Abdul Ghaffar Khan
Gandhi, Mahatma, 204, 322, 327, 405
'fourth-dimensional' way of satyagraha, 313
guilt-ridden and confused, 317
'Quit India' call given by, 199
struggle for the NWFP, 308
unequivocal approval to move for a free Pathanistan, 321
Gandhi, Rajiv, 326, 429
Gandhi–Irwin Pact, 136
Gardanne, General, 35
George VI, 246n
Germany's annexation of Czechoslovakia, 456
Ghafur, Abdul, 88n
Ghazni, 33, 38–40, 80n, 458–59, 463
Ghori, Muhammad, 27, 30
Gloomy Presentiments, 50–54
Goldsmid, Sir Frederick John, 51, 89n
Government of India Act, 10, 121, 281, 140n, 351, 382, 384, 405n
provincial autonomy under, 384
'Governor's rule', idea of, 211
Grace, Gilbert, 302
Graeco-Buddhist relics, 23
Great Calcutta Killings, 308, 323n, 336
'Great Game', dynamics of, 57
Griffin, Sir Lepel, 58, 91n
Grigg, Edward, 145–46, 159n
Guerrillas, 430
Gul, Ahmad, 297
Gul, Badshah, 125, 392
Gul, Sahibzada Ahmad, 296
*Gurkha*, 162

Hadda, Mullah, 107
Haq, A.K. Fazlul, 387, 405n
Haridwar, 324n
Harijans, 11, 281n
Haripur, communal riots in, 204
Hazara Public Safety Ordinance, 298

Hazara, 25, 33, 49–50, 65, 157, 161n, 209, 227, 289, 291, 293, 298, 361, 375–76, 430
   communal riots in, 226, 361, 375
   Sikh girl, case of, 361
Hazrat Mohammad, the founder of Islam, 26
Hejaz, 16n
Hekmatyar, Gulbuddin, 429, 439n
Henderson, Arthur, 164
Her Majesty's Government (HMG), 152, 184, 187, 196, 207, 228, 230, 238, 268–69, 271, 273–75, 288, 298, 308, 338, 342, 395–96, 413, 415–16, 418, 420–22
   3 June partition plan, 415
   partition India in 1947, 444
   policy announcement by, 231
   position on Afghan claims, 418
   transfer of power, 268
Herat, 26, 29, 38, 54, 56, 59, 78n, 96, 430, 440
Hijra, 139n
Hijrat, 101–3, 329
Hindu Congress, 113, 118, 171, 229, 361, 389
'Hindu-dominated' Government of India, 412
Hindu domination, 11, 149, 171, 196, 210, 220, 359, 389
'Hindu hate', trace of, 110
Hindu Kush, 22–23, 25–27, 33, 56, 76n, 331, 443–48, 457–64
Hindu Mahasabha, 248, 381
Hindu Sikh domination, 227
*Hindustan Times*, 272
His Majesty's Government (HMG), 196
Hitler, 410–11
Hizb-i-Islami, 429
'Homogeneous ministry', 340
Hoti Mardan, 87n
House of Commons, 11, 14, 420, 424
Huns, dominion of the, 77n
Hussein, Saddam, 16n

ICS, authoritarian habits of, 225
*Imamat*, 101
Imperial interests of Britain, 58
Imperial Russia, 56
'Independent Pathanistan', 400
India and Burma Committee, 146, 148–49, 155, 172, 228, 413
India Independence Act, 179, 185–87, 422
'India Independence Bill', 14
Indian and Burmese Round Table conferences, 245n
Indian Christian Association, 332
Indian Civil Service, 216, 239–40, 363
Indian frontier policy, 54
Indian Mutiny, 20n
Indian National Army (INA), 164, 208–9
Indian National Congress, 18n, 118, 166, 382–83, 405
*Indian News Chronicle*, 345
Indian Political Service, 216, 240, 252, 390, 451
Indian Reforms Act, 141n
Iran–Iraq war, 16n
Irwin, Lord, 120, 122, 124, 126
Islam Bibi, 107–14,
'Islam in danger', communal cry of, 234, 445
Islamic conception, basis of, 343–44
Islamic confederation, 391
Islamic Council of Afghanistan, 440n
Islamic fundamentalism, 429
Islamic State, Islamic radicalism of, 457
Ismay, General Hastings Lionel, 281n
Ismay, Lord, 210, 228, 240, 244–46, 268, 271, 274, 309, 316, 318, 323, 342, 347, 364–65, 394–95

Jalalabad, 27, 38–39, 42–44, 53, 78n, 100–1, 107, 409
Jallianwala Bagh massacre, 98–100, 138n, 326, 329
Jamaat-i-Islami (JI), 429, 439n
Jamait-i-Ulema, 107
Jamrud, 223, 258, 281n

Jandola, 257, 260, 281n
Jansson, Erland, 258, 262
Jenkins, Sir Evan, 229, 309, 324n
*Jihad against the British*, 96
Jihad, 96–99, 113, 194, 391, 429, 440
  'anti-Congress' propaganda, 388
Jinnah, Muhammad Ali, 10–11, 14,
  56, 113–14, 130, 136–37, 147–52,
  165, 169–72, 175–81, 184, 187–88,
  194–98, 204, 206–7, 210–11, 224,
  226, 234, 236, 240, 254–55, 272, 275,
  298–99, 305, 308–9, 312–21, 333,
  340, 342–47, 351, 367–69, 372–74,
  381–404, 419, 421, 445, 464, 466
  appealed to Pathans to vote for Pakistan, 346
  Bannu resolution, 344
  choice of ministers, 367
  cogent and eloquent pleading, 383
  collusion with Iskander Mirza, 392
  explain his 'Pakistan scheme', 340
  first mission to the NWFP, 385
  giving a call for Pakistan, 381
  Hindu–Muslim cooperation, 118
  in favour of elections, 395
  interventions, 381–82
  political relevance in India, 381
  principal player of India's partition, 466
  reconciliation efforts with Khan brothers, 399
  refusal to accept the Cabinet Mission, 336
  response to Gandhi's request, 398
  'sole spokesmanship' of the Muslims, 337
  strong votary of reforms in NWFP, 381
  two-nation theory, 288, 338, 375
*Jirga*, 37, 82n, 108–9, 113, 153, 156, 219, 222, 255, 257, 261, 293–95, 331, 372–73
Joshi, P.C., 12, 20n
*A Journal of the Disasters*, 40
Judicial enquiry, 158, 225

Jugal Kishore, Acharya, 232

Kabul, 76n
Kabul campaign, 38
Kafir King. *See* Khan Abdul Ghaffar Khan
Kafirs, 181
Kalat, 3, 17n, 391–92
Kandahar-based Taliban leadership, 432
Kandahar, 29, 32–33, 36, 38–41, 53, 55–56, 58, 80n, 98, 409, 432
Karlanri Tribal Confederation, 281n
Karzai, Hameed, 431
Kashmir, descended on, 211
Kaufmann, Konstantin Petrovich, 52, 89n
Kaur, Rajkumari Amrit, 315, 324n, 342
Keane, John, 39, 83n
*Kelly*, 162
Khalifas, 101–12
Khan Abdul Ghaffar Khan, 108, 113, 122, 129, 132, 136, 153, 253, 255, 258, 261–63, 272, 275, 280, 308–23, 326–47n, 351, 354–55, 357, 362, 366–67, 375, 384–85, 398–400
  boycotting the referendum, 343
  languished in a solitary cell, 332
  opposed to the 'grouping' scheme, 336
  as a political prisoner, 326
  popularity, 331
  role in the Indian national movement, 374
  stature of, 333
Khan brothers, 114, 219, 227, 254, 272, 274, 276–80, 313, 316, 323, 337, 339, 351, 385, 398
  reconciliation efforts with Jinnah, 399
  isolation of, 318
Khan, Abdul Qayyum, 113–14, 150, 179, 211, 234, 255, 289, 297–98, 339, 352, 357, 369–70, 372–74, 376–79, 384–85, 389
Khan, Abdur Rahman, 58–61, 91n, 423
Khan, Ajun, 50
Khan, Akbar, 41

Khan, Ali Gul, 197, 201, 355–56
Khan, Amanullah, 97, 411, 437
Khan, Aurangzeb, 32, 203–8, 300, 354–55, 372, 387–89
Khan, Bacha. *See* Khan Abdul Ghaffar Khan
Khan, Badshah, 249, 259, 311–15, 317–22, 326, 340
Khan, Colonel Mohammad Sharif, 261
Khan, Colonel Shah Pasand, 113–14
Khan, Daud, 429
Khan, Hayat, 387
Khan, Ismail, 257, 290, 293, 376, 431, 440n, 441
Khan, Khan Muhammad Abbas, 211
Khan, Khushal, 32, 445
Khan, Liaquat Ali, 180–81, 187, 206, 236, 245, 347–48n, 366, 377, 404
Khan, Majidullah, 262
Khan, Mirza Ali, 107–8, 110
Khan, Mohammad Akbar, 44, 85n
Khan, Muhammad Yakub, 91n
Khan, Nadir, 100, 330
Khan, Nasrullah, 97–98
Khan, Qazi Atta Ullah, 234, 292, 296, 357, 364, 366
Khan, Quli, 194
Khan, Raja Ghazanfar Ali, 136
Khan, Sanobar, 305
Khan, Sardar Abdur Rashid, 378–79n
Khan, Sardar Aurangzeb, 149, 203, 387–88
Khan, Sardar Muhammad Daud, 439n
Khan, Sher Ali, 51–53, 89n
Khan, Sir Aga, 328
Khan, Sir Zulfiquar Ali, 132
Khan, Swatai, 258
Khan, Wali, 328
Khan, Yakub, 53
Khanates of Khokand, 51
'Khani elite', 119, 199
Khanna, Meher Chand, 222, 234–55, 357, 364
Khattak, Khushal Khan, 32, 80n, 445
Khilafat movement, 102, 122, 329–30, 381, 405, 405n
Khilafatists, 102–3, 118
Khiva, 51
Khojak Pass, 83n
'*Khooni mushaira*' (blood recital), 375
Khudai Khidmatgar, 107, 121–36, 176, 181, 199, 203, 217, 223, 233–34, 249–51, 257–58, 272, 280, 288, 291–97, 298, 311, 314–16, 321–23, 327–28, 330–31, 334–35, 340, 343, 346–47, 354, 356, 365–67, 373, 375, 377, 384–85, 388, 394, 398–400
  agitation, 181
  contribution to civil disobedience movement, 250
  abstention of, 366
  ban on the, 130, 135, 137, 351, 384, 386
  boycott of the referendum, 322
  British ban on movement, 333
  movement, 122, 133, 330
Khyber Pass, 29, 33, 100, 126, 156, 229
Khyber Rifles, 99–100, 223
Kipling, Rudyard, 31, 34, 215
Kissa Khawani Bazaar firing, 297
*Kitab Futūh al-Buldan*, 27
Kohat, 28, 65, 93n, 103, 106–7, 227, 289–90, 293, 383, 433, 441
Kripalani, Acharya, 340
Kushan Empire, 77n

Labour Party, 7, 10, 19n, 146, 437
Lahore, 78n
Lahore Resolution, 195, 251, 331, 333, 385–87
Lahore Session, 324n
Lal Masjid incident, 434
*Lambardar*, 370n
Landi Kotal or Landikotal, 281n
Law, Edward, 85n
Lawrence, John, 46–48, 87n
Leopold (Leo) Amery, 146, 159n
Linlithgow, Viceroy, 195, 353, 387
'Lion of Herat', 441n
Listowel, Lord, 146, 172–79, 186–88, 210,

232–33, 236–37, 244–46, 271, 339, 419–20, 466
Lockhart, Rob, 92n, 62, 173, 175–81, 184–86, 188, 235, 237–38, 346–48n, 365–68, 399–400, 404, 420
Lodi, Ibrahim, 30
Lohia, Ram Manohar, 250
London Conference, 132
Looquitur, Attar Singh, 74–75
*Loya jirga*, 373, 379n, 430
   duty of the, 373
'Luftwaffe', 435n
Lyall, Sir Alfred, 53
Lytton, Lord, 51–52, 57, 65, 89n

Mackworth Young, 67–68
Macmillan, Harold, 14, 20n
Macnaghten, Sir William Hay, 40–42, 84n
Madras Presidency, 6
Mahmud of Ghazni, 27, 30, 458
Mahsud, Mohiuddin, 281n
Mahsuds, Shabi Khel, 152
Malakand, 76n
*The Malakand Field Force*, 65
Malakand incident, 257, 266, 281n
Malakand Political Agent, 225
Malang, 323n
Malang Baba, 308–9, 311, 315, 319, 321
Malik, 255–56, 258, 281n
Malik, Tori Khel, 305
Malviya, Madan Mohan, 382–83, 405n
Mamdot-Daulatana faction, 387
Mamund (Pathan tribe), 92n
*Manchester Guardian*, 13
Manki Pir's 'spirited speeches', 290
Marcuse, Jacques, 247
Martrys' Day, 121, 198, 294, 297
Mass migrations, 466
Mazar-i-Sharif, 90n
McMahon Line, 450, 460
Media campaign, 417
Menon plan, 272, 364
Menon, K.P.S., 451
Menon, V.K. Krishna, 7–8, 276, 281n

Menon, V.P., 150, 152, 180, 272–74, 281n, 339
Mesopotamia, 16n
Messervy, General Frank, 231
Metcalfe, H.A.F., 123, 133–35, 137, 217
Mieville, Eric, 12, 346, 395, 399, 405n
Millat, 290
Minto, Lady, 70–71
Minto, Lord, 68–69, 74
Minto-Morley reforms, 115
Mirza, Humayun, 390–91
Mirza, Iskander, 240, 353, 370n, 390–92
Mishra, Brajesh Chandra, 428, 438n
Mitchell, Sir Norval, 240
Modalities of holding the elections, 269
Mohajarin, 103, 139n
*Mohajir*, 102, 139n, 464
Mohmand, Khalil, 296
Mohmands, 80n
Mollie Ellis Affair, 103–7
Molotov-Ribbentrop Pact, 435n
Montagu-Chelmsford reforms, 115
Monteath, Sir David, 235, 237, 245n, 246
Montford reforms, 128, 132
Morley, Lord, 69, 71
Mountbatten, 6–8, 11–14, 56, 144, 146–49, 158, 162–88, 210–11, 227–28, 230, 232–40, 244–46, 268–75, 279, 297, 299, 301, 303, 305, 308–12, 316, 318, 322, 338–42, 347, 362, 364–65, 368, 393–404, 413, 422, 464, 466
Mountbatten, Lady, 304, 363
'Mountbatten Zindabad', 170
Mudie, Sir Francis, 309
*Muhajareens*, 329
Muhajir. *See* Mohajir
*Mujtahids* (experts of the sacred law), 96
Mullagoris, 281n
Multan, 4, 18n, 27–29, 33, 36, 38, 48
Murtaza, Maulvi Syed, 117
Musharraf, 432, 434
Muslim fanaticism, 126
Muslim League, 3, 9–11, 18n, 108, 113–14, 117, 148–52, 154, 156–57, 167–71, 177–84, 186–87, 195–96,

198–99, 201, 203–10, 219–21, 223, 226–29, 231, 236–37, 240, 248–49, 251, 253–55, 259, 261–63, 268–69, 271, 278, 281, 288–303, 305, 308–9, 313, 316, 321–23, 327–28, 331, 333, 335–37, 341, 343, 346, 351, 354, 357–63, 366–70, 372, 374–78, 381–82, 384–91, 393–94, 397–403, 413, 420
   aggressive propaganda, 171
   anti-Congress propaganda, 254
   anti-Nehru propaganda, 254
   apparent plan, 302
   communal ideology, 385
   demand of provincial autonomy, 367
   demonstrations against, 322
   electorate in the NWFP favouring the, 182
   friends of British government, 209
   interests remained protected, 184
   poor performance of, 209
   propaganda, 253, 361, 375
   representative only of Muslim India, 228
   successful in breaking the Congress stranglehold, 361
   supporters of, 257
Muslim League National Guard, 113, 292–93, 295
Muslim legislative tyranny, 116
Muslim National Guards, 255
Muslim revolt, 451

Naib-tehsildar, 281n
Napoleon, Pierre Louis, 35, 90n
National Congress, 118
'National identity', 465
Naujawan Bharat Sabha, 126, 131, 141n
Nazimuddin, Khwaja, 405n
Nazimuddin-Suhrawardy faction, 387
Nazi–Soviet (Molotov–Ribbentrop) Pact, 409
Nazi–Soviet venture, 411
Nehru, Jawaharlal, 14, 215, 279, 281n, 355, 438
   belief, 248
   concept of Indian nationalism, 249
   cosmopolitan and international in his outlook, 165
   'development' and 'freedom', 278
   external affairs portfolio, 252
   optimism about the future of communal politics, 248
   proclivity of, 276
   romantic notions, 258
   theoretical solution, 248
   wishful thinking and his pious intentions, 278
Nehru, Motilal, 118, 141n, 382, 405
Nicholson, John, 45–48, 50, 86n
Niedermayer, Oscar, 96–97
Nishtar, Abdul Rab, 169, 300–2, 305, 352, 389, 391
Nishtar, Sardar Abdur Rab, 297, 300, 370n, 389
'Noble sentiments', 62
Noble, Fraser, 298–300, 302
Noble, Sir Fraser, 362, 370n
Non-alignment policy, 8
Non-cooperation campaign, 353, 381
Noon, Feroz Khan, 113, 201, 297, 299–300, 327, 347n
North Atlantic Treaty Organization (NATO), 437n, 461
North Waziristan Agency, 107
Northbrook, Lord, 51
Novelty of Elections, 127–30
Nye, Sir Archibald, 6, 18n

'Offshore water defence', 455
Old Testament, 47, 251
One-sided referendum, 280, 345
'One unit scheme', 380n
'Open seas protection', 455
Operation Jubilee, 188n
'Operation Scuttle', 13
Ottoman (Islamic) political power, 101
Oxus river (Amu Darya), 22, 75n, 22, 459

*Pakhtun*, (journal), 329
Pakhtun tribal organization, 32
Pakhtunistan, 8, 219, 339–40, 343, 427, 429, 437–38n, 462–63
'Pakhtunwali', principle of, 109
Pakistan, creation of, 7, 194, 196, 237, 338, 426–27
Pakistan Air Force (PAF), 5, 18n
Pakistan Constituent Assembly, 178, 182, 187, 344–45, 397, 402
'Pakistan Day', 293
*Pakistan Times*, 296, 377–78
'Pakistan Zindabad', 170
'Pakistaniyat', 456
Panckridge, H.R., 122
Pandey, Sita Ram, 38–40, 82n
Pant, Govind Ballabh, 353, 370n
Panthic Akali Party, 335
Parliamentary Board, 121, 355
Parsons, Sir Arthur Edward Broadbent, 370n
Parthia, 77n
Partition plan, 7–9, 14, 231, 310, 312–13, 364–65, 394–96, 399, 418
Patel Committee, 295–96
Patel, Sardar Vallabhbhai, 254, 314, 326, 332, 384, 404
Patel, Vithalbhai, 122–23, 405
Pathan National Province, 234, 339
Pathan patriotism, 219
Pathan traits, 31
Pathanistan, 113–14, 149, 187, 219, 234–35, 238, 280, 312, 321, 343–45, 359, 364–69, 389, 399–400, 404, 415
*The Pathans* (book), 444
Peace Conference, 97
'Peaceful penetration' policy, 117, 372
Pearks, Stuart, 119, 126
Pennel, Theodore, 31
People's Liberation Army, 452
Persian Gulf, 8, 16n, 218, 392, 453
Persian Shah, 51
Peshawar, 76n, 94n
Peshawar riots, 121–27, 216, 361
Pethick-Lawrence, Lord, 155, 157

Pink plan, 409
*Pioneer*, 62, 65
Pir of Manki Sharif, 221, 224, 232, 252, 290, 295–96, 298, 346
Pir Sahib of Zakori, 289, 293
Pishin, 53, 58, 90n
'Pitiful pensioners', 223
Plassey, Battle of, 446
Plebiscite (1947), 423
Police ranks, demoralization in, 226
Political Agent, 152, 156, 158, 222–26, 238, 252–53, 255, 258–62, 265–66, 267, 329
  of Malakand, 161n, 225, 238, 260, 266, 329
  of South Waziristan, 252
Political reforms, 10, 114, 327, 382
Pollock, Sir George, 42, 85n
Poona Pact, 281n
'Population transfer', idea of, 465
Potsdam Agreement, 96, 138n
Potsdam Conference. *See* Berlin Conference
Powindah, Mullah, 107, 256
Prayer meetings, 106
Pro-Muslim League, 208
Pro-Pakistan elements, 268
Provincial assembly, 150–51, 182, 230, 257, 352, 358, 376, 378
Provincial autonomy, 120–21, 351, 358, 384
Provincial elections, 110, 209, 251, 384
Provincial League, 169, 172, 177, 198, 201, 205–6, 234, 297, 339–40, 387
Provincial Muslim League War Council, 290, 300
Public announcement of elections, 231
Punjab, communal riots in, 220, 226
Punjab Muslim Women's League, 296
*Purabia Nar Sanghar Katha*, 50
'Pushpapura', 76n
Pyman, H.E., 163, 189n

Qaid-e-Azam, 314, 319
Qasim, Mir, 30

Qayyum, Nawabzada Sir Abdul, 121, 351–52, 384
Qazi Abdul Wadi, 98
Qissa Khwani Bazaar firing, 123, 130, 348n
Queen Victoria, 162
Quit India movement, 10, 195, 199–200, 248, 334, 353–54

Rabbani, Burhanuddin, 429, 440n
Radcliffe Boundary Commission, 276
Radcliffe Line, 54
Rahimtoola, Sir Ibrahim, 328
Rahman, Amir Abdur, 60, 425, 443, 449
Rahman, Arbab Abdur, 355
Rajagopalachari, B., 314
Rajagopalachari, C., 324n
Rajputs, 88n
Ram Kaur. *See* Islam Bibi
Rangachariar, Rao Bahadur T.V., 116–17
Ranjit Singh, 35–38, 81n
    leadership of, 37
    Sikh territories of, 37
Razmak, 153, 222, 252, 255–56, 281n, 441
Red Army, 409, 455
'Red-hot cable', 145
'Red Shirt Camp', 200
Red Shirt volunteers, 292
Referendum, 7–8, 113, 169, 172, 174–78, 180, 182–83, 210, 228, 234–37, 239, 271–75, 277–80, 288, 292, 297, 308, 311–23, 326, 336, 338–46, 363–66, 374, 395–401, 403, 415–21
    boycott of Frontier Congress, 275
    boycotted by the Khudai Khidmatgars, 210
    Congress's acceptance of, 275
    Frontier Congress demanded a third choice, 277
    logic of holding a, 268
    results, 175, 179, 182, 210, 280, 395, 400, 402–3
Reforms Commissioner, 150, 339
Refugees, 430, 434
Resolution of Kashmir, 460

Right to self-determination, 197, 427
Roberts, Earl, 39
Roberts, Field Marshal Frederick Sleigh, 91n
Roberts, General Abraham, 39 Abraham, 83n
Rohillas, 30, 33–34, 80n, 459
Roos-Keppel, Sir George Olaf, 94n, 99
Rowlatt Act, 98, 329
Royal Air Force (RAF), 5, 100, 106
Royal Pakistan Air Force (RPAF), 18n
Russian advance in Central Asia, 51–52
Russo-Afghan border, 55, 449
Russo-Afghan Frontier Commission, 69

Sajdanashins, 251, 361, 445
Sakas (Scythians), 77n
Salisbury, Lord, 14, 56
Salt March, 331
Samarth, N.M., 116–17
Sandhurst, 93n
Sarangia, 458
Sarda Act, 119, 131, 141n
'Sarhad', 389, 405n
Sattar, Fazal, 262
'Scientific' frontier, 55
Second Afghan War, 65, 95, 99
'Seistan award', 51
'Seistan proper', 51
*Selected Works of Jawaharlal Nehru*, 258, 260–61, 263, 265–67, 276–79
Sethi, Ghulam Rabbani, 123
Shah Alam, 34, 81n
Shah Jahan, 32
Shah Mahmood, 36–37
Shah Muhammad Sulaiman, 122
Shah, A.S.B., 299–300, 305, 362
Shah, Ahmad, 30, 33–35, 37, 56, 458
Shah, Faridullah, 258
Shah, Mohammad, 33
Shah, Nadir, 22, 30, 32–33, 56, 75n, 437
Shah, Sayed Akbar, 48
Shah, Sayed Umar, 48
Shahid Gunj mosque incident, 108, 110
Shaht, Mohammed Zahir, 436n

'Shaitan Sirkar', 121–27
Sharia, 348n
Shek, Chiange Kai, 221
Shelton (Peninsular War veteran), 41
*Sher-e-Punjab, See* Ranjit Singh
Sherpao, Aftab Ahmad Khan, 432
Shia sect, 90n
'Shilly-shallying', 63
Shinwaris, 223, 258, 281n
Shuja, Shah, 35–42
Sibi, 53, 58, 90n
Sikh girl's conversion, revocation of, 362
Sikhs, rising power of, 35
Silk Road, 451, 455
Simla Conference, 167, 206–7, 373–74, 389
Simon Commission, 118
Simon, John, 140n, 146
Singh, Charan, 428, 438n
Singh, Gulab, 88n
Singh, Jaswant, 199
Singh, Master Tara, 205
Singh, Sri Krishna, 353, 370n
Smith, C.H., 301
Smuts, Jan Christiaan, 324n
'Socialist republic' model of India, 247
Socio-religious movement, 330
Soomro, Khan Bahadur Allah Bux, 405n
South East Asia Command (SEAC), 162–63
Soviet-aided Afghanistan, 4
Soviet invasion of Afghanistan, 409–10, 440, 453
'Specially Designated Global Terrorist', 439n
Spenser, Sir George, 181–82
'Spirited song', 62
Squire, Sir Giles, 413–19, 421–22
'Standstill agreement', 183, 366, 420
Starr, Lillian, 104–7
Steele, Flora Annie, 215, 241n
Stein expedition of 1926, 23
Stein, Aurel, 23, 25, 451
Stilwell, General Joseph Warren, 189n
Subsidies (bribes), 194–95

Sun Yat Sen's Kuomintang, 160n
'Surkh Posh (The Red Shirts), 130–37
Swaraj Party, 117, 382, 405n
Swat valley, 23–25
Swiss Constitution, 183
Syed Amir Hussain Shah, 295
Syed Murtaza Sahib, 382–83

Taliban, 429–34, 438–39n, 440, 456–57, 461, 464
Tashkent, 89n
Tehsildar, 141n
Terrorists attacked on Indian Parliament, 440n
3 June plan, 176, 234, 275–78, 311, 316, 340–41, 344, 365, 399, 415, 418
Third Anglo-Afghan War, 95–102, 115, 425, 444
Third Battle of Panipat, 33, 80n
Tibetan autonomy, 152
Timur Shah, 35, 79n
Tipu Sultan, 36, 81n
Tirah, 62, 65, 92n, 104–7
Tiwana, Khizar Hayat, 157, 232, 244n, 338
Toynbee, Arnold, 460
Transfer of power, 12, 14, 167, 169, 174, 185, 210–11, 215, 219, 229–30, 267–68, 272–74, 310, 362, 374, 394, 404, 412
'Treaty of Friendship', 101
Treaty of Gandamak, 53, 90n, 412, 435n
Treaty of Rawalpindi, 425
Tribal Areas, 56–57, 153–54, 220, 264, 296
Tribal *jirgas*, 219
'Tribal lawlessness', 372
Tribal mullahs, 361
Tribal treachery, melancholic reflection of, 42–45
Turkestan, 22, 30, 75n, 410–11, 448
Turkmens, 76n
Turko-German mission, 96–97, 409
Two boundary commissions, 281n
'Two-nation' theory, 288

acceptance of the, 445
triumph of, 445

Udaygram, 24
'Udyana', 23
Unionist Party, 231
Unpleasant memories, 265–80
Uprising of 1857, 57
Urdu nationalism, 464
Utman Khels, 125, 141n
Utmanzai, 135, 311, 324n, 328–31

'Vichy government', 362

Wakhan corridor, 449, 453, 457
War Council, 300
Warlike situation between India and Pakistan, 211
Wavell, Archibald, 44, 56, 145–58, 168, 205–9, 219, 221–22, 224–27, 254, 260–61, 264, 267, 359–60, 373–74, 413
Waziristan, 60–61, 65, 92n, 107, 110–14, 153, 218, 222, 255–59, 262, 290, 295, 305, 361, 376, 432–34, 441
'Wehrmacht', 435n
Weightman, J.G., 160n

Weightman, Hugh, 160n, 266
*Wells of Power*, 8
Western Neighbourhood, 426–35
White, Sir George, 62, 65, 92n
Whitehall, 2, 66, 93n, 147–49, 165, 424
Wood, Edward Frederick Lindley, 141n
World War I, 1, 16n, 68, 95, 163, 405

World War II, 1, 3, 5, 7, 10, 16n, 144–45, 148–49, 162–63, 194–95, 251, 333, 353, 386, 409, 437, 465–66

Xinjiang, 448–59

Yakub-ibn-Layth, 29
Young, Sir William Mackworth, 93n
Yue-chi confederation, 26
Yuldashev, Tahir, 434, 442n
Yunus, Mohammad, 385, 405n
Yusufzai, 28, 31, 78n, 203

Zalme Pakhtun, 233–34
Zaman, Shah, 35
Zeus, 189n
Zhob, 100, 139n
Zia-ul-Haq, 429, 438n–439n
Zionism, 8